Francis Cuthbert Doyle

Lectures For Boys

The Sundays of the year; our Lady's festivals; the Passion of our Lord; the Sacred Heart. Vol. 1

Francis Cuthbert Doyle

Lectures For Boys
The Sundays of the year; our Lady's festivals; the Passion of our Lord; the Sacred Heart. Vol. 1

ISBN/EAN: 9783742835895

Manufactured in Europe, USA, Canada, Australia, Japa

Cover: Foto ©Lupo / pixelio.de

Manufactured and distributed by brebook publishing software (www.brebook.com)

Francis Cuthbert Doyle

Lectures For Boys

LECTURES FOR BOYS.

THE SUNDAYS OF THE YEAR; OUR LADY'S FESTIVALS; THE PASSION OF OUR LORD; THE SACRED HEART.

BY
THE VERY REV.
FRANCIS CUTHBERT DOYLE, O.S.B.

'Sinite parvulos venire ad Me.'

VOL. I.

Second  Edition.

R. WASHBOURNE,
18 PATERNOSTER ROW, LONDON.
BENZIGER BROS.: NEW YORK, CINCINNATI & CHICAGO
1896.

TO

THE RIGHT REV. P. A. O'NEILL, D.D., O.S.B.,
Lord Bishop of Port Louis,

THIS SECOND EDITION

OF

'LECTURES FOR BOYS'

𝔦𝔰 𝔇𝔢𝔡𝔦𝔠𝔞𝔱𝔢𔡡

BY

THE AUTHOR

IN MEMORY

OF AN UNBROKEN FRIENDSHIP OF MORE THAN FORTY

YEARS' DURATION.

PREFACE TO THE FIRST EDITION.

ANY one who has had to deal with boys, will know how little hold on their attention the spiritual works seem to have which either are put into their hands, or are read to them for their instruction. It is not that such works are in nowise applicable to their age; nor is it because the matter of them is not in itself excellent, and better perhaps than anything that we can pretend to offer. Why then does it fail to catch their attention?

If we might venture to assign a reason, we should be inclined to say, that it is because the matter treated of, though in a certain sense applicable to them, is nevertheless seldom or never actually applied. It is above their heads, for it is oftentimes abstract and theoretical. Now anything of this nature, especially if it is introduced into religious teaching or exhortation, does not catch their attention. It puzzles and it wearies them.

This fact, though already well known to the present writer, obtruded itself in a special manner upon his notice some years ago, when his Superiors intrusted him with the care of the boys at the venerable College of St. Edmund's, Douai.

In his capacity as Prefect, a large share in the work of their moral training fell to his lot, and a very little observation served to convince him that his labour would be thrown away, unless the grand principles of the Moral Law were brought straight home to their hearts. But how was this to be done? By making the abstract—concrete, the theoretical—practical. A method whereby this might be brought about soon suggested itself to him, and he determined to test its efficacy at once.

This was, to address to the boys every morning a short, homely exhortation or lecture proportioned to their intelligence, and adapted to the circumstances of their lives as school-boys at College. The result fully answered his expectations; their attention was arrested; their curiosity was aroused; and it was gratifying to observe the earnestness with which they strove during the day to practise the lesson which they had been taught in the morning.

Now, as boy-nature in its main features is the same all the world over, that which interested and benefited one School, will in all likelihood interest and benefit many others.

It is with this hope, therefore, that the writer of these Lectures has ventured to publish a certain number of them, which will be followed in due course by the rest, should these prove acceptable.

If they serve to direct heavenwards the thoughts and the aims of the young—if they encourage them to walk in the narrow way, and help them, be it ever so little, to make their hearts the temples of the living God—he will consider any labour that he may have expended upon their composition, most amply repaid.

ST. MICHAEL'S PRIORY, BELMONT, HEREFORD.
September 29, 1879.

PREFACE TO THE SECOND EDITION.

SEVERAL years have now elapsed since the first edition of this work was exhausted. During those years frequent applications have been made to the Publishers, and to me, by persons in England and in America, for copies of the Lectures.

When these could not be obtained, urgent requests were sent to me from various quarters to republish them; but, for one reason or another, I have been unable, until the present year, to comply with the wishes of those who have been so kindly disposed towards me as to deem them worthy of this honour.

The leisure requisite for the task which they desired me to accomplish has luckily, of late years, been at my disposal; and a happy combination of circumstances has enabled me to see my way to reproduce the work, with such corrections as friendly criticisms have suggested.

For the greater convenience of those who may choose to use the Lectures, I have published them in one large volume, instead of in two small ones.

Another reason which has brought about this change, is the indulgent appreciation of those who hope that the present volume may be followed by a second. When I recoil from this labour, I am confronted with the promise which the preface to the first edition records. There I see that I have undertaken, on certain conditions, which I am told have been fulfilled, to complete the course; and I am urged, in certain quarters, to do so by the encouraging argument that I shall thereby be of some little assistance to my over-worked brother-priests.

The hope that this may prove true, emboldens me to carry into effect what so long ago I promised to perform.

F. C. DOYLE, O.S.B.

GREAT MALVERN,
August, 1896.

CONTENTS.

THE SUNDAYS OF THE YEAR.

ADVENT.

	PAGE
I. THE LAST JUDGMENT	1
II. STABILITY IN WELL-DOING	4
III. HUMILITY	7
IV. PREPARATION FOR CHRISTMAS	10
CHRISTMAS DAY	13
SUNDAY WITHIN THE OCTAVE OF CHRISTMAS—SCANDAL	17
THE LAST DAY OF THE YEAR	20

SUNDAYS AFTER EPIPHANY.

I. CONDUCT TOWARDS MASTERS	24
II. PROGRESS	27
„ THE MARRIAGE-FEAST OF CANA	29
III. THE LEPER	32
IV. TEMPTATION	35
V. THE SOWER OF TARES	38
VI. INFLUENCE OF A GOOD BOY	41
SEPTUAGESIMA—THE OBJECT OF COLLEGE-LIFE	45
SEXAGESIMA—THE SOWER AND THE SEED	48
QUINQUAGESIMA—BLIND BARTIMEUS	51

LENT.

I. THE TEMPTATION OF OUR LORD	55
II. ADVANTAGES OF COLLEGE-LIFE	58
III. THE RELAPSING SINNER	62
IV. MOTIVE FOR STUDY	66
PASSION SUNDAY—ABANDONMENT BY GOD	70
PALM SUNDAY—PREPARATION FOR COMMUNION	73

EASTER.

EASTER SUNDAY—SPIRITUAL RESURRECTION	76
I. LOW SUNDAY—FAITH	79
II. THE GOOD SHEPHERD	82
III. AFFLICTIONS OF THE JUST, AND JOY OF SINNERS	85
IV. MINDFULNESS OF OUR DESTINY	88
V. PRAYER	91
ASCENSION DAY	94
SUNDAY WITHIN THE OCTAVE OF THE ASCENSION—PERSECUTION	97
WHIT-SUNDAY	100

CONTENTS

SUNDAYS AFTER PENTECOST.

		PAGE
I.	TRINITY SUNDAY	104
II.	THE EXCUSES	107
III.	LOVE OF JESUS FOR SINNERS	110
IV.	PURITY OF INTENTION	113
V.	JUSTICE OF THE SCRIBES AND THE PHARISEES	116
VI.	TRUST IN GOD	119
VII.	WOLVES IN SHEEP'S CLOTHING	123
VIII.	THE UNJUST STEWARD	126
IX.	CHRIST WEEPING OVER JERUSALEM	129
X.	THE PHARISEE AND THE PUBLICAN	132
XI.	THE VICE OF DETRACTION	135
XII.	FALLEN AMONG THIEVES	138
XIII.	GRATITUDE	142
XIV.	TRUST IN PROVIDENCE	146
XV.	THE COMPASSION OF JESUS	149
XVI.	INSINCERITY	153
XVII.	CHARITY TOWARDS OUR NEIGHBOUR	156
XVIII.	LUKEWARMNESS	160
XIX.	THE MARRIAGE FEAST	164
XX.	GRATITUDE TO MASTERS	168
XXI.	FORGIVENESS OF INJURIES	172
XXII.	DUTIES TO SUPERIORS AND TO GOD	176
XXIII.	THE POWER OF FAITH	180
XXIV.	JESUS ON MOUNT OLIVET	183

OUR LADY'S FESTIVALS.

INTRODUCTION TO THE MONTH OF MAY	188
THE HONOUR WHICH WE PAY TO THE BLESSED VIRGIN	191
DEVOTION TO THE BLESSED VIRGIN	195
WHAT IS MEANT BY THE IMMACULATE CONCEPTION	198
THE POSSIBILITY OF THE IMMACULATE CONCEPTION	202
THE IMMACULATE CONCEPTION	206
HISTORY OF THE DEFINITION	209
THE NATIVITY OF THE BLESSED VIRGIN	213
PRESENTATION OF OUR LADY IN THE TEMPLE	217
THE ESPOUSALS OR MARRIAGE OF THE BLESSED VIRGIN	220
THE PERPETUAL VIRGINITY OF THE BLESSED VIRGIN MARY	223
THE ANNUNCIATION	227
THE VISITATION OF THE BLESSED VIRGIN	231
EXPECTATION OF OUR LORD'S BIRTH	234
THE PURIFICATION	237
THE FLIGHT INTO EGYPT	241
MARY DURING THE PRIVATE AND THE PUBLIC LIFE OF OUR LORD	244
THE SEVEN DOLOURS OF OUR LADY	248
THE ASSUMPTION	251
THE HOLY NAME OF MARY	255
THE ROSARY	259
THE MATERNITY OF THE BLESSED VIRGIN	264
THE PATRONAGE OF THE BLESSED VIRGIN	268
MARY, HELP OF CHRISTIANS	271
PURITY OF THE BLESSED VIRGIN	274
OUR BLESSED LADY 'DE MERCEDE,' OR FOR THE REDEMPTION OF CAPTIVES	278

MARY, OUR FAITHFUL FRIEND	282
MARY'S INFLUENCE UPON US	285
MARY, THE PROTECTRESS OF YOUTH	288
MARY, OUR ADVOCATE WITH OUR JUDGE	291
CONCLUSION OF THE MONTH OF MAY	295

THE PASSION OF OUR LORD AND SAVIOUR JESUS CHRIST.

ASH WEDNESDAY	300
THE TWO ASSEMBLIES	303
ARE WE CLEAN?	306
GRIEF OF JESUS FOR THE TREACHERY OF JUDAS	309
THE PRIVILEGE OF PURITY	312
PRESUMPTION OF ST. PETER	316
OUR LORD'S SADNESS	319
THE PRAYER OF OUR LORD	322
THE SWEAT OF BLOOD	325
THE TREASON OF JUDAS	328
THE ARREST OF JESUS	331
JESUS BEFORE THE HIGH PRIEST ANNAS	334
JESUS BEFORE CAIAPHAS	337
JESUS GIVEN OVER BY CAIAPHAS TO THE SOLDIERS	340
JESUS DENIED BY ST. PETER	343
THE DEATH OF JUDAS	346
JESUS BEFORE PILATE	349
PILATE'S CONDUCT TOWARDS OUR LORD	352
JESUS BEFORE HEROD	356
JESUS REJECTED FOR BARABBAS	359
THE SCOURGING OF JESUS	362
THE CROWNING WITH THORNS	365
'BEHOLD THE MAN!'	369
JESUS CONDEMNED TO DEATH	372
JESUS CARRYING HIS CROSS	375
INCIDENTS ON THE WAY TO CALVARY	379
CIRCUMSTANCES OF THE CRUCIFIXION	383
THE CRUCIFIXION	386
JESUS HANGING ON THE CROSS	390
'FATHER, FORGIVE THEM, FOR THEY KNOW NOT WHAT THEY DO'	393
'THIS DAY SHALT THOU BE WITH ME IN PARADISE'	397
'WOMAN, BEHOLD THY SON; SON, BEHOLD THY MOTHER'	400
'MY GOD, MY GOD, WHY HAST THOU FORSAKEN ME?'	404
'I THIRST'	407
'IT IS CONSUMMATED'	410
'FATHER, INTO THY HANDS I COMMEND MY SPIRIT'	414
MIRACLES AT OUR LORD'S DEATH	417
THE SIDE OF JESUS PIERCED BY A SPEAR	421
THE BODY OF JESUS TAKEN DOWN FROM THE CROSS	424
THE BURIAL OF OUR LORD	427
DEPARTURE OF THE BLESSED VIRGIN AND THE REST FROM THE TOMB	431

THE SACRED HEART.

	PAGE
THE OBJECT OF THIS DEVOTION	435
UTILITY OF DEVOTION TO THE SACRED HEART	438
IMITATION OF THE SACRED HEART	442
LOVE OF THE SACRED HEART FOR GOD	445
LOVE OF THE SACRED HEART FOR US	449
THE LOVE WHICH WE OWE TO THE SACRED HEART	453
PATIENCE OF THE SACRED HEART	456
KINDNESS OF THE SACRED HEART	460
HUMILITY OF THE SACRED HEART	463
MEEKNESS OF THE SACRED HEART	467
UNSELFISHNESS OF THE SACRED HEART	470
JOY OF THE SACRED HEART	474
SORROW OF THE SACRED HEART	478
FRIENDSHIP OF THE SACRED HEART	482
DEVOTEDNESS OF THE SACRED HEART	486
PURITY OF THE SACRED HEART	489
FERVOUR OF THE SACRED HEART IN PRAYER	493
COMPASSION OF THE SACRED HEART	497
ZEAL OF THE SACRED HEART	501
GRATITUDE OF THE SACRED HEART	505
OBEDIENCE OF THE SACRED HEART	508
THE SACRED HEART, CONSOLER OF THE AFFLICTED	512
THE SACRED HEART, A REFUGE OF THE TEMPTED	516
THE SACRED HEART, A PROTECTION AGAINST THE WORLD	519
THE SACRED HEART, A PROTECTION AGAINST THE FLESH	522
THE SACRED HEART, HELP OF THE DYING	526
DUTY OF REPARATION TO THE SACRED HEART	529
UNION WITH THE SACRED HEART	533
HOW WE OUGHT TO ENTERTAIN OURSELVES WITH THE SACRED HEART AFTER COMMUNION	536
CONCLUSION OF THE MONTH OF THE SACRED HEART	540

LECTURES FOR BOYS

FIRST SUNDAY OF ADVENT.
THE LAST JUDGMENT.

'They shall see the Son of man coming in a cloud, with great power and majesty.'—ST. LUKE xxi. 27.

1. As fear is the beginning of wisdom, the Church upon this day opens her ecclesiastical year, by recalling to the minds of her children the terrors of the great accounting-day, upon which neither saint nor sinner can reflect without a thrill of shuddering horror. It is no wonder that they fill us with dread; for the very shadows which that day of wrath shall cast before it, will be enough to make the strong man 'wither away with fear, and expectation of what shall come upon the earth.' The great globe beneath his feet shall rock to its very centre; the sun and the moon shall be darkened, and the stars shall not give their light; the sea shall pile up its tumultuous billows to rush in over the land; and the fires hidden in the bowels of the earth shall break forth to consume and to destroy.

It is, of course, uncertain whether you will be living when these things shall come to pass. The probability is, that centuries upon centuries will have rolled by, and that your ashes will have been scattered to the winds of heaven, before the coming of that day of darkness and of storm. Yet, though it is uncertain whether you will live to see the signs which shall precede the coming of the Almighty Judge, of this one thing you may be perfectly certain—that you, together with all the men who have ever breathed the breath of life, will be standing in the valley of judgment 'when the sign of the Son of man shall appear in the clouds of heaven.'

Your eyes will look upon Jesus Christ, coming with great power and majesty to judge the living and the dead. You will stand there, surrounded by those who have sat by your side in the study and in the class-room. You will be seen by the professors who taught you, and whom you loved so well. Your parents, your brothers, your sisters, your relatives, will all be there with you. You will be there, not as an indifferent spectator, but as a prisoner at the bar, to answer to Almighty God for all the deeds done in the body, whether they have been good or evil.

II. You may perhaps ask the reason why God, Who at the moment of death has already decided the eternal doom of each of us, shall once again cite the human race collectively before His dread tribunal. Many and grave reasons are given by theologians; but let this one suffice, for it is sound, and calculated, moreover, to inspire us with salutary fear : God shall summon the whole human race to a general judgment, because each of us owes to his fellow-men a debt of truth.* His life ought to have been so blameless as to have enabled him to throw open the secret recesses of his soul to the gaze of all around him, and to bear their scrutiny without a blush.

Has this debt of truth been paid by us to our brethren? With sorrow we must confess that it has not. For nearly everyone bears about with him two personalities: one which is known to God and to himself, the other which is known to men. The man, as he stands before the eyes of God, is most studiously concealed from view, and little more than a mask is presented to the gaze of his neighbour. Hence it often happens that a scoundrel goes down to his grave with the reputation of an honest man ; a libertine wears the garb of unspotted virtue ; and pride the most detestable lies concealed beneath the cloak of humility.

As a matter of fact, there is oftentimes as great a difference

* Nicolas, 'Études Philosophiques,' tom. iii., chap. xvi.

between the man as he really is, and the man as he appears to be, as there is between a smoothly-polished marble monument, and the rottenness and corruption which lie festering beneath it. God, therefore, has decreed that there shall be a great accounting-day, on which this debt of truth must be paid to humanity. He will then tear down the lying epitaph, and overturn the marble monument, and lay bare before the eyes of the whole world the rottenness and corruption of the soul.

The deeds which have been done in darkness shall be dragged forth into the light; the words which have been whispered in the ear shall be thundered forth by the Archangel's voice; the thoughts and the desires of the heart, springing into existence quick as the lightning-flash, multitudinous as the sands of the sea, shall all be made manifest and brought to judgment.

III. You are going this day to approach the Holy Altar, to partake of the victim which is there offered up for the sins of the world. You are going to receive into the tabernacle of your heart Him, before Whom you will one day stand in fear and trembling, to hear the sentence of your eternal doom. Therefore, look well into yourself, and see whether your soul is able to bear the searching glance of His all-seeing and all-holy eyes.

Is your life so pure that you could stand up fearlessly in the presence of your companions and professors, and let their eyes see you as you appear to the eyes of your God? Just examine into the nature of the thoughts which pass through your mind as you sit poring over your books. See whether your words are so blameless that you would not fear to utter them before your masters. Are your desires always lawful? Are your actions always so innocent that they might be done in the light of day?

If, after a careful scrutiny, you find that you have not harboured evil thoughts and desires, nor spoken wicked words, nor done anything that you would be ashamed of, you need not fear to approach the banquet in which Christ is received. For before God you are that which outwardly you appear to be before men, and therefore there is no debt of truth due from you unto them. But if you cannot do this—if you are conscious to yourself of not being what you seem to be—if you feel that you are like the whited sepulchre, fair without and foul within—stand back! Go, first, and pay your debt of truth. Reveal yourself before man, and let him see you just as you are before God.

Our merciful Lord does not require you to do this before *all* men, but only before one who holds His place. Before him you must manifest yourself as you are. At his feet weep over your sins, and your kind, merciful God will blot them all out for you. Then you need fear nothing; for on the dreadful Judgment-day the sins of the just shall not be made a spectacle to Angels and to men, because, having been washed away by repentant tears, they are, before God, as if they had never been. Do not fail, while Jesus dwells within you, to ask for grace to lead so pure and holy a life, that you will never be ashamed to let the whole world look into the most secret recesses of your heart. If you can do this, the day of wrath will not have any terrors for you. 'You will fear no evil, because you know no sin.'

SECOND SUNDAY OF ADVENT.
STABILITY IN WELL-DOING.

'What went you out into the desert to see?'—ST. MATTHEW xi. 7.

I. ALMIGHTY GOD ordained that the Baptist, who, in the Gospel of this day, is so highly commended by Christ, should be the pioneer, to go before and prepare the way for the preaching of His divine Son. In the fulfilment of that high office, while making the rough and crooked ways of men's hearts straight and plain, he at the same time showed forth in his own person, not only what manner of men they ought to be who are intrusted with a mission like unto his own, but what the character of those ought to be who are preparing to receive Christ into their hearts in Holy Communion.

Our divine Lord Himself, when speaking of John, proclaimed him to be no changeling who veered about with every wind that blew, but a man firm and tenacious of purpose, who, having once begun, went on perseveringly to the very end, without turning to the right hand or to the left. In his dealings with those to whom he announced the message of God, he did not respect persons, having one code of morality for the rich and powerful, and another for the poor and lowly. He had a character too open, straightforward, and truthful for that. Those who listened to him found that he did not mince matters, but told unpleasant truths, in an uncommonly outspoken manner, to those who least of all desired to hear them. He came to enforce upon a corrupt generation the necessity for penance, and his actions bore out the truth of his words. He did not lead an easy, self-indulgent life, but a life stern, austere, and laborious; for, in the fulfilment of the task imposed upon him, he flinched not from any pain, he shirked not any labour, however rude and unpalatable it might be.

With reason, therefore, did Christ tell the people that when they flocked out into the desert to John, they went forth, not to gaze upon a 'reed shaken by the wind,' nor to look upon a man 'clothed in soft garments,' but upon one 'greater than a prophet,' even upon him whom Divine Wisdom chose out from among men, to go before the face of the Redeemer, and prepare the way of the Lord.

II. For you there is in store this day a higher honour than that of preparing the way of the Lord. Christ Himself is going to visit you, and to abide in the tabernacle of your heart. Will He find you in any respect like unto him whose eulogy He pronounced this day, and who never had the honour and the privilege which you so often enjoy? Are you a mere reed that is shaken by the wind? Are you an effeminate being, clothed in soft garments, and always seeking your own ease? Examine yourself and see.

A mere reed shaken about by the wind is that boy who is not stable in his purposes. One week he will apply himself vigorously to his books, and the next he will fritter away hours of priceless value in foolish day-dreaming, or in frivolous and profitless reading. One day he will observe the College rules, and the next he will, without a reason, break through them. For a short time he will be fervent in prayer, and in visiting the Blessed Sacrament; he will be regular at Confession and Communion; then will come a period of utter carelessness and indifference. He will gape and wander at his prayers; he will avoid the chapel and put off going to confession; his whole conduct will be reckless. For a season he will take himself in hand, and try earnestly to curb his passions and to tame his rebellious nature; but then again, when the day of trial comes, after fighting for a time, he will throw down his arms, and, like a craven, yield himself up a captive to his enemies. He is never constant at anything, but is like the College weathercock, which veers about with every wind that blows.

Moreover, a boy of this character will shirk every duty that is in any way irksome to him. He will not study, nor pray, nor observe rules, unless it suit his humour and convenience to do so; but if these duties either run counter to that humour, or trench in any way upon that convenience, he will at once cast them to the winds.

III. If you find some, or perhaps a great many of these defects, in your own character, then you are one of those whom Christ would call: 'A reed shaken by the wind'; a soft, effeminate, unmanly creature, with hardly sufficient courage to meet the ordinary ills of everyday life. You are not in a fit state to receive Him into your heart. There are in it crooked ways which must be made straight, and rough ways which must be made plain, before He will enter it and dwell there.

Go, therefore, and weep over your defects and sins, and then approach humbly to your God. To stay away from Him will not better your condition. For He is the unchangeable One, from Whom all men obtain stability and strength. You need both these qualities, for youth is fickle and weak. Approach, therefore, to the strong and mighty God, in Whom is no shadow of change. He is your Father, and will take you lovingly to His bosom. While leaning your head against His sacred Heart, ask with confidence, and you will obtain. Say to Him : ' Father, let me not be so fickle, so inconstant, so like a reed that is shaken by every wind! Give me stability in well-doing. Make me go on perseveringly with my hard, dry lessons, because it is my duty, a debt which I owe to Thee. Make me constant in my service of Thee, even when I feel no sweetness in Thy company, but am obliged to fight with distractions and disgusts. Teach me to look upon the College rules as the expression of Thy will ; and finally give me that courage which will enable me not to shrink like a coward from difficulties, but rather with a brave and manly heart to face and master them.'

THIRD SUNDAY OF ADVENT.
HUMILITY.
' What sayest thou of thyself?'—ST. JOHN i. 22.

I. THE people who poured forth from the cities of Judea, and went down into the Jordan valley to hear the preaching of John, beheld a spectacle which had become a very rare one in their degenerate days. They came to the river's brink to look at, and to listen to a man who lived a life and wore a garb which brought before their minds the prophets of old. A garment of camel's hair clothed his emaciated body; a rough leathern girdle circled his loins; locusts and wild honey furnished him with food; the holes and caverns of the savage rocks with a solitary's rugged home.

His austerity inspired them, no doubt, with more of awe than of love; yet his fervid eloquence riveted their attention, and moved the central depths of their hearts as they had never been moved before. For he spoke to them no merely human word, but one inspired by the Spirit of God, a word which came from the Divine Intelligence, instinct with life and power, keen as a finely-tempered blade, and reaching to the division of even the soul and the spirit. He was, in fact, unto them the ambassador of God; and delivered his message with that prophetic fire which Israel had not known since the last echoes of Malachi's voice had died away, four hundred years before.

So high an esteem did his life inspire, and so wide-spread a reputation did his sanctity procure for him, that an embassy, composed of priests and levites, came from Jerusalem to put to him questions, which show us the deep veneration in which all classes of the people held him. They asked him: 'Art thou the long-expected Messias?' He answered: 'I am not the Christ.' 'Art thou Elias?' He said: 'I am not.' 'Art thou a prophet?' He answered: 'No.' They asked, therefore, in amazement: 'Who art thou, then? What sayest thou of thyself?' He said: 'I am the voice of one crying in the wilderness, Make straight the way of the Lord.'

II. Here is an example of humility, an example which it would be well for you to imitate, especially as you approach so frequently to Him Who is humble of heart, Who spurns the proud, and showers His favours upon the lowly. Attend, therefore, diligently to the lesson which the Baptist teaches you. Though possessed of virtues so exalted that men were led to regard him as Elias, or even as the long-expected Christ, he thought so little of himself as to say of himself: 'I am nothing but a voice crying in the wilderness.' That is John's testimony of himself!

But what do you say of yourself? Little, perhaps, in words, lest the odious epithet 'braggart' should be fixed to your name; but much, no doubt, in your thoughts and desires. For most boys are only too eager to be thought, and to appear to be, better and wiser than they really are. As soon as they are able to give a bald translation of Cicero or of Demosthenes, or to hazard an opinion about Homer or about Æschylus, they begin to assume airs and to talk, with a tone of authority, about matters of which they can know but very little. If they are able to produce a few wretched verses, which have no more poetry in them than the metre and the rhyme, they fancy themselves endowed with a high order of genius, and look upon their pitiful doggerel as sublime. When they either write an essay, or compose a speech, upon some trite subject, which they treat in the most commonplace way, and fill with empty platitudes and high-sounding phrases, they imagine that they are going to astonish the world with the irresistible rush of their impetuous eloquence.

There are others again, who, having nothing better to be proud of than a sweet voice, or a handsome face, or a well-knit frame, greatly admire themselves for these attractions, and expect that others will do the same.

Also, not a few act as if the chief aim of their life were to be the athletes of the College; to be the swiftest bowler, the surest batter, and the longest jumper among the boys; and, having once won for themselves these enviable distinctions, they fancy that they may, with justice, claim a very considerable share of public admiration.

Finally, almost all, without exception, though possessing none of the excellences which they suppose to be peculiarly their own, and even when conscious that they do not possess them, are nevertheless willing that others, at least, should suppose that they do possess them. How different is all this from the conduct of the Baptist! How unworthy of those whose Friend and Master, each time that they approach Him, bids them: 'Learn of Him to be humble of heart.'

III. Beware, therefore, of drawing nigh to Him, until you have humbled yourself in the very dust before him. He esteems nothing valuable but that which is *true*, and a proud boy is a living *lie;* for he presents himself before his fellows in borrowed or in imaginary plumes, and wishes them to believe that they are his own. Whatever excellence he has, comes not from himself, but from God. Therefore, to claim it as his own, and to wish others to believe that it is his own, and to take pride in it as if it were his own, is to be a liar before men. No upright and honourable boy would wish to bear so contemptible a character.

If, then, you discover that by your past proud and vain conduct you have deserved so odious an epithet, endeavour now to wipe out the stain from your soul. If you wish to know how this may be most easily effected, imitate the example which, in the Gospel of this day, St. John gives you. Should either your fellow students or your professors entertain a high opinion of your abilities, or of your piety, do not value yourself according to their estimate; remember that they can judge of you only by what they see. They cannot penetrate into the secret of your heart, and behold the many imperfections which detract from the worth of what seems so fair, and render it, perhaps, totally valueless before God.

When you obtain credit for anything which you do not possess, be the first to disabuse others of their mistaken notion. But should you be conscious that you really do possess certain qualities and abilities, for which you are praised and held in high esteem, be not forward in making these known; do not become the trumpeter of your own praise.

Above all things avoid that grave fault into which clever boys not unfrequently fall—the habit of contemning others who are not so highly gifted as they are. It is a good thing to be thus favoured by God; but it is ungenerous to look with disdain upon others who have not received so much as yourself. Finally, shun all affectation, and let it be your constant aim really *to be* what you seem to be, and never to *seem to be* what you are not.

FOURTH SUNDAY OF ADVENT.
PREPARATION FOR CHRISTMAS.
'Prepare ye the way of the Lord.'—ISAIAS xl. 3.

I. IN citing these words of the prophet Isaias, St. John the Baptist made use of a figure of speech taken from an incident with which most of his hearers were very familiar. For we read that in the East, whenever a prince or a governor went on a journey, men were usually sent before him to clear the ways, and make his progress as easy as possible. Also, the inhabitants of the district through which he travelled were called upon to assist in this act of homage and loyalty to their ruler.

As, then, the time for the commencement of Christ's public mission had now arrived, His great forerunner began to cry aloud, and to call upon all to make ready the way for His heavenly doctrine, that it might find an easy entrance into their hearts, and there meet with no obstacle to hinder its sanctifying influence from having its due effect upon their souls. He called upon them to pick out the rocks and the stones of sin and of evil habits. He urged them to be open, straightforward, and honest in their dealings with one another. They were not to bear about with them a deceitful mind, which would ensnare and mislead their neighbour by its tortuous windings. The hills of pride and of vanity were to be laid low by humility; the hollow ways to be filled up by good works; the rough ways to be made plain by penance; and then, all obstacles being removed, the Prince of Peace would come, and all flesh should see the salvation of God.

II. As the great prophet called upon the Jews to make ready for the coming of the Messias, so are you also called upon, by the near approach of Christmas, to make ready your heart to receive Christ, and to be enlightened by His divine teaching. The very preparations which you make at this holy season to celebrate with due solemnity that festival round which are grouped so many cherished associations, ought to bring before your mind the duties which God expects from you.

No sooner is your examination finished, than you set to work to make all things ready. You see that your playrooms are cleaned out with more than ordinary care. Everything is there furbished up, and made to shine with unwonted splendour. Evergreens are procured, and hung with artistic skill from the ceiling and the walls. Pictures, and clever devices, and transparencies, give an air of richness to the austere simplicity of the collegiate hall. The words of praise, which the Angels sang in the midnight sky, are blazoned forth in letters of gold. Each lends his aid willingly to the work, and every heart is happy in joyous anticipation of the great, the long-looked-for day.

There is about that day, and the eve which precedes it, something so sacred, something so interwoven with the best and holiest sentiments of our hearts, that it can never be forgotten; and could you see what Angels see, your eyes would range over the various quarters of the earth where the individual members of your College have been scattered, and you would behold the priest on his busy mission, the bishop in his diocese, the business man in his office, the doctor, the soldier, the lawyer, in their various positions of honour and of trust, pausing for a few moments, as this day draws nigh, to look back with fond regret to those scenes which for them will never return.

III. What, then, is the lesson which all this joyous preparation for Christmas ought to teach you? It should teach you to make a similar preparation for the reception into your soul of Christ Himself, in Whose honour the Church has instituted the festival. Do not confine that festival to your play-room, refectory, and theatre. Let it reach your heart, and be celebrated chiefly there. Be not less diligent in making it ready for the reception of your Lord than you are in decking out the room in which you amuse yourself.

Cleanse it thoroughly, and with more diligence than at other times, from every stain of sin. Resolve to avoid, in future, even those venial faults and defects about which boys are so careless, but which, nevertheless, mar the beauty of the soul. As for mortal or grave offences, let us trust that they are matters of rare occurrence in our Colleges. Fan into a brighter flame the fervour of your piety, which has perhaps either grown dull, or even become well-nigh extinct. Put away from you all deceitful, crooked ways. Detest lying. Be honest, open, and sincere. Bear no ill-will, no grudge against prefect, or professor, or companion. Be brave in meeting difficulties, patient in enduring them, and persevering in striving to overcome them.

Then in very deed will the coming of Christ be full of joy for you. Christ the little infant, Christ your little brother, Christ the lover of good boys, will come and abide in your pure heart, and His Angels will hover round you and sing, 'Peace on earth to men of good will.'

CHRISTMAS DAY.

'I bring you good tidings of great joy; for this day is born to you a Saviour, Who is Christ the Lord, in the city of David.'—ST. LUKE ii. 10, 11.

I. THE great day, for which you have looked forward with longing expectation, has come at last. It has brought with it, let us hope, that peace and joy which angelic choirs so many centuries ago announced from the midnight sky, when the infant Saviour first came into the world. Though your minds are familiar with the subject of the festival, yet, because it is one which, though old, is ever new, let us once again dwell upon it, that the lesson which it teaches may sink deeply into our hearts, and never be forgotten.

As we reflect, our minds travel back through the long centuries which have since elapsed, and we find ourselves actually spectators of what occurred. We gaze in spirit upon an aged, way-worn man, of humble and gentle aspect, who is leading towards Bethlehem his youthful bride, that they both may be enrolled there, according to the edict of the Roman Emperor.

They have come a long way; both are weary; and the city of their royal ancestor, seated upon its ridge of limestone rocks, and gleaming white in the rays of the setting sun, though close at hand, yet seems a great way off. They climb the ascent, and stand at last in its crowded thoroughfare.

Throngs of people have gathered there, bent upon the same errand as themselves. Every house is full: there is no room even in the public Caravanserai, where strangers usually found a resting-place. Yet shelter must be found somewhere, for the Virgin's time has come. Close by the Caravanserai there chanced to be a cave, at that time used as a stable. Thither Joseph conducted the Virgin, and there, in that cold, dark, and comfortless cavern, a little child was born at dead of night. That child is the Incarnate God!

The great, the rich, the wise, were totally ignorant of the stupendous mystery which had been wrought. But down upon the plain, and upon the hill-slopes of Bethlehem, there were poor shepherds keeping the night-watches over their sheep. They were probably looking towards the flickering lights of the town, and longing for the dawn of day, when suddenly the heavens above their heads were thrown open, a glory brighter than the sun shone around, and their ears were ravished with Angelic minstrelsy, singing, 'Glory to God in the highest, and on earth peace to men of good will.' As they listened, an Angel of the Lord stood beside them, and said: 'Behold I bring you good tidings of great joy, that shall be to all the people; for this day is born to you a Saviour, Who is Christ the Lord. And this shall be a sign unto you. You shall find the infant wrapped in swaddling clothes and laid in a manger.' After delivering his message, the heavenly visitant rejoined his brethren in the sky, and sang the praises of the new-born King. Then the shepherds, turning to one another, said, with joyful hearts: 'Let us go over to Bethlehem and see this word which has come to pass, which the Lord hath spoken.'

II. Like the shepherds, you also are going over to Bethlehem, not simply to gaze upon the infant Jesus, but to receive Him into your heart. For this is a day on which every College boy approaches the Holy Altar to eat of that sacred Bread which God has prepared for those who love Him. The same Jesus is there present, Who lay that first Christmas night upon a little straw in the manger. He will enter your heart to give you joy and peace, and to endow you with strength and courage to fight your way into that kingdom which He came down from heaven to throw open to you. But with what dispositions ought you to approach Him, Who so helplessly lies there, and so lovingly invites you to draw nigh unto Him!

In the first place, you must, like the shepherds, be found watching; for to you has been committed a treasure to care for, and to defend from the wolves of hell, who prowl about seeking to snatch it away from you. This is your soul. Vigilance on your part is necessary to defend it. To vigilance there must be joined earnest prayer, which is a weapon so formidable that, when wielded by the feeblest hand, it is able to inflict so terrible a wound that the most daring spirits of hell will flee away in order to escape it.

In the next place, you must have simplicity and humility of heart. If, like the great men of the world, you be full of proud thoughts, and high ideas of your own excellence; if you look with disdain upon others, or allow feelings of rancour or of hatred to dwell in your breast, no messenger will come from heaven to give you tidings of great joy, no angelic harmony will flood your soul with thrilling pleasure. The din of passion will drown the low, soft accents of celestial voices, and the vapours of worldly lust will veil their bright forms from your eyes.

Above all things, as you go not simply to gaze upon, but to take up into your arms and receive into your heart, the infant Saviour, prepare for Him there a resting-place which He will prize very highly—that is, a pure and spotless heart, the most fitting of earthly thrones for the God-man. Therefore, strive diligently to remove every stain from your soul; and, until you have thoroughly cleansed it from all defilement, dare not to advance one step towards the spot where Jesus lies. When you have done this, you may go over to Bethlehem, and you will be welcomed by St. Joseph and by the immaculate Mother. There throw yourself upon your knees. Jesus will stretch out His little hands and come to you. He will nestle in your heart, and you will feel that in very deed 'there is peace on earth to men of good will.'

III. During this Christmastide, you must not content yourself, nor imagine that Jesus will be content with one visit, made to Him upon the day of His birth. He wishes you to keep close to Him, because you have now greater need of His assistance than at other times. For, if you go home for the holidays, you will, of course, be free from all serious occupation and have much idle time upon your hands. Now, these are the days during which the devil gathers in his harvest. He finds work for idle hands to do. Therefore, you must be on your guard against him, and as you need more special graces to defend yourself from his attacks, you must be careful not to lose sight of God. You must frequently draw nigh to Him, and by earnest prayer merit His fatherly protection.

If, instead of going home, you remain at College for your holidays, even so there will be, comparatively speaking, very little to do. Discipline is relaxed; there are plays and various other kinds of amusement which distract the mind, and render the performance of spiritual duties more difficult than at other times. The soul begins to forget God, and to allow vain, foolish, and sometimes dangerous thoughts and images, to flash through the brain. This is for anyone, even at the best of times, a critical state, but it is fraught with much peril in times of idleness. Therefore, take care not to forget the Babe of Bethlehem. Do not omit your usual visit to the Holy Sacrament and to the shrine of our dear Lady. Jesus is lying in the narrow limits of the tabernacle, waiting for you to present yourself before Him. He longs to see you, and to confer His graces upon you. Therefore, do not begrudge Him a few moments every day, to pay Him your accustomed acts of worship. Make some little sacrifice for His sake, and He will amply repay you.

Furthermore, do not forget, in the midst of your festivities and your joys, that there are thousands of little boys—the brothers of Jesus and your brothers also—who are not so happy as you are. They are cold and hungry during these bitterly sharp days. The wind pierces through their worn and scanty clothing. They are oftentimes without bread, while you are surfeited even with luxuries. Therefore, do not let the joys of this Christmas-time make you forgetful of God's poor. Your pockets are full of money, which loving friends have given you, to make merry with. Let some of it find its way into the trembling hands of the poor. It will make them happy as well as yourself, and you will be doing a work most pleasing to your infant Saviour; for what you do to His poor, you do to Himself. If you feed them, you appease His hunger; if you clothe them, you warm and cherish His shivering members; and be assured of this, that He Who has promised to bestow an eternal reward on those who give even a cup of cold water in His honour, will not forget you. The child Jesus will smile gratefully and graciously upon you, and your heart will be filled with a heavenly peace and joy, far exceeding all that this world can give.

SUNDAY WITHIN THE OCTAVE OF CHRISTMAS.

SCANDAL.

'Behold this Child is set for the fall, and for the resurrection of many in Israel.'—ST. LUKE ii. 34.

I. AN aged man, whose daily prayer for years had been, that he might not close his eyes in death till they had gazed upon the Redeemer's face, uttered these words, as he pressed to his joyful heart the fragile form of the infant Jesus. They were addressed to that Child's Mother, whose heart beat high with exultation at the prophetic words which had been uttered about her Son: 'A light for the enlightening of the Gentiles, the glory of thy people Israel.' They were unto her the messengers of future woe, and they break in upon our jubilant antiphons, as the solemn peal of the passing bell breaks in upon the glad music of a bridal party. The Angels sang upon the night of His birth, and bade the fallen race of men rejoice, because a Saviour had been born to them. Will He, then, not be a Saviour unto all? Will He strike down some and raise up others? Yes; he will redeem all. He will pay the price of their redemption; but not all will accept His bounty; and because they reject His mercy, He will become unto them a rock of scandal and a stone of offence, against which they will strike their feet and stumble into hell.

Some will reject Him, because He will teach them that there is in Him a divine as well as a human nature, and that these two natures constitute one person—the person of God the Son, that is to say, the man-God, Christ Jesus. Men will not believe it. They will say: 'Either He is a divine person, with a merely fantastical body, or He is a man, with nothing divine about Him.'

Others will reject Him, because of His Church. They will not believe that He came into the world to set up a body of teachers, to whose care He would intrust the entire deposit of faith, remaining with them and their successors until the end of time, to guide and to preserve them from error. 'No,' they will say, 'it is not so. He taught the Apostles all truth, and they committed to writing whatever is necessary for salvation. From that collection of doctrine each of us is to seek guidance which will lead him to heaven.'

Others, again, will reject Him, because of His commands. They will not deny themselves. They refuse to walk in His footsteps; they cast off the Cross, and falling beneath the sway of their brutish appetites, make a God of their belly. The end of these is destruction: 'He is set up for the fall of many in Israel.' With that keen sword of anguish piercing her heart, the Holy Virgin received her Divine Child from the arms of Simeon, and went her way with these words of fearful import ringing in her ears: 'And thine own soul a sword shall pierce.' They thrust the iron into her soul. From that day forth she ever stood beneath the shadow of the Cross.

II. The words of Simeon about Jesus may, in a certain sense, be applied also to every boy at College. Of each it may be said, that in his own little circle of friends and companions 'he is set up for the fall, or for the resurrection of many.' For at College, just as in the great world which lies beyond its walls, each individual possesses an influence, for good or for evil, upon his fellows. He is able to build up or to destroy. His good example may lead them to God, by giving countenance to the weak and support to the wavering; or his bad example may turn them into evil courses, by breaking down some feeble barrier which still holds them on the narrow way. Therefore, it is necessary for him to watch most carefully over himself, that he may not, by word or by deed, become the occasion of fall unto his weaker brethren.

Especially ought this to be attended to by those who are high up in the School; for it is to the upper Forms that the younger boys look for models upon which to fashion their conduct. If they find their elders regardless of College discipline, they also will learn to contemn it. If they see them despising study, and sneering at those who labour conscientiously, they, too, will think it manly to be idle and to despise hard work. If they hear them grumbling at everybody and at everything, they, too, will catch their tone, and learn to snarl like their betters. To resist authority, and as a natural consequence, to live in a perpetual feud with those whose duty it is to maintain order, will also recommend themselves to the youthful generation, if they see those whom they consider the leaders of the School acting in this silly way towards their Superiors.

But if, in addition to bad example, the elder boys begin to take notice of, and to pet the younger; and especially if this be done in order to abet them in their misdemeanours, they will become so intolerably insolent, so mischievous, and so vicious, that no other course will be left open to the authorities than that of ignominiously expelling them from the School. Pray to God that it may never be recorded against you in the Book of Doom : ' This boy was set up for the fall of many in Israel.'

III. How, then, may you prevent so fearful a crime from ever being laid to your charge? By trying ever so to live that those who look up to you for example, may never see in your conduct anything that will help to weaken the good principles, or to undermine the piety, which they have brought with them from the sanctuary of home. Therefore, let it be your constant aim to regulate your words and actions with so much care, that they may always help to build up God's kingdom in the hearts of others, and never to pull down and to destroy it. Do not, however, attempt to do this by laying yourself out to edify. Strive rather to lead others to God, by fulfilling with scrupulous care all your duties towards Him. This purpose, fixed firmly in a boy's heart, will save him from that pharisaical self-consciousness, which is so justly held in abhorrence by all earnest and upright men. It will make him an example unto others, without any effort on his part to be an example. By his behaviour at prayer his companions will see that he is speaking to God; that he is in earnest about what he says; and that he is not hurrying through a meaningless formula. They will see by his strict observance of Rule, that he obeys, not because Superiors are watching him, but because he has a true sense of the presence and authority of God, Whose place they hold, and Whose will they make known to him. Hence also they will never hear from his lips a syllable to the disparagement of his professors, but only words which show that he highly values them, and keenly appreciates all the self-denial, which their difficult and responsible office imposes upon them. By his frequent use of the Sacraments, they will see his high esteem of these great means of grace, and will learn whence it is that he derives the strength of character which makes him what he is.

Furthermore, they will see that his piety actuates all his life. They will find that he labours hard at his books; that he is not proud, nor quarrelsome, nor passionate, nor vain. Let there be three or four boys of this kind in a School, and their influence will work wonders. They will be the means of resurrection to many. Boys will begin to pray fervently; the Rule will be observed through motives of obedience; no word of scorn against masters, nor murmur of discontent will any more be heard among them. Confession and Communion will be frequent; studies will be prosecuted with energy; a humble, charitable, Christian spirit will pervade the whole School, and it will thus become for the boys the house of God and the gate of heaven. Therefore, earnestly beseech Our Lord, when you this day receive Him into your heart, that you may never be a stumbling-block unto others, but rather a means to lead them to serve Him with their whole heart and soul.

THE LAST DAY OF THE YEAR.

'See, therefore, brethren, how you walk circumspectly : not as unwise, but as wise, redeeming the time, because the days are evil.'—EPHES. v. 15, 16.

I. As a traveller who has climbed to some lofty eminence, looks back upon the country through which he has passed, and tracing upon the plain below the dusty road along which he toiled so painfully, follows its winding course till it becomes a mere thread in the far distance, so on this, the last day of the year, do we also pause for a few moments to glance at it once again before it dies away and becomes a thing of the past. Yet a few short hours, and the year will have rolled by, like the waters of a rapid river, into the ocean of eternity. As we reflect upon the days and the months which were compressed within its limits, they seem but as yesterday. Such also will our whole life appear to us when we contemplate it from the brink of the grave, even though it should have gone beyond the limits marked out as the earthly span of mortal men.

During the course of this year, joys and sorrows have come to gladden or to depress us. They have been like the sunshine and the storm of the material world. One day a murky fog enveloped us, and on the next the gloom lifted a little, and gave us a glimpse of the azure sky. Perhaps we have suffered in mind or in body, and the Cross, instead of chastening, made us more fretful and impatient. Then, again, there were times during the year when the option of good or of evil, of life or of death, offered itself to us, and we may have stretched forth our hands to pluck forbidden fruit, and have greedily swallowed the tempting bait. Nay, more than this, not content with eating of the poisoned fruit, we may have persuaded others also to partake of it, and thus have involved them in our own destruction.

All these things have been, but now they are past and gone, together with the thoughts which flashed through our minds, the desires which grew out of these thoughts, and the actions which were begotten of both. They are past, indeed, but not one of them is forgotten, for an ever-wakeful eye has watched and marked them all. In God's great book they are recorded, and when the river of time shall have ceased to flow for us, that book will be opened, and these things will be brought to judgment against us.

II. If careful note has been taken by God's recording Angel of all that you have done during the past year, it is your interest to examine into your heart, and to see what charges he may have against you, in order that you may be able to answer them. For this purpose call to mind the reasons or motives for which God gave you the year which will so soon have passed away. He bestowed it upon you as a period of mercy, during which you were to prepare yourself for heaven, and by your conduct to prove that you deserve the reward destined for you. Certain talents were committed to your keeping, to be so employed by you as to increase their value, in order that God, seeing your fidelity and trustworthiness in small matters, may set you over those which are greater and more important.

These talents are the various faculties and powers of your body and of your soul. God intended your soul to rule your body, and to keep its animal instincts in subjection to His laws by sternly refusing to the sensual appetite every unlawful gratification for which it craves. Hence the soul must treat the body much in the same way as that in which a rider treats a horse which has not been broken in. He puts a bit into its mouth to restrain its impetuosity, and applies a spur to its sides to urge it forward when it would wish to be at rest. But, in order that the soul may be able to effect this, it must first bring *itself* into subjection to God. Its anger must be repressed, its pride humbled, its vanity trampled in the dust. When this has been accomplished, the soul becomes complete master of the body, and is able to rule it like an absolute monarch, whose slightest wish cannot be gainsaid.

Again, in your own particular case, God gave the year to you that you might develop your intellectual faculties, by diligent application to those studies which will mature the powers of your soul, and that you might learn discipline by the observance of Rule, by silence, by submission to authority, and by humble reverence for Superiors. On all these points there is room for much serious reflection, and the few remaining moments at your disposal, before the year is gone for ever, will be profitably employed in examining yourself, to see in what way you have corresponded with His wishes.

III. When you have impressed upon your mind the purpose for which God gave the year to you, in the next place, examine seriously whether you have used it for the ends which He intended. You had a work to accomplish, the outlines of which we have just sketched for you. How has it been done? Has it even been begun? Alas! very many utterly neglect it, and we must acknowledge with sorrow that the number of boys who do so is not by any means small. They do not take any pains to bring their animal nature into subjection to the spirit, and to submit the spirit to God. Some of them will not endure the slightest word of contradiction, but fly into a passion and lose all self-control. Others, through a cowardly fear of men, are neither truthful nor straightforward. Others set up 'self' as an idol, and most devoutly fall down and worship it. Others are disobedient to Superiors; they refuse to comply with their most reasonable wishes, and break through their most positive commands. Others are eaten up with pride and vanity, which, like canker-worms, consume the very heart of all their good works.

But, if so many neglect the cultivation of their souls, shall we not be able to say that by far the greater number attend, at least, to the culture of their intellect? Alas! no; this important part of their education—a part so essential for their worldly advancement—is oftentimes as much neglected as the all-important affair of their eternal well-being. They fritter away whole hours in useless reading, or in pernicious day-dreaming, and set at naught the College discipline, which assists so materially in the work of education.

If, upon examination, you discover that during the past year you have not taken any pains to curb your temper, to love truth, to subdue self, to obey cheerfully, to repress pride, to labour conscientiously at the work of your intellectual development, the work for which God gave you the year has not been done. But even now there is time. The year has not quite gone. Do not allow its few remaining hours to pass by without making your peace with God. Go to Him in all humility; cast yourself upon your knees before Him; be heartily sorry for the mis-spent past; blot out, by tears of sincere repentance, the handwriting of sin which the recording Angel has set down against you, and promise God to make a better use of the year which is about to begin its course on the morrow.

FIRST SUNDAY AFTER EPIPHANY.
CONDUCT TOWARDS MASTERS.

'They found Him in the Temple sitting in the midst of the doctors, hearing them and asking them questions.'—ST. LUKE ii. 46.

I. AFTER their three days of sorrowful searching, the parents of Jesus most probably found Him in one of the Temple courts, where the Hebrew youths were instructed in the Sacred Scriptures. If joy at His recovery did not master every other emotion, they must have been surprised at the scene which the Evangelist puts so vividly before us. Unlike the other scholars, who sat on the ground, or upon low stools 'at the feet of their Master,' they beheld the boy Jesus 'seated in the midst of the doctors,' who had gathered round Him, surprised at the depth of His questions, and struck with admiration at the answers which He gave. Though full of the Eternal Wisdom of the Godhead, He did not go among them to make an empty display of knowledge, but to begin that work which the Eternal Father had put into His hands. Hence the Scripture does not say that He either argued, or disputed with the doctors, but simply that He listened to them, and asked them questions.

At this early age He is the model of all boys. For the first work that God requires of them, is to 'attend unto learning.' In order to show them how they are to perform this task, He leaves His parents, as all College boys are obliged to do, in order to receive their education. He displays His eagerness for knowledge, though already possessed of the Divine Wisdom. In the presence of His masters, He conducts Himself with the greatest modesty and humility, and shows by this first and only public act of His boyhood, what manner of boys He would have you all to be.

II. Therefore, look well upon the child Jesus, and examine your own conduct to see whether it in any way corresponds with His. Like Him, you have a work intrusted to you by God your Father, which work is two-fold, consisting first in the sanctification of your soul, and secondly in the cultivation of your intelligence. Without at present inquiring how you perform the first part of that task, reflect for a moment whether you accomplish the second.

From the fact that you have been sent into the midst of the doctors or teachers 'to hear them, and to ask them questions,' you will understand that your education is not entirely the work of your masters. For you are not in their hands as a block of marble is under the chisel of the sculptor. You are living, intelligent beings, and, therefore, the chief part of your education must be performed by yourselves. Your masters may, indeed, give you precepts and show you how the work is to be done, but they cannot do it for you. You have to hear their instructions, and to ask them questions—to hear with dutiful submission and respect, and to question with humility.

Now what, as a general rule, are the sentiments of boys with regard to this part of the task intrusted to them by God? They are anything but those just mentioned; for their actions indicate that they practically consider their education to be the work of the master only. For how do they occupy themselves during the precious time of preparation? Instead of strengthening their faculties by serious labour, so that when they come to sit at the feet of their masters they may be able to hear them with profit, and to ask intelligent questions, too many of them fritter away the precious hours in absolute folly, or in pursuits which in nowise further the end for which they came to College. Some either stare idly at their companions, or, fixing their gaze upon vacancy, waste whole hours in profitless daydreaming. Others read works of fiction, which are well enough in their place, but mischievous if allowed to usurp the time assigned for serious studies. Others do almost everything except that which duty imperatively demands of them. They study geology, or botany, or history, or astronomy, but shirk Mathematics, Latin, and Greek.

The consequence is, that when these boys come to schools, and sit at the feet of their professors, they feel no interest in listening to them, and care not to ask them any questions. They do not imitate the boy Jesus. They leave undone the work which God has given them to do, and though it is their heavenly Father's work, they feel no zeal to see it accomplished.

III. If, in your student-life, you have not been imitating the boy Jesus, how will you dare to receive Him this day into your heart in the Holy Communion? You cannot expect that He will love you, or willingly come to you, or give you all the graces which He would otherwise bestow, unless you strive to liken yourself unto Him. He is your model, not only in virtue, but in hard work. Consequently you must labour as He did, if you desire to win favour from Him.

What then must you do? In the first place, you must fix this idea firmly in your mind: that the development of your intellectual faculties by serious application to dry and difficult studies, is as much a part of the service expected from you by God, as the sanctification of your soul. This idea will become for you a principle of action. It will invest with most attractive loveliness what is so hard and repulsive when looked at from the standpoint of self-ease and indolence, and will make you eager to accomplish your appointed task.

Though at times you may feel some repugnance to begin, yet this idea will act as a spur upon your sluggish will and rouse up all its energy. Immediately the prayers before study are ended, it will make you set to work without a moment's delay. You will not then substitute an easy branch or subject for one that is difficult. No, you will bravely look the difficulty in the face; you will grapple with it, and master it. When actually at school, and in the presence of your professor, you will pay the greatest attention to his words, in order to profit by them, and to make his difficult task as easy as possible. You will ask questions with the greatest respect and humility; you will never contend insolently with him, but remembering your model—the boy Christ Jesus—you will never do anything that would not meet with His approval.

SECOND SUNDAY AFTER EPIPHANY.
PROGRESS.

'And the Child grew and waxed strong, full of wisdom, and the grace of God was in Him.'

I. THOUGH Our Lord, in His boyhood and His infancy, was just as much God as He was in His mature age, and as He is now, seated in glory at the right hand of the Eternal Father, yet He chose to seem unto men like any other child. The shepherds who hung over Him as He lay in the manger saw but a helpless, wailing infant. The Magi, who bent their knees before Him, and presented their typical gifts of gold, frankincense, and myrrh, perceived no look of intelligence in the eyes which gazed so wonderingly upon them. Like other children, he grew up and became strong; like other children, His reason seemed to develop with His years. Yet all this time the plenitude of Divine wisdom and grace dwelt in Him.

There can be no doubt that God ordained this apparently slow and gradual advance in reason and in virtue, on the part of His Son, to teach boys that they too must advance in virtue and in intelligence as they advance in age. He wills them to keep the boy Jesus before their eyes as their model. Imagine, then, to yourselves a boy whose soul is without spot or stain; who is obedient and submissive; who ever thinks of others before himself; who is open, truthful, humble, sweet-tempered, affable, and mild. Picture to yourself one adorned with all these virtues, and yet in a way not to attract an extraordinary amount of attention—looked upon, indeed, with a feeling of veneration and love, but yet exciting no more of these sentiments than an upright and holy boy always excites in the hearts of those who know how to appreciate and cherish so priceless a treasure. Such a one was Our Lord Jesus Christ in His boyhood.

II. Such also ought each of you to be. Your progress in virtue and in favour with God, ought to correspond with your growth in years and in wisdom. But this is not always the case. Too many boys, alas! decrease in virtue in proportion as they advance in age. By their sins they lose the favour of God, while by their sharpness and their wit they gain the applause of men. Their early years give promise of a youth rich in virtues. We watch them expanding before our eyes like beautiful flowers, increasing every day in fragrance and in loveliness; but, unhappily, the cankerworm of vice sometimes creeps into those childish hearts, and eats away the very substance of their virtue, leaving behind nothing but the fair exterior. All that made them lovable and beautiful is withered and dead; and while in the eyes of men they appear worthy of praise and commendation, they are unto God and His Angels objects of detestation and of loathing. They grow and wax strong, and, it may be, display a brilliancy of parts which dazzles and astonishes their friends and their professors; but they are as weak as infants before an assault of the devil, and, like cowards, throw down their arms, and open wide their gates, when he first summons them to surrender. Alas! when that evil spirit enters their hearts, he not unfrequently enters them to take up there his permanent abode.

Hence it is that boys whom we have known to be pure and innocent of all evil become, as they grow older, prodigies of vice. Instead of being open and frank, submissive and humble, mild and unselfish, they become cunning and deceitful, rebellious and proud, vain and jealous, passionate and selfish. There is in them no thought about God, or about the purpose for which He sent them into the world. They begin to loathe virtue and the practice of piety; they shun the society of the good; they neglect the Sacraments; and thus their hearts, which were once the tabernacles of God, are changed into the abodes of the devil.

III. This must not be your case. It need not be the case of any boy, how weak soever he may be. For the devil is like the bully of a School—he masters only those who are afraid to show fight. From those who face him like men, and who are prepared to strike out in self-defence, he flees away with all speed. Besides, if you feel afraid, you have always near you the boy Jesus. He is your friend—nay, He wishes you ever to look upon Him as your brother. When, therefore, the devil comes to attack you, if you fear your own weakness, run at once to your loving brother. His arm is strong. His blow will make your enemy and tormentor reel and stagger, like a man who has been stunned; and then your arm, feeble though it be, will easily prostrate and defeat him.

But you must go to Jesus not only when the devil attacks you, but when anything troubles you. You wish to make progress both in virtue and in learning, and you find that there are many obstacles in the way, many difficulties to be overcome. Jesus, your brother, is ever at hand. Go to the silent chapel, where the lamp burns so softly before His altar-throne, and there speak to Him, and lay open the sorrows of your heart before Him—your weaknesses, your fears, your defects. Tell Him of your difficulties in study, and ask His help. Do this not once or twice, but regularly every day. What, think you, will be the result? You will, like the child Jesus, advance both in heavenly and in earthly wisdom, and the grace of God will be in you.

FOR THE SAME SUNDAY.

THE MARRIAGE-FEAST OF CANA.

'They have no wine.'—St. John ii. 3.

I. WHEN the wine failed at the marriage-feast, to which Jesus and His blessed Mother had been invited, our Lady's tender heart felt deep compassion for the newly-married pair, lest their inability to provide sufficient wine for their guests should cover them with confusion. Knowing her Son to be God, and able to do all things, she laid their necessity before Him, leaving Him to do what He might think best. Yet her heart pleaded for them, and besought Him to come to their assistance by the wonders of His divine power.

This action on her part drew from Jesus an answer which heretics look upon as a rebuke, and as an intimation, both to her and to us, that she can have no influence upon Him in causing Him to dispense His favours and graces. 'Woman,' said He, 'what is it to Me and to thee? My hour is not yet come.' But this cannot be the interpretation of these words, because, in the first place, the term 'woman' does not in itself imply any want of respect, since Christ upon the Cross used it when addressing our Lady, and also when commending the faith of the Cannanean woman. In the next place, He actually did grant the favour which she implicitly asked when she said, 'They have no wine'; and that, too, although the time for manifesting His power 'had not yet come.'

Therefore, the apparent harshness with which Christ almost invariably addresses His Mother must be accounted for in some other way. It is the opinion of grave theologians that the harshness of His words is for our instruction, while His acts with regard to all that she asked, put beyond the shadow of a doubt her immense power with Him, and His unbounded love and reverence for her. It intimates to us that as Redeemer He had severed all ties of flesh and blood, and that those whom He came to save were to be to Him, henceforth, both father and mother, both sister and brother. Those who wish to see this matter more fully discussed, and to learn what the theologians of the Church have written about it, will find the whole question treated of at considerable length in the able work of Nicolas on the 'Blessed Virgin.'*

II. The few words by which the Mother of Jesus made known the wants of the newly-married pair give you an admirable example of the way in which you ought to make your necessities known to God. These necessities are numerous, and press themselves upon your notice at almost every hour of your life; and though God knows them without being informed of them by you, yet, because prayer is one of the means ordained by His providence for the relief

* Tom. ii., chap. 17.

of these necessities, He wills you to make use of it when you wish to obtain His aid.

Observe, then, carefully the form of prayer used by His blessed Mother. She says, 'They have no wine.' These words tell us plainly what were the sentiments of the heart from which they flowed. She knew that Christ had the power to relieve the want; she fully believed that His loving, compassionate soul would make Him eager to do so. Therefore, with this faith and this knowledge, she simply states the want which she wished to have relieved. She does not argue with Him; she does not urge her request; she is content that Christ should know it, and quite resigned to acquiesce in whatever it should please Him to do.

Jesus answered her with apparent sharpness—'What business is it of ours whether they have wine or not?'—and gives as a reason for not complying with the implicit request which her statement contained, 'that the time for a display of power had not yet come.' In spite, however, of His apparent reluctance, there must have been in the tone of His voice, and in the expression of His eye, something which told her that her petition had been granted; for she said to the waiters, 'Whatsoever He shall say to you, do ye.' Her maternal instinct did not deceive her. He had heard and granted her prayer; for presently He ordered the waiters to fill the vessels with water, and, having changed it into wine, He bade them take it to the steward to be set before the guests.

Let your prayer have all the qualities which you see in this petition of our dear Lady. Let it be made with faith and confidence; let it be full of resignation and patient perseverance; and then Christ will at last give you the desire of your heart.

III. Jesus invites you this day to the banquet of His Body and Blood, in the Holy Communion. There you will receive into your heart Jesus, your Lord and your God. Do not fail then to let Him know all your wants. It will need but very little reflection to call to mind what they are. It may be that you are ill-tempered, passionate, and unable to brook contradiction. In the playground, you quarrel with your companions; in the class-room, you are out of humour with your master. Say then to Jesus: 'Father, I have no meekness.' Again, you may be awakening to the fact that you are not a lover of truth; that you are not sincere; and the shame of the disgraceful habit of lying may often cover you with confusion. The Truth itself is with you. Say, 'I have no truth; make me to love true speaking'; and He will give you grace to make both mind and speech be in accord. So, also, of the priceless virtue of purity, of sweet humility, of obedience, and the rest. 'Ask, and you shall receive.'

In the same way, ask God for help in your other necessities. If you are slow of understanding, and cannot master the difficulties of your lessons, call upon God, Who giveth understanding to little ones, and He will enlighten your darkness. You will not, perhaps, be conscious of His help, by any sudden and marvellous illumination of your intellect, but your unceasing cry to Him for aid will procure for you at least that power of patient industry which not unfrequently supplies the place of great talent. However, do not forget to imitate our dear Mother, not only in her prayer, but in her conduct after she had made it. Be ready to obey the injunctions and the inspirations of God, and, like her, you will have the happiness of seeing God comply with your wishes, and more fully accomplish them than you could ever either expect or desire.

THIRD SUNDAY AFTER EPIPHANY.
THE LEPER.

'Lord, if Thou willest, Thou canst make me clean.'—ST. MATT. viii. 2.

I. WE shall be able to form some notion of leprosy, if, in addition to the pages of Sacred Scripture, we consult the accounts which travellers in the East have given of it. From all that these men have told us, we may say, without fear of exaggeration, that it is the most terrible of bodily diseases, and may, therefore, be chosen to represent the horrible deformity of sin. It appears first like a little white spot upon the skin, and spreads rapidly, until the whole body is covered with it, and becomes quite corpse-like. In this diseased flesh there are formed swelling tumours, which in due time burst, and become hideous running sores. The hair and the extremities of the fingers and the toes fall off. In one word, the living man carries about with him all the horrors which, in the case of other men, lie hidden beneath the mould of the tomb.

Moreover, the leper, in his wretched state, has none of those consolations which lighten the burthen of other diseases. He is banished from his home; he is driven out from among his friends and kinsfolk; he is forced to herd with wretches stricken like himself by this terrible scourge of God. His neighbours and acquaintances pass him by with shuddering horror; and the stranger who incautiously approaches is scared away by the startling cry which the law compels the leper to raise: 'Approach not. I am unclean.' Worst of all, he is without hope; for though, from the ceremonial law of the Jews, it appears that this disease may be healed, yet all who treat of it affirm that, up to the present time, its cure has proved to be beyond the reach of human skill. Thus the leper is condemned to a living death. He is an object of loathing to himself, and of horror to his fellow-men.

II. Now, though we see not among ourselves any who are afflicted with this leprosy of the body, yet there are not a few among the sons of men whose souls are covered with the leprosy of sin. Their spiritual being presents to the eyes of God and of His Angels a spectacle as revolting and as hideous as the running sores and gaping wounds of these leprous outcasts presented to the eyes of their contemporaries. Therefore, beware of sin; but especially beware of that sin which is branded with the epithet 'unclean,' or you will speedily become loathsome and abominable to God. I say, beware! For do not imagine that you are safe from the infection of its virulent poison, because you are fenced in from contagion by the walls of the College. The devil found his way into Paradise, and it is vain to hope or to expect that any amount of vigilance can bar him out from institutions, the chief aim of which is to train up men to defeat and trample him under foot.

He will steal in like a thief in the night, and if he can but infect *one* soul with his poison, he will be content. For the chances are that the evil will spread. Like leprosy, it will show itself at first as a little spot, in the guise of an indelicate word. Flee away, then, with as much terror as if you heard the leper's cry: 'Avaunt! I am unclean.' If you suffer that word to rest in your imagination, it may take possession of your heart, and infect it so deeply, that all the foul following of the unclean devil will rush in and dwell there.

Oh! would that, like leprosy, this spiritual uncleanness could be easily detected! Then we might separate, and cast out the tainted from among those who are sound and healthy. Then might we prevent the infection of this subtle plague from working any mischief in the hearts of the young. For so great a horror of it would spring up in the breasts of all, that they would shun everything that might communicate its poison to their souls.

III. Whither, then, must you flee, if you wish to escape this horrible leprosy of uncleanness? What must you do, if, being tainted ever so slightly therewith, you desire to check its rapid and destructive advance? There is but one physician who is able to purge the impure taint from your blood, and that is Jesus Christ—' Lord, if Thou willest, Thou canst make me clean.' The remedy which He will give is not the mere contact of His sacred hand, nor the miraculous power of His efficacious word. It is His own most precious body and blood.

Therefore, like the leper, hasten to Jesus. Little children, so dear to the sacred heart, do you especially run to Him, that being shielded by His loving arm, and strengthened by His body and blood, you may be able to live untainted, even while breathing the infected atmosphere of this world. Go confidently, and with great love, to His holy Table; He calls upon His ministers not to drive you back; not to keep you away from Him. 'Suffer them,' He says, 'to come unto

Me.' It is only by clinging closely to Him, by nestling in His bosom, that your spotless robe can be preserved from stain, and your feet be made to trample upon the asp and the basilisk.

But should any child be so unfortunate as to have his heart already tainted with this dreadful leprosy, let him also run to Jesus. Let him cast himself down in all humility at the feet of Him Who never yet spurned the poor sinner from His presence, and then, with a heart full of sorrow, and a soul conscious of its shame, let him cry out to Him: 'Lord, if Thou willest, Thou canst make me clean.' You may be sure that He will stretch forth His hand—not simply to touch you, but to give you His body and blood. That remedy, and that only, both can and will make you clean.

FOURTH SUNDAY AFTER EPIPHANY.

TEMPTATION.

'Behold a great tempest arose in the sea, so that the boat was covered with waves, but He was asleep.'—ST. MATT. viii. 24.

I. AFTER a long day of wearisome labour by the Sea of Galilee, Jesus with His Apostles entered a boat, and bade them launch forth and make for the opposite shore of the lake. The mental toil of preaching and of teaching the people had so exhausted Him, that He laid Himself down upon one of the boat's cushions in the afterpart of the vessel, and fell asleep.

While the little bark ploughed her way towards the point indicated by Our Lord, the sky became overcast; dark masses of cloud loomed heavy and threatening over the hilltops, and the wind, rushing with impetuous violence down the profound ravines and wild gorges at the head of the lake, lashed its waters into fury, till they rose in foaming billows around the frail vessel, and dashing over it, filled it well-nigh unto sinking. The uproar of the elements did not awaken Jesus. While the hardy fishermen strained every nerve to right their little ship and bale out the invading waters, He slept calmly, as if unconscious of the peril which threatened them.

Every moment, however, the violence of the storm increased. At last the Apostles, seeing their efforts unavailing, woke Our Lord with that wild cry of fear: 'O Lord, save us; we perish!' Jesus arose at this appeal, and looking upon their white, terror-stricken faces, visible even amid the gathering darkness of the stormy night, rebuked them for their little faith; and then, stretching forth His hand over the tumultuous waters, which leaped and foamed around, He commanded them to be still. Straightway the wind fell, the surface of the lake became smooth as a mirror, and the little boat lay motionless upon its unruffled bosom. Seeing this astounding marvel, gratitude and astonishment took the place of fear in the minds of the Apostles, and, whispering to one another, they said: 'What manner of man is this, for the winds and the sea obey Him?'

II. In this miracle there is put before you an excellent image of your earthly career. For your frail, corruptible body is, as it were, the little bark which bears your soul across the wind-swept ocean of life, on which you are sure to encounter many a storm. It is, therefore, of the highest importance that you should be prepared for their coming. But nowhere can this preparation be made with greater facility, and with a more certain prospect of a successful issue, than within the precincts of your College. For the College is a miniature of the great world which lies beyond its walls. That world is the ocean on which you will have to sail; the College is an enclosed and sheltered haven, in which you may learn to navigate the storm-tossed ocean, and to pass with safety over its raging billows. For, though that haven is sheltered from the furious surges of the angry sea, yet it is not without storms and tempests of its own, which will serve to prepare you for the more serious and dangerous trials of the world.

These storms of school-life arise from two different causes: first, from the circumstances which surround you, and from the people with whom you live; and secondly, from the weakness of your own heart. Your companions, for instance, are not what you would wish them to be. They are perhaps rough, ill-tempered, and unkind. Their treatment of you is harsh and unfeeling. They taunt you with bitter words; they meet you with sour looks; they harass you with much petty tyranny. Again, college discipline weighs heavily upon you. Study is distasteful; masters are rigorous and exacting; in fact, all things seem to be awry—out of harmony with your notions of what is right and becoming.

But these are not the only storms that come to ruffle the tranquillity of your soul. There are others, arising from your own heart, far more grievous and dangerous. The devil knows well of what frail material you are made. He knows how easily that fund of concupiscence within you may be stirred up and set in motion; and therefore his constant aim is to lash it into fury by a perfect whirlwind of evil thoughts, in order that your soul may be swallowed up and lost amid the raging waters of ungoverned passions. To effect this, he will leave nothing untried, and his onslaught will be as sudden and as violent as are the storms which sweep down upon the Sea of Galilee. It is by bearing yourself manfully during these lesser trials that you will acquire the coolness, the steadiness of purpose, and the energy, which will carry you safely through the more serious difficulties and perils of your after-life.

III. In common with the Apostles, you possess one great advantage, one earnest of success, and that is, the company of Jesus Christ. In Holy Communion, He enters the vessel of your body, to make it firm and strong; He unites Himself to your soul, to make it courageous; and He is ever within easy call, that you may apply to Him when the waves arise and threaten to overwhelm you.

Therefore, be not afraid. Every Sunday morning, and oftener if you please, the Lord Who rides upon the whirlwind, and guides the spirit of the storm, comes into your heart. He comes to remain with you, bodily for a time, but spiritually for ever, if you will not drive Him thence by sin. While that actual bodily presence and union last, lay before Him all the storms which have burst upon you during the week; ask Him to be with you during the week which is to come, and to give you nerve and calm courage to meet bravely, and to conquer resolutely, every difficulty.

Remember that as Our Lord slept, and seemed to be unconscious of the peril which threatened the Apostles, so will He at times appear to hide His face from you. The storm will rage around you, and lash the sides of your little vessel. You will cry to Him, but He will seem deaf to your petitions. You will find no sweetness in the service of God, but rather disgust and weariness. Still, be not faint-hearted; cry aloud to Jesus, for He has not left you; He only sleepeth, to try your faith and patience. Be vigilant, persevere, call Him more earnestly, and He will at last show Himself. He will rebuke the angry storm, and say: 'Be thou still,' and there will ensue a great calm.

FIFTH SUNDAY AFTER EPIPHANY.
THE SOWER OF TARES.
'An enemy hath done this.'—ST. MATT. xiii. 28.

I. OUR Lord Himself explained the parable which is read on this day. 'The field,' said He, ' is the world; the wheat are all the good; the tares, the wicked; and the enemy who scattered tares among the good wheat is the devil.' It is therefore an easy matter to apply this to your own life, and learn the lesson which He intended it to convey. Your College, as you have already been told, is your little world. Your young hearts are the soil, in which the various professors are striving to plant both science and virtue. Their aim is to make you, first of all, and before everything else, good men; and then, if you have the ability, learned men. With this twofold object in view, they labour incessantly to instruct you, and to teach you how to develop the powers of your mind.

But all important in their eyes, as this object undoubtedly is, it is nevertheless secondary to the still greater and nobler purpose for which you are in the world, namely, to fit yourselves to be citizens of God's glorious kingdom. Hence they consider that the work of education is a failure, unless they have succeeded in teaching you to love virtue, and in inspiring you with the determination to be good men. They endeavour, therefore, to instil sound principles into your minds; they set before you the holy example of their own lives; and when they go to offer up the Holy Sacrifice, they bear you in their hearts before the altar of God, and pray that He Who giveth the increase may make their labours fruitful in your souls. They are glad, and rejoice as they see you springing up around them, with the grace of God sparkling in your eyes, and giving promise of a bright future.

But alas! there are times when their hearts are made heavy and sad with grief. For, they perceive here and there, on certain individuals among you, a blight which makes them fear for the future. The look of these boys has changed. 'It is not as yesterday and the day before.' There is sparkling in their eyes a light which we professors shudder to behold, for it is the reflection of a fire in their hearts most difficult to extinguish. We sigh, and ask with sorrow, not unmingled with indignation : ' Did we not sow good seed in this child ? Whence, then, hath he this crop of vice ?' Alas! the answer must too often be: ' An enemy hath done this.' *' Inimicus homo, hoc fecit.'*

II. Now, you will naturally enough wish to know who is this enemy, that so fearfully mars the surpassing beauty of God's grace in the souls of young boys like yourselves. We answer that, in your case, as in the case of grown-up men, it is the devil—but the devil, be it observed, working in such a way as not to let himself be either known or seen. He is far too cunning to unmask himself; for, if men could only see him beneath the various clever devices by which they are lured into sin, they would flee away from them with unfeigned horror. It is, therefore, the devil's policy always to keep out of sight, and to work through secondary causes, which are not likely to excite suspicion. Hence, when he wishes to rob a college-boy of his innocence, he does not present himself in the shape of some gross and foul temptation from which the boy would turn with disgust. No; he frequently effects his purpose by the agency of one of his schoolfellows, whose heart he has already corrupted.

From the abundance of that unclean heart, the mouth will speak. Its words will not be merely rude, coarse, and ungentlemanly, but, like the source from which they spring, foul, filthy, and impure. They will impart the knowledge of evil, and that knowledge, once acquired, can never be forgotten. At first the poor child who hears them is startled by the novelty of the light which is flashed into his mind. Then the fire of concupiscence, till that moment only smouldering in his bosom, is fanned into a flame. How anxiously the Angels must watch the next step that he will take! Will he extinguish it, or will he add to it yet fresh fuel, till it break forth into a conflagration which will consume and destroy him? Alas! the latter is but too often the case, and the temple in which God made it His delight to dwell, is reduced to ashes.

How truly, then, does the Psalmist say of those who utter words of uncleanness: 'Their throat is like an open sepulchre; with their tongues they have dealt deceitfully; the venom of asps is under their lips.' With what good reason may not we also say, as we contemplate the ruin which they effect: 'An enemy hath done this!'

III. How, then, is this frightful evil to be detected and cast forth from the College? Its discovery, we must confess, is a task of no small difficulty, because filthy words do not leave any visible stain upon the lips, and a wicked boy often-times wears as joyous and innocent a look as one that is pure as an Angel. But though it is difficult to distinguish the bad from the good, yet the mere fact that they are living together in any School ought to inspire Superiors with so keen a spirit of vigilance as will render it well-nigh impossible for a wicked boy to infect an innocent one with the virulent poison rankling in his own breast.

Watchful supervision, then, is the first step that must be taken to preserve a School from this pestilent evil. Great care, however, is necessary in the use of supervision. It must be exercised in a large-hearted and kindly way, not in a narrow and suspicious way, otherwise it will defeat the very purpose for which it is employed, and be productive of endless mischief.

The next means is the cultivation, among the boys themselves, of right notions about their duties towards one another. Many boys imagine that they ought never to tell the Superiors of anything that takes place among themselves, and that they would be guilty of a dishonourable act if they did. This is incorrect. They should, therefore, be taught that in all cases in which the moral well-being of the School is in peril, not only is there nothing dishonourable in making known the culprit, but there is something highly commendable in so doing; furthermore, that there is even a strict obligation, binding in virtue of the mutual charity which they owe to one another, to acquaint the Superiors with his wickedness.

Lastly, a most effective measure for the suppression of this evil, is the maintenance among the boys themselves of a high-toned public opinion about these matters. They should never suffer to be uttered in their presence words which even border upon wickedness, without at once expressing their disapproval, and turning their backs upon the individual who has so far forgotten his dignity, both as a Christian and as a Catholic. These three means will effectually stop this evil, if it have once entered a College; and if it have not already done so, will prevent it from ever gaining a footing among the boys.

SIXTH SUNDAY AFTER EPIPHANY.

INFLUENCE OF A GOOD BOY.

'The kingdom of heaven is like to leaven, which a woman took and hid in three measures of meal, until the whole was leavened.'— ST. MATT. xiii. 33.

I. IN the thirteenth chapter of St. Matthew, from which the Gospel of this day is taken, Our blessed Lord puts before us, under various images, the glorious kingdom of His Church, and the work which it is destined to accomplish in the world. Like the sower, it scatters broadcast over the whole earth, the treasures of its divine teaching. Its children are of a mixed character, consisting both of good and of bad, like the wheat oversown with tares. Its rapid diffusion, and the purifying influence of its doctrine upon the morals of men, are typified by the growth of the mustard-seed, and by the effect of leaven upon the mass of dough. The priceless value of the truth which it teaches is represented by the hidden treasure and by the pearl of great price; while the final separation of the virtuous from the wicked is shown to us under the figure of a net let down into the sea, and taking thence fishes of every kind—the good being reserved for food, and the bad cast back again as utterly worthless.

It is upon the comparison of the Church to leaven that you must specially fix your attention, and learn a lesson which will be profitable to your soul. By leaven is meant a fermenting substance, which is put into the mass of dough to cause it to rise, and make it fit to become light and wholesome bread. Like the barm which we use for the same purpose, it penetrates into every portion of the mass, and gives to it its own flavour. So has it been with the doctrine of the Church. It took possession of the corrupt mass of humanity, it penetrated and diffused itself throughout its every part, purifying it from vice, sanctifying it with heroic virtue, and raising it almost to the same height as that whence it had fallen.

II. If we may compare great things with small, we may say that similar in its nature is the influence which a good boy will exercise at College upon those among whom his lot is cast. That influence will in many cases prove to be even more powerful than is that exercised by the masters. For though the prefect and the professors are men of undoubted virtue, yet the boys do not receive from them so great an impulse towards good as they do from one of themselves. The reason is not far to seek; for boys take it as a matter of course that their masters should be upright and virtuous. It is their profession. It is their duty, and a part of their office, to teach virtue to others. Not so with one of themselves. They have a keener appreciation of the difficulty which a boy experiences in being good; and when a holy boy is brought before their eyes, his conduct makes a deeper impression upon them than does the example of those who are raised so far above them. The possibility of being thoroughly virtuous is brought nearer home to them, and they very naturally ask themselves, 'Cannot we do what that boy is able to do?' Added to all this, there is the natural beauty inseparable from virtue, a beauty which powerfully attracts the hearts of the young.

But now comes the question which each of you is sure to ask: 'What do you mean by a good boy?' We mean, in the first place, one whose heart is pure; who scorns deceit and lying; who is honest and straightforward in all his dealings with others. He is one who, to the utmost of his power, endeavours to be holy, and for that purpose tries to be reverent in all duties pertaining to the service of God, and frequently approaches the Sacraments. In his studies he is diligent, and does not squander precious time in silly pursuits. He respects and observes the discipline established by Rule. Towards his companions he is kind, affable, and obliging; and in all that concerns their welfare and happiness, flinches not from the performance of actions which entail much self-denial.

This is what we should call a good boy; and we affirm, without hesitation, that he will be a centre from which there will spread throughout the School a spirit which will speedily work wonders in the way both of internal and of external reform among the boys.

III. The thought of the great good which you may do to others ought to incite you all, and especially those among you who are in the upper Forms, to lead so holy a life, both secretly in your own hearts and openly before men, as will keep up in the School a high moral tone, and foster among the boys a frank, manly spirit. For the boy who is internally pure of heart, and externally all that we have mentioned, acts first as a disinfectant upon the circle of his schoolfellows, and secondly as a spur to urge them on to virtue.

In the first place, he acts as a disinfectant; for though purity is an internal virtue, yet it never fails to make its presence felt. It throws around its possessor a charm which gains for him respect and love. It encircles him with that odour of sanctity which banishes every unholy thought and feeling. Hence his very presence is a check upon vice, and his person serves to show those who are tainted with the corruption of sin, by the contrast which it will force them to make between themselves and him, how vile and abominable is the vice by which they are enslaved.

In the next place, he acts as a spur to urge them on to virtue; for when they see his devotion at Holy Communion, and his careful preparation for the Sacrament of Penance, their own hearts will whisper to them that it is thence he imbibes his courage and his strength, and that if they wish to be what he is they must approach and draw from the same source. While they are gazing listlessly about during study-hours, and inviting by their idleness the attack of the unclean devil, their eyes will perchance fall upon him as he sits absorbed in his books, and his industry will smite their sluggishness with so keen a lash as to rouse them from their torpor. His observance of discipline, too, will make them show to it, at least now and then, some little respect.

The whole School, moreover, will see that one can be a good Christian, and at the same time enjoy to the full all the happiness which many look for only in sin. For everyone will perceive that no one is more loved, respected, and sought after than the virtuous boy; because his heart, being free from care, makes him an excellent companion, full of merriment and of fun, eager to help others by sharing with them the happiness of his own breast.

Therefore let each boy, when he approaches Holy Communion, ask for those virtues which will make him a source of edification to his schoolfellows. Let him beg of Our Lord to give him a clean heart, from which will proceed pure thoughts, holy desires, and harmless words. Let him pray for diligence at his work; for a will to be obedient to authority; for a heart full of kindness and charity towards his companions. With all earnestness ask for these virtues; in your daily life try to put them in practice; and, like the leaven which the woman hid in three measures of meal, your holy influence will spread itself through the School.

SEPTUAGESIMA SUNDAY.
THE OBJECT OF COLLEGE LIFE.
'Go ye also into my vineyard.'—ST. MATT. xx. 4.

I. UNDER the figure of a vineyard Christ speaks this day of His Church, into which all are called to work for a reward, which is life everlasting. Some are labouring for this from their earliest childhood; others begin it in manhood; and not a few undertake this all-important task when their sun of life is setting, and the dark night of death is fast closing in around them. The great and common work which occupies each in that vineyard is the cultivation or sanctification of his own soul. But though the end which each has in view is the same, yet the means by which it is accomplished are various and different. In your own case, the means for your sanctification is a due attention to your education; and your education, as you doubtless know very well, is a work having two sides to it—the one moral, the other intellectual. Consequently, if you wish to make it a thoroughly finished work, you must ever keep this idea firmly fixed in your minds—that the cultivation both of your moral and of your intellectual nature is, for the present, the task which you have to accomplish in the vineyard of the Lord.

Your head and your heart are, so to speak, the soil which you have to plough, to harrow, and to sow; for, like the earth, they share in that primeval curse which dooms them to sterility, and makes them capable of producing nothing but ignorance and sin. Their cultivation is consequently a *work*, and a painful work. It is a *work*—a *labour*. Bear this well in mind. It is a part of that penance imposed on man for his transgression. For, immediately after his sin, God told him that, in consequence of his disobedience, the earth should not yield him any fruit except that which he should wring from it by the labour of his hands. So also is it with your intellectual and your moral nature. They will not yield you any harvest of learning or of virtue unless they be worked and made fertile by the sweat of your brow. Very little reflection will serve to convince you of this truth, and show you the necessity for serious and unremitting labour in this work of works.

II. In the first place, then, your moral nature or your heart needs cultivation; for it is a soil fruitful in nothing but briars, thorns, and thistles. You are, therefore, set over it, as God set the Prophet Jeremias over His people—' To root up and to pull down, and to waste and to destroy, and to build and to plant.' That is to say, to work at it with much labour, till you have cleared it of its rank growth of noxious weeds, and made it fruitful in all that is good. For you very soon perceive that its natural fruit is evil. Scarcely has the child entered upon the period of boyhood, than evil begins to show itself. There is a giddiness, amounting almost to recklessness, which leads him into a thousand misdemeanours. To hide these, and escape the punishment due to them, there spring up in his heart a craft and cunning fertile in slyness, deceit, and lies. He begins to worship self, to plot and to scheme, in order to obtain whatever is gratifying to his pride, and to shun whatever thwarts and contradicts his ease or his humour. He manifests violent passion, and rages furiously against both persons and things that dare to cross him. Not unfrequently, also, there is evident amid all this the first germs of impurity.

Therefore, bear in mind that a very important part of the work for which you have been sent to College is to learn how to root up these first-fruits of your corrupt nature. You have come to rid yourself of giddiness, and to plant in its stead a spirit of thoughtfulness. If you detect any inclination to deceit, to double-dealing, or to lying, do not spare yourself, but labour assiduously to cast out of your heart these dishonourable vices. Curb your bad temper by bearing patiently with the crosses which are very often the just punishment of your faulty character. Be ever ready to do for your companions little services which will cost you some slight inconvenience, and this abnegation will help to make you unselfish. But, above all things—for your own sake, for the sake of your family, for God's sake—ever hold in utter abhorrence whatever savours of uncleanness. Keep your heart free from that abomination of desolation, and your soul will become a fruitful soil, yielding rich harvests of virtue most pleasing to God.

III. In the next place, your work is to cultivate your intellect. The curse of the fall lies as heavily upon it, as it does upon the physical world around us, and upon the moral nature of man. It is without nerve, without power to do anything much except to fall into error. Ignorance enfolds it as with a pall, and causes it to stumble about in the dark, from one abyss of intellectual folly into another. Yet, bad as its condition may be, it is not utterly hopeless. For the intellect may be strengthened; the dusky pall be lifted from before its eye; and the light be made to shine upon, and guide it in the way of knowledge.

But, in order to effect this, much hard labour must be expended upon it. For the present, at least, that labour is intended, not so much to supply the intellect with a fund of knowledge which it does not possess, as to make it apt to acquire knowledge. In one word, it is to sharpen its faculties, and to render them capable of acting with all of power that is in them, upon the difficult matters which, at some future day, may be submitted to their examination. At present they cannot fix themselves steadily upon any given subject. They cannot retain the impressions of the thoughts presented to them; they cannot reason upon them. Why is this? It is because, through want of cultivation, the mind is giddy, shallow, inaccurate, and narrow. But the training to which you are subjected at College will remedy these defects. You are made to commit much to memory, till that faculty acquires a facility in fixing itself upon, and in retaining the words, the images, and the ideas which are put before it. You are made to work out slowly, from an unknown language, the thoughts of other men, and are, consequently, forced to hang for hours over words and sentences, till you have thoroughly mastered the ideas and the sentiments which they express. You are made to study the difficult problems of Mathematics, till you acquire the power of following out an intricate chain of reasoning, and the habit of accepting nothing upon the mere assertion of anyone.

The outcome of all this training, will be the acquisition by the mind of that power of attention, of concentration, and of grasp, a power which will enable it to go forth into the wide field of knowledge, and gather in from every side a rich harvest of science, profitable to itself, to others, and to the Church of God. Labour, therefore, with much earnestness at the task set before you. Go manfully through the heat and the burthen of the day; for the cool eventide will come at last, and the Master of the vineyard will pay unto you that exceeding great reward, which He reserves for all those who serve Him faithfully and well.

SEXAGESIMA SUNDAY.

THE SOWER AND THE SEED.

'The seed is the word of God.'—ST. LUKE viii. 11.

I. THE duty which your Superiors look upon as the most important in the high office committed to their charge, is that of sowing in your minds and hearts this seed of the divinely-inspired word. To teach you the sciences, and to send you forth into the world with an intellect as highly cultivated as its powers will admit, is, without doubt, an object of their earnest care. Yet, bearing in mind that the end for which God created man is not that he may become learned, they deem the mission intrusted to them unfulfilled, unless they have laboured with all their might to teach you to love and serve Him in this life, that so you may gain the one thing necessary—the possession of Him in the next. Hence, they are ever exhorting, entreating, and, if need be, reproving you. They are earnest, both in season and out of season, being ever spurred on to indefatigable zeal by the importance of the task which they have undertaken, and the rigorous account which they will have to give to Jesus Christ for the soul of each of you.

Hence their earnestness in teaching you to love God. This is why they do their best to paint sin before your eyes in its true colours. They bid you shun it as the most insidious and treacherous enemy that you have. They are ever watchful to keep you away from any person or from any thing that might be the occasion of entangling you in its meshes. They are always preaching to you the necessity for prayer. They exhort you to be honest, upright, and straightforward; to hate lying, double-dealing, cunning, and deceit; to love purity; to avoid with scrupulous care whatever might rob you of that priceless treasure, and to fight bravely and manfully against corrupt nature till, with the help of God's grace, you subdue it, and bring it into complete subjection.

II. You may ask, therefore, how it is that, in spite of all this care, there are occasionally some wicked boys to be met with at College. It cannot be that the word of God is at fault; it is good seed, full of power to strike its roots down deeply, to spread widely, and to bring forth fruit a hundredfold. Nor is it any want of diligence on the part of those who sow the seed. The fault, then, must be in the souls into which the seed is cast. Our Saviour mentions four kinds of ground, upon which the sower casts his seed: the wayside; stony ground; ground covered with thorns and brambles; and lastly, good ground.

Among college boys there are always to be found some whose hearts resemble the various kinds of soil which received the good seed.

First, there are boys whose hearts are like the wayside, beaten hard by oft-repeated sins, which have made them almost as impervious to grace as is 'the nether mill-stone.' They have become a public thoroughfare; all sorts of thoughts and desires are allowed to pass through them. When, therefore, the seed of God's word falls upon them, it does not penetrate, but is quickly snatched up by the evil spirits who hover round.

Then there are boys whose hearts resemble a rock, covered with a very thin layer of soil. These are weak, irresolute beings, who would like to be good, but who have not the courage to be so. They cannot resist evil, nor think, nor act for themselves. A sneering word, or a cold look, is enough to make them forsake God. The seed falls into their hearts, springs up, but, having no moisture, either quickly withers, or is blown away in the time of storm and temptation.

Again, there are boys whose natures are generous and noble; they are full of good impulses and high aspirations. But, as if to counteract these, they have strong passions, which they have not striven to control; rather, they have suffered them to get the upper hand of them, and are held in so slavish a bondage by them that they habitually fall into sin. These receive with joy the holy word of God. They form great and magnanimous resolutions, and, what is more, they keep them for some time. But the evil habits in which they have entangled themselves master their better nature, and hold them glued down in the mire of their vices.

III. Lastly, there is the boy whose heart is like the good soil, deep and rich, rid of stones, and thorns, and briars. He receives the word of God, the religious teaching of his masters, with a holy joy. That word penetrates into his soul. It strikes its roots deeply; it shoots up and spreads abroad, and brings forth fruit a hundredfold. Look at him, and behold the beauty, the richness, and the inestimable value of that fruit. Observe him during the time of prayer, whether he is in the study or in the chapel. His eyes either are on his book, or are closed to keep out distractions. His heart is fenced round with the memory of the divine presence; and whether he prays alone, or in company, no untimely nor unbecoming thought is suffered to disturb the sweet communion of his soul with God. Modesty clothes him as with a garment of honour, and the sweet odour of sanctity clings about his person like an indefinable perfume, making his companions to feel 'how beautiful with glory is the chaste generation.' He hates sin. He shuns the company of those who might be a source of danger to him. He is upright and straightforward. He scorns deceit and lying. He is brave and generous; and because his heart is the temple of God, it is full of charity and of kindly feelings towards all, without exception.

But do not for a moment suppose that the soil of his heart has been made fruitful without any labour or any trouble on his part. Like the heart of everyone else, it lay under the curse of Adam's sin. Of itself, it could bring forth naught but evil. Therefore, like a barren soil, it needed much labour and patient care. Nothing daunted by the difficulty of the task before him, he set vigorously to work, and, aided by the grace of God, made it what you now see it. He plucked up the weeds and the thorns; he cast out the stones; he filled up the hollows. Then he received the word with joy. He watched over it with care. He hindered it from being uprooted by the devil. He drove off the enemy who would have oversowed it with tares, and now he brings forth for God virtues which make him an object upon which the Lord from His throne in heaven looks down with boundless satisfaction.

Try, therefore, to be good soil. Enrich the barrenness of your hearts, by frequently planting in them the body and blood of Jesus Christ. This will speedily make them fruitful, and enable them to yield a golden harvest, which God will store up in His heavenly garners.

QUINQUAGESIMA SUNDAY.
BLIND BARTIMEUS.
'Lord, that I may see.'—ST. LUKE xviii. 41.

I. MANY of you have, no doubt, seen some poor creatures either standing at the church doors, or sitting by the wayside, whom accident, or disease, or natural defect, has deprived of sight. They are crushed beneath the double burthen of blindness and of poverty. They stretch forth their hands, and raise their piteous cry, to attract the attention, and to move the charity of the passers-by. The face of nature has become for them one vast blank. The golden sunshine is changed into murky night. The bright landscape, with its gay colour, its varied light and shade, its hills and plains, its waving cornfields and sparkling river, is wiped out, and is as if it were not. Friends, kindred, and brethren, are but so many voices. Their faces, which might say so much that the tongue leaves unsaid, are concealed from them by a darkness thicker than the blackest night. They hear the footsteps of the passers-by, and occasionally feel upon their palm the coin which they toss to them; but all the while they sit in darkness—we might almost say in the shadow of death.

Such a man was Bartimeus, who sat begging by the wayside which led into Jericho. But what is this that makes him quickly turn his head, and roll his sightless eyes in vain? It is the tramp of a great multitude advancing towards the city. He is filled with wonder to know what the unusual concourse may mean; and, raising his voice, inquires the reason from the foremost of the throng. Then his ear is greeted with the glad tidings, that Jesus of Nazareth is passing by. At the sound of that blessed name, his heart gives one exulting bound within him. This is that great wonder-worker, Whose touch has healed even leprosy, Whose voice has cast out devils, Whose shadow has driven away disease. Bartimeus is filled with faith and confidence; and lifting up his voice, tremulous with emotion and eagerness, he cries aloud: 'Jesus, Son of David, have mercy upon me!' The people bid him hold his peace; but he, nothing daunted, continues to cry out for mercy unto Him upon Whom no one hath ever called in vain.

Jesus, hearing his plaintive voice, stops in His onward progress, and orders him to be brought into His presence. One of the bystanders, therefore, straightway led him by the hand, and brought him face to face with Our Lord. The Redeemer, with voice as gentle, as reassuring, as compassionate as a mother's, asks him: 'What willest thou that I do unto thee?' And he said: 'Lord, that I may see.' Then Jesus said to him: 'Receive thy sight; thy faith hath made thee whole.'

II. Like Bartimeus, each of you may be said to be sitting by the wayside begging, and the alms which you ask is light: 'Lord, that I may see.' You are here at College to have the eyes of your intelligence opened, that you may be able to see things aright. From whom, then, may you, with greater propriety, ask this boon than from Jesus Christ, 'the Light of lights, that shineth in the darkness, and enlighteneth every man that cometh into this world?' You may, perhaps, think because you are young, and unknown to the world—unknown to many of even your schoolfellows —that therefore you are unknown to God. But this is not so. He knows you better than you know yourself, and will gladly make you share in that knowledge. What you need is to see yourself as He sees you, and then in very truth will the eyes of your intelligence be opened. Cry, therefore, unto Him, as Bartimeus did: 'Jesus, Son of David, have mercy upon me.' He will not pass you by. He will stand and say: 'My child! what wouldst thou have Me do to thee?' Then, from the very bottom of your heart, say to Him: 'Lord, that I may see.'

You want to see your weakness, in order that you may distrust your own unaided exertions. You need to be made conscious how utterly unable you are, without God's grace, to be upright, or truthful, or pure. You do not see the dangers which everywhere surround you. You do not understand the terrible malice of sin. You are not fully alive to the great malice there is in even a deliberate venial sin. Ask, therefore, to see all these things; and especially ask that your eyes may ever be kept open to this great truth— that you are in this world to save your immortal soul. If you lose sight of this, you will stumble about in worse than Egyptian darkness, and grope as the blind are wont to grope at mid-day.

III. Again, during study hours, let this prayer of Bartimeus frequently ascend from your heart; for, in answer to it, God will remove from your mental eyes that intellectual blindness, which veils from them the light of knowledge. You must not, however, either suppose or expect that He will do this for you in some miraculous manner, without any co-operation on your part. This is not the ordinary way of His providence, for He will have you first employ the usual means for removing mental blindness, and when you have done all that lies in your power, He will supplement what is wanting, and make your efforts fruitful.

The various branches which you are made to study, are the means for dispelling from the mind the darkness of ignorance. They do for its faculties what games and athletic sports do for the body; for they call forth and develop whatever of mental vigour there is in you, just as either cricket or football develops and strengthens the muscles of your bodily frame.

But, as we saw in our last lecture, the diligent use of these means is a part of that labour which is imposed upon man in punishment of sin; and, being a labour, it will at times be wearisome, and, like a load of lead, weigh heavily upon you. You will be made to feel, in spite of even unremitting toil, that you are intellectually blind, and need someone to aid you to remove the scales which obscure your vision. It is in moments like these that the cry of Bartimeus should rise from your heart—' O Lord, that I may see!'

God is intelligence itself. It is by His co-operation that our minds are able to understand. Therefore, ask Him with confidence, with earnestness, and with perseverance to give you intellectual sight. Now, what more opportune occasion can there be for presenting your petition than that happy moment when He comes to be your guest in Holy Communion? It is then that He enters your heart, and asks, with the loving affection of the tenderest of fathers, 'What willest thou that I do unto thee?' At that joyful moment remember your intellectual difficulties, and beg Him graciously to give you light to see your way through them.

Also, when actually engaged in mental labour, frequently invoke the aid of the Holy Spirit. While committing lines to memory, ask Him to make that memory quick and retentive. When you find yourself either entangled in the mazes of a Greek chorus, or brought to a dead stop before some involved and obscure passage in your Latin author, breathe forth that earnest prayer, 'Lord, that I may see!' If you are puzzled by some intricate problem in Mathematics, or if you are trying in vain to think out some theme which has been set for an English essay, cease not to say, with the Psalmist, 'O Lord, enlighten Thou my darkness.' Do this perseveringly, and you will find that your lively faith and childlike trust in God will meet with their reward.

FIRST SUNDAY OF LENT.
THE TEMPTATION OF OUR LORD.

'Then Jesus was led by the Spirit into the desert, to be tempted by the devil.'—ST. MATT. iv. 1.

I. ST. CHRYSOSTOM, commenting upon this passage, says that the Holy Spirit led Jesus into solitude in order to attract the notice of the devil, and give him an opportunity to try Our Lord; not, indeed, for the purpose of testing His virtue, which we know is beyond proof, but of teaching us how to quit ourselves like valiant soldiers in the warfare of life. The devil accordingly attacked Him in solitude; for it is when men are alone and unoccupied that his evil suggestions most easily find an entrance into their minds. Observe, also, that he began his assault when Christ had fasted forty days, in order that, taking Him at His weakest moment, he might the more easily effect His overthrow. But as the tempter knew not whether Christ was really God, or only a man of surpassing virtue, he tried Him by those three great temptations which, for the impressionable hearts of men, possess attractions that are apparently irresistible.

Therefore, drawing nigh to Our Lord, he said: 'If thou be the Son of God, command that these stones be made bread.' By these words he appealed to the sensitive appetite of Jesus, and put before His mind what at that moment seemed most needful for the sustenance of His life. To have complied with the tempter's suggestion would have shown a want of confidence in God, upon Whom Jesus, as Man, relied with unbounded trust for the supply of His temporal necessities.

In the next place, setting Him upon a pinnacle of the Temple, he bade Him cast Himself down, in order that the admiration of the people, when they saw Him miraculously upheld by the Angels of God, might stir up within Him vain glory and pride.

Lastly, by offering Him all the wealth, the magnificence, and the power of the world, if He would bow down and adore him, he appealed to that natural greed for worldly pomp and greatness, which impels men to labour incessantly with that patient zeal, untiring energy, and dogged perseverance, which are so conspicuously absent from their pursuit of far nobler and more worthy objects. But Jesus rejected all the baits held out before Him, and then routed His adversary with a contemptuous 'Begone, Satan!' which he dared not disobey.

II. If you keep the memory of this astounding scene ever fresh in your mind, you will not dare to repine or to complain when you are attacked and cruelly tempted by the devil. For if he ventured to suggest evil to the Son of God, we need not be surprised that he should lay his snares before the feet of mortal men. It is enough, therefore, for the disciple that he should be as his Master, and for the servant that he should be as his Lord. God, for His own wise ends and for our good, ordains it so, and tells us by the mouth of the Wise Man that when we come to the service of God we must stand in fear, and prepare our soul to encounter the temptations of the devil.

The trials to which you will be subjected will most probably come upon you in the same order as that in which they are narrated by the Evangelist. The devil will very likely try first to stir up that fund of sensuality which is within you, and make it rebel against the spirit. For you have now come to an age when the sensitive appetite, which ever seeks for pleasure, is fully alive within you, and manifests its existence not only by making you shrink from all trouble and pain, but by causing you to crave for that which in present circumstances the law of God, as well as right reason, most emphatically forbids. Before this appetite the devil will display, in their most seductive forms, all the sinful pleasures of a corrupt and wicked world. Fallen nature, looking with a covetous eye upon these, will urge you to accept them; and the law of God, written in your heart, to reject them with the disgust and the scorn which they deserve. Hence arises that mortal conflict between the flesh and the spirit—a conflict which so wearies and perplexes upright men that they long to be set at liberty from the body of this death. For they have to struggle, not against enemies of flesh and blood, who, when stricken down, cease to do mischief, but against spirits of darkness whose name is legion, who are never weary, never disheartened, but who still continue to fight on, till their adversaries have passed out of this world of conflict, and have received upon their brows the victor's crown of immortal glory.

III. In the next place, the tempter will try to entangle you in the meshes of vain glory. God may perhaps have given you great mental abilities, which enable you easily to outstrip all rivals in the race for intellectual distinction. Out of these gifts of God the devil will contrive a snare. He will paint before your eyes splendid visions of fame and glory which may be realized by these talents, lent to you from the treasury of God; and these phantoms will try to entice you from the narrow way, and lure you onwards to destruction, in the vain attempt to clutch their shadowy forms.

Later in life, ambition will beckon you to tread the steep and rugged path which leads to power and wealth, in order that you may satisfy your greed for these, as well as for the empty pageantry of earthly glory. The devil will promise all that a glowing imagination can picture to itself, if you will only bow down and adore him by setting at naught the holy law of God. That law, seemingly, is the only obstacle that blocks the way to power and wealth and glory. He tells you that you cannot clutch the glittering prizes which are so nearly within your grasp till it is removed. Only sweep it aside by one act of the will, and all these are yours.

This, in short, is the trial to which the devil will subject you. But, grievous as it is, still do not faint under it. Bear in mind, when he offers you the swinish food of sensual pleasures, that this garbage will never satisfy the cravings of your immortal soul. It may for a time intoxicate and stupefy it, but when the soul awakes from its debauch and sees the degradation into which it has fallen, anguish unutterable lays hold of it, and mercilessly rends it like some savage beast of prey.

Remember, also, that glory is a phantom. If you pursue it, it will lead you through rough ways, and along the brink of frightful precipices, and up to giddy heights where the head swims and the knees tremble; but when at last you stretch forth your arms to clasp it to your bosom and hold it as your lawful prize, you will find that you have infolded nothing but the empty air.

As for wealth and power, they are so worthless, that they forced one who had as much of them as earth could give, to cry out at last, with an almost despairing heart: 'Vanity of vanities, and all is vanity!'

Lose not sight of these great truths, but by frequent meditation keep them fresh in your mind and heart, and when Jesus comes to visit you in Holy Communion, ask Him to give you so great courage and strength that you may be able to prove yourself a worthy follower of your divine Captain—one who will ever rout His enemies with the words: 'Begone, Satan! The Lord thy God shalt thou adore, and Him only shalt thou serve.'

SECOND SUNDAY OF LENT.

ADVANTAGES OF COLLEGE-LIFE.

'Lord, it is good for us to be here.'—St. Matt. xvii. 4.

I. These were the words in which St. Peter gave expression to the ecstatic joy of his soul, when he beheld his Lord and Master transfigured before his eyes, and resplendent with the dazzling light of heavenly glory. That transfiguration had so entranced him, that he could do nothing more than express, in the simplest words, how good a thing it was to be there, contemplating that vision of wondrous beauty. Like him, you will break forth into the same joyous exclamation, if you reflect upon the many blessings of which you are made partakers, by being subjected to the salutary discipline of college-life. That life, if you will but take advantage of its opportunities, will make you so virtuous and so learned—will give you so great a mastery over yourself, that those who may hereafter be brought in contact with you will say: 'This is, in every sense of the word, a man.'

First of all, in point of virtue. The moral atmosphere of a well-regulated College is admirably adapted to nourish and develop the holy principles implanted in the hearts of young boys by their pious parents. For, besides the company and the example of the good, both which are powerful incentives to virtue, they are put under the guidance of men, whose constant aim is to impress upon their minds this first and most important principle—that they have come into the world, simply and solely to prepare themselves for a happy eternity.

As the most essential condition for securing this end is holiness of life, they are taught the necessity for having their hearts constantly imbued with its life-giving power. Hence it is that your Superiors keep your eternal destiny, as much as possible, before your eyes. They tell you that learning is but an instrument for helping you on in life—that it is a means to an end—not the end itself, or object for which you are to strive.

Your studies, as well as all your other occupations, are hallowed by prayer, and you are exhorted to employ it for all your necessities, whether they regard your soul or your body. You are taught not to gratify the ignoble cravings of corrupt nature, but to deny yourself, by refraining not only from wicked actions but from wicked thoughts, and from whatever could sully the purity of your heart. Pious reading, holy instruction, and good advice, like refreshing dew from heaven, keep your moral being ever strong and vigorous.

To crown all, there is at College frequent access to the

Sacrament of Penance, in which every stain is washed away. There, the young boy will always meet with a kind, loving, and compassionate father, to console him in his troubles, to counsel him in his doubts, to raise him if he have fallen, and to guide his feeble steps in the path which leads up heavenwards. Moreover, he may also frequently approach to eat the bread of life, which will strengthen him and enable him to resist the devil, to trample his evil suggestions under foot, and to triumph gloriously over fallen nature. You may therefore say with truth, because of the virtues which you are taught and which you may acquire at College: ' O Lord, it is good for us to be here!'

II. But, though this is the strongest reason which you have for rejoicing, and for giving God thanks that you are at College, yet there is another motive which, though inferior to the first, is nevertheless worthy of your most careful consideration. If you reflect upon it, your heart will overflow with grateful joy, and you will say with St. Peter: ' Lord, it is good for me to be here!' This is the opportunity which School or College affords you, for receiving a splendid education. Most boys take it so much as a matter of course that they are at College, that they scarcely ever give the magnitude of this benefit even a passing thought; and hence they rarely, if ever, thank God for this surpassing favour. Yet a stupendous favour it most certainly is, whether you regard it as a means for the development of your talents, or as a privilege which comparatively few are allowed to enjoy.

At College, every faculty that God has given you may be drawn out, strengthened, and made fit for the intellectual work which you may hereafter be called upon to perform. There are put into your hands the implements with which you may make your memory ready, tenacious, and faithful; your powers of perception keen; your taste correct; your judgment true; and your reason so well exercised, that it will be able to meet, and grapple with the more serious difficulties which it will have to encounter, when you go forth into the great world.

To have leisure for the cultivation of these faculties, is, as I have said, a privilege which few enjoy. Many of your own age, instead of being at School, are obliged to earn their daily bread; and while you are seated in your comfortable study, or are playing upon green lawns in the bright sunshine, or are resting beneath the shade of wide-spreading trees, they are shut up in murky offices, or in grim factories amid the incessant whir of machinery, under hard masters, and in the midst of companions whose conversation is neither pleasant nor edifying. Contrast your easy, happy lot, with their difficult and wretched life, and when you feel inclined to repine, to grumble, or to wish for the end of your career at College, reflect upon the blessings with which God has enriched you, and you will say from the bottom of your heart : 'Lord, it is good for me to be here!'

III. Finally, there exists in every School or College a wise code of disciplinary law, which plays no unimportant part in the great work of education. The purpose for which that code is enforced, is to stamp upon your character those qualities, which serve to enhance the virtue and the science, which you are at so much pains to acquire. In after-life, when you look back upon those laws which now perhaps are so irksome to you, you will on their account also confess 'that it was good for you to have been here.' A moment's reflection will convince you, that they force you to acquire habits which are necessary to make you a useful member of society, in that position in which it may please God to place you.

For, in the first place, they beget in you a habit of punctuality. They oblige you many times each day to be present in your place, in study, in class, in chapel, at a given moment which you must not anticipate, and after which you are not suffered to lag behind. They make you apply to certain studies, and forbid you to change them for others, or to invert their order. This cannot fail to give you a habit of perseverance in the performance of unsavoury work. In order to comply with the requirements of Rule, you have frequently to forego your own will; to stop in the middle of a game, or to interrupt a study which you would prefer to continue for some little time longer. Does not this accustom you to deny your own will, and help you to gain so great a command over yourself that nothing will be able to disturb you? Again, the very regularity with which you are compelled to perform all your actions, teaches you to be methodical, and gives you a love of order, the chief advantage of which will be that you will ever do the right thing, at the right time, and in the right place.

To crown all these advantages, you are taught to respect discipline, not merely for its utility, but chiefly because it is the expression of your Superior's will, which, if complied with through a motive of obedience, is by that motive supernaturalized, and made deserving of an eternal reward. Therefore, be careful frequently to thank God for the great privilege of being at College, and whenever you receive Him in Holy Communion, ask Him for grace to reap from your student-life all the advantages that have been enumerated, so that when you look back upon your college-life you will be able to say with truth: 'Lord, it was good for me to have been there!'

THIRD SUNDAY OF LENT.
THE RELAPSING SINNER.
'And entering in, they dwell there.'—ST. LUKE xi. 26.

I. WHEN Our Lord had cast out of that wretched man the dumb devil who had held him in bondage for so long a time, those who saw this act of divine power were filled with admiration. But some of Christ's enemies who also had been witnesses of it, though unable to deny the fact of the miracle, yet tried to render it useless as a proof of Our Lord's divine mission, by attributing it to the agency of devils. Jesus, however, speedily closed their malignant mouths by an argument which they could not gainsay, without exposing themselves to the ridicule of the crowd. 'Every kingdom,' said He, 'that is divided against itself, shall be brought to desolation. But, if Satan casts out Satan—as you say that he has done in the present instance—then is his kingdom at an end. This, however, cannot be the explanation of the act which I have just performed; for, as a strong man, armed and intrenched in his fortress, cannot be overcome, except by one who is still more powerful, so also Satan cannot be expelled except by One more mighty than he.'

Then He explained to His spellbound audience what the evil spirit does, when he is ejected from the soul of one over whom he has held sway. ' He goeth about seeking for rest, and not finding any, he saith: "I will go back to the house whence I came out."' When he is come, he findeth it cleansed from every stain, and adorned with the graces and the gifts of God. Then he goeth and taketh with him seven other spirits more wicked than himself, and they cease not to attack and molest that soul till either they are ignominiously routed, or, having once again persuaded it to throw open its doors to them, they enter it and dwell there.

See whether in these words Christ is not drawing a picture of what has happened in your own case. Boys sometimes come to School with evil habits, which they have contracted before they came; or while at School they meet with a wicked companion who teaches them evil; or they themselves, when tempted by the devil, yield to his suggestions. But the time of God's visitation comes, and then, by the words of the preacher during the solemn hours of a retreat, or by the voice of their Superior, or through the pages of some spiritual book, the Lord speaks to their hearts. Then the devil is cast out, and their souls, after being cleansed from the filth of sin, are adorned with God's choicest graces. For a time all goes on well. Soon, however, the evil spirit returns to test the sincerity of their conversion. But he comes not alone, for he now brings with him seven other spirits more wicked than himself; and if those boys break down during the assault, these devils will enter and take up their abode in their hearts.

II. How fearful is the state of a soul thus for the second time plunged into the mire, from which the merciful hand of God had drawn it forth! Its sin is now more grievous than it was before, because it is committed with greater knowledge and with more deliberation. The wound which it inflicts is more difficult to heal, because it is an old sore opened afresh. The dejection of mind, and the prostration of will power which it induces are harder to remove, because the sustaining force of hope is much diminished by this relapse into old disorders. But, if sin have grown into a habit by reason of oft-repeated falls, it will require little less than a miracle of grace to break up its empire over the heart. The poor sinner will make an effort to do so, but with only partial success. He will try again, and again will fail; and thus the greater part of his life will perhaps be nothing but a series of repentances and of relapses into sin. There is no apter figure of his miserable state than that wretched being in Hades, whose punishment it is, as poets say, to roll a mighty stone to the rugged hill-top, where it slips from his grasp and tumbles back again into the valley below.

This seems to be the task also of the relapsing sinner, who often tries to climb the mountain of God, but, losing his foothold, slips back and never reaches its summit. Oh, what a wretched existence must he drag wearily out in this unhappy world! He is ever promising, and never performing; ever making plans, and never carrying them into execution; ever feeling the pangs of penance, and never tasting of its ecstatic joys. If, then, any boy should find himself in this unhappy state, he must without delay search out the causes of it, and endeavour to remove them.

What are these causes? They are usually of two kinds: first, there are internal causes, which spring from the boy's own heart; secondly, there are external causes, which come from the persons and the things by which he is surrounded. Under the first head we may place that presumptuous confidence in his own strength—a confidence which springs up in his heart after a good retreat or a general confession. The natural effect of this presumption is to make him careless about keeping out of harm's way; he goes into danger, and perishes in it. Again, there is in all his religious duties a lukewarmness, which draws down upon him the displeasure of God, Who withholds from him that special protection which He grants to the fervent. Lastly, there is human respect, which makes him fearful of incurring the ridicule of the world.

The external causes which lead a boy back into sin are, on the one hand, all those persons and things that he knows from past experience to be what are called 'dangerous occasions'; and, on the other hand, there is the fellowship of the wicked. If, then, you wish to avoid a relapse into sin, you must carefully guard against the various causes which lead you into evil ways. Be vigilant; be brave; be prompt in resistance, and you will be preserved from again staining your soul with the filth from which you have been washed clean in the saving waters of penance.

III. You must not, however, imagine that the mere shunning of danger will altogether screen you from sin. True, it is a very efficacious means for escaping its polluting stain; but unless certain other precautions be taken, it will not suffice to preserve you from so frightful a calamity. These precautions shall now be set before you, and you will act wisely if you take them to yourself and store them up in the faithful memory, to be drawn thence and made use of in time of need.

In the first place, have a great distrust of yourself, because self-confidence is one of those pernicious weeds which bud forth in the heart after its conversion to God. The sweetness of His grace is then, ordinarily, so very great that the neophyte wonders how he could ever have taken delight in the husks of swine. He feels so strong that he imagines nothing will be able to move him from his fixed resolve. All this sensible fervour will, however, speedily pass away. Then the day of trial will come, when the enemy who has been ejected will return with sevenfold power, and lay siege to the heart. Therefore, distrust yourself, for your distrust will be your surest safeguard; because the consciousness of your own weakness will make you flee to God for strength; and this He will never refuse, if it be sought for by humble and earnest prayer.

In the next place, spiritual aid must be obtained from God through those two great channels of grace—the Sacraments of penance and the Most Holy Eucharist. The first conveys to the soul those cleansing waters which purge away the filth of sin; the second fortifies it with the Body and Blood of Jesus Christ. That food of Angels sanctifies the heart, and fills it with holy thoughts and pious affections. It chastens and purifies the body. It abates the fierce heat of concupiscence, and endows the will with power so great that it is able to subdue the rebellious flesh, and to hold in check the embattled forces of hell.

Therefore, have frequent recourse to Our Lord's life-giving Sacrament, in the refreshing waters of which you will be able to cool the burning heat of your youthful blood. As long as you neglect not to do this, there will be little fear of your relapsing into sin. For Jesus will hold you by the hand, as a father is wont to hold his little child. Either He will put to flight your bitterest foes as soon as they show themselves, or, if He suffer them to assault you, in order that you may win glory for yourself by routing them, He will stand by your side and cover you with His protecting hand. He will curb the strength of your adversaries, and never allow it to exceed your own. Thus guarded, and thus supported, you may be sure of victory. You will never again fall back into sin, and the evil spirit will never be permitted to enter your heart and dwell there.

FOURTH SUNDAY OF LENT.

MOTIVE FOR STUDY.

'Jesus therefore, when He knew that they would come and take Him by force, to make Him a king, fled again into the mountain, Himself alone.'—ST. JOHN vi. 15.

I. FROM the Gospel of St. Mark we learn that there were two reasons which urged Jesus to cross over the Sea of Galilee, and withdraw awhile from the publicity and the harassing labour of His missionary life. The first seems to have been the cruel murder of John the Baptist, whose head had been struck off in prison to salve over the wounded vanity of a malignant woman ; the second, that the Apostles might enjoy a little repose, for so great a number of persons had recourse to them that 'they had not so much as time to eat.' Jesus, accordingly, took ship, and, together with them, made for the opposite shore, where He intended to seek rest in the solitude of the mountains. But when the people learnt whither He intended to go, they set out for the same place, and, journeying round by the head of the lake, arrived at the spot where He must needs disembark, a short time before the vessel came to land. On reaching the shore, and seeing them gathered together to meet Him, He had compassion upon them, and, dismissing all thought of repose, spent the greater part of the day in preaching to them the word of God, and in healing their manifold infirmities.

When at last the evening drew nigh, the Apostles besought Him to dismiss the multitude to their homes, that they might buy bread to refresh themselves, for they had been listening to Him for a long time, and had had nothing to eat. Thereupon Jesus, after first trying their faith, bade them make the people sit down upon the grass. Then taking into His hands some bread, which it seems a boy had brought with him, He blessed it, and gave it to the Apostles to set before them. By a stupendous miracle, it multiplied in their hands, so as to be more than enough to satisfy the wants of the multitude, which numbered about five thousand.

As soon as the people saw what a wonder had been worked to relieve their necessities, their enthusiasm knew no bounds; they rushed forwards, to take Him in spite of Himself, and proclaim Him king. But Jesus, knowing their intention, fled from the honour which they wished to confer upon Him, and hid Himself in the solitude of the mountain.

II. This incident of Our Lord's life teaches us many lessons, chief among which is, perhaps, the loving care which God has for His children; for it shows us very clearly, that He literally fulfils His promise to those 'who seek first the kingdom of God and His justice ;' everything else that they desire is given unto them. But this is not the lesson which we would have you learn to-day; it is rather that which is contained in the concluding lines of the Gospel: 'Jesus hid Himself, and fled away into the mountain.' He shrank from the honour which they would have conferred upon Him, and withdrew from their sight. Now, what is your conduct when honour is put within your reach? Do you flee from it, deeming yourself unworthy of it? Do you not rather seek it with an eagerness amounting almost to the greed of passion? Do you not practically make the acquisition of it the *end* of your existence? Let us examine and see. In School or College there are three ways in which a boy may win distinction for himself: by studies, by games, and by social influence. We purposely leave virtue out of the question, because we hope that no boy will ever be so base as to cultivate it for the sake of the paltry honour which men can give.

Now, because these three things are the steps which lead schoolboys to eminence among their fellows, they are very often employed by them, not to accomplish the duty which they owe to God, but simply and solely to cover themselves with a transient halo of glory. Hence you shall see boys, who weary themselves well-nigh unto death in the pursuit of knowledge, in order to win the honour of being first in their School, to carry off the prize, and to have the esteem and the applause of their masters. There are others who, having no inclination for study, devote all their energies to excel in games. On their proficiency in this respect they dwell with much complacency; and, in order to outstrip all competitors, they employ in gymnastic exercises valuable time, which if rightly used for the purpose of intellectual labour, would gain for them no mean share of knowledge. Some few aim at distinction, by acquiring a certain amount of influence among their companions. Their chief aim is to have the management of everything that is started among the boys. If there is a cricket club, they must be at the head of it; if there is a debating society, they must organize its meetings, and perhaps preside over its discussions; if an entertainment is to be set on foot, it will never succeed unless they have the direction of it; and all this, merely to have the name of being the leading spirit in the School.

These ought not to be the motives which influence the actions of Christian boys. If our aim were to train them up to be merely natural men, we might content ourselves with instilling into them motives of this kind; but our purpose is a higher and nobler one. We wish to teach them how to raise their natural actions into the supernatural order, by performing them through supernatural motives. Hence, we never put before them the acquisition of honour, or of wealth, or of influence, as the objects at which they are to aim. Our constant injunction to them is, to make the honour and glory of God, and the salvation of their own souls, the main business of their lives; and we urge them ever to keep this in view in all their efforts to develop and cultivate the faculties which God has given them.

III. But someone will say: 'Do you not, by insisting very strongly upon these principles, crush all emulation out of the hearts of your boys, and by so doing remove from among them, one of the greatest incitements to sustained and vigorous exertion?' We answer, without the slightest hesitation: Most decidedly not! Far from taking away from them the spirit of emulation, we rather intensify it, by animating it with a higher and nobler motive. Our oft-repeated exhortation to them is this: Strive to the utmost bent of your ability, to outstrip one another in every department of learning. You are all running in the race, and though only one can receive the prize, yet the exertion of running is no small advantage to those who have entered the lists. Nevertheless, in the ardour of the contest, always remember what is the main object after which you are striving. It is not the first place, nor the prize, nor the applause of the School, and of the masters. It is to do the will of God; and that will is never so surely, nor so fully carried out by men, as when they steadily and faithfully accomplish their duty.

What is the duty of schoolboys? It is to develop their various intellectual faculties by close application to study. These faculties were given to them by God, in order that by the right use of them, they might promote His honour and glory. This, then, is the scope of all your labour and study. It is with this motive that you should be animated when you contend with others, and strive to outstrip them. Let it be the guiding principle of your life, and there will be no fear that the spirit of emulation will die out of your soul. It will rather glow with a brighter lustre, and save you from that petty jealousy, which not unfrequently mixes itself up with the praiseworthy spirit of rivalry, which naturally springs up among boys.

Therefore, when you receive Our Lord in Holy Communion, ask Him to give you this noble desire to work solely for Him. If hitherto your motive in study has been worldly honour, ask Him to enable you to change it. When either the devil, or corrupt nature, suggests to you lower motives, treat both the one and the other with the scorn which they deserve, and try to make God the first, the last, and the only object of all your thoughts, words, and actions.

PASSION SUNDAY.

ABANDONMENT BY GOD.

'They took up stones, therefore, to cast at Him ; but Jesus hid Himself, and went out of the Temple.'—ST. JOHN viii. 59.

I. THE discussion between Jesus and the excited crowd—narrated in this day's Gospel—took place under one of the porticoes of the Temple, before which there was a vast court, begun by Herod the Idumean, and not quite finished in the days of Our Lord. In this court were piled up all the materials requisite to complete the work, and thither, in their furious anger, the fanatical mob rushed for missiles to stone Him to death, when He clearly told them His divine nature in the solemn words: 'Amen, amen. I say to you, before Abraham was made, I am.'

He had borne patiently with their contradictions ; He had answered mildly when they called Him a liar ; and even when they outraged Him by shrieking out in their impotent rage, 'Thou hast a devil,' He had contented Himself with a simple denial of the monstrous accusation. But when they persisted in refusing to believe Him, and regarded as horrible blasphemy His claim to be the Son of God; when they even took up stones to put Him to death as a blasphemer, He hid Himself from their sight, and went out of the Temple.

They had repeatedly sinned against the light. He was the light which enlighteneth every man that cometh into this world, and when they shut their eyes and rushed blindly upon Him to destroy their Saviour, He had no other course left open to Him than to abandon them in the darkness which they had chosen in preference to the light. Thus also does God act with every soul that rejects His grace. He hides Himself and departs from it; and from that moment it ceases to be the abode of the living God.

II. From this departure of Christ from the Temple, you may learn a useful lesson. Like the Jewish people, it may be said of you that you are the vineyard of the Lord. He has chosen you out from among hundreds of thousands to be the objects of His special favour. He has sent you to College, where He has planted a hedge round about you, and built up a wall to protect you. He commits you to the care of men of tried virtue, who are animated with a spirit of large-minded and tender-hearted vigilance. They watch over you with a fatherly solicitude, and, by every means in their power, strive to ward off from you whatever might sully the purity of your soul. Hence no evil can pass the defences which their wise precaution has drawn around you, unless it is carried through them, concealed in your own hearts. In one word, God could do nothing more than He has done to insure your safety, and to make you good and virtuous. Therefore He has a right to expect that, thus fenced on every side from evil influence, you will listen to His voice, obey His commands, and bring forth much fruit of virtue.

But do you do so? Examine and see. God speaks to you by the good instructions which you receive from your Superiors; by the holy example which you see around you; and by that soft, low voice which makes itself heard in the depth of your conscience. Do you attend unto what He says to you? Do you not rather contradict Him? Do you not shut your ears to His admonitions, and, in spite of the earnest appeal of His sacred Heart, take up stones to eject Him from the temple of your soul? If you sin grievously, you do all this! You turn upon your benefactor, your Saviour. You eject Him from your heart, to make room for the devil. Not only do you cast stones at Him, as the Jews did, but you trample Him under foot, and by your sacrilegious act merit the punishment which God inflicts upon those who, like you, commit sin in the very Holy of Holies.

III. What is that punishment? It is to be left by God to wallow in the mire of sin; to be given over to a reprobate sense; and to have peace in the midst of iniquity. It is to have a conscience so dead to all that, in ordinary circumstances, fills most men with terror, as to fear none of God's judgments; to dread not His fierce anger, nor the endless years of eternity, nor the unquenchable fire of hell. It is to be unmolested, undisturbed, as being beyond hope of amendment.

How fearful is the state of a soul from which God has thus departed, may be gathered from the words which the prophet Isaias addressed to the Jews, in that parable in which he foretells their future reprobation and rejection by God. 'My beloved,' he says, 'had a vineyard on a hill, in a fruitful place; and he fenced it in, and picked the stones out of it, and planted it with the choicest vines, and built a tower in the midst thereof, and set up a winepress therein; and he looked that it should bring forth grapes, and it brought forth wild grapes. And now, O ye inhabitants of Jerusalem, and ye men of Juda, judge between me and my vineyard. What is there that I ought to do more to my vineyard that I have not done to it? I will show you what I will do to my vineyard. I will take away the hedge thereof, and it shall be wasted; I will break down the wall thereof, and it shall be trodden down. And I will make it desolate: it shall not be pruned, and it shall not be digged; but briars and thorns shall come up, and I will command the clouds to rain no rain upon it.'

Therefore, children of Jesus Christ, beware of abusing the manifold grace of God, given, perhaps, more abundantly to you, than to hundreds and thousands of others, who, had they been favoured by God, as you have been, would have reached an eminent degree of sanctity. Fear to sin in the sanctuary of College where God has placed you. Above all things, be afraid of contracting a habit of sin, by which you will be miserably enslaved and degraded. Fear this as you would fear hell itself; for it is when men have contracted a habit of sin that they are said to descend into the depths of iniquity, and to contemn the judgments of God. Therefore, whenever Jesus visits you in the Holy Sacrament, pray to Him with all the earnestness of your heart not to spare you if you should ever abandon Him by embracing sin, but to smite you with His chastening rod till you return to Him. Ask Him not to give you one moment of peace or of quiet in the false, fleeting pleasures of sin, but to harass you with remorse, to terrify you with visions of the dreadful judgment, and in this way to force you to abandon folly, and adhere to the only true wisdom.

PALM SUNDAY.

PREPARATION FOR COMMUNION.

'Behold thy King cometh to thee meek.'—ISAIAS lxii. 11.

I. WHEN the great feast-day of the Jews drew nigh, and the city began to fill with the crowds which came up to take part in the Passover, men gathered together under the porticoes of the Temple, and in the public places, and eagerly asked one another whether Jesus also intended to be present at the solemn festival. All had heard that He had raised Lazarus from the dead, though he had lain in the tomb for four days, and a burning desire to see and to hear Him had taken possession of every heart.

At last, on the first day of the week, a report went through the city that Jesus had left Bethany, and together with His disciples and a band of pilgrims, was coming towards Jerusalem along the road which wound round the foot of the

Mount of Olives. Straightway a multitude of people hastened forth to meet Him, and, ascending the slopes of Olivet, beheld Him drawing nigh, seated upon an ass. Full of enthusiasm at the sight of the great wonder-worker, thus approaching in modest triumph towards the Holy City, they climbed into the palm-trees, and, cutting down the huge branches, bore them in their hands as they advanced to meet Him. Then, as He drew near, their emotion broke forth into a joyous shout of welcome, and they cried: 'Hosanna to the Son of David! Blessed is He that cometh in the name of the Lord! Hosanna in the highest!'

Some stripped off their outer garments and spread them in the road that He might pass over them. Others cast their palm-branches upon the earth to adorn the way; and thus, with shouts of exultation and hymns of joy, they triumphantly conducted Him into the Temple. Seeing there the money-changers, the drovers, and those who sold oxen, sheep, and other animals for the sacrifices standing in the outer courts and carrying on their traffic, zeal for the glory of God's house filled His soul with a holy indignation, and, making a whip out of little cords, He drove them forth, exclaiming: 'My house shall be called a house of prayer, but you have made it a den of thieves.'

II. The same Jesus that rode thus in triumph into Jerusalem, comes frequently into your soul in Holy Communion. Is there as much eagerness on your part to receive Him as the multitude displayed who had come up for the festival? Is there as great joy when the happy moment draws near? Is there as much preparation to welcome Him? Alas! we must admit with confusion, that the Jews gave Him a more enthusiastic reception than we oftentimes accord to Him.

How many college-boys rush hurriedly from the playground, and, without much recollection, prepare for confession on the day preceding Holy Communion! When actually about to enter the sacred tribunal, they are filled with thoughts foreign to the act which they are going to perform. The same faults are repeated week after week. There is little or no amendment; perhaps they do not make even a feeble effort to correct the past. On the morning of Communion they go to the chapel to prepare for the reception of Christ. But what a preparation! They are full of distractions about their games, their studies, their various occupations and cares. They look about; they grow weary; they wish that the Mass would speedily end, that they may be at liberty to play. Oh, if they would only reflect Who it is that is coming! If they would but call to mind His love for the young!

When the Apostles wished to keep the little ones from approaching Him, He said: 'Suffer them to come unto Me, and forbid them not.' He is burning with eagerness to go to you, and you are cold towards Him. He wishes to press you close to His sacred Heart, and your heart is filled with the desire of miserable trifles. Oh, be ashamed of so much giddiness, which can be excused from base ingratitude only on the plea of youthful thoughtlessness! Resolve to amend conduct so disgraceful, and to return love for love.

III. What, then, must you do, in order rightly to prepare yourself for the reception of so loving a Lord? Observe what the Jews did, and try to imitate their conduct. In the first place, they were full of eager anticipation of the pleasure of seeing Jesus, of hearing Him speak, of having Him in their midst. Do you also, some days before Communion, call to mind that on the following Sunday you have to approach to receive your Lord.

As the Jews went forth from the noise and bustle of the busy city into the quiet and solitude of the country, so do you also make a solitude in your heart by means of recollection and prayer. You have many more opportunities for these than you imagine. There are times of silence, fixed for you by Rule. Take advantage of them to look into your heart, and to say to it, 'Jesus is coming to take up His abode within thee.'

Carry forth with you the palm-branch of victory over temptations. No offering can be more acceptable to Jesus than this. What a happiness will it be for you if, each time you go to Communion, you can say to Him: 'My dear Jesus! I have during the past week, by the assistance of Thy grace, gained several victories over Thy enemies, by not yielding to their suggestions.'

Then, too, you will be imitating the Jews in another of their acts; you will be spreading your garments under the feet of Jesus. For no one can resist temptations without at the same time casting off his evil habits, which, like garments, adhere closely to a man.

Also, your heart, thus freed from all impediments, will lift up its voice and its affections in joyful accents of prayer and praise, saying: ' Hosanna to the Son of David! Blessed is He that cometh in the name of the Lord!' How happy will be the Communions which are made in this way! What excellent fruit may we not expect from them! For from the souls of those who are thus careful to prepare for His reception Jesus casts out all wilful defects, all disposition to sin, and makes them the temples in which He delights to dwell.

EASTER SUNDAY.

SPIRITUAL RESURRECTION.

'Christ rising again from the dead, dieth now no more; death shall no more have dominion over Him.'—ROM. vi. 9.

I. AFTER the body of Our divine Lord had been cleansed from the blood and defilement of the Passion, pious hands lovingly and reverently carried it to the tomb. There it lay, motionless, pale, and lifeless, wrapped round in its winding-sheet. A ponderous stone closed up the mouth of the sepulchre, upon which the chief priests set a seal, and, in order to guard against any attempt at imposture, stationed there an armed band, to see that no one either approached the tomb or gained access to the body.

All that night and the whole of the following day Jesus lay in the grave. No sound broke in upon the silence except the measured tread of the guards who watched according to the strict orders which they had received, and rendered all access impossible. But very early on the morning of the third day the beautiful soul of Jesus returned to His body, rendering it thenceforth immortal and impassible, and endowing it with those qualities which shall be the special glories of our own sinful flesh, when death shall have been swallowed up in victory. Immediately, a heavenly splendour illumined the dark vault; the earth trembled at the majesty of the Man-God; and an Angel of the Lord, descending from heaven, rolled aside the stone from the mouth of the monument.

He had risen; He was not there. He came forth from the darksome tomb, glorified indeed, but still bearing in His body the marks of the wounds with which love for us had wounded Him. The guards, terror-stricken, half dead with fear, fell to the ground, and when they had sufficiently recovered from their stupor, hastened into the city, and there noised abroad the wonderful event. The whole people then heard that He Whom they had seen hanging dead upon the Cross, Whom they had mocked and scorned and rejected, had truly risen from the dead, and now moved about in their midst!

II. As the life of the risen Jesus differed from that which He had lived before His death, because lived under different conditions, so also must your lives be totally new when once you have risen from the death of sin to the life of grace. It may be that you have been living in sin—possibly in even grievous sin; but during the past week you have been called to repent, and to wash away all your stains in the tribunal of penance. You have obeyed the call, and have come thence white as snow, and radiant with the beauty of divine grace.

If your resurrection from sin is to be of any profit to you, your life after it must, like Christ's life, be a *new* one. It must be a new life not only by being altogether free from deadly sin, but by being free from all deliberate venial faults and sins. In your old life you may perhaps have made little or no account of lies told to excuse your bad conduct, or to screen yourself from well-merited chastisement. When teased or contradicted, or thwarted in any way, you may not have made any effort to control your temper, but suffered your passion to break forth. You were disobedient and sullen with your masters; you idled your time; you were critical, disobliging, and unkind towards your companions. As for your duties towards God, everything regarding His service was a positive source of annoyance to you. You were cold at your prayers, indifferent about the services of the Church, negligent in preparation for the Sacraments, and careless to improve your conduct in any way. To live thus was to be in a state of spiritual torpor, if not of positive spiritual death. From this God has raised you to a new life. You must, therefore, once for all, change the life which you were accustomed to lead. You must lay aside the trappings of the tomb, and, being brought forth from the darkness of death to the marvellous light of a new life, you must never again return to that land which is covered with the shadow of death.

III. How is this to be accomplished? It will be brought about by endeavouring, to the best of your power, to be just the reverse of what you were. Your own strength will be unequal to effect this, for it is a work requiring much untiring energy and persevering zeal. But you are not alone. You are about to unite yourself to the Conqueror of death and of hell. He Who by His own almighty power raised Himself from the grave will come to dwell in your heart; and to dwell in it not only for to-day, but for ever. You may renew His bodily presence within you as often as you please. Therefore, trusting in His strength, begin your new life with great confidence and hope of success.

Do not, however, suppose that you will never fail, or that your energies will never flag, or that you will never feel the whole undertaking to be hopeless. Such moments as these are times of trial, in which you must be ready to quit yourself like a man. Therefore, if you should again find yourself lying, in order to excuse yourself or to escape punishment, be determined that your weakness shall not get the better of you. Go boldly to your master and humbly acknowledge your fault, and even to your companions do the same. A habit of truth will soon be the result of so much determination and humility. When you feel your heart swelling with anger, and you at last give vent to your passion, do not on that account despair of ever curbing it. Punish yourself for this outbreak by asking pardon of him with whom you may have been unjustly irritated. Struggle also against idleness, disobedience, and sullenness. By degrees you will feel that these defects are gradually disappearing from your heart. But in your efforts to overcome self, do not forget that your strength is from God, and that it is obtained by prayer. Therefore, above all things, endeavour to serve Him fervently—not with coldness, nor with sluggish indifference, but with that ardent love which a good boy would feel for his own father. Do this, and you will soon see that you are truly risen with Christ, and are living with His new life.

LOW SUNDAY.

FAITH.

'Blessed are they that have not seen and have believed.'—ST. JOHN xx. 29.

I. THE Apostles were gathered together in an upper room in Jerusalem; the doors were carefully locked, and they themselves in grievous fear of being attacked and hurried off to prison, perhaps to death, by the Jews who had slain their Master. They were talking in subdued whispers of the wonderful fact which they had heard from the women, who had gone early that same morning to the sepulchre, and had not found there the body of Jesus. Peter and John testified to the truth of this, for they, too, had run eagerly to see whether this was really so.

They were full of doubt and fear. Had Jesus risen from the grave? Perhaps His body had only been taken away by the Jews, in order to excite public indignation against His followers, and by that means to procure their death. While they were in this state of doubt and fear, Jesus Himself suddenly appeared in the midst of them. The door had not been opened, and yet He had entered. Yes, Jesus really stood before them! The gracious form, the calm, majestic brow, the winning smile upon His lips, the wondrous light in His eyes—how could they be mistaken in them? Jesus Himself is with them once again! He speaks!—' Peace be to you.' They crowd round Him; they touch with wonder His hands and His feet; they kiss with loving adoration the print of the nails; and their hearts are filled with unutterable joy.

Only one of the Apostles had not the privilege of being present when Jesus came on that first Easter-evening. Thomas chanced not to be there on that ever-memorable occasion. When, therefore, the other Apostles told him what had occurred, he would not believe. Nothing could convince his incredulity but the actual putting of his fingers into the holes which the nails had pierced, and of his hand into the wide gash through which the soldier's spear had reached the heart of Our Lord. Eight days after this event he also happened to be present with the other Apostles, when Jesus again appeared in the midst of them. Singling him out from the rest, He bade him draw near and put his fingers into the holes in His hands and in His feet, and his hand into His side. The incredulous Apostle, falling down at His feet, and with a heart too full for many words, could do nothing more than acknowledge Him to be in very deed his Lord and his God. Then Jesus said to him: ' Because thou hast seen Me, Thomas, thou hast believed. Blessed are they that have not seen and have believed.'

II. Like St. Thomas, we also have not seen, and therefore there is an excellent opportunity afforded us of believing with simple faith, and of thus meriting the commendation of Jesus. The Church is to us what the holy women were to the Apostles upon that first memorable Easter. She is at once a witness and a teacher. She tells us not only that Christ is risen, but that He is still among us. Pointing to the most Holy Sacrament of the Altar, she teaches that He is as really present there as He was in the midst of the Apostles in that upper chamber, where they saw Him with the marks of His Passion still visible in His glorified flesh. Under the species of the bread, His Body and His Blood are present; and under the species of wine, that same body and Blood are likewise present; because the Body of Christ is a living body, no longer subject to death or to mutilation. The separate consecration is made to show forth in a mystical way the death which took place upon the Cross.

When the elements of bread and wine are either broken or divided, the body of Christ is not broken nor divided; only the species, or signs, or accidents suffer division. It may be eaten both by the good and by the bad, but with different effect: to the good it is the bread of life; to the wicked it is a mortal poison.

All this, and much more, the Church tells us; but we cannot see with our bodily eyes that it is so. That which we see, to our eyes looks like bread and wine. We behold the bread broken, and the wine poured forth. Both are consumed. Nor are we deceived, for our senses have not played us false; they have fulfilled their office, and have presented to us the appearance of things. To do this is all that they either are able or are expected to do. It is the office of the mind to judge of the *nature* of the things which lie concealed beneath these signs. Therefore it is to the mind that the Church addresses her teaching, and she does this with the authority of one commissioned by God. Consequently, though we may not, and cannot see that Christ is present in the Holy Sacrament, yet let us remember His words, 'Blessed are they that have not seen and have believed,' and, falling upon our knees, let each of us say, 'My Lord and my God!'

III. It is with these sentiments that you must approach the Holy Table. You will not derive thence half the benefit it is destined to work in your hearts unless you first stir up the faith that is in you. In your case it is not so much the absence of faith that we have to fear, as the want of due reflection. You believe most firmly that Christ, true God and true man, is there really present; but you allow the distracting thoughts of studies, of games, and of other trifles, to absorb your attention, to cloud the eye of your mind, and prevent it from seeing—as clearly as it would see if these things were entirely swept away—the Lord Who is stretching forth His hands to you.

Therefore, when you are preparing for Communion, banish every other thought from your mind, and represent to yourself Christ standing there before you, awaiting with all the fond eagerness of a most loving father, the moment when His little child shall rush into His arms and be folded to His heart. No earthly father can love you as He does. If you need proof, He says to you: 'Come hither, My child, and put thy finger into the places where the nails have pierced, and put thy hand into My side. Look at the rent which love for thee has made in My heart.' Oh, do not lose the precious moments when your head lies so close to that burning heart! Do not think of anything else than of the kind, good Father Who is clasping His child to His bosom, and bidding him ask for what he pleases.

Consider your necessities. Do you not wish to be pure —so pure that Jesus will be pleased with His little child? Do you not feel it hard to resist the devil? Do you not wish always to bear off the victor's crown? Above all things, is it not your desire never to be separated from that fond Father's loving embrace? Behold, now is the time to ask for all these graces. Do so with a firm belief that your whispered words fall upon the attentive ear of Jesus Christ; and animated with that faith, though you stand behind the veil and see not the reality, yet for that very reason, because seeing not you nevertheless believe, Jesus will bless you and give you all that you ask.

SECOND SUNDAY AFTER EASTER.
THE GOOD SHEPHERD.
'I am the good Shepherd.'—St. John x. 11.

I. THE allegory under which Our Lord represents to us His undying love and never-wearying care is drawn from a picture which is often looked upon in the East, and which may be seen there in all its minutest particulars, even at the present day. The shepherd in Palestine is a very different character from the shepherd whom we are accustomed to see among ourselves. He does not, as with us, drive his sheep before him, for to do so would in many instances be to urge them on to certain destruction. He goes before them to see that the mountain-paths are practicable, to remove obstructions, and to find for them suitable pastures. The sheep are so well trained by him that they know his voice; for if he sees them straying from the flock, or loitering behind, or climbing into dangerous places, he calls to them and rebukes them, and they know his voice. If a stranger calls to them, they at once lift up their heads, stand for a moment irresolute, and then perhaps rush off in alarm, and with headlong speed.

The shepherd goes before them well armed, and prepared to defend them from any ill that may threaten them from wild beasts or from robbers. Oftentimes he himself is in peril of death, and occasionally is actually overpowered and slain by the wild Arabs of the desert, who rush in upon him. His tenderness and gentle care are shown both by the way in which he accommodates his speed to the condition of the flock ·and by the love with which he lifts the weak and tender lambs into his arms, and bears them in his bosom. If he should miss one which has strayed, he forthwith goes in search of it, and, often at the risk of life or of limb, bears back the wanderer upon his shoulders to the fold.*

II. In these qualities of a good shepherd, you have a most faithful picture of Jesus Christ, the true Shepherd of your soul. Each of you is intimately known to Him, as intimately as if he were His *only* child. All your failings and shortcomings are before His eyes. All your necessities, your struggles, your difficulties, your aspirations, lie open before Him. All your past, whether it has been good or bad, is to Him as an open book, upon the pages of which are traced the thoughts which have coursed through your minds, the

* See 'The Land and the Book,' p. 201.

desires which you have conceived in your hearts, the words which you have spoken, the actions which you have done. There is no secret corner veiled from His sight. There is no depth into which His eyes do not penetrate.

He is well aware of the difficulties which stand in your way, and prevent you from being virtuous. He knows that it is mostly uphill work for you, with many a tangled, thorny thicket to be passed through, and many a slippery path to be carefully trodden, before you can stand in safety. But, remember, He goes before you, to clear a passage through the thorns, and to make firm the uncertain foothold. Whatever may cause you pain in your upward journey has first pained Him. You are the little ones of His flock. Oh, how tenderly does He love the young—the young boy whose soul is just looking out into the world of sense, and finding it so fair, so attractive; and the world of the spirit, so hard and so wearisome! Like the shepherd, He carries you in His very bosom, there shelters you from the storm, and beguiles the weariness of the journey. The wolves which prowl about to tear and to destroy, He keeps at a safe distance. He sustains your feeble life with His own Body and Blood, and should you unhappily stray, and become entangled in the briars and thorns of sin, He goes forth to seek you and draws you thence, more tenderly than the tenderest mother, and, bearing you back in His bosom, restores you to the fold in which safety and true happiness are to be found.

III. In return for this unutterable love, you owe to your Shepherd a very deep debt of gratitude. But how are you to pay it? You cannot give to God anything that He will accept more graciously than the entire and undivided love of your heart. If you love Him, you will keep near to Him by extreme purity of life, fearing to offend Him in even matters which to many would seem trivial. You will hearken to His voice by following the inward promptings and inspirations of His Holy Spirit, Who will secretly draw you after Him into yet more perfect ways. You will close your eyes to the tempting pastures which lie on each side of you, almost within your reach; you will turn away from them, be they ever so fair, and press onwards, treading in the footsteps of Him Who goes before you.

But if you love Him not, you will stray from His side, and put yourself beyond His reach; you will fall away from the body of the flock; and then the stealthy robber will seize upon and slay you, or the prowling wolf will rend and devour you. Jesus, your Shepherd, has put in His own place a visible shepherd, who must be obeyed and followed with the same docility as that with which you would obey Himself, if He were present and called you with His divine voice. This shepherd is your prefect or your master. He has at times to make you walk in hard and difficult ways—ways very displeasing to flesh and blood. Hearken to his voice, for the Good Shepherd has said: 'He that heareth you heareth Me.' Follow his counsels. Shun what he bids you avoid. Forego those pastures which seem to you so pleasant, so far removed from danger. Remember that your shepherd stands on the mountain-top. He commands the whole situation. He can see danger where you can see none. Therefore trust him, be very docile and obedient to him, and he will safely guide you to the Good Shepherd's fold, through the gate of which no robber can pass to steal, and over the fences of which no prowling wolf can leap to rend and to destroy.

THIRD SUNDAY AFTER EASTER.

AFFLICTIONS OF THE JUST, AND JOY OF SINNERS.

'You shall lament and weep, but the world shall rejoice: and you shall be made sorrowful, but your sorrow shall be turned into joy.'—ST. JOHN xvi. 20.

I. THIS is the lot which Our Lord promised to His Apostles, upon that night when He fed them, for the first time, with His own precious Body and Blood. He told them that their life would be a life of trial and of persecution. They were to be scorned by the great, derided by the learned, hated even unto death, by the powerful. They were to weep and lament, to feel all the ills of life, while those who maltreated them, because they were the followers of Christ, were to be glad and to rejoice.

By these words He did not wish them to understand that the cup of the wicked is one of unvarying sweetness, with which there is never mingled one drop of wormwood or of gall; but he intimated that His disciples would have to tread in the rugged path of self-denial, to which there would be superadded at times the bitterest persecution from the rulers of this world, and from their fellow-men.

The fate which Jesus predicted for the Apostles will to a certain extent be yours also, if you wish to lead a holy life. There is put before you now, in the spring-tide of your days, two kinds of life, either of which you may choose for yourself. The one is a life of virtue, the other is a life of sinful pleasure. If you choose virtue, you will in a certain sense 'lament and weep'; if you take vice, you will 'rejoice.' To choose the life of virtue means that you undertake to deny that self which you always and everywhere carry about with you. It means, therefore, many a sharp and bitter struggle. It means continual watchfulness, unwearied diligence, and unceasing effort.

On the other hand, to choose a life of sinful indulgence, is to carve out for yourself what is most easy, most pleasant, and most agreeable to flesh and blood. It costs no effort, it implies no struggle. It is simply like giving up the oars, flinging one's self back upon the cushions of the boat, and allowing it to glide smoothly and swiftly down the rapid stream, without a thought or a care whither it is going.

II. But is all the bitterness on the side of virtue? Is there nothing but sorrow and lamentation in the service of God? naught but pleasure and rejoicing in the pursuit of sin, in the service of the devil? Those who follow Christ can say that 'His yoke is sweet and His burthen light,' and those also who are the slaves of their own passions can tell us how galling is the tyranny under which they groan. The virtuous boy, it is true, will occasionally feel that it is a heavy and bitter thing to fight down the evil passions, which are striving within him for the mastery; but when the contest is over, there is the satisfaction of glory won, of duty accomplished; there is the thrilling thought that God has looked down upon him, and said: 'Well done, thou good and faithful servant!' Sometimes, indeed, he laments and weeps, but his mourning is ever turned into joy.

The wicked boy, on the other hand, who never resists, but gives a loose rein to his passions, rejoices in the pleasures of sin; but those pleasures are short-lived. They pass away in a moment, and then his joy is changed into mourning. For within him the small, still voice of conscience pronounces judgment, and makes its condemnation heard above the din of the most boisterous game, amid the gaiety of the most joyous festival. Then his heart is torn with anguish, and, looking back upon those few moments of pleasure, he sees that they were in reality a delirium—a short madness. He feels that his dignity is gone, that he is a degraded wretch, who has flung away his birthright for a foul mess of pottage, and basely surrendered the citadel of his heart to God's bitterest enemy.

If he strives to drown remorse by recklessly plunging still deeper into the mire, there is, from time to time, flashed into his mind the memory of the doom which awaits him, when once and for ever his joy shall be changed into eternal sorrow. Before his eye there looms dim and terrible that darksome land where, covered with the mist and gloom of death, he shall dwell in that outer darkness reserved for those who, in this world, have loved and served their passions rather than their God.

III. Which of these two sides will you choose? Will you join yourself to those who crown themselves with roses, 'who run riot'in every meadow,' and, with the words, 'Let us eat, drink, and be merry, for to-morrow we die,' encourage one another to lead a life of sin; or will you rather cleave to those who walk in rugged ways, where the flint cuts their feet and the thorn pierces their flesh? One party offers you a honeyed cup, the sweetness of which conceals a deadly poison; the other presents to your lips wormwood and gall, of which the healthful bitterness lasts but for a moment, and contains the elixir of everlasting life. Both stand before you now, in the bright days of your early youth, bidding for your immortal soul.

You are free. You may stretch forth your hand to which you please. But before you do so, look to the end. The present joy of sinners ends in weeping, wailing, and gnashing of teeth. The hard life of the virtuous is changed into everlasting joy, which no man can take from them. Choose, therefore, that which, though bitter for the moment, will afterwards become inexpressibly sweet. Be courageous enough to turn away from what is but a passing pleasure. Do not be misled by the thought of tasting this poisoned cup but *once* only, and only *one* little drop. He who raises it to his lips will not put it down again till he shall have drained it to the dregs.

But will that draught satisfy him? No; it will create within him a raging thirst, and, in order to satisfy this, he will trample upon all that is most holy. The chances are that it will so consume his vital powers as to drag him down to an early grave, where the vices of his misspent youth will sleep with him in the dust.

Therefore, be wise and dash that poisoned goblet from your lips. Taste not of it at all. Run to Jesus Christ, and ask Him to give you to drink of His precious Blood, which will slake the fiery thirst within you, and cause to spring up in your heart a manly determination to choose the better part, to lay hold of it, and having done so, never to look back till you can do so with safety, in that land where weeping and lamentation shall be no more; where every tear shall be wiped away from the eyes of those who mourn, and their sorrow be changed into never-ending joy.

FOURTH SUNDAY AFTER EASTER.
MINDFULNESS OF OUR DESTINY.

'None of you asketh Me: Whither goest Thou?'--St. JOHN xvi. 5.

I. OUR Lord seems to have been pained by the carelessness and the indifference of the Apostles concerning the place unto which He was going to make ready for them a heavenly home and a lasting city. He mildly reproves them for not manifesting more interest in what ought to have filled their minds with an earnest longing. The same reproach might, with good reason, be addressed to us. There is before us a great and glorious destiny. The same kingdom that Jesus went to prepare for His Apostles is awaiting us. Yet how few of us ever think of it! How rarely does the thought of it occupy our minds! How seldom does anyone pause amid the whirl of everyday employments to ask himself: 'Whither goest thou?' Nevertheless, it is a question that not only ought to be asked, but that must be asked, and asked frequently, if we would not miss the very purpose for which God created us. The constant memory of that purpose is the polar star which will guide us into the haven of everlasting rest.

Therefore, you must very often put to yourself the question: 'Whither goest thou?' It will prevent you from forgetting eternity and death; it will keep you from leading a careless, perilous life; and will preserve you from falling into sin.

'Whither goest thou?' You are hastening onwards with rapid stride to eternity! You have not here a lasting city, nor any permanent abode. Quicker than the waters of a river flow to the sea do you hurry onwards to the ocean of eternity. But there are *two* eternities: one of happiness, the other of unutterable woe. One with God, in the kingdom of His bliss; the other separated from Him in everlasting misery, in the company of the reprobate, under the tyranny of the devil!

II. 'Whither goest thou?' It is true, you are hastening to eternity; but, before you can enter that eternity, you must first pass through the portals of death. What does that mean? It means that a moment will come, much sooner than you expect, or, rather, when you *least* expect it, and then the painted scene of this life shall be drawn aside, and you will behold that real world for which you were created. It means that a moment will come when all that now completely fills your heart, and takes away its affection from the one object, upon which its undivided love ought to be concentrated, will lose its charm, and be seen by you in that light in which right reason would have shown it to you if you had only given yourself time to reflect. That moment will teach you that life is but a dark and wretched passage between time and eternity, and that everything in this world is but a means to gain the one thing necessary. Then this fact will obtrude itself upon you with a thrilling and startling novelty—that, after all, man is born only that he may die. The soul which gives him life and motion will depart from its tabernacle of flesh, and that flesh will become like the senseless clod which we trample beneath our feet. It will rot and decay, till at last nothing of it will remain but a handful of dust.

This is the reply which your soul will give to the question: 'Whither goest thou?' Also it will tell you that, as a happy eternity depends upon a good life, so a happy death is but the natural consequence of a good life. If an evil end does, at times, follow after a good life, it is an exception to the ordinary dealings of God with men, and ought to be regarded as one of those inscrutable acts of Almighty wisdom into which men should not search too closely, but adore with trembling awe.

III. 'Whither goest thou?' I go to eternity; I go to death. During the few moments of my mortal life I am borne onwards by time. It is a stream upon which I am floating swiftly, and surely, and inevitably towards eternity. My body is, as it were, the frail vessel in which my soul is embarked. The rudder is in my hand, to guide my vessel into a happy eternity. I am able to give to it an impetus which will carry it to the right hand or to the left—an impetus which will either bear it safely into the haven of eternal rest or hurl it into the dreadful abyss of never-ending woe.

What shall I do in order to reach the one and avoid the other? I must fix my eye steadily upon the point towards which I am sailing. I must keep it continually before me, by asking myself: 'Whither goest thou?' Vigilance must ever be in my mind and in my heart. No sleep, no forgetfulness, must steal over my senses. If I allow these to master me, I shall be whirled along without perceiving whither I am going. I shall awake at last to find myself upon the brink of destruction. Then the astonishment, the fear, the bewilderment, which will seize upon me, will render me powerless to do what is right, and I may suffer a miserable shipwreck.

Therefore now, while I am still able to think, I will avoid all carelessness and negligence. I will frequently ask myself, 'Whither goest thou?' But above all things, I will pray to Him Who guided the little bark amid the waves of the Galilean sea, and calmed the raging storm. I will beseech Him ever to stay with me in my frail vessel; to give me a calm heart, a strong hand, and a steady eye to guide myself safely into the kingdom of heaven.

FIFTH SUNDAY AFTER EASTER.

PRAYER.

'If you ask the Father anything in My Name, He will give it to you.'—ST. JOHN xvi. 23.

I. FEW duties are either more frequently or more earnestly urged upon you than is the duty of prayer. The ministers of God are ever striving to impress upon you its necessity; they never weary of recounting its advantages; and they recommend it at all times, and to everyone, as the sovereign remedy for every ill. In fact, the frequency with which it is brought before you will no doubt have made it a threadbare subject, hardly capable of arresting your attention. Nevertheless, you must not allow your mind to weary of it. All this urgency, on the part of those who have God's interest at heart, proves to you that you cannot over-estimate the importance of what they recommend, and that you ought to hold it in the highest esteem.

Your own experience, limited as it is, will have taught you that you stand in need of many things which only prayer can obtain for you. Moreover, these things are so essential for you that their place can be supplied by nothing else. God has therefore put prayer into your hands, as an easy means to procure for yourself everything of which you stand in need. Now, in your early youth, when your passions are just springing into life in all their freshness and vigour, ready to seize greedily upon what you fondly hope will feed and satisfy them, you require all the help that grace affords, to brace up and nerve your feeble will. To rule them aright you need calmness and courage, in order not to lose your head when they rage furiously against you ; and a strong and steady hand, to curb them and bring them into subjection. Corrupt nature, like a rich but uncultivated soil, is prolific in evil. Look into your heart, and see whether this is not so.

You will perhaps find yourself irritable, indocile, disobedient, untruthful, vain and proud. In addition to these noxious weeds, you will probably feel within yourself the first germs of sensuality, the first stings of that rebellious flesh which, unless tamed in its very infancy, will subject you to its tyrannous sway. Against this array of enemies, and of others which we have not mentioned, God has put into your hands a weapon of heavenly temper. Its trenchant blade flashes terror into the hearts of your foes. Use it manfully, and they will flee away terror-stricken and covered with the confusion of defeat. That weapon is prayer.

II. When Jesus gave it into our hands, He knew with what a host of enemies we should have to contend. He knew their power, their subtlety, their undying hate. In order, therefore, to put us upon an equality, or, rather, to make us superior to them, He endowed prayer with power to procure for us might so great as to render futile all the attacks which hell may make against us. We have but to lift up our voice in prayer, and straightway there is by our side a legion of Angelic Spirits. We have but to ask, and that which we wish for is given us : ' If you ask the Father *anything* in My Name, He will give it to you.'

See, then, the wonderful efficacy of prayer. If, in your dealings with your companions or with your masters, you find yourself ever ready, upon the slightest provocation, to fly into a passion, lift up your heart in prayer to God, ask for gentleness; and in due time you will be able to curb your anger. When you feel yourself disposed to resist authority, and to transgress the commands of Superiors, pray to God for a docile heart; and not only pray, but force yourself to do what you are told. God's grace obtained by prayer, co-operating with your good endeavours, will bend your stubborn will, and make you taste the sweets of obedience. Should you discover that you are in the habit of covering your delinquencies or your idleness with a lie, pray God to fill you with confusion for so disgraceful a sin, and you will in a short time obtain courage to tell the truth and shame the lying devil from your soul. If foolish pride and vanity make you the slave of public opinion, ask for the humility of the Child Jesus, and He will give you grace to strive to please Him only, by doing what your conscience dictates, and not what some worthless, giddy boy may fancy to be noble and manly. Especially when the unclean devil is trying to effect an entrance into the sanctuary of your heart, in order to rob you of the spotless purity of your soul, cry aloud to your Father Jesus, and He will come to your aid, and you will never feel how bitter a thing it is to have left the Lord your God by sin.

III. But you will say: 'There must surely be some proper mode of asking for what I need; for I often ask, and God remains deaf to my prayer.' If you do not receive what you ask, it is, as St. James observes, because you do not ask for it as you ought. Whatever you desire must be asked for in Christ's name—that is to say, it must be sought for from God through the merits of Christ; and you must add to all your petitions this condition: 'If what I desire is pleasing to God, and conducive to the salvation of my soul.' For oftentimes what we desire, if granted to us, would lead to our damnation; and therefore God in His wisdom, seeing this, refuses, like a good father, to grant that which, instead of being a favour, would be the severest of punishments.

If you ask for those spiritual gifts which have already been pointed out to you, you need not fear a refusal. God will be only too ready to bestow them upon you. But as for such favours as success in study and the like, you must leave all these to His good pleasure. Ask Him for quickness of intelligence, but always add, 'If it is profitable for me.' Then, even though you should not actually obtain that for which you pray, yet God will give you some spiritual gift which will be a thousandfold more advantageous to you.

Again, whatever you pray for must be asked with all humility; because God detests a proud man, and especially one who, besides being proud, is needy and poor, as we all are. Besides humility, you must have an attentive mind while you present your petition. Do not suppose for a moment that God will give anything to the boy who, while asking for what is so important for him, is thinking of his games or of his studies, and behaves with so much irreverence as to stare out of the windows, or to look at his hands, or at any object which may chance to catch his eye. Even your masters, with all their kindness and indulgence towards you, would drive you from their presence if you should dare to treat them in the same indecorous manner as that in which you presume to treat God.

Lastly, you must *persevere in asking*. You must not be content with once or twice praying for a virtue or a favour. If, after a hundred or a thousand petitions, your prayer still remains unanswered, do not lose courage; persevere knocking, and you will find that God, by withholding His favours for a time, does so only to test your virtue, and to see whether you are worthy of them. Prayer made in this way is sure to obtain from God whatever you ask; for Christ has said: 'Amen, amen I say unto you, if you ask the Father *anything* in My name, He will give it to you.'

ASCENSION DAY.

'And the Lord Jesus after He had spoken to them was taken up into heaven, and sitteth on the right hand of God.'—ST. MARK xvi. 19.

I. OUR LORD had accomplished the mission for which He came on earth. He had fulfilled to the letter all that had been written and prophesied concerning Him by the great men of old. The moment, therefore, had come when the Father should glorify Him, and adorn His humanity with that dazzling splendour which belonged to the Word before created things were made. But before manifesting that glory to the eyes of His Apostles, He stands once again, and for the last time, in their midst. He upbraids them for their hardness of heart, and for their incredulity in refusing to believe those who had told them of His resurrection. But why these words of reproof? We should naturally have expected that, having now only a few hours to remain with them, He would chide them no more, but would rather speak to them comforting words, calculated to inspire them with that courage of which they stood in so great need. Nevertheless, He acted otherwise, in order to show us how much He detests that sceptical frame of mind, so opposed to the childlike faith which He exacts from all who would be either His ministers or His disciples.

Having reproved them for their fault, He next gave them their great commission, to teach all nations whatsoever He had taught them. He bestowed upon them power to work miracles, as a testimony unto unbelievers that the hand of God ruled and directed them, and that the word which they spoke came from Him. Then, in order that they might witness the last great act of His earthly career, He led them forth from the city, and traversed the well-known and oft-trodden way towards Bethany. They crossed the brook Cedron, passed the Garden of Gethsemane, and climbed the steep of Olivet. Then, lifting up His hands, He solemnly blessed them, and ascended into heaven, where a bright cloud soon hid Him from their sight.

He had gone! Their friend, their guide, their master, no longer stood among them! No wonder that they remained, with tearful eyes, gazing up wistfully into the blue expanse of heaven. They were like children upon the seashore, straining their eyes after the ship in which their father is being borne away from them to some distant land. They wept, indeed, but their tears were tears of joy. For though Jesus no longer tarried with them, yet they knew Him to be present with them; and they felt sure that the Holy Spirit would come, to remain with them to the end of time.

II. St Augustine and St. Chrysostom, commenting on the seventeenth chapter of St. John, give several reasons why Our Lord did not choose to remain with His Apostles, but ascended into heaven. He Himself had said: 'It is expedient for you that I should go.' There was due to His humanity in heaven a glory which He went thither to receive. He departed from us to prepare for us a home, in which we shall live with Him for ever; and by so doing, He taught us that our hearts' fondest desire ought to be centred upon that celestial country, whither He, our treasure, has gone before us. By the fact of belonging to His Church we become members of a mystical body, of which He is the Head. As therefore He has ascended into heaven, so He would have us remember that thither also our thoughts must ever tend. Lastly, Christ returned to the kingdom of His Father to be our advocate before the throne of God, clothed in that very flesh in which He suffered and paid the penalty of our sins.

We offend in many ways, and sometimes very grievously. We deserve no mercy, and the anger of God is kindled against us. But Jesus is there with His pierced hands and feet, with His open side and thorn-crowned head. He stretches forth those hands to shield us, and shows unto His Father the infinite satisfaction which He paid for us. God is thereby appeased; the devil, our accuser, is covered with confusion; and we are pardoned and received back again to favour.

May Jesus plead for us, when we are summoned to the bar of divine justice, to give an account of our stewardship, and to answer for our many and grievous transgressions!

III. Christ has gone before us into heaven, to prepare a place for us. How are we to follow Him thither? If we are ever to enter into possession of that glorious kingdom, it can be only by making ourselves like unto Him. He has gone before to point out the way; we must follow in His footsteps, by fashioning our lives upon His, and by clothing ourselves with the virtues of which He has left us so many brilliant examples. As, then, trials and sufferings were the portion of His life, our lives also, in their measure, will not fail to be filled with many crosses, which will grieve and pain us too.

Consider what these are in your own case. Your companions are, perhaps, rude, overbearing, and tyrannical towards you. In order that you may nerve yourself to endure this, look at the mild behaviour of Jesus, under the most disgraceful and unmerited ill-treatment, and you will learn how to suffer with meekness that which human nature prompts you to resent and to repel; and to bear patiently with these, and the like trials, which are inseparable from public-school life. If you happen to be successful in your studies, if you easily outstrip all competitors, and bear off the honours which reward success, be not puffed up with pride. Remember that what you have belongs not to you. It is the gift of God, and is but a spark of that intelligence which He possesses in its plenitude. Even among men there are intellectual giants, whom you need not hope to equal, should you live to even a patriarchal age.

Also be careful to repress at once, and with vigour, all movements of corrupt nature. Keep your mind and heart pure, and be zealous to preserve them from every stain. By acting thus, you will be mortifying your fallen nature, purging it from the dross of earth, making yourself resemble, as far as possible, our great model, the God-man Christ Jesus. It is in this way that you will fit yourself to ascend after your Lord to that throne of glory which He has gone to make ready for you.

SUNDAY WITHIN THE OCTAVE OF THE ASCENSION.

PERSECUTION.

'They will put you out of the synagogues: yea, the hour cometh, that whosoever killeth you, will think that he doth a service to God.'—ST. JOHN xvi. 2.

I. WITH what sadness and dejection must these words of Jesus have filled the hearts of the Apostles! They had been dreaming all along of an earthly kingdom, of which

Christ should be the head, and they the princes. They had been picturing to themselves the triumph of their downtrodden race over the haughty conquerors, and the peace and prosperity which were for evermore to be the portion of God's people. But the great Master taught them, little by little, the mystery of the Cross; and before He left them, He had unfolded before them the real character of His mission, and had brought out into sharp relief before their eyes, the reformation which the ignominy and the sorrow of the Cross were to work in the world.

Not by earthly glory and power, not by earthly wisdom, not by ease and prosperity, but by scorn and derision meekly borne, by the 'foolishness' of the Cross, by a life of ignoble toil and poverty, were they to triumph over men, and gain the dominion of their hearts. They themselves were to stand in the foremost rank, and meet the full fury of the storm, which the powers of the world would stir up against the new order of things, about to be established by Jesus Christ. Though conscious of that sanctity with which Christ had endowed them, though convinced of the purity of their intentions, and of the blessings which they were offering to men, they were nevertheless to be cast out of the synagogues by their brethren, just as if they were the ministers of Satan.

They were to be hunted like wild beasts of the forest; they were to be loathed as enemies of the human race. The hands of all were to be against them, so that they would be forced to hide in the holes of the rocks, and to dwell in the fastnesses of the desert. Men would come to think so evilly of them, that they would consider that they were doing a signal service to God by slaying them.

II. Under one shape or another, the persecution promised by Christ to His Apostles must be the portion of every one also who strives to lead a holy life. By this, we do not mean that molestation which we experience from the temptations of the devil, and from the rebellion of corrupt nature; this is common to all men; but we mean, that the good and virtuous have to endure the enmity and the malice of wicked men, among whom they live; and what is still more difficult to bear—the hostility of the good, who oftentimes through some misunderstanding mistake their motives, and judge their actions amiss.

In your career at College, you may be sure that at some time or other you will suffer persecution. If you happen to fall among a certain class of boys whose delight it is to tease, bully, and tyrannise over the weak and defenceless, merely for the ignoble pleasure which base natures feel in inflicting pain upon others, you may console yourself with the thought that you are encountering the rough training of public-school life, and that in some roundabout way it will do you good. But persecution of this nature is easily borne. There are other and far more galling kinds of persecution, which will test your virtue and try it to the utmost.

You may, for instance, be wrongfully suspected by your companions of some base or of some mean act, which you detest and abhor as much as they do. They may accuse you of some dishonourable lie—not that every lie is not dishonourable—but of some lie which boys look upon with special loathing. They may taunt you with the meanness of tale-bearing, or with cringing to Superiors, or with courting their favour, or with hypocrisy, or with dishonesty at examinations.

On the mere suspicion of conduct of this kind, boys will cast you 'out of their synagogues,' by avoiding your company; they will hurl many a bitter gibe at your head; they will point the finger of scorn at you; and they will think that by acting thus, they are treating you with that measure of justice which you deserve. It is by enduring these persecutions with a brave and manly spirit that you will be proving yourself, in very deed, to be a true servant of Jesus Christ.

III. To bear this persecution is no easy matter. The mental anguish caused by these unjust, and oftentimes baseless suspicions, has before now forced bitter tears from the eyes of many a high-spirited boy, who would bear with unwincing stoicism the brutal treatment of a ferocious and cowardly bully. Yet, if a boy would imitate Jesus Christ, he must nerve himself to endure this whip of scorpions.

Let him first use all the means within his reach to justify himself, and to cast off himself the unworthy suspicion or the groundless accusation which is laid to his charge. Then, having done this, let him commit his cause to God, believing with firm faith that He will right him, and dissipate the dark cloud which for the moment has obscured his fair fame.

Let him not ruffle the calmness of his mind by dwelling upon the vile motives which may have urged his enemies to persecute him, nor upon the malice which lies at the bottom of their misguided zeal for justice. Leave those who act maliciously against you to the scourge of their own guilty consciences, and to the hand of God, Who in His own good time will avenge you, and bring down upon the heads of your persecutors the evil which they have meditated against you.

Look rather upon the calmness and the self-possession of Jesus, when He stood before an earthly tribunal, and false witnesses were blaspheming Him, and perjuring themselves to procure His death. He held His peace, so that even the pagan judge wondered at His forbearance, and did not believe his accusers. Think of your own sins, which may have brought this punishment upon you. Accept it in atonement for them. Humble yourself under the mighty hand of God. Bow your head to the storm, and when its purifying influence shall have accomplished its destined work upon you, God will exalt your head, and crown you with the glory of those who have bravely and patiently suffered persecution for justice' sake.

WHIT-SUNDAY.

'And they were all filled with the Holy Ghost.'—ACTS ii. 4.

I. From the Mount of the Ascension the Apostles, in obedience to the command of Jesus, returned to Jerusalem, there to await the coming of the Paraclete Whom He had promised to send to them. Their hearts were sad and heavy, for they had lost their Lord. Their guide, their counsellor, their defender, had been taken away, and, as it seemed to them, they were alone, in the midst of a fanatical people, who hated them because of Jesus, and who would be only too glad to treat them as they had already treated Him. They were, consequently, full of fear, and hid themselves in an upper chamber from the sight of the people. There, in humble prayer to God, and in holy converse with one another, they awaited the fulfilment of their Lord's most gracious promise.

At last, when the time ordained by God had come, they were startled by what seemed to them the impetuous rushing of a mighty wind; the whole house shook, and trembled as with an earthquake; and they beheld, shining over the head of each, a glittering tongue of fire. On the instant, they were filled with the Holy Ghost. The Comforter had descended from heaven upon them, and entered their hearts!

At once they felt themselves changed into other men. All fear, all weakness, all pusillanimity had vanished! The dark pall of ignorance hitherto enveloping their intelligences had been lifted and rolled aside; they arose perfect men. The whole plan of the redemption now unfolded itself before their eyes; and, perceiving themselves to be full of light, and zeal, and courage, to carry that plan into execution, they hurried forth into the streets of the city, and fearlessly preached Christ crucified.

II. This is the account which the Evangelist gives of the coming of the Holy Ghost. Like the mystery of the Blessed Trinity, there is in it little that is tangible upon which to rest our senses, and so make a standpoint for thought. But, though we may not be able so definitely to grasp what the Holy Spirit is, as we are, to conceive what Christ is, yet we may reverently seek for the reason of His descent upon the Apostles, and thus bring out clearly before our minds the purpose for which He comes into our hearts also.

In reading the Holy Scripture, we cannot have failed to

notice the fact that, though the Apostles were taught by Jesus Himself, they did not fully understand the truths which He put before them. Even so late as the Ascension day they had not grasped the scope of His mission upon earth. All that Jesus had told them lay in their minds like seed cast into the earth, and consequently needed a something to develop and bring to maturity the knowledge which He had imparted to them. That something was the life-giving presence of the Holy Spirit; and hence Our Lord, when speaking to the Apostles, said of Him: 'He will teach you all things, and *suggest* to you, all that I have taught you.'

But, besides this knowledge, the Apostles needed, for the success of their work, a *zeal* which would urge them to carry that knowledge to the ends of the earth. See, therefore, how that eagerness to make known the truth unto others sprang into life upon the advent of the Holy Spirit!

Furthermore, they required *courageous hearts* to enable them to face the dangers which bristled in their path, and to surmount the difficulties which stood in the way of the Gospel truths. This also the Spirit of God gave unto them. They who in the Garden had been terrified by the mere sight of the soldiers, now boldly face the whole people; and Peter, who shrank from speaking the truth before a servant-maid, now fearlessly, and before the Great Council, confesses Christ.

Therefore, the Holy Spirit descended upon the chosen band of teachers who, on that eventful day, formed the nucleus of the Church, to enable them to grasp the scope of Christ's mission, to teach the truths which He taught, and to carry those truths to the ends of the earth.

III. But, you will ask, why is the Holy Spirit given to us in the Sacrament of Confirmation? The Holy Spirit is given to you in Confirmation, and abides with you as long as you remain in the state of grace, because, like the Apostles, you need the same life-giving fire, the same ardent zeal, and the same unfailing courage that He imparted to them.

You have now arrived at that age when boyhood is merging into early youth. It is a critical period; for the line of demarcation between good and evil becomes sharply defined before your eyes, and, at the same time, the impulses of corrupt nature begin to make you feel their presence in your heart, and to urge you to cross the boundary-line between good and evil. This is a dangerous time. One step in the wrong direction may prove fatal.

Therefore the Holy Spirit is given to you by the ministry of the Church, in order that His vivifying grace may cause those guiding principles, traced in your souls by the finger of God, to stand out clear before your mind, so that when the seductive whisperings of corrupt nature strive to draw you away from God, they may be there to counsel what is right, and to point out, with unerring certainty, the way in which you should go.

Besides this, His presence in the soul imparts to it a strength which is not natural to it, making it cling to God, and to His holy law, with so tenacious a grasp that the powers of hell cannot loose its hold. He fills it with a zeal to defend the treasure of grace, given to it by God, which zeal makes it eager, not only to preserve itself free from every stain, but to inspire others with the like sentiments. Again, the Holy Spirit infuses into the heart in which He dwells, a supernatural courage which makes it proof against fear. It ceases to dread the persistent attacks of the devil, the lifelong enmity of the flesh, and the bitter persecution of the world.

Therefore, welcome Him into your heart, and pray Him with all the earnestness of your soul, to keep ever bright and clear before your eyes the law of God; to make you eager to preserve your innocence; to give you the strength and the courage necessary to go through the contest; and to prove yourself a true soldier of Jesus Christ; so that, when you have fought the good fight, accomplished your course, and kept the faith, He may place upon your brow the immortal crown, which He has promised to those who overcome in the strength of His name.

TRINITY SUNDAY.

'Glory be to the Father, and to the Son, and to the Holy Ghost.'

I. ST. PAUL tells us that man may come to a knowledge of God by contemplating the visible things that surround him, which are the works of His Almighty and creative hand. Chief among these visible things is man himself. Therefore, if we wish to penetrate into the nature of God, and learn what it is, as far, at least, as human ken can reach, we must look at our own nature; for of man only has God said: 'Let us make man to our own image and likeness.' This likeness is found chiefly in the soul. Therefore, from the operations of the soul, we shall be able to obtain some faint adumbration of the mystery of the adorable Trinity.

The soul by contemplating itself, and taking pleasure in its limited perfections, knows and understands itself. From the intelligence which does this, something proceeds, and that something is the concept of the thing understood. This, according to St. Thomas and St. Augustine, is called the interior *word* of our soul. In God also, Who is intelligence itself, a somewhat similar operation takes place. Contemplating, and taking pleasure in His infinite perfections, He knows and understands Himself, and thus begets a concept of Himself, which is called the Eternal Word of God.

Again: our intelligence in producing its thought—that is, its interior word—takes pleasure in itself, and loves itself in that word, and thence is produced in us love, or will. So also the Divine Intelligence in begetting its Word takes pleasure in that Word, and loves Itself in that Word, and thus from the depth of the Divine Nature, there proceeds will, or love, that is to say, the Holy Ghost.

As, therefore, the interior action of an intellectual nature, is the action only of the understanding and of the will, we see that all its operations begin in the understanding, and end in the will. Hence it is that there are three Persons, and not more, in the Blessed Trinity. Intelligence, thought —or reason—and will form the soul; infinite intelligence, eternal word, and perfect love form God, if, indeed, we may be allowed to use this expression when speaking of the Deity.

II. These three Divine Persons have one and the same substance. For, Spirit being simple and indivisible, reproduces itself entire, in the act of engendering its thought. The same thing must be said of the will. Hence, the soul subsists entire in its intelligence, entire in its thought, and entire in its will. Yet there are not three souls, but one and the same intelligent soul. Now God, Who is an immaterial and intelligent Spirit, in begetting His Son, communicates to Him His entire substance. The Holy Ghost also, in proceeding from the mutual love of the Father and the Son, has communicated to Him entire the same substance, and the same divine nature. Hence it follows, that the divine substance is entire in the Father, entire in the Son, entire in the Holy Ghost. Yet there are not three Gods, but one and the same God; for the *same* divine nature is found entire in the three Divine Persons.

The operations, however, which take place in the intelligent nature of God, are very different from those which take place in our souls. For we are, after all, only *images* of the Trinity. Consequently, in us, to understand is only an operation of the understanding. Our word, our thought, is not a reproduction of the substance of the soul which thinks; nor is it the same, in nature, as the soul which thinks; but in God, the act itself of understanding is God, and is the substance of God. The Word which is begotten by His intelligence, is a subsistent Being, of the same nature as the Divine Intelligence. The same must be affirmed of the Holy Spirit; for He also is a subsistent Being, of the same nature as the Father and the Son. Hence the three Divine Persons have the same substance; and since in a rational nature that which has subsistence, properly so called, is termed a person, it follows that in God there are three real and perfect persons.

III. These three Divine Persons are co-eternal; that is to say, one of them is not older than another. For, since God's

Intelligence and God's Will are His being; and since that Intelligence and that Will are eternal, it follows that the Son, Who is the outcome of the same Intelligence, and the Holy Ghost, Who is the mutual love of that Intelligence, and of that Word begotten by it, are co-eternal.

It is true that, in our method of speech, 'father' implies a priority to 'son,' both of time and of principle; but in the Trinity, the Father has, with respect to the Son, and the Father and the Son have, with respect to the Holy Ghost, a priority, not of time, but of principle. The Word is always with the Father, and the Holy Ghost is always with the Father and the Word. For, as man thinks his thought, or internal word, before speaking it, so God eternally thought His Word before speaking His thought; or in other words, God eternally begot His Word, that is, His thought. But when the fulness of time had come, God *spoke* His thought, that is, He sent His Word into the world, clothed in the nature of man, that He might be rendered visible to men, and be able to converse with, and teach them the way to heaven.

Yet, even then, the Word never left the bosom of the Father; just as our thought, though made manifest by spoken, or by written word, does not leave our mind; and as our word renders our thought visible, and our thought makes manifest the intelligence which produced it, so also the Word of God, Christ Jesus, makes known to us the Divine Intelligence. It is in the Word that the Divine Intelligence manifests itself—the Father in the Son, the Son and the Father in the Holy Ghost. Hence Our Lord said: 'He that seeth Me, seeth My Father also. If you knew Me, you would know My Father also. My Father will send you the Spirit of Truth. In that day you shall know that I am in the Father, and the Father is in Me.'—St. John xiv.

SECOND SUNDAY AFTER PENTECOST.
THE EXCUSES.
'I pray thee hold me excused.'—ST. LUKE xiv. 18.

I. THE Church has selected for the Gospel of this day a parable spoken by Our Lord in the house of one of the Pharisees, whither he had been invited to eat bread on the Sabbath. It seems from the words of the Evangelist, that the guests showed Him but scant courtesy, for they watched Him with critical eyes, to see whether they could detect anything blameworthy in His conduct. Also, in that unseemly contention for the place of honour, a contention upon which He comments in the course of His address, they no doubt withheld from Him the precedence due to His exalted character.

During the repast the eye of Jesus rested with compassion upon one of the guests whom He perceived to be grievously afflicted with dropsy. He healed him of his infirmity, justified his action, though done upon the Sabbath day, and then mildly rebuked His would-be critics for their pride and selfishness in contending for the chief seats at the feast. The host himself did not escape His censure. He told him that if he wished to receive an eternal reward for his charity, he must invite to his table the poor, as well as those who, being rich, could repay him by a return of hospitality.

Then one of the Pharisees, thinking perhaps that Christ's remarks were becoming somewhat unpleasant, tried to change their current by giving utterance to that empty platitude, which drew from the lips of Our Lord the beautiful parable read on this Sunday. 'Blessed,' said he, 'is he that shall eat bread in the kingdom of God.' Our Lord answered this inopportune remark, not because it had any bearing upon the subject about which He had just spoken, but because it expressed a widely-spread and deeply-seated conviction, especially among the Pharisees, that because they were invited to enter the kingdom of heaven, by being of the chosen race, they were, therefore, certain to gain possession of it. His parable taught them that, though invited, they might still not be suffered to enter; that though privileged to be of the chosen nation, the Gentiles might be preferred to them; yea, that even publicans and sinners might be introduced to partake of its joys, while they would be excluded from that unto which they had been called.

II. By the banquet, unto which all classes of men were so liberally invited, Our Lord, no doubt, primarily meant us to understand the heavenly Jerusalem; for He wills all men to enter, and to have a share in that blessed kingdom. In the next place, He would have us see in it a figure of the Catholic Church, in which are to be found those blessed Sacraments which impart to men strength and courage to tread the rough and difficult way which leads heavenwards. Now, though all are invited, yet not all are chosen, because not all will enter through the narrow gate, nor tread the rugged way, nor make use of the means which would help them to eternal happiness. You, however, have entered by the narrow gate; you are in the rugged way; but do you make use of the means which will without fail bring you safely to your journey's end? Let us examine a little, and see.

There is in the church of God a banquet prepared to give you strength and courage, and Jesus Christ, by the voice of His ministers, by the promptings of your conscience, and by His own loving invitation, cries out to you, 'Come to Me, you that labour and are heavily burthened, and I will refresh you.' How often do you answer, 'I pray Thee, hold me excused!' It is true, you may be willing enough to accept the invitation, so long as you have not to make any sacrifice; but should it happen that in order to approach Holy Communion you must give up some recreation, you say: 'I pray thee, hold me excused.' If you are a little wearied, you stay away. Some allege their studies; some their occupations; and some, alas! their sins and evil passions: 'Therefore, I cannot come.'

Beware of this! They who will not accept the loving invitation, do not receive that strength of which they stand in so much need. They halt upon the way. They totter and fall, and are left out in that exterior darkness, where there is unavailing weeping and impotent gnashing of teeth. The words of the great Master shall ring for ever in their ears: 'Amen, I say to you, none of those men that were invited shall taste of My supper.'

III. There is, however, a class of boys, differing widely from those who put forward these reasons to excuse themselves for staying away from Holy Communion. It is composed of those who have a real devotion to Our Lord, and who have tasted the sweetness of that heavenly bread which He gives unto those who deny themselves. Yet even they are tempted to allege certain vain excuses as reasons for abstaining from Communion. How often do we hear really good boys saying that they do not go every week to the Holy Table, lest they should become too familiar with it, and lose their awe and respect for that tremendous mystery! If they do not *say* this, how many of them are there who *think* it, and act upon it?

By a confusion of ideas, common enough at their age, they regard as the effect of the same cause two frames of mind which are the result of causes differing totally from one another. The first is that lassitude in the service of God which comes of negligence, and of habit which has fallen into a mechanical routine. The second is that dryness of spirit with which the holiest men are very frequently troubled. The former may well be feared, for it springs from a familiarity which has fallen into contempt; but the latter need not inspire us with alarm, for it is oftentimes either sent, or permitted by God, as a trial of virtue, or as a chastisement for venial sin. Weekly Communion, if it be made out of love for Our Lord, or a desire to advance in perfection, will never degenerate into that familiarity which breeds contempt; it will ever be a powerful means to draw down the dew of God's grace upon the barren soul, or to give it strength to bear patiently with the trial, when God is pleased to withdraw His favours.

Therefore, let not the vain fear of losing respect and love

for the Holy Eucharist keep you away from this heavenly banquet. Provided that you go to it with a heart full of love for God, of hatred for sin, and of eagerness to advance in virtue, you will never be wanting in those sentiments of respect, veneration, and awe, with which the upright of heart ever desire to approach the adorable Sacrament.

Should you be tempted to absent yourself because you invariably fall back into the same faults, meet this temptation with a little common-sense. Ask yourself this question: ' If, with the aid of the Body of the Lord, I am so unstable in virtue, how much worse should I be if I did not take this food, which imparts to me what little of spiritual life I possess ?' Look, therefore, upon all these excuses as so many suggestions of the devil, who wishes to deprive you of that food which will enable you to walk even unto the kingdom of God. Never say to Him Who invites you, ' I pray Thee, hold me excused.' With much eagerness, and with humble thanksgiving, accept His invitation, lest He should exclude you from the bright banquet-hall, and thrust you forth into the exterior darkness, where there is weeping and gnashing of teeth.

THIRD SUNDAY AFTER PENTECOST.
LOVE OF JESUS FOR SINNERS.
'This man receiveth sinners, and eateth with them.'—ST. LUKE xv. 2.

I. THE Pharisees openly complained of Our Lord's conduct, when they saw His kindness and gentleness towards those whom they, in their self-righteousness, regarded as incorrigible sinners. There is, in their complaint, a covert sneer which shows their contempt both for Jesus and for His followers. It says to us, as plainly as if they had spoken the words, ' This, forsooth, is the Messias, Who is to found a new kingdom of the Jews! Behold His adherents, the subjects of whom He is to form a new people. This man receiveth sinners, and eateth with them.' Our Lord, without noticing their unwarrantable assumption of spotless purity before God, mildly puts before them the mission of the Messias, and while so doing gives us a glimpse of the compassion of His loving heart for sinners.

He does this by bringing before their notice a fact of everyday occurrence among a pastoral people—a fact which would be familiar to every one of His hearers. 'What shepherd is there,' He asks, 'who having a hundred sheep pasturing on the hills, will not immediately, if he miss one of them, leave the ninety-nine, and go in search of the one that is lost? So it is with Me. I am the Good Shepherd. Men are My sheep. They who stray away from the flock must be sought after and led back again. It is the *sick* that need the physician. It is the erring that need a guide. It is the wounded and bruised that need a helping arm to sustain, and carry them back to their homes. These are they whom it is My mission to seek out and to save. I know all My sheep. I miss even one when it strays. I feel a void in My heart when it has left My fold; and as a mother weepeth over the loss of her little one, so do I lament over those who depart from Me. I go in search of them. I stretch forth My hands to them, and, with a gladsome heart, I bear them back in My bosom.'

II. How full of consolation to us all is this portrait of Our heavenly Father's character! It cannot but inspire our hearts with humble confidence in that Good Shepherd Who slumbereth not nor sleepeth in His unwearying watch over Israel. You especially may look upon yourselves as His flock by predilection; for the young are very dear to the heart of Jesus. Now, although you are favoured and loved by Him more than many others, yet there are times when even you must needs fear Him, in spite of all the confidence which His unbounded goodness inspires. For college boys occasionally stray away both from their Shepherd's side, and from the safe pasture in which He has placed them, in order that they may taste of other food from which He has wisely restricted them.

Some do this once or twice, and then, having by sad experience learnt wisdom, stray away no more. The devil tempts them, as he tempted Eve, to partake of that fruit, the taste of which will disclose to their view both good and evil. He puts it before their eyes, and asks them why they do not eat of it. He tells them that it will appease the hunger which is gnawing at the centre of their hearts, and craving to be satisfied. He promises to open out before them the wondrous fields of knowledge, through which they desire to roam at will. At last they yield to his suggestions, and with trembling eagerness stretch forth their hands to pluck the fruit. Then, indeed, their eyes are opened, but it is to see their own shame and degradation.

It is then that the poor child needs placing before him the picture of the loving Shepherd, Who straightway misses him from the fold. Oh! do not hesitate for a single moment, dear child of Jesus Christ! Lift up your voice to God; He will seek you. He will find you among the thorns and brambles of sin. He will not reproach you. No harsh words will escape His lips; but gently, tenderly, and with loving-kindness, He will extricate you from your wretched state, and on His shoulders bear you to the fold.

III. But there are other boys, who having once tasted the forbidden fruit, pluck and eat of it again and again, till its subtle poison has penetrated through all the veins and arteries of their moral nature, scorching up with a burning heat their spiritual life, and creating within them a raging thirst for sensual pleasure—a thirst which, in some sort, renders sin a necessity for them. They wander away farther and farther from their Shepherd. They put themselves beyond the sound of His voice. They strive to hide themselves from the searching glance of even His eyes.

Content with the garbage upon which the devil feeds them, they lose all taste for the pastures which they have left behind. But even so, they cannot withdraw themselves from the love of their Good Shepherd. Do what they will, it will find them out. His pleadings will soften their hearts, and draw from their eyes those penitential tears, the balm of which expels the poison of sin from their veins, reinstates them in the favour of their God, and raises them to the height from which they fell.

But terrible is the force of habit! They may fall again!

Again will the Good Shepherd bring them back, and again and again will they return to the pastures of the devil. O wretched state of the poor soul that is caught in the devil's meshes! Yet, do not lose courage! Look up to Jesus Christ! He is the Saviour Who came to seek out and to save the sheep of the house of Israel. He is the Physician Whom the sick man needs. Therefore, if you fall, call upon Him, and He will raise you up. If you fall again, again call upon Him. Do this till you cease to seek after those sinful fruits. Only persevere in the use of Christ's Sacraments, and you will obtain strength to cling to your Shepherd, and never to abandon Him till He shall have brought you into His heavenly home.

FOURTH SUNDAY AFTER PENTECOST.

PURITY OF INTENTION.

'Master, we have laboured all the night, and have taken nothing.'—St. Luke v. 5.

I. The events recorded in this day's Gospel occurred shortly after Our Lord's first appearance as a public teacher, when the fame of His wondrous eloquence and of His still more wondrous deeds, had gone forth throughout the whole of Galilee. Hearing that He stood even now on the shore of their inland sea, the people flocked thither in vast numbers, bringing with them their sick, their blind and their lame, to be healed by His touch, and to have their hearts moved by the magic power of His speech. In their eagerness to come near the great Prophet, they thronged upon one another, and strove for the privilege of being close enough to see Him, to hear Him, and it might be also to touch the hem of His garment.

Their well-meant, but not over-courteous behaviour somewhat incommoded Our divine Lord. Therefore, in order more easily to be seen and heard, during the lesson which He intended to teach them, He entered Simon's boat, and ordering him and those who were with him to withdraw a little from the land, He sat in the boat, and thence taught the people as they stood in circle above circle upon the shelving shore. When He had ended the lesson, He turned to Simon, and ordered him to launch out farther still, and to let down his net for a draught. Simon had been toiling fruitlessly all the preceding night, and in reply to the command of Jesus, said, with some little despondency: 'Master, we have laboured all the night, and have taken nothing; nevertheless at Thy word I will let down the net.' He did so, and a miraculous haul of fish, which well-nigh sank the little vessel, rewarded his faith and obedience.

Many, who have commented upon this incident, compare the sea to the world in which men are placed by God to fulfil their various and manifold duties. If they have God with them in their hearts, and work at His command, and in order to do His will, all their actions are good and meritorious of everlasting life. If they act without God, and without any intention, their actions are worthless, and will obtain no reward ; if with a bad one, they will be punished with rigorous justice. At their death they will appear before God with their hands empty, and with the despairing cry upon their lips : 'We have laboured all the night, and have taken nothing.'

II. How many a college boy is forced to repeat, with an aching heart, these words of the Prince of the Apostles! When he looks back upon the years which he has spent at College, and examines into the motives which actuated him in the performance of his many duties, he begins to realise that he has been 'labouring all the night, and has taken nothing,' and that, from a spiritual point of view, his hands are empty! For there is no supernatural reward attached to any action that has not been done for God ; and out of the multitudinous acts performed in the years that have gone by for ever, how few have had in them this life-germ, which will cause them to blossom and bear fruit unto eternal years!

Look at your everyday life! It is made up for the most part of actions which in themselves are indifferent, and which need the soul of a right intention to give them life and worth. What has been your intention? For the most part it has been but a natural one—to supply your wants, or to comply with the daily routine which you found established around you. You have gone to your meals, you have taken your rest, you have conversed with others, you have recreated yourself, without, perhaps, ever referring any of these things to God. If it is so, then, as far as supernatural reward is concerned, all this has been merely lost time. There is no merit; there can be no reward.

With regard to your duty of study, and the observance of college discipline, if the former has been pursued for pleasure, or for the excitement of outstripping others, and the latter to avoid punishment or to receive commendation, there can be no supernatural reward; because not only is there no supernatural intention in the acts, but at times there is one which vitiates and makes the action sinful. In this way many a boy loses the fruits of his labours at College, and at the end of his career discovers that his hands are empty, and that he has done nothing for God.

III. What therefore must be done, in order to make all your actions meritorious and profitable to you? In the first place, you must, like the Apostles, have Jesus sailing with you in the vessel of your soul. What, you will ask, is meant by that? It means that you should be in the state of grace, that your heart should be free from the guilt of grievous sin. For, as Our Lord Himself has said, the merit of our works is derived from their union with Him. Of themselves they are no more capable of merit and of reward than a branch, severed from its parent stock, is capable of bearing fruit.

In the next place, you must take care, in all your actions, to have a right intention. This, as ancient writers quaintly express it, 'is to cast your net upon the right side of the boat.' By this means you will gather to yourself, and render meritorious, that vast multitude of indifferent actions which constitute the staple of most men's lives. Hence, when you go to your meals, or to your rest, or to your games in the play-ground, say in your hearts: 'My dearest Jesus, I do this for Thee.' In the performance of what are strictly college duties have the same intention. When the bell summons you from the playground, cease playing, and keep silence, rejoicing that an opportunity is afforded you of denying self, and of doing something for God. When in the study, or the class-room, work conscientiously, not to gain praise or a reward, but to accomplish the duty which God has imposed upon you, saying in your heart, 'Father, I do this for Thee!'

As for your spiritual exercises, to have any other motive in the performance of them than purely and simply the fulfilment of God's will, is so abominable an act of hypocrisy, that it is to be hoped the natural candour and plain-dealing of boyhood will preserve you from conduct so detestable.

By observing these few counsels, you will not lose even one of the most ordinary of your actions. You will be turning into pure gold whatever you touch, and sending it before you into the heavenly kingdom, stamped with the approval of God, to form a treasure which will be your support and your glory throughout the endless ages of eternity.

FIFTH SUNDAY AFTER PENTECOST.
JUSTICE OF THE SCRIBES AND THE PHARISEES.

'Unless your justice abound more than that of the Scribes and the Pharisees, you shall not enter into the kingdom of heaven.'—ST. MATT. v. 20.

I. WHAT a startling effect must these words have had upon the minds of those who heard them from the lips of Our Lord! They were told, that their sanctity must surpass the sanctity of two classes of men upon whom they had been taught to look as the types of perfection; otherwise, they should never enter the kingdom of heaven! For, be it remembered, the Scribes were the people's recognised teachers —men to whom they naturally turned for guidance in the ways of truth and of justice; while the Pharisees were men who professed to observe every tittle of that law, which the Scribes undertook to expound.

We may learn with what scrupulous exactitude they performed the duties which it imposed upon them, from the graphic portrait of them which Our Lord puts before our eyes. They prayed much; they fasted often; they gave abundant alms; they frequented with punctilious regularity both the Temple and the Synagogue; they meditated upon the holy word of God; they bound it upon their foreheads; and were rigidly exact in the most trifling ceremonial observances which it inculcated, or which an unwise and illiberal criticism had fastened upon it.

Yet, Jesus Christ deemed all these devout practices insufficient to secure them a place in His kingdom. What is the reason of this? Because it was all mere outside show. These were but the 'trappings and suits of virtue'—actions that a man might play—actions performed to gain the empty applause of men, and not to satisfy the eye of God. For, though outwardly presenting an exterior which indicated an austere life, they were in the eyes of God, Who looks at the heart, nothing better than whited sepulchres. They were full of hatred, avarice, and pride; and while affecting a religious horror for any one who should eat with unwashed hands, 'they neglected the weightier things of the law—judgment, and mercy, and faith'; and thus while 'straining out a gnat, they swallowed a camel.'

II. Examine yourself, and see whether in some points, and to a certain extent, your conduct does not resemble that of the Scribes and the Pharisees. Their religious life, as we have said, consisted in mere external show. How much of your spiritual life, also, is made up of outward observance, beneath which there is no life-giving principle to infuse into it worth and merit? When you pray, are not your words sadly out of harmony with the thoughts of your mind, and the desires of your heart? You are oftentimes present at Mass; you frequent the Holy Sacraments of Confession and Communion; but are not these duties performed through habit? Alas! may we not justly fear so, when we see boys easily omitting these holy and necessary exercises, if, in order to perform them, they must either forego some amusement, or put themselves to some little inconvenience? See also, whether the motives of your actions spring from a desire to please God, or are not rather like those which induced the Pharisees to pray, to fast, to give alms, and to bear the intolerable burthen of the ceremonial law. If you cultivate piety, if you observe Rule, if you apply diligently to your books, in order to gain the esteem of your professors and of your fellow-students, your conduct is undoubtedly like that of the Pharisees. You may possibly gain that at which you aim; but it will be your only reward.

Again, examine whether there are not in your heart feelings of self-righteousness, and in your estimate of others a slight tinge of contempt, when you mentally compare them with yourself. Do you never feel within you that pharisaical pride which says: 'Thank God, I am not as the rest of boys—idle, untruthful, disobedient, rebellious, and the like!' Take care, while you indulge in this self-glorification, that they are not in the sight of God purer than you, and receive from Him abundant favours and graces, while you are sent away empty-handed: 'Thou thinkest that thou art rich, and made wealthy, and needest nothing; and thou knowest not that thou art wretched, and miserable, and poor, and blind, and naked. Therefore, buy of God gold, fire-tried, that thou mayest be made rich; and mayest be clothed in white garments, and that the shame of thy nakedness may not appear; and anoint thy eyes with eye-salve, that thou mayest see.'

III. If, then, you wish to be the dear children of Jesus Christ, and to enter His heavenly kingdom, your virtue must surpass that of the Scribes and the Pharisees.

In the first place, it must be *internal*. Do not get into the habit of always figuring to yourself what your masters or your companions will think of you. Put them altogether out of your mind, when you are about to perform any good action, and let your chief aim in the execution of it always be to gain the approbation of God. It matters little what men will think of you, for they see only the exterior, whereas God sees the heart. Consequently, when you pray, or go to Holy Communion, or visit our Lady, or the Most Holy Sacrament, do these things because they please God, and not 'that you may be seen by men.'

In the second place, studiously keep your mind from looking into the mirror of self-complacency, which the devil holds up before you, in order to fill your head with pride and vain glory. Any one who is tempted to gaze admiringly upon this flattering picture, will soon imagine himself to be more religious, more learned, and in general more excellent than are those around him. He will begin by depreciating, he will end by despising them; and there will grow up in his heart an overweening esteem of self, which will make him detestable in the sight of God and of men.

Lastly, let it be your constant endeavour to allow no evil passions to lay hold of your heart. For the first act of these tyrants is to put out the eyes of the soul. They will then easily make you accept counterfeit for real good. Like the Pharisee, you will be content if the outside of the cup be clean. You will lose the substance of virtue, and pursue its shadow. You will think that God is with you, whereas He has long ago said: 'Arise, let us go hence.' Therefore, keep evil passions out of your heart, and pray to Jesus Our good Father, that you may never be content to *seem* to be good, instead of *being* good. Let your motto ever be: '*Malo esse, quàm videri.*'

SIXTH SUNDAY AFTER PENTECOST.

TRUST IN GOD.

'I have compassion upon the multitude.'—ST. MARK viii. 2.

I. THE Scripture furnishes us with few facts which bring out before us in a more striking manner God's fatherly care for us, than does that great miracle which is recorded in the Gospel of this day. Our Lord upon another occasion, and in another place, had told the crowds who listened to Him that if, first and foremost, they sought the kingdom of God and His justice, all their other necessities should be provided for by His watchful providence; the miracle of this day is a complete fulfilment of that gracious promise. For the people, charmed by the eloquence and the attractive manners of this new Prophet, Who spoke to them 'as never man spoke before,' had abandoned all their worldly pursuits, and hurried to the place where report said that He would once again teach them lessons of heavenly wisdom. They remained with Him, forgetful of all else, even of their bodily sustenance.

Jesus, therefore, in order to reward their zeal for the good things of eternity, and their implicit trust in Him, determined to provide for their temporal necessities, because, taking Him at His word, they had cast 'all their care upon God.' For this purpose He resolved to work a great miracle, both to manifest His power, and to give them a foreshadowing of the bread of life, which in the fulness of time He meant to bestow upon them. Casting His eyes, therefore, upon the crowd around Him, He said to His Apostles : 'I have compassion upon the multitude, for behold they have now been with Me three days, and have nothing to eat.'

Seeing that He wished to refresh the people before dismissing them to their homes, the Apostles spoke of the impossibility of feeding them in the desert. Jesus did not notice their answer, but hearing that a boy in the crowd had with him five barley loaves and a few fishes, He told them to make the people sit down by tens and by fifties. Then He blessed the bread and the fishes, and bade the Apostles set them before the companies. Behold now what a marvel ensued ; these few loaves and fishes, multiplied by the blessing of Christ, sufficed completely for the four thousand men, so that the mere remnants ' filled twelve baskets.'

Learn from this, that Our Lord knows all your wants, whether they affect your material, bodily life, or the higher and nobler life of your soul. You can see, both from His words, and from His acts, that He is deeply touched by our miseries ; that He is willing to relieve them ; and that we may confidently expect that He will do so, if we seek first to please Him by a pure, virtuous life.

II. Now it may happen, that someone will say to himself: 'To the best of my ability, I *do* seek first the kingdom of God and His justice. If, then, God knows my wants, and compassionates me for the pain which I experience from them, and is ready to relieve me, how comes it to pass that I do not receive that help for which I crave, and which I await in vain? When I am involved in the difficulties of my Greek and Latin authors, when I am puzzled by the hard problems and theorems of Mathematics, I call upon God to help me; but no light is thrown upon the intricate sentences, and I wander helplessly and hopelessly through the torturing maze, where there is no order, and where all things seem to be in a state of inextricable confusion. In the same way, when I desire to be virtuous,—to overcome my bad temper, to hate falsehood, to be less selfish, more obedient, more charitable, and the rest,—I wish indeed for all these, and pray for them, but nothing comes of it. On the slightest provocation, I break forth into anger; I basely escape punishment by a lie; I seek myself first; I resist authority; and care not for the feelings of others. Therefore, I am inclined to think that there is much exaggeration about the providence of God in these matters, and also about the certainty of His coming to my relief, if I first seek His kingdom and His justice.'

How are these objections to be answered? An answer will easily be found, if we thoughtfully and carefully examine the way in which Our Lord performed this miracle. He might have infused so great strength into the people, that they would neither have felt fatigue, nor have been incommoded by the pangs of hunger. He might have ordered His Angels to provide them with food. He might have rained it upon them from heaven. But He did not do so. He used the bread which He found among the crowd, in the possession of a little boy. He made His Apostles take it, and set it before the people. In the same way, if you wish God to provide for you, you must use the means which you have at hand for meeting and overcoming your various difficulties, and then God will be moved to help you. When you have done all that you are able to do, you may confidently expect God to give you the aid of which you stand in need. But do you do this? Let us see.

You pray that God may enlighten your understanding; and

then, instead of concentrating all your energies upon the lesson before you, you allow your thoughts to wander; you look about you; you interest yourself in other things, and thus become hopelessly confused. No wonder that God does not assist you; for you do not first help yourself, by doing all that is in your power. So also is it with your spiritual necessities. You *pray*, as you say, against all the faults which you have mentioned; but what do you *do* to correct them? You make no effort to overcome yourself; you do not curb your anger; nor punish yourself for your lies; nor stifle your selfishness; nor consult the feelings of those around you. Consequently, no help comes from the Lord. Therefore, ever bear this in mind: 'God is always ready and willing to help those who are willing to help themselves.' Make some little effort, and no matter how small it may be, God will bless it, and cause it to produce happy results.

III. If, then, you wish Jesus, when He looks upon you, to be moved with compassion, to bless you, and to bestow fruitfulness upon your efforts, you must change your present method of action. By a holy life, keep close to your Lord; listen to His word when He speaks to your conscience; then crave earnestly for that assistance, and that blessing, which will render your desires efficacious.

You wish, as you say, to make progress in your studies; show Our Lord that you mean what you say, by doing all that is in your power to push forwards in the path of science. Let there be no waste of time, no staring about in the study, no attention to trifles, but concentrate your whole mind upon the involved and crabbed sentences of the author before you. Let no other pursuit be substituted for what you are obliged to study. Do not read English, when you should be reading Latin; nor Mathematics, when you should be translating Greek; nor Greek, when you should be studying History. For if you do your duty exactly and well, God will bless you, and your difficulties will melt away from before your face. Do what you are able, God will do the rest.

You are quick-tempered; keep a guard over yourself, especially over your tongue, and you will soon taste how sweet a thing is meekness of heart. You are inclined to tell lies; when you do so, acknowledge your fault before him unto whom you may have spoken falsely, no matter whether he is a master or a companion, and this moral obliquity will speedily be rectified. Determine each day to let your fellow-students have something in preference to yourself, and selfishness will soon disappear. Act in this way, and you will begin to feel that, one by one, these various defects are being rooted up and cast out of your heart. You will thus advance from virtue to virtue, and you will taste, as those only can taste who are willing to mortify themselves, the sweetness of God's fatherly love.

SEVENTH SUNDAY AFTER PENTECOST.
WOLVES IN SHEEP'S CLOTHING.

'Beware of false prophets, who come to you in the clothing of sheep, but inwardly they are ravening wolves.'—ST. MATT. vii. 15.

I. THESE words of warning were addressed by Our Lord to His disciples, concerning those false teachers who, under the guise of His sheep, should in later days, steal into the fold, and strive to make void the doctrine which He had preached. You may look upon them as addressed to you also. They convey to you a note of warning against those wicked and corrupt boys who may strive to lead you into sin. At times, boys of this stamp gain an entrance into the select fold of our Colleges. Outwardly, they seem to be clothed in the robes of innocence; but their apparent innocence is only a cloak, beneath which there is hidden a corrupt heart. It need not be matter of surprise to you, that there are boys who are thus perverse; nor that they should find their way even into College. Owing to the corruption of human nature, 'it must needs be that scandals should arise;' it is your business to guard against the harm which they may work.

For this purpose, there is need of much watchfulness;

because, as the devil can transform himself into an Angel of light, so are these, his agents, able to carry a smooth exterior, and wear all the semblance of great virtue. Their company is often most attractive; their conversation and bearing are agreeable; companions gather round them, go frequently with them, and become their bosom friends. Little by little they throw off the deceitful mask. As we have said before, from the abundance of their corrupt heart, 'their foul mouth speaketh,' and instils a subtle poison into the souls of those who listen. They impart the knowledge of evil; they open the eyes of the innocent. Alas! poor children, so unsuspicious of evil, how often does the knowledge thus imparted transform into the abode of Satan those souls of yours, which were once the temples of the Holy Ghost!

II. In order to prevent so great a calamity as this, the shepherd, appointed by Superiors to guard the youthful flock, must ever watch with unwearied diligence. His vigilance, however, must not be exercised in a narrow or in a suspicious spirit. This would wither up all confidence in the hearts of his boys, and deprive the shepherd himself of that peace which is the sunshine of the soul. You, therefore, who are the sheep of the flock, must aid him in his arduous task. It is your most sacred duty to raise the cry 'Wolf!' when you perceive that a wicked boy has crept in among you. By making him known to Superiors, do not for a moment suppose, either that you act dishonourably, or that you break faith with your school-fellows. In a case like this, in which your own virtue, as well as the virtue of your companions is in danger, to inform of him who is imperilling the well-being of the College, is so far from being dishonourable, that it is even an act of virtue, to the performance of which you are strictly bound in conscience.

In other matters that are not of so vital importance, as, for example, breaches of school discipline, there is no obligation whatever to make them known to Superiors. Be silent about them; for the maintenance of Rule and of order in no way concerns you. Stand faithfully by one another in all things in which you may do so without sin; and with all your heart, hate the weakness and the meanness of tale-bearing. But with regard to a wolf in sheep's clothing—there is no more dishonour in making him known, and in having him thrust out from your midst, than there is in crushing the head of a sleeping adder, or in dashing a poisoned goblet from the lips of a friend. Therefore, have no pity upon anyone whom you discover to be a wolf. When his works begin to betray him, with all speed flee away from him. Run to your shepherd, to your prefect, and tell him of the evil that is in the midst of you. His sage experience will teach him what course to pursue; and his strong arm will, if necessary, expel the intruder, before he has time to inflict a death-wound upon any of the flock.

III. Do not, however, while vigilantly on your guard against the influence of corrupt companions—do not suffer the devil to gain admittance into your own heart. For he ever goeth about seeking whom he may devour; and, as a wicked boy may disguise himself in the cloak of hypocrisy, so can the devil assume a pleasing shape, and appear to you as a very Angel of light. He is in the midst of you, and stands close by every boy. No vigilance on the prefect's part can keep *him* out. He is with you in the playground; he is by you in the study; he follows you into solitude; he leaves you not even when you kneel down to address your petitions to God. If he sees that you are idle, or that your mind is unoccupied, he whispers into your ear some evil suggestion. Therefore, be on your guard; for if you should listen to him, and allow the poison of his breath to enter your soul, you will become like to him.

Outwardly, indeed, there will be no change. You will, perhaps, seem to be as innocent as you were before. But there is wrought within you a change sad enough to make the Angels weep. You have become a wolf in sheep's clothing. You have ceased to be the child of God. You have lost your white robe of innocence and of honour. The glory with which you were crowned has been torn from your brow. You have no longer any right to the kingdom of heaven. Yet, though all this change has taken place, you are the same to the eyes of your school-fellows. But unless you speedily take yourself in hand, and sternly repress the evil that has poisoned your heart, the fury of passion will break forth, and make you a ravening wolf among your companions.

Therefore, beware of those corrupt boys who come to you in the garb of innocence, otherwise they will lead you to destruction. Fear not to make them known, and to have them expelled, should any of them chance to be among you. Also be ever on the watch against the wiles of the cunning devil. By unwearied vigilance, and by earnest prayer, keep him away from you; and when you approach the Holy Table to receive into your heart the Body and Blood of Jesus Christ, ask Him always to stand by you in the hour of trial; to check the fury of the ravenous wolf, and never to allow him to deceive and destroy you.

EIGHTH SUNDAY AFTER PENTECOST.
THE UNJUST STEWARD.

'And the Lord commended the unjust steward, for as much as he had done wisely.'—ST. LUKE xvi. 8.

I. WISDOM is so great a good, that we should be glad to learn it, from the lips of even our enemies. Hence, Our Lord does not hesitate to put before us, in the parable of the unjust steward, the criminal action of a dishonest man, that from it we may learn a lesson. He had enough foresight and skill to secure for himself a home and a source of maintenance for his declining years. From his conduct God would have us learn to be farseeing and careful about our eternal welfare. This steward, like many in his position at the present day, had probably lived far beyond his means, and in order to supply the deficiency of his income, had no doubt made free with his master's property. His delinquencies soon became known to his employer, who one day summoned him into his presence, charged him with his dishonesty, and called for his accounts, as it was impossible for him any longer to retain his office.

Hereupon, the critical nature of his position flashed upon him in all its horrible reality. Disgrace and beggary stared him in the face. But, if heretofore he had shown himself to be a fool, his worldly wisdom now did him good service. He bethought him of a plan which would free him from the necessity for labour, and from the disgrace of begging. Going to each of his master's debtors, he told one, who owed a hundred barrels of oil, to pay back only fifty. Another, who owed a hundred quarters of wheat, he bade restore only eighty; and so on through the whole list. When thrust out of his office, he knew that these men whom he had treated so generously would receive and maintain him in their houses.

The master heard of his steward's sharp practice, admired it, and praised him for it; much in the same way as we should admire and praise the dexterity of a thief who had cleverly purloined our watch or our purse; and Christ, turning to each of us, says: 'From this learn a lesson. Be ashamed to have less wisdom in securing your eternal salvation, than this wicked steward had in providing for his daily bread.'

II. A little reflection will point out to you what a startling similarity there is between the position of this unjust man and your own. Like him, you are simply the administrator, and not the proprietor of the various goods which you possess. Your memory, your understanding, your will,—your body, with all its powers, are not so entirely your own as that you can do with them what you please. They are given to you in trust, by God your Master, to be employed in His service, and for His advantage.

But, though this is an admitted truth, yet there is a notion in the heads of many boys, that the time for thus serving God with all their strength is not the period of youth. They look upon its bright and hopeful days as the proper season for having what they call their fill of the world's pleasures. There are, consequently, not a few who give themselves up to a life of sin, indulging their corrupt nature in all its desires; refusing not to eye, or to ear, or to heart the gratification for which it craves, and thus waste and destroy the excellent good things which belong not to them, but to the great Master and Lord of all.

They hope that the riper years of early manhood will bring with them greater facilities for employing God's gifts in God's service. But this is a delusion! Youth is the spring-time of life, when good seed may be sown in the heart. But if, instead of planting good seed, what the world calls 'wild oats' are sown in its place, what can be expected but a crop of sinful thorns and thistles, fit only to be burnt with unquenchable fire? For, as the Lord of the unjust steward came suddenly upon him, and caught him in the midst of his dishonest practices, so will the Master and Lord of the wicked boy, now grown into the still more wicked man, come at the time when He is least expected; He will touch him with the cold hand of death, whose summons no man can refuse to obey, and will call for an account of his stewardship, and then he will be steward no longer.

III. If you wish to escape a fate so terrible, learn wisdom from the conduct of that unjust steward. He showed himself to be keenly alive to his own interest, by making provision against the evil day. Do you act in like manner, by not neglecting your eternal interests, for the sake of a few moments of mad, delirious pleasure. You have in your hands all God's glorious gifts, which, if wisely put out to interest, will bring you in a hundredfold.

Therefore, keep well before your mind the position which you hold, and the purpose for which your various faculties have been given to you. You are simply God's steward. That which you have is His property, and not your own. You are in the world, to prepare yourself for the company of God and of His Angels in heaven; and you do this by gaining a complete mastery over yourself, and ruling your whole being as a sovereign prince. Your passions must be made to submit unconditionally, and for ever. There will then be peace in your heart, and where there is peace, a rich harvest of virtues will spring up. You will be pure, truthful, unselfish, generous, and charitable. You will enjoy the liberty of the sons of God, for you will be free from the slavery of sin. You will be crowned with glory and with honour, and you will have a never-ending source of joy in your heart, in being able to look back upon a well-spent youth, and forward to an eternity of bliss.

Gird up your loins, therefore, and accomplish the task imposed upon you by God. Serve Him now in the days of your youth, for He is worthy to be loved and obeyed at all times. Carry out, in act, this excellent principle, by never straying from the path of duty. Then, the peace and the joy which will fill your soul in consequence of the thought of a faithfully discharged stewardship, will repay you, even in this world, for the little struggle which a life of virtue necessarily entails.

NINTH SUNDAY AFTER PENTECOST.

CHRIST WEEPING OVER JERUSALEM.

'Seeing the city, He wept over it.'—ST. LUKE xix. 41.

I. COMMENTATORS are of opinion that the eyes of Jesus first rested upon the city of His great ancestor, the Prophet-King, at the point where the road from Bethany to Jerusalem sweeps northward round the shoulder of Olivet. Grand and soul-inspiring as that sight must undoubtedly have been, 'with the morning sun,' says Josephus, 'glittering so brilliantly upon the white marble and the burnished roofs of the Temple that the spectator had to avert his eyes,' it nevertheless sent no thrill of delight through the heart of the Man-God, upon this, the day of His triumphal entry into its gates. Seeing the city, He wept and lamented over it, and lifting up His voice He cried aloud: 'If thou hadst only known in this thy day the things that are to thy peace; but now they are hidden from thy eyes.'

What thoughts must have passed through His mind, as with streaming eyes He looked down upon the devoted city, the pride of His nation, while there came crowding back upon His memory all that God had done in ages past to sanctify and to save its people. Prophets and wise men had been sent to warn and to teach them; great kings had been raised up to rule, and mighty warriors to defend them; yet, with a perversity and a stubbornness that are without parallel in the history of the world, they had, as a rule, rejected the mercies showered so lavishly upon them.

At last God had sent to them His only Son. As man, as one of themselves, He had walked in their streets, taught in their Synagogues, and done wonders, to prove His mission. How did they treat Him? They contradicted, despised, and rejected Him: 'They would not have this man to reign over them.' Therefore, the time of their visitation had passed; the measure of their iniquities had been filled up; and the treasury of God's mercy, in their regard, exhausted. From the mouth of Jesus there consequently proceeded those sad words of lamentation and of prophecy, words which were afterwards so literally fulfilled. Fifty years had not passed away, before the Romans came. They dug a trench about the city, compassed it around on every side, beat it flat to the ground, and left not in it a stone upon a stone.

II. There is, then, as we learn from the mouth of Jesus Christ, both for individuals and for nations, a time of visitation. That is to say, there is a time of mercy and of patient long-suffering, during which God does everything to save man, except force the freedom of his will. But, when that day has passed, the season of mercy comes to an end, and there succeeds to it the time of justice and of judgment. This ought to make you tremble with fear; for if you look into your heart, you will perhaps see that Jesus has had reason to weep over you, for not having known the time of your visitation.

Like Jerusalem, you have been favoured with exceptional graces; for you enjoy privileges which are granted but to few. You are living in College, where your soul is sheltered from many dangers; where you have fixed times for prayer, for frequenting the Sacraments, and for learning all the science of the spiritual life. All evil example is, as far as possible, shut out, and prevented from exercising its baneful influence upon you. There is no one to jeer at, or to make you ashamed of your Religion. You hear nothing that will defile your heart; you see nothing that will bring a blush of shame to your cheeks. Added to all these spiritual advantages, there is that greatest of temporal blessings—a good, sound, solid education, which will fit you to occupy any position in life.

What return have you made to God for all these favours and graces? Alas! it happens sometimes that even in the sanctuary of College, there are those who do not know the time of their visitation. They give themselves up to sin, and allow that hideous tyrant to enslave them. They remain deaf to the voice of God, and to the reproaches of their own conscience. They shut their eyes, and will not see; and therefore the Son of God weeps over them bitter tears, and raises up His voice in sorrowful lamentation. For their enemies have gathered round, and dug about them the trench of evil habits. Very shortly they will rush in upon them, and pollute, set fire to, and destroy the temple of God in their soul. They will beat them flat to the ground, by making them adhere to earthly pleasures, and will leave behind nothing but a wreck of their spiritual being.

III. If, upon examination, you discover that you are one of those 'who have not known the time of their visitation,' do not turn away your eyes from the sorrowful face of Jesus, weeping so bitterly over your wretched state, and impending destruction! Listen with humility and with fear to the threats which fall from His lips. Remember that He does not threaten for ever, but follows up His cry of warning and call to repentance, with a crushing blow, if that merciful call is not listened to. Now is the time to make good what has been done amiss. Now is the time to redeem the past. Now is the time to change those terrible words of Christ into words of warning.

When Nineveh had well-nigh filled up the measure of her iniquities, and exhausted the treasury of divine patience and long-suffering, God sent unto her a Prophet, to proclaim in the name of the Lord: 'Yet forty days and Nineveh shall be destroyed.' Fear took possession of all hearts.

From the mightiest to the lowliest, they humbled themselves to the dust, and did penance in sackcloth and ashes. Then those prophetic words were changed into a mere threat; for God relented and turned away His indignation from them.

So will it be with you. Rise from your sins—break the chain of evil habits, and the wrath of the Lord will be appeased. When the voice of God sounds in your ear, listen to it. When conscience reproaches, hearken to its bitter words. There is health, there is life in them. They will be as a goad to your sluggish will; they will second the efforts of God's grace, and you will arise, so strengthened in the might of the Lord, that, like Samson, you will burst asunder the bonds that bind you, and walk abroad once again free—free with that freedom wherewith Christ hath made us free. Then will the tears of Christ be changed into tears of glad rejoicing. His threats will become words of praise and encouragement; He will call His Angels to be glad, and rejoice over one other sinner that has returned to Him and done penance.

TENTH SUNDAY AFTER PENTECOST.
THE PHARISEE AND THE PUBLICAN.

'I give Thee thanks that I am not as the rest of men.'— ST. LUKE xviii. 11.

I. IN this parable, Our Lord places before us for our instruction two men, differing as widely from each other in their characters, as did the respective classes to which they severally belonged: the Pharisee, on the one hand, as a type of the most strict and punctilious observance of the Mosaic Law; the Publican, on the other, as a type of godlessness and depravity; for he farmed the taxes from the oppressors of Israel, and enriched himself by the rapacity and the cruelty with which he extorted them from that already overburthened and down-trodden people. By selecting these two, Our Lord, as the Evangelist states, intended to give a startling lesson to those who trusted in themselves as just, and despised others.

Both these men went up into the Temple to pray; and

each of them, looking into his own inner consciousness, spoke to God words with which that secret examination inspired him. It filled the Pharisee with a high idea of his own excellence, as he called to mind his fasting and his prayer, his punctual payment of tithes, his almsdeeds, and the spotless integrity of his life. He boasted of being neither extortionate, nor unjust in his dealings with others; of being neither an adulterer, nor in fact anything else that was either wicked or profane. Therefore, he lifted up his voice and thanked God; but while doing so, cast a disdainful glance at the Publican, and numbered him among those of whom he could proudly say that he had never been one.

But what were the sentiments with which his self-inspection had inspired the Publican? The sight of his iniquities so confounded and humbled him, that he did not dare even to raise his eyes to heaven. He had not presumed to advance far into the Temple; 'he stood afar off.' His communing with himself found expression in that cry of shame and anguish, which breaks from a heart that is torn with sorrow for its sins: 'O God! be merciful to me a sinner.' He draws no comparison between himself and others. He is the last and worst. He is crushed, he is humbled; and God, Who searches the hearts of men, dismisses him to his home, enriched with grace and cleansed from every stain of sin, but spurns the proud Pharisee from His presence, more guilty and more displeasing in His sight, than he had been when he entered the Temple.

II. There is, perhaps, little either of the Pharisee's self-righteousness or of his self-glorification to be found among boys. Nevertheless the parable is not without its instruction for them, on other points about which they *do* plume themselves, and imagine 'that they are not as the rest of men.' You shall find some who are ever indulging in this mental act of thanksgiving for their physical or for their intellectual superiority to their fellows. They imagine themselves to be better looking, and better built than their companions; they are more polished, more gentlemanly, more courageous, more generous, more straightforward;

they can more elegantly translate a given passage, or solve more easily a difficult problem, or write an essay which will run more smoothly.

There are others who take great glory in their family connections. They are of gentle or of noble blood; and as this is perhaps the only excellence of which they can boast, they make much of it, and look down with lofty disdain upon those whom Providence has not so favoured. Hence that prying curiosity, on their part, to discover whether the parents of their schoolfellows are rich or poor; whether they are tradesmen, or follow some honourable profession. In their eyes, to be either poor, or lowly born, would almost seem to be a crime; if, at least, we may judge from the fervour with which 'they thank God that they are not, in this respect, like the rest of men.'

Yet, after all, how little have they to boast of, or to be thankful for! Often enough the boys whom they despise, surpass them in every other respect,—in intelligence, in honourable feeling, in virtue, in good looks, and even in that gentlemanly bearing upon which they set so great store. In after-life, these will be honoured for their inborn worth, and respected by men of sense, who will laugh to scorn, and sneer at the absurd pride, the impertinent pretentiousness, and the egregious folly of those who, though born of gentle blood, possess but few of those qualities which constitute the true gentleman.

III. Therefore, let every boy always bear in mind, that though spiritual pride, which constituted the Pharisee's guilt, may not have any place in his heart, yet it is more than probable that pride of another quality will take up its abode there. Of whatever kind it may chance to be, it is very displeasing to God; for, since it always makes us take to ourselves the glory and the credit of every good that we may either possess, or imagine that we possess, it thereby causes us to deprive God of the glory which is His due. For all those things in which we take pride are His. He has given us the use and the profit arising from them; 'but the glory He will not give to another.'

Whenever, therefore, we are led by the tempter, or by our own self-love, to look into our hearts and to take a self-complacent view of ourselves, we are acting like the Pharisee, especially if we cast a depreciating look upon our neighbour, and thank God that we are not like him. It is sinful to be proud of any virtue or of any good quality which we may think that we possess; but it is silly, as well as sinful, to glory in things so perishable as are strength and personal beauty.

Never boast about anything, but least of all about so merely accidental a good as nobility of blood. If God has given it to you, do not despise those who, with the exception of this, very likely surpass you in every other respect. To aim at being made much of on account of it 'betrays a pitiful ambition,' and betokens an emptiness of head closely bordering upon folly. Let it rather be your constant aim, to acquire those qualities of mind and of heart which constitute true nobility. Be humble and pure; be truthful, brave, and generous; then you will be noble indeed. Instead of instituting comparisons between yourself and others, try to think that all are more learned and more virtuous than yourself; and when proud thoughts arise in your mind, think of your many offences against God, strike your breast with humility, and say: 'O God, be merciful to me a sinner.'

ELEVENTH SUNDAY AFTER PENTECOST.
THE VICE OF DETRACTION.

'And the string of his tongue was loosed, and he spoke right.'—
St. Mark vii. 35.

I. Interpreters of Holy Scripture lay great stress upon these words, and see in them a deeper meaning than at the first glance reveals itself to a careless reader. The Evangelist, no doubt, by this phrase, meant to tell us, that after the touch of Our Lord's hand, and the word of power which accompanied it, the man who had been dumb, afterwards spoke correctly, with due articulation and right pronunciation. But they see far more than this in the words of the

Sacred Text, and would have them to signify, that he ever afterwards made a right use of his speech: 'He spoke right.'

How few there are who do this! The tongue is so slippery a member, and so hard to keep under control, that St. James calls it, 'an unquiet evil—a whole world of iniquity,' and considers him to be a perfect man who in his use of it does not offend God. By the tongue some sin in one way, and some in another, but we may say that nearly all sin by it in the way of detraction. In point of fact, there is no subject about which men are so fond of talking, as about their neighbours; and you shall rarely quit their society without either having heard them speak, or having yourself spoken, something to the discredit of your neighbour.

This is true, not only of men out in the world, but of boys living in the seclusion of College. What is your own experience on this score? You go into the play-room, or to the playground, and there you meet your class-mates, and straightway you hear something said about the professors, or the prefect, or your fellow-students which is injurious to their character. Their conduct is censured, their faults are picked out and ridiculed,—and where is the boy courageous enough to speak in their defence, or to refuse to join in the laugh raised against them? It is quite true that in all this there may not be anything that either severely wounds their reputation, or fastens upon you the guilt of a grievous sin; but yet you are thereby acquiring a most pernicious habit of detraction. It will cling to you, if you be not on your guard against it; it will lead you into many grievous sins; it will make you abominable in the sight of God, and detestable to the hearts of men.

II. In order, therefore, that you may understand in what the vice of detraction consists, you must know that, according to St. Thomas, it is defined to be: 'the unjust taking away of our neighbour's good name or reputation.' This may be done in various ways. If, for example, through spite, or dislike, or in order to screen himself from blame, one boy should accuse another of a theft which that boy has not committed, this accusation would be detraction, but detraction of a very grievous nature, which is called calumny, or imputing to another that which we know to be false.

Again; detraction may be committed by exaggerating the faults of others, and thus making them appear far greater than they really are; by putting an evil construction upon their actions; or by attributing to them base and unworthy motives. It is oftentimes a serious detraction to keep silence when another is highly commended, or to bestow faint praise, or to smile incredulously, or to raise one's eyebrows in feigned surprise.

But take notice, St. Thomas calls detraction: ' the *unjust* taking away of another man's character.' If there is a just cause for making known either his faults or his sins, that revelation ceases to be detraction; and, so far from being a sin, it becomes a positive duty; as for instance, when a boy discovers that one of his companions is corrupting the School by his filthy conversation. To make known to the proper authorities the wickedness of which he has been guilty is then no sin, for there is a just cause for taking away his good name. But in doing this, beware lest any motive of dislike or of revenge should prompt you to act. For, if this be the case, though you may commit no offence against justice, by taking away your neighbour's character, you will certainly sin grievously against charity, and fall away from God. Therefore, in order that you may be free from blame in taking away the good name of another, two things are requisite—a just cause, and an upright intention prompting you to act.

III. Having seen, then, in what the sin of detraction consists, conceive in your heart an honest hatred for an act so mean and so cowardly. You would look upon a boy who should strike another when his back is turned as a contemptible wretch to be scorned and spurned by every one in the School; well, detraction is a blow at your master's or your schoolfellow's honour, when neither of them is present to defend himself; and therefore, even from a worldly point of view, it is an act unworthy of a gentleman.

But there are higher and nobler motives to influence you, than the natural detestation which honourable boys feel for a mean and shabby act. There is the love of God, which cannot exist in one's heart without the love of one's neighbour. That boy, therefore, who pretends to love God, and yet feels not tenderly for the reputation of his masters and his schoolfellows, cannot be said to have any true love for God. The reasoning of St. John on this point is just and conclusive: 'If he loves not his neighbour whom he sees, how can he love God Whom he does not see?' Hence you may always measure your love of God, by your love of your neighbour; and as it is most important to love your God, judge how necessary it must be to love your neighbour.

Therefore, resolutely set your face against the vice of detraction. Give not ear unto anyone who is guilty of this sin in your presence. If you can adroitly turn the conversation to something else, do so; if you cannot, and the detractor is older than you are, keep silence, or think of something else, or leave the company. Shun those whom you know to be given to this vice, otherwise they will lead you to do as they do. Keep a careful watch over your tongue, and never permit a word of detraction to pass your lips; and since it is impossible to live in the world without hearing much that is to the prejudice of your neighbour, take this general rule for your guidance: be slow to believe evil of anyone, for men are prone to find fault with one another. On the other hand, you may generally believe whatever good they have to tell of one another, for they dole out praise, as the miser doles out his gold, only when driven to it by necessity.

TWELFTH SUNDAY AFTER PENTECOST.
FALLEN AMONG THIEVES.

'Who is my neighbour?'—ST. LUKE x. 29.

I. OUR Lord rarely refused to answer any question put to Him, even when those who asked it did so for the express purpose of puzzling, or of entrapping Him. In the present instance, a lawyer stood up among the audience which Jesus had just ceased to address, and asked Him that momentous question, which men, whose souls have been moved to their profoundest depths, will ask with a beating heart: 'What must I do to possess eternal life?' But in his case, anxiety to learn had not urged him to make the inquiry. Being himself a master in Israel, versed in the law and the prophets, and by his very calling bound to explain that law to others, he knew perfectly well what it required from those who would win the reward of heaven. He had, therefore, put the question in a spirit of captious criticism; and moreover, had probably done so with an air of conscious superiority, much in the same way as that in which a professor might interrogate one of his pupils.

Our Lord turned to him, and at once put him in his place; for, with that look of authority which made men call Him Master, He said to him: 'What is written in the law? How readest *thou*?' The lawyer gave the answer glibly enough, and Jesus commended him for it, just as a professor might applaud a little boy who had answered well: 'Thou hast answered right.' But He added with great significance: 'This *do*, and thou shalt live.' The lawyer at once saw the awkwardness of his position, and began to feel that instead of catechising, he had himself been catechised. Though somewhat crestfallen, he determined, if possible, to cover his defeat. He therefore asked: 'And who is my neighbour, whom the law says that I must love as my own self?'

Then Our Lord told of that man who, in going from Jerusalem to Jericho, fell among thieves, who robbed him, and left him wounded and senseless by the wayside. He put before His hearers the conduct of three men who travelled the same road and saw the unhappy man lying in his helpless and dangerous state. The priest and the levite looked at him, and passed on; but a Samaritan, between whose people and the Jews there existed a feud, embittered by the acrimony of religious controversy, saw him, and did not pass on. He knelt beside him; dressed and bound up his wounds; set him upon his own beast; and, taking him to an inn, paid for his careful tendance till he should have recovered. Then came from the lips of Christ another question: 'Which of these three men was neighbour to him that fell among thieves?' The lawyer answered: 'He that showed him mercy.' 'Go, therefore,' said Jesus to him, 'and do thou in like manner.'

II. From this you may learn that every one without exception is your neighbour, and has a claim upon your charity, whenever he is overtaken by any misfortune, and stands in need of help. Hence you may be called upon, even at College, to act the part of the good Samaritan. For though you may seem to be fenced in on every side from evil influences, yet, even at College, a boy, metaphorically speaking, may fall among thieves. For at College, as well as in the great world without, there is a way which leads from Jerusalem, the city of God, to the devil. It is infested with robbers, who lie in wait to shed innocent blood; and woe unto him who falls among them! The entrance to that slippery descent is idleness; and to fall among an idle set at College, is to take the first stride along that way of blood. For idle boys, in consequence of their idleness, are generally at war with their masters, who must, in conscience, use every effort to exact from them, by enforced industry, the work which a sense of duty should make them perform. Hence it is that the idle usually become discontented, and given to grumbling. They rebel, when they can do so with impunity, and systematically disobey even the direct and express orders of Superiors. When boys are in these dispositions, they are ripe for any work which the devil may think fit to suggest to them; and, therefore, we said that the idle, and those who consort with them, have taken the first stride along the way of destruction.

Again; a new boy may fall among a few wicked companions, who will dare to ridicule, and laugh at the piety which he has learnt, and brought with him, from his holy and happy home. Worst of all, he may fall into the company of those who will instil the poison that has made their own hearts desolate into his soul, which till that moment has lived in happy ignorance of its baneful existence. By these wretches he may be treated contumeliously, or robbed and wounded, or killed outright.

Your first duty, therefore, is one of charity towards yourself. Enter not upon that way of idleness which leads to the devil. Shun the company of those who either make light of piety, or speak sarcastically of those who practise it. Have the courage not to fear their words. What are these but the contemptible babblings of the most worthless boys in the School? Above all things avoid, just as you would avoid a leper, those who are corrupt in their words or in their actions. Should you discover any of this stamp among your companions, do not, for a single moment, hesitate to make them known to your Superior.. He will eject them from his innocent flock, lest the plague which has stricken them should infect all the little ones intrusted to his care.

III. Your next duty is to imitate the example of the good Samaritan, with regard to those who may chance to have fallen among thieves. There are occasions when this may be done, not only by those who are in the upper schools, but by even the youngest boy in the College. It is, however, from the elder boys that this work of charity is chiefly to be expected. You may, perhaps, have noticed some boy, who on his first coming to College had about him all the freshness and the fragrance of happy innocence. After a time you may, perhaps, remark that a great change has come over him. There is not the same light in his eyes, nor the same easy frankness in his manner. He has become a slouching, slovenly fellow, idle and mischievous, and afraid to look you in the face. There is about him an air of recklessness, a hardness of manner, a defiant boldness, which it is not pleasant to see.

If you take the trouble to search for the cause, you will probably find that he has fallen among a bad set: he has 'fallen among thieves.' Do not pass him by and leave him to his fate, as an incorrigible scapegrace! Do not say: 'It is no affair of mine; let Superiors look to it.' It *is* your affair. He is your neighbour. He is more—he is your little brother! One word from you may save him. Speak it, and there will be joy among the Angels of God! We have known cases of this kind, and have seen the wonderful change wrought in boys by a single kind word, or by a hand laid with friendly pressure upon the shoulder. There is a flash of gratitude from their eyes; there are a few faltering words, and then the flood of sorrow, long pent up in the heart, breaks forth.

Follow up this first victory by persistent, patient kindness, and you will bring back to Jesus Christ many a soul which would otherwise have perished miserably by the wayside, after being wounded by the hands of robbers. Especially let your kindness and your charity be poured out upon those boys who are not well-favoured, nor polished in manner, nor naturally lovable. You will oftentimes find that there is more true gold in them than in those who are externally more attractive. See in them only the children of Jesus Christ, and remember those blessed words of His: 'What ye did to the least of these little ones, ye did it to Me.'

THIRTEENTH SUNDAY AFTER PENTECOST.

GRATITUDE.

'There is no one found to return and give glory to God, but this stranger.'—ST. LUKE xvii. 18.

I. As Jesus journeyed through Samaria to Jerusalem, there met Him at the entrance to a certain town, the name of which the Evangelist does not mention, ten men 'that were lepers.' These wretched beings, drawn together by a common misery, which cut them off from all intercourse with their fellow-men, perceived Our Lord as He came onwards in the midst of His Apostles. Fame had, no doubt, carried to them the report of His miraculous power, and never-failing mercy; and their own pitiable, hopeless condition, prompted them to call upon Him to exercise that power and mercy in their behalf. Therefore, while Jesus was yet at a distance from them, they lifted up their voices and said: 'Jesus, Master, have mercy on us!' Never yet had He turned a deaf ear to that cry for mercy and compassion —a cry which the heavily-burthened always raised as He passed by. Now, also, pity moved His heart for these men, upon whom the hand of the Lord pressed so heavily.

As soon as their appeal reached His ear, He granted them what they asked, and bade them go and show themselves to the priests. Obedient to His word, they sped forwards on their way. But, lo! a sudden change comes over them as they go! Their sores dry up; the foul incrustation of their leprosy falls away from them; and, as the healthy blood goes coursing through their veins, they feel that in very deed they have been made clean! Joy beyond measure fills their hearts. It is so great that they can think of nothing but of their own happiness. Nay, they forget even Him Who had wrought this wonder in them!

But there is one who does not. As soon as he feels the joyous thrill of renewed health, filling his whole frame with gladness, he stands still. He thinks of that beautiful face, which had looked so kindly upon him; of that gentle voice, which had stirred his soul to its lowest depths. His heart overflows with gratitude. He turns back; he runs swiftly; he comes up with Jesus; and falling at His feet, adores and thanks Him. Then Our Lord, looking round upon those who followed Him, asks in a tone of reproachful sorrow: 'Were not *ten* made clean? Where are the nine?' Alas! they had forgotten their benefactor! One only, and he an alien, a Samaritan, had come back to give glory and thanks to God.

II. This incident ought to impress upon you the importance of, and the necessity for gratitude. You see that Christ expected the lepers to return, and thank Him, when they perceived the wonder which He had wrought in them. So also does He now look for gratitude from us, for the many graces and favours which He ceases not to shower upon us.

The reason of this is not far to seek. For gratitude shows that we appreciate the gift which has been bestowed, and that we are moved to love the person who has bestowed it. From this love and appreciation there naturally arises in the soul a desire to make a good use of the favour which has been granted to us. So that, after all, God, in wishing us to be grateful, is simply seeking our own advantage. He would have us find our obligation to love and serve Him, a light task and an easy yoke, that thus we may be led gently by the hand along the path of His commandments.

You ought, therefore, with all diligence to cultivate in yourself this much-neglected virtue of gratitude. A little thoughtful care will soon develop it in your heart. You might, for instance, begin each day by an act of gratitude for the repose which God has given you during the night, and for the life which He bestows upon you that day. Thank Him for being allowed to assist at Holy Mass, to make a meditation, and for being so often called during the day to sanctify your work by devout prayer. Then, as each of your studies comes round, they will one and all claim from you an act of thanksgiving for the inestimable advantage of a good education, and for the light by which you are enabled to grasp whatever you are taught. When you go to your meals, remember that it is from His hand you receive your nourishment; and be careful always to return thanks, with a devout heart and an attentive mind. Thank Him for your recreation, for the pleasure which you find in your games, and for the agreeable conversation of your companions. In fine, let the words '*Deo gratias*' rise frequently to your lips during the day; and when you retire to rest at night, again thank God for the sweet repose which He is about to give you, and ask Him to make you so love this virtue of gratitude, that your first thoughts on awaking may form themselves into an act of thanksgiving.

III. Another excellent means to acquire, and to keep a grateful mind towards God, is to be grateful to those also with whom we live. For if we are grateful to our fellow-men whom we see, it is likely that we shall be grateful also to God, Whom we do not see. For our reason will suggest to us, that if men deserve our gratitude for the little that they do for us, with far greater reason is God entitled to this, for the outpouring of His treasures into our hearts. You ought, therefore, to look upon it as a solemn duty, not only to be grateful to everyone that does you a service, but to give expression to your gratitude in their presence.

After your parents, those who have the greatest claim upon your gratitude are your masters, who, while you are under their charge, hold the place of your parents. A generous boy will bear in mind how patient they are with him, how painstaking, how eager to advance his interests. He will not know, perhaps, till he stand before the judgment-seat of God, how much of his virtuous life and of his good principles he owes to their exemplary conduct, and to their ceaseless prayer for him. Therefore, let him always express his thanks for every little act of kindness or of attention that they may show him, and always hold himself in readiness to do for them in return all the kindness that it may be in his power to offer.

To your fellow-students also you owe a debt of gratitude, and this in like manner you must always be willing to pay them. They often either do you a kindness, or show you particular favour. They defend you, perhaps, when you are spoken ill of; they go for your books; they execute your commissions; and frequently sacrifice their own pleasure and convenience to accommodate you. You should not, therefore, let slip any chance of repaying their goodness with its due meed of thanks. It will cost you very little to do this; but the advantages which you will reap from it are incalculable. It will attach all hearts to you, and thus widen the sphere of your power for good. Little by little, it will cast out of your soul all selfishness, and to do this, as you know, is no slight gain. It will, in fine, make God prodigal of His favours to you; eager on all occasions to come to your assistance; and will thus be a most powerful means to throw open to you the gates of the kingdom of heaven.

FOURTEENTH SUNDAY AFTER PENTECOST.
TRUST IN PROVIDENCE.

'Be not solicitous for your life what you shall eat, nor for your body what you shall put on.'—ST. MATT. vi. 25.

I. ALTHOUGH Our Lord has emphatically declared that no man can serve two masters so diametrically opposed to each other as are God and Mammon, yet there are many who make an attempt to reconcile the service of the one with the service of the other. They soon discover how futile is that attempt, and then, instead of throwing up the service of the world, and devoting their whole energy to the service of God, they excuse themselves for not so doing upon the plea that the claims of the world are so imperative and so absorbing, that they leave neither time nor inclination to satisfy those which importune them in the name of God. 'We must live,' say they; 'we must keep up our position in society; we must make provision for our children. This cannot be done unless we throw our whole energy into the work.'

Against reasoning so frivolous Our Lord directed a portion of His famous sermon on the Mount; for, knowing how easily men become blind to their eternal interests, when those which are temporal happen to clash with them, He wished to impress upon them the notion, that if they devoted their whole hearts to His service, casting all their care upon Him, He would most abundantly provide for their temporal wants. 'Be not solicitous for your life, He says, what you shall eat.' For which is deserving of greater care,—your life, or the food which sustains it? Without doubt it is your life. Which is worthy of greater care—your body, or the clothing which protects it from the inclemency of the weather? Undoubtedly it is your body. Why then do you waste your energies, and stretch them to their utmost tension, for a little food and raiment? If you make it your chief business to look after the welfare of that which is most precious to you, God will provide for your other necessities.

Look how He does this for the birds of the air! They do not sow, nor reap, nor gather into barns. Yet they never want, for God has a care of them. As for raiment, why should you be solicitous? Consider the lilies of the field how they grow! They labour not, neither do they spin. Yet, even Solomon in all his glory was never clothed like these! Now, if God provides so abundantly for the birds of the air; if he clothes so magnificently the flowers of the field, how much greater care must He have for His children, whom He destines to reign with Him for ever in heaven? 'Therefore,' He says to each of us, 'make it your chief aim to win that glorious destiny prepared for you, by ever pursuing after justice and sanctity, and then all your other wants will be liberally supplied for you by Almighty God.'

II. The solicitude which is reprobated by Our Lord rarely finds a place in a boy's heart; for the morrow troubles him but little. He has not to think about food or about raiment. When he is hungry, food is ready at hand; when he needs clothing, it is supplied as if by magic. But this does not prevent him from being troubled and solicitous about other matters, which, in a certain sense, subject him to the thraldom of Mammon. For, as in the world, men are drawn away from the service of God by the exigencies of their social position, or by the phantom of reputation, or by the pursuit of an absorbing profession—so also, boys at College are made to forget God by anxieties and cares, which, though small in comparison with those which weigh upon the breasts of their seniors, are nevertheless quite as destructive of their peace, and as effective in turning them from the one thing necessary.

Like men of the world, they have an ambition which craves to be satisfied. Like them, they have a social position which must be won, and a reputation which must be sustained. Hence it is, that a boy, in striving to be head of his school, and to preserve the esteem of his class-fellows, will oftentimes feel much of the anxiety which more serious burthens bring to the hearts of full-grown men. Now the danger is, that he may allow these anxious cares to take so firm a hold of him, that they will shut out from his soul the thought and the pursuit of more important things.

Therefore, for the college-boy also, the warning of Our Lord is necessary. He must not be solicitous for that which is of only secondary importance, and neglect that for which God created him. He must not make the pursuit of knowledge, though praiseworthy in itself, the main business of his life; nor again, must he regard the honour, or the reputation to be gained by its successful culture, as the chief object of his aims. Let him, then, first seek God and His justice, and those other things which are of minor importance—honour, reputation, and reward—will be given unto him.

III. Therefore, understand well what it is to seek *first* the kingdom of God and His justice. It is to make the service of God the main business of life, and to regard all other pursuits as only so many helps to enable you to transact that business well. It is to keep your heart detached from these less important things, and ever to bear in mind that they are valuable, only inasmuch as they help to procure for you the one thing necessary. The care and the anxiety which you may feel about other matters must be made subordinate to this; and if your look heavenwards should be in the least obscured by them, you must not hesitate to sweep them aside.

Therefore, do not allow anxiety about your studies to disturb your intercourse with God. When it importunes you during prayer, or meditation, or Mass, quickly set it aside; say that, at the proper time, you will give to these studies all the attention which they deserve. Be not over solicitous about what place you shall hold in your class. Work with all your might at the subject-matter put before you; then leave the result to God. Like the husbandman, wait in patience for the harvest. Your anxious trouble and foreboding will not advance it in the least.

As for repute among your class-fellows, for sharpness, or for learning, it is not worth striving after, and is frequently given to those who do not deserve it. Besides, always remember that even from an educational point of view, the first place, the prize, and the repute for learning, are not the objects to be aimed at in study. These are merely accidental things. They are the *enticements* to study, the *spur* to urge boys to greater exertion. Therefore, do not make them the chief end of your aims.

Do you rather always put God before you, as the great prize to be won; and consider the exact performance of duty as one of the best means for gaining that greatest of rewards. To do this, is to seek *first* the kingdom of God and His justice; and your heavenly Father, as an earthly recompense for your trust in Him, will take care that you want for none of those things which worldlings make the primary objects of their existence.

FIFTEENTH SUNDAY AFTER PENTECOST.
THE COMPASSION OF JESUS.

'Being moved with mercy towards her, He said: Weep not.'—ST. LUKE vii. 13.

I. As Jesus drew nigh to the city of Naim, travel-stained, weary, and footsore after a long journey of five-and-twenty miles, through a mountainous country, there issued through its gates a sad funeral procession. The hired mourners were wringing their hands, beating their breasts, and weeping as custom prescribed that they should weep over the death of an only son. Such truly was he, whom they were now bearing to his last resting-place without the city walls. Close behind the bier walked a veiled figure, bowed down with grief, and weeping bitter tears. This was his mother. Death had already once before visited her house, and taken away the father of her boy, leaving her desolate, indeed, but hopeful; for there yet remained with her an only child, upon whom she lavished all the love of her heart. She looked to him, as to one who would worthily fill the vacant place by her fireside, and become to her a consolation, and a staff to support her declining years. But, alas! the King of terrors had once again darkened her door, and stricken down the young man in the pride of his strength, and the bloom of his years. Therefore, with broken heart and tottering step she now followed him to the grave.

Jesus, and they who were with Him, stood still as the sad procession came slowly on; and seeing the poor weeping mother, His heart bled with pity for her awful affliction. May not her sorrow have brought to His mind the image of another Son going to His death, and of another heart-broken Mother following Him, as He staggered onwards under the heavy Cross? It may have been so! Compassion stirred His soul to its lowest depths, and as the sorrowing mother came near Him, He spoke gently and soothingly to her, and said: 'Weep not.' Then He laid His hand upon the bier, and those who carried it stood still. A hush came over the multitude as they looked towards Him, in anxious expectation of what was about to happen. The voice which had bade the mother weep no more, once again broke the stillness which had fallen upon the spectators. Clear and commanding, it rang out those startling words of power: 'Young man, I say to thee, Arise!' Obedient to the words of the Author of life, he who had been dead sat up, and began to speak. A stupor of amazement and of fear came over all, as they looked upon him, and while they lifted up their voices and cried aloud that God had again visited His people, Jesus withdrew from the midst of them, and entered the city.

II. The same Jesus is still among us, filled with the same sentiments of compassion, and ready to work the same astounding miracle, not perhaps for our bodies, but most certainly for our souls. The death of the body is to Him a matter of little moment. It is the gate through which the soul must pass to the embraces of her God. Hence He bids us not to fear it. But it is not so with the death of the soul; that death is followed by consequences which are frightful to contemplate.

Therefore, Jesus is anxious to ward off from us this kind of death, and eager to raise up those souls that have succumbed to it. He bids us fear only those who can inflict this death upon us. These are the evil spirits, wicked companions, and the unmortified passions of our own hearts. These last are within us, like the smouldering embers of a fire; evil companions, by their bad example, fan them into life; the devils feed the flame, and incite those around us and our own selves to add fresh fuel to the fire. If the young suffer themselves to be fascinated by the light which the first spark kindles, they speedily die the death of the soul. Then, like the young man carried forth through the gates of Naim, they are borne away from the company of the just, and from the city of God. Their hearts grow cold and callous to all that is left behind. They become powerless for good; sinful actions bind fast their hands, as with bonds of brass; and veil their eyes, that they may not see. Finally, they are hurried off into that dreadful state in which sin, having become habitual, holds them down in a narrow, darksome grave, crushed beneath the ponderous stone of their accumulated, and oft-repeated transgressions.

How sad is their state, and how awful are its consequences! But Jesus is full of compassion; though they are lying in the corruption and the rottenness of sin, they are His children, and His heart is moved with pity by the tears, and by the unutterable sorrow of those who follow them to the very brink of destruction. These are their Angel guardians; or it is the mother that bore them in pain and in sorrow; or they are the masters, whose hearts have been lifted up in prayer for them. Jesus sees their tears, and is not deaf to their groaning. The strong cry which goes up from their hearts, for the salvation of those whom they love, reaches the very centre of His heart. He lays His hand mercifully, but firmly, upon the bier—which interpreters explain to be the body—and either strikes it with some malady, or visits it with some misfortune, the healthful smart of which brings the soul to a sense of its peril. He flashes into its darkened interior a ray of His divine light, and then speaks that word of power: 'Young man, I say to thee, Arise! Arise from thy habits of sin. Burst asunder the bonds which hold thee fast, and cast aside the napkin which blinds thine eyes.' If the soul hearken to His call, He will pour His grace into her, cleanse her from all her filth, and restore to her that supernatural life by which we live unto God.

III. The Gospel is silent about the after-history of that young man, whom Christ raised from the dead. Therefore, we know not whether he fell away from the path of virtue, or persevered in the love and the service of Him Who had dealt so wonderfully with him. But we should imagine that the memory of what he had seen, in that land beyond the grave, would keep his feet upon the narrow way which leads to life, and that a deep sense of gratitude to Jesus would make his heart for ever steadfast in His love.

But can we say as much for those whom Jesus raises from spiritual death to the life of grace? Alas! no; they often voluntarily again seek death; and many there are for whom that relapse terminates in the flames of hell. God grant that this misfortune may never befall you! If He has ever, in His exceeding great kindness and love, stopped you upon the way to eternal death, and bade you rise once more to life, let gratitude arm you with a firm resolve never again to risk so terrible, and so irremediable a calamity.

This determination will be worthless, unless you at the same time most carefully avoid whatever has hitherto been for you the occasion of sin. If it has been the corruption of your own heart, keep a strict watch over it, and learn how to check and to mortify its desires. If your eyes have been a snare unto you, by reading what is unsuited to your age, or by looking at unbecoming objects, set over them a strict guard, for they are the windows of the soul, and through them the devil enters like a thief to plunder your treasures. If your ears have drunk in the poison of the knowledge of evil, close them henceforth against everything, except good.

But all these precepts will be of no avail to you, unless you obtain from God, by means of earnest prayer, the strength necessary to carry them into effect. Prayer nourishes and fortifies the soul. It prepares it worthily to receive the Sacraments, and to draw from those treasures of grace all the help that God intended them to impart.

Therefore, be earnest in prayer, and when restored to the arms of your Mother the Church, never again cause her a single pang, nor bring a tear of sorrow to the eyes of those who love you, and who are interested in your well-being.

SIXTEENTH SUNDAY AFTER PENTECOST.
INSINCERITY.

'When Jesus went into the house of one of the chief of the Pharisees, on the Sabbath-day, to eat bread, they watched Him.'—ST. LUKE xiv. 1.

I. ON the occasion when Jesus honoured the table of this chief of the Pharisees with His divine presence, He found Himself surrounded by a circle of that rigid sect, which ever showed so determined an hostility both to Himself and to His doctrine. Friendly feeling had evidently not moved them to introduce Him into their company. For, though their faces beamed forth looks of welcome, and their tongues uttered words of veneration and esteem, yet deep down in their hearts there lay hidden a budding germ of mistrust and of hatred. Their eyes were fastened upon Him to discover matter for censure: 'they watched Him.'

Also, be it remarked, the Evangelist tells us, that there sat in the presence of Jesus a man sorely afflicted with dropsy—a disease beyond the reach of the healing art. Many interpreters have thought that this man had been purposely placed there as a sort of bait to catch the well-known compassion of His loving heart, and thus entrap Him into healing him on the Sabbath-day. If, yielding to the impulse of His merciful nature, He should work a miracle to cure him, they would then be able to denounce Him as a transgressor of the law, and thus weaken His influence among the people.

The loving glance of Our Lord, naturally enough, fell upon the form of the swollen and disfigured creature before Him, and while every eye looked eagerly at Him, and every tongue made ready to cry out against the legality of the act which they saw that He would perform, Jesus startled them by putting as a question that which they were only waiting to formulate as an imperative prohibition. 'Is it lawful,' He asks, 'to heal on the Sabbath-day?' An ominous silence held every tongue mute. They were surprised and confounded. They dared not say, 'No'; they would not say, 'Yes.' We may easily picture to ourselves the look with which Jesus scanned the silent and discomfited assembly— a look of sorrow for their sin rather than of righteous anger for their insincerity and hypocrisy. Then, after healing and dismissing the dropsical man, He so justified His act that they dared not utter a single syllable against Him.

II. What you must specially remark in this Gospel is the absence of sincerity which is manifest in the dealings of the Pharisees with Our Lord. They pretended friendly and reverential feelings towards Him, that they might only the more easily ensnare Him. They did not dare openly to meet Him as an adversary; but hating Him as they did, and wishing for His overthrow, they thought to accomplish it without incurring the public odium which they foresaw would fall upon them if they tried to cast discredit upon one so beloved by the people. They were therefore insincere.

Now, as there are in the character of a man few blots which are held in more utter abhorrence by his fellow-men than is this want of plain dealing, it would be well for you most carefully to guard yourself against it. For this purpose, examine your conduct, and see whether you can detect in it the taint of insincerity. If in your intercourse with your masters, or with your companions, you pretend to be that which you are not, then you are insincere. There are some boys who, like the Pharisees, use their faces, their speech, their actions, to hide their real selves from others, in order that they may the more effectually carry out some end which they happen to have in view. They express with their lips sorrow, or joy, or indignation, but feel none in their hearts. Hence they deceive those who trust them; for they make them believe that they may be relied upon. But in the hour of trial the credulous discover to their cost upon what a hollow reed they have leant for support.

If it is bad to feign that which we do not feel, how vile

and detestable must it be, not only to play the hypocrite, but to boast of it before others! There are boys who are not ashamed to do this. By cunning, smooth-faced hypocrisy, they either obtain some favour, or escape some punishment, and then have the audacity to vaunt of their meanness, as of some feat of intellectual skill, by which—to use their own phraseology—' they twisted the Superior round their finger.' Happy would it be for them, if their school-fellows, instead of laughing at their knavery, were to arm themselves with canes, and beat these serpentine ways out of them.

Besides, it is very often a mistake, on the part of these youthful diplomatists, to imagine that they have deceived their Superior. As often as not he is only half-deceived, and that too, through a motive of charity; for although over-great plausibility in a boy raises in one's soul an amount of disgust which it is difficult to conceal, and makes one's fingers tingle to knock it out of him by physical force, yet one generally sets aside the impulse to use strong measures, as dictated by unworthy suspicions. Nevertheless we think that if, instead of listening with a half-angry, half-amused air to his cleverly devised approaches towards the object of his desires, each master were to dash straight across his tortuous paths, and tell him what he comes to ask for, he would do him a kindness for which that boy would in after years most sincerely thank him. Consideration for his feelings is altogether out of place here. He does not appreciate it, but attributes any forbearance to weakness or to folly.

III. Therefore, cultivate a spirit of straightforwardness in all your dealings with those around you. Always say what you mean, and mean what you say. If you have some object to gain, go straight to it. For, as the shortest way between any two given places is a right line, so the easiest and most expeditious way to compass any end which you may have in view, is to follow the straightest way that conducts to it, provided always that it is a just one. Impress this deeply upon your mind, and let it be one of your principles to be acted upon throughout life. By this simple strategy you will be able to outwit the most astute wriggler that ever wound and wormed himself to the end which he had in view. To dash straight across his zigzags and concealed approaches is for him the most disconcerting of manœuvres. Its very simplicity will seem, in his eyes, the result of most consummate skill, and he will fear you as an adversary against whom all his wiles are in vain.

Cast out of your heart the pitiful ambition of being thought the most knowing among your companions. They may laugh at you for it now, but they will scorn and hate you for it hereafter. Besides, in order to sustain so unenviable a reputation, you will be forced to practise insincerity till there grow upon you the habit—if we may use the expression—of aiming round the corner at every object; till hypocrisy will become so much a part of your nature that you will end by deceiving yourself.

Therefore, detest and loathe all deceit. Hate all double-dealing, sneaking, slimy ways. Be brave enough to endure the smart of the rod, or the cutting word of reproof, rather than be guilty of deceit. The rod will do you no harm; it touches the skin only; but deceit penetrates like a subtle poison into the heart. However, bear in mind that sincerity, like all other virtues, must be fought for and won with some little pain. Therefore, watch your conduct, and mercilessly cut out of your heart all insincerity. Let no day pass without earnestly praying to be freed from it. If you should fail at times, be not discouraged; go on struggling for it, and in the end the prize of a sincere and guileless heart will be yours.

SEVENTEENTH SUNDAY AFTER PENTECOST.
CHARITY TOWARDS OUR NEIGHBOUR.

'The second is like to this: Thou shalt love thy neighbour as thyself.'
—St. Matt. xxii. 39.

I. The Sadducees, who did not believe in the future resurrection of the body, brought to Our Lord what they considered a very puzzling case—that of the woman who had had seven husbands; and they asked Him with the air of men who deemed their question unanswerable: 'If there be a resurrection, as you maintain that there is, whose wife of the seven shall she be?' Our Lord's clear and luminous answer showed their interpretation of the Scripture to be so flagrantly erroneous that even His bitterest enemies cried out in admiration: 'Thou hast answered well!'

Among the crowd which had gathered round Our blessed Lord, there chanced to be a certain lawyer who, seeing how completely Jesus had solved this hitherto unanswerable difficulty, ventured in his turn to ask a question about which the Rabbis had indulged in much fruitless discussion. 'Which,' said he, 'is the *great* commandment of the law?' It is evident, both from the excellent spirit with which he accepted the answer, and from Our Lord's words of commendation for that spirit, that he had put the question with no malevolent intention; and though St. Matthew says that he asked it, 'tempting Him,' yet the expression does not mean that he did so with an evilly disposed mind, but simply with a desire to try Our Lord, and perhaps also to satisfy a very laudable curiosity.

In reply to his question, Jesus said: 'Thou shalt love the Lord thy God with thy whole heart, and with thy whole soul, and with thy whole mind. This is the greatest, and first commandment; and the second is like to this: Thou shalt love thy neighbour as thyself.' On hearing this, the lawyer expressed his satisfaction in words of heartfelt praise; and Jesus in His turn said to him: 'Thou art not far from the kingdom of God.' The whole law of God rests, therefore, upon these two precepts, and is comprised in them. To love God, as Our Lord has said that He must be loved, means that we give to Him our allegiance on all points, not excepting even the least; and to love our neighbour as we love ourselves, is to be just to him, and never in the slightest matter to do unto him what the law of God forbids.

II. Upon this second commandment, which Our Lord says is like to the first, take care to fix your special attention. It is the test by which you will always be able to discover whether you really love God with your whole heart, or not. For, as love of our neighbour is the outcome of our love of God, and bears the same relation to it as the blossom and the fruit do to the tree which brings them forth, so also the existence of fraternal charity in your heart will be a proof that the love of God is there too.

What then is it to love our neighbour as we love ourselves? It is, in all matters, to mete out to him the same measure of justice that we would have measured out to ourselves. It is to do unto him as we should wish that he would do unto us. Call to mind what those things are which you would not wish others to do to you.

First, you cannot bear unkindness in any shape or form. It wounds and lacerates you like a jagged weapon. You cannot bear your companions to be either rude or uncivil towards you. You writhe under their ridicule, when they raise a laugh at your expense, by pointing out your little weaknesses, or by laying their fingers upon your defects of mind or of body.

Again; you do not like to be teased, worried, and persecuted by those petty annoyances, which it is the delight of ungenerous natures to inflict upon those who are either younger or weaker than themselves. You are indignant when you find either that your confidence has been abused, or that the faults which you have committed have been revealed.

Lastly, to come to matters of minor importance, you suffer keenly when you are thrust from your place at the fire by some bully, who uses his strength to inflict pain and inconvenience upon the weak and defenceless. You are angered when those who copy his evil example either make you lose your place in the cricket-field, or do not suffer you to take your turn in the ball-alley, but, acting upon the principle that might is right, exclude you from these places as long as it seems good to them. It is like a thorn in your side to be obliged to witness their selfishness without being able to make them feel that the rights of others should be respected.

III. Having considered what kind of actions you would not like others to do unto you, be determined never to do any of them to your neighbour, and then you will be loving him, as you love yourself. Examine yourself, therefore, carefully, to see whether you mete out to others the same measure that you would have them mete out unto you.

On the score of kindness, how do you behave to those with whom you live? Are you disposed to do for the least of them those little services which politeness and gentlemanly feeling make men of the world do for one another, but which college boys are so apt utterly to neglect? Do you not often treat your companions with contempt and ridicule, forgetting how easy it is to say a smart thing, but how difficult to cure the wound which it inflicts? If you yourself have ever felt the keen edge of ridicule, do not gash and wound the hearts of others with it. Do not plague those who are younger and more helpless than yourself, by those practical jokes in the contrivance of which the juvenile mind is so ingenious. To do so is the sign of a cruel and tyrannical spirit, which develops itself to an alarming extent by indulgence. If any of your companions intrusts a secret to your keeping, inviolably guard it; and never abuse the simplicity of new comers by telling to every one that which in their guilelessness and inexperience they may have told to you either about themselves or about their homes. Above all things, study not to be selfish. Do not, at all times and upon all occasions, think and care only for yourself. It is positively painful for Superiors to perceive this unlovely trait of character in any one confided to their care; and it is their duty to point out and then to help their subjects to remove so ugly a blemish.

Therefore, aid them in this important branch of your education by trying to treat all, even the least of your companions, as you yourself would wish to be treated. Do not act upon that fallacy which we so often hear from the mouths of schoolboys: 'I myself used to be badly and mercilessly bullied, and therefore I must do to others as others have done to me.' But did you like it? No, you did not. How did you wish to be treated? Recall that wish now to your mind, and do unto others what you then so eagerly desired that others should do unto you.

EIGHTEENTH SUNDAY AFTER PENTECOST.

LUKEWARMNESS.

'They brought Him one sick of the palsy, lying on a bed.'—ST. MATT. ix. 2.

I. AFTER crossing the Sea of Galilee, Jesus went into His own city, and entered the house of some disciple or of some friend to refresh His wearied body. The report that He had come soon spread abroad, and in a short time a dense crowd had gathered in front of the house, eager to catch a glimpse of His sacred person, and to hear the words which fell from His mouth. Among the rest, there came four men, bearing in a bed one stricken with palsy. He could neither move, nor do anything for himself. Very likely he had not been able to ask these charitable persons to do this great act of kindness for him. Compassion for his wretched condition, and a firm conviction that Jesus could heal him, had probably moved them to lend him their aid.

On reaching the house, and seeing how vain would be the attempt to force a passage through the closely-packed throng, they made their way to the back; and as houses in the East are flat-roofed, and rarely more than one storey high, they found very little difficulty in mounting upon it, or in drawing up after them their sick man in his bed. Once upon the roof, they easily removed the tiles or the sods which covered it, and, having accomplished this, they lowered the palsied man down before the very feet of Jesus.

Their unwavering faith, as well as the wretched state of the sick man, excited the compassion of Our Lord. Looking at the poor, helpless being, He said to him: 'Be of good heart, son, thy sins are forgiven thee!' On coming into the presence of Jesus he had, no doubt, been moved by divine grace, and had recognised that his bodily ailments were but a figure of his internal maladies; sorrow had then touched his heart and cleansed it of its sins, and therefore Jesus told him that those evils which he had seen within himself had ceased to exist.

After thus healing the disease of his soul, there followed

next the cure of his body. For when the Pharisees had heard His words, they were horror-stricken, and mentally accused Him of blasphemy. But Jesus, looking upon them, said: 'Why think ye evil in your hearts? Whether is it easier to say: Thy sins are forgiven thee, or to say: Take up thy bed and walk? But that ye may know that the Son of Man hath power to forgive sins,' (then He said to the man sick of the palsy:) 'Arise, take up thy bed, and go into thy house.' Upon the word, he who had been helpless as a child stood up, and went forth in perfect health, so that fear and astonishment fell upon all, and they glorified God for having given so great power to one upon whom they still looked as a mere man like themselves.

II. Many are the lessons which this incident of the Gospel narrative might teach us; but let this one suffice—that the palsied man is but a material image of a soul which is lukewarm in the service of God. It is not dead, and yet it can hardly be said to live its spiritual life; for its power and its energy are gone. It is in an utterly helpless state, and may easily be pushed into the abyss of sin, in which it will inevitably die the death. See whether this frightful lethargy has not settled down upon your soul, and if you detect any sign of its presence, make a vigorous effort to shake it off. In order to assist you in this examination, consider attentively some of the signs which usually indicate the presence of lukewarmness in the soul.

The first sign given by spiritual writers, is a general disgust for all that concerns the service of God. If you are struggling against this, and feel sorry that you cannot be rid of it, you are not lukewarm; you are simply labouring under the trial of spiritual dryness, which is a very different thing from lukewarmness. But if, instead of giving it battle, you succumb to it, and take no pains to be rid of it; if you do not recall your wandering thoughts, when at prayer; if you indulge in a state of dreaminess during meditation, and look upon Mass and spiritual reading as wearisome impositions; if you avoid visiting the Blessed Sacrament, and set little store upon those various other exercises of piety, which are always encouraged among the boys of our Colleges; if you go rarely and with reluctance to Confession and Communion, and, in general, look upon all spiritual duties as something unpleasant which must be endured, rather than as a loving service of duty to God, you may take it for granted that you are in a state of spiritual lukewarmness.

The second sign is negligence in the performance of duty. All those things which we have already mentioned are duties more or less binding upon you. But besides these, there are other duties no less obligatory. These are study, obedience to Rule, submission to masters, and the like. Therefore, if you suffer the disgust which you feel for them so to lay hold of you, that it causes you to perform them with negligence; if you study only when under the eye of a Superior, and idle when beyond the reach of his surveillance; if you break and contemn the Rule; if you disobey the injunctions of your professors, and rebel against their authority, you may set down all these as indications of lukewarmness.

The third sign is the neglect of duty. If you read when you should study; if, laying aside the work prescribed for you, you take up that which you need not do at all; if you omit your prayers, or absent yourself from duty, or disregard Rule, or show a sort of indifference to all discipline, you are certainly in the state of lukewarmness. Be afraid of this state, for it is one of great peril.

If you were altogether cold, that is, given up entirely to sin, there would be some hope of your cure; but lukewarmness so deceives men by the appearance which it wears of spiritual life, and by the seeming absence of grievous disorders, that it causes no apprehension, and therefore is not attended to. Hence the general opinion, that the state of grievous mortal sin is more hopeful than that of lukewarmness: 'I would that thou wert either cold or hot. But because thou art lukewarm, I will vomit thee out of My mouth.'

III. If you should have the misfortune to be in this wretched state, how are you to rid yourself of it, and once more regain your former vigour? To do this, we must confess, is a matter of no small difficulty; for, a boy who, for some time, has been leading a life of lukewarmness, is much in the same state as that in which we find ourselves when just aroused from a deep sleep. We are without resolution, without energy; we are nerveless, helpless, and well-nigh glued to our beds. Now, if we would not fall back upon our pillows, and yield ourselves up again to our slumbers, what must we do? We must at once obey the first summons to rise. So also must he, unto whom the voice of God says: 'Arise, thou that sleepest.' There must then be no putting the matter off for a little longer time. If that be done, the drowsiness of sloth will master him, and he will lie helpless.

Therefore, the first thing to be done, is to attend to the call of God's grace; to stretch forth your hands to Him; and to ask Him to aid you. When once roused from your sluggishness, bestir yourself, and shake off your torpor, by the terrifying thought of the perilous condition in which you are, while in the state of lukewarmness. Then change the whole tenor of your life. Heretofore you have been sleepy and careless at prayer; henceforth be diligent and wakeful. Till now, meditation has been an intolerable burthen to you; from this day forth listen attentively to it, and exercise your mind and heart upon the matter which it puts before you. In the past, you have dreamed away the time of Holy Mass; but now, ever bear in mind that it is the open fountain of grace, at which you may slake your thirst, and in which you may be cleansed from your daily stains. Hitherto you have gone to Confession and to Communion without a previous careful preparation; henceforth be resolved never to approach the sacred tribunal, nor to sit at the Holy Table, without a most diligent search into the recesses of your heart, and a most fervent outpouring of prayer.

Finally, as a practical proof that you are really in earnest, work hard at your books during the time appointed for labour. Humbly submit yourself to discipline, and though at first you will feel weariness and disgust, yet do not grow faint-hearted on account of occasional failures. Gird up your loins like a man; face the difficulty, and you will conquer it. But, remember, that nothing can be done by a mere spurt. You must make a steady, persevering effort. It will at first be painful to you; and morally, you will feel what a man experiences physically, when he begins to take violent bodily exercise; he is stiff and sore in every joint, so as to be almost unable to move; but, if he go on regularly every day, all this will pass away. So will it be with you, in your spiritual life. At first, after your long state of inactivity and torpor, you will find everything in that life hard and painful; but if you persevere in your exercises, its manifold duties will shortly become as easy to you as it is to walk or to breathe.

NINETEENTH SUNDAY AFTER PENTECOST.
THE MARRIAGE FEAST.

'Friend, how camest thou in hither, not having on a wedding-garment?'
—ST. MATT. xxii. 12.

I. THE parable read in the Gospel for this day, is the last of a series. Christ addressed it to the members of a deputation, sent to Him from the chief priests and the ancients of the people. They came to Him as He taught in the Temple, and in a peremptory manner asked Him, by what authority He had ridden triumphantly into the city, cast the buyers and the sellers out of the Temple court, and received the loud acclaims of the people, greeting Him as the long-expected Messias. Jesus did not deign to reply to their question, for it had already been answered by His doctrine, His miracles, and His life. Besides, He knew full well that they came, not to learn the truth, but to entrap Him into saying something, which would give them a handle against Him.

In order, therefore, to punish them for their malevolence, He asked them concerning John's baptism a question which they dared not answer. Then he pointed out in parables, how they had always talked much, and had done little; had been honoured with a high trust, and had betrayed it; had been called by God, but had followed rather the counsels of the devil. Therefore He tells them, that, owing to their hardness of heart, and their fanatical opposition to grace, He will henceforth turn away from them, and their nation, to preach to the Gentiles, who will listen to His words and follow His counsels.

At this point the parable becomes interesting to us, unto whom He vouchsafed this great and unmerited mercy. For Our Lord goes on to say, that when the King came into the banquet-hall to look at the guests, whom his servants had gathered together, he noticed among them one who had not on a wedding-garment. This man either had neglected to bring one with him, or had refused to accept that which the servants offered to each as he entered the door. The surprised and indignant Monarch halts before him, and asks with some sternness: 'Friend, how camest *thou* in hither, not having on a wedding-garment?' To this question he received no answer, for the abashed and trembling wretch could not make any reply. Then the King, turning to his servants, said to them: 'Bind fast his hands and his feet, and cast him forth into the exterior darkness; there shall be weeping and gnashing of teeth!' Upon the word, they seized the intruder, bound him, and thrust him forth from the brightly-lighted hall, into the gloom of the lampless streets.

II. There is in the Church of God a great banquet, unto which all are invited, and at which the guests partake of the body and blood of Jesus Christ. To that Sacred Table the voice of your Superiors continually exhorts you to approach; and the heart of Jesus pleads earnestly for your company. Are there not times when you refuse the loving invitation, and petulantly say to Him: 'I pray Thee hold me excused!' Do you not also resent, as an unwarrantable interference with your liberty, the paternal advice of your Superiors, urging you to draw from this source of grace that spiritual strength of which you stand in so great need? Oh, how foolish are those boys who are so taken up with amusements, or so besotted with tepidity and indolence, or so given up to sin, that they will not attend to the voice of

Our Lord, inviting them with loving kindness 'to taste and see how sweet He is!' Their fate will be like that of those wicked men who not only refused the King's invitation, but maltreated his messengers. The wrath of God will be kindled against them, and their house will be made desolate.

Equally terrible is the fate of those who dare to sit at the King's banquet without the nuptial robe required by Him. What is that robe? Some interpreters say one thing, and some another; but you may say to yourself: 'It is purity of heart. If I have not that, I shall approach like Judas, and draw from the lips of Christ that sorrowful question: "Friend, for what hast *thou* come? How hast *thou* dared to come hither without that white robe, that spotless heart, that pure mind, that clean imagination, without which it would be a sacrilegious profanation to partake of My banquet?"'

Oh, let every boy most carefully avoid the guilt of so great a crime! For an unworthy participation of the Holy Eucharist has a terrible effect upon our moral nature. It binds in bonds of iron all the powers of the soul. It delivers it up helpless into the hands of its enemies. It brings down upon it the darkness and the gloom of the blackest night, and makes it grope like one that is blind, till it stumbles at last into that abyss of exterior darkness, in which there is 'weeping and gnashing of teeth.'

III. When, therefore, in obedience to the invitation of Our Lord, you venture to approach His sacred banquet, and to sit at His Holy Table, reflect seriously what that is of which you are about to partake. He invites you to eat of His holy eucharistic feast. The meat which He places before you is the body and blood which were offered up in sacrifice for you. It is the same Jesus that taught in the Temple, and went about Judea, and laboured, and died for you! It is God—the great, the incomprehensible. He is coming into your heart. He will repose there, as in His tabernacle. He will speak to you, face to face, as a friend is wont to speak to his friend,—nay, rather as a loving father is wont to speak with his little child. How pure, then, ought to be that mouth which shall receive the Lord! how spotless that heart which shall be His resting-place! He is the all holy God. He is infinite purity. He would not be born into this world but from a Virgin Mother. His delight is to feed among the lilies—that is, among pure souls.

It is necessary, therefore, that those who approach Him should be clothed in spotless purity of mind and of heart. You must consequently be most careful before Communion to acquire, and after Communion to guard with jealous care, this most precious and delicate of virtues.

Before Communion examine your conscience, to see whether any stains disfigure your soul. Say to yourself: 'Have my thoughts been pure? Have my words been innocent? Have my desires been in conformity with the law of God? Have my actions been modest?' If your conscience reproaches you upon any of these points, go straightway to the tribunal of penance, and with heartfelt sorrow acknowledge your sins; firmly resolve never to repeat them; and the blood of Jesus will cleanse you from every stain.

After Communion, remember that you have received into your heart the body and blood of the Lord. He is with you; and, as the Fathers express it, 'He is bone of your bone, and flesh of your flesh.' Do not, therefore, dishonour Him by sin, and thus trample under foot the blood which He shed for you. If you ardently desire that so dread a calamity may never befall you, go frequently to this divine banquet, in which is given you to drink that wine which 'springeth forth virgins.' Be specially careful to preserve unspotted the white robe which God gives you at this Holy Table, and then He will ever gladly receive you to that feast unto which He so lovingly invites you, saying: 'Come, eat and drink, and be inebriated, My dearly beloved!'

TWENTIETH SUNDAY AFTER PENTECOST.
GRATITUDE TO MASTERS.

'There was a certain Ruler whose son was sick at Capharnaum.'—
ST. JOHN iv. 46.

I. THE Ruler, mentioned in this day's Gospel, is generally supposed to have been one of Herod's courtiers. He had probably never given the humble carpenter of Nazareth more than a passing thought, till the chastening influence of sorrow had touched his heart, and forced him to reflect. A mortal sickness had stricken down his darling child, the hope of his house, and stretched him upon his bed of death. The physicians evidently held out no hope of recovery; for all that their medical skill could do had been tried, and tried in vain. In his distress, the father bethought him of the Prophet who had arisen in Israel. The whole of Galilee had now for some time been ringing with the stories of His wondrous power; and the praise of His gentleness and compassion was in every mouth. The father's heart bade him go to Jesus, and, obedient to its voice, he set out in the early morning, and at the seventh hour, or about one o'clock, reached Cana, where Jesus chanced to be staying.

With all the anguish of a father whose only child is in peril, he presented himself before Our Lord, and said to Him: 'Lord, come down, and heal my son, for he is at the point of death.' Jesus, seeing that the man had a merely natural faith or trust in His power—a faith that did not yet spring from a supernatural principle, said to him: 'Unless you see signs and wonders, you will not believe.' The seeming unwillingness of Jesus to grant his petition made the father's eagerness to obtain the favour which he came to ask only the more intense, for with even more earnestness than before he said to Him: 'Come down, Lord, before my son die!' Jesus then said to him: 'Go thy way; thy son liveth.' The Ruler doubted not for a single instant the word of Our Lord. He felt sure that what He said had already become an accomplished fact; and so certain did he feel of his son's safety, that he stayed in the town the whole of that night. This we gather from the words of his servants, when they met him upon his return : ' Yesterday,' said they to him, ' at the seventh hour, the fever left him.'

What must have been that father's joy when he once more clasped to his heart the son whom he had so nearly lost! How full of gratitude must that boy ever afterwards have been towards that father for having been instrumental in rescuing him from the jaws of death! That gratitude would form another link to bind them still more closely together.

II. This miracle should recall to your mind the tender solicitude of your masters, and especially of your Confessor, about your spiritual life. Boys, no doubt, oftentimes think that their masters do not care very much for them; that they look upon them as the great disturbers of their peace and comfort, and as the torment of their lives. This is not the case. For there springs up in the heart of the professors, and with greater reason in the heart of the Confessors, a great love for those under their charge. After a time they come to look upon them as their own children, and to feel for them that rational affection which, while it fills their hearts with tender love, does not blind them to the faults and the defects of those whom they love. You will, perhaps, never know all that that love of theirs has prompted them to do for you. If you have any notion of it, it is a very dim and misty one; and when at times their affection for you thrusts itself upon your notice, with the characteristic thoughtlessness of your age, you speedily forget it. In after-life you will more clearly understand it; and the thought of it will fill your eyes with tears.

As you emerge from boyhood, and from boyhood begin to tread the slippery path of youth, they watch you with an anxious and tender care. They fear lest you should slip and fall, or in other words, lest when your eyes are opened to discriminate between good and evil you should stretch forth your hand to the evil and should reject the good. Should that, which they most of all dread, actually come to pass—should you choose and pluck the forbidden fruit, and after partaking of it feel in your youthful blood all the maddening, fiery thirst after pleasure which its taste engenders—how earnestly, how passionately do they pray for you, and send up the strong cry of their affection before the throne of God! 'Come down,' they exclaim, 'O good Lord, before that my son die!'

You are perhaps going on thoughtlessly in sin, plunging deeper and deeper into it, and madly drinking of its muddy, poisonous waters, while they, on their side, cease not to cry unto God to snatch you away from them, and save you from the penalty of eternal death. Often in the dead of night they wake only to pray for you; and at early dawn your welfare is the first thought that enters their mind. When they recite the Divine Office, it is frequently for you. When they stand at the Holy Altar to offer up the spotless Sacrifice, they plead so earnestly, so vehemently for you, saying: 'Come down, Lord, before that my son die!' May it not be that you are now living the life of grace, and that you are what you are, simply and solely because of their unwearied prayers for you? Let this thought stir up in your heart a filial love for them, and inspire you with a determination to manifest your love by deeds which will prove your grateful appreciation of all that they have done for you.

III. A little reflection, aided by your own good common-sense, will point out to you the way in which you may show this gratitude. Bear in mind that the love which your Superiors have for you is a *rational* love. It is not that soft, effeminate love, which would blind them to your defects, and prevent them from administering correction. Consequently, though they tenderly love you, yet they do not hesitate to chide you with wholesome severity, and at times to inflict upon you great bodily as well as mental pain. On these occasions do not, like some silly and ungenerous boys, blot out from your recollection their patient forbearance, and the thousand kindnesses which they have done you, and treasure up this one act of real love in order to repay it by sour looks and swaggering insolence. Receive the correction with silent submission. Lay it to heart. Profit by it, and it will become another link of that chain which binds the hearts of your masters to you.

In the next place, give them all your confidence. Towards your spiritual Father this is absolutely necessary. Let there be nothing secret between you and him, and let your heart be to him as an open book, in which he may read all that you feel and think. This confidence will enable him to guide you with greater certainty, and will beget in his heart a still greater affection for you. You will thus be shielded from dangers, and kept out of grave sin. Your heart will be at peace; all your little trials and sorrows will be lightened by being shared with another, and no harassing doubt will trouble your mind.

Lastly, try always to receive with respect their sound advice; and as far as possible endeavour to put it in practice. They oftentimes warn you against evil; do not on these occasions prefer to trust to your own light. Even should they order you to withdraw yourself from the society of some one whom you tenderly love, do not hesitate to obey, even though the severance of that tie should cause you great pain. You do not, and you cannot see now, the why, or the wherefore; but later on in life you will, and then you will bless them for their sage conduct in your regard.

Love your Superiors, and show your love not by words only, but by deeds also. Respect them from your heart, and prove that your respect is genuine, by the strict and willing observance of that etiquette which the Rule requires to be shown to them. Also, never forget them in your prayers to God. They have procured for you many a grace, and many a favour from the throne of mercy; do you on your part do all in your power to repay them for their love and zeal for you, and never cease to ask Our good God to give them light and grace to guide you safely along the slippery path of youth.

TWENTY-FIRST SUNDAY AFTER PENTECOST.
FORGIVENESS OF INJURIES.

'And the lord of that servant being moved with pity, let him go, and forgave him the debt.'—ST. MATT. xviii. 27.

I. OUR Lord took occasion, from a dispute which had arisen among the Apostles, to warn them against injuring their neighbour, particularly by the sin of scandal. After speaking of the injuries done unto others, He naturally spoke of the injuries which others might do unto them, and counselled them to endure all these with unvarying meekness. At this juncture St. Peter struck in with a question which gave Christ an opportunity of speaking about the pardon of injuries, which is perhaps one of the most difficult of the precepts of the New Law. In order to imprint it more deeply upon their minds, He exemplified it by a parable, which forms the Gospel for this Sunday. 'How often,' asks the impetuous Apostle, 'shall my brother offend against me, and I forgive him? Shall it be till the seventh time?' Jesus turned to him and said: 'I say not to thee till seven times, but till seventy times seven times.' By this answer Our Lord did not intend to measure out, with mathematical nicety, the precise number of times that we are to pardon our neighbour. He simply wished to tell us that we are *ever* and *always* to forgive our brother, no matter how often or how grievously he may sin against us.

To illustrate His meaning, He put before them what may possibly seem an extreme case. It is that of a steward whose accounts, when examined, convicted him of having defrauded his master to the enormous amount of ten thousand talents. If we take the talent at its lowest value, this sum would not fall far short of two millions sterling of our money. He had not wherewith to pay, and therefore falling upon his knees asked for time, and promised to refund what he had foolishly squandered during the absence of his lord. The sight of his servant's grief and humiliation softened the master's heart, and not content with simply giving him time to repay that of which he had robbed him, he did far more —he generously forgave him all the debt.

While the steward's eyes were still dim with the tears of gratitude which had burst from them at generosity so unparalleled, he met a fellow-servant who owed him a hundred pence, which would be equivalent to about three pounds of our money. Totally forgetting the mercy which had been shown to himself, he seized him roughly by the throat, and demanded instant payment. In the self-same words that had shortly before broken from his own lips, in the presence of his master, that poor servant fell upon his knees, and besought him for yet a little time, and he would pay him all. But he turned a deaf ear to his prayer, and, taking him, cast him and his family into prison, till he had paid the last farthing. The master hearing of this dastardly conduct, summoned the unfeeling wretch before him, upbraided him for his tyrannical cruelty, and thrust him into a dungeon till he could refund the whole of this enormous debt. 'So also,' said Our Lord in conclusion, ' shall My heavenly Father do to you, if you forgive not every one his brother from his. heart.'

II. Look into that heart of yours and see whether it has not much to reproach you with upon this head. God is your King, and Lord, and Master. You are His servant, intrusted by Him with the government of your immortal soul—a region wide enough to exercise to the full all the ruling power that is in you. Have you not, in the administration of that province, contracted debts to an enormous amount? Reflect upon the thoughts which throng multitudinous into your mind during the course of a single day. Multiply them by years, and then ask yourself for how many of them you stand accountable before the eyes of an all-seeing God! The very words which have passed your lips may have made you His debtor, not only on your own account, but on account of those who heard you, and who were scandalised by your speech. Your actions have been many—some of them, no doubt, have been offensive to God. Your omissions have been grievous, your good deeds few— and those few vitiated by unworthy motives. When all these things rise up before your mind, and stand like so many witnesses at the throne of God, clamouring for your condemnation, what can you say? You have not wherewith to pay your debts, and what is more, you never will have wherewith to do so. You can do nothing but throw yourself upon the mercy of your Master, craving for a little time to redeem the past, and to atone by humble penance for a mis-spent life. You have, no doubt, done this, and God in His loving kindness has forgiven you all your debt, simply because you asked Him. This has happened, not once or twice, but many times. God has dealt mercifully with you; and you—how have you dealt with those who become your debtors on account of some paltry, trifling matter which is hardly worth your notice?

A companion has made a sarcastic remark which wounded you; he has opposed you in your designs, either in the playground, or in the school-room; he has thwarted you in the execution of some little scheme which you had at heart; he has teased you; he has behaved towards you in a rough, unkind, rude manner. This is the sum of his offending; and likely enough you have not forgiven him! His offence rankles in your heart like a poisoned arrow. You treat him coldly. You do not speak to him. You malign him before others; you exaggerate the injuries which he has done you; and with very bad grace, you at last relent somewhat towards him, only after a most humble apology. Your cry to him is: 'Pay what thou owest.'

Only reflect a little! In the course of a whole year, your worst enemy does not offend you so much as you offend God during the course, perhaps, of morning prayer or of meditation! Yet He forgives you! Have compassion, therefore, upon your fellow-servant, even as God has had compassion upon you! Fear lest His fierce anger be enkindled against you, and He smite you, and destroy you for ever.

III. The meanness, the selfishness, the total absence of every generous sentiment, evident in conduct which betrays an unforgiving spirit, ought to inspire every noble-hearted boy with a horror of it. But there is a motive far higher than this, a motive which will perhaps incite you to fight down this cruel disposition, and make you earnest in your endeavours to pluck it out of your heart. This is the memory of the judgment of God. Both you yourself, and those who offend against you, shall one day stand before the tribunal of your common Lord and Master. There are times when, even amid the whirl and excitement of every-day life, there is flashed into your mind a light, which reveals to you the number and the enormity of your manifold transgressions. But when you stand in the presence of the eternal light, how the graves of the past will give up their dead!

Every act, thought, and word will stand up before you, like a mighty host, in multitude more numerous than the sands on the sea-shore. 'When the Lord shall arise to judge, what shall I say? and when He shall question, what shall I answer?' You will be able to *say* nothing. You will be able to *do* nothing, but throw yourself entirely upon His boundless mercy and crave for pardon. But will the Judge listen to you? Will He not point to your fellow-students, and ask you how you have treated them when they offended you? Did you not scorn, contemn, and hate them; and that, too, for a few words spoken, probably in jest; for a mere look, a laugh, a childish trick? 'I have forgiven thee,' He will say, 'not once, but a thousand times; thou hast been offended, and thou hast not shown mercy. Thou wicked servant, oughtest not thou to have forgiven them, even as I forgave thee? In thy daily prayer thou didst petition Me to forgive thee, in the same measure, and to the same degree, as thou didst pardon others. Now I will hear and answer thy prayer. Thou wouldst not forgive others, I will not forgive thee! Begone, accursed, into that outer darkness, where there is naught but wailing and gnashing of teeth!'

Bear this in mind when you have been angered by your brother; and remember that justice without mercy shall be meted out to him who hath not shown mercy. Therefore, learn well the rule of forgiveness which Our Lord has taught: Forgive ever and always; forgive from your heart, and not from your lips only; and God will do unto you as you have done unto others.

TWENTY-SECOND SUNDAY AFTER PENTECOST.
DUTIES TO SUPERIORS AND TO GOD.

'Render unto Cæsar the things that are Cæsar's, and to God the things that are God's.'—ST. MATT. xxii. 21.

I. AMONG the Jews, a certain class of men, laying aside the national hopes to which their countrymen so fondly clung, had attached themselves to the fortunes and the service of the Idumean king whom the Romans had set up to govern Judea. These were popularly called Herodians. The Pharisees, on the other hand, were most intensely national, and looked with contempt upon those who favoured Herod, as fawning sycophants, and base traitors to their country and to their God. Both parties hated Our Lord; and upon that common ground met together in a confederacy of wickedness to destroy Him, or at least to undermine His influence with the people.

They came, therefore, to Him, while He taught in the Temple, and pretending that a discussion had arisen between them, upon that frequently contested point whether a Jew might lawfully pay tribute to a Gentile—they put the question to Him, with all the art of skilful diplomatists. Like the base hypocrites that they were, they first flattered, that they might afterwards the more easily destroy Him; yet, in spite of themselves, they were forced to pronounce upon Him the most splendid eulogy that human lips could utter. 'Master,' they said, 'we know that thou art a true speaker, and teachest the way of God in truth; neither carest thou for any man. Tell us, therefore, what dost thou think: is it lawful to give tribute to Cæsar, or not?' They looked at Him eagerly, intently, with a gleam of anticipated triumph in their eyes. If He answered—Yes, that reply would for ever destroy His credit with the people; for they would not, and could not believe Him to be the Messias. If

He said—No, the civil power would soon lay its iron hand upon Him.

But Jesus could not be deceived. He tore off their mask of pretended respect, and of anxious search for the truth, with one withering word of well-merited scorn. 'Hypocrites!' He exclaimed, 'why do ye tempt me? Show me the coin of the tribute.' They at once put into His hand a Roman denarius, or penny, bearing the effigy of Tiberius Cæsar on the one side, and on the other, his proud title 'Supreme Pontiff.' Pointing to the image on the coin, and to the legend which ran round its edge, He asked: 'Whose image and superscription are these?' They answered: 'Cæsar's.' Then with divine wisdom and prudence, He escapes both horns of their cunningly contrived dilemma, by saying: 'Render therefore to Cæsar the things that are Cæsar's, and to God the things that are God's.'

II. By this luminous answer, Our Lord has taught us that the civil power has a claim upon our dutiful obedience, in all matters in which its enactments do not infringe the divine law. But, as the college-boy does not come in contact with the civil power, he must for the present look upon the authorities who rule over his School, in the same light as that in which the ministers of the civil government are regarded by those who are living out in the great world.

The disciplinary rules which Superiors enact, for the maintenance of order among their youthful subjects, call upon him for the same obedience and respect that the laws of the State claim from its citizens, in return for the privileges which the governing power enables them to enjoy. Therefore, when the college-boy submits cheerfully to discipline, and complies conscientiously with all that it demands from him, he renders to Cæsar the things that are Cæsar's. As it would be out of place here to enumerate all these things, we will point out only a few of the most common duties which loyalty to discipline requires from you.

In the first place, it claims internal as well as external respect for all Superiors. Hence, when passing by, or when addressing any of them, you must courteously salute them.

Your words, when speaking to them, should be modest and submissive; and when out of their presence, all conversation about them should be respectful, and full of charity.

In the next place, it requires a willing, prompt, and cheerful obedience to be paid to all their commands; for it is needless to remark, that none of these will ever prescribe anything that is sinful.

Also, it wishes you to receive their correction with silence, their punishment with submission, and to observe with punctilious honour the bounds marked out for you.

When the bell gives the signal for the cessation of play, college discipline would have you leave off at once, and go straight to the duty to which it calls you. It bids you keep silence at all times, and in all places in which silence is ordered, unless there is some reasonable necessity which calls upon you to speak. It enjoins the observance of self-restraint in your relations with one another, and also of those minor regulations which insist upon personal cleanliness, about which some boys are apt to become very careless.

The exact compliance with these little laws, established by college authority, goes far to make the will submissive to the great laws of God. If the former are diligently observed, they become for the latter like a string of outworks stretching far away, and rendering it difficult for the enemies of our salvation to make a sudden irruption into our hearts.

III. Besides rendering to Cæsar, or to lawfully constituted authority, that obedience which is its due, you are told, moreover, to give unto God that which upon so many titles He justly claims from you. To do this is to satisfy a most important obligation. It is your chief work; and your life at college, if it is worth anything, must teach you to give unto God what is His due.

The first of God's claims upon you, is that you should uphold His authority in the little kingdom of your heart. You are the governor of that kingdom; and it is your duty to keep in subjection to God's law the various conflicting powers which strive there for the mastery. This is an arduous task; but to assist you in the accomplishment of it, He has put at your disposal the great power of prayer.

A right use of prayer is the next of the duties which God requires from you. It is a duty that has to be attended to very often in the course of each day. But though the frequency with which you are called upon to perform it, ought to make it easy, yet prayer is one of those religious exercises in the execution of which the majority of boys fail most miserably. Look, for instance, at the manner in which they go through the prayers both before and after study, as well as at the beginning and the end of class; observe how they say the Angelus and the grace both before and after meals; take notice of the way in which they make the visits to the Blessed Virgin, and to the Most Holy Sacrament, and you will be obliged to confess, with sorrow, that these duties are performed, for the most part, with the lips only, while the heart is far away, occupied with its own thoughts and desires. This carelessness ought to fill you with shame, and inspire you with a well-grounded fear of God's chastisement.

Again: look at the way in which you prepare to receive the Sacraments! Is there not neglect, coldness, and indifference with respect even to them?

Furthermore, to return to the duties imposed upon you as governor of your heart, God requires of you, in that capacity, to bring into subjection to Himself the unruly passions which your corrupt nature causes to rise in rebellion against Him. How do you quit yourself of this obligation? What efforts do you make, for example, to curb your temper? Is it not a source of annoyance to yourself, and a very thorn in the side of your companions?

Then, with regard to pride, do you not continually plume yourself on some imaginary perfection? Do you not very often escape punishment by violating truth? Yet, God looks for meekness, humility, and truthfulness from you, as well as for charity, purity, and the weightier matters of the law. Do you find these virtues in yourself, and see their fruits manifest in your dealings with others? If you do not, then you do not give tribute where tribute is due. In one word, you are withholding yourself from God, for you yourself, both body and soul, are the coin stamped with God's holy image. Give, then, to Him the entire service of that soul and of that body. Be just in your dealings with others, and you will thus be giving to God the things that are God's, and to men the debt of service which you owe unto them.

TWENTY-THIRD SUNDAY AFTER PENTECOST.
THE POWER OF FAITH.

'If I shall touch only the hem of His garment, I shall be healed.'—
ST. MATT. ix. 21.

I. THE Gospel of this day brings before our notice two instances of human misery, which are common enough even in our own times. The first is that of a father mourning over the death of his only child; the second is that of a poor woman who for twelve long years had languished under the ever-increasing burthen of a grievous disease. In her fruitless attempts to obtain a cure she only added to her misfortune, by reducing herself well-nigh to beggary.

The bereaved father was a man of wealth and influence, being the chief ruler of the Synagogue. He had, no doubt, both seen Our Lord and listened spell-bound to His wondrous words of power. In the agony of his grief he, therefore, sought out this great Prophet; for he felt convinced that Jesus had the power, and, if made acquainted with his heart-rending grief, would have also the will to help him. Coming, therefore, into His presence while He taught the people, he fell down at His feet, and, in a voice broken by the vehemence of his emotion, besought Him to come down with him, and call back to life his daughter, who had just breathed her last. Jesus rose at once and went with him, followed by the multitude, eager to witness the miracle which they felt sure that He would perform.

Among the crowd which thronged Him on every side, there struggled onwards with the rest, the poor, emaciated, sick woman. Sorrow filled her heart also; but now it began to beat with hope. 'He is so kind,' she said within herself, 'so compassionate, so powerful, that if I but touch the hem of His garment I shall be healed.' With this idea in her mind, she makes her way little by little through the throng, and coming at last quite close to Him, stretches forth her hand and timidly touches the hem of His flowing robe. At once she feels the joyous thrill of renewed health and vigour pulsing through her veins, and shrinks back amid the crowd, rejoicing within herself, and glad to have escaped notice.

But lo! Jesus stands still! He is speaking. He asks who it is that has touched Him? Then trembling, at once with joy and fear, she came forwards, cast herself at His feet, and proclaimed aloud the wonder which had been wrought in her. Jesus looked at her with all the tenderness of a father for his daughter, and spoke those words, which she never afterwards could forget: 'Be of good heart, thy faith hath made thee whole.'

Having come to the Ruler's house, they told him that the maiden had died; and Jesus again spoke of faith: 'Fear not,' said He, 'only believe.' Then entering, He took the dead child by the hand, and said to her: 'Maid, arise!' and, on the word, she returned to life. How great is the power of faith! It procures favours from God, not only for ourselves, but for those whom we love. Fear not, therefore, only believe.

II. It may be that there are some who are very near and dear to you, over whom you are often forced to weep bitter tears, because they are dead to God, and sleep the death-sleep of sin. Sometimes it is a father that for long years has ceased to practise his religion. The Sacraments have become for him sealed fountains. He has left off assisting even at the Holy Sacrifice of the Mass. Yet, withal, he is a good and loving father, kind, generous, devoted. The only drawback to the complete happiness of your home is that he kneels not with you at the Holy Table, and does not worship before God's Holy Altar.

Or it may be that one of your parents does not belong to the Catholic Church, and while cheerfully allowing and encouraging you to practise your faith, does not believe in what that faith teaches. What, then, are you to do? Do what the Ruler did for his little daughter. Go to Jesus, and pour forth the desire of your heart before him. He will hear you. Nay more, He will come with you, and raise up those for whom you pray, provided that you have a living, active, long-suffering faith, which will not grow weary and faint-hearted if the grace which you ask be deferred.

Or, again, it may be that there is some friend whom you love very dearly, and who has fallen into evil courses—has become wild and careless, has abandoned the Sacraments, and shown in his conduct those signs which indicate that he has left the narrow path, and is striding rapidly along that broad, slippery road which leads to destruction. If he is one of your school-fellows, do your utmost, by kindness and affection, by winning words and sage counsel, to lead him back to God. Like the Ruler, go to Our Lord and plead earnestly with Him for His own little child. He waits for you in the narrow chamber of the Tabernacle. There cast yourself upon your knees before Him, and amid the unbroken stillness of the chapel, speak to His sacred heart. Speak to Him with faith. Believe that He is able to help you, that He is willing to help you, and that He earnestly desires to help you, and He will do what you ask Him to do. 'Fear not, only believe.'

III. On the other hand, it may be that you yourself are like the poor woman, whom that languishing disease so grievously tormented, at one and the same time consuming her bodily strength and devouring her worldly substance. If you have contracted a habit of sin, and thereby entangled your feet in the meshes of the devil's net, the similarity between her case and yours is most striking. A spiritual disease has laid hold on you, a disease which is most difficult to shake off. It saps the strength of your will, and makes you feeble for good. Now and then, when a sense of the terrible nature of your disorder flashes upon you, you struggle against it; you make efforts to rid yourself of it; but you strive in vain. You feel yourself daily growing more and more the slave of passion. You feel that every sentiment of uprightness, every high aspiration, every noble feeling, is fading out of your heart, and that you will very soon become an utterly degraded being. You then seek out those physicians who have already so often warned you that you would come at last to this pass. In times gone by you laughed at their warning, and discarded their advice. But now you go to them again. You try to recover. But, alas! how many relapses does the habitual sinner experience!

Ah! if ever you needed faith, it is surely now! Yes—faith in the power of God—faith in His willingness to help you—faith in His patient long-suffering. Yet even so, look at the faith of the sick woman, and do not despair. Like her, be humble, and come to Jesus with the same sentiments as were those which animated her heart. Touch His heart by the completeness of your trust in Him. If you should fall back into evil ways, return again and again to Him; go to those who hold His place; explain your malady to them; follow their advice; and, with God's help, you will be freed from your disease. If from time to time your good resolutions fail, be not down-hearted; still trust and believe in God. But, at the same time, remember that you must help in your own cure. Therefore, avoid occasions of sin; pray very humbly, and very earnestly; frequent the Sacraments, and you will most certainly be cured. Christ will say to you: 'My son, arise! be of good heart; thy faith hath made thee whole.'

TWENTY-FOURTH SUNDAY AFTER PENTECOST.
JESUS ON MOUNT OLIVET.

'There shall be great tribulation, such as hath not been from the beginning of the world until now, neither shall be.'—ST. MATT. xxiv. 21.

I. AFTER a day of more than usual contention with His bitter enemies, Jesus turned His back upon them and left the Temple, never again to enter within its hallowed courts.

But before He did so, He first completely silenced and confounded the Scribes, the Pharisees, and the Herodians, and launched forth against them those well-merited anathemas, which brought matters to an open rupture between Him and them, and raised in their hearts that thirst for His blood, which eventually brought Him to the disgraceful Cross.

As He left the sacred precincts of the Temple, His disciples called His attention to the beauty of its architecture, and to the richness of the material out of which it had been built. Turning to them, He bade them mark these things well, for that the day drew now close at hand when not one stone of this magnificent structure should be left upon another. Then, while the evening came on apace, He led the way to the summit of Mount Olivet, followed by His sad and dejected Apostles.· There they sat down, and looked upon the city which lay beneath them.

What a scene of beauty must have met their eyes, as the setting sun bathed with its splendour the public buildings and the glorious Temple—one of the world's wonders, and their own nation's proudest boast. With aching hearts they looked upon all this magnificence, and asked, with fear, when these things of which He had spoken should come to pass.

Then Jesus told them the signs which were to precede the overthrow of their nation, and put before their eyes that terrible picture of their city girt round by a besieging army, and torn by bloody factions within the walls. He spoke of the famine and the pestilence, which were to consume what the sword of civil discord should spare. He told them of the assault, the capture, and the destruction of their city; of the burning of the Temple; of the overthrow, the subjugation, and the dispersion of their race.

Passing next to the still more distant future, He spoke to them of the final destruction of all earthly things; of the signs in the sun, the moon, and the stars; of the famines, the wars, the pestilences; of the sea rushing in upon the land; the earth bursting asunder and vomiting forth fire; men withering away for fear and expectation of what should come upon the world. 'Then,' said He, 'shall they see the

Son of Man'—now despised, rejected, and soon to be crucified—'coming in the clouds of heaven, with great power and majesty.' The Angels shall go before His face, to summon from the four corners of the world all the dead, and call them to judgment. For every man, without exception, shall manifest himself before the throne of Jesus Christ, to give an account of all the deeds done in the body, whether they have been good or evil.

II. From both these terrible predictions, you may gather much that will teach you lessons of spiritual wisdom, on this the last Sunday of the ecclesiastical year. Your soul, like Jerusalem, is the city and temple of the living God. Upon it have been lavished multitudinous favours and graces, from the treasury of His mercy. To it there have been granted secret inspirations of the Holy Spirit, urging it on to greater perfection. God's servants and God's ministers have carried His message to it, and have been sent to guide and direct it. It has been a garden enclosed, a fountain sealed up, and protected on every side against evil. Nay, God Himself has come down and taken up His abode in it. He has set a seal upon it, by the unction of His Holy Spirit, and given the care of it to His Angels, that they may keep and defend it from evil.

All this has God done for your soul. What return have you made for His loving condescension? Just reflect a little! Can you say that you have gratefully received all these favours, and that you have tried to make Him some little return? Alas! how many are there whose conscience will force them to strike their breasts with sorrow, and to acknowledge with bitter remorse, that they have abused the grace of God, and trampled it under foot, by profaning the channels which conveyed it to their souls. When the Holy Spirit either gently pleaded with them to follow the lead of grace, or sternly reproved them for their sins, they drowned His voice amid the tumult of unruly passions. When God's servants and ministers instructed them in their duties, and warned them against the snares of the devil, they laughed them to scorn. When either duty, or the great festivals of the year, brought them to the Holy Table, they gave Jesus the traitor's kiss in that banquet of love, and received Him into their polluted hearts. Those hearts were once the temples of God, but now they are the abodes of furious passions. They have broken down the gates of the Sanctuary; they have suffered every unclean beast to enter; they have set up the abomination of desolation where once there stood the throne of God. They have done all these things, and God has been silent.

III. But will God be silent for ever? No; for there is no evil deed committed for which a reckoning of some kind or other has not to be made. Though the accounting-day is long a-coming, yet it comes at last. At present it seems but a mere speck in the far-off future, for you are now in the heyday of youth. You have health, and strength, and buoyant spirits; you fear nothing; no unpleasant consequences follow; and therefore, like the fool in the Scripture, you begin to think that there is no reckoning to be made, that there is no God to notice these things.

But what says the Wise Man? With the bitterest irony he thus addresses the youthful sinner: 'Young man, give a loose rein to thy passions. Refuse thine eye nothing that it covets, nor thy heart aught that it desires. Satisfy to the full all the base passions of thy nature, but remember that for all these things thou shalt answer before God.' When the measure of iniquity has been filled up, and while the wicked repose in fancied security, dreaming only of still further gratification—the Son of Man will come to judgment. There will perhaps be no warning. But as lightning coming out of the east, and, in the twinkling of an eye flashing across the whole expanse of the heavens unto the west, so shall the coming of the Son of Man be.

What would be your lot for all eternity if He were to come at this very instant? What would it have been, had He come at a certain time which you can well remember? The very thought of this makes you shudder! If you desire never to be taken unawares, let the memory of the day of wrath be ever present to your mind. Think frequently of it

—how the heavens shall roll aside, like the curtains of a tent, and disclose to your view the Son of Man, Christ Jesus, coming with great power and majesty. You will be standing in the valley of judgment, awaiting His coming, either among the blessed or among the reprobate. If among the blessed, you will fear nothing; but if among the reprobate, you will call upon the mountains and the hills to fall upon you and hide your turpitude from your fellow-men and from the piercing glance of God's all-seeing eye.

Keep this dreadful scene before your mind, and it will keep you out of all evil. If you should now be in the state of sin, reflect that for you personally the judgment-day may come at any time; for if death were to strike you with his merciless dart, your eternal lot would be decided in a moment, and your position fixed for that last great day of terror and of wrath. You have now to blot out, by tearful sorrow, the black catalogue which is written up against you. Do not allow this season of grace to slip through your hands. Be converted to the Lord, turn away from the wickedness of your sin, and ask God to fill your heart with so salutary a fear of that day of calamity and of misery, that it may keep your feet for ever in the narrow way which leads to life. Say to Him from the depth of a contrite heart: 'Pierce, O Lord, my flesh with Thy fear, and direct my steps in Thy sight.' That fear will teach you to tame your unruly passions and bring them into subjection; that guidance will support your tottering footsteps and lead you to the golden gates of His eternal Kingdom.

OUR LADY'S FESTIVALS.

INTRODUCTION TO THE MONTH OF MAY.

I. THE month of May, which Christian piety has dedicated to the honour of our Blessed Lady, is with us once again. It has come to gladden our hearts with its beauty, and to strengthen our souls with the graces which God will shower upon them, if during these fleeting days we not only meditate upon the life and the privileges of His holy Mother, but strive to imitate her virtues. As loving children of that gentle Mother, Jesus calls upon us to join in the universal hymn of praise which will ascend before the throne of God, from every part of the world in honour of her whom the King of heaven delighteth to honour. He wills that we should listen to and obey that call; because the admiration and the love which this devotion excites are no barren sentiments, but lead to the practice of every Christian virtue.

In order, therefore, that our hearts may be disposed to obey this call, let us reflect upon some of the motives which should induce us to enter with earnestness into the devotions of the month of May.

During this month the whole Catholic Church throughout the world is united in honouring and praising her, in giving to her that inferior and relative worship, which in no way detracts from the honour which we pay to God. As members of that great Catholic body, the head of which is Christ, it is fitting that you should not be out of harmony with any of its impulses or its motions, but should correspond at once with the direction given by the head. Moreover, since this is a time when all Catholics are engaged in works of piety, in prayer, and almsgiving, it must of necessity follow that it is also a season of great graces. This should be a weighty reason with you for not allowing the sentiments of your heart to be out of harmony with those of the Church; for you know from personal experience how much you need the aid of grace, and how ill you can spare the slightest increase of its efficacious power.

But, in addition to these motives, there is one other which will have no slight influence with the hearts of college boys; this is the fact that your devotion to the Blessed Virgin will please your Lord and Master Jesus Christ. As a most dutiful and loving Son, He gave His heart's fondest affection to His Mother. He honoured, He loved, He obeyed her. Next, therefore, to obeying His own commands, you can give Him no greater pleasure than to love and imitate her, for by so doing you will become like her—all in all for God.

II. These, then, are some few of the motives which ought to influence every boy, and cause him to make a generous effort to spend this month well. If he will devoutly go through its various exercises of piety, it will do him good. For, no matter to which of the three classes he belongs, into which any School may be divided, the month, we repeat, will do him good, if he will but take pains to profit by it.

First, there are those—and God grant that their number may be very small—who are living in a state of sin, careless of their eternal salvation, forgetful of God, blind to the existence of hell, and intent only upon satisfying the cravings of their youthful passions.

Then there are those who have been leading good and holy lives; who have tasted how sweet it is to weep over, and to blot out their childish sins, and to unite their hearts to Jesus in the Holy Sacrament. But, unfortunately, they have lost their first fervour, and have become remiss in their duty, performing most of their religious exercises merely through routine, without either affection or earnestness. Lastly, there are those who have steadily trodden the path of virtue, in spite of great dryness of spirit, and of many temptations to fall away; who still pray, and communicate, and visit the Holy Sacrament, though these exercises have lost their savour; who, through a sense of duty, prosecute their studies, and know by experience that those who wish to follow Christ must deny self, and daily bear the weight of the Cross.

Now, what will the month of May do for the boys who may chance to belong to any one of these three classes? If they enter heartily into its devotions, it will benefit them all. For those who are so unfortunate as to be living in enmity with God, it will procure the grace of repentance. They will make a good confession, and be reconciled to their Father. Thus the month of May will be for them the beginning of a new life. The lukewarm will be roused from their lethargy, will begin to serve God in a manner worthy of His infinite goodness, with all the ardour and the affection of which their hearts are capable. As for the good boys, they will receive an increase of grace, to aid them to ascend into the higher paths of perfection, paths in which God invites His chosen friends to walk, in order that they may be made worthy of a more intimate union with Him, and of favours greater than those which they already enjoy.

III. Let each, therefore, be determined to take advantage of the opportunities offered to him by God for advancing the interests of his immortal soul. God does not force you to accept His grace; He merely offers it to you, and moves your will to receive it. Hence, you may, if you please, reject it. But be not so unwise. Rather take up with spirit all those practices, which your Superiors with the approbation of the Church, suggest to you as so many props to support your weak nature in the arduous work of your soul's salvation.

You know what these practices are. They are the hymns which you daily chant at the end of the Holy Mass, telling of our Lady's greatness, her virtues, her tender love for sinners, and her powerful intercession with Almighty God; the Rosary, which imprints deeply in your soul the knowledge of that mysterious chain of wonderful events by which Our Lord accomplished the Redemption; the visit to her altar, when the toil of day is done, to offer up your love, and to seek her intercession; the act of virtue to be practised on the following day, which virtue you learn, as from a heaven-sent letter taken from her shrine; the short instruction usually given in the chapel before you retire to rest; and finally, Benediction of the Blessed Sacrament, in which Jesus, Mary's Son, raises His hand to bless you, and sends you to your rest enriched with grace, and full of good resolves to spend the following day to the honour and glory of God.

Be earnest, therefore, in the performance of all these various practices of piety. In after years the memory of them will twine your affections round this venerable home in which your youthful mind and heart were trained in science and in virtue, and will play no unimportant part in keeping your feet in the ways which lead unto everlasting life.

THE HONOUR WHICH WE PAY TO THE BLESSED VIRGIN.

I. At the very outset of these Lectures, it is but fitting that there should be laid before you, as briefly as possible, the reasons for which the Church calls upon her children to pay homage to the Mother of God. These reasons will enable you to give to yourselves and to others 'a reason of the faith that is in you.' For you are sure to be asked: 'Why do you honour the Virgin Mary?' When this question is put to you, you will be able to say: 'We honour her because God has thought fit to honour her more than any other creature. By following His example we can do no wrong, but we are able, moreover, to obey the mandate of St. Paul, who tells us "to imitate God as most dear children." Therefore, as God has honoured her, so do we her children pay her honour.'

But how has God honoured her? He has honoured her in this way: having preordained her to be the Mother of His Son, He sent an ambassador from His heavenly court to ask her to become a participator in no less a work than the redemption of the world. He sent no ordinary ambassador or Angel with this message, but one of those mighty Seven, who ever stand before the throne of God. As ambassador of heaven, that Archangel did not speak his own sentiments of admiration, but uttered the words and the sentiments of the Almighty. What were these? They were words expressing sentiments of the most profound respect. 'Hail,' he said to her, 'full of grace! The Lord is with thee. Blessed art thou among women.' Well might he thus begin his address to her, for God had furthermore commissioned him to say: 'Thou shalt conceive and bring forth a son, and thou shalt call His name Jesus. He shall be great, and shall be called the Son of the Most High. The Lord God shall give unto Him the throne of David, His father. He shall reign in the house of Jacob for ever; and of His kingdom there shall be no end.'

Mary, however, mindful of her virginity, and unwilling to sacrifice it to become the Mother of even God's only begotten Son, ventures to tell the Angelic messenger that this cannot be done, except by the intervention of God, and in some extraordinary way. He at once reassures her: 'The power of the Most High shall overshadow thee. And therefore, the Holy, which shall be born of thee, shall be called the Son of God.'

If, then, the great Archangel, speaking as the mouth-piece of God, and uttering the sentiments of God, paid so great honour to our Virgin Queen, why should not we also be allowed to pay homage to the Mother of Our Lord and God—of that Jesus, Whom we are striving to love with our whole heart, our whole strength, our whole mind—more even than we love our life?

II. But besides those who quarrel with us for paying homage to the Blessed Virgin, there are others who do not find fault with us for this, so much as for praying to her, and asking her to intercede for us with God. 'Why pray to her?' they say; 'she cannot hear you. Then, by asking her to intercede for you, you make her your mediator, whereas St. Paul says: "There is one mediator of God and men, the man Christ Jesus."'

You may answer that you pray to her because you believe that the Saints, though enjoying the vision of God, have not lost their interest in their brethren who are still in the world. For, if Our Lord, in one of His parables, makes even one of the lost in hell solicitous for his brethren whom he had left behind him, with far greater reason may we argue that those who are ever contemplating the face of the God of love will not be unmindful of the salvation of those who are still engaged in the conflict. This, however, is not simply an inference of reason. It is a Scriptural fact, for the Sacred Writings very frequently represent the Angels of God as knowing, and taking an interest in that which passes upon earth; as offering up the prayers of the faithful; praying for and sympathising with men in their sorrows and afflictions.

If, then, the Angels can know what happens here below, and can feel an interest in those who are their brethren, it is but rational to infer that those also who now are like to them in heaven will share in their knowledge and in their interest, and most of all others, Mary, the Mother of God, who loving Jesus so tenderly, will consequently love most ardently the souls of men for whom He died.

'But how,' you may ask, 'does she know these things?' Like the Angels and the other Saints, she knows these things by contemplating the face of God. In the light of His countenance the Blessed see, as in a mirror, all that it is necessary for them to know; and they acquire this knowledge, as St. Gregory teaches, 'not naturally by their own power, but supernaturally by the intuitive vision of God.'*
Or, as the same truth is explained by St. Augustine: 'They know by the revelation of the Holy Spirit what is necessary for them to know—just in the same way as that in which the

* St. Greg. Mag., Lib. Moral., i. 12, c. 14.

Prophets, while living here on earth, knew what God in His providence revealed to them.'*

Therefore, as the Angelic Spirits know, by contemplating the face of God, that some sinner has turned from the evil of his ways, and thereupon a thrill of joyous delight passes through the Choirs of heaven, so will the Saints and the most holy Mother of God be able to know when we poor sinners ask for her, or for their intercession with God.

III. As for the third objection—'that by thus praying to, and asking her to intercede for you, you make her your mediator with God, in direct opposition to the words of St. Paul'—you may answer it thus: In the text just cited, St. Paul is speaking of Christ as the mediator of *redemption*. In this sense there is no one, whether Angel or Saint, that can claim to be, or that can be said to be, our mediator; for Christ, and Christ only, has redeemed us. But there is another sense in which the word *mediator* is used, namely, to signify any one who intervenes between two parties as an intercessor.

In this sense the Catholic Church has always taught that the Angels and the Saints may be called mediators. Mediation of this kind can in no way be injurious to the mediation of Christ. For His office of mediator is only then injured, when men apply to other sources for aid, because they deem the power of Jesus insufficient to save them; but not when, looking at the virtues and the merits of those who are God's dearest friends, they beseech them to intercede with God for them. This they do in consequence of a well-grounded fear that, through their own great unworthiness, He may not so readily hearken unto them.

No one thinks that he dishonours God by asking a good man to pray for him; nor does he for a moment dream that by so doing he is, in any way, trenching upon the mediation of Christ. If, then, our natural reason tells us that these prayers are acceptable to God, and induce Him more readily to grant our petitions, surely we may argue that the prayers of those who have left this world, and who, being now

* Cura pro Mort., 15.

purged from all stain, live face to face with God, will be far more pleasing to Him, and have much greater weight with Him.

Therefore, we conclude, that by praying to the Blessed Virgin, we in no way interfere with the mediation of Christ. He is the mediator of *salvation;* the Saints, the Angels, and more particularly, the most Holy Virgin, are mediators of *intercession,* powerful with God, by means of prayer, by which they move Him to grant, in His infinite mercy, that which our unworthiness does not deserve to obtain.

DEVOTION TO THE BLESSED VIRGIN.

I. THERE is due to the Blessed Virgin, as we have seen, a certain meed of honour, in consequence of her exalted dignity, and of the love and respect entertained for her by Almighty God. How, then, are you to pay her this honour? You may quit yourself of this debt in her regard, by a most tender and filial devotion. But, as there is a devotion which is false, as well as one which is true, it is necessary that you should carefully distinguish the one from the other. False devotion to the Blessed Virgin is that which contents itself with certain external practices of piety, without attending to that inward amendment of life and manners, which is the real end of all devotions.

It is false devotion, therefore, to imagine that the Blessed Virgin will, in some way or other, bring about your salvation, if you recite her Rosary, or be enrolled among the number of those who wear her livery, or show reverence to her statues and pictures, or bear about you medals stamped with her effigy, while all the time your soul is given up to sin. The Blessed Virgin, as you know, is only a creature. Though most exalted and highly favoured by God, still she is only a creature, and consequently her power falls infinitely short of the power of God. Now God Himself, all-powerful as He is, could not save a soul so disposed; because, though He created us without our consent, yet He will not save us without our co-operation. Hence it would be absurd, as well as impious, to expect that our Lady, who is only a creature, can do more than God. She may pray for you, and God may offer you His grace, in answer to her prayers; but without an effort on your part to correspond with it, that grace will remain inefficacious, and you will go on in your sins.

Remember, therefore, that the boy who is disobedient, or vain, or proud, or idle, or given up to the slavery of his baser passions, is not devout to the Blessed Virgin; no, not though he may recite the Rosary, and sing hymns in her praise, and bow to her statues, and put himself to much inconvenience in order to pay visits to her shrine. These holy practices may move our dear Mother to turn upon him her eyes of mercy, and to procure for him the aid of divine grace to begin his conversion. But even so, unless he correspond to the movement of grace so obtained, his devotion will profit him nothing.

II. On the other hand, true devotion to the Blessed Virgin consists in ardent desires and in earnest efforts to imitate her holy life and sublime virtues. The boy who wishes to have true and solid devotion to her must put her before him as a painter or a sculptor sets before his eyes the model from which he is about to copy. All the practices of piety instituted in her honour, must be to him so many calls to direct the eye of his mind to her, and to move his will to fashion his life upon the example which he sees traced out in hers.

As he examines closely into the various details of that life, what will he find? He will find it to have been a life of labour, a life made up of a round of the most ordinary duties, faithfully and perseveringly discharged. He will see that the bright robe of spotless purity adorned her with its glory; that her heart, freed from all ambitious aims, ever bowed itself down in deepest humility before the infinite perfection of God, compared with Whom, she considered herself to be but as an atom floating in the sunbeam; and that a most tender love of God animated her every action.

Furthermore, he will see her deep gratitude to God, for all the mighty deeds which He had accomplished in her;

her burning zeal for His glory; her unshaken faith, and her unwavering confidence in God. Look, therefore, long and well at this life in which every virtue shone resplendent, and earnestly pray God to give you grace to reproduce in your own life all the excellences which you perceive in hers.

III. You can, therefore, easily understand that if you wish your devotion to the Blessed Virgin to be solid and advantageous to you, you must not be content with that merely external homage, which many mistake for true piety. Aim rather at a devotion which shall manifest itself by vigorous action within your own heart, and shall thence cast out whatever is either contrary to the law of God, or displeasing to her whom you desire to love and reverence.

Consequently, do not imagine that your acts of devotion are pleasing to the Holy Mother of God, so long as you manifest a decided distaste for your books, and idle away the precious time appointed for labour, in silly day-dreaming, or in frivolous reading. The disobedient and stubborn boy, who is ever at war with authority, can lay no claim to devotion to our Lady. Nor can he who is vain and proud, either of his abilities, whether real or imaginary, or of any other excellence that God has bestowed upon him. Least of all others can he be said to have this devotion, whom Satan has tied down with the chains of evil habits.

He only is devout to our Lady who, besides performing acts of piety in her honour, looks into her life, and tries to make his own like unto it. If his constant effort is to keep his heart pure by never suffering wicked thoughts to remain in his mind, and by ever scrupulously observing the laws of Christian modesty—he is devout to the Blessed Virgin. If he stifles all silly thoughts of pride, and remembers that whatever he is, or whatever he can do, comes from God—he is devout to the Blessed Virgin. If he obeys his masters' wishes—if he is grateful to them for their unwearying efforts to improve his mind—if he is brave and truthful, never shrinking from punishment if deserved, and scorning to save himself by a disgraceful lie—he is devout to the Blessed Virgin. If he courageously sits down to his books, and diligently applies himself to master their difficulties, conscientiously employing all the time appointed for lessons in accomplishing his duty—he is devout to the Blessed Virgin.

His homage to her is then not a mere lip-service, for he tries to do what he knows will be pleasing to her; he tries to serve God in his little way, as she served Him, by a holy life, and by the scrupulous discharge of all its duties, no matter whether they are pleasant or not. Like her, he looks upon them as the will of God, and by doing that, he tries to serve his Father Who is in heaven. Every other kind of devotion is a delusion. It does not please God, and it is consequently profitless to man.

WHAT IS MEANT BY THE IMMACULATE CONCEPTION.

I. WHEN Pius IX. defined 'the Blessed Virgin to have been immaculate in the first instant of her conception,' he did not add a new dogma to the creed of the Church. He simply formulated the belief of the faithful, a belief implicitly contained in the deposit of faith, declared it to be free from all error, and to be held from that time forth with the unwavering assent due to the revelation of God. Like all the doctrines of the Church, it is expressed in the most precise and clear terms; and yet, while non-Catholics rail at it, without knowing even what it means, there are not a few, among the faithful, whose knowledge of it is either altogether incorrect or hazy in the extreme.

Some imagine that our Lady conceived Our blessed Lord without detriment to her virginal integrity. This is perfectly true; but it is not the Immaculate Conception. Others, that the power of the Holy Ghost overshadowed St. Anne, the mother of the Blessed Virgin, and that she conceived her highly privileged daughter in the same way as that in which the Blessed Virgin conceived Jesus Christ. This is false, and is not the Immaculate Conception. It is neither of these things. Its nature will best be understood by defining it in the exact words of the dogmatic decree. 'We define,' said the Pope, 'that the doctrine which holds that the Blessed Virgin Mary, in the first instant of her conception, by a singular grace and privilege of Almighty God, and in view of the merits of Christ Jesus, Saviour of the human race, was preserved intact from all stain of original sin, has been revealed by God, and must therefore be firmly and constantly believed by all the faithful.'*

Before proceeding to establish the doctrine enunciated in this proposition, there are three things to which theologians call our attention. In the first place they point out that the conception spoken of is that which is called passive. Then they bid us observe that the stain of original sin is contracted neither from the body only, nor from the soul only, but from the union of the two, by which union the individual is constituted a child of Adam; consequently, that the Immaculate Conception was wrought at the very instant of the soul's union with the body by the positive influx of divine grace upon the soul, by which grace it was made pleasing to God. Lastly, they carefully notice that the Church does *not* teach that the Virgin did not *need* redemption; for the decree states that God bestowed upon her this stupendous privilege '*in view of the merits of Jesus Christ, Redeemer of the world.*' This, in a few words, is the teaching of the Church about the Immaculate Conception.

II. 'But,' we immediately ask, 'what is the scriptural authority which can be adduced in support of this doctrine?' The most famous is that contained in the words uttered by Almighty God, after having heard the excuses of our first parents for their disobedience. For, turning to the serpent, He cursed him for having deceived them; but while so doing, He promised them a deliverer. For, addressing the evil one, the cause of their ruin, He said: 'I will put enmities between thee and the woman, and between thy seed and her seed. She shall crush thy head, and thou shalt lie in wait for her heel.'

No one will dare to deny that the deliverer here spoken of

* Constitutio, 'Ineffabilis Deus.'

as the seed of the woman, is Our Redeemer, Christ Jesus; and that the woman, whose seed or offspring He is, is the Blessed Virgin. As, therefore, God proclaimed by the words, 'I will put enmities between thee and the woman, and between thy seed and her seed,' that the hostility between the serpent and the woman is identical with that existing between the serpent and her seed, it must follow as a logical consequence that, as the enmity between Jesus Christ and the devil is an enmity absolute, perpetual, and precluding all antecedent friendship whatsoever, so also the enmity between the Virgin and the devil must likewise be absolute, perpetual, and exclusive of all foregoing friendship with, or subjection to him.

Moreover, by the words, 'She shall crush thy head,' or, according to the Hebrew version, 'He, or it, that is to say, the seed, shall crush thy head,' God foretold the effect of that enmity against the devil, both on the part of the woman's seed, and on the part of the woman herself. They were both to obtain a full and complete triumph over him. If we take our version, it will mean that the woman will obtain this triumph by the power of her Son. If we take the Hebrew version, it will mean that Christ will gain this triumph over the devil—a statement which comes to the same thing. This triumph must be *full* and *complete;* if the devil had infected the woman with his poison—that is to say, if the woman had not *always* been free from stain—instead of her having crushed the head of the serpent, it would be the serpent that had crushed her head. That which is said of the woman must with still greater reason be said of her seed, since the triumph to be gained by the woman and by her seed is foretold by God, as the fruit of the enmity between the serpent and the woman, and between the serpent and the woman's seed.

Therefore, as the enmity in both cases is said to be identical, it must follow that the triumph also over the devil will be identical and common to the woman and to her seed —with this difference, however: the seed of the woman gains the victory by His own *inborn* power; the woman, only in virtue of her Son's omnipotence.* This is one out of many Scriptural authorities for the doctrine of the Immaculate Conception.

III. Besides the text from Genesis—a text which, even if it stood alone, would furnish a sufficiently solid foundation on which to build this dogmatic truth—there are in the Sacred Scripture other passages, which, though weak, if taken by themselves, nevertheless acquire no inconsiderable force, when viewed in the light which that wondrous oracle throws upon them.

Of this nature, for instance, is the Archangel's salutation, when sent to ask the Virgin's consent to be the Mother of Our Lord. His greeting has in it much meaning: 'Hail!' he says to her, '*full* of grace.' Such, again, are the words which he uses, when the Virgin, disturbed at the appearance and the address of her heavenly visitant, began to ponder, in some trepidation, upon the meaning of his embassy. 'Fear not, Mary,' he says, ' for thou hast found *favour* with God.' Also, her cousin, St. Elizabeth, filled with the Holy Ghost, at the approach of Mary cried aloud in words inspired by that Holy Spirit: '*Blessed* art thou among women, and blessed is the fruit of thy womb.'

This *fulness* of grace, this *favour* with God, this special *blessedness*, greater than any woman had ever before enjoyed, what do they point to, when we bear in mind that *enmity* put by God between the Mother of the Redeemer and the infernal serpent, except to that special privilege, to that immunity from the original stain—an immunity which God, from a prevision of the merits of Christ's Passion and death bestowed upon her, that she might be the Mother of Jesus Christ, Our Lord and Saviour? This is the scriptural basis of the dogma, defined in our days.

Now, what is the lesson which you are to learn from it? It is that sanctity, the greatest, the most exalted, becometh the house of God. Your heart is often made the throne, the resting-place, the house of Jesus Christ, when He comes to you in Holy Communion. Therefore, let the consideration

* Perrone, De Deo. Creat., Pars III., cap. iv.

of Mary's Immaculate Conception inspire you with the resolution to keep your heart clean, pure, free from every stain of sin—but most especially from the slightest taint of that sin which is most hateful to the purity of God, and most opposed to His awful and unapproachable sanctity.

THE POSSIBILITY OF THE IMMACULATE CONCEPTION.

I. FROM what has been said, it will be seen that the Immaculate Conception signifies that, by a special privilege, Almighty God exempted the Blessed Virgin from the stain of original sin. On hearing this, it is natural for us, with all reverence, to ask whether this is possible? We ask it without for a moment supposing that there can be any limit to the power of God. Yet, in the face of St. Paul's positive assertion 'that all men have sinned in Adam, and that all in his person have died the death of sin,' how can it be that the Blessed Virgin has escaped the infection of that poison which flowed from him into his descendants?

In the words of the Church, we answer: 'She escaped it by a special privilege.' This privilege is one of those exceptions to those general laws of God which may be suspended, or reversed, or altogether abrogated, whenever it pleases Him to manifest His supreme dominion over created things. The record of these exceptions is frequently to be met with in the pages of Sacred Scripture. For instance: God preserved the three children from the fire of the Babylonian furnace; He rolled back the waters of the Jordan to allow the Israelites to pass over to the Promised Land; He called back Lazarus from the tomb. Yet, it is a general law of nature, that fire should burn, that rivers should flow onwards from their source, and that the dead should not return to life. Therefore, as God has, at certain times, and for His own wise purposes, held in abeyance the ordinary laws of nature, we argue that He could also hold in abeyance the law by which the original stain is transmitted by parents to their children. Nay, we are emboldened to go a step farther, and to say, that since He has already made so many, and so stupendous exceptions to His ordinary laws, in favour of His blessed Mother, it is but logical not to deny that He could make this other one also.

What has He not done for her? The great St. Augustine says, 'that He made her so pure as to be exempt from those involuntary defects into which the saintliest men fall many times each day.'* According to the teaching of the most approved Doctors, He freed her from the rebellion of the senses; exempted her from the pains of child-birth; gave her flesh free from all frailty; and—greatest and most indubitable of all others—worked in her person a marvel, 'whereat,' says Bossuet, 'nature stood amazed, in momentary expectation that all her laws were about to be reversed—He caused her to conceive, and to bring forth Our blessed Lord, without the intervention of a human father, and to have the glory of maternity, without losing the bloom of virginity.'

If, then, God could do all this, it is little to say that He could also make an exception to the general law, by which all men died in Adam, and by which they were infected with the stain of his primal transgression.

II. If, then, Almighty God had the power to make this exception, as everyone will admit that He has, let us, in the next place, consider whether it is not becoming that He should exercise that power. For, suppose for a moment that He had not done so; then, it would not be quite evident that He is omnipotent over evil, and that there is no limit to His power.

In order to bring out this truth in its clearest light, we will use the argument which Bossuet† employs, to reassure those who imagined that the sinlessness attributed to Mary by St. Augustine detracts somewhat from the special prerogative of Jesus Christ. After first pointing out that God conferred upon her the innocence spoken of by the great Doctor of the Western Church, whereas the sinlessness of Christ is His by nature, and not by gift or by privilege, he

* St. Augustinus, Nat. et Grat., Num. 42, tom. x.
† Bossuet, Sur la Concept., Sermons, tome iii., Paris, 1841.

establishes, in the first place, that Jesus surpasses Mary in an infinite degree. He is God, Mary is but a creature. He then goes on to say: 'Yet she is the most favoured of His creatures, and consequently must in point of sinlessness, have over them an advantage, to which no other can lay claim. You will admit,' he says, 'that God sanctified her in her mother's womb. But that is not enough. This privilege He granted to St. John the Baptist, and, according to the opinion of some Fathers, to the Prophet Jeremias. Great as this favour undoubtedly is, it does not satisfy me. Mary must have some privilege which does not trench upon the prerogatives of Christ, and yet is hers, in a way in which no one else can share it with her. This is no other than the Immaculate Conception. By conferring upon her this privilege, God has proved to us that His empire over evil is *infinite*. For, when man is born into the world, he enters upon the stage of life, stained with the sin of Adam's rebellion. Over this God triumphs by baptism, which washes away the guilt of sin, without, however, ridding man of its baneful effects. But, even before man is constituted a wayfarer, that is to say, while he is still in his mother's womb, the devil has an empire over him, and sets his mark upon him. Consequently, God has there also shown His power, by freeing from the devil's dominion, even before their birth, some of His special favourites, and most distinguished champions. Of this number is the great forerunner of Christ, the austere and saintly Baptist.

'But, notwithstanding this and other exceptions to the ordinary law, there is still one intrenchment, behind which the devil holds sway, and where the arm of God does not reach him. This is the very instant when the soul is joined to, and animates the embryo body, and thus constitutes the individual a child of Adam. If God did not prevail over evil, even in this first instant of conception, the devil could boast that he had been able to vitiate the root, though he could not vitiate the rest of the tree. Hence, every rational man will see how suitable it is, that God should exercise His power, by choosing out at least one solitary creature, the Mother of His Son, to preserve her, even from the beginning, from ever passing under the power of the devil.' He had the power to do so, and we have seen, from the argument of Bossuet, how becoming it is that He should exercise that power.

III. St. Anselm, arguing in the same way, very beautifully illustrates how it is at once both possible for God to make this exception, and consonant with sound reason, that He should be willing to make it. 'If,' he says, 'God is able to endow the chestnut with this property, that it is formed within a thorny covering, and there lodged, nourished, and brought to maturity, without suffering any puncture, why should He not be able to cause that the human temple, prepared by His own hands, to be the dwelling-place of His Christ, should be conceived under the thorns of sinners, without receiving from them any wound? Most certainly He could do so.' Then this enlightened Doctor, this profound philosopher, this devout client of Mary, going a step farther, devoutly says: 'He had the power to do so; He willed to do so; and, being God, with Him to will is to do; He did so.' *Potuit, voluit, fecit.**

As, therefore, the whole doctrine of the Immaculate Conception seems to bring out before our eyes, in the boldest way, the awful sanctity of God, let it be your aim, daily to purify yourself more and more. You will feel, no doubt, the bitter and wearying nature of the struggle requisite to effect this; but do not, like a coward, yield to the devil. Do not listen to that lying spirit, saying: 'It is impossible.' No, it is not impossible; for God is able to make you pure, holy, and spotless. Moreover, it is His will that you should be so: 'This is the will of God, your sanctification'; and, being able and willing, He will make you holy, on one condition, which is, that you yourself *will* it. Pray, therefore, to God to strengthen your will. You can be as pure as an Angel; *will* to be so, and that which is wanting to your strength will be supplied by the almighty power of God. He is able to make you pure, He wills to make you pure, He will make you pure.

* De Concept. Mariæ, cap. iv.

THE IMMACULATE CONCEPTION.

I. EVERYONE will admit, that Almighty God has the power to exempt the Blessed Virgin from the stain of original sin. Also, that it is becoming that He should free her from that blemish, in order to make her worthy, in some degree, to be the Mother of His Son. Furthermore, we have seen that a kind of necessity impelled God to exercise this power, in order to show that there is no limit to His dominion over the devil. We come now to examine two facts—the Maternity, and the Incarnation—facts which in a way necessitate the Immaculate Conception; and though these, as well as the reasons already adduced, are not direct and positive proofs of the dogma, yet they serve to show us how consonant it is with reason, and how admirably it fits into the plan of redemption. More than this we do not need, since the Holy Spirit has spoken by the mouth of the Church, and defined it with the infallible certainty of faith.

We maintain, therefore, that the fact of the Maternity of the Blessed Virgin implies the Immaculate Conception; for, the same reason that made Our Lord be born of a Virgin Mother, would also make Him be born of an Immaculate Mother. Why, then, did God will that His Son should be born into this world of a Virgin? He willed it, in order that the sanctity due to the sacred humanity of Christ should already exist in His Mother, and throw the halo of its beauty around His sacred person. But, if God required that this sanctity should be the foregoing and preparatory condition which fitted her to become the Mother of Our Lord, we can see at a glance that its spotless beauty ought, logically, to take its rise from the very conception of the future Mother of the Redeemer. For if the reverence due to the sanctity of Jesus Christ urged Almighty God to work a marvel, 'at which nature stood amazed,' namely, that a daughter of Adam should be at once a virgin and a mother, the same reverence required that Mary should be as free from every stain or blemish, at the first moment of her being, as when, upon the explanation of the Angel, she said, 'Be it done unto me according to thy word,' and the only begotten Son of the Eternal Father entered her womb, and there took flesh of her sinless body. That flesh, which He took from her, not only must be free from stain, but must never have been subject, at any time, or for the shortest instant of time, to the defilement of sin. Thus we see how the fact of Mary's Maternity, or motherhood, claims for her an Immaculate Conception.*

II. Furthermore, the fact of the Incarnation, or of that act of divine power by which God took upon Himself our human nature, implies the Immaculate Conception. For it would be derogatory to the infinite holiness of God, to imagine that He would take upon Himself flesh, which at one time, though but for an instant, had been defiled with the serpent's venom. Therefore, what has been said of the Maternity, will apply with equal force to this other great fact of the Incarnation, considered in itself. But no slight weight is added to the argument, when we reflect upon the end which Christ had in view in becoming man. A rapid glance at the plan of redemption will bring this out clearly before your mind.

Man had offended a God of infinite majesty. The offence thus committed could not be adequately atoned for, except by a being equal to God. Yet, the being making the atonement must belong to the guilty race—must be a man. The Incarnation solved this difficulty; because Christ is truly God, equal to the Eternal Father, and yet at the same time truly man, being one of the race which had prevaricated. The purpose, therefore, or end for which Christ became man, was to redeem us from sin, to burst our bonds asunder, and to open for us a fountain in which those who wish, may wash away their stains in His precious blood. Therefore, if Christ came into the world to redeem us, both from that original sin and from our own personal sins, His coming, or the Incarnation and sin, must mutually exclude each other. But, if this is the case, as all will admit that it is, then we must also admit that Mary, who is associated with Christ in

* Nicolas, 'La Vierge Marie,' chap. v.

the work of the Incarnation, as the seat, and the instrument of that divine mystery, is also excluded from that stain of original sin. For, if she is not, then we must say that she, through whose instrumentality the malediction pronounced upon Eve has been reversed, lay under its ban like the lowliest of Eve's daughters; that she, through whom every blessing came into the world, has been infected with the original curse; that she, who brought the priceless ransom of our redemption, has herself once been a bond slave, and tributary to the tyrant, whose throne her glorious offspring came to overturn and grind into powder, to be trampled upon by the sons of men.*

III. Thus we see that both the Maternity of our Blessed Lady and the Incarnation of Our Lord necessitate, in a certain sense, the dogma of the Immaculate Conception. Furthermore, this dogma, while pointing out to us the admirable congruity with our reason, which runs through the whole plan of the redemption, cannot fail at the same time to teach a lesson which every thoughtful boy will do well to impress deeply upon his mind. This lesson is the lofty notion of God's awful sanctity which it brings home to us. God is so holy, that before lowering Himself to assume human nature, He did not consider it enough to be born of a virgin, but that virgin must be one who is spotlessly pure, and so fair that He can call her His beloved, and summon heaven and earth to witness that there is no stain in her. She must be free, not only from all actual sin, but from even the blemish of any venial sin. Yet, pure and holy as she is, the Church, when speaking of the Incarnation, seems to be amazed at the condescension of God, in taking upon Himself human nature, and says to Him: '*Non horruisti Virginis uterum*'—' Thou didst not *abhor* the Virgin's womb.'

What a lesson does this teach you! God does not disdain to come to visit you in the Holy Sacrament. He enters your bosom. He unites Himself to you! Oh, what purity, what spotless purity does He require from you, in order that you may be, in some degree, worthy of this

* Nicolas, 'La Vierge Marie,' chap. v.

union! Yet you are but flesh and blood, exposed to many temptations, and prone to evil! So great condescension on His part cannot but urge you to make a strong and generous resolution to win for yourself that cleanness of heart with which He is so well pleased. The task, no doubt, is a difficult one, but still it is not impossible. A courageous heart, and a determined will, sustained and aided by the grace of God, will be able to accomplish it.

Therefore, be not afraid. Go frequently to Jesus in the Holy Sacrament. Unite yourself to Him. Take Him into your heart, show Him its corruption, and ask Him to cure it. When you reflect upon the Immaculate Conception, and upon all the miracles which God effected in that mystery, through His love of purity and His hatred of the opposite vice, fall upon your knees, adore the sanctity of God, and beg of Him to make you at least a faint image of His holy Mother, by giving you grace to be spotlessly pure.

HISTORY OF THE DEFINITION.

I. AFTER treating of the Blessed Virgin's Immaculate Conception—so justly regarded by us as one of her greatest privileges—it will be well for us to learn something about the history of that dogma, which has received the authoritative sanction of the Holy See, and which has been declared to be of faith, only in our own day. Those who know nothing of it, except that which may be gathered from the shallow and flippant criticism of newspaper correspondents, or from the still more shallow expositions of men hostile to the Catholic Church, sneer at us for our credulity, and charge the Church with adding to her creed a dogma never before heard of, till Pius IX., in 1854, defined it to be an article of faith. The sneers of these men may be passed over in silence; their calumnies against the Church must be met and refuted.

In the first place, it is incorrect to say that the Church has *added* a new article to her creed. The Church does not add to the deposit of faith; she is simply the guardian and exponent of that deposit of religious doctrine intrusted to her keeping by Jesus Christ, and watched over with jealous care by the Holy Spirit. Hence it has been pithily said that the dogmas of the Church are not defined by her in order to make them be believed, but they are defined because they *are* believed, and held generally by the faithful. This is specially true of the dogma of the Immaculate Conception. For though the Pope took the chief part in bringing about its definition, yet, true to the usual method pursued by the Church in these matters, he scrupulously adhered to the rule laid down by his glorious predecessors, and carefully inquired whether this belief, which eminent and learned men all over the world called upon him to define as an article of faith, ' had always, and everywhere, and by all, been held and professed,' though not, it might be, with that unfaltering belief which is given to an article of faith.

Therefore, in the year 1849 he issued an encyclical letter to the Bishops of the Catholic Church, calling upon them to send to him, in writing, their own belief, and that of the Churches over which they ruled, concerning the Immaculate Conception of the Blessed Virgin. This wish all obeyed with scrupulous care, each Prelate sending his own belief, and the actual belief of his Church upon the point, and in many cases, also, the belief of his Church in past ages. These testimonies were found to be well-nigh unanimous; and almost every Prelate expressed an earnest desire that what ' had always and everywhere, and by all been believed,' should at last, by the authoritative voice of the Vicar of Christ, be declared to be an article of Catholic faith.

Theologians of world-wide repute carefully examined and thoroughly sifted this mass of evidence, and at last, after the space of five years, when all that could be adduced either for or against the dogma had been duly weighed, the Pope, surrounded by upwards of three hundred Bishops from all parts of the world, defined it to be an article of faith henceforth binding on the consciences of Catholics.

Thus we see that the Church, by her action, has not *added* to her belief. She has only declared what was held and believed by the faithful upon this point to be true and implicitly contained in the deposit of faith committed to her keeping by Jesus Christ.

II. Nor is this a *new* dogma, and unheard of, before the days of Pius IX. For, omitting the scriptural authority, which has already been considered, we may adduce in testimony the document known as the 'Acts of the Martyrdom of St. Andrew the Apostle.' St. Augustine, St. Gregory the Great, the Menologium of the Greeks, and a great number of other credible witnesses, approved of this and held it to be authentic.* In that document we find the following words, said to have been uttered by the Apostle, when confessing the faith before the Proconsul Egeus: 'The first man by the wood of prevarication brought death into the world; it was necessary that by the wood of the Passion death should be expelled from the abode which he had usurped. As, therefore, the first man was formed from *earth which was still immaculate*, it was necessary that from *an immaculate Virgin* the perfect man should be born, by whom the Son of God, Who first created man, should repair that eternal life, which man had lost in Adam.'

This belief is not confined to the Western Church; it is held by the Greek Church also; and although that Church is in schism with the Roman See, and has been separated from communion with it for more than ten centuries, yet it clings with a tenacious grasp to the dogma that Mary is the Virgin Immaculate.

The testimony of the Bishop of Nicopolis shows us that the same belief is held among the Abyssinian schismatics, who have retained the dogma in spite of their heresy and infidelity.†

The Mahommedans also add their voices, to swell the chorus of those who bear witness to the antiquity and the universality of this belief. In the third chapter of their Koran, we read these words: 'The Angels said to Mary, God hath chosen thee, and *made thee exempt from all stain*, and selected thee from among all the women of the universe.'

* Nicolas, 'Vierge Marie,' tom. ii., chap. v., p. 134.
† Recueil, etc., par son Em. le Card. Gousset.

The same belief is wide-spread among the people of Chaldea. Of this, the Patriarch of Babylon informed the Holy See, in his letter upon the definition of this dogma. He cites the words of one of the Mahommedan doctors, who says: 'Of the whole human race, there were no creatures that were not ruined by the devil, except Mary and her Son.'*

If these testimonies do not satisfy us about the antiquity of this belief in the Christian Church, even before heresy and schism had torn it asunder, let us still further strengthen our faith by searching for proof of it, amid that array of Saints and Doctors whose holy lives and prodigious learning have edified and enlightened the Church even unto our own times.

III. However, 'as their name is legion,' and their testimony on this point unanimous, it will be best to divide them into five classes, that we may thus escape the weariness of listening to a multitude of witnesses, each saying the same thing.†

The first class comprises all those who, explaining the third chapter of Genesis, assert that the enmity between the woman and the serpent, therein predicted, must be understood of that natural and perpetual war, which existed between the Virgin Mother of the Redeemer and the infernal spirit whose head her heel should crush ; or, as some versions have it, whose head her divine and spotless Seed, the Man Christ Jesus, should trample upon.

The second class is made up, first, of those who explain the salutation of the Angel: ' Hail, full of grace,' as indicating that Mary is more pure than are the heavenly hosts, and free from all spot and stain ; and secondly, of those who treating of the words, ' Thou hast found favour with God,' explain them to mean a perpetual favour, and address her with the words, ' O thou who art *altogether* free from stain.'

In the third class, we put those Fathers who exempt the

* Recueil, etc., par son Em. le Card. Gousset.
† Perrone, ' De Deo Creatore,' vol. ii.

Blessed Virgin indefinitely, and without any exception, from any blemish.

The fourth class comprises all those who grant this privilege to the Mother of Our Lord, if not in so many words, at least in those which are equivalent.

The fifth class consists of those who, whenever they institute a comparison between our first parents and the Blessed Virgin, declare that she is free from their sin.

Therefore, from all that has been said, we conclude that the accusations of the ignorant, both against us and against the Church, are ill-founded. The Church does not add to her doctrine. What non-Catholics regard as additions are nothing more than the logical developments of doctrine implicitly contained in that original deposit of faith left to her keeping by Our Lord. In this sense, therefore, we may say: It has always been believed in the Church; it has everywhere been believed, and, since the number of those who either disbelieved it, or deemed it to be inopportune is so small, we may also add, it has been believed by all. We, in our day, have been privileged to hear that which many Saints and devout men have desired to hear, and have not heard it; and we have seen what they desired to see, and have not seen it.

THE NATIVITY OF THE BLESSED VIRGIN.

I. In the little village of Nazareth there dwelt two most holy servants of God. Their names were Joachim and Anna. Being already far advanced in years, they had wellnigh ceased to hope that their union would be blessed with a child, when God accomplished the desire of their hearts and gave them a daughter to console them, and to shed an undying lustre upon their race. To this child they gave the name Mary—a name to be held henceforth by all men in everlasting benediction. This was the chosen one of Adam's seed, destined by God to be the Mother of His Son, and for that end preserved by Him from the stain of that first transgression which lost us Paradise, and became for us a fruitful source of every woe.

As she lay in the arms of her mother, filling with unspeakable joy the heart against which she nestled, nothing in her appearance indicated that there had entered the world a child more wondrously favoured of God than any other that either had ever, or should ever, see the light, except, indeed, the Son to be born of her in the fulness of time. She was unnoticed, undistinguished, because 'all the glory of the King's daughter is from within.' Yet, external glory was not wanting to her. For of her God had spoken when, summoning before Him the guilty pair who had transgressed His commands, He passed upon them sentence of death, and condemned them and their posterity to a life of pain and toil. With the hope of her coming, He mitigated the severity of the sentence, and broke the full weight of the blow. They were told to look forward to a future Eve, who should give birth to One Whose heel should crush the serpent's head.

Of her the Patriarchs spoke, as they gathered their progeny around them, and faithfully handed down the tradition, and the hope of a future Deliverer. For her advent, the world, disgusted and affrighted with its own wickedness, sighed and prayed. In their prison of Limbo, the Just, who were detained till the Mighty One should come to burst their bonds asunder, waited and longed for the birth of Mary; for she was the dawn preceding the Sun of Justice which would presently shine upon them, and turn their darkness into the brilliant light of eternal day. Yes, heaven and earth, and the departed Just, sighed and prayed for her coming, and on her entrance into the world broke forth into transports of joy.

II. No one has more reason to be glad and rejoice on this the birthday of the Blessed Virgin than you have, who, from your infancy, have been taught to look upon her as your mother, your model, your advocate. If you ask for motives which on this day will make your heart beat in unison with the hearts of all good men, you will find them in these three titles, which ought to have a special significance for you, now that you are undergoing your moral and your intellectual training. For the mother's influence in training the child is all-important. No one else can supply her place in giving to it that love, that tenderness, and that care which helpless infancy demands, and which her heart only can adequately bestow. In your college career, in the moral training which you undergo during its course, you are, as it were, in your spiritual infancy, and therefore you need one who will be full of a mother's never-dying love and patient forbearance. It is true, you meet with God's representative in the person of your confessor, who manifests a mother's tenderness towards you; but there is also that most loving Mother Mary, to whom you are intrusted, and from whom you may always look for all that your own mother would give you, and for a great deal more besides. In trouble, you may have recourse to her; in dejection, you will be lifted up by her; in trials and difficulties you may apply to her for the aid of her powerful prayers, and for the sweet comfort of her protection.

But more than this, you need a model upon which you may look, in order to copy into your own heart the virtues which you perceive in it. You have this in our Lady. For in her you see purity, obedience, and humility; unflagging industry and unwavering fidelity; never-varying gentleness and considerate kindness towards others. Therefore, let it be your aim to copy and to put in practice what you see, just as good children copy and imitate their parents.

If you look upon Mary as your model, and try to imitate her, you will feel the power of her advocacy. You stand in need of much that you do not deserve to receive; she will ask it for you, and with you. You are compassed with enemies whom you cannot conquer if you stand alone; she will aid you and be at your side, asking God's grace for you. You feel your weakness in temptation, and in the practice of virtue; she will lift up her spotless hands, and plead with a mother's strong cry unto Him Who has never yet been deaf to her prayers.

III. You have, however, another duty besides that of rejoicing at the birth of one who is your mother, your model, and your advocate. It is a duty that every grateful boy is glad to perform towards those who have done him a service; that is, to return thanks for benefits received. You must, therefore, unite yourself in spirit with the Patriarchs, who during long centuries sighed for the coming of the Just One, and besought the Lord to rend the heavens and come down to save them—with those venerable Seers who, enlightened by the rays of God's fore-knowledge, lifted the curtain of the future, and peering through the vista of coming ages, saw in the far distance the advent of the King of peace. You must stand amid the company of the priests and the just men, who, beside their smoking altars, slew and immolated the victims, which typified the Lamb of God and the sacrifice of Calvary, and, in their heart of hearts, prayed that He would make speed and come. All these have watched and prayed to see what you have seen, and many of them, like Abraham, saw it in spirit only, and were glad.

Therefore, in a transport of gratitude, lift up your heart to God. Thank Him for sending Mary into the world, and thus *beginning* the work of redemption. Thank Him for making her the link by which He united Himself to our human nature, thereby ennobling and purifying it. Thank Him for first making her pure and spotless; preserving her from the ingress of sin; and constituting her the one solitary boast of our fallen humanity. Thank Him for making her your spiritual mother; for giving her to be your guide during your student life, your model in virtue, the shield and guardian of your purity. Put yourself under her protection; ask her to intercede for you with God; to defend you in time of temptation; to aid you in the development of your intellectual powers; and never to cease praying that you may always devote them to the honour and the glory of God. Finally, present to your Mother a gift which she loves right well—a firmly-rooted determination to keep your heart pure and spotless, in order that it may become the abode of Jesus Christ.

PRESENTATION OF OUR LADY IN THE TEMPLE.

I. It has ever been a pious belief among the faithful that Joachim and Anna took our Blessed Lady when but three years of age to the Temple in Jerusalem, and there solemnly consecrated her to God. The tradition upon which this belief is based is one for which there are good grounds in the Sacred Text itself, since we know that children, under the old dispensation, were thus early devoted to the service of God. Also there are not wanting historical testimonies by which we may trace it back to the very commencement of the Christian era.

As early as Apostolic times we find Evodius, Bishop of Antioch, recording in a letter, preserved by Nicephorus, the fact of our Lady's Presentation. Grave authorities, such as St. Jerome, St. Gregory Nazianzus, and St. John Damascene, have followed in his footsteps, and held it to be true. Traces of it are to be found also in the Koran, in the nineteenth chapter of which it is recorded, 'that Mary withdrew from her family, and going to the east side of the Temple, covered herself with a veil, which hid her from their sight.'

The Greek Church, as early as the twelfth century, celebrated a festival in honour of the 'Presentation'; but only in the year 1464, during the pontificate of Paul II., did the Latin Church admit it into her calendar. We are told, therefore, that not only the parents of our Lady, but our Lady herself made the oblation, for on that day she for ever dedicated herself to God by the vow of perpetual virginity. Nor need we feel any surprise at this action in one so young. For, if with St. Bernardine of Siena, and the great theologian Suarez, we may piously believe that at her conception God endowed Mary with such a use of reason as is required to elicit an act of faith, we may be able to understand that she was fully aware of the great step which she then took, and with her whole heart made the sacrifice of herself to God.

Nor is she singular in being thus, from her mother's womb, privileged with the use of reason; for, if we may believe the Scripture, St. John the Baptist, even before his birth, leaped with joy and exultation at the close proximity of the Saviour, which act presupposes a knowledge which indicates the use of reason.

Therefore, young as our Lady was on the day of her Presentation, she knew the significance of what her parents were doing for her, and on her part gave herself up to God entirely and for ever. She gave up home, family, and friends. She gave up earthly pleasures, and finally she sacrificed that which is dearer to man than all else, namely, her own will; so that what is said of her Son might with justice be said of her—she was obedient unto death.

II. Like the Blessed Virgin, you may, in a certain sense, look upon yourself as presented to God by your parents. In sending you to College they have intrusted you to the care of others to be brought up under the very shadow of the Sanctuary in the fear and the love of God. You are sent there to be trained and disciplined by secular studies, so that your mind may grow, expand, and be made fit to grapple with the difficulties of those sciences which you may afterwards be called upon to study. This, it might be supposed, is the chief and only end for which they suffer you to leave the shelter of home. But, side by side with this, and far more important than this, is that other end for which they sent you to College.

Your soul must be prepared to fight God's battles; it must be taught to defend itself, and to make itself proof against the fiery darts of the most wicked one. Therefore, do not neglect this most important part of your education. Like the Blessed Virgin whom you are proud and glad to address by the fond name 'Mother,' you must present yourself to God; for it is by giving yourself to Him in your youthful years that your soul is made strong enough to bear His yoke, and your heart courageous enough to resist His enemies.

Therefore, train your heart to love purity; keep yourself free from evil thoughts and imaginations; and when these come unbidden into your mind, make speed to eject them by the aid of prayer. By prompt obedience make your will submissive to the requirements of discipline, and to the wishes of Superiors; and lastly, if you desire to make it an easy thing for yourself to keep your heart as the tabernacle of God, and your will as His loyal subject—be unwearied in your application to study, even though it is distasteful to you. For as long as you are busy and well occupied, there will be only one devil to tempt you; but if you be idle, there will be a whole legion to lay siege to your heart; and even if they made no effort to seduce you, still, because you are idle, you would be a source of temptation to yourself.

III. All this you will, no doubt, admit to be perfectly true. You will say: 'It is a good thing, like the Blessed Virgin, to devote one's self from one's earliest years to the service of God; it is good to be pure and obedient; also, the hard work of study helps greatly to ensure this self-immolation unto God. But it is so hard! There is no pleasure in it, and I am so young! Will it not be much easier for me to attend to these things when I am older?'

I say most emphatically, No! You think that it is hard, and *very* hard, to be what is called *a good boy*. But tell me candidly whether you have ever tried to be one? You will perhaps say that you have. But for how long? No one would call that a serious effort which lasts but for a day, or a week. Let it be persevered in for some months, or for a year, and if you then say it is hard I will believe you. Boys who have made this effort found it *hard* only at first; but each attempt became easier; each victory over self made the next more easy; it added to their strength and courage, till at last they were able at once to put the devil to flight; to detect him before he could effect an entrance into their hearts; and so they found that, far from being difficult, the task of being good is easy, easier even than that of being wicked.

You may say: 'There is no pleasure in being good.' Again let me ask: 'Do you speak from experience?' I should be inclined to think that you do not. For what pleasure can be compared with that which comes from a pure heart, and from a conscience perfectly at rest? Sinful pleasure, as it is called, is a delirium, which for a time deadens the heart to sorrow; but when that delirium has passed away the soul awakes, more keenly alive to suffering than it was before. Hence, there is neither joy nor peace for a boy who gives himself up to sin.

Again, be not deceived with the notion that virtue will grow easier as you grow older. Virtue grows easy only to those who practise it from their youth. Vice grows into a habit, and a habit soon becomes a second nature. It twines itself round one, as ivy twines itself round an oak. At first, a child might pluck it away; but in the course of years it crushes the very life out of the gigantic tree to which it has attached itself. So is it also with vice. It grows with our growth. It waxes strong with our years, till at last naught but a miracle of grace can free us from its grasp.

Therefore, be wise in time. Be pure, be obedient, be laborious in your early boyhood's years, and then in your manhood, and in your old age, you will bless God for having given you grace to bear His yoke from your youth.

THE ESPOUSALS OR MARRIAGE OF THE BLESSED VIRGIN.

I. WHEN some great monarch has chosen for himself a partner to share his throne, it often happens that circumstances prevent him from going in person to accept her hand, and receive the blessing of the Church. On these occasions, a minister of state is deputed to go in the king's name, and act as his representative; but when the ceremony is over, his only duty is to conduct the bride to his master, and having done that, his office is at an end. Thus did God act with the spotless Virgin, whom he had chosen to be the Mother of Our Lord and Saviour Jesus Christ. He selected as His ambassador the meek and lowly St. Joseph. To him, the guiding hand of Providence gave the Virgin to wife, when she had completed her education in the courts of the Temple. With him she lived in their humble home at

Nazareth, in that mutual love and reverence which we may fancy the Angels feel for one another; for, though he undoubtedly possessed all those marital rights, which the husbands of other women enjoy, yet we know that, in his case, they were never exercised. The Virgin had given her consent to be his wife, only because she felt sure that her virginity would be safe under the shadow of his protecting presence.

That she held this position in the house of Joseph may be gathered from the pages of the Sacred Text; for we read in the first chapter of St. Luke's Gospel, that 'in the sixth month, the Angel Gabriel was sent from God into a city of Galilee, called Nazareth, to a Virgin, espoused to a man whose name was Joseph, and the Virgin's name was Mary.' Twice in this passage does the Evangelist call her a virgin, though living in the bonds of wedlock. But, setting aside this induction, the reply which she made to the Angel, when he told her that she should be the mother of a Son greater than any that the world had ever seen, puts the matter beyond all doubt. 'How,' she asks, 'shall this be done, because I know not man?' A still stronger proof that at this time she lived in wedlock with Joseph, and had not been simply affianced to him, is to be found in the pages of St. Matthew's Gospel, in which Joseph is represented as sorely troubled and perplexed, on perceiving that his immaculate spouse, of whose virtue he had not the shadow of a doubt, would nevertheless soon become a mother. These passages make it evident that Mary and Joseph, though married, were living in the state of holy virginity, which state, as we shall see later, they never exchanged for the ordinary married life.

II. It may be asked why the Eternal Father so studiously concealed from the eyes of men the miraculous conception of Our Lord? Why did He not at once proclaim to the world that Jesus had been born of a virgin? Why did He rather so mask His introduction among men, that they were led to look upon St. Joseph as His father, and to ask in after years: 'Is not this the Son of the carpenter?'

The most learned theologians of the Church give various reasons, which may all be reduced to the following: In the first place, we may say generally, that God had fixed the times and the moments in which to work His stupendous mysteries, and that He did not deem it suitable, all at once, to make manifest the wonderful Incarnation and birth of His son. That stupendous work He, slowly and by degrees, revealed to men, in order that its marvellous nature might not dazzle and overwhelm them.

Then, by giving a husband to Mary, He most jealously guarded her virginal honour in the eyes of the people; for, had Our Lord been born of her without any putative father, the carnal-minded Jews would have looked upon her as an adulteress, and would very probably have stoned her to death. But, besides hiding from the world the mystery of the Incarnation, Joseph had other offices to fulfil with regard to our Lady. For God had appointed him to be her guardian, guide, and consoler, in the midst of her afflictions and her journeyings both to and from the land of their exile. Moreover, He willed him to be the support of that little family of which Jesus was the centre; and upon him He imposed the task of providing bread for the sustenance of the upholder of the world. Lastly we may assign, as a final reason, the desire of Almighty God to do honour to the lowliness, justice, and simplicity of this descendant of David, by committing to his care the two beings that were dearest to Him, and by so doing to make him His own representative upon earth.

III. We venture, once again, to remind you of the lessons which the espousals of our Lady, as well as all the other events of her life, teach you. From the circumstance of her virginity, from the hesitation, and, we might almost say, the determination which she evinced not to part with that priceless treasure, to be the Mother of even the Messias, you may learn what were the esteem, and the honour, in which she held that most beautiful of virtues.

Learn also the great love which God Himself has for it, from the fact of having prepared for His Son an immaculate mother, and of having wrought the astounding miracle of that Son's conception in order that His human nature might be circled with the halo of its glory. Surely there can be few stronger proofs of the desire which God has to see it held in high esteem among men.

Therefore, if you wish to be very pleasing to God, if you wish to have the privilege of being one of His elect children —one of those who, like St. John, are allowed to approach and lean their heads upon the bosom of the Saviour—love and cultivate in your heart the holy virtue of purity. It is a virtue that makes a boy most lovable. It throws around him an indescribable charm which attracts and fills with admiration and love the hearts of those who know him. It shines through his eyes; it is seen in the modesty of his looks; in the composure of his gait; in the quiet happiness which smiles through him. It sits upon him like sunshine upon a beautiful landscape.

Oh, love it then with all your heart, and strive with all the strength and the determination of your will to keep it untarnished in your soul. If you feel, as we all feel, that you carry this priceless treasure in an earthen vessel; if you experience the assaults of the devil; if you undergo the cruel persecution to which he subjects those who try to preserve this, and carry it safely through the slippery paths of life, do not lose courage! That tender Mother, who loves purity so well, will pray to Jesus for you. Cry to her when you are assailed by the devil; she will lift up her voice with you. She will cause the powerful arm of Jesus to smite those who assail you, and, with the help of God, you will save your precious jewel of purity from the hands of the evil one.

THE PERPETUAL VIRGINITY OF THE BLESSED VIRGIN MARY.

I. THERE are some minds so gross and carnal, so little alive to the reverence due to the sacred humanity of Jesus Christ, that they tread in the footsteps of Helvidius, a heretic of the fourth century, and maintain that, after the birth of Our

Lord, the Blessed Virgin lived the ordinary married life of other women, and bore children to St. Joseph. Some have done this quite recently, and you will probably meet many who will side with them, though admitting that all antiquity is against them. In order, therefore, that you may have something more than your strong Catholic instinct to repel and detest so gross and revolting a heresy, it will be well to put before you the grounds upon which Helvidius and his followers base their argument—if, indeed, it may be called an argument, and not rather, as a deep Catholic thinker has put it, 'the most gross ignorance of grammar.' Having done this, the answer which St. Jerome and other great lights of the Church have given, will be put into your hands as a weapon to destroy the shallow sophisms of a perverse and unbelieving generation.

In the first place, Helvidius maintained that the Blessed Virgin and St. Joseph lived together as man and wife *after* Our Lord's birth, because St. Matthew, in his Gospel, says that they had not done so *before* that time. He draws his second argument from the words which the same Evangelist makes use of, after narrating the Angel's message to St. Joseph bidding him not to fear, but to take unto himself Mary, his wife: 'And he knew her not,' says the Evangelist, '*until* she had brought forth her first-born.' The heretic, seizing upon the particle *until*, argues from it that Joseph and Mary *did* live together as man and wife after that event, and that other children were born to them, because Jesus is called the *first-born*, which He could not really be unless there had been others born after Him. To confirm this conclusion he appeals to the testimony of the Jews themselves, who, struck with wonder at the learning which Jesus displayed, exclaimed: 'Is not this the son of the carpenter? Is not his mother called Mary, and his *brethren*, are they not called James and Joseph and Simon and Jude? And his sisters, are they not all with us?' Upon these grounds is based the heretical and condemned opinion which would destroy the perpetual virginity of the immaculate Mother of God!

II. To meet this attack, which Calvin stigmatises 'as the result of excessive ignorance,' the simplest method will be to adduce, from the Sacred Text, passages similar to those cited by Helvidius and his followers. These, if interpreted in the same manner as that in which the phrases are interpreted whereon his sophism is built, will at once lay bare the unsoundness of his argument, and compel those who uphold these views to adopt the one or the other of these alternatives: either to abandon them altogether, or to adhere to a blunder in grammar so gross, that a fourth-form boy would be soundly whipped for having been guilty of it.

What schoolboy does not know, that when the priority of one act is stated with reference to another, the phrase does not imply that the latter act really *did* take place afterwards, but only that it did not take place before? Hence St. Jerome, when explaining the passage in question, observes: 'By the word *before*, the Scripture points out to us what *did not* take place. Therefore, when it says: "Before they came together," it does not mean that they afterwards *did* come together.' The same must be said of the particle '*until*,' in the other passage, in which Joseph is said 'not to have known her, *until* she brought forth her first-born.'

In order, therefore, to prove that the meaning of these particles is really what we assert it to be, let us take at random, out of the Scripture, two or three passages in which they are employed. In the hundred-and-ninth Psalm David represents God as addressing His Only begotten Son, and saying: 'The Lord said to My Lord: Sit Thou on My right hand, *until* I make Thy enemies Thy footstool.' Shall Jesus Christ, then, sit at God's right hand and reign only *until* His enemies shall be humbled under His feet? In the first Book of Samuel, commonly called the first Book of Kings, it is stated, in the concluding verse of the fifteenth chapter, that Samuel saw the face of Saul no more, *till* the day of his death. Will anyone venture to say that the Prophet saw the face of that disobedient Prince on the day of his own dissolution? Again, in the fifth verse of the twenty-seventh chapter of Job, that holy patriarch protests thus to his would-be comforters : '*Till* I die, I will not depart from my innocence.' Surely this cannot mean that at his death he intended to curse God for having afflicted him, and then die the death of the reprobate !

Hence, we conclude with St. Jerome, that by these expressions, in which the Evangelists state that one thing did not take place *before*, or *until* another had taken place, they did not mean to intimate that that latter act did really occur, but rather that it never took place at all. As for the term '*first-born*,' it would be idle to maintain that it has any weight in proving that after Our Lord other children were born to our Lady. The expression simply means, as Grotius very well remarks, 'that no one *preceded* Him, but not that any other *followed* Him.'

III. It now remains for us to discuss the question of Our Lord's '*brothers*,' as the Scripture calls them ; for, if it could be proved that those mentioned in St. Matthew's Gospel were really what we understand by the word 'brothers,' the position of Helvidius would be unassailable. But this is precisely what cannot be demonstrated. It is a well-ascertained fact, which even the bitterest opponents of our doctrine cannot gainsay, that among the Hebrews, *cousins*, and even those who were more distantly related, were oftentimes styled 'brethren.' Let us see whether this was not so in the case of Our blessed Lord. Luckily for us, the names of those who are said to have been His brethren are given in the Scripture. Therefore, let us search the pages of the Sacred Text for the clue which will lead us to discover who these men were. One of the Evangelists gives their names. In the thirteenth chapter of St. Matthew's Gospel they are called James, Joseph, Simon, and Jude, and are styled 'the brethren of the Lord.' In St. Mark's Gospel, James and Joseph are mentioned as the sons of a Mary, different from Mary the Mother of Jesus. St. John, in the nineteenth chapter of his Gospel, calls this Mary the *sister* of the Mother of Jesus. From this, therefore, we gather that as the Church has ever believed, as the Fathers have ever taught, and as the custom among the Jews warranted them in believing and in teaching, the men who were called the brothers of Our Lord, and the women who were called His sisters, were really nothing more than the children of our Blessed Lady's sister, and consequently cousins of Our Lord. The only exception that can be taken to this proof is, to raise a doubt whether Mary, the mother of James and of Joseph, is the same person as Mary, the sister of the Blessed Virgin. But this doubt is speedily dissipated, because, as Grotius remarks, there is mention in the Gospels of only three Maries—Mary the Mother of Jesus, Mary Magdalen, and Mary the mother of James and Joseph. Therefore, we say again, that the young men mentioned in the Gospel as brothers of Jesus were only His cousins, and styled, according to the Jewish custom, brothers of the Lord.*

Thus falls to the ground the impious attempt of heretics to tarnish the splendour of our Lady's virginity. Detest and abhor their carnal views; ever defend the fame of your glorious Mother's brightest ornament and privilege; and strive to the utmost of your power, by prayer, by self-restraint, and by watchfulness, to imitate by the purity of your life, the untarnished and incomparable purity of her, who is the purest of God's creatures.

THE ANNUNCIATION.

I. WHEN 'the fulness of time' had come, for which the fallen race of men had been sighing during well-nigh four thousand years, the decree went forth from God that 'the desired of all nations should at last rend the heavens, and descend upon the world.' There, all things were now prepared for His coming. The sceptre had fallen from the feeble grasp of the tribe of Juda, and men, wearied with crime, were looking about wistfully for some one to lift them out of the frightful abyss of depravity into which they had fallen, and to reconcile them with God.

The favoured being, destined from all eternity to be the

* Grotius, Annot. in Matth.

connecting link between the Divinity and our human nature, had been made ready for that great work, and nothing more remained to be done than to send an ambassador to make known to her the will of Heaven, and announce to the world the dawn of redemption. For this high office God selected no ordinary messenger, but despatched one of the mighty Seven, who ever stand before His awful throne. Gabriel, the Angel of the Incarnation, brought the glad tidings which he had foretold in vision to Daniel, by the waters of the river Tigris, in the time of the evening sacrifice. God did not send him to any of the great and renowned cities of the world, but to Nazareth, a place so insignificant that men used to ask in contemptuous surprise, 'Can any good come thence?' Among all the maidens of Nazareth God commissioned him to convey His message to her who, deeming herself the least of the daughters of Sion, had for that very reason drawn down upon herself the admiring and reverential gaze of Almighty God.

The Angel, having entered the humble abode of the village artisan who had espoused Mary, addressed to her the words which God had commissioned him to speak: 'Hail, full of grace, the Lord is with thee! Blessed art thou among women.' He told her that she had found favour with God; that she should conceive and bear a Son, Who should be called Jesus, the Son of the Most High God; that He should reign in the house of Jacob for ever; and that of His kingdom there should be no end! Alarmed at the tidings thus conveyed to her, and solicitous for the virginity which she had vowed to God, she asked how this could be. But when the Angel explained to her the divine nature of the generation of Christ, she meekly bowed her head to the decree of God, and on the instant the Holy Ghost overshadowed her, and the Incarnation, looked and longed for by Sage and Patriarch and Prophet, became an accomplished fact—Mary stood before heaven and earth as the Mother of God. The Holy of Holies dwelt among us.

II. This, in a few words, is the great mystery accomplished in what we call the Annunciation. It is a mystery in which we are taught by God, and by His holy Mother, lessons of the greatest utility. For, if we ask ourselves what it is that God there does for us, we are told by St. Augustine,[*] that He takes upon Himself the form of a slave, to confound our pride. He impoverishes Himself, and bestows Himself upon us, together with all that He has, to make us rich. Look into your hearts, and you will find that one of your chief enemies is that wretched pride which makes you displeasing in the eyes of God and robs your actions of nearly all their worth. Your constant wish is to ascend; to appear before men; to pretend to more than you have; and to seem to be more than you are. This runs through your whole life, and, if you aim at pleasing God, you will discover what a ubiquitous enemy this is with which you are forced to grapple. Look at Jesus, however, Who being God, did not disdain to assume our human nature, to take the form of a servant, and to be reputed a sinner. Look, and let very shame cast all pride out of your heart.

Yet, lest the sight, and the intimate knowledge of your many meannesses and weaknesses should too much deject you, Jesus, in this mystery, brings before your mind another great fact, namely, that He assumed all the miseries of your nature which were compatible with His Divinity. Consequently, by impoverishing Himself in this way, He has been able to prove to you that He knows by experience all your miseries—sin alone excepted—and is able to compassionate you, who feel all their weight.

Hence, when dejected by the ills of life, and by your apparent inability to stand against them, you may look at Jesus, and gain courage by the thought that you have a kind and merciful brother, Who will compassionate your miseries, and Who will be able to relieve them. This will lift up your lowliness, and make it capable of doing great and even heroic things.

Furthermore, when you reflect that this same God, by thus humbling and impoverishing Himself, has been able to give Himself to you and to unite Himself most closely

---

[*] In Psalmum ci.

to your nature, you may with joy ask yourself: 'How hath He not with Himself given me all things?' In Him you have wisdom, and virtue, and strength. Therefore, strive by holiness of life ever to be united with Him. Then His wisdom will guide, His strength will defend, His virtue will enrich you; so that after having in this world given to you Himself, veiled as it were, and under dim, shadowy figures, He will in the next life give to you Himself, no longer under figures, but openly, fully, entirely.

III. But in this mystery, besides the lesson which you receive from God, there is another which you may learn from His holy Mother, by reflecting upon her conduct during the whole scene which the Gospel narrative puts before you. This also is a lesson of humility. She is told by the Angel that she is full of grace; that among all the women of the earth she is the blessed one, the most favoured and loved by God; she is told that God is going to work in her a most stupendous miracle—no less a miracle than that of making a creature the Mother of His own Son—the Redeemer of the world—the Great Messias, so long looked for, so vehemently desired. All this does not elate her, though, surely, never before had God so highly honoured any human being. Yet she utterly forgets herself, and is absorbed only in the thought of the condescension of that great God Who vouchsafed to work in her wonders so astounding. No sooner did the Angel explain that the virginity, which she prized so highly, would not be lost by the conception of the Son of God, than she bowed her head, and in words of the deepest humility submitted to the decree of heaven: 'Behold,' said she, 'the handmaid of the Lord; be it done unto me according to thy word.'

This teaches you the lesson of humility, a lesson which all are so loth to learn. Try to learn it well; and when you are commended for anything that you may have done, in the way of studies, or of games, or of general conduct, be not puffed up with pride. Do not attribute the excellence to yourself; let all the glory and the honour go to God. Say to that spirit of vanity, which would make you dwell with self-complacency upon yourself: 'I am but the servant of the Lord.' Also, be careful to check all undue pleasure which you may feel from the natural satisfaction of having done something commendable. Try to forget self, and to thrust it out of sight. Let your aim ever be to have for yourself nothing but the labour of your actions, to give to God the glory of them, and to your neighbour the profit arising from them.

THE VISITATION OF THE BLESSED VIRGIN.

I. Mary had heard from the Angel that her cousin, St. Elizabeth, had conceived. Therefore, immediately after the work of the Incarnation had been accomplished in her, 'she went with haste into the hill country of Judea,' where Zachary lived with his holy spouse, Elizabeth. It must not be supposed that she undertook all alone this long and wearisome journey; the customs of the country, and the perils of so hazardous an undertaking, make it evident that this could not have been the case. Either Joseph accompanied her—though this fact is not mentioned—or she availed herself, very likely, of one of those companies of devout Israelites who usually went up to Jerusalem to worship at the Temple, and joining herself with them, travelled in safety towards her destination. Her way lay through Galilee, where Jesus should one day work miraculous wonders; through Samaria, the people of which were so much detested by the Jews, that the enemies of Our Lord taunted him with the odious epithet 'Samaritan'; and over the rocky wastes of Judea, till she came at last to the hamlet where Zachary resided.

Hastening forwards to the abode of this venerable priest, she entered his dwelling, and greeted with loving cordiality her holy relative. Mary saluted first; and in accordance with the custom of the country, laying her hands upon her own heart, said: 'Peace be with you.' Elizabeth gazed with a look of joyous surprise and of deep reverence upon her youthful cousin, for, as soon as the gentle voice of Mary reached her ears, feeling herself filled with the Holy Ghost, and gifted with prophecy, she cried out with a loud voice and said: 'Blessed art thou among women, and blessed is the fruit of thy womb.' It seemed as if she had caught the echo of Gabriel's words, and had felt some of his admiration and reverence. Then, struck with the condescension of the Blessed Virgin, she continued: 'And whence is this to me, that the Mother of my Lord should come to me! For behold, as soon as the voice of thy salutation sounded in my ears, the infant in my womb did leap for joy. And blessed art thou who hast believed, because those things shall be accomplished that were spoken to thee by the Lord.'

Then Mary, filled with gratitude for all the mighty and wondrous works which God had wrought in her, poured forth the joy of her heart in that sublime canticle, in which she thanks God for having looked upon one so lowly as herself, and for having had mercy and compassion upon poor fallen man.

II. There are two things which this mystery does for us: in the first place, it brings out more clearly before our minds, the Virgin's characteristic virtue of humility; in the second place, it gives us a startling proof of her power with God. Her venerable and holy cousin openly expresses her astonishment at the favour conferred upon her house, by the visit of one so exalted, and so closely united with God. 'The Mother of her Lord and her God had actually come to visit her!' 'Blessed art thou,' she exclaims, 'among women! Because of thy great, thy simple faith, that which the Lord God hath promised will assuredly come to pass.'

Mary, in her deep humility, makes no reflection upon her own incomparable dignity. There is no return of her thoughts upon self; for she is wholly absorbed in the contemplation of God's condescension to one so lowly. Her soul and her heart were full only of God, and without giving a thought to herself, unless, indeed, it were to speak of her lowliness, and to predict that on account of the favour which He had done to her, all generations should henceforth call her blessed, she gave up her whole being to the praise and glory of His Name. Behold in her that complete forgetfulness of self, that deep abasement of soul, and that confession of nothingness, which are so pleasing to our Creator, because they are the truth, that they win for us His affection. They are the virtues which God looks for from us. Therefore, to obtain them we should empty ourselves of ourselves, and never suffer our thoughts to contemplate our own fancied excellence, nor to revel in self-complacency, which, being a species of spiritual luxury, is so abominable in the eyes of God.

III. In the next place, the power displayed by our Lady in this mystery is most startling. It is startling, because, though we know her influence with God by means of prayer to be very great, yet that influence does not very forcibly strike us, until there is brought before our notice some such manifestation of its efficacy as is that which we see in the mystery of the Visitation.

Through her instrumentality, God made known the redeeming power of His Son, Jesus Christ. The mere tone of Mary's voice, in whose chaste bosom Jesus lay enshrined as in a temple, was so thrilling, that the future Baptist caught the echoes of its marvellous sweetness, as he lay imprisoned in the womb of his mother, and being thus made conscious of the proximity of His Lord, leaped for very joy; because, as the Fathers teach, the Author of all grace then cleansed him from the original stain, working this miracle through the instrumentality of Mary.

Furthermore, the efficacy of God's presence in that house, and the plenitude of the Holy Spirit residing in the ever Blessed Virgin caused the sound of her voice to fill the sainted Elizabeth with a like spirit. God, for the time being, gifted her with the spirit of prophecy; she saw the marvel which had been accomplished; she felt that the Messias resided under her roof, and looking through the vista of future ages, she beheld Him seated upon the throne of David His father, established King in the house of Israel for ever and ever.

If, then, God through His Virgin Mother wrought miracles so stupendous, we may be sure that He has not diminished her power of procuring the like favours for those who love and reverence her. Therefore, strive to have in your heart love and reverence for the holy Mother of God. Try so to live that she may often visit you, and seeing in your soul those virtues which Jesus delights to find in young boys—a burning love of Himself, and a high esteem of purity —she may say: 'Peace be to you,' and by her intercession obtain of Jesus the grace which will preserve and augment still more and more these admirable virtues.

EXPECTATION OF OUR LORD'S BIRTH.

I. AFTER spending three months with her cousin St. Elizabeth, the Blessed Virgin returned to her own home at Nazareth. There she occupied herself in the humble offices of the household, awaiting in prayer and faith the accomplishment of the Archangel's words. At last the time drew nigh, when God had decreed that the 'expected of all nations' should enter the world, and be visible to the eyes of men. We may well conceive with what eagerness His holy and virginal Mother looked for His advent, now that it might happen at any moment. She longed to behold with her own eyes Him, after Whom the race of men had been sighing for the last four thousand years. He was to her that which He could not be to any other created being —her Son, bone of her bone, flesh of her flesh; and therefore, as her love for Him exceeded that of all others, so also did her wistful expectation of His coming immeasurably surpass theirs.

She would think, no doubt, of those weary centuries which had rolled so slowly by, during which devout men had sighed, and prayed, and pined away for His coming—had wished to see the day, and had not seen it. She would reflect upon those early patriarchal times, when the shepherd-progenitors of the great David prayed for Christ's advent, as they kept the night-watches over their flocks.

She would see, in spirit, the prophets and the wise men of Israel, lifting up their hands to heaven, and with tearful eyes imploring God to rain down the Just One, as a refreshing dew upon the thirsty earth. By the flowing waters of Babylon's great river she would see the captive children of her people, weeping as they thought of Zion, and praying with aching hearts for the great Messias to appear, and free them from the oppressor's yoke. She would think, at last, of that great Prophet, who longed so vehemently for her Son, that as he prayed by the Tigris, at the hour of the evening sacrifice, an Archangel sent by God stood before him, and revealed to him the moment when the Liberator should present Himself, because he had with so extraordinary an ardour desired to know it.

The combined longing of all these now filled her breast. The hour was close at hand, and all that patriarch, sage, and prophet had wished for, lay enshrined in her maternal bosom. There Jesus awaited the moment of His birth, conscious of that baptism wherewith He had to be baptised, and sorely straitened with eager longing for the pre-ordained moment, when the waters of suffering and of sorrow should close over His head, and flood His soul with woe unutterable.

II. You will, perhaps, be able to conceive some notion, faint though it may be, of the intense ardour with which the holy Virgin longed for the visible presence of Jesus Christ, in order that she might press Him to her bosom, if you call to mind the eagerness with which you yourself desire something, to which you look forwards with more than ordinary anxiety.

Without any irreverence, we might suggest to you, as an example, the day when studies are to cease, and you are to go home for your holidays. When you contemplate that much-desired event, while it is still at some distance, you look at it with a sort of sickening sensation, as at an object which is hopelessly beyond your reach. The time seems to *drag* itself slowly and wearily along. Weeks look like months, and months lengthen themselves out into years.

Fancy, then, what must have been the holy impatience of our Lady for the coming of Him for Whom her soul longed, with all the intense burning love of her spotless heart! When you reflect upon this, let it stir up in your heart a little of that glowing fire of love, which ought to burn in the heart of every boy who is preparing to approach the Holy Sacrament. This is the lesson which the Church tries to impress upon you, by establishing a special festival in honour of this holy longing.

Try, therefore, to learn it well. When you are about to partake of the body and blood of Jesus Christ—when you are to have the happiness of receiving into your heart the very same Jesus for Whom our Lady sighed and prayed, do not be so cold! Do not be so careless, so indifferent! Remember the weary centuries through which priests, and sages, kings and peoples, wept and watched, and prayed to see the day which you see, and did not see it, and to enjoy the privileges which you hold so cheap, and did not enjoy them. Apply yourself vigorously to prayer. Beg of the Holy Spirit to come into your soul, and to set it on fire with His love, that you may begin to thirst after the presence of Jesus, as vehemently as the hart panteth after the cool refreshing water-brooks.

III. But do not confine this longing of your heart, to the days when you have the happiness of communicating. It is good to sigh, to weep, and even to faint away with languor after that heavenly banquet. Yet do not think that God will be satisfied with this. Those who love Him feel no less ardour for all that is dear to Him. Now, if there is one thing more than any other, which God specially desires, it is the advancement of His glory among the children of men. This is the wish of the most sacred heart of Jesus. Therefore, if you love Him, and desire to be of one spirit with Him, try to long ardently for that after which He sighed with so great vehemence during His mortal pilgrimage. He wished for the sanctification of men's souls. You must do so likewise.

First of all, begin by purifying and adorning your own

interior. Then strive, as far as in you lies, to help your fellow-students to sanctify themselves, by giving good example, by letting them see how sweet a thing it is to bear the yoke of Christ, and above all, by praying earnestly and continually that God may preserve both them and you from all stain of sin.

Again; Jesus desired that we should do the will of His Father. Try to accomplish it first in your own heart. Be submissive to your Superiors, who make known to you the will of God, for of them He Himself says: 'If you hear and obey them, you hear and obey Me.' Be resigned when there happens to you anything which is contrary to your will; and in all the events of life, let your prayer ever be: 'Thy will be done.'

Lastly: God wishes that His kingdom may prevail over the kingdom of Satan, that virtue may be practised, that vice may be held in abhorrence, and that justice may reign upon the earth. Try to correspond with His wishes, by making your own heart a kingdom, of which He shall be King, and then, by word and by example, by fervent prayer and by constant desire, labour to establish that kingdom in the hearts of others.

THE PURIFICATION.

I. SINCE we have already in another place treated of Our Lord's birth, and of the principal events which followed it, it will be unnecessary here to consider them in detail. Therefore, passing over the adoration of the Shepherds, the circumcision, which took place upon the eighth day, and the advent of the Magi from the far East, we come to the next great incident in our Lady's life. This is what is called 'the Purification.' The law of Moses regarded every woman after giving birth to a child as unclean for the space of forty days. During that time it excluded her from the Temple, and forbade her to touch anything reputed to be holy. Moreover, the child born of her it made 'sacred to the Lord.' If a first-born, and of the male sex, the parents had to redeem it from the hands of the priest by means of a sacrifice, which the law itself prescribed. When this obligation had been fulfilled, the law considered the uncleanness to be purged away.

Joseph, therefore, went up with Mary his spouse unto the Temple at Jerusalem, in order to comply with these requirements of the Levitical Law. Though their observance by no means bound her, because by giving birth to Jesus she had contracted no defilement, but after that event was more a virgin than before its occurrence, yet, because God thus willed to hide from the eyes of men the great mystery of the Incarnation, she humbly acquiesced in the decrees of Heaven and obeyed. She accordingly presented herself before the priests in the Temple, and delivered up her child Jesus into their hands. Joseph then made the poor man's offering to redeem Him from them. He gave them two doves and five pieces of silver. The doves were sacrificed, and the priests then restored the Child Jesus to the bosom of His Mother; but not before the dim eyes of the aged Simeon had gazed in rapture upon His infant form, and the soul of Anna, the prophetess, had been gladdened by the vision of the Redeemer.

The ceremony of the Purification being over, Mary returned with Joseph into their own village of Nazareth, pressing more closely to her heart the infant Saviour, for the words of Simeon were ringing in her ears, and the shadow of the Cross threw its darkness over her life. Thenceforth she must abide in its chastening gloom, and wait in humble submission for that dreadful day when the iron should in very deed enter her soul.

II. There is a very practical lesson taught by this incident of our Lady's life. Like her, you go up, not once, but frequently, unto the Temple to be purified; but with you this is no mere ceremony; it is a positive necessity, if at least you have any care to please God. Like her again in this act of religion, you have to give up or sacrifice what is as dear to every one as a child is to its mother—that is, your own perverse will, and by giving it up to receive it back again changed into one which has been made straight according to the rule of God. Very probably you have nobly made this offering to God, and now feel what a blessed thing it is to be spotlessly pure in His sight. But bear in mind that, having once done this, you go away from the feet of Jesus with the shadow of the Cross upon you. To give up sin is not an act which is over as soon as the sacrifice has been made: it is not an act that causes you to suffer but one sharp pang, and is then done with for ever. No; it is a life-long renunciation, or giving up of that will of which you have once for all made a sacrifice to God. It is a *state*, not an *act*, of suffering, but yet of suffering that is full of happiness and sweetness. Young as you are, you will no doubt have felt both its sweetness and its pain; therefore the example of our Lady ought to spur you on to choose the nobler state of suffering—if indeed it can be truly so called—in preference to that wretched, sinful life which fools deem pleasant.

Hence when once you have made your choice, and given up your will into the hands of Jesus Christ, never desire to recall your gift. Daily and hourly it may be, you will be solicited to turn aside from the narrow path, and to take at least one short run in the broad way. Your spiritual enemies will tease you and worry you; they will try by every means in their power to exhaust your patience, and to break down your resolution. But do not give way. Do not become a foolish changeling. Patiently endure. It is the shadow of the Cross that is upon you. Only be faithful, and the gloom will change into a halo of glory, the momentary suffering into an eternity of joy which eye hath not seen, nor ear heard, nor the heart of man conceived.

III. A no less important lesson is given to you by the mere fact that our Lady submitted to the requirements of the ceremonial law. By so doing she has taught you to respect and submit yourself to the laws of the place in which you chance to be. For the present moment your law is the Rule of the College in which you live. No doubt, at times, its requirements are somewhat harassing; but the Rule should not, on that account, be set at naught. For the present, then, we will give you a few reasons which will inspire you with respect for your Rule; in its own due place the whole question of College Rule and discipline will be gone into more minutely.

In the first place, then, your Rule is worthy of the profoundest respect, because it represents to you the will of God. It has been made with due deliberation, and for a wise end by your Superiors, to whom your parents have intrusted you. From the fact of giving you into their hands they have, for the time being, transferred to them their own authority, and consequently when you deliberately transgress the orders, or the Rule made for you by your Superiors, you are guilty of an act of disobedience. True it is slight, and in a matter of little moment. Yet it is disobedience all the same, and consequently displeasing to God, Who says to parents and to Superiors, as He said to the Apostles: ' He that heareth you, heareth Me.'

In the next place, your Rule is worthy of your respect, because, if you obey its injunctions in the spirit and for the motives which we have put before you, it will be productive of sanctity in your soul. For every act performed through love of God merits an eternal reward, and procures from Him a certain measure of grace, which enables us to perform with ease and alacrity other and more difficult duties.

Lastly, your Rule is deserving of respect, because it is necessary to ensure that quiet and that order without which any attempt at education is rendered futile. If, then, you wish to advance in the love of God and to make progress in your studies, you will maintain, to the utmost of your power, the authority of the Rule, by observing it and by showing others that you esteem and think highly of it. Do this, and you will be nerving yourself for the observance of more difficult precepts; you will be sanctifying your soul and daily rendering yourself more pleasing to God.

THE FLIGHT INTO EGYPT.

I. THE prophetic words of Simeŏn gave the first blow to the loving heart of Mary. Not long afterwards a second fell upon her, and made her realise in all its stern and bitter truth the sorrowful prediction of the aged Seer. While she slept peacefully by the side of the slumbering Jesus, her holy spouse gently awoke her and bade her arise and follow him into the land of Egypt. During the night an Angel of the Lord had stood by him, and given him the order of heaven. It was short and peremptory: 'Arise,' said the Angelic visitant, 'and take the Child and His Mother, and flee into Egypt, and be there until I shall tell thee. For it will come to pass that Herod will seek the Child to destroy Him.' Without a word of remonstrance he did as the Angel told him, and with blind obedience and a child-like trust in Providence, turned his back upon his peaceful home, his friends, his kindred, and set out with speed for the land of the stranger.

Our Lady, filled with the same spirit, acted in the same heroic manner. She did not hesitate for a single instant. She manifested no unwillingness, she made no delay. To her, Joseph represented the person of the Eternal Father, therefore his word must be obeyed like the sacred law of God. Her faith knew no bounds. She did not ask whether this could really be God Whom she carried in her arms, and held so closely to her bosom that she could feel the beatings of His tiny heart. She did not waver when she beheld Him thus weak, helpless, and fleeing from the face of the persecutor. Within her there arose no petulant questioning about the propriety of this proceeding, no demanding why the Angel, who gave the message, could not lend his helping arm to protect them from injury in the obscurity of their own home. No; for she had penetrated into the folly of the Cross, and seen in it the deep wisdom of God. She understood 'that God is then truly *great*, when He makes Himself *little*; truly powerful, when He appears in the eyes of men weakness itself; truly wise, when to them His actions seem foolish; and truly royal, when He annihilates Himself, and acts as the servant of all.' In all these things she said to herself: 'The finger of God is here.' It would be no wonder, no miracle, that God should act magnificently, or gloriously, or in a way to dazzle the eyes of men. But that He should humble Himself, that He should be an infant, poor, weak, a fugitive—this pointed Him out to her as God. She bowed to His decree and went into Egypt.'*

II. Very obvious are the lessons which you are to learn from conduct like this. The first is a complete and unbounded trust in the guiding hand of Providence. You are the children of a good Father Who loves you with all the intensity of His divine nature. He is the Lord and Master of all things, infinitely rich and powerful. He knows all your wants, He sees and has compassion upon them. If, then, you believe this—as you most undoubtedly do—it will follow as a natural consequence that your trust in Him ought to be without limit. Nothing can happen to you without His will, or, at least, without His permission. Whatever, therefore, befalls you must, in some way or other, be for your good. Even those things which seem to be positive evils and misfortunes, are very often sent to you for your good. Hence you must never repine, nor grow impatient when you are in adversity, or when things appear to be going wrong with you, or when you have not all that you wish. Remember that God is infinitely wise; that He sees farther and more deeply than you do; and just as a child often asks for a thing which would be hurtful, and even fatal to him, and weeps and rebels when it is not given, so is it frequently with us. We regard things as misfortunes, and writhe under and revolt against them, when in reality they are for our advantage.

Therefore, in all that happens, whether it wears the appearance of good or of evil, whether it comes to you as a friend or as a foe, receive it as the messenger of God. Bow your head humbly before it. Thus you will imitate Mary, who arose in the night and departed from her home without asking either why or wherefore. She knew that God orders

* Nicolas, Etudes, etc., tom. iii., chap. ix.

all things for the best. She accepted the will of her Superior for the time being, as the will of God, and without a remonstrance followed blindly in the way which he pointed out to her. Oh, may we always bear within our breasts hearts as submissive and obedient to the decrees of God! Therefore, when that which we regard as evil comes upon us, let us encourage ourselves to endure it by the thought which nerved holy Job to be patient in misfortunes: 'If we have received good things at the hand of God, why should we not receive evil?'

III. The second lesson is no less obvious than the first. It is to flee away in all haste from the face of those enemies, that seek to destroy your immortal soul. As long as you are in the state of grace, Jesus remains in your heart as in a sacred tabernacle. He sits there as on a throne, filling you with holy thoughts, and clothing you with strength against the attacks of your enemies. But nothing is more hateful to the devils than a good boy, who is eager to love God, and to keep his soul free from stain; for they know well, that he is not good for himself only. He is the source whence good flows unto others. If he happens to fall among a wicked set, he becomes unto them like a well in the midst of the desert. He creates around himself a fertile spot, which attracts and charms those who are parched with the heat of passion, and sometimes makes them turn their eyes to God. Hence it is the aim of the wicked spirits to cast Jesus out of his heart. They try to make the holy youth commit some sin from which Jesus will flee, as He did from the face of Herod. Consequently, they leave nothing undone in order to compass this detestable end.

It is your duty, therefore, to learn from the flight of the holy family, the great wisdom of fleeing from sin, and from all that might lead you into it. The devil strives, in various ways, to lead boys into sin. He suggests to them evil thoughts, and filthy imaginations, which are very dangerous —but only to those who do not flee away at once. If there is either any delay or any hesitation, these thoughts are as nets which entrap birds, or as the lime which holds them fast, till they are secured by the hand of the fowler. Again: he tries to catch and destroy them by means of wicked companions, who either speak wicked words, or do wicked actions. From all these, your only safety is flight. Stop up your ears, close your eyes, and flee away as Lot fled from Sodom; as Jesus, Mary, and Joseph fled from Herod. Think of that holy flight; and, if the devil should ever try to destroy your soul's life which is Jesus Christ, by inducing you to be guilty of sin, at once call to mind the Angel's words to Joseph: 'Arise; get thee hence.' If you do not obey, both the Child and His Mother will be taken from you.

MARY DURING THE PRIVATE AND THE PUBLIC LIFE OF OUR LORD.

I. THE Angel, when ordering Joseph to conduct Mary and her divine Child into Egypt, told him to remain there, until another message should be sent to recall him from the land of exile. With humble submission to the divine will, and a firm faith in God, Joseph obeyed, and patiently awaited the decree of heaven, which should authorise his return to the land of his fathers. The missive came at last, when the tyrant who sought the life of the Child had been summoned to his account.

Joseph obeyed the order to return, with the same simplicity as that with which he had obeyed the order to depart; but fearing to settle in Judea, where Archelaus reigned in the place of Herod, he retired with the holy family into the obscurity of Nazareth. There, Mary lived with the Child Jesus, watching Him as He advanced in wisdom, in age, and in grace, before God and men. Nothing occurred to break the even tenor of her life, except the yearly visit to Jerusalem, at the great feast of the Passover.

On one of these occasions, when Jesus had now reached His twelfth year, they lost Him for the space of three days, and at last found Him in the Temple, seated in the midst of the Doctors, hearing them and asking them questions. After that wondrous manifestation of His divinity, He returned with them to Nazareth, and was subject to them. The Gospel is silent about our dear Mother from that time till the first miracle wrought by Our Lord shortly before entering upon His public life.

What did she do during those eighteen years? She did what another Mary did, whenever Jesus came to her house to visit her. She sat at His feet, listening to His heavenly doctrine, and advancing in grace and in holiness day by day. She occupied herself in working for Him Whom she knew to be the Incarnate God, while all the time her heart became more and more inflamed with His love. She contemplated Him as she beheld Him labouring for her, working at a humble trade, and obeying her slightest wish, with all the loving alacrity of the best of sons. She kept thinking, too, of those words of Simeon, and looking forward with a sad and aching heart to that awful day which loomed dark and terrible, in the rapidly approaching years. All the while Jesus was there before her; and as He raised His beautiful face to kiss her, or to twine His arms about her neck, or to speak in those thrilling tones which afterwards were wont to hold the multitudes spell-bound with their unearthly sweetness, she thought of the thorny crown that should circle His brows, of the blows that should disfigure His face, of the nails that should pierce His hands, and worst of all, she bore in mind that she should stand by and see it all with those very eyes wherewith she now gazed so lovingly upon Him.

II. This was the life of Mary at Nazareth; a life of holy contemplation, at the feet of Jesus; a life filled with that chastening sorrow which prepares holy souls to do and to suffer great things for God. At last the moment came for Jesus to begin His mission. He took leave of her, and went upon that 'business of His Father,' for which His heart had been pining these long years past. This period of labour for the salvation of men opened by the working of a miracle, which her prayers procured, although the time had not arrived for the manifestation of His divine power. From that day she had to bear the anguish of a mother who is no longer allowed, except at rare intervals, to gaze upon the child whom she loves as dearly as her own life.

We hear of her but twice, till it is recorded that she stood beneath the fatal tree of the Cross. The first time was when she came with His kinsfolk, seeking to speak with Him, while He preached and called unto Him all those who were labouring under, and were heavily burthened with, the ills of life. The mere mention of earthly ties, and of earthly affections at that moment, and in those circumstances, drew from Him words which appear somewhat harsh and unfeeling: 'Who is My mother?' He exclaims, and 'Who are My brethren? He that doth My will, he is My father, My mother, My sister, and My brother.' But though seemingly wanting in tenderness, yet they were not really so. They held out an inducement to those unto whom He spoke, to practise what He had been teaching, in order that they might share in that love which He promises to those who obey His commands. He will love them as if they were as dear to Him as a mother is to her son.

The second occasion on which we hear of Mary is likewise one when Jesus happened to be addressing a vast crowd of people, inviting them to heavenly happiness and to fidelity to His word. A woman, amid the throng, filled with admiration at His marvellous eloquence, and thinking what a happiness it must be to be the Mother of so excellent a Son, cried aloud: 'Blessed is the womb that bore Thee, and the breasts that gave Thee suck.' Jesus answered her, and said: 'Yea, rather, blessed are they that hear the word of God and keep it.' Some, who hate the ever Blessed Virgin, would have it that these words are derogatory to her dignity, and that they were spoken by Our Lord as a caution against paying to her that honour which throughout all ages the Church has given to her. But this is not so. Look at the text of the Gospel; look at the idea of the woman who spoke, and at the words which Jesus had been uttering. The woman, admiring the wonderful work which He had just performed in expelling the dumb devil, and carried out of herself by hearing the crushing reply which He had made to the envious Pharisees, restricted the happiness of belonging to Jesus to the mere earthly condition of being related to Him. Jesus spoke out at once, in order to correct this notion, but not to humble His Mother, nor to make little of her unapproachable dignity—'Yea, rather, blessed are they that hear the word of God, and keep it.' Far from humbling her, far from lowering her dignity, He pronounces upon her a splendid eulogium. He blesses those who have heard and kept His word! What had Mary done? She had heard and 'kept all these words, revolving them in her heart.'

III. From this, as from the other parts of our Lady's life, you may learn lessons very applicable to the circumstances in which you are at present. Your college career is for you what the seclusion and the humility of the home at Nazareth were to our Blessed Lady. You have in the tabernacle the same Jesus that Mary looked upon in her little house. The virtues which He displayed before her eyes, He manifests to you also. He is content with the poverty of the tabernacle. He is so obedient that He comes from heaven, at the voice of a creature! When once under the sacramental species, He is passive in the hands of His priests. How wondrous is the silence which He there maintains! How stupendous are the works which He there performs—sanctifying the perfect, leading back the erring, consoling the hearts that mourn, guiding and wielding the destinies of empires and of kingdoms, crushing down some into the dust, exalting others—doing in fact the work of God within the little round of the host. All this Mary knew, as she looked upon Him at Nazareth. The thought of it sanctified her. Let it sanctify you also in your seclusion.

From His lowly state, learn to be humble, to think very little of yourself, not to plume yourself upon any fancied excellence, but to say frequently to your heart, which throbs with pride or with wounded vanity: 'Be still—Jesus is here. He humbled Himself—I live with Him, let me be like to Him.' Learn to obey. A word from Mary made Him eager to do her bidding.

In the Sacrament He does the bidding of a man. For His sake, therefore, look upon your masters as the representatives of God, and promptly submit to their will. Never dare to give them impertinent answers, nor to utter against them words of derision or of scorn. Soften for yourself the rigour of discipline, by contemplating the labour and the silence of Jesus. Spur your sluggish will to make vigorous efforts to study, and to do the work allotted to you, by reflecting upon the labour of Jesus. Above all things learn not to thrust yourself into the notice of others; and when you are tempted to do so, in order to gratify the pride of your heart, remember the obscurity in which Jesus lived so long, and in which Mary buried herself during His public life. Be content to abide in humble obedience, submission, and laborious work, till God shall have prepared you to come forth into the sight of men, to do for Him that work which He has prepared and destined to be accomplished by your hands.

THE SEVEN DOLOURS OF OUR LADY.

I. ONE of the Wise Man's most pathetic exhortations is, that a son should never forget the travailing and the sorrows of his mother. In order, therefore, that we may bear in mind the bitter anguish which lacerated our Lady's heart, we must reflect to-day upon that scene of woe in which her seven-fold sorrow culminated, in which the waters rose up around her, and closed over her head in a sea of anguish, such as never before flooded the heart of mortal man.

Jesus hung on the Cross, the outcast of His nation—a mark at which the vile rabble, and their still viler leaders, hurled their bitter taunts, and aimed their clumsy scorn. A galling wreath of thorns circled His head; His eyes were filled with blood; His hands and feet nailed tightly down to the cruel wood. The wickedness of a sinful world pressed heavily upon Him, and its ponderous weight well-nigh crushed Him Who upholds the universe. During His death-agony, men scoffed and jeered at Him, taunting Him with impotence, and blaspheming Him most vilely; and all the while there stood by that death-bed of shame, Mary His Mother! He was Her Child; her blood flowed in His veins; her heart beat in unison with His. Those sacred features, now so sadly bruised and disfigured, were the exact counterpart of her own. That head, now crowned with thorns, had often nestled in her bosom. That tongue which now and then spoke through the darkness, had been taught by her to lisp its first accents. Between Him and her there had passed all that interchange of fond affection and tender love which takes place between a mother and the child of her bosom. Add to this the intense love with which she loved Him as her God, and we may truly say, there never could be love between mortal man and God greater than the love which existed between Jesus and Mary.

If, then, the natural effect of love is union, and if the greater the love the closer the union, we may form some idea of the agony which the sufferings of Jesus caused her heart. The thorns which made His temples throb with acute pain were as a circle of fire upon her brow. The nails which pierced His hands and feet fastened her also to His Cross. The foul language, the revilings, the scoffings, the blasphemies uttered against Him, were as a hail of fire upon her heart. Verily she was filled with His reproaches, and the revilings of them that reproached Him fell upon her. To what shall we compare her, or to what shall we liken the sorrow of this Virgin daughter of Sion? It is great as the sea. Who shall heal it? 'O! all you that pass by the way, attend and see if there be sorrow like unto her sorrow.'

II. As we look at that ocean of sorrow, the bitter waters of which inundate her soul, we are forced to acknowledge that human words are but faint and inadequate symbols by which to indicate its depth and its breadth. Yet, though we may not be able to do this, we may at least turn our eyes with compassionate tenderness upon her, as she stands beneath the Cross, to see how she bears herself under its crushing weight, that so we also may learn how to suffer.

There are some to whom misfortune deals a blow so terrific that they are stunned and dazed by it. The insensibility which its violence produces, shields them from feeling the poignancy of the pain. It was not so with Mary. Though the magnitude of her grief surpassed all other human sorrows, yet she did not allow it so to master her as to make her swoon away, and thus be unable to feel the keenness of the sword which wounded and tortured her. Her grief, being calm and self-possessed, was on that very account all the more terrible, all the more bitter, because her mind fully adverted to all the circumstances which aggravated and brought it home more closely to her heart. Not one circumstance of those three cruel hours, during which the Saviour of the world slowly died before her eyes upon His Cross of shame, escaped her notice. Her chalice was indeed a deep and bitter one, but she drained it to the very dregs She *stood* beneath that Cross!

Yet she was neither hard nor insensible. She sighed and wept, and would not be comforted; but her grief did not *overwhelm* her. Strong men had fled away from that spectacle. Some had turned away their eyes, that they might not witness the terrible anguish which that mutilated Victim endured. But Mary *stood* by Him to the end, and her tearful eyes looked up into His pallid face as it sank in death upon His breast.

O broken-hearted Mother! by the grief which then wrung thy maternal heart, by the fidelity which made thee stand by the Cross of Jesus, and bravely associate thyself with Him in His hour of ignominy and of pain, pray for us to God, that our hearts may be torn with true contrition for our sins. Mayest thou stand by us in the last hour of our life, and give us courage to pass through the portals of death to the feet of Our Judge.

III. From the sorrows of the most holy Mother of God, learn that all sorrow is the effect of sin. The first tears that ever dropped from the eyes of man were wrung from him by the bitter loss which he sustained on account of sin; and every tear that has since fallen, and gone to swell the tide of human woe, has had its origin in sin. Mary had never been guilty of sin. But sin seized upon and murdered her only Child; and therefore sin made her weep, we might almost say, tears of blood, upon the place dyed with the blood which she had given to Jesus Christ.

Look back at your life, and call to mind the numberless times in which you have sinned against your Lord. Each of these sins had its share in causing Mary's bitter tears. They helped to strike down that thorny wreath upon the brow of Jesus; to wield the cruel scourge; to dig through the delicate hands and feet; to murder Him upon the Cross. They gave nerve to the executioner's arm, and malice to the hypocritical Scribe, and words of scorn to the rabble that screamed and yelled around the Cross.

When, therefore, you contemplate the sorrows of our dearest Mother, fall upon your knees before her, look up into the face of your Saviour, smite your breast, ask pardon for having been the cause of His and of her sufferings; and promise that by resisting evil for the future, and by living a holy life, you will endeavour to blot out the evil of the past. If the merciful but just hand of God should chastise you for your sins by sending you sorrow to wring your heart with anguish, and to draw bitter tears from your eyes—Oh! lift up those eyes to the Cross on which Jesus hangs, beneath which Mary stands, and learn patiently to bear the trial. Weep with her over the work which your hands have done. Those tears are a sweet balsam to the wounds of Jesus; they are a consolation to the heart of His Mother; they are a health-giving fountain which will wash away the filth of sin, 'and heal the stroke of its wound.'

THE ASSUMPTION.

I. AFTER the ascension of Our Lord it is generally believed that the Blessed Virgin went with St. John to Ephesus, where the beloved disciple fixed his See. There she lived in the strictest retirement with him, to whose protecting arm and gentle heart the best of Sons had confided her, in the last moment of His bitter agony. Years rolled on in that peaceful retreat; weary years, no doubt, to a heart so closely united to God, and so ardently desirous of seeing Him face to face; but yet, years made sweet by loving submission to that divine will before which her own will ever bowed in profoundest adoration.

At last the summons came. Three-and-twenty years had passed since she had seen Jesus rise gloriously above that mountain mentioned in the Acts, and had gazed upon His receding form till the bright cloud hid Him from her sight. The Virgin Mother had now reached her seventy-second year. Though she had run the course meted out to mortal man, time had traced the record of his passage but faintly upon her calm and peaceful brow. She went to the grave well-nigh as bright and beautiful as she had been in the days of her early youth. Tradition says that St. John took her to Jerusalem, when he became aware that death should soon separate him from that glorious Mother. She wished to die where she had seen her Child, her Lord, her Saviour pay the bitter price of man's redemption. There, in that city, so full for her of sad and of glorious memories, death came to lay his icy hand, ever so gently, upon her pure and spotless heart.

By a special providence, as tradition says, the Apostles were all, with one exception, assembled round her couch. They looked once more upon that face which so forcibly reminded them of Jesus. They heard again the sweet accents of that gentle voice. They knelt again to receive the parting benediction of her whom they regarded as their Mother and their Queen. As they gazed, a smile of heavenly joy illumined her face, the lips parted, and her bright spirit had gone—Jesus once more clasped Mary to His heart. Her sacred body having been first embalmed, after the manner of the Jews, with rich and precious ointments, was then carried by the Apostles, and deposited in one of those cave-tombs which are so common about Jerusalem.

Some days elapsed before the absent Apostle, St. Thomas,

arrived. Being filled with grief because he had not seen the face of his Queen, he at last prevailed upon his fellow Apostles to withdraw the stone from the mouth of the sepulchre, that he might gaze upon her in death whom he had loved so tenderly during her life. His wishes were complied with; but when they had entered the tomb, they found not there the body of the holy Virgin. The linen cloths which had wrapped it round were folded and laid together in one place, and the flowers upon which it had reposed were scarcely faded. All present bore witness to the miraculous fact; and the universal sentiment which has ever prevailed in the Church, is that God united her spotless soul to her virginal body, and assumed it into heaven, where she now reigns, seated nearest of created beings to the awful throne of God.

II. This is the tradition which has come down to us, of the crowning event in our Lady's life—a holy death, followed by the glorious assumption of her virginal body into heaven. This may provoke a smile from the sceptic, or a blasphemy from the unbeliever; but the child of the Church will see in the festival, which has been instituted to celebrate this mystery, a sufficient guarantee for his belief. Also the fact that no relic of the Blessed Virgin's body exists, either in the East or in the West, is no slight proof that God assumed her body into heaven, as tradition maintains. For if her body had remained in the tomb, it would have been preserved most religiously by the pious reverence of the faithful.

However, be this as it may, we may strengthen our faith by noting the congruity of the mystery, and seeing how admirably it fits in with the rest of her life. Death, as we are told so often, is but the echo of life. Now the life of Mary was a miraculous one, and therefore it would not have been in keeping with itself, if the end of it had not been of a piece with all that had preceded. We should, therefore, naturally expect that her death would differ from that of ordinary mortals. Furthermore, if we reflect a little, we shall see that there is between our entrance into life, and our exit from it, a certain relation; because there is in both terms something that is similar. This is mortality. In our conception, death is in germ; our departure from this stage of life is but the completion, the development of the first seed of destruction. The germ of death in our conception is original sin, which is transmitted to us by our parents; the death which extinguishes our spark of life is the daughter of sin. Grace delivers us from both species of death—from sin, by baptism; from the consequence of death, by the resurrection. Hence we are able to see how it is that the Virgin's destiny may differ from that of other men.

In her conception God preserved her from original sin, that is to say, from the death of the soul; and He ought, therefore, to preserve her from the consequence of death, which is corruption. Like her Divine Son she passed through death, but stayed not in it. In her, as in Him, death was the fact of sin, but not its effect. He rose again to life by His own power—He raised her from the tomb through grace.* Therefore, with St. Augustine we may reason thus: 'If God had the power to preserve the virginity of Mary, while enriching her with the fruitfulness of a mother, He had the same power to preserve her body incorruptible in the tomb. If he had the power to do so, He had also the will, and if He willed it, He did it.'

III. Rejoice, therefore, with the whole Church of God upon this day, when Mary, the Mother of Jesus, after her weary pilgrimage, was summoned to her eternal rest. Represent to yourself the whole court of heaven going forth to meet her with canticles of joy, with sound of harp and of psaltery, while choir answered choir in ravishing strains of celestial minstrelsy. Angelic natures, looking at the beauty of that soul which came to them from the earth, cried out in astonishment: 'Who is she that cometh up from the desert, flowing with delights, leaning upon her beloved?' Jesus is there by her side, conducting her to that kingdom which His blood had opened for her and for all His other children. 'Lift up, therefore, your eternal gates, O! bright

* Nicolas, 'Vierge Marie,' tom. ii., chap. xvii.

kingdom of God, and the Lord of glory shall enter in !' He takes His Mother by the hand, He seats her nearest His Almighty throne, and amid the acclamations of Angels and Archangels, of Thrones, Dominations, and Powers, of Cherubim and of Seraphim, the ever Blessed Trinity places upon her head the crown of glory, which she had merited by her marvellous virtues, by her humility, her submission, her piety, and the large share which she took, while here below, of Christ's bitter chalice of suffering and of sorrow.

On that exalted throne, Mary our Mother is seated. The King of heaven is her Son. She is powerful with Him, and when she intercedes, His loving heart will never say nay. Therefore, be of good courage! When you feel how worthless, and how little deserving of attention, are your own petitions for grace, ask her to pray for you and with you, that God, out of the love which He bears her, would deign to listen to your prayer. Look into your heart, and see what you need most. You need all those virtues which will make you like Mary, and also, in some degree, like her Son Jesus. Ask her to pray for you, that you may be obedient; that you may be submissive to God's holy will; that you may fight manfully against the devil; that you may lead a most pure and holy life. Ask all this with confidence, and at the same time do not forget to pray for final perseverance, that having led a good life, you may crown your days by a holy death, and deserve to enter that kingdom where she is reigning with Christ her Son, invested with that power and glory which He purchased for her at the price of His own most precious blood.

THE HOLY NAME OF MARY.

I. In the year 1683 the Hungarians, having rebelled against the Emperor Leopold I., invited the Turks to come to their assistance, and help them to withstand the forces which their angry Sovereign had prepared to lead against them. In answer to their appeal, the Turks marshalled against the

Empire an immense army, consisting of about two hundred thousand men, and after a short time actually laid siege to Vienna. Pope Innocent XI. did everything in his power to stop this flood of barbaric invasion. But after his most strenuous efforts, only seventy-four thousand men could be gathered together under the standard of the Cross. Nevertheless, trusting wholly in God, and calling upon the powerful intercession of Mary, Help of Christians, the hero Sobieski led the Christian host against the Infidel, and gained a complete victory over the forces opposed to him. To commemorate so auspicious an event, Innocent instituted, in honour of the Blessed Virgin, a festival, which is called the feast of the Holy name of Mary.

You may, perhaps, be surprised that a festival should be instituted to do honour to her name, and may feel inclined to ask with our great Poet: 'What's in a name?' Let us try to see, in order that we may appreciate the piety and the wisdom which that act indicates. A name is, as it were, a compendious expression or term which embodies all that is good, or lovable, or odious in the person whom it serves to designate. When it is either whispered in our ear, or written before our eyes, it has a talismanic power, and conjures up before us him whom we love and respect, or him whom we despise and hate. We behold his wisdom, and his generosity, his fidelity, his strict integrity, his tender heart, his open hand—in fine, all that makes our blood course quickly through our veins, and our eyes sparkle with pleasure when we call to mind his worth, and the many amiable qualities by which he has endeared himself to us. Or, it tells us of one who is base and mean, selfish, cruel, and vindictive, from whose detestable envy and malice we have suffered much. Then our cheeks either grow pale with fear, or burn with resentment when it is mentioned, and a vision is presented to our eyes, from which we turn away with horror and disgust.

Hence it is that there are names which, when uttered in the assemblies of men, will melt their hearts with tenderness, and bring the glow of honest pride to their cheeks;

they leap to their feet and applaud them to the echo. Again, there are other names, which are received with a loathing and detestation which it is fearful to witness. They raise a very storm of groans and hisses, and disclose to us hatred so intense, so concentrated, that our blood runs cold as we reflect upon it. From this, you see that there is a great deal in a name; and however men may sneer at us for honouring names, they themselves do that which they so foolishly deride. They honour the names of those whom they love, by giving them to their children, by calling their streets and their towns after them, by applying them as titles of distinction to those whose genius they admire. What is this but acknowledging that there is a great deal in a name, and that there are some names which deserve honour, and others which are to be held up to universal execration and scorn.

II. Mary's name is therefore held in high honour among us, and receives from us a reverence inferior only to that which we pay to the greatest of names—the sacred and ever blessed name of Our Lord Jesus Christ. For her name is to us all that the names of great heroes, statesmen, generals, and benefactors are to the nation at large, and a great deal more besides. What does it bring before us? It brings out before our mind's eye the image of her, whom Almighty God deemed worthy to be the Mother of Jesus Christ. We remember, as we fondly gaze upon her figure, that the Incarnate God, in the days of His mortal life, looked up to her, loved her, and obeyed her, just as we ourselves obeyed, loved, and reverenced our own dear mother, only with a degree of love of which our feeble natures are incapable. His lips have kissed her face; His arms have been twined round her neck; His head has nestled in her bosom. As then we love Him more than all else—more than our life— we must love what to Him is so surpassingly dear.

That name 'Mary' tells us of one so faithful in her love to Our God, that she clung to Him in His ignominy and shame, and stood by Him as He hung upon His Cross. It puts before us the image of her, who, as the poet says, is

'Our tainted nature's solitary boast.' While, therefore, we deem her name so sweet, so lovable, so worthy of honour, we must not forget that it is a name of power with God, and of terror to all His enemies. She obtained from Him, in the days of His mortal life, all that she chose to ask; with much greater reason, therefore, will she be able to do so now that she reigns with Him in glory. She is the Woman who crushed the serpent's head, through the might of that all-powerful One, Whom she gave to the world, and consequently her very name must be a terror to the devils.

When, therefore, you are assailed by these enemies of your salvation, call upon that holy name; it will remind them of the Almighty arm which crushed their strength, and ground it into dust beneath His chariot-wheels. It will bring before your mind a most sweet image of holy purity, of the tenderness and undying ardour of a mother's love. It will inspire your heart with unwavering fidelity to God. It will be to you a tower of strength against the face of your enemies.

III. Therefore, as men pay honour to the names of those whom they love, and manifest it in various ways, so also does God desire us to honour the name of His Mother. If you wish to know in what way you should do this, look around you, and see what men do to honour a name. If it is the name of the nation's hero, it is received with acclamations of applause and delight. If it is that of a beloved child, or of a revered parent, the eye kindles with love and the heart beats with pleasure when it is mentioned. People call their streets and their squares, their ships and even their societies by the name of him whom they love. If a suppliant ask them for a favour in the name of a child, or a father, or a dear friend, they will do deeds of mercy, out of the love which they bear to that child, or that father, or that friend. Their anger is appeased, their firmly-set purpose is changed, the treasury of their money is opened wide by the magical power which lies in the names of those whom they love.

Will it not be so, think you, with Our good God, if we make our petitions to Him in the name of her whom He loves so well? Will He be able to refuse us anything, if we be lovers of that sweet Mother, and do her homage? Certainly not. We have not a God Who cannot feel as man feels. He has a human heart, and is touched by whatever appeals to human sympathies. He will love those who love His Mother, and be generous to those who strive to do her honour.

Therefore, always reverence that holy Mother, and hold her name in benediction. Bow your head slightly when it is mentioned; utter it with respect; frequently use it, to recall to your mind an image of all that is most pure, most holy, most tender, and most endearing in human nature. Use it when harassed by temptation, when oppressed with gloom, when burthened with sorrow. Especially use it when you kneel to ask some favour from Jesus, the source of all grace. Remind Him of her who is your Mother and your advocate with Him. Ask that kind, good, merciful Jesus, through the love which He has for Mary, to grant your petition. By doing this, you perform an act pleasing to Him, because you acknowledge that you are unworthy even to approach to Him; that you do not dare to present your petition, unless it is signed with the name of her whose slightest wish He never refused to obey. In fine, cherish in your heart so tender a devotion to her, that, like those who love in this world, the name of your beloved Mother may be, metaphorically speaking, written upon your heart, and then it will rise frequently to your lips, and be pronounced with that respect and that love which are its due.

THE ROSARY.

I. No devotion to the Blessed Virgin is more familiar to the Catholic school-boy than the holy Rosary. He recites at least some portion of it every day, and is frequently a member of some society, the object of which is to keep alive this pious practice. He bears the chaplet about upon his person, and testifies his love for it by wearing it round his neck while he sleeps. As the Church celebrates a festival in honour of the Rosary, it will be suitable first, to trace out here the origin of this devotion, and then to consider its many advantages, in order that our love for it may increase more and more.

We are told that it is usual in the East, for anyone who entertains for another great sentiments of love and veneration, to present to him a crown of roses. The Christians learnt this custom from those among whom they lived, and expressed the devotion of their heart to our Lady, by crowning her altars and her statues with these circlets of sweet-smelling flowers. In the fourth century, St. Gregory Nazianzus conceived the idea of substituting for these material crowns, a spiritual one, consisting of beautiful prayers which he composed and circulated among the faithful. But as this species of prayer could be used only by those who knew letters, some other means had to be discovered, in order to extend the holy practice to the faithful at large.

The honour of doing this is due to St. Bridget—that illustrious and holy virgin of the fifth century—whom the Irish people styled ' The Mary of Ireland.' She substituted for the prayers of St. Gregory, the Our Father, ten Hail Maries, and the Creed, which were to be recited while the various incidents in the life of the Blessed Virgin, and of Our Lord, were revolved in the mind. To her, also, is due the honour of having introduced from the East, the practice of counting these prayers upon beads, or pieces of stone, after the manner of the Solitaries of the Thebaid.

Not, however, until the beginning of the thirteenth century, did the Rosary receive its present form. The guiding hand of Providence then led St. Dominic to give to this beautiful devotion the form which it bears at the present day. During his life a fearful heresy infected France. This heresy, from Alby, the place where it chiefly displayed itself, is called the Albigensian heresy. Those who professed this form of error admitted two Gods, attacked the Sacraments, and denied the use of baptism, penance, and matrimony. Their actions were so vile, their doctrines so horrible, that they had, at last, to be suppressed by force of arms. While labouring for their conversion, St. Dominic received in a vision from heaven an order to introduce among them the practice of the Rosary. He did so, and marvellous results immediately followed. The hearts of the people were softened; they gave up their heresy; abandoned all the abominable practices into which it had led them; and purged away their guilt by humble penance.

Finally, to honour the devotion of the Rosary, St. Pius V. ordained that a festival should be celebrated on the first Sunday in October, to commemorate the victory over the Turks, gained at Lepanto, by the Christians, on the seventh of that month, in the year 1571. This victory he attributed to our Lady's powerful intervention on behalf of the Christian people, who during the engagement were occupied in reciting the Rosary, to obtain a successful issue to the war.*

II. This, in short, is the history of the Rosary. Its many excellences are often overlooked for want of thought; but a very little reflection will suffice to make them manifest to us. The chief prayers of which it is composed have the singular advantage of being well-nigh purely scriptural. The Our Father is the work of our Divine Lord; the Hail Mary is made up of the Angel's salutation, and of Elizabeth's inspired words, to which the Church has added a beautiful petition for Mary's powerful intercession in the perils of life, and at the supreme moment when we are summoned hence to the life beyond the grave. The 'Glory be to the Father,' which completes each decade, expresses in a concise form our belief in the mystery of the Most Holy Trinity.

In addition to the excellence of being made up of prayers which are almost entirely scriptural, the Rosary has another great advantage, from the fact that it combines meditation with vocal prayer. For, as you know, the person who recites it must put before his mind and dwell upon the various mysteries of which it is composed. By this means we pass in review, and imprint upon our hearts the chief events connected with our redemption.

* Sambucy, ' Manuel du Chapelet.'

We behold the Angel conversing with the Virgin at Nazareth, and revealing to her the great design of Almighty God. Next, we see her hurrying through Judea to the hill-country, to visit and congratulate her cousin upon the great mercy which God had shown to her. Then we are introduced to the stable at Bethlehem, and gaze upon the new-born King. The scene in the Temple is next brought before our notice, when Mary there presented Jesus, in accordance with the decree of the Mosaic law, and those sad words of Simeon's prophecy pierced like a keen weapon into the tender heart of the Virgin Mother. These joyous mysteries are brought to a close by that wondrous manifestation of divine power which Jesus gave on that day, when His astonished parents found Him at Jerusalem, seated in the midst of the Doctors, hearing them and asking them questions.

The succeeding part brings before us the sorrowful scenes of Our Lord's Passion. Jesus is presented to us, praying in the Garden of Olives, undergoing that mysterious agony of disgust and fear which seized upon Him when He contemplated the sins of men, and all that tide of bitter suffering which swept over Him on the following day. He stands in the Hall of Pilate to be scourged, crowned with thorns, laden with His Cross of shame, and finally to go thence to Calvary—there to die the death of a slave.

After the sorrowful scenes we are bidden to look upon the glories of His risen life. Jesus bursts asunder the chains of death, and issuing from the tomb, ascends, after a sojourn of forty days upon earth, to the kingdom of His Father. Thence, according to promise, He sends the Holy Ghost to be the consoler, the guide, and the teacher of His Apostolic College. Finally we contemplate the reward of her who during her mortal life had so faithfully served Jesus; Mary is assumed into heaven, and there receives that crown of glory which her Divine Son placed upon her head, and thereby constituted her Queen of all the heavenly hosts.

Thus, the chief facts of the Redemption are ever kept before the mind of him who devoutly recites the Rosary.

They teach him to love the virtues which our Lady practised; to hate sin, which so cruelly murdered Our Lord and Master Jesus Christ; and to look forward with confidence to that reward which, beyond the grave, awaits those who here below faithfully serve God.

III. Having seen the many excellences of the Rosary, resolve to love it, and to make good use of it. Do not contract the habit of reciting it merely with your lips; for this will cause it to become for you the most wearisome and monotonous of devotions. But while you recite the words of the Hail Mary, represent to your mind the various mysteries, and reflect upon them. By this means your attention will be fixed, and the mysteries themselves be made familiar to you.

At the same time, let each mystery be said by you for some particular intention. When you recite the first five joyful mysteries, ask Almighty God, through the intercession of His holy Mother, to make you, like her, submissive to His holy will, full of charity for your companions, humble and lowly in your own estimation, devoted to God's service, and eager in the pursuit of that knowledge which you were sent to College to acquire.

During the sorrowful mysteries, ask Him to give you a contrite heart to weep over those sins which made Jesus recoil and shudder in the Garden of Gethsemane. As you call to mind the scourging, ask for courage to lead a life of mortification. When you meditate upon His crowning with thorns, firmly resolve to avoid and detest bad thoughts. Bear all inconveniences with a manly spirit, in order that, like Him, you may feel the weight of the Cross. Finally, be most scrupulously exact in the observance of His holy law, and your fidelity to its precepts will fasten your whole being with Him to the Cross.

The glorious mysteries will make you pray, that as Christ rose again from the dead, and dieth now no more, so you also may never return to the grave of sin, with its fearful rottenness and corruption. His ascension will teach you to have your thoughts ever fixed upon the glorious kingdom of heaven. The descent of the Holy Ghost will remind you continually to ask His assistance to open out your intellect, and enable you to understand and retain what you learn. This ought to be the special prayer of every boy engaged in study. The assumption, and the crowning of our Lady in heaven, will make you frequently reflect upon the glory and the joy of that happy home, and cause you to despise the slight discomforts, and the petty trials, through which you have to pass, to that never-ending reward.

If in this way you recite the Rosary, it will cease to be what many find it—wearisome and monotonous. It will become your cherished devotion. It will procure for you the virtues of which you stand in need, and will help you to rid yourself of any evil habits which you may have contracted. Only persevere in saying it well, and it will be as a golden chain uniting you more closely unto God.

THE MATERNITY OF THE BLESSED VIRGIN.

I. THE word 'maternity' signifies motherhood; and when we use it in reference to our Blessed Lady, we mean by it that she is the Mother of Jesus Christ. Let us, therefore, try to understand, as far as may be, all that is implied in that word, for it will enable us to appreciate the vast importance of the fact which it indicates.

In order that we may grasp the full magnitude of Mary's dignity, let us ask ourselves: 'Who is Jesus Christ?' If we had been living during the reign of Tiberius Cæsar, and had gone to Jerusalem, we should probably have seen in the Temple courts a man of grave and dignified aspect, Whose voice, when He began to speak, brought a hush of silence upon the vast crowds which gathered round Him whithersoever He went. We should learn, if we asked about Him, that most men regarded Him as a prophet, who had done wonders greater than any man had ever worked before, and spoken words of wisdom not unworthy of Solomon, and had aims and aspirations which pointed to something, about which the people were not quite agreed. We should learn that He came from a city of no repute; that His neighbours regarded Him as the son of a poor carpenter; and that His mother bore the name ' Mary.'

This is about the sum of what we should hear concerning the man Jesus Christ, upon Whom our eyes would be riveted with a sort of fascination for which we should hardly be able to account. We now know Who He is. We know that we could kneel down, and prostrate ourselves upon the earth in profoundest adoration before that Man, for He is God!

Yet Mary is His Mother! The Mother of God? Yes, as truly, and as really as she who bore us is our mother. Jesus is not a mere man, to Whom God united Himself, as He might unite Himself to one of us. He is a Man-God, and the divine and the human nature did not, in Him, constitute two individuals, but one individual or person, the person of God the Son, Jesus Christ, Our Lord and Saviour. Mary is His Mother, and therefore is the Mother of God. True, she did not give to Him His Divinity; but does our earthly mother give to us our soul? No, that comes from God; and yet she is our mother. So is it with Mary. She is truly and really the Mother of God. Deny this, and you overturn all Christianity.

II. From this you will see why it is we say, that after grasping the idea of the Maternity, you will begin to understand the importance of the fact which it expresses. It is *so* important, that we may call it the bulwark of Christianity. For every blow struck at Jesus Christ can reach Him only by first breaking through and destroying the motherhood of Mary. It is the rock upon which all heresies have split, and against which they madly dash themselves. Hence the Church inserts in the Office of our Lady, an antiphon which seems exaggerated, but which is nevertheless strictly and most theologically true. Addressing the Blessed Virgin, she says: ' Thou alone hast destroyed all heresies throughout the world.'

Examine for yourself and see whether this is really so. In the early ages of the Church there rose up men, who taught that Jesus had not a real human body, but only a mere phantasm—a body which appeared to be like a human body, but which was not really one. This heresy is met and refuted by the fact of Mary's motherhood. Later on there sprang up the Arian heresy, which denied that Jesus Christ is one and the same substance with the Eternal Father. This, as you may see at a glance, can be maintained only by first depriving the Maternity of its incomparable dignity. Nestorius followed close after Arius, and taught that Jesus is a mere man, to whom the Divinity allied Itself. Like his predecessor, he first struck at Mary. He must first rob her Maternity of its chief glory, before he could reach Our Lord ; for he had to maintain that she had given birth to a mere man, before he could assert that the Divine Nature is not hypostatically united to the human nature. Pelagius, by denying original sin, and the necessity for grace, could not logically hold his ground, without at the same time denying the necessity for the Incarnation, and Mary's Maternity.

So it has been with all the heretics that have risen up against the Church. If they try to deprive the Blessed Virgin's Maternity of its true glory, they cannot do so unless they first dishonour Christ. If they attack Jesus, it cannot be done unless they first attack His most holy Mother. Her Maternity is therefore the rampart which circles the Man-God, Christ Jesus, and protects from assault the mysteries of the Incarnation and of man's Redemption. If Mary cannot be called the Mother of God, then Jesus Christ cannot be called God. If He is not God, then is Christianity a delusion. Consequently the fact of Mary's Maternity is one of the most important in the whole range of the Christian economy, and its defence ought to be as dear to us, as is the defence of the Divinity of Christ.

III. If then, you love Jesus Christ, if you believe that He is God and Man, if you maintain that He redeemed us —cherish and defend the Maternity of your dear mother. Call it to mind every time that you utter those words which the Church has added to the inspired words of the Angel and of St. Elizabeth: 'Holy Mary, Mother of God.' Let them be your watchword in contests against those who do not believe in Christ's Divinity: 'Jesus Christ is God, and Mary is His Mother.'

Also, let them recall to you another fact—that she is the spiritual Mother of all the faithful. Jesus, Our Lord, when hanging upon the Cross, looked down before His eyes were closed in death, and saw His Mother standing beneath, looking up into His face, and weeping over His terrible sufferings. She had been a faithful Mother to Him, upon Whom all future believers were to fashion themselves. He knew that His children would need a tender Mother to educate their souls, to care for them, and to pray for them, just as the tender age of our infancy needs a heart as loving as is a mother's, to cherish us in our helplessness. He looked down and He saw her, and standing near her that disciple whom He loved best. Making one last effort, He said to her: 'Woman, behold thy son;' and then addressing the disciple, He said to him: 'Son, behold thy mother!' John, at that moment, represented the whole Christian family; and, in bidding Mary look upon him as her child, Jesus bade her take us all to her motherly heart, and regard us thenceforth as her children. Therefore, we hold His place in her regard, and if we stand in the place of Jesus, we may confidently look for that love, and that fidelity, which she bestowed upon Him. We may expect from her a mother's love, a mother's devotion, a mother's intercession.

What then need we fear? If we have irritated Our God, and sinned against Him; if we have taken the portion of substance which belonged to us, and going into a far-distant country, have there expended our fortune in riotous living, we may well fear the just anger of God. But we have for our mother that being who stood by the Cross of Jesus. Have recourse to her, then, because you are unworthy to approach your Lord. She will enter His presence with you; she will hide you under her mantle; she will kneel before Him with His penitent child; she will join her petition to yours, and He will not turn away His face.

Oh! strive ever to be a true and devoted son of Mary, to be like her in your purity of life, in your love of God, in your devotion and fidelity to Jesus, and in the midst of the wickedness of this world you will be a bright object upon which He will look down with complacency.

THE PATRONAGE OF THE BLESSED VIRGIN.

I. EVERY school-boy will have a tingling recollection of his first introduction to collegiate life. On that ever-memorable day, he found himself thrown for the first time into the midst of more than a hundred inquisitive and not over-considerate youths, of various ages and dispositions, from the grave, dignified sixth-form boy, to the noisy youth who had barely left off weeping for his comfortable home. Though in the midst of noise and bustle, yet he stood completely alone; for he knew no one, and he was convinced that no one either knew or cared for him. He felt the need of some one to lean upon; some one who would give him the sense of protection. No doubt God sent him a friend, who performed both these offices for him. He gave him a *patron.*

All school-boys will know what that means, and most have, no doubt, experienced the comfort which it brought to their own hearts. Some one, out of the confused mass around the new-comer, looked kindly upon him, took him by the hand, and became his friend. Very probably he was older than the poor, forlorn youth, whom the strange life seething about him stunned and bewildered. He had experience of the ways and the customs of the School. He knew the temper and the public opinion of the little world in which he lived. He had perhaps succeeded in winning for himself even its respect and goodwill. He stepped to the front and took the sad freshman under his protection. His eye caused the most forward of the youthful tormentors to fall back; his word closed the lips of those who would have exercised their wit at the expense of his *protégé;* and his strong arm bade those beware who would have played off their clumsy jokes upon him.

What a consolation to find so influential a friend when

entering upon the sharp probation of college life! The little world around us lost its dreary look and smiled upon us. We felt a sense of rest and of security in the thought of our friend. He became a refuge in danger, a terror to our enemies, an increase to our joys, a consoler in sorrow, a shield in the time of battle. Oftentimes, too, he later on proved to be a counsellor in doubt, a monitor in critical moments, and a stern reprover, if we happened to stray from the path of duty. This is the true idea of a patron.

II. What this patron is to us at College, that, and much more besides, is the Blessed Virgin in the Court of Heaven. We are here in this land of exile, at a great distance from our true home, undergoing a probation which is to fit us for heaven. We are in the midst of enemies, whose aim is to make us lose the great prize of eternal glory, which is awaiting us in the life to come. They are strong, we are weak; they are subtle and cunning, we are dull and inexperienced. They hate us because we are made after God's image, and they are aided and abetted in their murderous designs by the corrupt world in which we live, and by the fallen nature which is our inheritance.

Surely we need a patron to uphold us, to take our part, to bid these strong ones fall back, to counteract their plots, and to break their great strength. We need a patron, and God in His mercy has given us one, in the person of His own most blessed Mother. She is most kind, most tender, most loving. She is to us all that a mother is to her child. But, in addition to these qualities, which are calculated to endear her to us, she has one other, without which a patron is of little use—she is very powerful. Her Son is Jesus Christ. He is God Almighty, and therefore can do all things. He obeyed her when He lived upon this earth of ours. He yielded to her request, made in favour of those who were in difficulties, and worked a miracle though His hour had not yet come. Surely, now that she is in heaven, now that she is the first in His celestial court, He will not be less generous. Her intercession with Him is all-powerful; He will not deny her request.

Furthermore, she is a terror to all our enemies. There is an eternal enmity between her and them, an enmity which can never be appeased. Her heel is ever crushing the head of the infernal serpent, which lies in abject terror at her feet. This is your patron in heaven, full of love for you, most powerful with God, and terrible to your enemies.

III. Young and inexperienced as you are in the warfare of the Spirit, you nevertheless feel keenly enough the need in which you stand of her patronage. The time has come for you when the tempter holds out before you the forbidden fruit. It appears fair to your eyes, sweet to your palate, and the taste of it promises to unfold to your gaze the wide fields of knowledge. There is within you a hungering after it, which it is a species of martyrdom not to satisfy. Outside your heart there are agents innumerable, soliciting your acceptance of what the devil offers. If you stretch forth your hand and take it, your eyes will, indeed, be opened to fresh knowledge, but it will be knowledge that will fill you with confusion. Your hunger will not, however, be satisfied, because it is a hunger the nature of which is like that of fire —it is only increased and intensified by that which feeds it.

You need a patron to preserve you from following the evil counsel of your enemies, and to restrain their attacks by the power of his arm. You need one who will help you up if you have fallen, and be patient with you in the long and wearisome malady which is the consequence of the poison of sin. Mary is that patron. Have recourse to her, therefore, in the struggle which takes place between your corrupt nature and grace. When evil is presented to your choice, flee to her and beg her powerful prayers for you with God. If you should unhappily fall, humbly ask her to bear patiently with you, and to obtain from God the grace of a sincere repentance, courage to keep on the narrow way, resolution to deny yourself, and patience under the Cross, which the observance of God's law imposes upon you. Be not afraid of the struggle which is before you. Fight on bravely against yourself and the devil. God is watching the contest, and if there is on this earth a spectacle upon which

He looks with love and satisfaction, it is upon a young boy who is striving to curb his rising passions and to keep His all-holy law.

MARY, HELP OF CHRISTIANS.

I. POPE PIUS VII. established the feast which, under this glorious title, is celebrated in honour of our Blessed Lady. It is usually kept upon the twenty-fourth of May. Upon that day the much-enduring and saintly Pontiff, after an exile of several weary years, returned to his capital, whence the violence and tyrannical injustice of the first Napoleon had banished him. Almighty God, in a most unexpected and almost miraculous way, restored him to the arms of his exulting flock, and the holy Pope ever afterwards attributed that restoration to the intercession of Mary, the Help of Christians. In order to show his gratitude to her he ordained that this feast should be kept throughout the Church.

Already at several critical junctures in comparatively modern times, had she proved herself the buckler and defence of the Christian people. When, in the sixteenth century, the Turks were threatening to pour down their devastating hordes upon Europe, and sweep away the civilization bequeathed to us by many generations of patient toilers and men of genius, another Pius—the fifth of that glorious name—like a watchman upon the towers of Israel, roused up the nations to a sense of the peril which threatened them. They responded to his call; gathered together their forces, under the leadership of John of Austria; and invoking the aid of Mary, Help of Christians, began, in the Gulf of Corinth or Lepanto, that famous sea-fight which ended in the destruction of the fleet destined to bear the forces of Islam into Europe.

In the following century the same inveterate foes of Christianity had actually invested Vienna, and were, to all human appearances, sure of an easy victory. The Christian people once more invoked Mary's aid, and another Christian hero led the insignificant army of Christ, to a glorious triumph over the forces of the false prophet.

Thirty years later, the Emperor Charles VI. smote them once again at the Island of Corfu, and by the powerful intercession of Mary, snatched victory from the warlike sons of Mahomet.

It is with reason, therefore, that we look upon Mary as a tower of strength against the face of our enemies, and as the helper of the Christian people. Though she is bright as the sun, and beautiful as the moon, yet, to those who would trample upon the people whom her Son willed to save, and crush out the faith which He came on earth to establish, she is terrible as an army in battle-array.

II. As in the past, Mary has proved herself to be the powerful helper of Christians, so will she still prove herself to be their protectress, at the present day. The power of her intercession with Jesus is as great now as it was then. For, as He is always the Almighty, so is she always our powerful advocate, able to obtain from Him an opportune intervention of His mighty arm, to avert the danger which threatens to overwhelm us.

First, there is the Church of God, over which she stretches the shield of her all-helping hand. The powers of the world gather together, and take counsel against it. They look upon it as an antiquated institution, which is no longer of any use in the world. They imagine that it is an obstacle to the march of what they call 'modern progress'; that it is a galling fetter upon the political and the intellectual well-being of man. Consequently, they unite together and say to one another: 'Let us burst her bonds asunder, and cast her out from before our face. Let us thrust her aside as a worthless piece of machinery, which must make way for the modern improvements invented by a more enlightened wisdom to overawe and rule the souls of men.' So they bring to bear upon her all the force and all the cunning that worldly wisdom can array upon its side. They stop at no calumny, they shrink from no injustice to compass their ends. They lash themselves into fury, and dash themselves madly against her; but in the very fever-heat of their rage, we remain calm and fear not, for their efforts are vain. Like the billows of the sea, foaming, and chafing, and hurling themselves upon the rocks which bound our coast, they may seem, for a time, to overwhelm her, but when they retire she still stands there unmoved—victorious, and triumphant over every storm. For, in the midst of persecution, we cry to the Help of Christians, and her powerful intercession gives worth to our prayer, and wins God over to listen to us, and to look upon our trouble. Then does He arise in His strength; He laughs our enemies to scorn; and scatters them with the breath of His fierce anger, as chaff is scattered before the storm.

III. Mary is the helper not only of the great Christian commonwealth of the Church, but of the individual members who constitute that vast body of which Christ is the head. For what is true of the great body of Christians in general, is true also of each individual Christian man. If the great mass suffers persecution and bitter trial, the individual member is not left unmolested. There are enemies who combine against his individual soul, just as the powers of the world unite their strength, in order to divide and conquer the mighty army of which he is but a private soldier. Some of these attack him from without, and others from within. Against each of these he stands in need of help.

Examine your own life and you will see that all this is perfectly true. Is not your peace of mind often disturbed by the envy and the jealousy of companions; by the ignorance and the prejudice of those who misinterpret your actions, ascribe to you unworthy motives, and perhaps punish you for that of which you have never even dreamed? Have you not also much to suffer from yourself? Are there not cares, which though small in themselves, nevertheless harass and worry you? Have you no passions to keep under control; no evil habits which hold you in bondage, and make you feel what a bitter thing it is to be a slave?

Added to all this, do you not feel that there are powers

of darkness surrounding you and laying snares to entrap your soul? Whither shall you turn for help? You feel that you are not worthy to approach to God, that your sins render you displeasing in His sight. Whither shall you go in your anguish but to the Mother of Jesus, that Mother who is so pleasing to Him, and so spotlessly pure? You know that she loves you, that she feels for you, and that she is ready to help you. You call upon her and she hears you. She unites her prayers with your's, and Jesus listens. You become patient of suffering and of wrongs; you accept the ills of life, as penance for past sin; you courageously resist the devil; you acquire virtues; you become fixed in your resolve to love and serve God. In one word, you triumph over the enemies of your soul, through the powerful intercession of the 'Help of Christians,' who by praying unto God for you, makes Him more ready to hear your cry, and more willing to grant your petition.

PURITY OF THE BLESSED VIRGIN.

I. WHEN we think of the Blessed Mother of God, our mind pictures to itself the figure of one to whom Jesus might have said: 'Thou art all fair, my beloved, and there is no spot in thee.' She is that one solitary daughter of Eve, between whom and the arch-enemy of mankind, God has put hostility which is absolute and infinite. Next to God, though at an immeasurable distance from Him, she is the purest, the most holy being that it is possible for the mind to conceive. For, as St. Thomas teaches, the nearer we approach to God, and the more closely we are united to Him, the farther do we recede from sin, and from whatever is hostile to His sanctity. But between God and His creatures, no union has ever been so intimate as that which existed between Mary and her Creator. For the Divinity entered her most chaste womb, and there assumed from the immaculate flesh of the second Eve the substance which formed the body of the Man-God, Who gave Himself up for our redemption. He dwelt there for nine whole months.

His heart beat in unison with hers; He breathed with her breath; He lived His human life by her life, being flesh of her flesh, bone of her bone.

Hence, as no union with God could be more close or more intimate than this, it follows that no creature could possibly be more pure, or more holy, or more resplendent with divine gifts and graces. From this, judge of her spotless purity. The Angel styled her 'full of grace' when he came to announce to her the wondrous work of the Incarnation; how that purity must have been increased by contact with the source of all purity! Even then she set that jewel at so high a price, that she hesitated to part with its virginal lustre to become the mother of even the Messias! What must her esteem of it have been, after she had given a part of her substance to form the earthly tabernacle, in which the God of heaven might make Himself visible to men, and deliver Himself up to death for their redemption!

O Mary! most pure Mother, look down upon us and draw our hearts to love dearly what thou didst prize so highly! Thou art all fair, and there is no spot in thee; pray for us, that we may be cleansed from defilement, and be made less unworthy to appear before the face of Our dearest Lord.

II. A great love of holy purity is one of the fruits which a college boy ought to gather from his devotion to the Blessed Virgin. When he contemplates its wondrous beauty and its excellence in her, a longing desire to have it in his own heart ought to be the outcome of his meditations and of his prayers. Look, therefore, and see what are the advantages which you will gain by the cultivation of this queen of virtues.

The boy who is pure, is the friend of Jesus Christ. Jesus loved, and smiled upon, and blessed with His holy hands, and kissed with His sacred lips, the little children who were presented to Him—because they were innocent and pure. He will do the same to you. He will smile upon you, and bless you, and dwell in your heart, if you cherish the virtue which makes it a fragrant tabernacle for the abode of God.

It will make you very dear to Mary, for, in her eyes, it will cause you to be like unto what Jesus Christ was, when, as a little boy, He called her by the sweet name 'Mother.' The Angels will cluster round you if you be pure, because purity makes you like unto them—makes you their brother. They will lift you in their hands, and take from your path the stone of offence and the rock of scandal. It will circle your youthful brow with glory and with honour. The beauty and the fragrance of the sanctity which dwells in your heart, will shine through your eyes, and be a source of attraction unto others to tread in your footsteps and to love virtue.

Yes, the boy who is pure is a very centre of holiness, and the fire of divine love which burns in his heart, will inflame the hearts of all with whom he comes in contact. His companions will see in the modesty of his gait, in the chaste brilliancy of his eyes, in the indescribable charm of his person, a something for which they will hardly be able to account — a something which will attract, which will charm, which will lead them to think, and from thinking to conclude that it is the presence within him of that pearl of great price which makes him what he is. They will emulate him in good, and he will thus be the means of leading many to God.

As a final blessing, the pure boy will enjoy a heavenly calm, and taste a happiness which human words are inadequate to express. For he bears about in his heart Jesus Christ, the joy of the elect, Who will give to him that peace which surpasseth all understanding, and will flood his soul with pleasures, of which the slaves of sin can have no conception.

III. Therefore, let one of your resolutions after this lecture be, to cultivate in your heart a great love for the angelic virtue of purity, which is so bright a jewel in our Mother's crown. For, if you do not possess it, your heart is like a casket from which the precious stone has been taken, or a flower which has withered, or a body from which the soul has departed. It is a worthless and loathsome object in the eyes of God. Be determined, therefore, to preserve your purity with still greater care. If you should unhappily have lost it, strive to win it back by the labour of penance. Do not, however, imagine that you will feel no difficulty in recovering it, or in holding it when once you have won it back. You will feel much difficulty in so doing. Therefore, like a brave boy, you must be prepared to meet it; for to gain and preserve purity, the sacrifice of even your life would not be too great a price to pay.

It is difficult to win, because the devils hate it, and surround the soul with countless snares, and put before it most enchanting objects, to draw it away from the pursuit and the love of this virtue. It is difficult to preserve, because they cease not to attack, to worry, and to torment him who wishes to keep it. The treasure is a priceless one, but it is placed in a vessel of clay, and the poor child has to carry it through slippery ways, and along the edge of frightful precipices, where the head grows giddy and the feet slide.

What, then, is the boy to do who feels within him, and around him, the fierce rage of the devils, and sees the perils of the way? He is to call for help unto Him Who is never deaf to the prayer of those who from their hearts cry to Him for aid, to keep the treasure of their purity from the robbers that infest the way of life. He is to put himself under the protection of her who is the spotless Virgin, the purest of God's creatures. She will plead for him before God, she will shield him from the assaults of the enemy, and obtain for him that strength which will make him despise them.

But besides praying, the boy who wishes to be pure must act. He must guard the entrance to his soul, like 'the strong man who keepeth his court,' and then all his interior will be at peace. Let him not allow his eyes to wander, or to fix themselves upon dangerous objects. Let him keep his ears closed against dangerous discourses, and eject at once those evil thoughts and suggestions which are like the fiery darts flung of old by hostile armies into beleaguered cities. Finally, let him look upon the statue of the Immaculate Mother, which stands midway between the study and the playground, and read the inscription which is placed beneath it. It has been put there to act as a monitor: '*Posuerunt me custodem.*'—'They have put me here as a guardian—a guardian over your purity.' Lift up your heart to the Virgin of virgins, at the same time that you raise your cap to salute her statue, and say to her: 'Dearest Mother! guard faithfully for me the treasure of my purity, and suffer it not ever to be taken from me.'

OUR BLESSED LADY 'DE MERCEDE,' OR FOR THE REDEMPTION OF CAPTIVES.

I. THE appropriateness of this beautiful title, given in 1218 to our Lady, will best be understood from a narration of the events which led to the institution of this festival in her honour, and to the foundation of a Religious Order under the same glorious appellation. In the year 1189, there was born in Languedoc a nobleman named Peter Nolasco, whose soul God filled, even in his earliest years, with a great love of virtue, and with a tender compassion for the poor. At the age of twenty-five he made a vow of chastity, and joined himself to Simon de Montfort in his crusade against the Albigensian heretics. After the defeat of these latter, James I., King of Aragon, appointed him tutor to his son, whom he accompanied into Spain. At that time the Moors had seized upon certain parts of the Peninsula, and the sight of the misery to which Christians were reduced in slavery under these cruel task-masters, filled the heart of Peter with a desire to lighten their heavy burthen.

While revolving in his mind how his good-will might best be carried into effect, our Lady appeared to him, in a vision during the night, and intimated to him that it would be very pleasing to her Divine Son, if an Order of religious men were established for the redemption of captives. On the following day, Peter went to his confessor, St. Raymund de Pennafort, to tell him of the vision with which he had been favoured; but to his great surprise, he found the Saint already acquainted with the fact, for the same heavenly visitant had graciously signified her wish to him also. Moreover, she had revealed to the King that this project had the blessing of her Divine Son. These three, therefore, at once determined to establish a Religious Order for the purpose of redeeming captive Christians from the tyranny of the Moors.

In addition to the usual vows of religion, they by a fourth vow bound themselves to remain, if necessary, in captivity till ransom could be procured for the liberation of the slaves. Pope Honorius III. by word of mouth approved of this Brotherhood, and Pope Gregory IX. in 1235, solemnly confirmed and established it as a Religious Order. He gave its members the Rule of St. Augustine to guide them to perfection, and a white habit to remind them of the purity to which they were to aspire under the patronage of the most pure Virgin. Thus, under the auspices of our Lady of Redemption, these holy men set about their heroic work, and while rescuing the bodies of Christians from the slavery of the Moors, they did their utmost to free their souls from the slavery of the devil.

II. You may judge from this indication of Mary's love for the Christian people, and from her eagerness to free their bodies from the tyranny of cruel and infidel masters, what must be her zeal to free them from the still more cruel slavery of Satan. They are her children, committed to her care by Jesus Christ, loved by Him with unutterable tenderness, and purchased at the price of His bitter Passion. In her eyes they are, so to speak, invested with the personality of Jesus Christ. They are, in a measure, unto her what He was, and therefore the love which she bore to Him is transferred to them. Judge therefore of her sorrow, when she beholds them in the jaws of the wolves of hell. When men lose their liberty, and fall beneath the yoke of a foreign power, it is their bodies only that are in chains; their minds, their souls are free. No dungeon can darken their light, no manacles, no fetters can bind down their thoughts or their aspirations. The tyrant may threaten, may kill; but he cannot compel the will to bend. If, as a last resource, he strike with the sword, one sharp pang will for ever free the poor wretched prisoner from his clutches.

It is far otherwise with the tyranny of the devil. He enslaves the *souls* of men. With a tempting bait, he first allures them into his nets, and having once entrapped them, he holds them fast. Very speedily sin enfeebles the will, darkens the intellect, and fills the soul with disgust for heavenly things. Hence, when from time to time grace urges it to rise again, it may do so for a season, feeling all the while how terribly strong is the hold which the devil has upon its powers. It struggles against him for a while, and then falls back. Thus the evil one, by his tyranny, succeeds in destroying not only the bodies of his slaves, but their immortal souls. Therefore, Jesus bids us not to fear those who can destroy only the body: 'I will tell you,' He adds, 'whom you shall fear. Fear Him who can destroy the soul.'

Our dear Mother is, therefore, full of tender solicitude for her children. When she beholds them in the power of this cruel enemy of her Son, she lifts up her pure and spotless hands before the throne of God, and continually pleads with Him for them, that the ransom of the precious blood may be applied to them, that their chains may be broken, and that they themselves may be restored to liberty.

III. Knowing, therefore, the great love of your holy Mother Mary for poor sinners, you must strive to the utmost of your ability to second her desire for the redemption of souls from the slavery of sin. In order that your zeal may be according to knowledge, you must begin with yourself; for otherwise you will present to the eyes both of Angels and of men the ridiculous spectacle of one who saves others, but destroys himself; who points out to others the way to heaven, but will not himself walk in it.

Do not be so foolish. Let not sin dwell in your soul; suffer it not to enslave your heart. Be not of the number of those fools who fancy that they can for a time walk with the devil, and then easily withdraw from his fellowship; who imagine that they may float with the stream, and then return in safety to the pleasant shore. Those who think thus, little know the tenacious grasp with which sin holds a man down in its iron fetters, nor the velocity with which the stream of iniquity whirls him beyond the reach of help or the hope of return. If you are wise, learn this in time. Withdraw your feet at once and for ever from the fetters of sin, and turn your back resolutely upon the glitter of the tempting stream. After thus manifesting zeal for your own soul, you may venture to be zealous for the souls of others; for he who is in safety may strive to help others, and he who is not sick may with propriety try to heal those who are.

But how are you to do this at College? You can do it by the good example of a pious and holy life, for there is nothing that so powerfully moves young boys to be virtuous as the blameless conduct of some fellow-student. If he is really good, there is about him a something which leads them to holiness. It makes them feel unworthy to be in his company, if their conscience is not at rest; and the repose which sits upon his happy face, makes them long to taste and see how sweet are the chaste joys of a virtuous life. The college-boy may help to redeem captives from sin and from the devil, by saying a word in season to those who are not in the narrow way; by upholding right principles; by rejecting and scorning those which are wrong; by never blushing at anything except that which is dishonourable and sinful; and, by loudly and uncompromisingly protesting against that which is wicked.

Therefore, stand by those who are weak; spur on the pusillanimous; and let your own life be your strongest argument for what is virtuous and upright. Lastly, ever have in your hands the powerful weapon of prayer. Let not a day pass without lifting up your heart to God, and imploring Him to preserve both yourself and your companions from ever falling under the tyranny of sin; and if you are a member of Our Lady's Sodality, which is established in most Colleges for this very purpose, recite her Office with great fervour, and beg of her who is the Mother of the Redeemer, to pray with you and for you, that by the grace of God your own heart may be preserved from the bondage of the devil, and the hearts of your schoolfellows be made firm and loyal in the service of Jesus Christ.

MARY, OUR FAITHFUL FRIEND.

I. THE author of the 'Imitation' says very wisely: 'Without a friend thou canst not well live.' This is true, in a greater or in a less degree, of everyone of us without exception. We need someone to whom we may freely and openly speak out our mind, in whom we may confide, and upon whom we may lean with unbounded trust. Happy is the boy who can find among his companions one who is worthy of trust like this, and who will prove unto him a faithful friend! For in every boy there is much that requires a genial influence to draw it forth and bring it to maturity; otherwise it will wither and die, like seed hidden too deep in the earth, and therefore unable to reach the air, the light, and the heat. There are high aspirations, noble resolves, lofty aims, which, if shut up within his own bosom, remain there like so many phantoms. Let him but find a true friend, into whose patient ear he may pour the thoughts which stir within him, and they will take some definite shape, and grow into actions which will give glory to God and bring help unto men.

For his spiritual necessities he finds this friend in the ghostly father, to whom he gives his whole confidence, and from whose tender, loving heart he has no secrets. But besides him there is another friend, of whose considerate kindness and faithful love he stands in much need. This is that friend who will abide with him amid the continual struggles which he must maintain against his unseen foes, and plead unceasingly for him before Jesus Christ. It is Mary, the Mother of Jesus, the college-boy's patron and friend. He has at heart interests which very closely affect her also. He has his purity to defend against those neversleeping robbers, who, like beasts of prey, rage furiously around him, watching for an opportunity to snatch it away. He has his studies to care for, and to treat of with the Seat of Wisdom. He has his trials to speak of—the temptations which harass him, the weariness and the dejection which weigh him down.

With whom can he, with more ease or with greater confidence, speak of these things than with her who watched over the holy boyhood of Jesus? She has the true notion, the true ideal of what a boy should be ; and when he makes her his friend, and trusts in her, he is sure never to lose her, and furthermore to be made like unto her Divine Son Jesus.

II. There is, in the friendship of our Mother Mary, one quality, upon which you must specially fix your attention, because it will fill your heart with love for her and with great confidence in her. This is her fidelity. No characteristic is more strongly marked in her. It stands out boldly and clearly in the Gospels, and it is one that cannot fail to strike us, if we reflect at all.

We can see it in her throughout all the stages of her life. Her fidelity to Our Lord never wavered for a single instant. It began at the first moment of His conception ; it lasted till He expired before her eyes upon the Cross ; it still endures ; it will end only when God ceases to be. We may predicate this fidelity of all that hidden period, over which the veil of silence has been drawn by the sacred writers, as well as of those few special instances recorded in the Gospels ; for these are but so many glimpses vouchsafed to us, glimpses from which we may judge of the general tenor of her life. All her fidelity culminated in that one grand act by which she stands for ever before the world as the most faithful of God's creatures. She shrank not from His Cross of shame. She was His Mother! Yet, there she stood on Calvary, where He died in agony greater than ever human frame endured before. She saw the fanatical fury of His adversaries ; she saw their rage against Him ; their fiendish delight when they had nailed Him to the accursed tree, and by that act had made Him, as they imagined, for ever infamous. She heard the blasphemies, the taunts, the revilings. Her eyes looked into the dying eyes of her Son. She saw all His sufferings, and bravely bore the pain which the sight of them inflicted upon her. She *stood* heroically by His Cross. Apostles had fled away from that terrible spectacle of human woe; disciples had staggered in their faith; but she, faithful *even unto death*, neither fled, nor wavered for an instant in her belief. She stood there till pious and loving hands loosed from the Cross the dead body of Jesus, and laid His thorn-crowned head upon that bosom which, having been His first pillow in this world of sin and of sorrow, rightly became His last resting-place in death.

III. You may confidently look for the like fidelity from her, if you succeed in securing for yourself her friendship. How are you to do this? By endeavouring to the best of your power to make yourself an exact copy of her Divine Child Jesus.

First, let it be your chief aim, chief above intellectual proficiency and everything else, to be pure in mind, and heart, and body. How spotlessly pure must have been the boy Jesus, in Whom the Divinity dwelt corporally! In your measure and in your degree you can become like Him. He has Himself been a boy, and therefore has sanctified that age. Call upon Him, then, by the surpassing holiness of His youth, to save you from the tyranny of your passions, which now begin to stir within you, and strive to gain the mastery over your heart.

Next—in order to fence round this precious virtue, this jewel of boyhood—study to be very humble. Think nothing of yourself or of your family, of your abilities or of your prospects; but, looking upon all that you have as God's gift, take no glory to yourself therefrom, but say: 'I am nothing, I can do nothing, I have nothing except that which has been given to me by the bounty of God.'

Finally, obey your Superiors, as Jesus obeyed Mary and Joseph. Then you will be an image of Jesus, and His holy

Mother looking upon you, will love you because you resemble Him. You will then in very deed be her child, and you may expect from her all that faithful love which she gave to Jesus Christ. She will be by your side when the devil comes to tempt you; she will aid you in your studies; she will comfort and console you in grief, and in dejection; in one word, she will be your faithful friend.

When you come to die, she will be at your bedside looking into your eyes and encouraging you. She will defend you through the gates of death, and you will appear without dread before your Judge, because Mary will conduct you to His feet.

MARY'S INFLUENCE UPON US.

I. THE influence which a mother exercises in forming the character of her child, is very great. It is so great, that we might almost say the work is entirely hers. For, those who, in after years, help to build up his character do nothing more than either develop or modify the work which she has begun; or, to speak more correctly, they simply foster the germs which she has planted. The reason of this is obvious. A child, during those early years in which he is under the loving care of his mother, is like a piece of clay in the hands of a modeller. He will take whatever impressions she pleases to give him. These, being the first, sink down deepest, and last the longest.

Now, God, in His infinite wisdom, while providing for us an earthly mother to tend and care for us during our helpless infancy, did not forget that our soul would need some one just as gentle and as tender, to watch over its well-being, and to impress upon it those characteristic marks which make it an exact counterpart of Jesus Christ. Though our own earthly mother does this to the best of her power, yet there is wanting in her work a something which can be supplied only by one who is herself the living image of Jesus. Therefore He gives us, as the mother of our spiritual life, His own most blessed Mother.

She had opportunities of studying and of transforming herself into His likeness such as no one else could possibly have had. Till His thirtieth year, He lived constantly before her eyes. He daily and hourly conversed with her. He confided to her the thoughts, the feelings, the longings of His sacred heart; and when we bear in mind that her pure soul loved Him with all the tenderness of a mother, intensified by her ardent worship of Him as her God, we may form for ourselves some idea of the effect which that love would have upon her character. She would think as He thought, and feel as He felt; she would love what He loved, and be zealous for what He had most at heart; in one word, she would become the exact image of Him, and thus be best fitted to influence and train the souls of those whose end in life is to be conformed to the likeness of Jesus Christ.

II. If then, the college-boy, knowing this, put himself under the protection of the Mother of God, look upon her as his mother, and regard himself as her son, she will exercise over him that influence which an earthly mother exercises over her child. She will exert all her power, and use all her weight of intercession to fill his soul with those virtues, and to impress upon it that character which will make him somewhat like Jesus; and the boy himself will be moved to imitate the excellence of the Mother whom he loves and reveres. For, if we contract a certain degree of resemblance to those with whom we live, as is evident from the stamp which is perceptible upon those who come from the same College, we may naturally expect that Mary's devout client, who always sets before his eyes her holy example, and frequently revolves in his thoughts her life and actions, will come in time to resemble her.

He will be distinguished by the two great marks which characterised her, and which she received from her Divine Son. These are, great purity, and ardent zeal for the salvation of men. What a happiness it will be for you, and with what glory shall you be crowned, when you have your heart filled with the love of that heavenly virtue! You will feel yourself animated with the strength which it inspires, and all on fire with the noble, lofty aims which it generates. You will taste its sweetness, and will share in the beauty with which it circles the brows of the chaste generation. It will cast out of your heart all selfish motives; it will fill you with a noble desire to seek out and to save those who are rushing headlong to destruction, because they close their eyes to the beauty upon which you are gazing. You will be animated with the spirit of Jesus Christ, which you will imbibe by being under Mary's influence, and which that influence has made you love and tend unto, with all the eagerness of a soul whose eyes have been purified and made to gaze upon the entrancing loveliness of God.

III. But you will ask: If I am to be filled with the spirit of Jesus, as a consequence of being a client of His holy Mother, upon what, or upon whom shall I be able to exercise my zeal, within the narrow bounds of the College?

You must exercise that love for souls, with which you will be inspired, first of all upon yourself. You will find that your own heart is like a fruitful soil, which ever needs the constant care of the husbandman. Its very richness is one reason why it demands greater attention. For there are weeds which constantly crop up, and which must be uprooted at once, lest they multiply and scatter their germs abroad. The very flowers of virtue need to be trimmed, and the vines of good works to be pruned, in order that the flowers may be richer and more choice, the fruit more abundant and of a more excellent quality. You will be sensible of this if you carefully search into the principles from which your actions flow. Many of these you will discover to be selfishness, vanity, a desire of praise, and the like. Moreover, you will feel within yourself slight movements of anger and of jealousy, little meannesses and untruthfulness, a will to disobey, to murmur, to set aside duty—all which will give you matter enough upon which to exercise your zeal.

Then, with regard to others, you may confine your exertions, for the present, simply to saying and to doing nothing that would hinder them from being good. Do not encourage those who rebel, who break Rule, who are idle and mischievous, by any foolish commendation of their daring, or of what some would call 'their manly spirit.' Do not yourself set them an evil example in this way, and if you ever have an opportunity of dissuading any one from doing anything that is wrong, or of expressing your strong disapproval of any delinquency which happens to come under your notice, do not fail to do so. On these occasions a rebuke, or a look of disapproval from a boy, is often more salutary than the sternest denunciation from the lips of a master. Be regular and exact in the performance of your duty; study well; love discipline; be good-tempered with your companions; be constant in frequenting the Sacraments, and you will be exercising and showing a zeal for souls, a thousand-fold more true and more useful, than if you set yourself up to preach to others, to give gratuitous advice, and, in a word, to be what every one would call 'an intolerable nuisance.' Do this now, and God will in after life fit you to serve His cause in a more active way, either by giving you a vocation to His glorious priesthood, or by making you a good, influential layman, who, in his own sphere, will do very much for the glory of God.

MARY, THE PROTECTRESS OF YOUTH.

I. THE period of youth is a precious time, during which a boy ought to be growing in the knowledge, love, and practice of every virtue. It is a time that bears the same relation to his spiritual life as infancy does to his bodily life; and, therefore, just in the same way as that in which the tender years of his childhood need the loving care of a mother to protect from harm, and to develop the strength of his bodily frame, so does the time of his boyhood need the watchful care of a gentle mother to bring to maturity, and to preserve from premature harm, those seeds of virtue sown in his heart during the happy days of his innocent childhood.

There is in this idea reason enough to show you why our Blessed Lady should be the protectress of your youth.

But there is another reason, and that is, the intense love which Jesus ever manifested for children. His eyes always looked upon them with loving kindness, and His face wore an expression of unspeakable tenderness whenever He turned towards them. Hence you will find that in the crowds which surrounded Him, children ever contrived to be near Him. Nothing in His bearing either terrified or overawed them; and they evidently perceived, with that natural instinct which they possess in so remarkable a degree for discovering those who love them, that His heart overflowed with tenderness for them. He proved that these were His sentiments, by the gentle rebuke which He administered to the Apostles who tried to thrust back both the children and those who strove to bring them to Him: 'Suffer little children,' said He, 'to come unto Me, and forbid them not.' Also, by the fact, that when the disciples were disputing among themselves about preeminence and dignity, He took a child by the hand, and setting him in the midst of them, proposed him to them as a model: 'Unless you become as this little child, you shall not enter the kingdom of heaven.'

Now, if Jesus ever manifested so tender an affection for children, this fact became one reason the more why our Lady should imitate Him in this respect also. They were dear to His sacred heart, and as her heart ever beat in unison with His, they must be dear to hers also; the Mother cannot help loving and caring for that which is so dear to her Son.

II. When we begin to examine more closely into the reasons which could thus attract the love of Jesus, and of His holy Mother to little ones, we find that another motive, besides that of being their Father and their God, moved the sacred heart to love them. He loves them because they are so innocent, and so much exposed to lose that innocence.

Their innocence and their helplessness likewise attract the love of our dear Mother Mary. What do her eyes behold in the boy who has just left his home, and who is making his first trial of life at College? She sees a soul which is radiant with divine grace, fresh, bright, and beautiful, unconscious of evil, unsullied as the lily, and fragrant as a golden casket filled with aromatic spices. That soul is to her as a polished mirror, into which God is looking with wondrous complacency. She sees there an exact reflection of His divine perfections. His sanctity, His peace, His calm, are mirrored there as the heavens are reflected in the unruffled bosom of some inland lake. That soul is to her what that little boy was, of whom we read in the history of the persecutions. The body of Our Lord, in the Most Holy Sacrament, was put into his bosom to be carried to the suffering confessors in prison. What wonder is it, then, that she should love and wish to protect and save from profanation so precious a treasure, especially when she sees how easily that beauty and that heavenly fragrance may be swept away. A word may do it, a glance of the eye, a passing thought!

What, then, would that youthful soul be before her eyes, and before the sorrowful eyes of Jesus Christ? As a fair garden, over which the desolating blast of a whirlwind has swept in all its fury. Its beauty and its fragrance, its fair and goodly show of fruit and of flowers are all gone! So is it, also, with the soul. Instead of the God Who dwelt there, there comes a tiger spirit of desire, which will never say 'Enough.' That evil spirit will drag the child through the mire of sin, till his white robe be utterly spoiled, till the bloom, the fragrance, and the glory of sanctity have departed, and left behind not a single vestige of their presence.

III. Bear in mind, then, what a thing of beauty the soul must be, when it is innocent and pure. Ever look upon the holy Mother of God as the protectress of that priceless treasure, during the days of your helpless youth, when your very inexperience and ignorance of evil expose you to the cunning devices of the devil. Be determined to keep your heart in the state of grace, for it is grace that makes it so pleasing to God. Let the happiness of so blessed a state encourage you carefully to guard it. You bear Jesus in your heart; you have the image of the Blessed Trinity mirrored in your soul; you are an object upon which the great God of heaven, from the height of His awful throne, looks down with loving complacency.

But because you carry this treasure in an earthen vessel —beware! You are clad in a white robe, and have to walk through muddy ways, and yet keep it from all spot and stain. How shall you be able to do this? By looking upon the Mother of Jesus as your protectress, and by ever trying to deserve her loving care. In temptation, cling to her. Cry to her for aid. Beg of her to shelter you from the heat of the battle, and to be close at hand when your enemies rise up against you.

But if, unfortunately, you have already lost that treasure, and have fallen upon the muddy way, do not be discouraged. Rise with great confidence, and do not, like a coward, lose heart at the first reverse. Stubborn resistance will at last carry the day. Therefore, pray fervently; shun occasions; be humble, and God will give you grace, by the aid of Mary's powerful intercession, to withstand the enemy. Your stains will be purged away, your robe will be made white in the blood of the Lamb, the treasure will be restored to your heart, and God will once more regard you with love. Oh! ever look upon your sweet and loving Mother as your protectress! Ask her to guard your treasure with and for you, and 'you will be protected under her covering from the heat, and will rest in her glory.'

MARY, OUR ADVOCATE WITH OUR JUDGE.

I. If ever a man stands in need of an advocate to plead for him with all the earnestness which love inspires, it is surely when he is summoned into the presence of Jesus Christ, to give an account of his stewardship. This manifestation of ourselves before the judgment-seat of God, is one of those certainties which await us in the life to come, and no man can reflect seriously upon it without a shudder of genuine terror. For truly, 'it is a fearful thing to fall into the hands of the living God'—to close our eyes upon the world, and upon all that is dear to us, and to open them in the dread presence of that awful Majesty Who is holiness itself. In His sight the Angelic spirits themselves are not pure; His power is unlimited; and from His sentence there is no appeal.

If we bear these things in mind, and then give a glance at the life which we have been leading, we shall rouse up our sluggish senses, and begin to feel keenly the need that we have of an advocate so powerful as our dear Lady is. Look back upon the past! What has been your behaviour, for example, towards that trusty guide, conscience, which God has given to you, to direct you aright, to cry out with a warning voice when your feet begin to wander from the straight path? Have you not closed your ears to its reproaches, and drowned its accents with your loud excuses? If so, it will stand at the bar of divine justice, as a witness against you. Its words will be heard there, and its testimony will be beyond suspicion.

You will perhaps say: 'I have confessed all my sins.' But have you had true sorrow for them? Alas! what do you think of your confessions, now that you call to mind how carelessly you prepared for them, and how little heed you afterwards took to amend? If they have not been well made—if your negligences have been gross and culpable, 'what will you say to the Lord when He shall arise to judge?' Has your conduct been any better with regard to even the Most Holy Sacrament? It may be that your sluggishness and your carelessness have made you profane the body of the Lord. If to these things we add your actual sins, your sins of thought, your sins of word, your sins of deed, is there not good reason for you to fear and tremble, in anticipation of the rebuke which will break from the lips of your Judge, and of the terrible sentence of condemnation which will follow it?

With truth, then, may each of us exclaim: 'What shall I do when God shall arise to judge, and when He shall question, what shall I answer Him?'

II. At the hour of death, the remembrance of a careless and sinful life is a fruitful source of well-grounded fear; but at the same time, if we have turned to God from our sins, and have tried to make reparation for them, we need not lose courage, for we have, in the person of our dear Mother Mary, a very powerful advocate with Jesus. She will not, in that trying moment, desert us. It is the last time that her influence can be exerted in our behalf, and she will use it with our Judge to make Him propitious to us.

Her influence is indeed very great. It is the influence of the best of mothers, with the most loving and dutiful of sons. Can that Son withstand the prayers of His Mother, when He beholds her at His feet, with pleading look and streaming eyes, asking mercy for those whom He disdained not to call, and to look upon as His brothers? He hears the thrilling tones of her low, sweet voice. It is the voice of her whose word of humble submission to the decrees of God, drew Him from the heights of heaven, and clothed Him with our human nature. He beholds those pure and spotless hands outstretched in supplication. They laboured for Him; they tended and cared for Him; they were laid with caressing fondness upon His head in childhood, and pressed His infant form with loving tenderness to her burning heart.

Surely Jesus will not turn a deaf ear to the pleadings of so beloved an advocate! He will smile graciously upon the trembling child who appears before Him. He will not remember the past. He will blot it out from His records, and we shall then be able to approach His awful throne, to give an account both of the good and of the evil that we have done. The evil, He will forget; from the good, He will take away all its imperfections; and will then crown it with an everlasting reward.

III. We must, however, remember that, if we wish to have the most holy Mother of God for our advocate, it will not be sufficient for us merely to say that we desire this. Action must be joined to will, and then some result will follow. For, just as it would be useless for us to wish for a lawyer to plead our cause, unless we also took the trouble to seek one out and to explain our case to him, so is it equally futile to wish for our Lady's advocacy, unless we take measures to secure it. What then, you will ask, are we to do, in order to make her an earnest pleader for us, at the bar of divine justice?

The first step to be taken is to give up all habits of sin. She will not interest herself in anyone who will not do this, unless, indeed, it be to pray for him unto God, that his heart may be moved to make this most necessary resolve. For sin is continually scourging, crowning with thorns, and crucifying that Jesus, Whom she loves most tenderly. Therefore, in her eyes, sin is a most hideous monster—the most abominable of evils. Hence, the boy who hugs to his breast this offspring of hell need not expect her to exercise her influence with Jesus, nor to plead his cause before the throne of mercy, when he is summoned to give an account of the deeds which he has done in the body.

After giving up sin, the boy must ever put great confidence in the Blessed Virgin. Out of humility, he must deem himself unworthy of any favour from God, and frequently ask our Lady to pray for him, and to present his petition to Jesus. He must look upon her as his model, and try to tread in her footsteps. She practised humility and had a low esteem of herself. Therefore, he must not take pride in his family, nor in his talents, nor in his appearance. She gave to all, an example of mildness and gentleness. She sought not her own profit. She loved truth and honesty. Therefore, he also must aim at these virtues. Let him be kind to his companions, and restrain his anger. Let him be unselfish, and ever scorn lying, cunning, and deceit. In the midst of a corrupt world, she lived a most pure and holy life, being without either spot or stain of any kind. Let him also try to keep his heart pure. Let him fight down his unruly nature, reject evil thoughts, stifle evil desires, and, like a noble boy, scorn to do anything that would disgrace him in the eyes of God and of His holy Angels.

He who does this, or at least tries to do this, though with

numberless failures, will be very dear to the heart of the Blessed Virgin. If he be weak and fail, she will still love him for his goodwill, and by her powerful intercession will obtain of Jesus that grace which will at last make him a strong and perfect Christian. She will stand by him in the day of trial; she will aid him against his enemies; and he will soon be able to lead a sinless life. Then when death comes to usher him into the presence of his Judge, she will be by his side; she will lift up those spotless hands, and plead with that eloquent voice, to which Jesus never yet turned a deaf ear. Happy will he be, for when she raises her voice in prayer, God will not remember his sins. He will deal leniently with him, and with a smiling face will receive him into His heavenly kingdom.

CONCLUSION OF THE MONTH OF MAY.

I. In a few hours more this month of May will be a thing of the past; it will have flowed into the ocean of eternity. If we look back to its commencement, it seems like yesterday. It has come, and it has gone; there are thousands for whom it will never return again. We may be of this number. When next it comes with its sunshine and its flowers, other boys will gather here to pray; other voices will sing the hymns which we have sung; and other ears will listen to the words of exhortation which we too have heard—but we may not be here. It is thoughts like these that make each of us pause and ask himself, 'What benefit have I derived from all the pious exercises of this month?' It is a month of special favours and graces, and its devotions are intended by the Church to be productive of practical results Therefore, let us examine ourselves, in order that we may see unto which of the three classes we belong, unto whom God has offered this grace of the month of May.

Do I belong to that blessed company who have received the gifts offered to them? If my heart can say, 'I have tried to be one of them,' then will it be a joyous thing for me to look back upon the days which have gone, and I shall taste some of that satisfaction which men of the world experience, when they look over their accounts and find that they are in good order. This joy will be mine, if I can say that I have been careful to go, at the close of each day's labour, to offer up at the shrine of our Lady the studies, the recreations, and the trials which have filled up its fleeting hours.

All the more genuine will that joy be, if I have not failed to do this when wearied and well-nigh exhausted by the work of the day, and when dryness of heart, and sluggishness of will, have counselled me to withhold my wonted service. For then only can we say that our devotion is not mere sentimentality, when it exercises a practical influence upon our ordinary life. If it has made us study more diligently, and be more observant of Rule; if it has withheld our hearts from murmuring and disobedience; caused us to be gentle and charitable to others; opened our eyes to our defects, and inspired us with a firm resolve to conquer them—then may we, with reason, rejoice, for our gain has been great, and we have done something to promote the glory of God. We have laid up for ourselves treasures in heaven, where the moth cannot destroy, nor thieves break in to steal.

II. If, however, our conscience cannot give us this good testimony, but tells us that we have not done that which, as faithful children of Mary, we ought to have done, we must class ourselves among the number of those who have neglected to receive the grace which God offered to them.

When the other boys went to visit her shrine, we stayed behind in the playground. We would not sacrifice five minutes of our recreation; it would have been too great a privation. While other voices joined in the canticles sung in her honour, only our voices were silent. While others made some effort to imitate her virtues, her industry, her truthfulness, her submission to authority, and, in order to excite themselves to the exercise of these virtues, were careful to remember the pious practice which fell to them by lot, we would not submit to the restraint which these efforts put upon us, and did absolutely nothing in her honour. We were as idle, and as giddy during study-time, as we were before the month began. We disregarded Rule, and, as often as we could, without incurring punishment, infringed the discipline of the College. We made no effort to be truthful, to be gentle, to be kind; while all the time those, perhaps, who sat by us were trying to practise these virtues, and, in consequence of their efforts, were advancing in the love of God.

Yet, God did not ask of us anything very great. All the devotions of the month, and all the acts of virtue, were small things, within our reach, not going beyond either our strength, or that which is suitable to our years. But we would not make an effort. Why was this? Because we allowed a spirit of sloth and indifference to creep over and to take possession of us. The sooner, then, this spirit is shaken off, the better. A spirit of this kind is most opposed to all self-denial. It does not take up the Cross. It rather casts it away. But, if any one will not take up the Cross, and deny himself, he cannot be Christ's disciple. If he be not the disciple of Christ, there will be no kingdom of heaven for him. That kingdom is only for those who are willing to do violence to themselves, to take up their Cross, and to conquer their slothful spirit.

III. Let us suppose, however, that we have neither received with joy the graces of this month, nor yet neglected during its course to avail ourselves of the many favours which God has offered to us; we must then class ourselves among those who have gone with lukewarmness through all its devotions and pious practices. We have not been in earnest about anything, but have lazily drifted along with the tide of custom. What we have done, has been done because others did it. We have simply kept pace with the crowd. We have visited the shrine of the Blessed Virgin, we have sung canticles in her honour, we have assisted at Benediction, and performed various other acts of piety; but all has been done in a careless, slipshod, indifferent manner, without spirit, without attention, without earnestness.

What have we gained by it? Nothing! What we were

before the month began, that we are at its close. We were slothful at our prayers, careless about confession, and sluggish at Communion; and we remain so. We wasted our study-time in foolish, giddy tricks; we broke through discipline, without either reason or scruple; we were impertinent and disobedient to professors; and such we continue to be, without any sign of improvement. We are neither hot nor cold. We do not commit any great sins, and we do not cultivate any great virtues. We halt half-way between God and the devil, or, at least, we try to do so. It is of men of this stamp that the Holy Ghost says, 'I would that thou wert either hot or cold; but because thou art lukewarm I will vomit thee out of My mouth.' This rejection by God is almost invariably the end of those who live a tepid, careless life. They fall, at last, into some grievous sin, which either opens their eyes to their wretched state, or is the beginning of their final reprobation.

It is a matter, then, of great importance, that we should bestir ourselves, even now, when the last few hours of the month are fast gliding away. It is never too late to begin to do good. Hence, after seeing in what class we ought to place ourselves, we should try to the best of our power, not to be of the number of those who are lukewarm; nor yet of those who do not avail themselves of the opportunities of grace afforded them by the goodness of Almighty God. Let those who are tepid, and those who manifest culpable indifference to the things of God, be on their guard, and remember what the Holy Spirit said to that Bishop whom He rebuked for similar faults: 'Be mindful whence thou art fallen. Do penance and do the former works; or else I come to thee, and will move thy candlestick out of its place.' Be sorry, therefore, for the carelessness and the indifference of which you have been guilty, and try to atone for them by more watchfulness, and by greater fervour in the service of God.

But if you have conscientiously done your best to make this month what God intended it to be—a month of graces —rejoice with all your heart, because you have good reason to be glad. For, though there is some little sadness in the thought that these days of blessing and of spiritual joy are gone—it maybe for ever—yet that sorrow must be outbalanced by the satisfaction of duty accomplished, defects corrected, and the foundations of a life of virtue and utility laid deep in the soul—a life so fruitful in good works, that there will be given to it in the next world that reward which 'Eye hath not seen, nor ear heard, nor the heart of man conceived.'

THE PASSION OF OUR LORD AND SAVIOUR JESUS CHRIST.

ASH-WEDNESDAY.

I. THE Church on this day opens the holy season of Lent, by reminding us in a very impressive manner of the origin whence we sprang, and of the end to which we must inevitably go. For the priest of God, taking ashes in his hand, signs with them upon our foreheads the sign of the holy Cross, and says: 'Remember, man, that thou art dust, and into dust thou shalt return.' This, indeed, will be the lot of our mortal body, but not of our immortal soul; for that shall live for ever. If its life is to be a happy one, the soul must first deserve its beatitude by its entire submission to the laws of God; and, as experience will teach you, this obedience to His just demands cannot, without mortification, become a permanent habit in the soul. It is your duty, therefore, to impress upon yourself this truth, and to find out what mortification is best suited to your age and position.

In the beginning God created man, in what is called original justice, one prerogative of which endowed him with a complete mastery over himself, enabling him easily to control his animal nature, and make it follow the dictates of reason. But when he sinned against God, his act of rebellion weakened that control, so that man at present, even though aided by God's grace, cannot, without a painful struggle, hold his own against the cravings of the flesh. As, then, the instincts of man's animal nature are ever urging him to do what is contrary to the law of God, he cannot observe that law without contradicting and fighting against his unruly passions. To do this, is to mortify one's self.

Hence, in keeping the law of God, you have to endure a bitter contest with your own corrupt nature. You have to deny yourself; and he who, day after day, and year after year, goes on perseveringly doing this, is treading in Christ's footsteps, and mounting the steep ascent into the kingdom of heaven. As, therefore, the salvation of your soul is the one thing necessary, you will be able to estimate the importance of mortification, without which the soul cannot bring itself into subjection to the law of God.

II. From this you will see, that the first step in mortification is to observe the law of God; it is to be pure in thought, in desire, in act; to do your duty to God and to man; to be truthful, obedient, humble, meek, forgiving, and the rest. But, besides this, there are various other practices of mortification, which, if exercised, will enable you more easily to give to God that complete service which, upon so many titles, is His due. Some of these shall now be suggested to you, and you will find that they are all within your reach, and may be practised without attracting the attention of anyone. They are simply the ordinary duties of your college-life; but to perform them, will entail a little mortification.

In the first place, you are expected to rise from bed at the first signal in the morning. But what does self say to you at that early hour? It craves yet a few moments longer! It dreads the cold lavatory, the hasty toilet, prayer, meditation, and mass, followed by the long morning's study. Seeing all this in prospect, it is hard to rise at once. Here, then, is an excellent opportunity for mortifying self. Take advantage of it, and signing yourself with the holy Cross, offer your heart to God, shake off all sluggishness, and face the duties of the day, like a brave Christian boy.

In the next place, college discipline at times will weigh heavily upon you. It is hard to keep silence during the long study hours, and you would like very much, now and then, to have a few words with your neighbour, just to exchange ideas, to communicate a thought which strikes you, to ask the solution of a difficulty which has brought you to a full stop, or to obtain some information of which you stand in need. If you repress your desire to speak, and forego the little convenience which you would experience by a short conversation, you will be practising a good act of mortification.

Again; there are times during the study hours when you feel weary, and when the desire comes into your heart to relax your efforts a little, and to divert yourself, either by doing nothing at all, or by reading a more interesting work, than are those which the old classical authors have left us. If you either overcome, or at least endure, the uneasiness, and keeping your story-book closely shut up in your desk, go on with your hard but profitable studies, you are fighting against self, and performing an excellent act of mortification.

III. Besides these acts of mortification, there are many others, which are every day thrown in your way, and of which you lose the value, either because you do not accept them, or because you accept and bear them through merely natural motives. Your class-fellow, for instance, speaks angrily to you; he slights you; he either underrates your abilities, or utters some sarcasm which raises the laugh against you. Do not resent this, nor fly into a passion with him, and especially do not let what he has done to you rankle in your heart.

Again; the weather is cold and drizzly, and you cannot go outside for exercise. Do not complain of it, but say rather, that it is God's weather, and thank Him for giving you an opportunity to suffer something for His sake. Now and then your food, perhaps, is not all that you could desire. Do not grumble at it, but receive it with thanks, and reflect that there are hundreds of thousands who would regard as a luxurious feast, that of which you find so much reason to complain. Occasionally, also, it will happen that there is imposed upon you some penalty, which you have not deserved, or which, though well merited, you consider far heavier than the fault demanded. Well—either silently bear the injustice, as an expiation for those faults of your's which have escaped punishment, or remonstrate humbly and respectfully with the Superior who has imposed it upon you. If there be any mistake, he will, no doubt, be only too glad to correct it.

These are a few of the acts of mortification which are frequently thrown in your way. They are admirably suited to your present position at College, and will afford you many an opportunity of expiating past faults and sins. Do your utmost, therefore, to take advantage of them; and as your age hinders you from joining in the fast of Lent, let your fast be a fast from sin, and a patient endurance of the inconveniences and the hardships of your college life. In the spirit of penance, offer these to God. He will graciously accept them from you, and in return will bestow upon you many signal graces.

THE TWO ASSEMBLIES.

I. DURING the season of Lent, the origin of which may be traced back to Apostolic times, it is the custom of devout men to meditate in detail upon the various incidents of Our Lord's Passion, in order to fill their hearts with love and gratitude to God, and to turn them away more effectually from sin, the cause of all Christ's bitter sufferings. You must, therefore, take part in this pious practice, in order that you may share in those wondrous graces which it procures for all who, with a devout mind, apply themselves to it. We shall, therefore, day by day, ponder upon each of the remarkable incidents in the pathethic story of man's redemption.

First, then, let us go back in spirit to those eventful days, which preceded that on which Our Lord had resolved to pay the penalty of our many transgressions. There were gathered together, in the same city of Jerusalem, two companies of men, differing as widely from each other in character as they did in the purpose for which they had each been assembled. One of these had been summoned, on the fourth day of the week, by the High Priest Caiaphas. It consisted of the most bitter enemies of Our Lord,—the chief priests and the elders of the people: 'And they consulted together, that by subtlety they might apprehend Jesus, and put Him to death.' Over the other, Christ Our Lord presided. He had called together His Apostles, on the night before His Passion, to feed them with His precious body and blood, to confer upon them stupendous powers, and finally, to make them fit instruments for aiding Him in the regeneration of the world.

Do not these two assemblies bring out clearly before your mind, the antagonism which has always existed between God and this wicked world? Do they not bring back to you the thought that you yourself have oftentimes imitated the Jews, by doing your utmost to frustrate God's designs on your behalf? He wishes to make you virtuous and learned; to develop, by college training, both your moral and your intellectual life. What do you do to carry out His designs? By sin, you mar the beauty of God's image in your soul, and, by your persistent idleness, you dash to the ground all hopes of intellectual progress.

II. While the Jews, then, were contriving ways and means for the capture and the death of Our Lord, He was preparing to bestow upon the Apostles, and, through them, upon us, the priceless gift of His body and blood, in the Holy Sacrament. But before He carried out His design, He performed an act which is full of instruction for us. Rising from the table at which He had been reclining, He girded Himself with a towel, and having poured water into a basin, He, the Lord and Master of the universe, knelt before those rude fishermen to wash their feet, as if He were the lowest of menial servants.

Now, we are the children of Jesus Christ; we call Him Lord and Master, and we do well, for He is so. If, then, He humbled Himself so far as to do for His creatures what many a servant would refuse to perform for us, we ought not to shrink from a little humiliation for His sake, Who so deeply humbled Himself for us. It is not much that is asked of us. It is simply to repress proud and vain thoughts, to be generous and condescending to our inferiors, and to perform for one another little acts of charity, which though somewhat humiliating to a proud nature, are nothing more than those offices of good fellowship and of kindly feeling which one gentleman is glad to perform for another. Do not, therefore, think that it is in any way lowering to do these offices for your schoolfellows. If you do, stifle the foolish notion.

Hence, if anyone asks you to take his book to the study, or to fetch a cap from the stand, or to carry a bat to the cricket-field, or a pair of skates from the skating-pond, be ready to oblige him; and even if he does not trouble himself to ask, but unceremoniously commands you to do these offices, be ready cheerfully to obey. Do all these things for God's sake, in imitation of the mildness and the humility of Jesus Christ. This motive will take the sting out of the rudest and harshest command. It will change all that in these services would be degrading and unbecoming, into glorious deeds worthy of an eternal reward.

III. But in addition to the lesson of humility, there is another, and perhaps still more important one, which this action of Our Lord teaches us. He was about to give to His Apostles His own body and blood. They were to be most closely and most intimately united to the Holy of Holies. It was therefore necessary that they should be spotlessly pure, in order that the awful sanctity of God might find in them nothing defiled. This necessity Our Lord wished to make manifest to them by this extraordinary act. For, when He came before St. Peter and knelt at his feet to wash them, the heart of that great Apostle revolted against this act of humility. He knew Christ to be God, the Creator of heaven and earth. He knew himself to be a weak, sinful man, and therefore in amazement he said to Him: 'Lord, dost Thou wash my feet? Never shalt Thou wash my feet! Thou art my Lord and my God! It is not becoming that Thou shouldst perform for me so menial an office.' What does Our Lord say? 'Unless I wash thee, thou shalt have no part with Me.'

If we remember that with the exception of Judas, all the other Apostles were free from grievous sin, this saying of Our Lord's will teach us what great purity He requires from those who approach the Holy Eucharist. It is your happy privilege to partake very often of that sacred feast; see, therefore, that you cleanse your heart from every stain of sin—I mean from those lesser faults of which boys make so little account—for it is to be hoped that you never incur the guilt of a grievous sin. Purify yourself from all slight animosities; from coldness towards your class-fellows; from little jealousies. Ask pardon of God for wasting time, by idling away the study hours; for waywardness and disobedience to Superiors. Lament over your distracted prayers, your tepid Communions, your listless thanksgivings, and your general lukewarmness in God's holy service. Then with all humility approach Our Lord, and from the Sacrament gather strength to endure future trials, and courage to fight against and to overcome your many faults.

ARE WE CLEAN?

I. WHEN Jesus had washed the feet of His Apostles, He rose from His knees, and looking upon them, uttered a few significant words, which will furnish you with much matter for serious thought. 'You are clean,' He said to them, 'but not all.' Even among the chosen twelve, He found one whose heart had gone over to His enemies. This defection flooded the soul of Our Lord with bitter sorrow; for, as He was about to give them His body to eat, and His blood to drink, He must have contemplated with shuddering horror the frightful sacrilege which Judas would commit by receiving Him into his traitorous heart; and, therefore, He uttered these startling words, to save him from so great a profanation: 'You are clean, but not all.'

Does it never occur to you to ask yourselves, 'Can these words be ever with truth addressed to us?' We are far more numerous than the Apostles were; and we frequently eat of the same Holy Sacrament with which Our Lord fed them. Does He, then, ever say to us: 'You boys of this College—you, My children—you are clean—but not all.' It is quite possible, and because it is possible, you must take care that in your particular case it may never pass from a bare possibility to an actual fact. The words of Christ might be addressed to you for one of these two reasons: either because you have sinned, and have not confessed your sins, or because you have confessed them without being truly sorry for them.

Boys, unfortunately, sometimes fall into grievous sins, and do not confess them. The devil tempts them to sin, and encourages them to the commission of it, by the ease with which they may afterwards, by confession and hearty sorrow, blot out the wicked act. But when the evil has been done, an overwhelming shame fills them with confusion, and seals up their lips. If they do not, by the aid of God's grace, overcome this, they will not acknowledge their guilt, and therefore, instead of leaving the sacred tribunal free from all stain, they will go forth blacker and more hateful to God than they were when they entered it. The morning comes for Holy Communion. They approach with the rest, but it is with a heart torn with bitter remorse, for a voice keeps repeating to them: 'You are unclean. He that eateth and drinketh unworthily, eateth and drinketh judgment to himself, not discerning the body of the Lord.'

II. Or again: it may be that a boy who has sinned goes to confession, acknowledges his transgressions, repeats the act of contrition, and promises never to sin again. But, in spite of this promise, deep down in his heart, there is lurking a determination to repeat the act for which he has apparently been sorry. If this is so, his repentance is no repentance at all. It is a mere sham. For repentance means that there is a complete conversion of heart, a turning away from sin, with a firmly fixed determination never again to fall into it. It means that there is a detestation of the past, and a real wish that that past may be undone, and blotted out for ever.

In addition to this, it means that the various remedies for healing past wounds shall be applied, and all those persons, places, and things that have either inflicted or brought about the infliction of these wounds upon our immortal souls, shall be for the future most studiously avoided. Therefore, if while confessing sin, you do not sincerely make up your mind to have done with it for ever, but have a sort of understanding with your heart, that either after a short time, or after even a considerable interval, you will again indulge in those prohibited thoughts, or words, or desires, or actions, your conversion to God is only apparent; your sins are not blotted out; you are still unclean.

If in these dispositions you approach to Holy Communion, you profane that divine Sacrament, and trample under foot the blood which Christ shed for you. Of course, all this must be understood of grievous sins; for venial faults of slight anger, impatience, vanity, lies of excuse, and the like, are not of so grave a nature as to kill the soul, and hence do not render it unfit to approach to God in Holy Communion. An act of sorrow, or an act of love, will blot out these defects, and all that is required is a general determination to avoid them. Be thoroughly convinced of this, and always try to keep your detestation of mortal sin, and also of deliberate venial sin, strong, vigorous, and full of life within you, and then God will never say to you: 'Thou art unclean.'

III. After having dwelt upon the two reasons for which these few and terrible words of Our Lord may be addressed to boys in general, it now remains for you to look back upon the past, and to consider whether you yourself may not have deserved so scathing a rebuke.

If, in recalling the time which has gone by, you can remember a day on which you were guilty of an unworthy Communion, through the wilful concealment of some grievous sin, these words were then actually addressed to you by

Our Lord. If you have not already repented of so fearful a crime, do not hesitate for a moment to make all things right, by a good confession. Some time or other the sin either *must* be confessed, or there will be no salvation for you. Therefore, to delay so necessary an act is foolish; but besides being foolish, it is criminal; for each confession, each Communion, adds to the guilt of the first sacrilege, and fans into a fiercer flame the wrath of God against you. Have courage, therefore, and put not off till to-morrow that which ought to be done to-day. First of all, go to God, and ask Him to give you grace to overcome your foolish shame and fear; then, with a contrite heart, cast this heavy load from your soul at the feet of God's minister, and you will taste how sweet a thing is the peace of a good conscience.

Again; if upon examining past confessions, you discover that they have been defective, through want of a firm determination not to sin again, of which want you were conscious at the time, go at once to your director, seek his advice, and begin at last to lead a new life. By earnest prayer, and by strict watchfulness over yourself, seek from God grace to rid yourself of sin; and having once got rid of it, never again, under any pretext, allow it to gain a footing in your heart. Say to it: 'I have done with thee for ever. Never again, with the help of God, shall it be said to me, "Thou art unclean."'

GRIEF OF JESUS FOR THE TREACHERY OF JUDAS.

I. THE heart of Our Lord must have been deeply grieved at the treachery which Judas meditated against Him; for the gloom which it cast over His soul, manifested itself upon His usually serene and tranquil countenance. The keen eye of the beloved disciple detected at a glance the anguish which it caused Him to suffer; for he tells us in his Gospel, that Jesus, being troubled in spirit, said: 'Amen, amen, I say unto you, one of you shall betray Me.' You will be able to bring home to yourself the intense suffering indicated by these words, if you try to put yourself for a moment in Our Redeemer's place.

Suppose that you have among your schoolfellows a friend whom you tenderly love, and for whom you have performed numberless acts of kindness, which entailed much inconvenience and self-sacrifice. You have always taken his part in troubles and difficulties, defended him from danger, and frequently borne the disgrace and the punishment which ought to have fallen upon him. Between you and him there have been no secrets, and you have been to him what a true friend ought to be—the very half of his soul.

Now, if after all your trust and affection, he were to turn upon you, and betray you; to publish your faults and your weaknesses; to blacken your character with your schoolfellows and your masters, what a blow would his dastardly conduct give your heart! How terrible would be your grief, and how fierce your indignation! His ingratitude would wound you like a viper's tooth. It would stun you, and deprive you of words strong enough to give vent to your outraged feelings. If anyone else had treated you a thousand-fold more contumeliously, you would have borne it. If your enemy had acted thus, you would not have marvelled at it: such conduct might have been expected from him. But for a friend—and for a friend so dear to you—to be guilty of the like baseness, quite vanquishes you, takes away the very power to defend yourself, and makes you ready to sink down upon the earth, and give vent to your grief in a flood of unmanly tears.

II. Think, therefore, of the unutterable anguish which the treachery of Judas caused to the sacred heart of Our Lord. What friend ever loved his friend as Jesus loved that wretched man? He chose him from among hundreds of thousands, just as He chose St. Peter and St. John. He must, therefore, have had for him a special predilection. For well-nigh three years, He admitted him to the closest intimacy. Day by day He spoke to him, taught him, and opened out to him the mysteries of the kingdom of God. He allowed him to witness many of His most astounding miracles. He gave him power, in common with the other Apostles, to perform wonders in the might of His own most holy and adorable name, destined him to be one of the pillars of His Church, and to sit as judge upon one of the twelve thrones, judging the twelve tribes of Israel.

Yet, notwithstanding all these favours, his heart had conceived the design of selling that loving Master, Who had done so much for him, and Who loved him so tenderly that He admitted him, as one of His dearest friends, to kiss His sacred face. Jesus knew his intention perfectly well. Yet He knelt before him, as He did before the other Apostles, and washed his feet. He did all that God could do to a human heart, except force its free will, in order to make him change his intention; but to no purpose. It had become as hard as the nether mill-stone, and God's grace fell upon it as fruitlessly as the gentle rain falls upon the arid rocks.

All these circumstances added to the treachery of Judas, a sting which Our Lord would never have felt, had the betrayal been wrought by another hand. If a Scribe or a Pharisee had ensnared, and delivered Him up to His enemies, it would have been only natural; for they were His open and most inveterate foes. But that this should have been brought about by a *friend*, by a chosen *Apostle*, this made his act so wantonly cruel, that it wrung from the lips of the Royal Prophet this bitter wail of grief: 'If mine enemy had reviled me, I would indeed have borne it; but that *thou*, my friend, my familiar friend, who didst sit at my table and eat *sweetmeats* with me—that *thou* shouldst do this thing, hath dealt me so heavy a blow that it hath broken my heart.'

III. From these words we may conclude, that the sins of those, who like ourselves, have received signal favours from God, cause the sacred heart of Jesus more acute suffering than the transgressions of men who have not experienced at His hands bounty so exceptional.

Reflect, for a moment, upon all that God has done for you. You have been born of good parents, brought up in easy circumstances, and sheltered from the privations and the dangers which are usually the lot of the poor. Before you there is a bright and honourable career, for which you are being prepared by an intellectual training, which will enable you to meet all the demands which your position in the world may require of you. You are protected from the allurements of vice, and from the contagion of evil company. The priests of God's Church watch over you, guide you, and pray for you.

With all these advantages, God may reasonably hope that you will give unto Him that service of head and of heart which is His due. He has done for you so much that He has not done for others, that He looks for a more grateful service. But what is the case? Alas! alas! it sometimes happens that those who are thus highly favoured are corrupt to the very core, while other boys, who live in poverty, surrounded by bad example, with naught before them but a life of hard labour and privations of every kind, are pure before God, and lead lives of more than ordinary sanctity.

Has not Our Lord good reason to grieve? Is not His sacred heart most sorely tried by the ingratitude and the treachery of those upon whom He has heaped the greatest benefits? Oh! if you find that you are among the number of these, be ashamed of your black ingratitude and heartless treachery to your Lord and Master, and promise Him that, if in the past you have thoughtlessly sold His love and friendship for what the Prophet calls 'a handful of barley and a little bread,' you will for the future prove yourself worthy of His love and friendship by unswerving loyalty, which will keep with scrupulous exactitude every tittle of His sacred law.

THE PRIVILEGE OF PURITY.

I. IT is consoling for us to remember, that if the heart of Our Lord suffered unutterable anguish because of the treachery of Judas, it found some relief in the loving devotion of the other Apostles, and especially of him whom Jesus honoured with marks of more than ordinary affection. This was the youthful Apostle St. John, whose virginal purity is generally supposed to have been the bond which united him so closely to the Redeemer, and made him the special favourite of the Lamb of God.

Jesus, then, in this the hour of His bitter grief, felt the need of human sympathy, and therefore drew close to His bosom the disciple whom He loved so well. It is St. John himself that puts before our eyes this beautiful picture; for immediately after recording the trouble of Jesus at the treachery of Judas, and His startling announcement that one of them should betray Him, he adds the words: 'Now there was leaning on the bosom of Jesus one of His disciples, whom Jesus loved.' This is a picture which you boys ought to study long and well. Jesus always showed great affection to little children, because they are generally innocent and pure. For the same reason He allowed the head of St. John to rest upon His bosom.

If you wish to be His special favourites, and to be drawn with unutterable tenderness to His sacred heart, you also must be spotlessly pure. You must keep your fresh young hearts clean from all defiling stains of sin. You must make them a sanctuary in which no wicked thought shall ever be suffered to abide. Permit not unruly desires to find a lurking-place there, and jealously guard all its hallowed precincts from the mere approach of what is unclean. Then you, too, will be allowed to go very frequently to Jesus, and rest your heads upon His bosom, close to His sacred heart, whence there will flow out upon you, grace to keep you free from the terrible vice which is so opposed to God's sanctity, and so hateful to Him. That priceless pearl of purity will be set by Jesus in your heart, and will invest you with so wondrous a charm that men will cry out in admiration: 'Oh! how beautiful with glory is the chaste generation!'

II. While St. John leaned thus upon the bosom of his beloved Master, there occurred an incident which gives us a still clearer knowledge of the privileges reserved for the pure of heart. The words by which Our Lord announced that He knew full well the treason of Judas, very naturally filled the hearts of the other Apostles with anxiety and alarm.

Experience had taught them their own weakness, and they knew that it is precisely when a man seems to himself to be as unshaken as a rock in his fixed resolve, that he is very near some shameful fall.

Each, therefore, dreading lest he himself might be the traitor, kept a painful silence. They did not dare to ask their Master, lest the awful 'Thou hast said it!' should break from His lips, and wither them up where they sat. But the impetuous spirit of St. Peter could not endure the suspense; he knew one who would not fear to ask, and to whom Jesus would give a most gracious answer. Beckoning, therefore, to St. John, he whispered to him: 'Who is it of whom He speaketh?' He, therefore, leaning upon the breast of Jesus, said to Him: 'Lord, who is it?' Jesus at once answered, and pointed out the wretch, by giving him a morsel of bread, which He first dipped in the dish before Him.

From this, learn how complete is the trust which exists between the pure soul and God. How intimate are their relations, how close is their union! God gives to it favours for which others would fear to ask. He shows it special marks of affection and love. He more clearly discloses Himself to it than to others, and more abundantly imparts to it the light of His own Holy Spirit. Nor should we wonder at this; for the pure soul is a joy to the heart of Jesus. It is a bright spot upon the earth, a spot towards which His eyes turn with love. It is a garden enclosed, filled with delightful lilies; and it is of those that possess this treasure that He says: 'My delights are to be with the children of men.' To them, in a special manner, He addresses these consoling words: 'We will come to him, and will make our abode with him.'

III. By the consideration of these extraordinary privileges, stir up within yourself an ardent desire to make yourself worthy to receive them from the hand of Jesus Christ. Let it be your firm resolve this day, ever to be of the glorious company of those who keep their white robes free from every stain. If it has been your good fortune never to have slipped and fallen into the mire, give God thanks, and with all the earnestness of your soul, daily beg of Him to keep His hand upon you, and to direct your feet in His paths. But if through human frailty, or through evil influences, you have come to know by sad experience the difference between good and evil, do not grovel in the mire into which you have fallen.

Lift up your head, and view your position; the sight will fill you with horror, but it will also nerve you to make one grand effort to free yourself. You will see that each new act of sin plunges a man deeper and deeper into the mire; that it forms a new link in the chain which keeps him in bondage; that it extinguishes, one by one, the few remaining embers of Christian sentiment left in his heart, and thus renders well-nigh hopeless the chance of his return to God.

You may, after a time, liken his condition to that of one who has plunged into a swiftly-flowing river which rolls its rushing waters over some mighty cataract. Every stroke that he takes carries him nearer to destruction, and makes it less possible for him to turn back and reach the bank.

Let each of you, therefore, fear to enter the waters of sin. If you should have done so, turn back at once; for though you can no longer hope to be of the number of those who have never fallen, you will be at least of the number of those who, after staining their white robes, have by tears of repentance washed them clean in the blood of the Lamb. But remember—both you who have never known sin, and you who, having known it, have escaped from its bondage—that you bear this treasure of purity in earthen vessels. If you wish to carry it safely, you must do two things: you must go frequently to confession, and, above all things, very frequently to Communion. It is in Communion that you are closely united to Christ, that you lay your heads upon His bosom, and receive Him into your hearts to purify and to strengthen them.

Never forget these two things: the Sacraments of Penance and the Holy Eucharist, very often and worthily received, will in the first place restore lost innocence, and then preserve it from being lost again.

PRESUMPTION OF ST. PETER.

I. By giving the morsel of bread to Judas, Jesus pointed him out as the traitor; but with his characteristic gentleness, the beloved disciple seems not to have shared his knowledge with the other Apostles, though his heart, no doubt, burned with righteous indignation against the sordid wretch, who could thus sell the best and most loving of masters. He remarks, however, in his Gospel, that after the morsel, the devil entered, or took possession of Judas, and that he arose from the table and went forth: 'And it was night.'

Then Jesus gave vent to His grief, and told them that they should all abandon Him that night. 'I, your Shepherd,' said He, 'shall be stricken by God; and you, My sheep, shall be scattered.' The conduct of St. Peter, on hearing this prophecy, merits our attention; for it will teach us a useful lesson of self-distrust, which will save us from many a grievous fall. He had just partaken of that sacred banquet in which Christ is received, body, soul, and divinity. Being full of fervour and devotion to his Master, He thought that nothing could shake his fidelity. Trusting, therefore, in his own strength, he made no account of Our Lord's words, declared himself stronger and more loving than all the rest, and boastfully exclaimed: 'Even though *all* shall deny Thee, yet I will not deny Thee.'

In these proud words, we see the effect of religious fervour not tempered by humility. It made this Apostle, in the first place, dare to contradict his Divine Master. 'You will all prove unfaithful to Me this night,' said Our Lord. 'You are mistaken,' exclaims St. Peter; 'we shall not. None of us is so base as to follow Thee only when all things smile upon Thee, and to flee away, like a coward, in the day of storm.' In the next place, it led him to depreciate his fellow-Apostles, and to exalt himself. 'Even though all should desert Thee, yet will not I.' He did not say, in his heart: 'I hope to make good what I say, through that strength which God gives in time of need.' No; he forgot this, and imagined that he should be able, by his own personal bravery and innate strength of character, to do what he had promised. He trusted in himself—and fell. Before the cock crew that night, he had thrice denied his Lord.

II. Look into your past life, and you will probably discover that many of your falls have been brought about by presumption similar to that which inflated the heart of St. Peter. It may have been after a retreat that this pernicious trust in your own strength sprang up within you. During the holy days of that period of grace, you may have felt the finger of God upon your soul. The eternal truths stirred your heart to its lowest depths, and those precious tears which blot out sin, flowed freely from your eyes. You felt experimentally how sweet a thing it is to belong to God, and to serve Him with all the strength of your will. In the fervour of your heart you said: 'From this day forth I have done with sin. Never again shall it darken my soul with its hateful presence.'

No doubt you really intended to be true to this sincere resolve. But, joined with it, you had not that knowledge of your own weakness, and that trust in God alone, which would have given it stability. You believed too much in yourself, and God might have addressed to you a warning like that which He gave to St. Peter: 'A single month shall scarcely elapse before you will deny Me—not once or twice—but many times.' Your spiritual father told you to beware, to distrust yourself; but you deemed his caution superfluous. He told you to pray, to avoid evil company, and every occasion that might imperil the safety of your soul. These injunctions you thought needless for one so firmly fixed in his good resolve as you were. 'Others may need this advice, and may with advantage make use of it; but I can answer for myself.'

In what did this foolhardiness end? It ended as all similar temerity must inevitably end. You went back to the company which you were told to avoid; you met the occasions which had previously proved fatal to you; you struggled against them for a time, but found to your cost that in their presence you were feeble as a child in the grasp of a powerful man. Alas! like all those who love danger, you found in it your own destruction. You said: 'Though all shall deny Thee, yet will not I,' and in punishment of your proud presumption, you became a traitor to Jesus Christ.

III. Like the wise and prudent, learn to profit by the experience and the misfortune of others. Be not like the fool, who never learns wisdom except at his own cost. When you read, or when you are told of an example similar to that which has been put before you this day, argue thus with yourself: 'I am not stronger in my love for Jesus Christ than St. Peter was. I have neither so much light nor grace. If then he fell, through trusting too much in himself, and too little in the aid of divine grace, how can I expect to be more successful, if I imitate his conduct? Therefore, I must shun what was the occasion of his fall.'

You cannot more effectually do this, than by frequently reflecting upon your own weakness. From the lessons which these meditations will teach you, you will learn that in God alone is your strength, and that both the will to act, and the act itself, come from Him. Consequently, put very little trust in those fervid sentiments which naturally spring up in the heart after the stirring thoughts of a retreat, or the devout reception of the Holy Eucharist. Resolves formed on these occasions, are often mere sentiment, and not the fixed determination of the will. They lead boys to presume too much on their fancied strength, and to think that nothing can shake their purpose. They forget to tread cautiously. They lose their keenness of vision for danger, and as a natural consequence, they find out when it is too late, that they have fallen into the snare of the enemy.

Therefore, always distrust yourself. Go not wilfully into danger. Never imagine that sin has lost its power to attract, because for a great many years you have not yielded to its seduction. Keep away from it. It is not dead, but sleepeth; or, rather, it only feigns to sleep. If either curiosity or carelessness should bring you within its reach, it will spring upon you with the strength and the ferocity of a tiger, and your soul will die the death in its cruel fangs.

OUR LORD'S SADNESS.

I. AFTER the last supper, Our Lord addressed to His Apostles a most touching discourse, and at its close, raising His eyes to heaven, poured forth for them to His Eternal Father a prayer every word of which is fired with the love of His sacred heart. He prayed for each priest who should succeed them in the sacred ministry, and for all those who should be brought by their labours to the knowledge of the truth. Then rising from table, He went forth, followed by the eleven, and crossing the brook Cedron, directed His steps towards the Garden of Olives, there to spend some hours of the silent night in fervent prayer. Having entered the Garden, he ordered all, except Peter, James, and John, to remain near the entrance; but taking with Him these three who had witnessed His glory upon Thabor, He went forwards out of the moonlight into the deep shade of the olive-trees. Yet even the favoured three were to be spectators of His humiliation only at a distance. He had given to them upon Thabor a glimpse of His Divinity to sustain their faith in this His hour of weakness.

As they went, the Evangelist remarks, that 'He began to grow sorrowful and to be sad.' He could not hide His grief within the sanctuary of His own heart, but said to them : 'My soul is sorrowful, even unto death.' This sadness arose from a foreboding of that fearful storm of sufferings and of cruel indignities which, on the following day, burst upon Him. He experienced all that sinking of heart, that nervous, agonising dread, that shuddering repugnance which men feel when they anticipate some great calamity that is impending over them. This is oftentimes a source of keener torture than the actual misfortune which they dread, and sooner than endure it, some have put an end to their existence. We all know very well what the sufferings of Our

Lord were like, and we are able, therefore, to form some idea of the horror with which He anticipated them, and of the bitter anguish with which they pierced His soul. The cruel agony which it caused Him made Him exclaim: 'My soul is sorrowful even unto death.'

II. In order that you may appreciate more feelingly the weight of mental agony which Our Lord endured, by thus contemplating His sufferings, you must call to mind the torture which you yourself have experienced from the anticipation of some grievous pain. During the course of your life you have been obliged, in all probability, to undergo some surgical operation. It may have been as great as the resetting of a broken limb, or as insignificant as the extraction of a decayed tooth.

You will doubtless, then, be able to remember the pain which the mere thought of these operations inflicted upon your nervous system. Your imagination invested them with terrors, which made your flesh creep and your heart beat with quickened pulse. You recoiled from, you revolted against the suffering, and in your mind underwent a hundred times the hateful operation. It was a positive relief to you when the much-dreaded moment arrived, and you felt the actual pressure of the surgeon's hands, and experienced the wrench of his instrument which, by one sharp pang, put an end to your agony of suspense.

Or, again, your young life has perhaps been darkened for months, and for even years, by the fear of a parent's death. Day after day the dread of it has hung over you and clouded your soul with sorrow. When at last the blow fell, and the kind, indulgent father, or the beloved mother, ceased to be, the pain seemed less acute than the continual dread of it in which you had been living. Think, therefore, what must have been the agony which Our dearest Saviour underwent during those long hours when He put Himself face to face with His dreadful Passion.

There loomed before Him an awful night of indignities and outrages, to be followed by a day of sufferings so intense, that we shudder even now at the bare recital of them. He knew every incident that would happen. He heard every taunt and gibe that would be spoken, and felt every blow that would be struck. He saw the mock trial, the bloodstained pillar, the thorny crown, the disgraceful Cross, and the three hours of lingering agony. In that foreknowledge and in that anticipation, He endured beforehand all the tortures of His bitter Passion.

III. In this mental agony of Our Lord, as well as in His other sufferings, each of you has, perhaps, had a hand. The sins which you have committed hovered round Him in the gloom of the olive-trees, and, like hideous spectres, glared upon Him with savage eyes. He saw them all. He knew that they were the creation of your wicked hearts, and He prayed His Father to forgive you. You have been sorry for the sins which brought into existence these torturers of Jesus. You have promised Him never to repeat them, and your love of Him tells you that you would not wish again to afflict His sacred heart. But remember that there are now in the world men who in your regard hold the place of God, men who have the most intimate relations with you. They are His representatives, and because your parents have intrusted you to their care, they have by that act given them, for the time being, their own authority over you.

Hence, to cause them to endure the mental torture of fear for your future well-being, whether temporal or eternal, is indirectly to afflict with heavy sadness the heart of your Lord. You fill the hearts of your Superiors with dark forebodings, when you begin to manifest those traits of character which, like straws upon the surface of a stream, indicate whither you are tending. When you are idle, when you hate application, and waste your opportunities of learning, they fear that your listlessness will cling to you through life, and mar your worldly prospects. When they see that you are passionate, wayward, headstrong, and take no pains to correct these defects, they fear for the future of a heart which has so little self-control. If they find that you are loth to go to confession, that you rarely approach to Holy

Communion, and show a general indifference about your religious duties, they are apprehensive lest this youthful neglect of Religion, growing with your years, may lapse at last into downright unbelief. But should they perceive that vice has entered your heart, then it is that their soul undergoes an agony of grief and of fear. Therefore, out of compassion for Our Lord's sadness, resolve to avoid inflicting the like mental torture upon those who in your regard hold His place.

THE PRAYER OF OUR LORD.

I. JESUS did not take the three chosen Apostles with Him to the spot where He had determined to grapple with His natural repugnance to the cruel death which awaited Him; but after cautioning them to watch and pray, withdrew from them to a more secluded part of the Garden, that He might more freely pour out His soul in prayer to God. There, casting Himself upon His knees, He sought relief for His overburthened heart, in loving communion with His Father. But no heavenly consolation flooded His soul, for He had shut off from it all that refreshing spiritual sweetness which might have come to it from His divine nature. He therefore tasted to the full all the bitterness experienced by a soul which ardently longs to speak to its God, but which is compassed with darkness, and is dry and barren as earth, parched by the fierce heat of an eastern sun. 'Weeping,' says the Prophet, 'He has wept in the night, and His tears are upon His cheeks.'

See how humbly He kneels there in the presence of His Father! Hear with what earnestness He urges His petition, and mark how resignedly He commits the issue of it to the disposition of the Eternal Wisdom, though He ceases not, all the time, to repeat with most persevering and indomitable energy, the desire of His human heart that the chalice may pass away from Him. But the heavens above Him are as brass. There is no response to His prayer. He rises, therefore, from His knees, and goes to His Apostles to seek for some little consolation in their sympathy. But He finds them asleep—unconscious and apparently careless of the pain which He is enduring.

An hour before they were full of fervour, and had promised great things, and lo, they could not watch *one hour* with Him! Jesus Himself seems to be surprised at this, and addressing Peter, who had been loudest in his protestations of devotedness, said to him, in a tone of reproachful astonishment: 'Simon, sleepest *thou?*' Then, with another word of warning to be vigilant and prayerful, He left them, and withdrew into the dark shadow of the trees, there to struggle against the repugnance of His human will, to take upon Himself, and to suffer for, the crimes of a sinful world. No friendly voice encouraged Him. No gentle hand soothed Him. He knelt alone. He wept in the night, and the tears were on His cheeks. He looked upon the right hand and upon the left, and there was no one to pity Him.

II. This abandonment of Jesus in the hour of His direst need, by those who ought to have been by His side to support and encourage Him, will teach you where you should put your trust. A day will most likely come upon you, as it does upon most men, when either sickness or misfortune will strike you; and when, staggered by the blow which has been dealt, you will stretch forth your hands for help and support to those whom you have loved, perhaps too well. God grant that you may not have to clutch at the empty air, but may meet with a strong arm to catch you, and lovingly to bear you up. But even though God should send you a helper, who will come to visit and console you, as you lie stretched upon your bed of pain—crushed with the weight of your misfortune—yet, after doing what is in his power to aid and comfort you, he will have to go his way and leave you to yourself.

The friends who fluttered round you in the days of your strength and prosperity, and who were friends—as far as human nature would allow them—these will pursue their ordinary business, and amid the bustle of every-day life will forget you; or if they think of you, will speedily banish from their minds the afflicting thought of your malady. They will not watch *one hour* with you, but will leave you to lie in sorrow, till the shadow of death creep over and hide you from the sight of the living. To these you also will cry, in angry surprise: 'Could ye not watch one hour with me?'

Dearest children! there is One Who will never desert you. He is always at hand. His eye is ever upon you, and His ear is ever open to your prayer. He will watch with you in your sorrow and affliction, and, therefore, let it be your main study now to make Him your chief and only friend. By their love of earthly friends, boys sometimes lose the friendship of God, because they prefer to offend Him rather than thwart or disappoint or displease His creature. But do you cling to, and never separate yourself from your God. Trample under foot all love for others that is incompatible with the love of God. Be faithful to Him. Prefer Him to all earthly persons and things whatsoever. In reward of your fidelity, He will send you trusty friends, and chief among these He Himself will be your strength, your consolation, and your support when the day of calamity and of misery shall come upon you.

III. Another lesson which Our Lord's conduct upon this trying occasion ought to teach us, is humble resignation to the divine will. Let us be assured that nothing either happens to us or can happen to us, without the will of God. Men may be employed as instruments, and may take occasion through their evil passions to injure or to grieve us; but though God does not wish the evil, nor in any way countenance it, yet He suffers it to befall us, in order for our greater glory, to draw good from it.

Keeping this steadily in view, resolve, in imitation of your Divine Lord, patiently to endure whatever trials may happen to you in this mortal life, and bend your will to accept them with resignation. Now, the trials of college life are not very great; but yet, they are for you, what the misfortunes of the world are for those who are engaged in the great battle of life. Therefore, look upon them as sent to you by the hand of God, and by your submission to the divine will, endeavour to turn them to your advantage. No doubt, you have in your mind many projects which miserably fail. Your hopes are dashed to the ground; you are straitened by anxieties; and you feel losses which cause you great grief. These may be the loss of your place in class, your failure to win the prize, or the fear of that mishap. Bear the grief, the disappointment, and the failure, like a Christian. Say to yourself: 'It is God's will, and for my good.'

Nevertheless, while submitting to the will of God, do not grow faint-hearted. Like Our Lord, return again and again to prayer. Ask that help may be given you to win what you aspire after; that your hopes may be realised; and your projects crowned with success. Go on perseveringly, and faint not, and then you will imitate your Lord and Master. You will be heaping up for yourself treasures in heaven; you will be preparing yourself to act like a Christian hero in the world; and, even though God may not give you what you ask, yet by being in conformity with His will, you will obtain favours of far greater value, and win for yourself a bright crown in heaven.

THE SWEAT OF BLOOD.

I. JESUS returned to the spot where He had been praying, and, casting Himself upon His knees, renewed the petition to His heavenly Father that the bitter chalice might pass away from Him. But this could not be. 'In the head of the Book it had been written of Him, that He should do the will of God.' That will had decreed that He should take upon Himself the iniquities of us all, and pay the penalty due to them. Behold Him, therefore, kneeling upon the earth, in the gloom of the overhanging trees. What is it that makes Him shudder, and shrink, and groan so piteously? His whole frame quivers and sways to and fro, while His broken words intimate the intense earnestness with which He appeals to God. His brain reels; He grows faint and giddy; He falls flat upon the earth, moaning like one straitened and oppressed with anguish beyond the power of human nature to endure.

What is it that so unmans Him, Who is, of all the other sons of Adam, the most manly? It is not the contemplation of the physical pain that is so soon to torture His human frame as never flesh of man had been tortured before. Yet even that, clearly as He sees it, is enough to appal the stoutest heart; for He beholds with a vividness greater than human fancy can depict, all the blows, the stripes, and the indignities which the fierce anger of a race proverbially malicious and revengeful, is about to heap upon Him. No, it is not this, for there is something else from which Jesus shrinks with unutterable loathing, something more intensely torturing to His holy soul than the sharpest and keenest pain could be.

This is sin. He is to take upon Himself the iniquities of us all. The men of all times are to come and cast their burthens upon Him. They are to pile upon His head their accumulated crimes, till He lies crushed beneath their monstrous weight. Then the Eternal Father is to look upon Him, thus bearing the sins of the people, and to strike Him so fiercely, that from the crown of His head to the sole of His foot there shall be no soundness in Him.

II. This thought produced in His soul a horror so great, that it gave rise to a struggle between His sensitive nature and His human will; a struggle which caused the blood to burst its natural channels, and, forcing its way through the pores of His skin, to trickle down in great drops to the ground. Nor need we wonder at this, if we remember that Our blessed Lord did not *clothe* Himself in the leperous garment of the world's iniquity, as Jacob covered his neck and hands with the skins of the kids that had been slain. He took upon Himself the *guilt* of sin, and allowed His heart to feel all the *sense* of its guilt—its shame, its remorse, its separation from God.

Call to mind the iniquities of those who perished in the great Flood. They were so abominable that God repented of having ever created man. Think of the crimes which made a merciful God sweep from the earth by a storm of tempestuous fire the cities of the Plain. Think of the heretics who have torn the Church with falsehood and schism; the persecutors who have slain the Saints of God; the murderers and the robbers who have shed innocent blood; the unclean, the hypocrites, and the rest who have caused God's name to be blasphemed upon the earth. The guilt of all these Jesus took into His heart; and, not of these only, but of all the men that either have breathed, or shall ever breathe the breath of life, from the sin of him who first brought death into this world and all our woe, down to the sin of him whose iniquity shall cause the cup of man's transgressions to overflow, and provoke God once again to let loose His wrath and destroy the world.

This enormous weight of guilt crushed Jesus to the earth. There He lay, overwhelmed with shame and confusion, before the all-holy eyes of His Eternal Father. Though the sins which He bore were not His own, yet the thought of having them imputed to Him, as if He had actually committed them, so tortured Him that He would have died, had He not been sustained by His divine nature, in order to immolate Himself upon the Cross, as an expiatory victim for the sins of the world.

III. Each of you stood among the number of those who forced from the sacred body of Jesus, that agonising sweat of blood. As He lay prostrate upon the earth in the bitterness of His anguish, He saw you all. He felt all the sins that you have committed, knowing well their circumstances and their malice, just as if you had been guilty of them in His presence. You pitilessly flung them upon Him in His hour of terrible sorrow, and He neither resisted nor resented your cruel act.

He bore the guilt of every evil thought that you have thought, of every evil word that you have spoken, of every evil desire that you have cherished, and of every evil deed that you have done. Each knows, to a certain extent, the long catalogue that is scored against him in the book of the recording Angel. As our minds travel back through the past, and catch a glimpse of its dark pages, the number and the enormity of our sins dawn upon us for a moment with a vividness so startling, that we shudder and turn away sick at heart. If they fill *us* with confusion, think of the agony which they caused to that spotless and all-holy One.

Cast yourself, therefore, upon your knees in the presence of God, and humbly implore Him to pardon you the share which you had in His sweat of blood. Pray that the precious drops which fell from Him, on that awful night, may blot out your offences, and promise Him never to sin again. Beg of Him that, when you have to struggle against the seductive whisperings of corrupt nature, He would call to your mind the sharp contest which covered His sacred body with that crimson sweat, and the memory of it will enable you to fight manfully against the evil one, and to win for yourself and for your King a glorious victory.

THE TREASON OF JUDAS.

I. JUDAS had not been idle during the interval which had elapsed since he left the company of the Apostles. He had hurried off to the priests and the elders, and, together with them, had arranged everything for the apprehension of Jesus. He took the precaution to give them even a sign by which they might recognise Our Lord amid the company of the Apostles : 'Whomsoever I shall kiss,' said he, 'that is He ; hold Him fast.' Then, having received from the priests a company of armed men, he led the way to the Garden of Olives, followed by a motley crowd, armed with staves and clubs, and bearing lights, in order more easily to discover Him if He should flee, and hide Himself in any of the numerous caves which abound in the vineyards round Jerusalem.

Jesus had risen from His knees, and coming to His sleeping disciples, had roused them from their slumber, at the moment when Judas, at the head of these ruffians, entered the enclosure of the Garden. The traitor at once eagerly ran towards Him, and saluting Him with the words, 'Hail,

Master!' imprinted upon His sacred face a kiss, which makes us shudder with horror, when we reflect upon the treachery which it concealed. Jesus patiently endured it, and did not spurn him from His presence. He uttered no word of reproach, but, with gentle sadness, whispered to him: 'Friend, for what purpose art thou come? Dost thou betray the Son of man with a kiss?'

These words, coming from the mouth of the Redeemer, ought to have softened the hardest heart. But they fell upon the ears of a sinner, grown callous by oft-repeated sins, of a sinner who had made his heart as hard as steel, and as impervious to grace as the flinty rock is to the gentle rain that falls upon it. Judas heeded them not, and having accomplished his treachery, slunk back among the crowd, and hid himself from view.

II. The treason of Judas is one of those startling manifestations of human frailty, which occur at times even among those who seem to be the pillars of God's Church. They rouse us from our dream of security, pealing into our affrighted ears those solemn words of warning: 'Let him that thinketh himself to stand, take heed lest he fall.' Surely, if we might anywhere look for stability, it would be among those whom Jesus Himself selected to be His representatives among men.

He saw the hearts and the dispositions of those whom He gathered round Him, for this purpose, and therefore Judas must have been a man who, if he had persevered in the way in which God called him to walk, would at last, like the rest of his colleagues, have laid down his life for Christ, and sealed a glorious career by a still more glorious death. He had the privilege of daily intercourse with the incarnate God. His great familiarity with Him, entitled him to salute Him with the kiss of friendship. He had been taught by Jesus, counselled and directed by Him, and, no doubt, had often been the subject of His long and fervent prayers. Yet, though sealed with the Apostleship, and privileged as few men have been either before or since, he fell away from the service of Jesus Christ, and perished most miserably.

Since that time, very many have imitated his treason, and sold their Lord and Maker for a sum as paltry as was the blood-money which he received from the iniquitous priests. Heretics and unbelievers use them as examples with which to illustrate their arguments against our holy Religion, and many of the simple faithful find in them a rock of scandal and a stone of offence.

But, instead of doing us any hurt, the fall of even the holiest men may be turned for us into a signal benefit, if we learn to regard their prevarication, as a warning of what may happen to ourselves. We are all weak, and liable to err from the path of duty; therefore, when we see those who are more perfect than ourselves turning traitors to their God, let us remember to stand in fear, not to be high-minded, not to be censorious, but humbly to ask God to guide our steps in His paths, to keep His hand upon us, and not to suffer our feet to slide from the narrow way into the broad road which leads to perdition.

III. Each of you may, perhaps, think that he will never be base enough to desert Our Lord, as the wretched Apostle did. But be on your guard! You are now pure and innocent. You taste to the full that sweetness which God gives to those who faithfully follow Him. You are filled with noble aspirations, and delight in the honour and glory of unsullied virtue. You feel a horror of everything vicious, and the shadow of iniquity, flitting for a moment across your mind, makes you shudder. Furthermore, you deal familiarly with Jesus Christ, as one of His most cherished children. You approach Him very frequently in His Most Holy Sacrament; you kiss Him as your Father; you are pressed by Him close to His sacred heart.

Again I say, beware! for this love may not last. It is the constant prayer of your Superiors that it may, and that when you are flung into the fierce *mêlée* of the battle of life, you may not be thrust into the mire and trampled beneath the feet of your enemies. Remember, however, that there have been many who were as carefully nurtured as you have been, and who were as full of good and noble sentiments as are those which now animate your breast; nevertheless, they have shamefully belied the early promise of their youthful years. What has happened to them may happen to you.

But, if you wish the blossoms of virtue which clothe you now with so much beauty never to be blighted, but to develop into the rich clusters which God, in the autumn of your life, will gather into His garners, you must try to put in practice these few precepts.

First, have a lowly opinion of yourself, and a thorough conviction of your own weakness, believing firmly that unless you take care to correct yourself, you will fall into most grievous disorders. In the next place, be not careless about *venial sins*. Little sins have brought to a miserable end many who were far advanced in sanctity. Lastly, do not imagine that you can sin with impunity; then repent; and then sin again. These repentances are very doubtful. But having once repented, never repeat your sin; and then, by assiduous daily prayer, beseech God to have His hand upon you, and to keep your footsteps in His paths.

THE ARREST OF JESUS.

I. It seems, from the Gospel narrative, that though Judas gave the preconcerted sign which pointed out to the soldiers the person of Our Lord, they did not at once rush on Him and seize Him. Either their eyes were blinded, so that they could not see, or the traitor had been so precipitate in performing his villainous part, that they had not observed his salutation. As they stood irresolute, Jesus advanced towards them. All signs of weakness and of fear had now vanished from Him. With unfaltering step He came to them, and asked, in a voice free from the slightest tremor of apprehension: 'Whom seek ye?' They answered: 'Jesus of Nazareth.' Then He uttered these few simple words, 'I am He,' with so majestic a dignity of mien, and with so quiet an intrepidity of tone, that His would-be captors reeled backwards and fell to the earth.

Amazement and fear held them spell-bound. They dared not lay a finger upon Him. Again, therefore, Jesus said to them: 'Whom seek ye?' and again received the same answer. 'I have told you,' replied Jesus, 'that I am He. Therefore, if ye seek Me, let these go.' By these words He gave them permission to seize upon Him; for the soldiers at once advanced, and with them the servants of the High Priest. Whereupon St. Peter drew forth his sword, and, aiming a blow at the most forward, struck off his right ear.

Jesus somewhat sternly bade him put back his weapon into its scabbard, as the use which he had made of it seemed to imply a want of faith in the power of God, Who, on a word from His beloved Son, would have sent to His assistance ten legions of Angelic Spirits. Then, with compassionate tenderness, He healed the wound inflicted by His over-zealous Apostle, and, as the hour granted by His heavenly Father to the powers of darkness had come, the hour in which they might wreak their malice on the sacred flesh of the God-Man, the soldiers rushed forwards, laid their unholy hands upon His person, and bound Him with ropes like a common malefactor.

II. Reflect now in what way you may make the contemplation of this incident in Our Lord's Passion, bear upon your daily life. There are, in your college career, seasons of trial and of difficulty, when all things seem to be turning against you, and when, in addition to the trouble which molests you on every side, there is added the enticement of the devil to abandon the service of God, and to give yourself up to the pleasures of the flesh. That evil spirit wishes to draw you out from the city of God, in which you are protected from harm, into the dark night; and, under shadow of its all-covering mantle, to make you seize, bind, and carry off Christ your Lord to a disgraceful death.

When you are on the point of sinning—when your will is hesitating, trembling, as it were, in the balance—Jesus Himself comes before you, and says: 'Wherefore art thou come? Is it to betray Me? Is it to hand Me over into the power of My enemies? to bind Me? to drag Me away? to condemn, scourge, crown Me with thorns, once again to crucify Me, and to trample under foot the blood which I shed for you?' He speaks to you with a gentle voice, half sorrowful, half reproachful, and utters those magic words which ought to arrest you, even though standing on the brink of the precipice, and about to plunge headlong down. 'My child,' He says, 'it is I. Do not, I beseech thee, do this thing! Do not outrage Me! I have tenderly loved thee, with more than a mother's love. I have watched over thee. I have seen thy struggles and thy trials. I have borne thee up in the wearying heat of the conflict. I have given thee all that I have; more I could not give, for I gave thee Myself. I have shed the last drop of My blood to redeem thee. What, therefore, art thou about to do?'

Reflect upon it, and let the horror which the magnitude of so great a crime will flash into your soul, bring you to your knees, in humble supplication for pardon, for mercy, for strength. Ask Him ever to be at your side in time of conflict and of trial, and when the battle rages fiercest round you, to cheer your flagging courage and rouse your failing energies with the words: 'Fear not; it is I.'

III. But there is another aspect under which we may look at these words of Jesus Christ. Like the soldiers and the Jews who apprehended Jesus, there are some who are in no way impressed by the words which Christ addresses to them. They are deaf to the gentle pleading of His loving heart. All that He has done for them, all that He promises to do for them, is forgotten. The attractions of sin flaunt in so glaring a fashion before their view, that they see not the tearful eyes and the blood-stained face of their Saviour. His outstretched hands are unheeded by them. They fling Him aside; they thrust Him into the clutches of His enemies; and satisfy their hearts' desire. There is no hand raised to smite them for their impiety; because it is their hour, and the hour of darkness.

But that hour will pass away; and then it will be God's day—a day of calamity and of misery, a day of whirlwind and of storm. For the sinner is not suffered to go on for ever in his sins. The measure of his iniquities is filled up, and then the hour of doom strikes the knell of condemnation for him. He shall be snatched from the midst of his sins, and hurried into the presence of his Judge. Then he shall hear these words of Jesus, thundered into his astonished ears by the voice of an angry God: ' It is I, Jesus of Nazareth. It is I, Whose words you have despised, Whose counsels you have set at naught, at Whose threats you have laughed. It is I, Whose laws you have broken, Whose sufferings you have made unavailing, Whose person you have profaned. Now the day of vengeance has arrived. Thou mayest call upon the mountains to fall upon thee, and to cover thee, but they cannot hide thee from My wrath. Therefore begone, accursed one, into everlasting fire! Never again shalt thou look upon My face, but henceforth and for ever My hand shall be heavy upon thee. Thou shalt groan in thy anguish, but the thorn shall be fastened, and the gnawing worm of conscience, which tells thee that all this is through thy own fault, shall feed upon thy heart for ever.'

JESUS BEFORE THE HIGH PRIEST ANNAS.

I. It must have been close upon midnight when Jesus with His captors reached Jerusalem. Yet, so eager were the priests to be rid of Him, that they did not wait until the morning, but had Him ushered at once into their presence, that the preliminary trial might be gone through, and the way prepared for His condemnation and death on the following day. The soldiers, therefore, led Him straight to the house of Annas, the father-in-law of Caiaphas, the High Priest.

This Annas presided over a tribunal of seventy-two ancients, before whom all cases of false doctrine were tried. More than twenty years before this, he had been High Priest, but had been deposed by the Roman Procurator. Old age had now come upon him, but his heart had not grown tender with his years, but rather harder and more unfeeling with avarice and pride. It has been suggested that the ferocious hatred displayed both by him and by all the priests and the elders against Our Lord, arose from the fact that Jesus had so publicly, and with so vehement indignation, driven the buyers and the sellers from the Temple Courts, and had thus cut off from them a fruitful source of pecuniary gain.

We may, therefore, picture to ourselves the glare of fiendish triumph which shot from his eye, as Jesus, bound like a common felon, stood before him. He began at once to question Him about His doctrine and His teaching; but the time for answering these inquiries had passed, even had they been asked for the sake of instruction, and not rather to entrap Him. Jesus, therefore, mildly referred him for information upon these points, to those who had listened to Him. 'I have spoken nothing in secret. Ask those who have heard Me.' Upon this, one of the menials standing by struck Our Lord a violent blow upon the mouth, saying: 'Answerest Thou the High Priest so?'

That vile mockery of a judge allowed this breach of justice and of common decency to pass unrebuked, for the indignity offered to Jesus gratified his malicious heart. It elicited from Our Lord nothing but a mild and dignified expostulation with the wretch who struck Him, for his injustice and barbarity: 'If I have spoken evil, give testimony of the evil; if well, why strikest thou Me?'

II. At the present day men dare to cite Jesus before their tribunals in somewhat the same spirit as was that which animated the infamous High Priest so many centuries ago, and for reasons almost similar. The doctrine of Jesus is a curb upon fallen nature. It reins in the fiery impulses of its fierce passions; and these, feeling the curb, chafe against it and strive to be rid of it. His teaching keeps within due bounds the reason of man, as well as his untamed nature. Consequently, all those who do not wish to be restrained by the law of the Lord, hate Him for imposing it upon them, and do what lies in their power to destroy Him. Hence it is that we find men calling in question the very existence of

Jesus—looking upon the whole Gospel narrative as a tissue of fables, and upon the divine law as a code invented by priests to subject the credulous to their sway.

They summon Jesus before the tribunal of their reason. He appears there, always prejudged, with His hands tied, and if possible with His mouth gagged. They question His doctrine in a sneering, captious, half-critical, half-bantering sort of way, as if they hardly deemed it rational. If a crushing answer is given, they fly into a fury, and allow the speaker practically to be struck on the mouth, contrary to the prescriptions of law and of justice. Beware of this. It is the outcome of a spirit of irreverence, which is born of rebellion against the law of God. No one calls in question the existence of God, or the right of the moral law to man's obedience, except those who have first revolted against the moral law, and persevered so long in their revolt, that it is their interest to deny the existence of a guardian of the law who will sharply avenge every infringement of it.

Let them, then, first heal the wounds of their hearts, and they will soon see that reason will find nothing illogical in the scheme of divine government which has been revealed to us. Let them conscientiously observe all the precepts of God's law, and they will never desire to call Jesus Christ to the tribunal of their reason, to show cause why He should dare to claim, and still more to exact, from them dutiful allegiance.

III. There is, however, in this unjust trial one incident from which a lesson may be learnt more suited to your years than is that which teaches you to shun an irreverent and critical spirit. This incident is the blow which Jesus received upon the mouth. It is with the mouth that men very often most grievously offend Almighty God; for with it they give utterance to all the wickedness that is generated in their corrupt hearts. Look, therefore, to yourself, and see what use you make of it.

How do you speak of your masters? You cite them before your tribunal, and pass in review their characters, their conduct, their persons, their abilities. Then you venture to judge them, to criticise them, and to condemn whatever in their actions seems displeasing to you. Very often—in fact, nearly always—your judgment is a very partial one, being influenced mostly by personal pique against those who have, perhaps, done you a real kindness by being severe with you.

Your own companions are next brought to the bar, and treated in the same way. With regard to them, you may sometimes have gone so far as to reveal important secrets which they confided to you. Perhaps, out of spite, you have invented and spread abroad groundless accusations against them, detrimental to their good name and character.

How often is your mouth sullied by lies? Of some sins of the tongue, God grant that you may never be guilty! But though your offences in point of speech may not be grievous, yet remember that to atone for them Jesus received so patiently that brutal blow upon His sacred mouth. Therefore, often ask Him, through the pain and the confusion which He then endured, to teach you to set a gate of prudence before your lips, so that no unseemly word, no sharp and bitter saying which might wound your neighbour and soil your conscience, may ever escape your mouth. When you feel tempted to speak anything that would leave even a slight stain upon your soul, think of the blow given to your Lord, and for His sake keep silence.

JESUS BEFORE CAIAPHAS.

I. ANNAS and his associates deemed the case of Jesus to be one which came within the province of the Sanhedrim, and accordingly sent Our Lord to Caiaphas. The attendants, therefore, led Him straightway across the courtyard to the hall in which the worthless High Priest sat with his colleagues, waiting with ill-concealed impatience, to proceed with this nefarious trial. The Evangelists state, in a marked manner, that they conducted Him to Caiaphas, *bound* as a criminal, worthy of condemnation. In this ignominious plight, Jesus is once more presented before

His judges. Not one among them looked favourably upon Him, for He stood in their way as a hated obstacle which must be removed. They thirsted for His blood, and all were agreed that that thirst must be satisfied to the full.

But how to gratify their desire, without openly declaring to the world that they were about to commit an abominable crime, became now the object of their greatest anxiety. Gladly would they have dispensed with all forms of justice, had they not dreaded to offend against public decency. Therefore, they instituted a mockery of a trial, and, in the terribly straightforward words of the Evangelists, they sought false witnesses to destroy Him.

All the old accusations which had already been scattered to the winds by Our Lord, were once more trumped up against Him: 'He had healed the sick upon the Sabbath day; He had cast out devils by the power of the evil one; He had consorted with publicans and with sinners; He had refused to give tribute to Cæsar,' and a whole host of similar charges, the mere statement of which was their best refutation. There was so much discrepancy between the testimony of the different witnesses, that none of these charges seemed sufficient to convict the prisoner.

At last there came two men, whose story seemed a little more coherent than were the accusations of the rest, and who at least reported the same thing. They declared that He had said: 'Destroy this Temple, and in three days I will build it up again.'

II. During the whole of this trial, Jesus stood in the presence of the High Priest, His hands tied behind His back, His eyes modestly cast down. No shadow of displeasure passed across His features, as the witnesses uttered perjury after perjury against Him. No flash of indignation shot from His eye; no word escaped from His lips. He stood there and listened, as if the calumnies uttered, were spoken against some other man. His dignified silence disconcerted the judges, and filled them with confusion and rage. If He would only speak, they might vent against Him their pent-up hate. His calm bearing lifted Him far above their petty spleen, and enabled Him to look from a lofty height upon them and upon their villainy.

His silence became intolerable. It could be borne no longer. It filled Caiaphas with so great rage that, starting to his feet, he exclaimed: 'Answerest thou *nothing* to the things that these witness against thee?' Passion distorted his face; hate sparkled in his wicked eyes as he peered into the countenance of Jesus, and waited amid breathless silence for an answer to his question. But not a word passed the lips of Our Lord. Then, lifting up his voice, he uttered that solemn adjuration which his crafty soul knew full well would extort an answer from his prisoner, and, at the same time, give the judges something upon which to fasten an accusation. 'I adjure thee,' he said, '*by the living God*, that Thou tell us, if Thou be the Christ, the Son of God.' Amid the deep silence which followed so solemn an appeal, there issued from the hitherto sealed lips of Jesus the startling response: '*I am.*' Then He added: 'And you shall see the Son of man, sitting on the right hand of the power of God, and coming with the clouds of heaven.'

The wily Sadducee, unappalled by this thrilling announcement, gladly seized upon His words as the most damning evidence of guilt, and, crying out with well-assumed horror, 'He hath blasphemed,' rent his garments, and, appealing to his assessors, received from them the long-expected answer, 'He is worthy of death.'

III. There are two ways in which you may make this sad episode in Our Lord's Passion very advantageous to yourself. The first, is when you happen to be wrongfully accused either by your masters, or by your companions, and upbraided for that which you have not done. Mistakes of this nature often occur at College, and are the cause of much suffering to those upon whose heads the imputation falls. On these occasions, bear in mind the conduct of your Saviour. Be calm, and do not lose your head in a whirlwind of indignant denial, which will only agitate you, and perhaps confirm an ungenerous and naturally suspicious character in his notion of your guilt.

When the charge has been stated, firmly and quietly deny it, if you are innocent, and then say no more. If you are guilty, at once admit your guilt, and atone for your fault by bravely submitting to the punishment which may be inflicted. This conduct will gain you respect and affection from your masters, and your fault will be forgotten in admiration of the frankness with which you confessed it.

The next lesson which this trial should teach you, is that every sinner treats Jesus in precisely the same way as that in which Caiaphas and his wicked crew treated Him. When you sin grievously, you bind the hands of Our Lord; you drag Him into the midst of His enemies; you bring forwards all sorts of frivolous, vain, and foolish reasons to excuse yourself for wishing to put Him to death. When you are asked by the devil, or by your passions which urge you to thus contumeliously treat your Lord and your God, ' What think you of the Christ?' by your conduct you cry out, ' He is worthy of death.' Bear this in mind, and reflect how often you may have acted thus towards Jesus. Humbly crave His pardon for the past, compassionate Him for having been treated thus by the priests, and promise never again to reject Him, nor to choose the devil as your master in His stead.

JESUS GIVEN OVER BY CAIAPHAS TO THE SOLDIERS.

I. By the loud acclaim of the whole assembly, Jesus had been judged worthy of death. In consequence of that sentence, the people would now regard Him as an impious heretic, upon whom it would be pleasing to God to heap every indignity. It is very likely that Caiaphas, on hearing the unanimous verdict of his colleagues, rose together with them and left the hall. If he did not do so, but remained behind and looked on approvingly while the bystanders subjected Jesus to the treatment which the Evangelists describe, this fact will brand another note of infamy upon his deeply-stained character, marking him as a vile wretch, who, to his many other evil qualities, added the degrading vice of malignant cruelty. For the fanatical wretches immediately began to maltreat the helpless Victim who stood defenceless in their midst. These were the soldiers, the menials, and the hangers-on of the High Priest's palace—men whose souls the devil seems to have entered, and filled with diabolical rage and cruelty against Jesus Christ.

Some of them spat in His adorable face, 'upon which,' says St. Paul, 'the Angels desire to look.' Others plucked at His hair and beard. Others, clenching their fists, dealt upon His face blows which stunned and staggered Him. With derisive shouts and laughter, others struck Him with the palms of their hands, and, in allusion to His prophetic character, asked Him to tell them 'who it was that struck Him.'

We know, or at least we may have heard, of what vile conduct the roughs of our own country are capable; but we can hardly think it possible that men could have so lost every sentiment of manliness, as to be guilty of conduct so cowardly as this, unless devils had entered their very bodies, and filled them with some of their own hatred for all that is upright, honourable, and pure.

Our Lord stood among these wretches, with His hands tied behind Him! No one, therefore, but the vilest coward, and one dead to every sentiment of humanity, would have raised his hand against that unresisting Man, from Whose person, though treated with so great ignominy, there shone forth a calm dignity, which must have awed, while it maddened His assailants to commit upon Him still greater outrages.

II. This treatment lasted during the whole of that dreadful night. The Evangelists have drawn a veil over the secrets which its darkness conceals, and have contented themselves with saying: 'And, blaspheming, many other things they said against Him.' Ah! reflect upon the thoughts which cannot fail to rise within you, as you pass in review all these cruel ignominies which were heaped upon your Saviour! By sin, the Catholic boy pronounces sentence of death upon his Lord. To procure that sentence, he appeals to his own passions, which he ought to rule and guide. He says to them, when Jesus stands before him, 'What think you?' They cry out, 'He is worthy of death.'

If that boy gives way to the clamour of these unholy and unjust advisers, he does what Caiaphas did—he leaves Jesus a prey to the vilest of His enemies. For by sin, the sinner strikes Our Lord upon the face. He insults Him as foully as did the cowardly ruffians who dared to void their filthy spittle upon that meek, unresisting face, upon which the whole world shall one day be forced to look with trembling awe—and woe unto him who shall see it in its anger! He covers those all-seeing eyes with a filthy rag, when he wishes them not to see his own wicked actions. He strikes and buffets His sacred person, by his frequent and oft-repeated sins. He fills His ears with his wicked words, and stabs Him to the heart, by his evil desires and abominable thoughts. In one word, he does what in him lies to renew again all the bitter Passion which Jesus endured so patiently. In the mad delirium of his sins, he forgets that Jesus felt his hand amid the pluckers and the strikers, and saw his face amid those who spat upon, scorned, and flouted Him.

III. If, then, in the past you have been one of those who grossly and shamefully insulted Jesus Christ, remember that the moment is fast approaching when you shall stand before Him face to face. Your eyes shall look into those eyes of His, from whose piercing glance no darkness can hide you. You shall see that face which was defiled by spittle and disfigured by blows. Your ears shall hear the accents of that wondrous tongue which has kept silence for so long a time.

Therefore, hasten now while you have time, to undo that which you are sorry for having done. You cannot, indeed, *recall* the past, but you may, at least, wipe out from its record the charges written up against you. You cannot live over again the years which you have wasted, but you may redeem the time by more than ordinary diligence and fervour. Lose not a moment, therefore, in setting about this all-important work, for you know not how much of daylight yet remains before the dark night shall set in, during which 'no man can work.'

Casting yourself, therefore, upon your knees before your Redeemer, Who stands there wearying out by His patience, the rage and the malice of His enemies, ask pardon for your share in their wickedness. Wash away from His face, by your repentant tears, their filthy spittings. Make amends for their hatred, by your fervent love. Shield Him from their blows, by your diligent observance of His law. Drown their blasphemous shouts, by your humble prayers; and, as you look upon your Lord and your God, thus abandoned, thus maltreated, thus trampled under foot, make a strong resolution that, come what may, you will for the future, both with body and with soul, most faithfully serve Him. For your sake He gave His body to the strikers, and His soul to the bitterness of sorrow; therefore, let your body and your soul serve Him all the days of your life.

JESUS DENIED BY ST. PETER.

I. A REALLY good boy has this advantage over one that is indifferent and lukewarm—he profits both from the good which he sees others perform, and from the evil of which they may be guilty. An indifferent boy, on the other hand, shuts his eyes to the example of the good, and is only the more confirmed in his tepidity, by the evil which he sees others commit. When a good boy hears of anyone's fall into grievous sin, the fact fills him with fear, and makes him cautious and humble. Try, therefore, to be animated with his sentiments, and you will derive the greatest advantage from the consideration of St. Peter's miserable denial of Christ.

After Our Lord's apprehension in the Garden, Peter fled away like the rest of the Apostles; but shame for his cowardice, as well as the burning love which he bore to Jesus, induced him to turn back and follow Him 'afar off,' even to the house of the High Priest. Through the influence of a disciple, well known to the High Priest, he gained admittance into the hall, in which the servants were standing round a fire warming themselves, and talking upon the events of the evening. Peter drew nigh to the fire, anxious perhaps to hear news of his Master. As the red glare of the light fell upon his face, one of the maid-servants suddenly addressing him, said: '*Thou* also wast with Jesus the Galilean.' Completely taken by surprise, he straightway denied her assertion, almost before he had time to think of the enormity which he thereby committed.

Alarmed at the fact that he had been discovered, he drew back out of the light of the fire, and made towards the gate; but as he went, another maid-servant looking into his face said to him: 'Thou also wast with Jesus of Nazareth.' Fear had taken possession of his heart, and he once again denied all knowledge of Our Lord.

Dreading lest, if he hastened away, the bystanders might be confirmed in their suspicions, and apprehend him as a follower of the Galilean, he seems to have come back again towards the fire. Then those who stood round, and who had heard his second vehement denial, turned upon him and said: 'Surely thou also art one of them; for even thy speech doth discover thee.' Then Peter, for the third time, denied with an oath that he knew Jesus, and immediately the cock crew. He then remembered the words of Our Lord. His heart throbbed with an agony of sorrow for his sin, and rushing forth into the court-yard, he wept bitterly over his lamentable apostasy.

II. From the downfall of this pillar of Christ's Church, learn not to be high-minded, but to stand in humility and in fear. It may be that, at this present moment, you are living a pure and holy life. Evil of every kind is far removed from you. You delight in prayer, in holy reading, and in the devout reception of the Sacraments. Vice is hateful to you, and in the strength of your present favour, you imagine that nothing in the world can separate you from the sweet love of Jesus Christ. Nevertheless, be on your guard! Stand in fear! You think yourself to stand, take heed lest you fall.

There have been many boys as good, as virtuous, and as fully determined to continue in the path of virtue, as you are at this moment; yet we have seen them fall away, and make shipwreck, not only of their virtue, but of their faith! They trusted too much in their own strength. They ventured to go within reach of sin. They drew near to the fire, convinced that they could not be drawn into it. They poised themselves upon the edge of the abyss, confiding in the steadiness of their heads, and in the iron strength of their nerve; but, alas! they fell, and some of them never to rise again.

They found their way into pleasant company. They made friends, and were indulgent towards their weaknesses. They began to fear lest they should offend them; and then a bantering word, or a taunt, or a sharply-barbed witticism, stung them into doing something which made them totter upon the brink of the abyss, lose their footing, and at last fall down headlong. Then they floated with the stream, and made no effort to struggle against it. They lost sight of all that before they fondly cherished, and soon grew not only not to care for it, but positively to dislike it, to banish the inconvenient memory of it from their minds. Thus they went from bad to worse; from negligence to indifference; from indifference to forgetfulness; and so to total oblivion of God, of hell, of eternity.

III. Moreover, from Peter's fall, learn how important it is for you to keep close to Jesus Christ, and not to follow Him, as the Apostle did, 'afar off.' It is always a very dangerous thing for a college boy to be lukewarm in his service of God. For, in that state, he is at a distance from God. What advantage does he, then, derive from prayer? If you examine the way in which he quits himself of that solemn duty, you will see. He looks about, he thinks of his games, of his studies, of his neighbours, in fact, of everything but of his own necessities, and of God, Who is able to relieve them. How does he prepare for confession? Carelessly, distractedly, and more for the purpose of escaping study, than of cleansing his heart and strengthening his soul. It is the same with Holy Communion. As he is at his prayers, so is he also at his studies—idle, negligent, listless. Therefore, since he does not ask for grace, and offends God by his pretence of service, God withdraws Himself from him. He, consequently, becomes weak, unable to resist his enemies, and falls an easy prey to them.

Beware, also, of the company into which you go. Avoid those who are idle, and who show no respect to their masters. Keep away from grumblers—those discontented beings whom nothing can either please or satisfy, and who make everyone around them wretched in the extreme. Run from those who make sport of Religion; who speak disrespectfully of its priests; and mock those who are pious and good. You will find in their company nothing but evil. Join yourself, rather, to those who are devout, studious, respectful, and contented. Their conversation will be full of innocent mirth; it will edify you; it will spur you on faithfully to serve God, and to work for the purpose of pleasing Him. Finally, always pray to God to give you a distrust of your own strength; to make you humble, and fearful of yourself. Commit yourself to the care of the Angel whom He has placed over you, to guide you in all your ways. That loving Spirit will bear you up in his hands, and hinder you from striking your foot against a stone.

THE DEATH OF JUDAS.

I. AFTER the apprehension of Jesus, the traitor Judas very probably mingled with the crowd, in order to escape observation. Curiosity, however, would, no doubt, impel him to follow the concourse into the city, to see how matters would end. He would hear, from the remarks which were let fall by those who had been present at the preliminary trial, of the vile treatment which his Master had received from His captors; and also of the general impression current among the people, that He would most certainly be put to death. He had, in all likelihood, never calculated upon this; but had thought that Jesus would find means to escape unharmed from their hands, as He had already oftentimes done before.

But now that He seemed to be wholly in their power, Judas knew full well how little chance of escape there was for Him. As well might he expect a pack of famished wolves to loose their prey, as hope that the priests, the Scribes, and the Pharisees would show any mercy to Jesus. The wretched traitor then began to see, in all its appalling magnitude, the atrocity of the crime of which he had been guilty. Remorse, like a ravenous vulture, kept rending his heart. He could not rest. To be still for a moment, caused him to endure the agonies of hell. The calm, pale, sorrowful face of Jesus, Whom he had given over to death, haunted him like a spectre. All the numberless acts of love which He had done to him, in trying to soften and change his heart, now rose up before his mind like so many avenging furies, hounding him on to the brink of the abyss.

Hearing, therefore, on the following day, that Jesus had been scourged like a common slave and condemned to the awful and disgraceful death of the Cross, despair took possession of him, and, entering like a maniac the hall in which the priests were assembled, his face pale and haggard, his eyes bloodshot, his garments in disorder, he flung down the paltry sum of money which they had given to him for his treachery, and cried out in the bitterness of his soul: 'I have sinned in betraying innocent blood!' The priests, with cold superciliousness, looked upon his misery, and cynically replied: 'What is that to us? look you to it.' Stung to madness, the wretched traitor rushed from their presence. No thought of repentance entered his mind. He hastened out of the city, and, going into one of the olive-yards in the suburbs, hanged himself with a halter. What an end for one who had been an Apostle of Jesus Christ! An Apostle —a traitor—a suicide!

II. Besides the lessons of humility and fear, there is another which this total downfall of an Apostle will teach you. It is, that sin, even in the present life, is always followed by punishment. We do not allude to those temporal chastisements which are unseen by men, or which, if seen, are attributed by them to natural causes; but to that internal torment of soul which is called remorse. It is the voice of conscience upbraiding men with their wickedness; and though it is 'small and still,' yet no dissipation, nor pleasure, nor whirl of excitement, is able effectually to drown its tone.

Hence the boy who makes himself the slave of sin, is always tortured, as Judas was, by bitter remorse. The tongue wherewith it utters its reproaches is keen as a viper's tooth. In the midst of games, it cries aloud to him: 'What hast thou done?' When he is forced to be quiet in the still hours of study, it whispers in his ear its accusations, till the very words of the author before him re-echo its taunts. At night, when he lies down to rest, it frights him with the terrors of death. While his companions are laughing and enjoying themselves in all the glee of happy innocence, he hears it saying in the very centre of his heart: 'There is no joy for thee! Thou art God's enemy. The abyss is under thy feet; and, if thou wert to die, hell would be thy portion for ever.' Oh! how true is that saying of the 'Following of Christ': 'If there is joy in the world, the man whose heart is pure enjoys it; and if there is anywhere tribulation and anguish, an evil conscience feels the most of it.'

III. Furthermore, learn wisdom from the treatment which Judas received from the priests. When he first presented himself before them to make that vile compact, which ended in the betrayal of Our Lord, they eagerly received him, and showed him marked attention. They encouraged him to do what he proposed, and gave him reasons which, perhaps, smoothed away any conscientious qualms which might have deterred him from his crime. But, as one of your authors very truly remarks: 'No one expends money upon a traitor, with a view to further that traitor's interest; but as soon as he becomes master of what he sought to gain, he hates and distrusts and reviles him.'*

* Demosthenes; *De Coronâ*, par 59. Oxford. 1870.

So also did these priests act towards Judas. They employed him as a tool which served their wicked purpose. When they had accomplished that, they threw him away with disdain. He had betrayed innocent blood! But what did it matter to them? He had lost his peace of mind. What cared they? His crime had driven him to despair and madness. They thought nothing of it. They laughed at his misery, and sneeringly said to him: 'What is that to us? look you to it.'

So it is also with all those who would lead you into sin. Beforehand, and while they are tempting you, they pretend the greatest friendship and love for you. But afterwards they hate and despise you. There can be no true esteem, no true friendship, no real love that is cemented by sin. You can expect no lasting regard from anyone who urges you to sin. It is himself that he loves, not you. When these wretches have compassed their ends, they laugh heartlessly at the misery which they have created: 'What is that to us? look you to it.' Yes, dear children, look to yourselves in time! Never betray Jesus Christ to His enemies. Above all things have Him for your friend. He will always be faithful. He will never desert you. Never offend Him, and you will never feel with how keen a tooth remorse can bite; and you will never hear from false friends the bitter gibe: 'What is that to us? look you to it.'

JESUS BEFORE PILATE.

I. DURING the whole night, Jesus suffered the most outrageous treatment at the hands of the brutalised menials, to whose keeping the priests had consigned Him. Wearily as the hours of darkness dragged on, they came at last to an end; and with the dawn, there appeared a messenger from Our Lord's inveterate foes, summoning Him before a full assembly of the Sanhedrim. That tribunal passed upon him the sentence of death. But as the Jews no longer possessed the power to inflict capital punishment, they were obliged to hand Jesus over to the Romans, before their vengeance could be glutted to the full. Accordingly, after a few hours, they dragged Our Lord through the streets of the city, to the palace of Pontius Pilate, the Roman Governor.

As he went along, the people and the strangers who had come up for the festival of the Passover, were told that this man, whose fame had gone throughout Judea, had been at last discovered to be nothing better than a cunning cheat, who, by sleight of hand, had gained for himself the reputation of a prophet and a worker of wonders. The people, therefore, insulted, derided, and reviled Him as He passed along the crowded thoroughfares.

On arriving at the Governor's palace, they sent Jesus into the hall, most likely with some of the soldiers, or the Temple guards; for the priests feared to incur ceremonial uncleanness, by entering the house of a Gentile. Pilate, in order not to offend the fanatical prejudices of this stiff-necked, turbulent people, came down to them to the place where they stood without. The accusations brought by these hypocrites against Jesus, were 'that He fostered seditious designs among the people; that He wished to overthrow the Roman power; that He persuaded men not to pay tribute to Cæsar; that He set Himself up as the King of the Jews.' The clear-headed Roman saw, at a glance, how matters stood. He had heard enough of Jesus to know that the charges of these vindictive priests against Him, were the outcome of their jealousy and wounded pride; and he felt convinced that, if the accusations had been true, these men would have been the first to join themselves to anyone who opposed the Roman dominion. After listening to their story with ill-concealed scorn, he left the accusers to question the accused.

II. Here let us pause, and try to fathom the abyss of mental suffering endured by Our Lord, on account of the falsehoods which were uttered against Him. He heard the iniquitous reports of His character, which were industriously circulated among the people, and He knew also the foul lies which the priests were even now uttering before the Governor. Calumnious lips had blackened His fair fame, and He stood before the people, no longer as a holy prophet, a man of God, one who had worked wonders the like of which no man had ever worked before, and spoken words beyond the power of human tongue to utter, but as a clever cheat, a man who had cunningly imposed upon the simple, and by dexterity, or by the power of the devil, had performed those miracles, the fame of which had filled all Judea with a stupor of amazement.

Think what acute anguish must have wrung His heart, as He heard the execrations, the gibes, and the jeers of the crowd exulting over Him as they would have exulted over the detection of a wicked charlatan. You may realise somewhat of His pain, if you try to put yourself in a similar situation. What would be your own torture of mind, if you were falsely accused before the whole School of some disgraceful act, and if your companions believed you to be guilty of it? Suppose, for a moment, that someone had accused you—let us say—of opening another boy's desk, of reading his private papers, and of stealing thence some object of value. What shame and confusion would fill your soul, when you either saw your companions avoiding you, or heard their taunts, and the terrible epithet 'thief,' with which they would brand you? Your heart would quiver with indignation, and be ready to burst with grief, for you would feel that you were spurned and despised by all. Of a somewhat similar nature must have been the feelings of Our Lord, as He stood pale and haggard, with His hands bound, and the traces of His ignominious treatment fresh upon Him, the priests all the while falsely accusing, and the people raging against Him.

III. From the sin of those wicked priests, endeavour to learn something for your own edification. Envy goaded them on to murder Jesus Christ, for, His holy, austere, and laborious life, cast a reproach upon their effeminate indolence; the light of His wisdom threw all their knowledge into the shade; and His miraculous power gained Him the credit and the reverence of the people. The priests, therefore, feared that all men would run after Him and desert them, and hence their continual opposition to His teaching, and their rage when He silenced and humbled them in presence of those before whom they wished to pose as the guides and teachers of Israel.

Now, as envy caused them to commit the frightful sin of putting to death the Son of God, it may likewise hurry you away into many grievous disorders. You must, therefore, by contemplating their awful crime, conceive a detestation for that base passion which led them into it.

It is one that very easily gains the mastery over schoolboys. For, among them, there must, of necessity, be a spirit of emulation. They are, so to speak, pitted one against another, and the scope and aim of all their striving must be, both physically and intellectually, to surpass one another.

This being the case, it is your duty to watch yourself, and see that this spirit of rivalry does not degenerate into one of envious and envenomed contention. For, when you see others outstripping you in the race, there is danger lest you should begin to dislike them, to hate them, and to grow sad at their success. Therefore, carefully guard your heart against this abominable vice. When you are defeated in any respect, quietly admit the fact, and try to be glad with those who have gained the victory. Do this on all occasions, and instead of inflicting injury upon your own soul by grieving at their good fortune, you will share in all their good works by rejoicing with them, and giving God thanks for their success.

PILATE'S CONDUCT TOWARDS OUR LORD.

I. The Roman Governor, after hearing the accusers of Jesus, left them without, and entering the hall, stood face to face with Our Lord. Though the wild fanaticism, and the narrow exclusiveness of the Jewish priests filled him with a contempt which it cost him a hard struggle to conceal, yet fear of an impeachment at Rome forced him to treat them with a certain amount of deference. Looking, therefore, upon Jesus, standing there, pale and weary—with the marks of the preceding night's ill-treatment still upon Him—he began with the chief accusation against Him, and said: 'Art thou the King of the Jews?' His tone, half of pity, half of incredulous surprise, made Jesus look up and ask him in return: ' Sayest thou this of thyself, or have others told it thee of Me?' Pilate answered: 'Am I a Jew that I should believe anything so improbable? Behold, thy own nation and the chief priests have delivered thee up to me. What hast thou done?'

Jesus, putting aside this question, spoke of His kingdom, saying, ' My kingdom is not of this world, else would not I be standing here bound and defenceless.' Again, therefore, came the question from Pilate: ' Art thou a king, then?' Yes—but one far different from those who rule over the transitory affairs of this lower world—a king of the truth. From this conversation, Pilate judged Our Lord to be a harmless visionary, and going forth to the eagerly expectant multitude, told them very plainly that he found in Him no cause for condemnation.

This announcement the Jews received with loud clamours, and fresh accusations and wilder cries for blood rose from them, as the priests went about among them, hounding them on to cry for His blood. Had Pilate been a man of equitable mind and firm resolve, he would have ordered out a company of soldiers and cleared the square of these shrieking fanatics; but, fearing to offend those whose accusations at Rome might rouse the susceptibilities of his imperial master, he hesitated, and took refuge in that asylum of all irresolute minds—a temporising policy, which staves off a difficulty only for a time, but does not permanently remove it.

II. You should study now, in the days of your youth, to form for yourself a habit of mind totally different from that which guided the conduct of Pilate. For this purpose, accustom yourself upon all occasions when there is a question of right and of wrong, first to discover, if possible, what is right, and then to follow it, cost what it may.

Hence, during your college career, always be ready to

take advantage of every opportunity that presents itself for acting in this manner. These opportunities cannot fail, from time to time, to offer themselves to you. For the life of a great public School is sure to bring to the surface the conflicting elements of right and of wrong. It does this in small matters as well as in great. In both instances, the right and the wrong become centres round which two opposing parties group themselves, and you will be obliged to declare yourself for the one or the other of the two camps which are formed in the School. Each of these cannot have right on its side; and the chances are that, on the wrong side, there will be a majority of the loudest talkers, and of those who are looked upon as the leading spirits of the School. In your secret heart you may feel that right lies with the minority; but, at the same time, there will arise the fear of offending many who are your friends, the fear of incurring the ridicule and the sneers of those whom you love, and whose good-will you desire to cultivate. Hence there will be a contest within you, as to which side you should take.

Do not try to be half with one side and half with the other. Choose rather what you think to be right, and adhere to it, no matter how great may be the outcry against you. By acting in this way, you will accustom yourself to fear nobody but God, and to dread nothing but evil. This will make you a good, honest man, faithful to your conscience, and loyal to your God.

III. Some few instances will, perhaps, enable you to understand more clearly what we would have you do. Let us suppose, for example, that a number of your class-fellows, including yourself, are implicated in some piece of boyish mischief, which is detected by your masters, and brought home to you. A lie would avert the punishment, and some are found base enough to urge that the circumstances of the case are of a nature to justify you in screening yourselves, by that means, from the anger of the authorities. Public opinion inclines in that direction; and the finger of ill-merited scorn would be pointed at you, if you should oppose the judgment of the majority. What are you to do? What says your conscience? That it is not right, and, therefore, that it is not lawful to tell a lie. Do not, then, hesitate for a moment, but meet the disdain, or the anger, or even the blows of your schoolfellows rather than offend your God.

Again, there are times, perhaps, when a proposition is made, and a sort of conspiracy is entered into among your companions, to take from the College what does not belong to you. Some would call this a boyish freak, but your conscience tells you that, no matter what name may be given to these acts, they are, after all, pilfering, and, therefore, dishonest and unlawful. Be not weak enough to yield to public opinion, through fear of being called cowardly and spiritless. The thing to be looked at, is whether the action is right or wrong. If it is wrong, let no power on earth force you to go against that inward voice which says to you, 'Non licet'—'It is not lawful.'

Finally, suppose that the actions of Superiors, or of some particular master, meet with the disapproval of the School, and that those who feel themselves aggrieved, call upon the boys to show their displeasure in a marked manner by playing some trick, by way of revenge, upon the person or the persons who are supposed to have invaded their rights. What are you to do? Are you to be hurried away by the tide of public opinion? You know very well that the judge, in these matters, is neither the individual boy, nor any number of boys who may fancy themselves aggrieved. The Superior is a man of mature judgment. What he has done has been done with good reason, and very probably with justice, not in the slightest degree exceeding the fault. Therefore, suffer not yourself to be swept away with the crowd. Firmly hold your ground, and steadily oppose the private pique of a few noisy grumblers. Side with authority, especially if you fear to go with the crowd, because your inward monitor tells you that you would be doing wrong. If, while you are at College, you act in this way, you will acquire that strength of character which will enable you to conduct yourself as a Christian should, in those contingencies in which things of greater moment are in question. Ever strive to take the right side, in spite of feeling, of affection, and of respect for those who, blinded by passion, take the wrong. You will thus accustom yourself to take God's side in every question, and will never condemn Jesus Christ, in order to win the favour of His enemies.

JESUS BEFORE HEROD.

I. PILATE, in his perplexity and fear, caught eagerly at any semblance of a reason to rid himself of this most embarrassing trial. As soon, therefore, as, amid the other accusations, there fell upon his ear that one which indicted Jesus 'for stirring up the people from Galilee even to Jerusalem,' he remembered that Herod, who happened just then to be in the city, held jurisdiction over that province, and ought, consequently, to try the case which had been brought before him. He accordingly sent Jesus to Herod, thinking thus to wash his hands of the matter, without giving offence either to priests or to people. The Jews, therefore, once again dragged Jesus through the streets of the city, and with imprecations, blows, and insults, conducted him to the palace of the Idumean Prince, and ushered Him into his presence.

Herod, seated amidst his licentious courtiers, received Our Lord with joy. Like other men, he had heard much of Jesus, and of the wondrous works wrought by Him—how He had opened the eyes of the blind, made the lame to walk, cured lepers, and raised even the dead from their graves. It gave some fresh excitement to his sated and debauched heart, to see this wonderful Man, Whom he expected to satisfy his vulgar curiosity by performing in his presence one of those astounding miracles which had made all Judea ring with His praise.

Herod, therefore, at great length questioned Our Lord. But his questions drew no response from the poor, despised, and deeply-injured Man, Who stood a prisoner before him. An angry flush mounted to his face, as he perceived that Jesus had set him at naught; and though the Jews stood by, earnestly accusing Our Lord, he did not deem their clamours worthy of notice. He had been set at naught in his own palace; but He that had dared to do this thing should be treated with galling contempt. He therefore ordered a white garment to be thrown about the shoulders of the prisoner, and, seated amid his courtiers, jeered at Our Lord as a fool, and sent Him back to Pilate.

II. What were the reasons which induced Jesus to remain silent in the presence of Herod? There is a very obvious one, which will strike even the most thoughtless. The inquiries of Herod were made simply to satisfy an idle curiosity; and his desire to see Our Lord sprang from nothing higher than the craving of a weary and worn-out libertine for some new stimulant to excite his deadened senses. No fruit could be hoped for from one so disposed. To answer him would have been as criminally wasteful of holy things, as it would be to cast pearls before swine.

But spiritual men see other reasons for this silence— reasons which will not be without a warning lesson for us all. They observe, that by Herod's adulterous marriage with his brother's wife, he had been cut off from the communion of the Jewish Religion, of which he made a nominal profession. He had led a most licentious life, and though sternly rebuked, on that account, by the saintly Baptist, had not heeded his reprehension, but, in order to gratify the wounded vanity of a wicked woman, had basely caused him to be murdered in his prison. Jesus, therefore, in a heart so corrupt, could find no healthy spot on which to cast the seed of His life-giving word. The fierce fever of sensuality had pulverised it into dry and barren ashes. The heavens would drop no dew upon it, but left it desolate, awaiting that day when the hand of the Lord should for ever seal its barrenness, by setting upon it the mark of eternal reprobation.

As Jesus would not speak with Herod, so is He silent also with those who, like him, live in uncleanness, and in the habitual abuse of divine grace. At first He speaks to them both by His inspirations and by the voice of His ministers. But when, by oft-repeated sin, every particle of good soil has been burnt up in the heart, He desists from this fruitless labour. He speaks no more by conscience, by inspirations, or by the voice of ministers. There is a profound silence, more dreadful than the frightful peal of the prophetic voice, threatening and calling to repentance. Oh! sad indeed is the fate of him unto whose questioning Jesus will not answer even a single word.

III. Therefore, learn to fear, as well as to love, Jesus Christ. You represent Him to yourself as a most tender Father, Who looks with unutterable compassion upon the errors and the wanderings of His little children; Whose face is ever wreathed in smiles of affection; Whose hands are outstretched to receive and to take to His bosom those who wish to return from their evil ways. All this is perfectly true. But, at the same time, you must never forget that He is a Father Who can be angry, as well as loving; Who can punish, and Who does punish with appalling severity, when it seems good to Him.

Jesus is what you represent Him to be, unto all those who though they sin, do so through frailty, rather than through malice; who blush for their sin and their ingratitude; who rise again speedily, and return with hearts broken with sorrow. But, do you think He looks favourably upon those who sin, and go on sinning without the slightest remorse—who sin because He is good, and who after repentance, and even while pretending to repent, determine after a time to sin again? Certainly not! With these He will be silent. He will leave them in their sins.

Beware, therefore, and do not provoke Him to be silent with you, for sins like those which Herod committed—for uncleanness and for rejection of grace. Never stifle that voice of conscience, which, like another Baptist, cries out to you, from the centre of your heart: 'It is not lawful for thee to do this thing.' Pray, rather, that it may often speak to you, and warn you against sin. Ask Jesus to uphold you in temptation, and to speak to you trumpet-tongued, should you ever fall into evil ways. Say to Him frequently: 'Be not silent with me, dear Jesus, but speak to me as Thou didst speak to the child Samuel, and grant that when Thou callest to me, I may always answer, "Speak, Lord, for Thy servant heareth."'

JESUS REJECTED FOR BARABBAS.

I. FROM the court of Herod, the Jews once more led Our Lord back through the streets of the city, dressed in the garments of a fool, and greeted on every side with the derision of the fickle crowd, who but a few days before had welcomed Him as the long-expected Messias. Not a gibe, nor a jeer, nor a cutting taunt escaped His notice. He drank in their bitterness, and drained the chalice to the very dregs.

Behold Him now once more in the presence of the Roman Governor, awaiting with unalterable meekness the sentence which the priests were urging the rabble to extort from the vacillating ruler. Pilate, with his Roman instinct of justice, dared not yet sacrifice a prisoner so manifestly free from guilt. But rather than take the straight path, and pursue it in spite of the insane clamours of a fanatical people, he again temporised. He recollected the immemorial custom, on the paschal solemnity, of releasing, at the request of the people, some criminal for whom they might choose to petition. There happened, at that time, to be in custody a malefactor of the worst description—a man who was at once a robber, a rebel, and a murderer. Pilate, therefore, eagerly grasped at this last opportunity of saving the life of Our Lord.

Coming forwards, and standing upon the platform above the heads of the surging throng, he put this question to them: 'Whom will ye that I release unto you—Barabbas, or Jesus, Who is called the Christ?' At once there uprose a unanimous shout: 'Not this man, but Barabbas!' Pilate, astonished at their injustice, and enraged at their vindictive cruelty, exclaimed: 'Why, what evil hath He done?' They answered him by still more furious shouts for the release of the robber and murderer. 'What, then,' he cried, 'shall I do with Jesus?' 'Away with Him!' they screamed. 'Crucify Him! Crucify Him!' 'Shall I,' he answered—while his whole frame quivered with scorn and indignation—'shall I crucify your King?' Maddened into a very paroxysm of fury by this taunt, and by the delay which he had made in satisfying their thirst for blood, they shrieked out that most humiliating admission for a Jew: 'We have no King but Cæsar'—acknowledging thereby that the sceptre had indeed passed away from Juda, and that they were now under the Gentile yoke.

II. How awful an insult did Pilate offer to Jesus, in thus putting Him upon a par with a robber and murderer! But what must have been the anguish of Our Lord, when on being compared with Barabbas, His own chosen people gave their deliberate preference to this outcast, to this human beast of prey? Jesus the holy, the wise, the great Prophet, the worker of deeds which no man had ever done before, the speaker of words which no human intellect could devise, and no human tongue bring forth with so much eloquence and power—even He, the reputed Messias, had been set below a wretch stained with deeds of the darkest dye— whose hands had even been imbrued in Jewish blood! Jesus heard the Governor ask the people this question. He heard their frantic cries for His death, and for the release of the robber. He stood there silent, crushed with shame, despised, rejected, the outcast of His people!

You yourselves have, perhaps, tasted how bitter, and how galling a thing it is, to be set aside by your companions, and to see one whom you looked upon as in every way inferior to yourselves, chosen out and thought to be superior to you. The verdict of your companions upon you and upon him may have been about nothing more important than your respective proficiency in games. Yet, even in so trivial a matter as this, the thought of your own worth, and of the injustice done to you, has made tears of indignation start from your eyes, and caused your heart well-nigh to burst with the effort which you were obliged to make, in order to keep down your anger, and prevent it from breaking forth.

Think, then, of the agony of suffering which Jesus endured, and learn from Him, that sweet humility which keeps the rebellious heart quiet, restrains the angry tongue, and holds back the storm of winged words in which your wrath would otherwise expend itself.

III. Examine into the secrets of your heart, and see whether you have ever dared, like Pilate, to propose to your soul the choice between Jesus and mortal sin. See whether you have not, like the Jews, taken to yourself a Barabbas, and rejected Christ. As your mind travels back through the past, you will, perhaps, remember either some particular day, or hour, when circumstances put before you the fascinating charms of sin, and the less gaudy but more enduring beauty of virtue. In your ears a voice whispered those words, which, either sooner or later, are addressed to everyone: 'Which of these two do you wish to be given to you? Which of them do you choose for yourself?' If, incited by the frenzy of passion, you preferred the more showy attractions of sin, you were guilty of as great an insult to Jesus Christ as the wretches, who in their savage delirium, chose the robber and murderer in preference to the adorable Son of God. For, by rejecting virtue, you rejected His law; you rejected Himself; and cried aloud: 'Not this man, but Barabbas.'

Alas! how often is this the case with boys! As soon as the light of reason has given them power to discriminate between good and evil, they unfortunately, in but too many instances, choose the evil, and reject the good! 'We will not have this man to reign over us,' they cry, we prefer the charms of our own passions. The ignoble gratifications which they can give, we prefer to the sweets of virtue. We are too young to be tied down to the hard ways of what you call a holy life; later on we will, perhaps, try it, when we have sated ourselves with sin; but not till then: 'Not Christ, but Barabbas!'

O! what a choice! That vile robber will turn upon them and make them his wretched slaves, and they will find that he is an exacting and cruel task-master. He will not be satisfied with their service ; nothing but their life's blood will suffice for him. Oh ! if this has been your choice, melt, by the hot tears of true repentance, the chains which bind you ; flee to the bosom of Jesus, and never again abandon Him.

THE SCOURGING OF JESUS.

I. Though Pilate's effort to save Jesus had thus far proved of no avail, he did not, on that account, give up all hope of ultimately delivering Him from the hands of His enemies. As soon, therefore, as he had released Barabbas unto the Jews, he did not straightway condemn Our Lord, but having once again protested that he found in Him no crime worthy of death, he nevertheless declared himself ready to enter so far into their views with respect to Him, as to give Him a most severe correction, and then set Him at liberty.

Upon this, the soldiers led Jesus away from the presence of the Roman Governor, into the Pretorium. There they stripped Him of His garments, and, having bound Him to a pillar, grasped in their cruel hands the much-dreaded *flagellum*. This was not the ordinary *virgae*, or rods, with which, according to Roman law, malefactors were usually flogged. The *flagellum* consisted of leathern thongs tipped with lead or with iron. To be struck by it, was looked upon as the lowest degradation, and none but the worst criminals were ever punished in this way. Nevertheless, with this instrument, and by the hands of brawny ruffians, Our Redeemer was now to be tortured.

Swinging these whips over their heads, they brought them down upon the virginal flesh of Jesus, with all the might of their muscular arms. Each lash left upon the white, delicate skin a long bloody weal, and, as the fury of the torturers increased, the flesh was broken, torn, and, in places, whipped from the bones, till the blood ran down upon the pavement, bespattered the walls, and crimsoned the hands of His merciless tormentors.

Forty stripes save one were all that the law sanctioned ; but the revelations of the Saints tell us, that the soldiers struck till their hands grew weary. Then, and not till then, did they desist, and leave Jesus quivering with agony, fainting from loss of blood, a spectacle at which the stoniest heart would have melted with pity.

As we think of this flagellation, our flesh creeps with horror, and the blood curdles in our veins. But this terrible chastisement did not satisfy the vengeance of Christ's enemies. Naught would content them but His heart's best blood.

II. Pause and reflect, for a few moments, upon this awful torment which Jesus endured for you. At the present day a punishment, somewhat similar in kind, but incomparably lighter in degree, is inflicted upon those who are guilty of robbery with personal violence. Generally speaking these are burly, hardened ruffians, apparently void of feeling, and oftentimes little better than the brute creation. Nevertheless, there is no punishment, with the exception, perhaps, of death, from which they shrink with more horror, not because they feel that it degrades them, but because of its intolerable pain. Yet the number of lashes inflicted upon them, rarely exceeds thirty! These, moreover, are administered by one of the prison officials, who bears no ill will to the culprit, and a physician stands by to stay his hand from inflicting more punishment than the wretch is able to bear. In spite, however, of all these mitigating circumstances, the boldest ruffian shrinks and shudders at the first touch of the biting thongs. Few go through the punishment with sufficient fortitude to repress their shrieks of agony. Many swoon away after it is finished; many even before the tenth stroke!

What, then, must have been the agony which Our Lord endured during His merciless flagellation? His judge did not give Him into the hands of a cool, unimpassioned minister of justice; no one in authority stood by to restrain the ferocity of those who tortured Him; no one even to restrict the blows to the legal number. His torturers were brutal by nature, and, amid the lawless license of their soldier-life, had lost what little of pity they ever possessed.

They were many in number, and were lashed into fury by the devil, and hounded on by the rage and the hatred of Our Lord's enemies. They struck Him with all the might which fury lends to a powerful arm. They struck Him till they tore the flesh from His bones. They struck Him so long and so heavily, that, had He not been supported by His divine nature, He would have died. Yet no cry of pain escaped from the lips of that unresisting Victim. Like the sheep which is led to the slaughter, He opened not His mouth.

What a spectacle for us to look upon! Torn, mangled, disfigured, quivering with the agonising smart of the cruel throngs, He stands there, well-nigh fainting with the keenness of a punishment more severe than mortal flesh had ever felt before. Truly, 'God did put upon Him the iniquities of us all, and for them hath He struck Him, till He has become a very worm, and no man.'

III. Yes, for our sins God, suffered wicked men to strike the sinless flesh of His only-begotten Son, till He became like unto a leper, disfigured with bloody weals and gaping wounds, as the leper is with the loathsome corruption of his foul disease. Sin is a leprosy with which men disfigure their souls, till, in a spiritual sense, they become the exact counterparts of that torn and disfigured body of Christ, leaning against the pillar, now all crimsoned with His blood.

Think of this, ye children of Jesus Christ, and remember why your Lord and your God thus suffered shame and degradation. He allowed Himself to be publicly stripped of His clothing before a crowd of vile wretches, to atone for all the immodesties which are committed in the world; to be publicly whipped like a common slave—like the worst criminal, like the most ferocious human wolf, whom society is about to cut off from the face of the earth—in order to satisfy, by the agony of His lacerated flesh, for all those sinful delights by which men defile their hearts, and change them from the temples of the living God, into the abodes of the devil.

Therefore, let it be your aim, after reflecting upon the

torture which your Lord endured in His cruel scourging, to obtain, by means of humble, earnest, persevering prayer, a great love for modesty, a deeper and more determined resolution to preserve yourselves from the stain of uncleanness. To wash away this stain, and to provide a healing balsam for our gaping wounds, He suffered His sacred flesh to be torn open, and His precious blood to leap forth. But, at the same time, He wished us to bear Him company in His sufferings, and to share in His Passion, by mortifying our sinful flesh. If we have not the courage to smite ourselves with those scourges, with which the love of God has armed the Saints, we may at least strike ourselves with the equally galling whip of self-denial. If we cannot resist unto blood, we may at least endure the pain of turning away from what the flesh so eagerly covets, and sacrifice, for the sake of Jesus, some little of that ease which, by reason of our many and oft-repeated transgressions, we do not deserve to enjoy.

THE CROWNING WITH THORNS.

I. The inborn cruelty of the brutal soldiers who tortured Jesus, suggested to them one other means by which they might add insult to the degrading injuries which they had already heaped upon Him. Calling to mind that His enemies had accused Him of styling Himself King of the Jews, they said one to another, 'If He is a king, He must be crowned'; and, going forth into the gardens which surrounded the palace, they cut off a branch from the acanthus thorn, and, having twisted it into a wreath, returned into the hall where Jesus stood. Rudely pushing Him into a seat, they brought forth an old, tattered, purple cloak, and threw it over His bruised and bleeding shoulders. Then, placing the torturing wreath upon His head, they struck it down with their mailed fists, so that the sharp thorns penetrated to the bone of the skull. Finally, they put into His hand a reed for a sceptre, and thus completed the derisive coronation.

Now began a scene of insult and of mockery—a scene

so full of diabolical cruelty that, were it not recorded in the Sacred Scripture, we should deem it to be the invention of a poetical fancy rather than the sober record of historic truth. The whole band of soldiers gathered into the hall to witness the sport. Some of these wretches approached Him, and, bending the knee with mock reverence, said : 'Hail, King of the Jews!' Others thrust out their tongues at Him, and leered in His face. There were some among them cowardly enough to spit upon that adorable face, upon which the Angels desire to gaze, and to strike Him with the palms of their hands as He sat there bound, defenceless, and writhing with pain. The pitiless spectators received each insult with shouts of laughter. Every clumsy joke made at His expense, and every piece of coarse buffoonery played upon Him, excited still more their rude hilarity, and their cruel desire to plague and ridicule Him.

Oh! how hard must have been the hearts of those men who could look into the face of that unresisting Victim, and thus smite and flout Him! His eyes were filled with blood, His face was pale with the intense agony of His thorny crown, His whole body seamed and torn with the thongs of the scourges; yet, in spite of this, they ceased not to add to His sufferings, and to trample upon His fine sense of honour, by their vile words, their scorn, their gibes, and vulgar jests, till even they wearied of their sport, and felt relieved when the Roman Governor once more summoned Jesus into his presence.

II. In the Canticles, the inspired writer cries out : 'Behold King Solomon in the diadem wherewith his mother crowned him in the day of his espousals'; but let us say to ourselves : 'Behold Jesus, Our Lord and Our God, in the diadem wherewith our sins have circled His brows.' Yes, for there is a terrible significance in this coronation of the head of Jesus with thorns. The head is 'the palace of the soul.' In that palace, reason and the other intellectual faculties are supposed chiefly to reside. There it is that the soul brings to life and indulges in all those thoughts and imaginings by which God is so often and so grievously offended. The

Eternal Father, therefore, deemed it fitting to lay upon the Redeemer's head all their crushing weight.

As the sharp points of the thorns pierced through His flesh, rending and tearing His sacred temples, He thought of those who, being filled with an overweening esteem of self, look down upon and contemn others. He thought of the countless millions who revel in that spiritual luxury of pride, and strive to rob God of the glory which is His due. He thought of those who pine away with envy and jealousy at their neighbour's good. He thought of those who sit brooding for years over some petty wrong, or some fancied slight, hatching thoughts of revenge. But, most of all, He thought, with shuddering horror, of those who admit into their heads, and cherish in their hearts a troop of wicked thoughts, thus turning the temple of God into an abode of the devil, and defiling the throne of the Lamb with the filth and mire of carnal sins.

Ah! look at Him as He sits there, exposed to the insults and the rude laughter of those pitiless monsters—so gentle, so patient, so uncomplaining—and then reflect upon the share which you have had in this cruel business. Through the mist of blood which is darkening His eyes, He gazes wistfully upon you, and asks for compassion, or at least for one tear of sorrow for your share in striking down upon His head that crown which burns His brows like a circle of flame. Think upon the thoughts of your soul, and, if they have ever been of a nature to torture your Lord, weep over them; kneel before Jesus, not to deride, not to mock, not to strike, not to spurn Him, but to tell Him the sorrow of your heart, and your determination never again to offend Him.

III. In the present condition of our corrupt nature, we cannot always exclude from our minds these various thoughts of pride, envy, jealousy, revenge, and the like. Our nature is a fallen one, ever tending to corruption; the devil watchful and cunning; the world attractive; and all these combine together to tempt us from our allegiance to God. But, though we cannot altogether exclude these thoughts from our minds, we have the power always to eject them, as soon as our intelligence adverts to their presence. One vigorous act of the will, aided by divine grace, is sufficient to do this; and a most efficacious means to remind us of our duty, is the recollection of that pale, agonised face, and of those wistful eyes, which from beneath the thorny crown look out so beseechingly upon us. Therefore, bring that picture before your mind, when the images which excite these various passions are presented to it by the devil, or by corrupt nature.

It may be that you have met with some signal success, either in your studies, or in the games which are played at College; and you begin at once to swell with pride, to look with disdain upon your less fortunate and less gifted comrades. Think of the thorny crown which the pride of men has fixed upon your Saviour's brow. Others have perhaps carried off the prize for which you have laboured so hard and striven so well; you envy them their success; you are jealous of their talents; and your heart, like a frail vessel, is tossed about by the storm of these passions. Oh! think of the thorn-crowned head which throbbed with most acute pain for you! You are injured, grossly, wantonly, and you pant for vengeance; or, worse still, you are harassed and tormented with troops of evil imaginations, wicked thoughts, and the desires which spring from them. They give you no rest; they weary you; they seem to cling to you. But fear them not! Look upon the thorn-crowned head of your Lord. Remember His bitter pain, the throbbing of His temples, the sickening agony, the burning pangs which shot through His sacred head, and beg of Him, by all that He suffered then, not to allow you to be unfaithful to Him. Bear patiently with the disgust which these temptations cause you. Loathe and detest them, and, in order to increase your horror of all that they suggest to you, bear in mind that to blot out, and to atone for their wickedness, Jesus suffered Himself to be crowned as a mock king, to be derided by the brutal soldiers, and to be scorned as never man was scorned before.

'BEHOLD THE MAN!'

I. It seems, from St. John's Gospel, that Pilate had given orders to the soldiers to conduct Jesus into his presence after they had scourged Him. For he still entertained a hope that the pitiable spectacle of Our Lord's torn and bleeding body might soften the hearts of His enemies, and induce them to let Him go. With this object in view, he brought Jesus forth upon the balcony of his Palace, whence He could be seen by all the people, and pointing to Him, cried aloud: 'Behold the man!'

These words, few and simple as they seem, have in them a depth of meaning which we must try to fathom. Coming from the lips of the Roman Governor, they were meant to convey to the people some such ideas as these: 'Here is the man who called himself your king; who made himself equal to God; who threatened to overthrow your temple, and in three days to build it up again. For these offences, frivolous as I deem them to be, I have punished him with the utmost rigour, in order to satisfy you. Look at him! Behold the man! He is clothed in his royal purple; his body is torn with numberless wounds; his face is swollen with blows and defiled with spittle; his eyes are full of blood; his head is crowned with thorns; he is bound like a criminal; he has been degraded and punished severely. Be satisfied, therefore, with the punishment which I have inflicted upon him; for he has suffered enough to atone for his folly and his offences.'

But that piteous spectacle moved not their stony hearts. The words of the Governor were received with one long and piercing cry for His life's blood: 'Away with him!' they shrieked; 'crucify him, crucify him!' Jesus stood there facing the angry mob. He heard their fierce shout for His death. He heard Himself rejected by the voice of His people: 'We will not have this man to reign over us!' He heard them protest in the face of heaven and of earth 'that they had no king but Cæsar.' The time had come; the prophecy had been fulfilled. A ruler of the tribe of Juda no longer held the sceptre.

There stood Jesus, 'without comeliness, without beauty; a worm and no man, the reproach of men, the outcast of the people.' Nevertheless, do you look at Him, and as the words of Pilate ring in your ears, ' Behold the man !' adore Him as the God-Man, Christ Jesus.

II. There are two ways in which you may make these words useful to yourselves. In the first place, you may regard them as addressed to you by God, in order to make you fully understand the sad condition to which sin has reduced our human nature. Jesus Christ, as He stands there before you, presents to your view an image of the soul ravaged by sin. Sin has weakened it, in all its faculties and in all its powers. It has wounded the soul, and by wounding has drained it of its vital force. It has filled it with the thorns of unrest and of remorse. It has darkened its intellectual vision. It has marred the peerless beauty with which God adorned it, left it well-nigh a mere wreck, and made it like a creeping thing of the earth—an outcast from the sons of God.

In the next place, you may look upon the words of Pilate, as addressed to you by Our Lord Himself; and, so regarded, they will become to you like a shield of defence in the time of temptation. Therefore, in the day of bitter trial, imagine that you hear Jesus say to you: 'Behold the Man! Look, and see what I have endured to cleanse you from sin, and to preserve you from ever again falling into it. You are tempted to disobey your masters—look at Me. I have been obedient, even to the death of the Cross. You are, perhaps, filled with proud and vain thoughts, proud of your abilities, vain of your personal appearance. Look at Me! there is no beauty nor comeliness in Me, and I have been treated as a madman and a fool. Your heart is full of angry thoughts and resentful feelings; I have borne patiently with spittings, revilings, and degrading blows. Do the evil spirits and your own rebellious flesh tempt you to debase yourself? Ah! I beseech you, look upon Me! From the crown of My head to the sole of My foot there is no soundness in Me. My temples are wreathed with thorns, My eyes are blinded with blood, My tongue is parched with burning thirst. I am giving up My life for you, My friend, My child! Do not therefore scorn nor revile Me, nor spit upon My face, for I am your friend, your Father, your God. Look well at Me. I am what I am, through love of you. Do not add to My pains. Let not your hand strike down My thorny crown, nor wield the cruel lash, nor drive home the nails into My quivering flesh. Look upon Me, and spare Me.'

III. In your past life, brief as the time has been, between the dawn of reason and the present moment, there have, perhaps, been occasions about which your heart will feel a pang of sorrow when you make considerations such as these. It may be that, like the Roman Governor, you have stood between Christ and your own passions, willing, on the one hand, to defend Him from them, and yet not courageous enough, on the other, to crush them, rather than either offend or injure Him. While looking upon the face of Christ, you have, perhaps, allowed the wild cries of your passions to prevail, and, like a coward, yielded up your Saviour to their savage and brutal treatment.

Or, again, you may be able to call to mind certain moments when, like the Jewish people, who called so loudly for the blood of the Redeemer, there came before the eyes of your soul the sad spectacle of Jesus—thorn-crowned, scourged, derided, and yet so patiently, so meekly looking at you, and pleading with you for your love and your fidelity. Like the Jews, you may have cried aloud: 'Away with him! Crucify him! I will not have this man to reign over me!'

If in your life there have been moments of so great madness, now is the time to atone for them by heartfelt sorrow. Kneel in spirit before that much-enduring, much-derided Man of Sorrows, and weep over the share which you have had in bringing Him to so sad a pass. Recall those words with which you sentenced Him to death, and resolve never again to deliver Him up to His enemies. Promise Him that, when the time comes for proving your fidelity to Him, when you must either deny yourself, or renounce and crucify Him over again, you will picture Him to yourself as He

stood that day before the Jews, and will say to your heart:
'Behold the Man, Christ Jesus, such as my sins have made
Him.'

If you do this when the devil, or the world, or your own
flesh tempts you to forget and to forsake God, you will
never be among the number of those who answer the cry
of conscience bidding them 'Behold the man!' with the
frenzied shout: 'Away with him! Crucify him! Crucify
him!'

JESUS CONDEMNED TO DEATH.

I. THE Roman Governor at last began to see that all his
efforts to deliver Jesus were vain. The wild rage of the
populace startled him, and made him fearful of the consequences which might flow from their fanaticism, if he should
attempt any longer to thwart their wishes. Though he had
repeatedly pronounced their prisoner free from guilt, yet he
now weakly gives way before the clamours of an excited
mob, and delivers Him up to their pleasure. Therefore,
seating himself upon his tribunal, he ordered water to be
brought, and, in the presence of all, caused it to be poured
upon his hands, calling them to witness, by this strikingly
symbolical act, 'that he considered himself to be guiltless of
the blood of this just man.'

Upon the word, there uprose from the crowd that fearful
shout which sealed the doom of the Jewish nation, and even
at this distance of time sends a thrill of horror through our
hearts, when we call to mind its dreadful import: 'His
blood,' they cried, 'be upon us and upon our children.'
Then Pilate pronounced a sentence of death, the most
iniquitous ever uttered by the lips of man.

Strange and unheard-of spectacle! Here is a judge who
repeatedly testifies before the assembled multitude that the
prisoner at the bar is one whose conduct has ever been free
from blame. He knows full well that the accusers, though
making a great show of zeal for Roman authority, hate it
with all their hearts, and are really actuated by malice

against the prisoner, whom they are hunting to death to glut their own private revenge. The witnesses, too, are lamentably at variance with one another, and give contradictory evidence. Yet he has not manhood enough to stem the tide of public prejudice, and, through a love of justice, dash it aside as a something formidable only to a cowardly heart. He weakly yields, and, while proclaiming Jesus to be innocent, basely condemns Him to death.

Nevertheless, he would salve over his conscience by an empty ceremony. He would wash away the murderous stain from his hands by a little water! Vain sophistry! His knowledge of law would tell him that he who incites another to do some deed of injustice, is responsible for the act which his agent commits. Vainly did the people offer to take the whole guilt upon themselves. Their willingness to do so could not free him from the stain of innocent blood-shedding. His hands were as deeply crimsoned by the deed done upon Calvary, as were those of the men who drove the nails through the hands and the feet, and pierced the side of Our Lord. Upon him, as well as upon the Jews, fell the awful weight of that precious blood.

II. The evil example which upon that memorable day Pilate gave to men has been faithfully copied by them, and there are many who dare to treat Jesus, as that cowardly wretch, in the brief day of his power, treated Him. They know perfectly well the justice and the goodness of God's ordinances. They have for them even a sort of barren admiration, as for a something which is, in the abstract, good and beautiful. But when they are forced to confront their fierce, tumultuous passions, they shrink from the labour and the difficulty of subduing them; and, rather than undertake so arduous a rask, they trample under foot the sacred claims of truth and of justice. Have you yourself never done so? Reflect for a moment and see.

In College, as in the world, there are virtues which all admire. Public opinion expects them from each individual, and God also requires them from those who would be His servants. Let us take, for example, the virtues of truthfulness and honesty. Every one admires and praises these two virtues, and would think himself grossly insulted, if he were told that he is a liar, or a thief. But now, put some college boys to the test upon these points, and see whether their boasted love of truth and of honesty will stand the trial.

Let us suppose that a boy finds himself forced to choose between truth and falsehood. He has done something for which he deserves punishment, and is detected. His only means of escape is a lie. If he tells that lie, his conduct, to a certain extent, resembles the conduct of Pilate; for he acknowledges the justice and the goodness of truth, but sets it aside, and chooses instead, a foul and disgraceful lie.

Again; let us suppose that he stands in need of money, that money is thrown in his way, and that he takes what is not his own. He acknowledges the beauty and the goodness of honesty, but he rejects it for dishonesty; because, in this case, as in the preceding one, his passions cry out against the impulse of his better nature, and 'their voices prevail.'

So it may fare with the other virtues. To set them aside, and to choose in preference those things for which corrupt nature craves, is to be guilty of an act similar to that which Pilate committed. It is to say, in the face of heaven and of earth: 'I know that this virtue is good, and that to love it, to adhere to it, is to obey the law of God; yet, because my passions clamour for its destruction, I will hand it over to them to be destroyed. It is their fault, let them look to it.'

III. If we imitate this wretched example, upon us will fall that curse which fell both upon the Jewish people and upon him who weakly yielded to their fanatical rage. The blood of Jesus will be upon us for our destruction, and its crimson stain will mark us out for punishment, more dire than was that inflicted upon the cities of the Plain, which God overthrew in the hour of His fierce anger. 'It will be more tolerable for Sodom and Gomorrah in the day of judgment than for us.' But let us not incur so wretched a fate. Let us strive rather to make the blood of Jesus fall upon us for our greater good in this world, and for our eternal welfare in the world to come.

In spite of ourselves, that precious stream has flowed in upon us and over us. At our Baptism, the priest poured it upon our heads to wash away the stain of the original transgression. When the Bishop, at our Confirmation, imposed his hands upon us, and gave us the Holy Spirit to enlighten and to guide our steps, the blood of Christ purchased for us that inestimable boon. That same blood is given us to drink, when we kneel at the holy altar to partake of the body of the Lord. When we are stretched upon the bed of death, the priest of God will be called in to wipe away the last relics of our sins, with that holy unction which receives its power and its efficacy from the precious blood of Jesus. God's minister, who is for us the representative of Christ, derives his wondrous power from the virtue of that blood. Our very parents were joined together in the bonds of holy matrimony by the blood of Jesus Christ, which cemented and sanctified their union, and filled their hearts with undying love for us.

Since, then, we cannot escape the stream of blood which issued from our Saviour's heart to save us, let us do our utmost to hinder it from having been poured upon us in vain. Let us bear in mind that in Baptism God sealed us with it; that in Confirmation we swore allegiance to Him, and became His soldiers; that in the Holy Eucharist He feeds us with it; in Penance, washes us from the filth of our sins with it; that in the sacrament of Holy Orders He procures for us teachers and guides; and in the sacrament of Matrimony infuses into our parents' hearts, with that same blood, strength to be faithful to each other, and to bring us up in the fear of God. Oh! may that precious blood fall upon our hearts like a fertilising rain, which will make them bring forth fruit unto everlasting life.

JESUS CARRYING HIS CROSS.

I. WHEN the fatal words of condemnation had passed the lips of Pilate, the ministers of his tribunal made all speed to carry the sentence into execution. They hastily constructed a rude Cross, and brought it to the place where Jesus stood. Roughly tearing from His lacerated shoulders the purple robe of scorn, they put on Him once again His own seamless garment. Then they laid upon Him the instrument upon which He was to die; the Centurion in command of the soldiers gave the word to advance; and Jesus set forth upon the last weary journey of His mortal life.

Everywhere the streets were thronged by a multitude of people, eager to see Him pass to His death. There were some who exulted over Him, either because His tongue had not spared their wicked lives, or because His heavenly wisdom had brought confusion upon them, when they attempted to contradict His teaching, or to gainsay His word. Others were indignant that they had been carried away and deceived by a man, upon whom they were now taught to look as a mere charlatan. Some few compassionated Him. They were the women and the children, who were laughed at and despised for their weakness and simplicity.

There, in the midst of His enemies, with their gibes, scoffs, and bitter taunts ringing in His ears and piercing His heart with sorrow, Our Redeemer slowly drags His tottering limbs along, under the weight of the heavy Cross. A strong man would have found its burthen as much as his strength could bear; but Our Lord, in His pitiable condition, after so many hours of mental and of bodily torture, and after so great a loss of blood, must have been well-nigh crushed beneath its weight.

Behold Him, as His weary eyes look sorrowfully around searching for one friendly, compassionate glance. The sweat of death is trickling in great beads down His face, as it does from those who are exhausted by sickness or by overmuch labour. It is purple with the blood which flows from His many wounds. His hands are trembling; He is panting with fatigue; the whole scene swims around Him; and He falls under His burthen, not once only, but again and again. Is there no heart of flesh there to pity Him, no eye to weep over Him, no hand to help Him? None! He is lifted up, and pushed forwards. There is no more rest for Him in this world, for He is bearing the heavy load of our sins. It must crush and torture Him till He has breathed forth His holy soul into the hands of His Eternal Father.

II. As we call to mind the image of Our dear Saviour, thus wearily staggering along under the weight of the Cross, let us remember that if we would be followers of Him, as we pretend to be, we must, like Him, take up our cross: 'If any man would be My disciple, let him deny himself, take up his Cross, and follow Me.' Every one, whether he wills it or not, must bear the Cross during his mortal life. But it is not unto all men an instrument of salvation; for they do not fulfil the conditions which make its burthen light, sweet, and meritorious; they will not deny themselves, they will not follow Christ. The Cross nevertheless is upon their shoulders—a crushing and hateful burthen, from which they try by every expedient to rid themselves. They murmur against it; they cast it off; but in one shape or in another it meets them again, and galls their unwilling shoulders.

Since the Cross, then, cannot be avoided, it is only common-sense, on our part, to try to turn it to advantage, and to make a virtue of that which is a necessity. How are we to do this? By willingly accepting our Cross; for, by so doing, we shall be denying ourselves, and treading in the path which Jesus trod before us. In your life at College, there passes not a day in which you do not meet with your Cross, and find occasion to deny yourself, and to follow in the footsteps of your Lord.

It comes to you from external causes, as well as from your own self, and from your spiritual enemies. It is, for instance, a grievous Cross to you to rise from your bed in the morning, in obedience to the call of duty. It is hard to be tied down to your books, to be obliged to keep silence, and to limit yourself to the bounds marked out for you by Rule. It is difficult to be striving at all times to accommodate yourself to the imperfect characters of those with whom you have to live. Many of them, it may be, are sources of annoyance unto you, and if there are not many, there is sure to be at least one from whom you have much to endure. To use a common expression, he is a thorn in your side, and a daily source of suffering. Your Superiors, your equals, your inferiors, all in their turn, may add to the burthen which you are obliged to bear.

If you fight against your Cross, it will but gall you the more. Bear it, then, patiently, for God's sake. Do not try to cast it from you, for then another, and very likely a heavier one, will fall to your lot. Therefore, in imitation of Our Lord, bear that one which is laid upon you; it will furnish you with many occasions of daily and hourly denying yourself, and of treading in His footsteps.

III. Furthermore, do not forget that even though all external sources of annoyance were actually removed, you would nevertheless be a heavy Cross to yourself. As a matter of fact, what is it that most frequently makes a boy's life burthensome to him? Sometimes it is his own ill-humour, which, causing him to be disagreeable to his companions, draws down upon him their well-merited resentment; or it is his critical spirit, which makes him find fault with everybody and with everything around him, till others, in self-defence, pick out his faults and defects, and parade them before the public gaze.

Is he not frequently for days, it may be for weeks, made quite unhappy through fits of childish jealousy at the success of a rival? If he would only frankly acknowledge his inferiority, he might be as light-hearted and as gay as are the most successful of his schoolfellows. What greater source of misery can there be to a boy than is that ridiculous vanity, which makes him so sensitive to some slight check, or fancied wrong, or the thoughtless rudeness of his companions?

Again, supposing for a moment that, being free from these defects, he is also screened from the misery which they draw after them, yet even so, he cannot escape the Cross. For if he be striving to become holy and virtuous, he will have to suffer unceasingly from the assaults of the devil. True, it is a glorious warfare, and the satisfaction of victory amply repays us for the trouble and the anxiety engendered by the conflict; nevertheless, the persistency of the persecution, and the harassing nature of the devil's temptations are so great, that it is of all other Crosses perhaps the most difficult to bear.

Therefore, fix your eyes well upon Jesus, as He totters along under the weight of His heavy Cross. That spectacle will give you courage to bear your own. It will give you strength to carry it in the footsteps of Our Lord; and should you ever grow weary, and be well-nigh fainting under your burthen, you have but to look at Jesus, and you will persevere. Say to yourself: 'Can I not bear this light and easy weight for the love of Him, Who from beneath the crushing weight of the Cross, looks at me with weary eyes, and asks me to keep Him company?' Surely, after all that He has suffered for you, you will not refuse Him this little consolation. Courage therefore! If you wish to be His children you must deny yourselves, take up your cross, and follow in His footsteps.

INCIDENTS ON THE WAY TO CALVARY.

I. ON the way to Calvary three incidents befell Our Lord, from which we may gather profitable instruction. Two of them are mentioned in the Gospel; for the third we have no other authority than that pious tradition for which St. John's Gospel furnishes sufficient grounds. The first of these incidents is that which the Sacred Text records about certain pious women of Jerusalem. St. Luke tells us that as Our Lord toiled up the steep way leading to the place of His death, His face all disfigured by blows, defiled by spittings, and stained by blood, some holy women who looked upon Him and saw His pitiable condition, burst into tears and bewailed His misery. Jesus turning to them said: 'Daughters of Jerusalem, weep not over Me, but weep for yourselves and for your children.'

The second relates to Simon of Cyrene, who happened to

be coming into the city from the country, as the *cortège* which led Our Lord to execution passed through the gates. Jesus had probably stumbled under His heavy burthen and fallen to the earth, and His executioners, fearing lest He should die before reaching the appointed spot, seized upon Simon, and compelled him to carry the instrument of torture after Our Lord.

The third is that tradition which tells us that the Mother of Jesus, led and protected by the beloved disciple, stood by the roadside to catch a glimpse of her Only One as He went to His death. This is, to say the least of it, very probable, since she must have trodden that way of sorrows, to stand, as she did, by His Cross of shamê. We are told, then, that as Jesus staggered along under the crushing load of His painful burthen, and drew nigh to the place where His Mother awaited Him, He raised His weary head and looked into her face. Their eyes met, and the sword of sorrow, foretold by Simeon, entered her soul. There, before her eyes, her Child and her God slowly and painfully laboured onwards to the place where He must die! He had ever been so loving, so obedient, so gentle to her; and now she saw Him disgraced, reviled, and insulted. She heard the bitter taunt of priest and of Scribe; she saw the savage blows, and the merciless soldiers goading onwards the unresisting Victim.

As Jesus looked into her white, agonised face, and saw the speechless woe stamped upon her features, He trembled in every limb, His little remaining strength forsook Him, and He fell crashing to the earth. Who can doubt but that the Mother in an instant flew to the side of her Son, and imprinted upon His brow her parting kiss? No priest, nor Scribe, nor soldier, hardened and brutal as he might be, would dare to arrest, or to lay a hand upon her in that last act of maternal affection.

II. From each of these incidents we may learn a useful lesson; for we may take it for granted that they were allowed to happen for our instruction. The words of Our Lord to the holy women, teach us that the grief excited by the contemplation of Christ's sufferings must not be a grief of mere sentiment, a grief which might be produced by the perusal of some pathetic story. If it be of that nature, it will be fruitless. Our sorrow must be made to spring from grief at the cause of His sufferings. It must be a sorrow for our sins, and for our unmortified passions. 'Weep,' He says to us, 'for yourselves and for your children—for those passions which are the offspring of your will, and of your self-love.' To shed tears over Our Lord, for any other motive than this, is to indulge a morbid sensibility which is tickled and gratified by contemplating the moving spectacle of human woe. Solid piety is rarely generated by it. It is for the most part a mere matter of nerves, and does not affect the will so as to move it to action.

Of Simon of Cyrene we are told that he made a virtue of necessity, and willingly carried Our Lord's Cross, so that he thereby changed what would have been a disgraceful imposition, into a source of merit and salvation. In the last lecture, we said enough upon this subject to induce you to turn to account the various Crosses which must of necessity fall to your lot. But we may add here, that the example of Simon will furnish you with one reason the more, for patiently enduring the little trials and contradictions which are thrown in your way. By so doing you will, like him, be made to share in the suffering and the shame of your Redeemer. You will be bearing the Cross with your Lord, and atoning for your sins. Think of this when you are refused some favour for which you ask. Bear it in mind when you feel inclined to pursue some branch of study which is out of place at the time. Remember it especially when the burthen of daily routine presses heavily upon you, and seems to be wearing you away, like galling manacles upon the wrists of a prisoner. Look up; Jesus is before you—faint, weary, panting with exhaustion. Take up your burthen cheerfully—it is the Cross that you are helping your Saviour to carry.

III. From our holy Mother, we may learn never to be ashamed of Our dearest Lord. At the moment when her eyes met His, the priests had succeeded in branding Him as a public malefactor. They had said to the people: 'He is not a prophet; he is not even a just man; he is not the expected deliverer. We have unmasked him, and found him to be nothing more than a clever cheat, whose imposture and cunning failed to serve him, just at the very moment when he hoped to carry away with him the minds and the hearts of all.' Men pointed at our Lady as the Mother of this notorious criminal whom the Roman Governor had condemned to death. They looked upon it as a disgrace to have known Him, or to have been in His company. What must it have been in their eyes to be His Mother?

But that spotless, loving Mother acknowledged Him in the presence of them all. She followed in His footsteps. She stood faithfully by Him to the very end. Learn, therefore, from her, never before men to be ashamed of Jesus, that He may never have cause, before the face of heaven and earth, to disown you, upon the great accounting day.

You will find occasions for exercising this sort of fidelity to Our Lord, even within the precincts of your College. For sometimes, through a want of moral courage, boys are led to assent to, or to connive at, what is wrong. When, for instance, either their neighbour is spoken ill of in their presence, or their masters are ridiculed and detracted, they foolishly laugh with the crowd, not being bold enough to stand up resolutely, and openly to take God's side. They violate Rule, through fear of being thought cowardly; and alas! sometimes also, they countenance unbecoming conversation, through dread of giving offence. What is this but to be ashamed of Our Lord? What is it but a prelude to that still more culpable denial of Him which they will make later on before the giddy and unbelieving world? What is it but that shame of the faith, and that indifference to high principles, which are the ruin of the young men of the present day?

Therefore, always endeavour, even in the smallest matters, to stand up courageously for the right. Disregard the tittering and the sneering of the moral cowards who cover their want of manhood by a foolish laugh. Never do wrong to please some so-called friend. He is unworthy of that honoured name, if he strives to turn you from the path of duty, which your conscience bids you follow. Therefore, go not into his company, for if you do, he will speedily make you like himself. But if, carefully shunning all those who make light of God's law, you boldly, on all occasions, declare yourself for it, you will soon fear no one but God; and as a reward for your fidelity, that good God will, before the whole world, acknowledge you as His son.

CIRCUMSTANCES OF THE CRUCIFIXION.

I. BEFORE we contemplate the last cruel act of this sorrowful drama, we must reflect upon a few of the circumstances which accompanied it. These will be brought out clearly before us, if with St. Thomas we ask: Why did the Jews crucify Our Lord upon Calvary? why did they choose the mid-day hour? and why, of all other times in the year, did they commit that crowning sin upon the greatest of their solemnities? In each of these circumstances there is a mystical reason, which we must try to understand, and turn to our spiritual profit.

The first thing that strikes us in these various adjuncts of Our Lord's death, is that they served to make it more ignominious. Calvary, in His days, lay beyond the walls, a conspicuous spot, visible from every part of the city. Hence, when the executioners lifted Christ up upon the Cross, He became an object upon which every eye might gaze. Being, moreover, the place where criminals suffered the extreme penalty of the law, all who saw Our Lord hanging there would conclude that He was some notorious malefactor, who had been guilty of a great crime, for which outraged justice had let loose upon Him her direst wrath.

Furthermore, they crucified Him at mid-day, God having thus ordained it, to give us to understand that as the sun then reaches his meridian height, and shines with greatest splendour, so did Christ's love for us burn with its most intense ardour, when the sins of a wicked world were putting Him to death.

Lastly, they crucified Him upon the greatest festival of the year, when, in memory of their deliverance from Egypt, they were immolating the Paschal Lamb, in order that a greater multitude might be witness of His ignominy; but God willed it so, in order that Our Lord's followers might see that now the real Paschal Lamb, the Lamb of God, had sacrificed Himself, to free mankind from the slavery of sin, and to throw open unto them the gates of the kingdom of heaven. Thus, the very means employed by His enemies, to cover Him with ignominy, served only to bring out into clearer light, His humility, patience, and undying charity for us all.

II. After dwelling upon the reasons which lie hidden under these circumstances of Our Lord's death, we have next to try to learn from them the lessons which He intended them to convey. Do we, like Him, seek for public humiliation? Alas! we are very far from these holy dispositions. In fact, we are so far from seeking humiliation, that we are ever on the watch to obtain honour. We like to make a figure before the eyes of our little world—to be talked of, to be admired, and to be eagerly sought after. If we dare not, like Our blessed Lord, seek for occasions of humbling ourselves, we ought at least to shun publicity, and to be content to live a hidden life at College, by not wishing to be the leading spirit, the prominent character among our fellows.

Again; in imitation of that fervent love with which the heart of Jesus ever burned for us, we must try to lead a life of fervour in His service. Let us not imagine that this means being always in a state of spiritual sweetness, and never feeling any difficulty in accomplishing our duty to God. This is a false notion of fervour. For, though these delightful consequences often enough flow from it, they do not constitute its essence, but are rather its accidents. Fervour is nothing more than the exact fulfilment of our duties both to God and to our neighbour. The fervent boy does not omit these duties when they cease to be pleasing, nor sluggishly perform them when they have lost their novelty. In one word, fervour is a steady, equable, persevering, common-sense service of God. It is founded upon this simple truth, that God being always the same, our service of Him ought consequently, at all times and in all circumstances, to be the same.

Strive, therefore, to pay to Him this debt of fervent service, not only on great feasts, and on days of Holy Communion, but at all times. Give this to Him in the dark, dull, and dreary days of study and of labour, as well as in the bright, joyous holiday-time, when the genial sunshine and the anticipation of coming pleasure gladden the heart, and make it susceptible of pious emotions. But piety which has not a more solid foundation than this, is not lasting. It passes away with that which gives it birth. In imitation, therefore, of God's abiding love for us, let us endeavour to pay to Him every day of our lives the service of duty conscientiously performed, no matter at what sacrifice to personal feeling or to personal convenience.

III. Lastly, out of gratitude to Our dearest Lord, for having offered Himself in sacrifice for us, let us nerve ourselves to make every day some little sacrifice of our self-will, and of our personal convenience. To a good and piously-disposed boy, opportunities for so doing are never wanting at College.

The obedience due to college rule and discipline, calls upon him each day and each hour to sacrifice his self-will and his convenience. If he gladly endure the restraint which this imposes upon him, remembering the goodness of Him Who came to teach us obedience and submission, he will frequently, each day, offer up a sacrifice of self to God.

In his intercourse with his fellow-students he will also meet with much to try his temper, and to humble his pride. On these occasions let him not retaliate, nor strive by brute force to win for himself a very precarious peace. This frame of mind would soon beget in him a temper which would brook no contradiction, and unfit him to deal, in after-life, with the men among whom his lot may be cast.

Let him always put himself in the lowest place, and try to treat others as he himself would wish to be treated. Then there will not pass a single day upon which he will not feel the keen knife of self-sacrifice.

Let him patiently endure the hardships which most boys meet with at College—the cold of winter, the heat of summer, rough fare, early rising, and close application to difficult and distasteful studies.

Let him unite these to the sacrifice which, during His mortal life, Christ made of all that could please flesh and blood. By doing these things he will learn that lesson of self-denial without which a spiritual life is impossible, and he will make his college life resemble that which Jesus led for his sake in this world—a life of humility, of fervour, and of continual self-denial.

THE CRUCIFIXION.

I. JESUS at last reached the spot where the law appointed that He should suffer the worst punishment that His enemies could inflict. In order to degrade Him in the eyes of His nation, they caused Him to be led thither in company with two malefactors, who were about to receive the just reward of their crimes. By this piece of malignity, however, they unwittingly fulfilled the prophecy of Isaias, who said of Our Lord: 'He was reputed with the wicked.'

As He stood upon Calvary, meekly awaiting the completion of the arrangements for His death, the executioners offered to Him, according to custom, a draught of wine mingled with myrrh. This they gave to criminals who were about to die, for the purpose of deadening their senses to the agony of their torments. Our Lord just put His lips to the cup that He might taste of its bitterness, and then refused the draught, that He might be able to drain the chalice of suffering to the very dregs.

They then stripped Him of His garments. This inflicted upon Him a two-fold torture—one of physical pain, by reopening once more all the wounds which He had received in His cruel scourging; the other of moral pain, by exposing Him naked to the gaze of the multitude.

Being thus made ready for the sacrifice, they threw Him down upon the wood of the Cross, and the revolting scene of His crucifixion began. Fixing a huge nail upon the palm of His hand, they drove it home by the blows of a hammer, through the quivering flesh and muscles, into the wood of the transverse beam. Then seizing the other arm, which had shrunk up in the agony of this cruel torture, they stretched and pulled it till the hand reached the spot marked out in the wood for the nail. Again the blows were struck, and again the nail was driven into the wood of the Cross. The sacred feet of the unresisting Victim were then drawn down and fastened to the place marked for them. How fearful must that spectacle have been! We cannot look upon even a trivial surgical operation; how should we have been able to stand by while Jesus suffered this terrible agony for us? There He lay, silent and uncomplaining, crushed beneath the weight of the world's iniquity. After a few moments the soldiers came, and, raising the Cross aloft, carried it to the hole which had been made in the ground to receive it. There they firmly secured it, and the disfigured, scourge-torn, bleeding form of Our Lord appeared high above the heads of all, a spectacle unto Angels and unto men.

II. Look at your Lord and Master as He hangs upon the Cross, and learn from Him a lesson of patience and resignation. No word of repining, no murmur, no complaint will ever break from the lips of him who fixes his eyes upon that torn and bleeding Victim. It matters not how sorely he may be tried, by anguish of mind or by pain of body, his sum of woe cannot even be compared with that ocean of sorrow which deluged the heart of Jesus. 'Oh! all ye that pass by the way, attend and see if there be sorrow like unto My sorrow.'

You may be tempted severely by the devil; he may give you no rest by day or by night, but fill your mind with foul images, whisper filthy suggestions into your ears, and affright you with his illusions. This is a sore trial, but it cannot equal the Cross.

Your heart may be oppressed with despondency; your spirit may faint within you, and all hope seemingly die out of your soul; yet dark and God-forsaken as your life may be, it cannot equal the gloom and the abandonment of the Cross.

Even when all that you undertake fails miserably, and a blight falls upon plans which ought to have succeeded—yet reflect that your life cannot possibly seem to be a greater failure than the life of Our Lord appeared to be when it closed amid the horrors of a public execution.

If corporal infirmities should attack your mortal frame, and fill it with searching pains, look at the Cross, and you will endure them all with patience.

In the loss of all that is dear to you—when parents are called away, or property is lost, or friends prove unfaithful, look at the Cross; Jesus is there, stripped of all that He possessed; deprived of His good name; abandoned by His disciples; without a spot on which to rest His dying head, or a friendly hand to wipe away the gathering sweat of death. There is no one nigh to Him but His loving Mother, whose presence does not assuage, but rather augments His pain; and as for the few friends who with her have not feared to stand by the Cross, their grief serves only to cut Him to the heart.

Verily, then, does Jesus hang before us as the man of sorrows. Looking upon Him, the most afflicted of the sons of men may find consolation in the midst of the direst misfortune. He can point to Him and say: ' There is no sorrow like unto His sorrow. It is great as the sea. Who shall heal it?'

III. We must not, however, contemplate Jesus hanging on the Cross, merely for the purpose of making our own misfortunes tolerable. We must meditate upon His sufferings, in order to obtain from Him, through their merits, that courage which will enable us to support the ills of life with that holy resignation which He displayed in the midst of His bitter Passion.

In times of temptation, when our wearied and harassed souls begin to sigh for rest, and to think that perhaps it would be better to yield, than to go on enduring this merciless persecution, the sight of Jesus hanging on the Cross will inspire us with a willingness to suffer that which, after all, is a mere nothing compared with the misery of sin. It will tell us to be brave and generous, and not to fling down our arms under the very eyes of our Captain, Who has stood the brunt of the fight, and broken for us the might of our adversary's arm.

In times of dejection it will bid us hope on, and wait confidently for the moment when God shall again visit us. Did not the dark pall of disgrace and of death hang gloomily enough over the crucified form of Our Lord on Calvary? Yet there lay in store for Him the glorious day of His resurrection. So will it be with us also. We are now in darkness and in sorrow, but let us wait patiently for the Lord, and He will give us the desires of our hearts.

If our projects always fail, even so, we must not lose courage. The recollection of Our Lord's perseverance in a career, which to the eyes of men seemed to be an utter failure, ought to enable us to go on hopefully and perseveringly, till we win our crown.

In sickness and in pain, a glance at the Cross will remind us that for our sins God struck His only Son; and we shall be comforted and strengthened to bear patiently with our malady, by the thought that we are making some little atonement for our transgressions, and helping Our Lord to carry their heavy weight.

Should death take away those who are dear to us, or should false friends desert us in the days when fortune smiles not upon us, still, when we look at the Cross, we feel assured that there is One at least, Who will stand by us to the last, to soothe and comfort us, because we have ever turned to Him, to learn patience in our sorrows and trials, and have made them tolerable by seeing that none of them can be compared with His.

JESUS HANGING ON THE CROSS.

1. IF we may judge of the temper of the Jewish crowd which gathered to witness Our Lord's death, from that of the rabble which a few years ago used to assemble round the gallows upon the day of a public execution, we should give them credit for at least some few sparks of humanity. For no matter how great might be the public indignation against a felon's crime, the mob which came to witness his death-agony rarely reviled him at the supreme moment.

It was not so in the case of Our Lord. While He hung upon the Cross, they passed in front of Him and blasphemed Him. They wagged their heads, shot out their tongues, and pointing the finger of scorn at Him, said: 'Vah! thou who destroyest the Temple of God, and in three days dost build it up again, save thyself! If thou be the Son of God, come down from the Cross.' The soldiers who stood by to keep order, joined with the people in jeering at Him and taunting Him. Nay, even the two robbers, who were suffering the same punishment, outraged Him by their words, though, as we shall see later on, one of them, being converted by the patience of Our Lord, afterwards repented, and publicly atoned for the sin which he had committed against Him.

Some one may say: 'It need not be matter of wonder that those who attend public executions should show themselves brutalised to the last degree, and should be capable of gloating over and of insulting the dying, in their last hour of shame and pain.' But this excuse has no force when we reflect that those who uttered these revolting taunts against Our Lord were not merely the dregs of society—the scum and sweepings of a great city. They were the polished, well-educated men of Jerusalem. For listen to the words of St. Matthew: 'In like manner, the chief priests and the Scribes and the Ancients, mocking Him, said: "He saved others, himself he cannot save. If he be the King of Israel, let him now come down from the Cross, and we will believe him. He trusted in God; let Him deliver him, if He will have him; for he said, I am the Son of God."'

What a spectacle is this! Men who ought to have learnt how to control their passions, men in whom we should have thought that the fire of hate had been slackened by the snows of age, so far forgot both themselves and the sanctity of their office, as to mingle with a crowd of ruffians, in cursing and reviling their now helpless enemy. They put the word of scorn, the bitter taunt, the cutting gibe, into the mouths of those who had not wit enough to frame them for themselves, and so led the chorus of hate and malignity which struck upon the ears of Christ dying upon the Cross.

II. How deeply must these insults have wounded the heart of Our Lord! The priests and the Ancients jeered at Him for four things, in which He took the greatest glory. In the first place, they derided His power. 'If He was, as He pretended to be, the Son of God, where was that omnipotence which must have been His, in consequence of His divine nature? He had not been able to frustrate the treacherous designs of a false disciple; nor to burst the feeble bonds which held His hands; nor to escape from His captors. He could not ward off the blows which were showered upon Him; nor avoid the sentence of death; nor loose Himself from the accursed tree. He saved others; Himself He could not save. Therefore all His miraculous works were nothing better than cunning impostures, contrived and executed by the aid of the devil.'

In the next place they sneered at His royalty: 'If he be the king of Israel, let him come down from the Cross. There he hangs, this so-called king! A king without subjects, crowned with thorns, with a reed for his sceptre, and a gibbet for his throne.' They forgot that He had said: 'My kingdom is not of this world'; that the day should come when they should see Him seated upon the throne of His majesty. Their shouts of rage had drowned all this. Yet He had spoken it. Heaven and earth shall pass away, but that word shall not pass away. Little as they recked of it, that moment kept swiftly advancing upon them, even while they stood there and made little of His royalty.

Furthermore, they dared to jeer at Him for even the confidence which He placed in God. ' Where,' they cried, ' is that boasted trust of his in the Lord ? If such a man as he ever had any trust in God, let God now give to us a proof of this much-vaunted reliance on Him. Let Him prove that this criminal is innocent, by coming to deliver him ; for, if he be the Son of God, God will surely claim His own.'

Finally, to crown all their profane and blasphemous injuries, they insult Him for having said : ' I am the Son of God.' At His trial they charged Him with blasphemy for having uttered these words, and shrieked out : ' He is worthy of death for daring to usurp that title.' Now they taunt Him with it. Jesus, upon His bed of pain, could dimly see them through the mist of blood and the shadows of death which were falling over His eyes. He could hear their laughter and their rude jests. He was dying to save them, and they were looking up at Him, jeering at Him, wagging their heads in bitter mockery, and gloating over Him in the agony of His death. All the time the red drops were falling one by one upon the earth. He generously gave all His blood to save them, but they would not have it. They trampled it under their feet in the dust.

III. Do not imagine that the mockers of Jesus have ceased to exist. The impiety of those who dared to insult Him in His death has been imitated, and is still imitated, at the present day. Some, like the Roman soldiers, deride Him by their unbelief; others, like the Jewish people, by their wicked lives ; and others again, like the priests and the Ancients, by turning the special gifts and favours which God has bestowed upon them, into so many instruments with which to offend Him. College boys, who give themselves up to sin, belong to this last and most guilty class ; for upon them God has showered His choicest blessings, and bestowed, both for the purpose of knowing and of serving Him, innumerable advantages which are denied to multitudes of others.

Take one rapid glance at the past and the present, and see whether you ought to count yourself among those who reviled and jeered at Our Lord! If the past has had upon its records many a dark account scored up against you, let us hope that tears of repentance have long since cancelled your debt. But look well to the present, and see whether you are not hurried away with the crowd, and mixed up with those who jeer at Christ. Beware, lest, like them, you come at last to scoff at your Saviour, by trampling under foot His holy law. If your past has been wicked, tremble lest the seeds of evil habits have been sown in your heart. It is against these that you must specially guard, if you wish not to be of the number of those who derided Our Lord.

Beware, therefore, of ever again giving yourself up to sin. Do not flatter yourself with the notion that when you grow older, you will be better able to master your passions. You will not be able to do so. For if you indulge them now, you will make them master you, and they will bind you in fetters which nothing but a miracle of grace will be able to break asunder. Now, in the days of your youth, root out of your soul all vices while yet they are feeble, and in your riper years you will be master of your own heart. But if you cherish them, and weakly yield to them, you are preparing for yourself a wicked manhood and a cynical old age—evils which are oftentimes the earthly punishments of a misspent youth. Pray God to avert from you so dire a fate, and beseech Him that by a virtuous college life, you may avoid being of the number of those who have made their souls a desert, scorched by the fiery heat of passion, and swept by all the storms that torment an undisciplined heart.

'FATHER, FORGIVE THEM, FOR THEY KNOW NOT WHAT THEY DO.'

I. No insult, nor sarcasm, nor taunt, however bitter, had been able thus far to exhaust the patience of Jesus, as He hung upon the Cross. He made no retort, He uttered not a syllable in answer to the outrageous conduct of the Jews. Their hour had come, the hour of darkness, and they might consequently both do and say to Him what they pleased. But yet, being mindful of us, He wished to teach us a lesson by word of mouth, as well as by example, and, therefore, from the Cross, uttered a few words which show us the sentiments animating His heart in that supreme moment, when the iron had entered His soul, and the waters of tribulation had well-nigh closed over His head.

They were not words of indignation, nor a cry for vengeance, like that which broke from the lips of Elias, and brought down fire from heaven to consume his enemies. He did not, like the prophet Eliseus, curse those who reviled Him. Being the Saviour, His heart overflowed with gentleness and mercy, which found expression in the first words that He uttered: 'Father, forgive them, for they know not what they do.' Forgetful of Himself, He thought only of His tormentors, whom He could dimly see passing before Him. He prays for them, and thus literally fulfils His own grand precept of charity. They had struck Him upon one cheek, and He had not averted the other. They were cursing and reviling Him, and He blessed them. They had stripped Him of everything that men hold dear, of property, of friends, of reputation; they were about to take away even His life, and He prayed God to shower upon them His choicest blessings.

What goodness, what magnanimity is here! In His deep humility He sets aside His Godhead, and says not, 'I forgive you'; but, speaking from the lowliness of His humanity, He says, 'Father, forgive them, for they know not what they do.' He screens them from guilt by attributing their sacrilegious acts, their blind hatred, their malignant and persistent persecution, to ignorance: 'They know not what they do.' Their blindness, it is true, is wilful. It had been brought on by the indulgence of their wicked passions. Their hatred is irrational. Their persecution is undeserved. But He remembers none of these things. He seizes upon the slightest shadow of excuse to palliate their guilt, and obtain mercy for them, that, their eyes being opened, they may see their wickedness, and blot it out with bitter tears of repentance.

II. This lesson of the sublimest charity is one which you can never learn too well. Therefore, listen attentively to it. Repeat it over and over again. Meditate upon it till it sinks down deeply into your heart, and becomes a part of your being—one of the motive principles of your life. For there are few virtues which you are called upon more frequently to practise, and there is perhaps none which it is more difficult to preserve and exercise to the full extent of the Gospel requirements.

In your every-day life at College, little differences are sure to occur between you and your companions. They become complicated, and the breach between you widens daily more and more. You think yourself injured by reports which are circulated concerning you, and you feel that your heart is full of vengeful thoughts against him who has set the malicious story afloat. It is a pity that these things should ever occur at all; but it must needs be that they should happen. For since no one is perfect, it is morally impossible that our mutual failings should not now and then come into collision. What, then, are you to do? Are you to stand upon your dignity? Are you to treat the offender with coldness, or to repay with interest the injury which he has done to you? If you pursue this line of conduct, you will never be at peace.

Look rather at Jesus upon the Cross. Mark well how grievous are the insults and the injuries heaped upon Him. Can your wrongs be compared with His? Has He not just cause to flash forth His lightnings, and smite those who so foully maltreat Him? Yes; but His heart is full of charity, for He is God, and 'God is charity.' Listen, therefore, to His words: 'Father, forgive them, for they know not what they do.'

How true is it, in the case of those who wrong you at School, 'that they know not what they do!' There is too much generosity in the boy-nature to do, out of pure malice, an injury unto any one. The evil which they do to one another is the result of the waywardness and the thoughtlessness of youth. If they reflected for a moment, they would not do to you what would cause you pain. Be generous, then, towards your school-fellows, for Our dear Lord's sake. Make no account of the slight offences which they commit against you, and looking at the figure of your crucified God, say with Him: 'They know not what they do.'

III. There are one or two other motives, which it will be well to suggest to you, since they are very efficacious means for moving the will to act in a forgiving spirit towards those who offend against you. In the first place, remember that your college companions do not, in the course of a whole year, commit against you one tithe of the offences which during a single day you commit against God. Just consider the matter for a moment.

What is it that you have most frequently to complain of in your companions? It is oftentimes nothing greater than some little act of coldness, or contempt, or indifference. A sharp word escapes them, or they are rude, or sarcastic, or impolite towards you; they are disobliging, ill-tempered, and the like. But how do you treat God, your Lord and Master? When you approach to speak to Him in prayer, you are indifferent, cold, and irreverent. Would you dare to behave to one of your masters, when you go to speak to him, as you do to God? Do you not sin against Him by anger, and disobedience, and untruthfulness? Do you not in many other ways offend and grieve Him? What are your companions' faults against you, compared with your sins against God?

In the second place, you may take it for granted, that as you find some of your companions very troublesome and offensive to you, so there are doubtless others in the School who find you a very disagreeable person to live with. To them you are rough, unkind, morose, sharp-tongued, and altogether very unlovable in character.

As, then, you yourself are full of faults, bear in mind that others also are not Angels. If, therefore, they have to put up with your imperfections, and to suffer from them, justice demands that you also should tolerate their shortcomings. Consequently you must resolve, after the example of Our Lord, to be ready and willing to forgive the little faults of which your schoolfellows are guilty towards you. Call to mind this resolution when you repeat that petition of the Lord's prayer: 'Forgive us our trespasses as we forgive them that trespass against us.' In this way ' you will bear one another's burthens,' and, in the words of the Apostle, ' you will thus fulfil the law of Christ.'

'THIS DAY SHALT THOU BE WITH ME IN PARADISE.'

I. To render the death of Our Lord more ignominious, there were crucified with Him two thieves, the one on His right hand, the other on His left. Their association with Him, while it satisfied the revenge of His fanatical enemies, also fulfilled the prophecy of Isaias, who said of Jesus: ' And with the wicked He was reputed.' For the sake of one of these men Our Lord opened His lips for the second time, and spoke from the Cross.

Three of the Evangelists record that, at first, both these malefactors reviled and insulted Jesus as He hung between them. Only St. John gives us the good tidings that one of them afterwards repented, and won for himself eternal life. He very probably owed his conversion to the patience with which he saw that Jesus suffered His cruel torments, and the magnanimity with which, forgetting Himself, He thought of and prayed for His persecutors.

It seems, then, from the narrative of the beloved disciple, that when the impenitent thief again took up the words of the mockers and blasphemers who stood around, taunting Our Lord with His inability to save Himself, the other turned upon his former associate and rebuked him for his impiety. ' Is it possible,' he said, ' that thou dost not fear God, seeing that thou art in the same condemnation ? We, indeed, suffer deservedly; for we receive the just penalty of our deeds; but this man hath done no evil.' Then, with all faith and humility, addressing himself to Jesus, he said: ' Lord, remember me when Thou shalt come into Thy kingdom.'

By these words he professed his belief in the divine nature of Jesus. Looking into his own heart, and seeing his guilt, he did not deem himself worthy to share in that heavenly kingdom, over which he believed that Christ should one day rule as Lord and Master. He feared not to say, in the presence of priest and of Pharisee, that they had unjustly condemned Jesus to death. He confessed Him openly before men; and Jesus, breaking the silence of His agony, openly acknowledged him as His son, and promised him a share in the glory and the happiness of His heavenly Father's court: ' This day,' said He to him, ' shalt thou be with Me in paradise.'

II. It is a terrible thing for us to reflect, that by the side of Jesus dying upon the Cross, and pouring out His blood for the salvation of men, there hung two human beings, one of whom was saved and the other lost. It is but natural that we should ask ourselves how this came to pass. For, looking at the matter from a rational point of view, we should expect that when the same cause is operating upon two men of a similar class, the same effect will be produced. Both ought, therefore, to have been responsive to the movement of divine grace and have been converted to God. Yet they were not; for though the same cause operated upon the souls of both, it did not work in both the same effect. How, then, are we to account for this, since we believe that God wills all men to be saved, and gives unto all, grace sufficient to accomplish that object?

We can account for it by this simple reason: one of these men put no obstacle in the way of grace, and the other did. One of them, as soon as he heard the whisperings of God's Holy Spirit in his heart, listened to them, and allowed them to sink down deeply into his soul, to stir up his better nature, and to turn it to God. The other did not do so. When that gentle voice first made itself heard, and bade him look at the evident signs of a divine nature which shone through the torn and bleeding figure hanging so near to him, he thrust back the thoughts which began to throng in upon him. He had heard, in a confused sort of way, of miracles, the like of which no prophet had ever wrought before; of blind men restored to sight; of the lame, to the free use of their limbs; of the loathsome leper, to complete soundness of flesh; of the very dead, to the life which they had lost. These things had been told to him of Jesus, Who now hung beside him upon the disgraceful Cross. He could see the derisive crown of thorns upon His head; His face becoming rigid at the approach of death; His body quivering with agony. The shouts of the crowd, cursing and blaspheming Him, reached his ears. He saw all this, and would not believe, but said to himself: 'This cannot be the Son of God.' Then, with that strange, irrational, and unaccountable rage, which not unfrequently takes possession of the wicked at the sight of the just, he opened his mouth to curse and to revile. He died impenitent, untouched by grace, within reach of its source, his very body stained, it may be, with the precious blood which Jesus shed for him in vain.

III. Can we assign a reason why this wretched man should have been so hardened? We can; and the thought of it ought to be a warning and a lesson to each of us. The probability is that he had been going on for a long course of years in the habit of oft-repeated sin, which banished from his heart all fear of God, and all shame of evil. In course of time, custom so deadened his moral sense that evil lost for him its hideous nature, and assumed the appearance of good. His soul being cased, as it were, in armour of proof, received no refreshing dew of divine grace, and his heart, consequently, became hard and barren as the unproductive rock. The blows of adverse fortune made no impression upon it, and the strokes of human justice might break, but could never soften it. Thus it came to pass that this hardened sinner did not accept the proffered pardon of Almighty God, though the source of grace poured out its crimson stream at his very side.

Here is a warning lesson for each of us. Say not: 'There is much time yet before me. Youth is the time to give a loose rein to the soul,' or, as the world has it, 'To sow one's wild oats.' This language is foolish and impious. The silly dupe of the devil thinks that, by sowing his wild oats, he is burying them like dead things which have in them no germ of life. But he is sowing seed which will produce a harvest such as the devil will eagerly gather into his barns. Sin added to sin induces a habit, and a sinful habit becomes a heavy chain which is not broken in a day. Nothing but long years of patient, unwearying effort can burst its links asunder.

Shall you have the strength and the courage to go on perseveringly in that effort? It is very doubtful; for you will have to keep at bay a whole troop of ferocious passions, which like wild beasts will cry savagely for their food of sin. Fettered with your heavy chain, weakened by self-indulgence, how shall you be able to hold them in check? How shall you, as you are obliged to do, strangle and destroy them? Either you must destroy them, or they will destroy you. Therefore now, while you are young, carefully guard yourself against contracting a habit of sin. Take upon yourself now, in your boyhood's happy years, the yoke of Jesus Christ. In your early manhood it will be an easy burthen to bear, and in your old age a crown of glory upon your head.

'WOMAN, BEHOLD THY SON; SON, BEHOLD THY MOTHER.'

I. 'THERE stood by the Cross of Jesus,' says the Evangelist, ' Mary, His Mother,' and close by her side that disciple whom Jesus loved. Both were looking up with streaming eyes into the face of the dying Saviour. They could dimly see it through the gathering darkness of the miraculous eclipse; and though the deepening obscurity concealed its increasing pallor from their view, they felt that the end could not now be far off.

Jesus, also, from His Cross looked down upon them. His failing eyes were fixed first upon His own dear Mother; and no doubt the memory of His childhood, and of the countless times He had nestled in her bosom, came back upon Him, flooding His soul with anguish unutterable. He thought of her standing there by His Cross of shame, watching the life-stream slowly ebbing away from His pale and disfigured body. He thought of the sword of sorrow which had pierced her heart; of her surpassing love for Him; of her unswerving fidelity; and compassion for her added one other ingredient of bitterness to the gall of His chalice. At last He opened His parched lips, and, with feeble voice, addressed her: 'Woman,' He said, 'behold thy son.' By these words He intimated that He willed her henceforth to be a mother to His beloved disciple, and to transfer to him all that wealth of earthly love which she had hitherto lavished upon Him as her Son. 'How great,' exclaims St. Bernard, 'is the exchange here made! She receives the disciple, instead of the Master; the servant, instead of the Lord; the son of Zebedee, instead of the Son of God.' In very truth, the iron had now entered her soul.

Then Jesus, slowly turning His dying eyes, and fixing one last parting look of love upon His young disciple, said to him: 'Son, behold thy Mother.' He gave to him the only earthly treasure dear to His heart. He gave him His own Mother, to be to him what she had been unto Himself. He gave the spotless Virgin to the pure and virginal Apostle. He committed the care of the Virgin to one who was himself a virgin, and by that same act He made us the children of His holy Mother; for St. John is generally looked upon, by the Fathers, as having represented, upon Calvary, all Christian people; and they argue, that by saying to Him: 'Son, behold thy Mother,' Jesus addressed Himself also to each of us.

II. Since, then, Jesus has willed that the ever-blessed Virgin should be the Mother of those whom He disdained not to call His brethren, it is our duty to learn what are the obligations which, by that bond of kindred, we have contracted towards her, and also what are the offices which she will perform for us, if we be faithful to our part of the contract. If she is our Mother, we owe to her love, honour, and obedience. Love is the first duty that she claims from us. Let us remember that, according to the interpretation of the Fathers, Mary is looked upon, in the economy of the redemption, as the second Eve, and is consequently Mother of all the faithful. The words of Jesus to her made her, in a spiritual sense, the Mother of those who should be born of His redeeming blood, and associated to His Church. As, therefore, we owe a debt of love to the mother who bore us —a debt which we must continue to pay till our last breath —so do we also owe a similar debt to our Mother Mary for her spiritual maternity.

From the love which we bear to her, there will spring up in our hearts a chivalrous sentiment, which will incite us to manifest our love by certain external marks of honour and veneration, to which her peerless dignity, as Mother of God, in every way entitles her. When we remember that the incarnate God took flesh of her; that she cherished Him in her arms; that He loved her as never son loved a mother; that He obeyed, that He honoured and respected her, we cannot adduce any authority either higher or more trustworthy to give its sanction to our honour and veneration.

If, then, we love and honour the Mother of God, we shall, like all dutiful children, be most *obedient* to her wishes. Her will is that all men should ever be obedient to the most holy law of God. By endeavouring to observe that law, we shall be rendering to our Mother's wishes an obedience which will please her beyond measure. Therefore let us strive to be pure in heart and in mind; to be humble in our thoughts and in our bearing towards others; to have charity with all, even with those who show none to us; and we shall thus be loving, honouring, and obeying her whom Christ gave to us to be our Mother.

III. After having learnt what our duties are towards the

Mother whom God, in His loving-kindness, has given us to watch over the growth and the development of our spiritual nature, we may, in the next place, ask what are the offices which we may expect from her in return for our obedience, veneration, and love.

If we do what she requires of us, we may look with confidence to her for an ever-constant, ever-faithful love. That love of hers for us will never vary, because as long as we observe the law of her Divine Son, we are in the state of grace. Now, the child who has that inestimable happiness, is conformed to the image of Jesus Christ. Hence the Blessed Virgin, seeing us made like to her beloved Son, will love us as His brothers, and as her children. She will be able to obey the injunction of her Son when He said: 'Behold thy son.' As, therefore, her love for Him never varied, it will never vary in our regard, so long as we preserve His image in our hearts.

But suppose it should happen that her earthly child should mar, by wilful sin, the beauty of God's image in his soul, does her love at once cease? No; for she remembers the sad plight of Jesus, when He bore upon Himself the iniquities of us all. She calls to mind the blows and the outrages, and she sees again the gentle look of His eyes when He lifted up His head to pray for His tormentors. Poor sinners! be not afraid! The heart which beats within Mary's bosom is most conformed to the heart of Jesus. If He so prodigally bestowed His love upon you, if He bore so patiently with you, she also will remember that unspeakable gentleness and forbearance, and will lift up her spotless hands before the throne of grace to pray for you; and as she faithfully followed Jesus during the last hours of His life —as she did not desert Him when He hung like a malefactor upon the Cross—so will she prove herself a faithful Mother to you. She will stand by you, to pray for you, and to defend you.

'MY GOD, MY GOD, WHY HAST THOU FORSAKEN ME?'

1. The shadow cast upon the circle of the dial marked the hour of mid-day, when the Jews filled up the measure of their iniquities by hanging Jesus aloft upon the Cross. His enemies had at last gained their wish, and were now rejoicing over Him in the agonies of His ignominious death. But the sun, shining in meridian splendour, hid its face when they had accomplished that awful deed, and a preternatural darkness settled down upon the world. This was not the result of a mere eclipse, for the paschal moon was at the full; but God had worked a stupendous miracle, by which He wished to show His horror at a deed of darkness, the like of which the world had never seen before. A deep fear, an indescribable awe, took possession of all hearts. Men groped about, unable to see whither they were going, and remorse for the share which they had had in crucifying this just Man, began to gnaw like a serpent at their hearts.

There, high above the heads of the hushed and awe-stricken multitude, hung the tortured frame of Our dying Saviour. It could be seen, gleaming white against the murky darkness of the sky; it hung motionless, save when the drooping head wearily moved from side to side, vainly seeking a little rest. At last He once more raised His voice, and its mournful accents were heard from out the darkness, saying: 'My God, My God, why hast *Thou* forsaken Me?' Only extreme anguish could have wrung this complaint from Him; and these words give us a glimpse of the utter desolation of His soul. Centuries before, by the mouth of His prophet, He had spoken of that sad hour, beseeching God to pity Him in the day of trial: 'Save Me, O God,' He had said, 'for the waters are come in, even unto My soul.'

His cry of agony proves to us, that the material wounds of His body did not pierce His soul with one tithe of the anguish with which the withdrawal of those heavenly consolations tortured Him, consolations from the enjoyment of which He had shut Himself off by a heroic act of His own will. Hence He became like one abandoned by God, to spiritual darkness and despair. His soul had no comfort. It had become like unto a land scorched by the fierce heat of a tropical sun.

II. There are two ways in which God forsakes the children of men. The first is when He withdraws Himself from them on account of their sins; the second, when He hides Himself from them, only for a time. In the latter case it is to try their virtue, or to punish their negligence, and so to take off their affections from what might prove very prejudicial to them. When anyone sins grievously, he is instantly abandoned by Him, and straightway becomes the abode of the devil. His soul is buried in the profoundest darkness, because the light which enlighteneth every man that cometh into the world has gone out of his heart. Hence he is no longer able to see the beauty of that virtue in which he used formerly to take so great delight. He begins to despise it, and to think that it is nothing more than a figment of the mind—a poetical fancy. He begins also to be blind to the hideous deformity of vice, and very soon is guilty of actions which would once have filled him with shame and horror. To the eyes which are thus darkened, vice assumes the livery of virtue, and is mistaken for it. It is received into the heart and cherished there as a friend.

Alas! how many a boy has thus been abandoned by God, and taken possession of by the devil! A wicked companion, it may be, makes him acquainted with sin. At first he recoils from it with horror, and then, perhaps through a miserable shame of being laughed at, grows bold in wickedness, and loses all fear of it. He casts God out of his heart. He becomes blind, and sees not whither he is stumbling. Therefore, O child of Jesus Christ! be watchful and given to prayer, lest so sad a fate should ever befall you! Flee from all evil companions, and never be ashamed to stand up boldly for God. Blush not to serve Jesus Christ. Speak out fearlessly for Him, and turn your back upon those who are so wicked as to laugh at you for your innocence.

By acting thus, you will encourage the weak to resist, and

to do as you have done. You will put to the blush those who would dare to laugh at piety and honour, and they will feel in their inmost soul that *they* are worthy of scorn, and *you* of praise and glory. Act thus, and you will always walk in light, for you are following Christ, and ' he that followeth Him, walketh not in darkness, saith the Lord.'

III. But the darkness which God sometimes allows to envelop His children, is far different from that which is the result and the punishment of sin. For, though they cannot see His face, through its thick and heavy pall, though they are made to feel all the anguish that men experience who have lost a great treasure, yet they are confident that He has not quite abandoned them. They are simply in the dark, and Jesus, though hidden from their view, is nigh to them all the while, just as upon Calvary He remained nigh to our Lady and to St. John, though concealed from their eyes by the miraculous darkness. This happens to all Christians, and oftentimes without any fault on their part. When this is the case, it is sent as a trial to purify them from hidden defects, and make them more perfect.

You who are at College will no doubt have had some slight experience of this. You will have felt the sweetness of God's actual presence in your soul, especially when you were doing your best to love Him, and to keep His holy law. Prayer then delighted your heart; you felt no difficulty in exercises of piety; Holy Communion filled you with ecstatic joy. But suddenly all this changed. Prayer became a torture. You knelt down, and straightway a whole crowd of idle thoughts about play or about study rushed in upon you, and you were surprised to find that the prayer had come to an end, and that you had not been with God. You arose from your knees abashed and dissatisfied. Your daily meditation became an impossibility. It cost you an effort to go to Communion, and that holy mystery lost all its savour for you. Doubts about your confessions filled your mind, and scruples arose, peopling the past with hideous phantoms of sin, the recollection of which seemed to have completely escaped your memory.

In addition to this, the devil perhaps assaulted you with many and grievous temptations. Hence you imagined that you were abandoned by God, that you were left in the midst of your enemies; and there arose to your lips that cry of anguish which broke from the lips of Our dying Lord: 'My God, why hast *Thou* forsaken Me?' But yet God stood nigh to you all the time. Should this trial again come upon you, first examine whether you have not perhaps deserved it by your careless conduct, and by the commission of a multitude of venial faults. If you discover this to be the case, humble yourself, renew your fervour, make generous efforts to be faithful to Jesus Christ, and, after a time, the darkness will be dispelled, and the brightness of God's countenance will once again shine upon you. But if you cannot see that there has been any fault on your part, look upon this privation of God's sensible presence, as a cross sent to try your courage; and remember that a good boy must love God for His own sake, and not for the sensible sweetness which is sometimes to be found in His service.

'I THIRST.'

I. In reading of the battles which are recorded in history, you cannot have failed to remark, that the pain of thirst is always mentioned as one of the greatest tortures of the wounded. What must the sufferings of Our Lord have been, after His many and so grievous wounds! No drink had passed His lips since the preceding night, when He had supped with the Apostles. Every circumstance that had happened to Him in the interval, served only to add fresh fuel to the raging thirst which consumed Him.

No sleep had closed His eyes during the preceding night. On the following day the Jews had wearied Him out with journeys from one tribunal to another; and had subjected Him to the most cruel treatment ever endured by man. His flesh had been rent and torn by scourges; His head tortured by a thorny crown; His hands and feet pierced by nails; His body well-nigh drained of its vital stream.

Consequently, the thirst engendered by all this suffering and loss of blood must have been intense. So notable did this feature in Christ's bitter Passion seem to the Royal Prophet, that he thought fit specially to mention it in the twenty-first Psalm: 'My tongue,' he says, 'hath cleaved to my jaws, and Thou hast brought me down into the dust of death.'

In order, therefore, to fulfil another prediction of this same Prophet: 'In my thirst they gave me vinegar to drink,' Our Lord once again lifted up His voice, and by saying, 'I thirst,' made known the anguish which He suffered. Hearing this, one of the soldiers ran to a vessel filled with vinegar, which lay near the Cross, and dipping a sponge into it, fastened it upon a stalk of hyssop, and raised it to the mouth of Jesus. Our Lord tasted the vinegar, but would not drink it. His Mother stood by, and saw this. She knew what torture her dying Son endured, but she could not give Him any relief. He cried for a little water to moisten His lips, and she could not procure it for Him. Gladly would she have forced her way through the dense crowd which covered the place of Calvary, and gone for water to allay His thirst; but she knew that Jesus did not wish for it. He spoke merely to let us know what He suffered, and probably would have refused the draught had it been raised to His lips.

II. Our Lord endured the torment of excessive thirst, and purposely made known the anguish which it caused Him, in order to give us courage to curb our thirst after three things, for which our corrupt nature is ever craving. We thirst to satisfy our own will; we thirst after honour; we thirst after pleasure. Christ, by making known the torment which He endured, brought about the fulfilment of His Father's will; for His words reminded the executioners that there remained yet one pain which He had not felt, and so caused it to be inflicted upon Him. Thus He denied His own will, and accomplished that of His Eternal Father.

How very different is our conduct! The aim of our life is in all things to do our own will. We rarely ask ourselves whether that which we wish to do is conformable to the holy will of God. Nay, we very frequently wish that God would make *His* will conformable to *ours*, and we sometimes do what we wish, even though we know it to be directly opposed to the law of God. This must not be. Jesus has given us a very different example; let us try to imitate it, by being obedient to the will of God. As this is made known to us by the commands which our Superiors impose upon us, let us do what they wish, whether it is pleasing to us or not; and then we shall be suffering like Our Lord; we shall be athirst to do something which we very much desire, and yet we shall deny our own will, in order to do His.

When, therefore, your Rule prescribes that you should employ your time upon a certain branch of study, be very exact in obeying its injunctions. Do not disobey rules which your Superiors have made, because these rules happen to be somewhat galling to you. If you feel inclined to be idle when your manifest duty is to work at your books, yield not to the thirst for ease; rouse up your indolent nature, and force it to do the will of your master, which in that particular instance is the will of God. Do not look upon disciplinary rules as mere restraints put upon your liberty, restraints which must be shaken off whenever an opportunity presents itself, but rather as indications of God's holy will, to be obeyed for His sake.

III. Again; there is in the heart of every one a thirst for honour. There is no boy that does not wish for distinction, in some way or other, and that does not erect for himself airy castles, in which he disports himself, vested in all the splendour of that particular kind of excellence after which he aspires. Of his own powers and abilities he has a certain estimate, upon which he builds the entire structure of his fancied greatness, whether it is that of a distinguished physician, or an acute lawyer, a stately bishop, or an able general. Of these things he dreams, and for them he thirsts with all the intense avidity of nascent ambition. But do not indulge in these day-dreams, for by not so doing you will mortify to a certain extent, your thirst after honour. Be awake and active; be up and doing! Study rather what is set before you; and in that study let your aim be, not to gain those honours to which you aspire, but to fit yourself to fill that position in life for which God destines you. If you act thus, He will give you that which will be most advantageous for you.

Finally, the devil will not fail to strew in your path the fascinating snares of sensual pleasures, and to kindle within your heart, if you listen to his solicitations, a raging thirst for them. But do not give ear to him. Listen to the advice of the prudent, and fix not your eyes upon his allurements. What he offers to you looks very tempting, and promises much happiness. But do you resolutely turn away from it. It is nothing more than a lying cheat. You will perhaps find it hard to do this, and you will feel the torture of a raging thirst which craves to be satisfied. Yet if you be wise, you will not satisfy it, and in due time God will give you to drink of the torrent of His heavenly delights. Even in this life you will taste a sweetness, and enjoy a tranquillity, compared with which the delirium of sensual pleasures is but as a sickly dream.

If you need courage to nerve you to despise the present delights of the senses, look up to the Cross. Behold how the lips of Jesus are parched with burning thirst. He endured that torment to teach you a little forbearance. Surely, you will not refuse to endure some little mortification for the sake of Him Who endured so much for you!

'IT IS CONSUMMATED.'

I. THAT last act of barbarity by which the Jews gave Our Lord vinegar and gall to drink, caused Him to speak once again. For, after tasting the bitterness of what they had offered to Him, He said: 'It is consummated.' These words, coming from the mouth of Our dying Redeemer, are full of a deep meaning, upon which we must meditate. From them we learn that before breathing His last, He cast back one rapid glance upon the life which He had spent upon earth. He called to mind the lowliness of His birth,

His life of poverty and toil, the wearisome journeyings of His missionary career, the contradictions and malignity of His enemies, and the torrent of woe unutterable of which He had so plentifully drunk during His bitter Passion. Looking into every circumstance of His earthly career, He could say: 'All that My Father hath ordained for Me to suffer, I have suffered. I have drained the chalice to its very dregs—" It is consummated."'

Considering the end for which He had come into the world, He could also say: 'It is accomplished.' He came to expiate the disobedience of Adam—He had done so; for He was obedient unto death, even to the death of the Cross. He came to crush the serpent's head, and to conquer death and hell. He came to open the gates of heaven, and to teach us the road thither, both by word and by example. By that example He established evangelical perfection upon a firm and solid basis, showing men in His own person how to despise the joys of earth, how to preserve the jewel of purity, even in vessels of clay, how to submit their stubborn will to the yoke of obedience. All this His Father had willed Him to do, and having accomplished it, He said with triumph: 'It is consummated.'

Finally, He saw that all the figures by which He had been typified had in His person received their fulfilment. Therefore, He announced all these things to the world by saying: 'It is consummated.' The night with its darkness was fast passing away; the dawn was at hand, when the Sun of justice, bursting through the clouds which had obscured His splendour, should triumph for ever over death and hell. Only those shall share in that triumph, and reign with Him in His glory, who shall be able to say of the task which God gave them to accomplish during their mortal life: 'It is consummated.'

II. For each of us also a moment will come, when, standing upon the confines of eternity, we shall cast a glance backwards over the course which we have run. As we look through that past, the diorama of our life will unfold itself to us, till every incident of our brief career shall have passed in review before our eyes. We shall see the enemies whom we encountered, and the persecutions with which they assailed us. Memory will give up the records of the contests which we have had with the powers of darkness, and will represent to us once more the many bitter struggles which we have undergone in the warfare of life. Our works, our plans, our schemes—the thoughts of our minds, the desires of our hearts, the evil and the good—all will start up again into life and appear before us. We shall look upon them all, and say: '*Consummatum est*—It is finished.'

Shall we utter these words with satisfaction and joy, or shall they escape our lips while we sicken with regret over what is past, and shudder at the dark future which is swiftly advancing, and which has already cast its shadows upon us?

If we have led evil lives—if in the pride of our strength we have said, each to himself: ' Young man, rejoice in thy youth! Give free course to the desires of thy heart. Refuse thine eyes, thine ears, thy hands, nothing that will gratify them '—alas! with what horror and despair shall we utter these words : '*Consummatum est*'—It is all ended now! Yet a few moments more, and all that earth and creatures can give will have passed away! What will it profit us then to have lived in the enjoyment of sinful pleasures? They have vanished like smoke, and have left behind naught save the burthen of guilt and the sting of remorse.

Do not wait until that last moment to think these thoughts and to say these words. Reflect upon them *now*, and repeat to yourselves the words with which they will inspire you. They will teach you that true happiness consists in waging an unceasing war against the unruly desires of the heart. They will make you resolve to set a guard before your eyes, to hedge round your ears with thorns, to put a bridle upon your tongue, and to answer all the foolish invitations of the world, the flesh, and the devil with these words of wisdom : ' What will it profit a man if he lose his soul ?'

III. Moreover, these words of Our Lord ought to suggest to you, that like Him, you have come into the world to finish a work which has been marked out for you by your heavenly Father. Ask yourself therefore now: 'Shall I, at the end of my life, be able to say of that work, "*Consummatum est!*"'—It is finished?

Put clearly before your mind now what that work is. God gave you life, and sent you into the world, to prepare yourself for an eternity of happiness; you are to show yourself worthy of so high a destiny, by fidelity to God's holy law, during the short span of your mortal life. Have you kept this end of your existence before your eyes? Have you thus far, even so much as realised, and brought home to yourself, what is the meaning or purport of your existence? Alas! there are very many who do so for the first time, when a voice is heard in the night crying: 'Behold the Bridegroom cometh; go ye forth to meet Him.' Conscience then wakes up and cries in their terrified ears: 'You have a soul to save. This is the end of your being. All other pursuits are unimportant and secondary.'

You have reversed the order, and, putting out of sight the only object for which God created you, have pursued with avidity unimportant trifles. Now the end has come: '*Consummatum est!*' The night has closed around you; you cannot work. God clearly pointed out to you the means by which you might easily have accomplished the task imposed upon you. You had to mortify yourself; to tame your flesh; to subdue your pride; to bend your stubborn will. The accomplishment of these things was that Cross, which He commands all His disciples to take up, and to bear after Him. But what have you done? You have shunned everything that could either pain or thwart you. You have indulged your imperious passions. You have been proud, disobedient, selfish, and greedy of pleasure. You have angrily cast from your shoulders the Cross which God put upon them. You have turned aside from the path traced out by His footsteps, and have followed the guidance of corrupt nature. God grant that you may not have to listen to these reproaches in that terrible moment, when your lamp of life is feebly flickering, and the dark curtain is about to lift from before your eyes, and to throw open to your gaze the boundless ocean of eternity.

May each of us be able to look back then upon a life well spent, a race bravely run, and a work entirely and faithfully accomplished.

'FATHER, INTO THY HANDS I COMMEND MY SPIRIT.'

I. JESUS would not consent to die until He had fully accomplished the work appointed for Him by His heavenly Father. That being done, His day of life had ended. The moment had come when He must yield His spotless soul to God. Gathering up, by a supreme effort, all His remaining strength, He cried with a loud voice, 'Father, into Thy hands I commend My Spirit, and bowing down His head, He gave up the ghost.' Men had done their worst; they could now injure Him no more. While, therefore, His lifeless body hangs before us, gleaming white amid the darkness, let us ponder upon the significance of these His last words.

We also shall one day have to look into the face of Death, that king of terrors; but shall we be able at that moment to turn to God, and say as Jesus did, 'Father, into Thy hands I commend my spirit'? These words can come with truth only from the lips of those who have looked upon God as their Father, and proved their love for Him by obeying His holy law. But they will be sadly out of place in the mouths of those who have practically regarded Him as a hard taskmaster, and treated His commands with contempt, unless, indeed, God touch their hearts with sorrow, and so cause them to utter these words from the depths of a contrite spirit.

To those, however, who will not repent, God does not show Himself as a loving Father, eager to welcome them to His heavenly home, but rather as a severe and angry master, who is about to exact from them a rigorous account of all that they have done. Learn, therefore, from these words of Christ, whither you are to direct, during your mortal life, all the energies of that soul which He has intrusted to your care.

God is your Father, and your last end. In Him, therefore, put your trust. During your life, seek for rest and happiness in Him, and at the hour of death you will find Him a refuge, a consolation, and a reward exceeding great. Remember, also, that only your soul is worthy of the greatest care. See what a lesson Our Lord gives you in this respect. He does not commit His sacred body to His Father's care, nor His reputation, nor His honour. He gave up all these to His enemies, as of little worth compared with His soul. Hence impress deeply upon your mind that saying of Our Lord's, 'One thing is necessary,' and that is, to save your soul. 'What doth it profit a man if he gain the whole world, and lose his own soul?'

II. As all Our Lord's lessons were intended by Him to be eminently practical, it is our duty to turn to the best account those which He taught us with His last breath. The first of these is to regard God as Our Father; for if we can imprint this idea upon our hearts, its influence upon us will be productive of many virtues. As Our Father, there is due to Him from us a debt of love and of confidence, in return for that everlasting love with which He loved us. This love is not to be a mere sentimental emotion, but a love which will show itself in act by the faithful discharge of duty, and by the strict observance of God's commands, no matter at what cost to our poor fallen nature. A college-boy loves God as his Father when he applies himself steadily, hour after hour, to lessons which are difficult and distasteful, whereas, if he chose to shirk his duty, he might employ himself more pleasantly. Again, he loves God as his Father when he manfully endures some punishment which he might easily escape by basely telling a lie, but does not do so, because this would offend God. One act of this sort of love is worth a whole lifetime of mere sentiment. Sentiment promises much, but does very little. It is full of pious affections, but cannot bear a sharp word. It spends much time in prayer, but it does not urge him to study. Distrust all devotion of this kind. It is no sign of the love of God. It may exist in the soul, together with a will rebellious to God's commands, and a heart wide open to the inroads of His enemies.

To the love of God you must join confidence in Him, such as a dutiful boy puts in his father or in his dearest friend. To excite this in your heart, you have only to consider how good God is. You have been told that the love of a mother for her child is but a faint image of the love which God has for you, His dear child; that His heart is ever yearning for you; that His eyes are ever open to see your wants, His hands ever stretched forth to succour you. Now, as it is one of the greatest pleasures of those who love, to bestow gifts and favours upon those whom they love, so there is nothing that gives God greater pleasure than to shower His blessings upon those whom He loves. Therefore, have a great confidence and a boundless trust in Him. If your heart, at times, feels weary and faint with the struggle which a Christian must maintain against his enemies, do not despair—trust in God; He will uphold and defend you, and bring you safely through the fiery ordeal.

III. Besides loving God, and confiding in Him, you must aim at possessing Him in your heart. This is the work which God gave you to do, and by accomplishing it you will save your soul. Therefore, he who wishes to gain possession of God, must be determined to thrust aside whatever may come between him and the object at which he aims. The obstacles to the possession of God are your own self, or your companions, or the perishable goods of this world. These were never intended by God to be hindrances to your salvation. They were given to you by Him to be helps, and they cease to be helps only when you no longer use them as *means* to an end, but rather rest in them as the *end* itself.

Hence, just in the same way as that in which your studies were not meant to be the end of your existence, but only the means or instruments to train your mind, and fit you to take your position in the world, so also the various created objects upon which you so often fasten your affections were never meant by God to be the end or purpose for which you are in the world, but only the aids to assist you in winning the great prizes of life, which are God and a happy eternity.

Therefore, if you wish to obtain possession of God, you must make all things else subservient to this aim. If they start up before you, and stand in your way as obstacles, you must, without hesitation and without remorse, sweep them from your path. If you have not courage enough to make this paltry sacrifice, you will lose your soul. Surely that precious jewel for which Christ died is worth more than a little earth, than a vapour which appears for a while, than a momentary pleasure, which is gone like a lightning flash.

Therefore, let nothing be more precious to you than is your immortal soul. Be ready, for its sake, to sacrifice the love of father and of mother, the comforts of home, the ease of riches, nay, even life itself, rather than imperil its safety. Let not human respect, nor the love of some friend, ever lead you away from God. Keep ever in your mind those words with which every Catholic boy is so familiar: 'Whatsoever I lose, if I gain Thee, all is gained, and whatsoever I gain, if I lose Thee, all is lost.' Let your heart, then, for ever set up its rest in God, and it will undervalue all things else to gain the eternal reward. He who acts thus during the pilgrimage of his mortal life, will be able to look fearlessly into the face of death, and to say with confidence to God: 'Father, into Thy hands I commend my spirit.'

MIRACLES AT OUR LORD'S DEATH.

I. An event so extraordinary as the death of a God-Man, necessarily gave birth to portentous signs by which God intended to glorify His Son, to manifest His anger against those who had crucified Him, and to express, in a material way, the spiritual effects which were to flow from His death.

The first of these miraculous portents occurred in the Temple. Between the Sanctuary and the people, there hung a great veil to shut out the gaze of the vulgar from the Holy of Holies. At the very moment when Jesus upon the Cross, bowing His head, breathed forth His soul into the hands of His Father, an invisible hand rent this huge curtain in twain throughout its entire length. Caiaphas, to mark his pretended abhorrence of the blasphemy which he impiously fastened upon Our Lord, rent his garments in the sight of the people, and God now rends the veil of the Sanctuary, to manifest His abhorrence of the sacrilege which the confederates of that hypocritical priest had committed upon the person of the Lord's Anointed. Also, He worked this miracle to intimate to mankind that the gates of the sanctuary were unlocked by the blood of Jesus; that the law of fear had passed away; and that henceforth His people might with love and confidence approach their God.

The next miracle consisted of the quaking and shuddering of the earth, which seemed to tremble at the deed which had been done. In many places the rocks were split asunder, the graves yawned and gave up their dead, who glided about the dark streets, appeared in the Holy Place, and filled with terror the awe-stricken people.

Lastly, the Centurion, and some of the pagan soldiers who stood around guarding the place of execution, hearing the loud cry with which Jesus had given up the ghost, feeling the earth quivering beneath their feet, seeing the rocks splitting, and the weird figures of the sheeted dead flitting to and fro, struck their breasts with sorrow for the part which they had played in this iniquitous drama, and went away, openly confessing their belief in Him Whom they had crucified, and fearlessly proclaiming: 'He is, in very deed, the Son of the Most High God.'

II. If these were the effects produced in inanimate nature, and in the hearts of pagan soldiers, by the death of Jesus Christ, what, let us ask ourselves, ought to be the effects which the contemplation of that great sacrifice of love should produce in the hearts of Christian boys? These effects ought, in a spiritual sense, to be the exact counterpart of those which took place in the sight of the people of Jerusalem.

First of all, there is sometimes hanging before the eyes of boys, a veil which prevents them from seeing things in their true light, and from attaching to them that importance which they deserve. Hence, they often mistake shadow for substance, falsehood for truth, and consequently waste their energies in the pursuit of a phantom which always eludes their grasp. This veil, in their case, is nothing more than a spirit of carelessness, of slothful indifference, and not, as in the case of worldlings, a darkening of the intellect, sent by God in punishment of sin.

Boys frequently do not pray, or, if they pretend to do so, their very prayer becomes offensive to God. They do not attach sufficient importance to the duties of religion, and consequently do not receive the grace which is necessary to curb the uprisings of their nascent passions. Hence it is that they oftentimes plunge headlong into sin, and go on from bad to worse, till they become frightful examples of youthful depravity. If any boy wishes to avoid the spiritual darkness induced by these disorders, a darkness which will fill his youth with vices, and his mature age with a brood of savage passions, he must at once tear down this veil of careless indifference about the things of God.

He will be moved to do so, by careful meditation upon the Passion of Our Lord. It will convince him, by the example of Christ, that life is not given to him as a time in which to amuse himself, but to do a particular work marked out for him by God—that is, to save his soul. It will teach him that he must not, in this world, look for what is easy and pleasant, but prepare himself to do much that is hard and distasteful; to be humble, to be pure, to be true to God, faithful, and loyal; in a word, to be like those children of whom Jesus told His Apostles, that unless they resembled them in humility, purity, and simplicity, they should not enter the kingdom of heaven.

III. A second effect of meditation upon the Passion of Our Lord, will be somewhat analogous to that which His death produced upon inanimate nature. It will make the college-boy tremble and quake with fear, when he beholds, in the person of Christ, the awful severity with which God punishes sin, or rather, the shadow of sin; because Jesus did no sin, but simply took upon Himself the guilt of all our iniquities. Nevertheless, God struck Him with a severity which makes all who reflect upon it shudder with terror.

Let your heart, therefore, picture to itself, if it is able, the storm of wrath which will sweep down upon those who sin against God by thought, by speech, by desire, by act; who lead others into sin, and thus become well-springs of evil—the poisonous waters of which may never cease to flow till the day of doom. Do not turn away from this startling thought, for its influence is most salutary. Fear will burst asunder the hard rock of your heart. The deeds which you have done, and which, like dead men, are locked up and buried in its depths, will be cast out of their graves. They will stand up before you in all the horror with which they are invested. Then you will weep over them; you will be sorry for them; you will strike your breast with compunction, and determine that they shall never again be admitted into your heart.

This is that true sorrow which breaks the hardest heart, or rather softens it, and prepares it for the influence of divine grace—and this is the third effect of the contemplation of Our Lord's Passion. Let the memory of what He suffered for you never depart from your mind. Frequently call up before your imagination that blood-stained figure of Our Lord—bruised, broken, abandoned, despised; and, as you think of the darkness, the earthquake, and the risen dead—startled from their graves by the death of Life—strike your breast as the Centurion and the affrighted soldiers did, and, grieving over the share which you have had in His sufferings, resolve, once for all, to break with sin, and never again to incur its frightful guilt.

THE SIDE OF JESUS PIERCED BY A SPEAR.

I. THE Jews feared very much lest Pilate should leave the bodies of the three crucified men upon their respective crosses all the next day which, being the Sabbath, and the most solemn day of the great Paschal festival, would be desecrated by their presence. To prevent so great a profanation, they sent a deputation to the Governor, beseeching him to remove them as speedily as possible. Pilate immediately gave an order to this effect, and the soldiers proceeded at once to execute upon the crucified the extreme penalty of the law.

One of them grasping in his hand an iron bar, dealt each of the thieves a tremendous blow both above and below the joints of the arms and the legs, and then crushed out what little life yet remained in them, by one finishing blow upon the chest or the stomach. On coming to Jesus, he found that death had rendered any further punishment in His case superfluous. Deeming it, therefore, useless to treat Him in the same way as that in which he had treated the two thieves, he did not break His bones, but taking a lance, drove the point through His side into the sacred heart. Instantly there flowed out through the gaping wound a little blood and water—all that remained of moisture in His lacerated body, which had been trodden like grapes in the wine-press of the wrath of God. Jesus made no movement as the soldier inflicted upon Him this last outrage. The body hung there still and lifeless.

But though He had already passed far beyond the reach of pain, there stood beside the blood-stained Cross one whose heart felt most keenly the pang intended for Him. Then, in very deed, did that sword of sorrow spoken of by holy Simeon, transfix the virginal heart of Christ's afflicted Mother. The bright steel which pierced His flesh inflicted upon her soul a most cruel wound. Like her Divine Son, she could now say with truth: 'It is consummated. I have stood here and seen all the prophecies that related to my Son accomplished to the full. They wished to break His bones, and yet did not dare to do it; for it is written: "You shall not break a bone of Him." They have, indeed, in wanton cruelty opened wide His sacred heart; but in so doing they have but fulfilled another prophecy, which said: "They shall look upon Him Whom they have pierced." '

II. Let us now try to penetrate into some of the reasons for which God allowed this last outrage to be perpetrated upon His Son. One of these was doubtless to anticipate and refute an objection which would be urged against the Divinity of Our Lord. Some unbelievers have maintained that He did not really die upon the Cross, but only swooned away through loss of blood, and that careful treatment afterwards restored Him to life. They tried, in this clumsy way, to account for the resurrection, which Christ always appealed to, as a proof of His divine nature and mission. Their blasphemous assertion is, however, rendered not only untenable, but absolutely absurd, by the seemingly wanton cruelty of some nameless Roman legionary, whose lance pierced the side of Christ, penetrated into His heart, and drew forth that blood and water which make the fact of death indubitable.

But though this reason may serve to strengthen our faith, we will pass it over, to dwell more particularly upon another, which will appeal more directly to our hearts, and be more productive of spiritual advantage to our souls. Jesus wished to be stricken and punished, not only externally, but even in the very centre of life, in order that He might atone by the rending of His heart for all the evil that proceeds from the hearts of men. It is the heart, or the carnal nature of man, that is the source of the greater part of our errors and sins. By it the Sacred Scripture understands all those sensitive faculties which men gratify by the criminal indulgence of their flesh. From it, as from a well-spring, there issues forth that stream of iniquity, the fatal waters of which Christ referred to when He said to His Apostles: 'From the heart come forth evil thoughts, murders, adulteries, fornications, thefts, false testimonies, blasphemies'; in one word, all those things which defile the soul.

By suffering His heart to be opened, He caused to flow thence a healthful stream, of which we may drink, in order to purify that source of evil which we carry about within our own breasts. Go frequently to that well of life, in the Holy Sacrament of the Altar. Drink deeply of its saving waters, and they will fertilise your barren heart, and make it bring forth virtues which God will crown with glory in heaven.

III. Another reason urged Our Lord to allow this wound to be inflicted upon His side, and upon His sacred heart. He wished to give us one last proof of the boundless generosity of His love. When the soldier's spear had pierced His lifeless body, the Eternal Father could call upon us to look at Jesus nailed to that Cross, and tell Him whether He could do anything more to prove to us how much He loves us. There hung His only begotten Son, consubstantial with Him, eternal, almighty. He had given His body to the strikers, His cheeks to the pluckers. He had not turned away His sacred face from those who spat upon it. He had most plentifully given His blood, and, lest we should say that He had made any reserve of it, He willed that its very source should be drained. He had done all that God could do, to write upon the heart of man: 'I have loved thee with an everlasting love.'

All that He asks in return, is that we should love Him with our poor, weak, human hearts, and as a proof of that love, give our obedience to His holy Son. He does not ask much, and He gives us strength to do even the little that He *does* ask. He nerves us to encounter self-denial, by the sight of His crucified body; He gives us courage to face slight persecutions, by upholding us with His own strong right arm; and when we are hard pressed by our enemies, we shall ever find a sure refuge, a place of rest, in the wound of His sacred side. When sorrow wrings our heart, we can look upon Him and we shall see that our sorrow is not equal unto His. When the world turns against us, when men despise us, and treat us with harshness and injustice, we may look up with confidence to that white figure hanging upon the Cross. We can see the gaping wound of His side; there is our sanctuary; there our harbour of rest; for over it is written that loving invitation to all the downtrodden, weary wayfarers of earth: 'Come unto Me, all ye that are heavily burthened, and I will give you rest.'

THE BODY OF JESUS TAKEN DOWN FROM THE CROSS.

I. IF the laws usually observed in the execution of criminals had been carried out, the body of Jesus would have been left in the hands of the ministers of justice, and upon them would have devolved the task of committing it to the grave. But since He had now fully accomplished the end for which He had come into the world, the hour of darkness, during which the wicked were suffered to work their will upon Him, had passed away. Their hands could never again be laid upon Him. God, in His fatherly providence, had prepared for the burial of His Son two men, noble of birth, and upright of heart, who had loved and reverenced Jesus, but through timidity of character had up to this time done so only in secret. The spectacle of Our Lord's cruel torments, however, had upon them an effect similar to that which the descent of the Holy Spirit had upon the Apostles. It filled them with courage to face any danger, and nerved their hearts to make any sacrifice for Him, Who had given to them so noble an example of devoted love.

As soon, therefore, as they knew that Jesus had breathed forth His soul, one of them, named Joseph, a rich man of Arimathea, went boldly to the Governor and asked him for the body of Our Lord, that he might bury it with the honour due to One so holy, and held in so high repute by the great mass of the people. How keen a lash did this petition apply to the soul of the irresolute, time-serving Pilate! Here there came before him a man of spotless integrity and of high standing with his nation, asking for the body of Him Whom he had handed over to the blind fury of a fanatical mob. The contrast between Joseph's courage and his own vacillation and weak acquiescence in the wishes of the profane crowd, cut him to the heart. He did not refuse the petition, but ordered the body to be delivered up to Joseph's care.

Armed with this warrant, the loving disciple hastened to Calvary. There he found Nicodemus, who had brought with him precious unguents, balm, and sweet-smelling spices, with which to prepare the body of the Lord for burial. These two devoted men, assisted by the pious women, drew forth the nails from the hands and the feet; disengaged the thorny crown from the tangled hair; and then the sacred body was gently, tenderly, and by the hands of those who loved and reverenced Jesus, lowered from the Cross, and laid in the arms of His Mother. His head reposed in death upon that bosom which had been His first resting-place upon earth.

II. Let us now draw nigh to that broken-hearted Mother as she sits at the foot of the Cross, and look upon Him Whom God has stricken for our sins. There He lies without sense, without motion; His eyes are closed, His limbs are rigid, His flesh is gashed, torn, and rent with cruel wounds. There is now no beauty nor comeliness in Him. From the crown of His head to the sole of His foot there is no soundness. He is like a leper, and one stricken by God and afflicted. Truly He hath borne our infirmities and carried our sorrows, and because it hath pleased Him to take their guilt upon Himself, the Almighty hath exacted from Him the great debt of justice which we were unable to pay.

O children! so dear to Jesus Christ! look well at this piteous spectacle! Let the boy whose heart is proud, and whose head is full of vain thoughts, study attentively the picture which lies before him. There is Jesus, Who on account of our pride, bent down His own sacred head, that the billows of the world's scorn and contempt might roll their tumultuous waters over Him; that the lowest rabble might laugh at, and insult, and flout Him.

Let him who is revengeful—who resents the smallest

injury, and treasures up enmity in his mind, approach and look upon Jesus. Those upon whom He had heaped countless benefits have brought Him to this sad plight, and yet He prayed for and forgave them.

Above all, let him before whom the devil displays the allurements of the senses, and who feels tempted to swallow the glittering bait—let him look upon the dead body of Jesus. Where is the faculty of mind, where the power of sense that has not been strung to its utmost tension by torture, the keenest that could be devised by the mind of man? His head is all wounded by cruel thorns, to atone for our sinful thoughts; His eyes are blinded by blood, to expiate the wicked indulgence of our lascivious eyes; His ears are stunned by blows, to satisfy our sins of hearing; His mouth is swollen by blows from the horny fists of His enemies, to make amends for our wicked speech; His hands are pierced, to wipe away our evil deeds; His feet are bored through, on account of the speed with which we ran in wicked ways; His heart is well-nigh cloven in twain, to wash away the unholy desires of our hearts; His whole body is one vast wound, to pay the penalty due to our sinful flesh for the carnal delights in which it has indulged.

III. What are the thoughts suggested to you by the contemplation of Jesus lying thus in the arms of His most holy Mother? Are they not bitter recollections of the share each of you has had in making Him what He is? There is not one of us that cannot point to some scar upon that sinless flesh and say: 'It was I that did that!'

Have not our thoughts, at times, struck down the points of the thorny crown into the sacred head and temples of Our Lord? Have not our deeds filled His eyes with tears of blood? Our words have perhaps dealt Him blows, which were as heavy as the one which He received from the servant, who, in the house of the High Priest, struck Him upon the mouth. Our sinful acts have been unto His flesh as the thongs of the biting scourge, as the nails which burnt like red-hot iron, as the keen point of the lance which drank the last drop of His heart's best blood.

Looking upon the work of our hands, can we gaze unmoved upon the lifeless form which with mute eloquence appeals to us? Oh! let not our hearts be harder than were the very rocks which burst asunder at His death. Let us look upon the body of Our Saviour, resolve to atone for the past, and by tears of sorrow, to blot it out from the memory of God. Let each of us determine never again to reopen the wounds of Jesus.

When evil thoughts, whether of pride or of revenge, whether of vanity or of wickedness, come into our minds, let us reject them, and we shall thus be plucking out the thorns from the head of Jesus. When we refrain from the commission of sin, we shall be warding off from His sinless flesh the thongs of the galling whips. When we walk in the narrow path of virtue, we shall be taking out the nails from His hands and feet; we shall be holding off the lance from His side; we shall be fastening ourselves to the Cross in His stead, and thus deserve to bear in our flesh the marks of His glorious Passion, by crucifying our vices and concupiscences.

THE BURIAL OF OUR LORD.

I. Before consigning the body of Our Lord to the tomb, Joseph and Nicodemus, aided by the holy women, performed for it all those offices of piety which their faith and love prompted them to bestow. Having first cleansed it from the foul stains which the rage and brutality of the Jews had left upon it, they next, with the most profound respect, anointed all its gaping wounds, pouring over them sweet-smelling spices, and covering the whole body with myrrh. They then wrapped round the lifeless form a clean winding-sheet, and covered the sacred head with a linen cloth. Naught else now remained to be done except to bear that precious burthen to the grave, which Joseph had hewn out of the rock as a resting-place for himself. No one had yet been buried there, so that it had not been defiled, but had been providentially reserved as a receptacle for that virginal body, which, though lifeless, yet remained hypostatically united with the Divinity.

But before the grave closes over the body of her Son, Mary kneels once again by the shrouded form. Her face is bent over the veiled features of her Child, once so beautiful, and now so cruelly disfigured by the savagery of the Jews. She again presses to her bosom that sacred head, which had so often nestled there in the happy days of childhood. The tears break forth from her eyes. She imprints one farewell kiss upon the brow, now, alas! concealed from her view, and feels, in that supreme moment, all the agony of a broken heart.

By her side there kneels the beloved disciple, the spotless St. John, whom Jesus had given to her as a son instead of Himself. His tears fall fast, as he tries in vain to comfort her. Magdalen, deeming herself unworthy of aught else, stations herself at the feet of her Lord, and performs for them in death that office of love which she had not feared to perform in life, when He sat in the midst of His jealous and ever-watchful foes.

With unspeakable gentleness and tenderness, Joseph, Nicodemus, and John take the body of Jesus from the arms of His Mother, and bear it into the cavern. They lay it upon the ledge of rock prepared for its resting-place, and having closed the entrance of the sepulchre with a great slab of rock, all withdrew, to await in sorrow, and yet in hope, for the dawning of the glorious resurrection morn.

II. There are mystical meanings attached by devout men to the various incidents of Our Lord's burial, and upon these we must reflect, in order to draw thence matter for our own edification. In the preparation of Our Lord's body for the tomb, special mention is made of the use of myrrh. Its specific property is its power to preserve bodies from corruption. By spiritual writers it is always looked upon as a symbol of Christian mortification, which is so bitter, and yet so beneficial to human nature. From the use of it in the embalming of Our Lord's body, they would have us understand that, as the sharpest mortification entered so largely into His whole earthly career, so also, if we pretend to be His followers, should we make it hold a prominent place in the service which we render to Him. Bear in mind that without mortification no one can lead a holy life; and the best mortification for you who are at College, is to keep your hearts free from the taint of sin, and to do your duty exactly and well. In the accomplishment of this you will find bitterness enough to preserve your soul from the poison of this world's corruption.

Again; from the fact that Our Lord's friends wrapped His body in a clean winding-sheet, spiritual writers take care to point out to us the love which Jesus always manifested for purity. As He made it the darling virtue of His life, so He would mark His love of it, even in the grave, by causing His body to be enveloped in a cloth of dazzling whiteness, to symbolise the virtue which He so highly prized. See that your love of it be also very great. Be willing to suffer much from the assaults of the devil and from the rebellion of your corrupt nature, in your struggle to guard it from all spot or stain. Let your courageous defence of it be a pledge to God of your love for Him, and of your desire to serve Him.

Lastly, from the new sepulchre, in which no one had yet been laid, learn a further lesson of purity. Your heart, when you go to Holy Communion, becomes in a certain sense the tomb of Jesus Christ; for the true body and blood of the Son of God are laid up there as in a tabernacle. Therefore, see that your heart be always pure and clean. Let there be no filth nor rottenness of corruption in it, nothing that is unclean, for then Our Lord would shrink from all contact with it, with as much horror as that with which we should flee away from the loathsome tomb. Therefore, let the cry of your heart to God always be the Royal Psalmist's fervent prayer for purity: 'Create in me a clean heart, O God!'

III. Apart, however, from the mystical lessons which Our Lord's burial presents to us, there is a very solemn thought which it ought to raise in our minds. This is the thought of the nothingness of the present life, and of all the seeming good that it can give to us. To say that it passes away more quickly than an arrow, which divides the air and leaves not a trace behind, is to say what everyone knows, but what few are able to realise. Yet, whether we are able to bring this home to ourselves or not, the day will inevitably come, when it will be forced upon us. The grave will close over us, as we have seen it close over others; our friends will drop a few tears upon the mound which covers our remains, and, with a final 'May he rest in peace,' will depart, and so life and the world will have ended for us.

Look at that newly-made grave, in which one of your schoolfellows is laid to rest. You knew him well—his thoughts, his aspirations, his future hopes. To him they are now at an end for ever! You go away from his tomb awe-stricken, as you reflect that he has looked upon the face of God, that he now knows the secrets of the unseen world, to which you also are hastening. What does it avail him to have been nobly born, to have been rich, clever, beloved by all, flattered, sought after, admired? Nothing— unless he aimed at those unseen goods for which God created him. If he has not done so, his life has been a mistake, his end is the beginning of eternal sorrow, and his occupation will be to weep over lost opportunities, which will never return. A fate like this may be yours. It is in your power to prevent it, by making a right use of the present time. Time is now given to you to prepare for that future life which alone deserves the name life.

Therefore, regulate all your actions now with an eye to that future existence. See that no thought be harboured in your brain, and that in your heart no desire be suffered to find a resting-place, which desire might develop into an evil deed, and bear the fruit of eternal death. Your days will thus be passed with God, and when your allotted time shall have run its course, you will close your eyes upon this perishable world, with the firm hope that when you open them again, it will be to look into the face of God your Father, welcoming you with a smile of approval to His heavenly home.

DEPARTURE OF THE BLESSED VIRGIN AND THE REST FROM THE TOMB.

1. THE ponderous stone which closed up the mouth of the sepulchre, shut out the weeping Mother from the body of her Child; yet she still tarried by the spot, as if fascinated, till the beloved Apostle, who held the place of Jesus in her regard, gently and lovingly led her away. Her body, indeed, he might withdraw to a distance from her Son, but her heart remained with Him in the grave, for where her treasure lay, there also her heart rested. How great must have been her desolation, how bitter her sorrow, as with head bent down and faltering step, she walked away from the spot where they had entombed Him! She must, perforce, pass by the Cross, crimsoned with His blood. There she would carefully tread the ground, lest she should trample upon that which had lent its regal dye to the wood.

But, though plunged in a sea of sorrow, her heart would doubtless not forget those who had been so generous, and so courageous in their love, as to honour and care for the body of her Lord. They would not be suffered to depart to their homes from that scene of sorrow before they had heard from her lips the expression of her deep gratitude, for the noble part which they had played towards Him. How sweet must have been those words of commendation which issued from that Mother's lips, and how entrancing the thrill of spiritual joy which the glance of her tearful eyes shot through their hearts!

Then the Apostle St. John took her to his home, where she passed the night. There, no doubt, the rest of the Apostolic band gathered round her, full of grief for the loss of their Lord, and of shame for their cowardly desertion of Him in the hour of danger. Sad and desolate as her own heart must have been, she had yet to comfort them and to lighten the burthen of their sorrow. Thus did those whom Jesus loved so well, mourn over their grievous loss, and pass in review all the incidents of His bitter Passion, which they either had themselves witnessed, or had eagerly

gathered from the narratives of those who were present :
'Weeping, they wept in the night, and the tears were upon
their cheeks.' Among them were sounds of lamentation
and of great mourning over Him Whom they loved: they
would not be comforted, because He was not.

II. When we look back into the past, we may perhaps
be able to call to our remembrance certain occasions when
we, like our Lady, were separated from Christ. But how
different was our separation from hers! We had slain
Our Lord, cast Him out of our hearts, and buried Him
beneath the heavy load of our sins. We had turned our
backs upon Him, and had gone away with smiling eyes,
and a heart made delirious by the poisoned draught of the
devil's chalice. Gentle hands were stretched forth to seize
and draw us back from the brink of the precipice whither
we were hastening, and warning voices cried aloud to us,
' Beware !' We saw, we heard, but we heeded not. Our
proud hearts resented their interference, and we hurried
forwards with a swift step and a defiant glance.

Yet, what had we done to be proud of? or what had
happened to fill us with exultation? Like cowards we had
deserted our Leader in the day of trial, thrown down our
arms in the midst of the battle, and yielded up our persons
to the power of His and of our enemies. We gave Him
up to the fury of His bitterest foes, and basely sold Him for
a reward more vile than were the thirty silver coins for
which Judas betrayed Him to the Jews.

Oh! if thoughts like these come back like avenging furies
to torture your soul for the deeds of the past, and if the
devil should try to make you think so unworthily of God
as to despair of pardon, call to mind all that He endured
for you in His Passion, and you will feel what were the
depth, and the length, the height, and the breadth of His
undying love for you.

Do not, like the traitor Judas, distrust that love, but
rather, like the other Apostles, return sorrowing to wait
for pardon and to weep over your weakness. Like them,
draw nigh to the ever gentle Mother of God. Ask her to

intercede for you with her Son. Beseech her, by her neverfailing love, and by her unwavering fidelity, to obtain your pardon, and like a loving mother, she will present your petition to Him Who never refused her any request. He will take you back to His heart, and with the help of divine grace, you will never again desert Him.

III. Now that we have come to the end of these holy days of Lent, now that we are preparing to celebrate with joy the glorious feast of Our Lord's resurrection, let us cast a rapid glance at the stirring thoughts which have been placed before us during this penitential season. Christ is God, and He became man for love of us; He lived upon this earth of ours, and felt, so as to learn experimentally all our miseries, sin only excepted. Like a common labourer, He toiled at an ignoble handicraft, and by so doing invested labour with a dignity which has made its sharp penance for ever honourable. He came forth from His obscurity and taught a heavenly philosophy, which lifts men out of the mire of earth into the kingdom of God. He taught them to look upon this world as a place of exile, this life as a pilgrimage. To solace their misery and to strengthen their weakness, He gave them Himself to be their food during the days of their banishment. To blot out the handwriting against them, the Eternal Father had decreed that He should die. He submitted to His Father's will. The time for the fulfilment of that divine decree arrived, and Christ entered upon His bitter Passion. Over His whole being there crept a dread of death, so intense that it filled His soul with a mortal agony, and caused Him to sweat blood. One of His disciples basely betrayed Him; one of His creatures condemned Him to death, and handed Him over to the ungovernable fury of an angry mob. His people rejected Him, and chose in His stead a robber and murderer. They scourged Him like a malefactor, nailed Him to the disgraceful Cross like the vilest slave, and there —between two thieves, amid the cruel jeers of His own nation,—He died a lingering death of the most acute pain.

Reflecting upon all this, each of us can say: 'Christ

died for *me*, and delivered Himself up for *me*.' Surely, greater love than this no man hath, that he should give up his life for his friends. Therefore, let us not be behind-hand in generosity of love to Him. Let us give to Him all that we have, our hearts, our souls, our faculties, our powers. Henceforth let us be determined to serve Him only. But as we cannot do this without His assistance, we must ask Him for it, and He will give it to us. Let us ask Him so abundantly to bestow His grace upon us, 'that neither life nor death, neither Angels nor men, neither principalities nor powers, neither things present nor things to come, may ever be able to separate us from the love of God, which is in Christ Jesus our Lord.'

THE SACRED HEART.

THE OBJECT OF THIS DEVOTION.

I. In order that you may be able to appreciate the motives which induced the Church not only to sanction devotion to the sacred heart, but very earnestly to recommend it to her children, it will be necessary at the outset to tell you what the precise object is towards which she directs your adoration. A clear knowledge on this point will preserve you from every shadow of error, will anticipate and refute objections, and make you eager to practise the various acts of piety instituted to do honour to the loving heart of Our dearest Lord.

What, then, is the object towards which the piety of the faithful is directed in devotion to the sacred heart? It is not the heart of Our Lord, considered apart from His human nature, or abstracted from His body. It is not the heart of Our Lord, looked upon as separated from His divinity. Nor is it that same heart regarded as a mere symbol or sign of the immense and undying love of Jesus for each of us. In none of these respects is the sacred heart the object towards which the Church turns the devotion of her children, and bids them offer to it their adoration and their most ardent love. These are the errors and the misrepresentations of men whom either party spirit or the demon of heresy has so blinded that they do not wish to see.

The object which the Church proposes to her children's devotion, is the real and physical heart of Jesus Christ, the heart which is now living and beating in His breast, and therefore the heart of a divine Person. When we adore it, our adoration is directed to it as being a part of the Man-God, Christ Jesus, and consequently, in adoring it, we adore by one and the same act the whole Person of Jesus Christ; that is to say, we adore the Person of the incarnate Word, and in that Person the whole humanity, and the most sacred heart, living, animated and hypostatically united to the Word, considering it as the heart of a divine, incarnate Person.

Therefore, the material object of our adoration is the material heart of Our Lord, not separated from His humanity or from His divinity, but the living heart of the incarnate God.

II. But besides this material object of our devotion, there is also a spiritual one, of which the sacred heart of Our Lord is a symbol. This is the burning love of Jesus for men, as well as all those internal sentiments which filled the human nature of the God-Man. No tongue can tell the intensity of that love which burned in the heart of Jesus Christ. When we contemplate it, we are forced to lift up our hands in amazement, and silently to gaze upon the proofs which He has left us of its length and its breadth, of its height and its depth. That love laid Him as a helpless, wailing infant in the manger. It made Him toil in obscurity at a humble trade. It exposed Him to the envy, the contradictions, and the malignant hatred of a proud and fanatical priesthood. It nailed Him to the Cross, and rent wide open His sacred side. It holds him still among us in the solitude of His eucharistic prison.

Of all this the sacred heart is to us a symbol, inasmuch as it is what theologians call *the object of the manifestation* of that boundless love. For, though the heart cannot strictly be said to feel either love or sorrow, either anger or resentment, because these are really acts of the will, yet, because the heart is the organ upon which the movements of our intellectual and our physical nature make their chief impressions, it is natural for us to attribute these acts to it, though they are in reality accomplished by the will.

Hence, as the heart of Our Lord felt all the intense energy and vehemence of the acts of His will, by which He either loved or grieved, by which He suffered anguish, or fatigue, or bodily pain, it has become for us the object by which all these actions and affections of Our Lord's internal nature are made known to us. As such, it is the symbol of His love. By adoring it, therefore, we, in a spiritual way, pay homage to all that tenderness and compassion which He felt for the infirmities of our human nature.

III. Having learnt, then, what the precise object is towards which the Church, in her devotion to the sacred heart, directs the adoration of the faithful, we must next inquire into the motives which urged her to sanction that devotion, and wish for its wide diffusion among her children.

First, she intended by this means to meet and counteract the pestilential spirit of Jansenism, which made salvation well-nigh impossible, by cutting men off from the Sacraments, which are the channels of grace. This spirit had already diffused itself far and wide in France, when the vision vouchsafed to the Blessed Margaret Mary gave a *fresh* impulse to this devotion. For we must not suppose that the devotion is an entirely *new* one. It is really as ancient as that sorrowful day when the brutality of a Roman soldier pierced the side of the dead Christ, and threw open to us the portals of that sanctuary of love.

Secondly, she desired that the love which the devotion excites in the hearts of those who practise it, might enable them to resist that materialistic spirit, and that total indifference to religious teaching, which seem to be the characteristic marks of modern society. These, we may say, were the Church's two great motives in wishing for the wide diffusion of this devotion among the faithful.

But besides these, there were numerous other motives for the encouragement of a devotion which is now so popular. Of these we will mention one or two, and then suggest a few pious practices in honour of the sacred heart.

The sacred heart is the most noble part of that immaculate body which is united to the divine Person of Christ. That body paid the price of our redemption; it is the food of our souls, and the victim of propitiation, daily offered for our sins. Therefore, it is only right that we should adore the most noble part of it, as forming one whole with it.

Furthermore, since ungrateful men, instead of repaying the immense love of the sacred heart, pierce it anew with sorrow by their indifference and their sins, and so frequently outrage it in the Holy Sacrament, the Church, by sanctioning this devotion, gives to all an opportunity of making reparation by their fervent love, for the injuries which are heaped upon this uncomplaining Victim.

Therefore, let no day pass by without saying some little prayer to the divine heart of Our Lord. Assist more devoutly at the holy Sacrifice of the Mass, in which that sacred heart is daily immolated for you. Neglect not to visit the most Holy Sacrament in which Jesus waits so lovingly to receive you, and you will thus be complying with the wishes of His Church; you will atone for the ingratitude and the indifference of men; you will give pleasure and bring consolation to the heart of Our Lord; and He will pour down upon you in return those spiritual blessings which will finally bring you to your true home, close to that heart which has so tenderly loved the poor sinful race of men.

UTILITY OF DEVOTION TO THE SACRED HEART.

I. DEVOTION to the sacred heart recommends itself to all classes of the faithful without exception; but to none with more reason than to college-boys. For it procures for them, in the spring-tide of their life, three qualities of which they stand very much in need, to enable them to win their crown. These are strength, courage, and steadiness of purpose to fight down their carnal nature, and to gain the upper hand in their struggle with the powers of darkness.

They need strength; for they have arrived at that critical

period of life, when they become conscious of the existence within themselves of passions which fight against the law of their mind. They begin to know that their nature is partly carnal and partly spiritual; that their spiritual nature must either subdue and make their carnal nature its bond-slave, or be itself brought under subjection. The flesh is strong, and the spirit weak. The visible things which surround them appeal to them through eye, ear, and sense, urging them to revolt against the salutary, but stern, rule of their spiritual nature. Faint, however, is its voice, amid the loud clamours of carnal nature; feeble and ineffectual its resistance, unless the powerful aid of grace comes in to curb the imperious demands of the flesh.

That grace will be communicated to the boy, if he be devout to the sacred heart. For, whenever he feels his own heart parched with the fire of conflicting passions, the memory of the beauty and the holiness of Our Lord's sacred heart will be as a balmy dew, and as a cool, refreshing breeze to the fever-heat of his youthful blood. The majesty of its spotless purity, and the calm serenity of its unruffled peace, will charm him and inspire him with a love for all that it loves, and with a desire to possess some faint shadow of its virtues. The love engendered by this desire will bring about a union between his soul and the sacred heart, and that spiritual union will make him long to unite himself to Jesus, not in spirit only, but in reality, by means of Holy Communion. Thus united to the source of sanctity and of purity, he will be armed with the might of Jesus Christ, which will make him able to cope with the powers of darkness, who are plotting his destruction.

II. But the possession of strength alone will not ensure victory, for, in addition to strength, a boy requires courage in order to be able to face difficulties and dangers, to bear up against the weariness of sustained effort, and not to lose heart even in the ignominy of defeat. For in the path of virtue which the love of the sacred heart has inspired him to tread, there are many obstacles which cannot be removed by mere strength, many enemies who cannot be scattered by the fury of a single onslaught. They stand up before him, and obstinately contest his passage. They are not to be disposed of out of hand, nor dispatched at a single blow. Their destruction is a very tedious work indeed, requiring much patience and continual hard labour, with scarcely a moment of repose or a day of security. He must ever be on the alert, with arms in his hands, and a will determined to hold his own. This prolonged effort, this tension of all his powers, is wearisome in the extreme. Still it is most necessary, and even with all this watchfulness and good-will to do battle for Christ, there may at times steal over him moments of weariness, in which he grows careless, and is off his guard. Then the foe creeps in upon him, and by snatching from him a decisive victory, forces him to retreat with great loss. Against this also it is necessary for him to bear up, and not to despair of ultimately defeating his enemies.

Now where, except in the sacred heart of Our Lord, will he be able to obtain this courage to hold his own, to face difficulties, to persevere in his resistance, and not to despond, even after some signal defeat? In Jesus Christ he will find what always inspires great courage, a kindly heart which takes a deep interest in all that concerns him; a considerate heart, which will bear patiently with his faults; a sympathetic heart, which knows how to feel for him in trouble and in failure; a heart to which he can go with confidence, and from which he may expect naught but consolation and sweet words of encouragement.

After communion with that heart of Jesus, the boy who has grown weary of the incessant struggle against a bad temper, a vain heart, a proud spirit, an untruthful, deceitful disposition, departs from the Holy Table with renewed strength and a will firmly resolved not to yield to the enemies of God, nor ever to give up His sacred cause, though it may be full of difficulties and trials which are very hard to bear.

III. In addition to spiritual strength, and courage to make use of that strength against his foes, the college-boy will need a determined will to ensure his perseverance in good. It is easy to make a beginning, and to go on for some time with the work which has been undertaken; but the true test of genuine piety, is perseverance in that way which we are convinced will lead us to everlasting happiness. This steadiness of purpose is difficult to secure. For, after a time, the novelty of God's service wears off. The sweetness, too, which we experienced at the beginning, disappears, and leaves us with a daily recurring round of duties which have lost their savour, and have become a most wearisome task.

How insipid do those duties now appear to us, duties which we once performed with so great relish! To rise from bed, to observe Rule, to apply to distasteful studies, to live apart from the family circle, and to subject ourselves to the rough discipline of public school-life, are now so many acts against which we internally revolt. At prayer, too, there is no longer a consciousness that we are speaking to Our Father, that He is looking at us, and blessing us. Our communions are dry and barren; our confessions seem never to make us any better; and then, added to this, there are troubles from without, and troubles from within. Surely, to remain steadfast in our resolve, and not to give way in these circumstances, requires a fixedness of purpose bordering upon the heroic.

Nevertheless, you will secure this for yourself by devotion to the sacred heart. That heart is human as well as divine. It felt all those very miseries—sin alone excepted—to which you find yourself subject. There were times when the work of daily life became distasteful to it; when it sighed for relief; and yet persevered under a weight of depressing cares, which none but a divinely human Person could have borne. In the Garden of Olives, and upon the Cross, all sweetness departed from its prayer, and anguish unutterable wrung its every fibre, till the agony which this caused forced Jesus to cry out in the excess of His sorrow: 'My God! My God! why hast Thou forsaken Me?'

That is the heart to which you go in your trials and in your difficulties. Can you fail to be spurred on to fresh and more vigorous exertion, when you know that your Saviour before you felt all these miseries? No; you have too much generosity to make yourself unworthy of so trusty a friend, of so kind a master. You will pluck up fresh courage; you will make strong efforts; you will put self out of sight; and, remembering that it is the duty of the creature to accomplish his appointed task, and to serve God, not for his own pleasure, but for the pleasure and the satisfaction which that service gives to God, you will be content to persevere in darkness and in storm, as well as in sunshine and in calm. The example and the encouragement of the sacred heart will inspire you with this fortitude; and thus strengthened, thus encouraged, thus made steadfast in your resolution, you will persevere to the end, and receive the reward due to those who have fought the good fight and kept their faith.

IMITATION OF THE SACRED HEART.

I. To the college-boy, the utility of devotion to the sacred heart is beyond dispute, inasmuch as it furnishes him with the very weapons of which he stands most in need at the outset of his career. He needs strength to cope with his passions, courage to subdue them, and a determined will not to be turned aside by difficulties, till that desirable end is gained. All this is secured to him by devotion to the sacred heart, provided always that his devotion is practical, and induces him to imitate that heart which he strives to love. This is a necessary condition, without which devotion itself is of little worth. The boy must strive to make his heart resemble, in its sentiments, the sacred heart of Our Lord. By the heart, we mean, of course his moral nature. If he look well into that, he will see at a glance that it needs much cultivation. Like his intellect, it is a barren soil that must be diligently tilled, otherwise it will produce nothing but those evil passions which Our Lord says spring up there in rank luxuriance. It will be without nerve to resist evil, without courage to meet difficulties, without any high or any noble aspirations after good.

Consequently, it is a matter of the first necessity that the heart of each boy should be cultivated by modelling it, as far as possible, upon the sacred heart of Jesus Christ. In that process it will, like a diamond under the skilful hand of a lapidary, be freed from the foreign matter which obscures its beauty and lessens its value. Like the golden ore, it will be purged from dross. Like the marble block, it will be chiselled into shape, smoothed, and polished, till every vein be brought out clearly in all its wealth of colouring. It will be cleansed from selfishness, from unholy desires, and will be made to beat in unison with the heart of Jesus, by obedience to the divine law. This is what St. Paul asks us to do, when he says: 'Be ye imitators of God, as most dear children.' This is what he means when he bids us, 'Put on the Lord Jesus Christ.' By obeying that injunction, we are also accepting the sweet invitation of Our Lord, Who says: 'Learn of Me, because I am meek and humble of heart.'

II. Now that you are fully alive to the necessity for modelling your heart upon the likeness of the heart of Jesus, you will perhaps ask, 'How is it to be done?' We answer. By so chastening and subduing your heart, that it will become one in sentiment with the heart of Jesus. For, as all true friendship as well as all true love consists in the union of wills, so that the two individuals may be said to will and not to will the same thing—'*idem velle et nolle*'—so, when the heart of a boy has come to esteem and love what Jesus esteems and loves, and to hate what Jesus hates, he may be said to have made his heart like unto the sacred heart of Our Lord.

Therefore, consider attentively what are those qualities which Jesus loves in a boy, and make it the aim of your life to acquire them. Does He set great value upon strength of limb, or beauty of form, or nobility of birth, or elegance of manners, or high intellectual ability? Not unless these things are accompanied by virtue. They are His gifts, it is true; and some of them are the external trappings which we are accustomed to regard as the marks of a gentleman. As such they ought to be duly valued. But what He esteems most are lowliness of heart, unselfishness, truth, purity. These constitute the real gentleman, for they beget that noble and generous feeling, that lofty courage, that heroic fortitude, to which all pay homage.

Aim, then, at the acquisition of these. Be not high-minded. Set not too great store upon mere externals. These are the things which base spirits worship with so much servility. Never imagine that you have made even the first step towards true gentlemanliness, until you can recognise it under a rough exterior and dressed in tattered garments. Seek not self. Be attached to truth. Scorn all that is false and deceitful. Keep your heart pure.

Esteem, honour, and love these things, and then your heart will love what Jesus loves, and will hate all that He hates. You will hate pride, deceit, self-seeking, and everything that could sully the purity of your heart, and make it the abode of God's bitterest enemy. To a heart like this, Almighty God will love to unite Himself, and around it the Angels will cluster in admiration and in love.

III. There is no royal, no easy method to accomplish this much-to-be-desired likening of our hearts to the heart of Jesus. It is a work of some difficulty; but yet not of so great difficulty that the youngest boy at College may not hope to succeed in it. He cannot, of course, succeed by his own unaided efforts, but with the help of God's grace it will be easy for him to do so. Therefore, the first means that every boy must employ in the accomplishment of this necessary and important work is prayer; because by prayer grace is obtained from God. Hence, whenever a boy unites himself to the sacred heart in Holy Communion, he must ask Jesus to transform him into His likeness. No opportunity is more suitable for obtaining this favour; for in that divine banquet he leans his head upon the loving heart of Our Lord, just as St. John did at the last supper. He may then address Him and say: 'Dearest Lord, make my heart like unto Thine.' He must lift up his voice for this same purpose when he kneels before the tabernacle at his daily visit. He must do it frequently during the day, by short ejaculatory prayers, which like fiery darts will reach the heart of Jesus, and draw thence the strength which will enable him to trample under foot all that is displeasing to God, and make him love and esteem everything of which God thinks highly.

To prayer he must add his own individual efforts to make his heart one in sentiment with the heart of Jesus. For this purpose, let him frequently ask himself: 'What would Jesus do if He were put in precisely the same position as that in which I am, at School?' Sometimes I feel weary and inclined to waste the study hours in folly or in useless trifling. What would Our Lord do in these circumstances, if He were here as a boy seated at this desk? In spite of weariness, He would go on with His work; so will I. If He were sneered at, and ridiculed, and despised, what would He do? He would bear it patiently, and would not break out into a fury of passion; therefore, under the like provocation, I will crush down my temper. If He were wrongly accused, and had base and unworthy motives attributed to Him, what would He do? He would modestly and firmly exculpate Himself, and then let the matter rest. In this respect, likewise, I will try to imitate Him.

By these practical means a boy will, in a short time, make his heart in all things like the heart of Jesus. Therefore, knowing how necessary it is to do this, resolve to take up every practice that will assist you in so glorious a work. You know what virtues you have to aim at in order to accomplish it; make the attainment of them the object of your life, and with the help of God's grace, and the powerful assistance of our dear Lady's prayers, you will become like your divine Lord. As a dear child, you will imitate your God; you will put on the Lord Jesus Christ; and learn the great lesson which He came on earth to teach.

LOVE OF THE SACRED HEART FOR GOD.

I. It is necessary, as we saw in our last lecture, that the college-boy should *imitate* the sacred heart of Our Lord, if he wishes to derive any benefit from his devotion to it. But in order to imitate, he must first *know* the sacred heart. He must understand its virtues and its sentiments, its wishes and its aims. This knowledge, however, can be obtained only by meditation upon that adorable heart. For by meditation the boy puts the heart of Our Lord before his mind, just as an artist keeps before his eyes the model from which he is copying, while he either transfers its beauties to his canvas, or makes them stand out in bold relief from the marble block at which he labours. Let us then, to-day, try to learn the great, the most prominent virtue of the heart of Jesus, namely, its love of the Eternal Father.

That love is the love of a human heart, but of a human heart which is deified, for it has been assumed by a divine Person to be the heart of a Man-God. Hence, there is in its perpetual act of love, an intensity of ardour which it would be impossible for a merely human heart to feel. Love fills and wholly occupies it. All its affections, all its desires, all its thoughts, all its aims are centred in God. His glory is the object which makes it beat within the bosom of Jesus. As that glory can in this world be given to God, only by making His infinite perfections known to His creatures, it is the desire of Our Lord's heart that men may know Him, and by knowing may learn to love, and by loving may glorify Him ; since that love will make them strive to express in their own hearts the beauty of holiness which they perceive in His.

This work Jesus, as man, undertook to accomplish. He laboured at it as no one ever laboured at any work before. Yet in that work He had no thought of self. He sought not glory, nor renown, nor fame among men. 'He sought not His own glory.' 'There was one who sought it for Him.' He looked not for ease, nor for gratification, in the accomplishment of His task. The good pleasure of God, and the fulfilment of His wishes, were to Him what glory, honour, and a world-wide reputation are to other men. Hence, His whole heart lived and laboured only for God. Its pleasure consisted in doing the will of God, and in doing it to spend itself and to be spent. It is thus that the sacred heart loves God.

II. As we contemplate this burning, this all-absorbing love of Jesus for God, and then compare with it our own love for Him, what a contrast is presented to our eyes! It is so great that each of us may well ask himself: 'Do I love God at all? and if I do, what sign is there in my daily life to prove that I do?' For, if love of God exists in the heart, it is of its own nature so absorbing, as to leave no room there for any other love that is not of God. It carries the whole heart away with it. It seizes upon all its thoughts, upon all its desires, and fixes them upon its treasure. Hence, where that treasure is, there also is the heart. Can you say this of your love of God? If you could, then would your love resemble the love of the sacred heart. God's interests would then be your interests. You would consider them first, and most important. They would be the theme of your thoughts, the burthen of your words, for your tongue would speak from the abundance of your heart. You would labour for His glory, and in that work of love, self and self-interest would be forgotten. You would hail even suffering as a welcome minister come to put to the test your burning love for God, and prove that it is not a mere passing emotion, that your protestations of undying affection are not the vain vapourings of a coward heart, which flinches at the first touch of pain, loses courage at the first difficulty, and despairs at the first reverse of fortune.

But what is really the case? The interests which absorb your whole heart and soul are your own. You shun trouble, difficulty, and inconvenience when the cause of God requires you to meet them. In the little world which surrounds you, you seek to advance your own reputation and glory. You work for yourself, you study for yourself. You wish to be thought clever, brave, upright, and honourable, for your own gratification, and care little, perhaps, whether you possess the reality, provided that you can assume the shadow of these things.

As for God's interests, alas! how ill it fares with them in

your heart; and yet God intended that heart to busy itself chiefly about them—to know Him, to love Him, to serve Him—in one word, to glorify Him. But do you seek to bring about so happy a consummation? If so, why do you not work at your heart in order to root out from it pride, ill-temper, untruthfulness, and the first germs of sensuality? He who truly loves God would do this. But what do you do? Look first into your own heart, and then contemplate the heart of Jesus, and you will see what you have to amend.

III. The vast difference which you will perceive between the love of the heart of Jesus for God, and your own love for Him, will clearly point out to you what you have to do. You must reform your heart, by modelling it upon the heart of Jesus. This reformation will be effected, by withdrawing its love from the objects to which it has learnt to cling, and the modelling of it upon the heart of Jesus will be accomplished, by inspiring it with a love for all that He loves and values highly.

In order to effect this, you must first ignore self, and deem it worthy of only a secondary place in your affections. When you have learnt this lesson, you will have made much progress in the science of God. You will discover, however, that the task of putting self in its proper place involves a great deal of work. It is, in fact, no less a work than that of changing most of your affections, and your motives of action. At present, you look upon your life only as a preparation for your career in the world. You study, simply to fit yourself for some office which will bring you honour and emolument. Most of your thoughts are directed to gain these ends. In the meantime, how fares it with your eternal interests? Do you ever think of them, and of that future world to which you are hurrying with a speed of which you take so little account? Do you try to shape your life, and the motives with which it is actuated, by those views which will direct you to your only true and real end?

Perhaps these things do not strike you, or at least have not yet struck you. Let them do so now. Deem nothing worthy of real esteem, except that which tends to the interest and the glory of God. Look upon your life as a preparation for the eternal life which awaits you beyond the grave. Though you may regard your studies as a work which is to fit you for your duties in the world, yet always look upon them as subordinate to that all-important task which God has sent you into the world to finish.

In fine, let everything that in any way either touches you, or occupies your mind, first be looked at in its bearing upon eternity, to see in what way it may be directed to the glory of God. By acting thus, you will be breaking loose your affections from the things of the world, and fastening them upon the things of God. You will be filling and occupying yourself with God's interests. You will be working for His glory, and in your measure and in your degree, you will come at last to love God with your whole heart.

LOVE OF THE SACRED HEART FOR US.

I. As love is one of the most powerful levers for moving the human will, it is natural that its influence upon the impressionable boy-nature should be well-nigh unbounded. It is for this reason that all educators who are worthy of the name, strive to win for themselves the love of their boys. If they succeed in doing this, their task will be an easy one; for when a boy loves those who teach and guide him, his character may be moulded by them into whatever shape they please. Hence we consider that one of the best methods to make you practise the virtues of the sacred heart, is to inspire you with a love for Jesus Christ; for if you love Him, you will do all that He desires. We will, therefore, in this lecture, bring before you the love of the sacred heart for you, in order that, seeing how great it is, you may strive more earnestly to make that heart a return of love.

If we look about for any special manifestation of that love, we can find none better than the most Holy Sacrament of the Altar. There the sacred heart dwells, and is present as really as it was to St. John when he leaned upon the bosom of Jesus, and heard its rapid pulsations, while Our Lord gave to His Apostles a manifestation of love, whereat the whole court of heaven stood amazed. That same heart is in the silent Chapel, within the narrow limits of the tabernacle, often with no other company than the flickering lamp and the adoring Angels who cluster round His altar-throne. He thinks of each of you, and loves you. He sees your thoughts, He observes your actions, He knows your difficulties, trials and temptations. He is full of the most tender compassion for you. His heart yearns for you, and goes out towards you. He wishes to have you quite close to Him. He desires you to go to Him and to receive Him into your hearts, that He may dwell there and make you love Him.

He does all this for you, and you remain cold and indifferent. He is burning with love for you, and how do you treat Him? You sit at your desk, you pore over your books, and never give Him a thought. You amuse yourself in the playground, without ever casting a glance at the Chapel where He is thinking of you, and whence He is looking at you. Perhaps you do not go for even a few minutes to pay Him a visit, and lay before Him the necessities which press upon you, and weigh down your young heart with sorrow. Yet Jesus does not cease to love you, to wait for you, to call you to Him. His love is patient, because it is eternal.

II. Examine, therefore, more deeply into the nature of the most Holy Eucharist, and try to learn what God's love for you has caused Him to do in that wondrous Sacrament. He wished to be with you in His humanity and in His divinity. He desired that His sacred heart should be given to each of those whom He loves. But in order to accomplish this, He had to lower Himself, not, as St. Paul says, 'by taking upon Himself the form of a servant,' but by lying concealed under the species of bread and wine. He puts Himself into the power of every priest throughout the world, and, at the bidding of His creature, He descends from heaven. He remains quite passive in the hands of that creature, and awaits, with all the longing of a fond father, for his little ones to come and be clasped to His sacred heart. His priests are ordered to call all men unto Him, to press them, to compel them to approach this feast of love. His children need not there fear the intolerable glory of His Divinity, nor the majestic dignity of His humanity. He has veiled them both from their sight, that they may draw nigh with greater ease and confidence.

Besides this, He makes Himself, in the Holy Eucharist, a Victim to be offered up in sacrifice, as an atonement for your sins, and as an acceptable peace-offering to the offended majesty of God. For the Victim which is immolated in the Mass, is identically the same as that which was offered upon Calvary, the manner only in which it is offered constituting the sole difference between the two. In the unbloody sacrifice, the same Jesus offers up His sacred heart, and, in a mystical way, pours forth His precious blood for each of you. He does this daily and hourly, upon every altar throughout the world, so that there is no limit to His immense, His infinite love. He offers Himself for you individually, just as if no other soul existed in the world.

Judge, then, from this, the love of the sacred heart for you, and when you look at the tabernacle, where His love holds Him a prisoner, let St. Paul's words come into your mind, and fill you with unbounded love for Him: 'Christ died for me, and delivered Himself up for me.'

III. What return, then, will you make to that sacred heart for its boundless love of you? Surely your gratitude will not fail to do something which will prove that the treasure of God's affection is not spent upon you in vain. You can do nothing better than try to make your love for Him resemble that which He bestows upon you. He is ever thinking of you, and planning for your welfare. Try not to let an hour pass away without sending forth your heart to Him in His prison of love. Lift up your thoughts to Him while you sit in the silent study, labouring at your appointed task, and offer it to Him Who laboured so hard for you. When you are arrested by difficulties, ask Him for help; when tempted to idle your time, call to mind His laborious life; and endure the mortification of hard work for the sake of Him Who tasted so much bitterness for you. During your hours of recreation, and even while playing at your games, turn to Him for a single moment, and tell Him that you are recreating yourself for His glory, and ask His blessing upon yourself and upon your companions. If either dejection or sorrow falls upon you; if the devil raises up a storm of temptation about you; if your companions either malign or maltreat you, seek your consolation in the sacred heart, and you will thus learn to think frequently of Him Who so often thinks of you.

In the next place, as Our Lord abides with you, and is living in the very house in which you dwell, never let a day pass without paying Him a loving visit. There are some boys who repair to the Chapel three times in the day to visit their Lord: in the morning, to ask a blessing on their studies; in the afternoon, to offer them to Him; and at night, to thank Him for all the blessings of the day. Do you go, at least once each day, to visit Him. Ask for grace not to sin; never to yield to temptation; for success in your studies, and for courage to persevere faithfully in the service of God. This will be some return for the unspeakable blessing of having God so nigh to you.

Lastly, since Jesus in the Blessed Sacrament invites you with so much earnestness to receive into your heart His body and blood, His soul and Divinity, let not sluggishness, nor self-convenience, nor any other excuse, keep you from accepting His pressing invitation. The college-boy must know, that if he would be holy, if he would be pure and acceptable to God, he cannot be so without partaking of the body and blood of Jesus, Who is the source of all sanctity.

Therefore, go frequently—once a week is not by any means too often—and unite yourself to the sacred heart. That heart will purify you from your defects; it will give you the strength of God to resist the devil; it will encourage you in your pursuit of virtue; it will console you in time of dejection and of sorrow. You can give to Our Lord no better proof of your love, than to approach and receive Him in Holy Communion. Therefore, in return for the love of that holy heart, learn to think willingly of its love, to visit it every day in the tabernacle, and to receive it into your heart, to be your strength, your light, your consolation, and the pledge of that future life in which you will be for ever united to it.

THE LOVE WHICH WE OWE TO THE SACRED HEART.

I. THE sacred heart of Jesus most tenderly loves each of us, and awaits with unwearying patience for us to make Him a return of love. We must, therefore, imitate Him in this respect also, as in so many others; and our love for Him must resemble that which He lavishes so bountifully upon us. Of what nature, then, is the love of the sacred heart for us? It is what theologians call a love of *preference;* that is to say, a love which causes a man to prefer the object of his love to all other things whatsoever. Is not this the nature of that undying love with which the sacred heart loves us? Let us examine and see.

There is not the slightest doubt that Our Lord might have redeemed the world in a way altogether different from that in which he effected it, and without that total 'emptying of Himself,' as St. Paul expresses it. He might have come among us, as the Jews expected that He would come, clothed in all the power and the majesty of an irresistible conqueror. He did not do so, because He chose to win our love. He preferred our love to power, wealth, and the obsequious obedience which ever attends on kings. Therefore, He came as a poor despised Galilean, of humble birth and lowly presence. He came from a city so despicable, that men who afterwards heard of His wondrous deeds, used to ask, in scornful surprise: 'Can aught of good come from Nazareth?' He did this, because He preferred our love to the glory and the honour which were due to the noblest, the wisest, the best man that ever trod this earth.

What is more precious than a good name? Yet Jesus

preferred our love to it. He suffered Himself for our sakes to be called a liar, a deceiver, a blasphemer, an enemy of God.

What do men strive after with more intensity of purpose than they do after honour? Yet Jesus preferred our love to His own honour. For us He did not disdain to be despised, rejected, and counted worse than one who was a murderer and robber.

What do men value more than ease, and wealth, and friends? Is it not life? Yet Jesus set it aside and esteemed it of no value compared with our love. He preferred our love to all that men hold dear; and in order to win it for Himself, He sacrificed all that we cling to with so great tenacity, and that we sometimes prefer to the love and the obedience which we owe to God.

II. Jesus loved us, and still loves us with a love of preference. How do we love Him? If we cast ever so rapid a glance over our daily life, we shall see that our preference is given in most, if not in all cases, to mere perishable things, rather than to that God Who has been so prodigal of His love to us. In grave matters, let us hope that we shall never suffer anything to be dearer to us than are the love and the friendship of God; but this should be so in matters of minor importance likewise. Unhappily this is not the case, as a moment's reflection will show.

Let us call to mind some of these lighter matters and see. We know, and we are always taught, that in obeying our Superiors, and in following the rule of life which they have traced out for us, we are doing the will of God. Yet when called from recreation to study, we are slow to give up our play, or our conversation, or our reading, and in consequence we fail in our duty; we follow our own will; we prefer it to the will of God, manifested to us by the will of our Superiors, whose wish it is that we should obey at once. When our own ease and convenience are in question, do we not prefer them also to the will of God? How else can we account for our reluctance to rise when called in the morning, and for our sluggishness during study time, when we should give up our own convenience and ease at the summons of duty.

Again; we have, perhaps, a very false notion of honour, and consider that we are obliged to quarrel with our companions, because some vain, empty-headed boy will consider us to be cowardly and spiritless, if we do not resent every slight and injury that we receive. We do this, because we prefer our honour to the honour of God. Furthermore, we study and perform our various actions, to gain applause from our masters and companions, and not to do God's will. Why? Because we prefer our reputation to the good pleasure of God.

In these, and in many other ways, our conscience will tell us that our love of God is not what it ought to be, and hence our chief aim should be to make it resemble, as nearly as possible, that love of preference which the sacred heart has for us. Then we shall, in small things as well as in great, put God first, and prefer His will and His good pleasure to our own ease, honour, reputation, and everything else that self would bid us love.

III. From this contrast between the love which the sacred heart has for us, and our love for the sacred heart, we shall be able to put our finger upon the defects which mar the beauty of our soul's love for God. It will teach us what we have to do, in order to have for God that love of preference which He has for us. Let it, then, from this time forth, be our fixed purpose to put God in the first place in small matters as well as in great, and we shall soon discover that this purpose, if pursued with determination, will, little by little, weed out that self-love which makes us prefer our own ease to the will of God.

At our studies, when tempted to relax our efforts, or to cease from them altogether and give ourselves up to the luxury of idleness, let us call to mind that God wills us to work during the time allotted for study, and that if we idle, we are preferring ourselves to Him. If at times it is somewhat galling humbly to obey the command of a Superior, let not that spirit of resistance which comes of pride, stiffen our necks, and harden our hearts, and make us do our own will. Let us repress our heart's uprising, and force it to be docile to another's will. We shall thus be preferring the will of God to our own. As for the foolish idea that we must upon all occasions defend our honour, and by ill-temper and pugnacity cause others to respect it, let us set this down as a pagan notion to be got rid of as soon as possible. It is an overweening love of self, rather than a care for what is right, that keeps alive these false principles among boys. Let us be ready to give up our own will, our own ease and convenience, our honour and the reputation which we enjoy among our schoolfellows, whenever by retaining any of them we should prefer ourselves to God.

Thus we shall love God in preference to all other things, and if we persevere steadily in this course from day to day, from year to year, it will beget in us so strong a habit of self-denial, that it will cost us very little to sacrifice self to God, and the result of this will be, that our love for the sacred heart will resemble that love of preference with which the sacred heart so generously and so unselfishly loves us.

PATIENCE OF THE SACRED HEART.

THE great Apostle, mindful of the infinite tenderness and love of God for man, thought that he could delineate His character for us in no better way than by that one, short, pregnant phrase: 'God is charity.' The love of God for us made Him take upon Himself our nature, and appear among us in human flesh. Hence the sacred heart of Our Lord may be said to be the incarnation of the charity of God. Now St. Paul, in his eloquent eulogium upon that divine virtue of charity, enumerates its various attributes, and, first among them, places the virtue of patience: 'Charity,' he says, 'is patient.'

How true is this of the heart of Jesus! If there is a model of patience, it is surely Jesus Christ. We know, at least in some degree, the burning zeal, the wistful eager longing of His heart for the salvation of men. We can guess its intensity, from the vigour and the force of the divine will, which energised His human will; and yet for thirty years He bided His time, and continued patiently waiting for the moment decreed by the Eternal Father to begin that work, the accomplishment of which threw open to us the gates of the kingdom of heaven.

Then, when He had begun His work, and had chosen out the men who were to be the pillars of that Church, by means of which He intended to reform and purify the world, see how patiently He bore with their imperfections! They were rude, unlettered fishermen; they had low views of His aims; they were slow of intellect, and full of petty jealousies and childish rivalries. Yet He kept them close to Him, and with imperturbable patience, taught and trained them. The heroism requisite for a task of this kind, will be feelingly appreciated, only by those who have had to bear up against the weariness and the disgust inseparable from teaching boys, who are either too dull or too idle to learn.

Furthermore, when He actually came before men to call them to Himself, and to deliver unto them the message which He had received from His Father, His enemies, the priests, the Scribes and the Pharisees, opposed, and hated, and maligned Him. They contradicted and reviled Him. They called in question the purity of His motives, and met all His advances with the most fanatical hostility. Yet no word of impatience escaped His lips, so that even pagans and His bitterest opponents marvelled at Him.

But this wondrous patience shone forth most conspicuously, during the short day of darkness during which His enemies had Him completely in their power. A menial struck Him on the face; lying witnesses falsely accused Him; a time-serving judge unjustly condemned Him; and yet He remained patient. His people rejected and finally crucified Him. Throughout all this He continued to be patient. No murmur, no complaint, no harsh word against His enemies passed His lips. Before this endurance, before this superhuman patience, we bow down in homage and reverence, for it is the patience of the God of charity.

II. When we contemplate those manifestations of patience, they surprise and strike us with awe. But when we come to examine the patience of God with regard to ourselves, it is no less startling, no less wonderful. Just consider, for a moment, the infinite patience of the sacred heart, with yourself personally. Look at the period of your childhood when you first began to be able to distinguish good from evil. Did you turn away at once from that hideous monster sin, and cleave, like a true child of God, to Jesus Christ? God grant that you did, and, furthermore, that you have persevered in your allegiance. But, if you did not, reflect for a moment in what meshes of evil you were entangled by your newly-awakened passions. God pitied your inexperience, and patiently bore with you. He waited for you, and did not, as He might have done, and as He has done in the case of so many others, punish you after the first transgression.

Later on you may have been led into more grievous sins. Still He patiently waited. How long-suffering has He been with you, in your sins of ungovernable anger, in your selfishness, your pride, and disobedience! Has He had nothing to rouse His indignation in your use of His Sacraments? Have you always been sincere in the tribunal of penance; and with respect to the most holy and tremendous mystery of the Eucharist, in which Jesus gives Himself to you, have you always been in a fit state to partake of it? May it not have been that, like those of whom St. Paul wrote, you have there eaten and drunk your own condemnation? If so, has not the sacred heart had a great deal to bear from you?

Even now, when you are at your best, what are you to think of your coldness in the service of God, of your carelessness at prayer, your giddiness in church, your sluggishness in confessing and in communicating? Does the heart of Jesus feel no smart of pain from your conduct in these matters? Dearest children! when you think of these things, the pale, blood-stained face of Jesus seems to look reproachfully at you, and to chide you for your want of love. Let it stir up within you every feeling of generosity, and make you resolve to be better for the future, and never again to trespass upon the infinite patience of that loving, sacred heart.

III. Therefore, the practical lesson which you must learn from all this, is to make your own heart patient, like the sacred heart of Jesus. Living as you do, and as you must do to the end of your days, among those who are very imperfect, occasions will of necessity present themselves, when your companions will be a source of grave annoyance and of even positive pain to you. But do not suppose, when others make you feel the weight of the Cross, that they, in their turn, have nothing to suffer from you. They see and feel the defects of your faulty character, just as you see and feel the defects of theirs. Consequently, on the principle of 'bear and forbear,' you must make up your mind to endure and to be patient. Hence it is that the Apostle says: 'Patience is necessary for you.'

You must, therefore, brace up your will, and nerve yourself to meet and to bear with patience the many trials which are unavoidable in your college life. For instance, those with whom you live may not be all that you would desire; they may be rude, selfish and despotic. They may take a pleasure in contradicting what you say, and in tnwarting your wishes, no matter how reasonable they may be. They may satisfy their cruel disposition, by teasing and causing you all the petty annoyance which it is in their power to inflict. Yet do not storm, and break forth into a fury of passion. Be good-humoured, and for God's sake endure the passing inconvenience.

It may happen that you will meet with some who will go so far, and be so malicious, as wrongfully to accuse you of some fault of which you are wholly innocent, or to attribute to you some meanness which you utterly detest! Try to bear with patience even this, because the heart of Our Lord had to taste of this bitter chalice also, and to drain it to the very dregs.

Nay, there are occasionally to be met with in Colleges, certain characters who regard as hypocrites those who are trying to lead lives of piety. They insult them, and try to fasten upon them this odious epithet. Should you ever encounter these contemptible wretches, be firm, in spite of their raillery and bitter scorn. The best proof that you are not a hypocrite will be, not to notice the vile accusation, but to bear it with patience. On these, and the like occasions, keep down your rising anger, and restrain the hand which is tingling to do battle in defence of your honour. Remember whose child you are! Look on the patient heart of Jesus, and bearing in mind all the scorn, insult, and contumely, which He endured for you, be patient under these little trials, which are sent to test of what metal you are made, whether you are true gold, or only lead, which yields to every impression.

KINDNESS OF THE SACRED HEART.

I. Our Lord once said to those who were listening to His preaching: 'From the abundance of the heart the mouth speaketh.' This proverb will furnish you with a measure by which you will be able to gauge the height and the depth, the length and the breadth, of His kindness towards the young. For, if you examine the words which He spoke about children, you will be able from them to form some notion of the wealth of kindness which is stored up for them in the treasury of His sacred heart. How, then, did Jesus speak of little children? He spoke in so tender a way as to put before you a true picture of His unutterable love for them.

On one particular occasion, numbers of them were gathered round Him. Either their parents had brought them to receive His blessing, or they themselves had forced their way through the crowd, and found places quite close to His sacred person. The Apostles, observing this, wished to thrust them back, thinking, no doubt, that they incommoded Jesus, and held the ground which would have been better occupied by those who had wiser heads. But Our Lord did not think so; He prevented them from expelling the children, and said, with great gentleness: 'Suffer them to come unto Me, for of such is the kingdom of heaven.' These words express the kindness of His heart for the young.

But He did not restrict that kindness to mere words. He called them to Him, laid His hands upon their heads, took them into His arms, embraced them, and placed them close to His sacred heart.

From these words and acts, judge of the kindly thoughts which Our Jesus must have entertained about children! With what sweetness must these thoughts have manifested themselves in the kindly glance of His eyes, and the sweet smile with which He met their upturned gaze! These drew the little ones to Him, for, with the quick instinct of childhood, they saw that He loved them, and hence they feared not to go to Him, to take Him by the hand, and be raised up to receive His loving caresses.

II. From the kindly words, actions, and thoughts of Jesus about the young, you ought to conceive a great love for the sacred heart, whence they have all flowed, as from an inexhaustible well-spring. This love will lead you to Him in all your necessities. You are now young; you are inexperiencd; you are weak. It is for these very reasons that the heart of Jesus goes out to you with all the unutterable tenderness of the great, omnipotent God. If you are perplexed by the evil to which your eyes are but just opening, ask Him, Who so fondly loves you, to avert it from you, and to keep your feet from its snares. If the bait which is held out to seduce you from the narrow way makes you feel weak and giddy, and about to yield to the fascination of evil, go to Him Who loves you. He is the mighty One, and in His strength you will be able to grapple with, and to overcome, the most potent champion of hell. By thus fleeing to Him in your hour of weakness and peril, you will show Him that you love Him with your whole heart.

Again; let the kindness which He has invariably manifested towards the young, inspire you with that childlike confidence, which always springs up in the hearts of those who come under the fostering influence of a kindly man. Be not afraid of your Lord! Confide in Him, as you would confide in a loving and tender-hearted father. Let not the thought of your many present defects, of your shortcomings, of your failures, and of even your sins, keep you away from His heart. He has seen and known them all. But He is your Father. Look up, therefore, into those eyes which speak so eloquently to you. Stretch forth your hands to Him. Run to Him. He will not receive you frowningly. He will not reject you. He will open wide His arms, and catch you to His heart, and you will thence draw strength tenderly to love Him, trustfully to confide in Him, and never again to cause one moment of anguish to His kind, fatherly heart.

III. But, if the heart of Jesus is so full of kindly feeling, and of so unspeakable tenderness for you, it is but right and just that you should try to fill your own heart with similar sentiments for those whom God loves, just as much as He loves you. Your little world of College is often enough made sad and intolerable to many a heart, because of the unkindly disposition of certain boys. They both think and speak unkindly of one another; they do unkindly and unbrotherly acts to one another. Now, out of love for that sacred heart, which is so full of kindness for us all, make a resolution this very day to try to imitate it, by being kind to those with whom you live.

First of all, do not think harshly of them. You cannot penetrate into their souls, and hence you cannot know the motives which have prompted either their words or their acts. You often, in fact, see their actions through a false medium, which only distorts and makes them appear monstrous. What you deem evil, may be good; what you regard as unmanly, may in reality be most courageous; what you look upon as mean and ignoble, may be the result of some high principle. Therefore, interpret all that you see, in the best sense that it will bear, and what you cannot defend, try at least to excuse.

If you are kind in your thoughts, you will be kind in your

words also. Never let a harsh, or an insulting expression escape your lips. Do not be either biting or sarcastic in your speech; words of this kind are like barbed arrows; they stick in the heart; they rankle there for years; and inflict a wound so deep, so painful, that no length of time can heal its smart. Therefore, be kind in your speech, for kind words fall like balm upon a wounded spirit. They fill with joy many a dejected heart, and spur on to fresh exertion many a despairing soul. One kind word has before now arrested a poor sinner on the brink of hell, and made him a happy, loving child of God. Therefore, speak these words to your companions, and you will be among them as an Angel of God, filling their hearts with confidence and with love for Him.

Also, do kind actions for them whenever you are able. Many an opportunity for the exercise of these will present itself during the course of each day. Anticipate the wishes of others; help them in the difficulties of their lessons; go on their messages; look upon yourself almost as the servant of all, and you will win the hearts of all, not only to yourself, but to God. At the same time, you will be laying up for yourself in heaven treasures which never fade, and adding many a bright jewel to that crown of glory which will grace your brows for ever.

HUMILITY OF THE SACRED HEART.

I. Honour, glory, power, and praise are due to Jesus Christ, because though clothed in human flesh, He is nevertheless really and truly the great, almighty God, before Whom all the hierarchies of heaven bend the knee in trembling adoration. But as He came to redeem us from our miseries, He brought with Him, in His human heart, the antidote of that poison which had been our ruin. Pride cast us down from the lofty eminence to which God in the beginning had raised our human nature; and, therefore, humility must be planted in our hearts to restore us to our dignity, and to induce us to imitate Him in this most necessary virtue.

Just consider in what way He has given us, in this respect, a most glorious example. He cast aside the glory and the obsequious homage which were due to His nature and to the dignity of the Messias, and chose rather to be born in the utmost poverty. His parents were very poor and very lowly. His reputed father held no higher position than that of a common workman. They were so poor, that they could not send Him to the schools in which the wealthy and the noble were educated. They, therefore, brought Him up in illiterate toil, and He earned His daily bread in the sweat of His brow. He ought to have been the king and ruler of men, and, had He so willed it, all creatures would have stood waiting to catch the faintest whisper of His will. But being humble of heart, He preferred to obey rather than to command. He submitted Himself to His Mother and to St. Joseph. He fulfilled all the requirements of the civil and of the ecclesiastical law. He yielded Himself up to the hands of His enemies, and obeyed them, even to the ignominious death of the Cross.

The profoundest veneration and respect were His by inalienable right; yet, through love of humility, He waived His claim to the homage of His people, and chose rather to endure their contempt and their bitterest scorn. They loaded Him with the most atrocious calumnies. They looked upon Him as a blasphemer, a liar, a cheat, and a seditious demagogue. They preferred to Him a thief and murderer, and caused Him to end upon the Cross, between two malefactors, the days of His mortal pilgrimage. Thus did Jesus love humility. He chose it as the instrument by which to regenerate the human race. We fell by pride; we are raised to our former dignity by humility.

II. Do you love humility, and try to foster its growth in your heart? Alas! how far removed are boys generally from the lowly sentiments which filled the heart of Jesus! They are so far from them, that they take pride in those very things which Jesus rejected. There are some who pride themselves so much upon either their noble or their genteel descent, that they seem to think that they have conferred upon the world a signal service by deigning to come into it. Upon all those who cannot boast of blood so pure as their own, they look with a degree of scorn which is laughable to behold, and deem them to have incurred disgrace, by being born of parents 'who commit the enormity of living by an honest trade.' Had they been brought in contact with Our Lord during His youth, they would probably have contemned and despised Him for being the son of a carpenter. In their eyes He would not have been a gentleman.

Others, again, upon whom God has bestowed great intellectual ability, while by a law of compensation He has withheld from them what is called genteel parentage, plume themselves unduly upon their powers, and laugh cruelly at the stupidity which is sometimes the distinguishing feature of those who boast of, and set too great a value upon their gentle blood and their high connections. Not a few are silly enough to glory in matters of such minor importance as are personal appearance, strength, height, and prowess in the football or in the cricket field. Finally, all without exception, who in a greater or in a less degree, sin against God by pride, look for repute among their fellows, and expect to receive from them a certain amount of consideration, for the various excellences which they have, or which they imagine themselves to have. They are full of conceit, which manifests itself in their looks, their walk, their every gesture; and when those who are wiser than they endeavour both by word and by deed to correct them of their folly, they rage and storm, and talk about their honour and their dignity, and play such fantastic tricks before the whole School, as call loudly for the vigorous application of the birch-rod, to whip the offending Adam out of them.

III. Boys of this stamp are certainly very far from having their hearts like the sacred heart of Jesus. If, then, you have any desire to resemble Him, any wish to be pleasing to Him, and to find a place in His most holy heart, you must root out from your own all the faults which we have mentioned, for they disfigure it, and make Jesus turn away from it with displeasure.

Do not, therefore, set very great store upon gentility of blood, if God has bestowed it upon you. It is certainly very often a great advantage—the source of many and inestimable blessings, for which God must ever be thanked and praised. But, at the same time, do not be so foolish as to despise those who do not possess the like privilege. God does not regard you with one whit the more favour on account of it; and, if it be the *only* recommendation that you possess, sensible men will treat you with but scant courtesy on its account. They look for something more than high birth to command their esteem.

Let those also who are sharp-witted, and gifted with a clear head, a far-reaching mind, and a ready tongue, set not their hearts on these favours of God, nor take pride in them as if they were their own. They are not their own. They are God's gifts; and, to regard them as one's own, and to glory in them as if they were one's own, is to deprive God of what is His upon so many titles, that He never will suffer it to be given to another. Besides, it is as silly for a boy to be proud of his intellectual power as it would be for a man to be proud of the clothes which he has borrowed from another. Therefore, let each boy attribute to God all that he has, and never scorn others for not possessing those gifts which God has conferred upon him, but has not thought fit to bestow upon them.

As for the foolish pride which inflates some boys for their personal beauty, or for their strength and their dexterity, let it find no place in your heart. A slight sickness will deform the fairest face, just as a blight destroys the most beautiful flower. A fever will paralyse the strongest arm, and render futile the most consummate skill. Therefore, glory not in these transitory goods. ' Let not the wise man glory in his wisdom, nor the strong man in his strength,' but let it be your aim to glory in the humility of Jesus Christ. Look upon all that you have, in intellect, in social position, in wealth, in strength, or in health, as the pure gift of God. Thank Him for it, and give Him whatever glory and consideration may accrue to you from its possession.

MEEKNESS OF THE SACRED HEART.

I. Besides the fundamental virtue of humility, there is, very nearly akin to it, another virtue which Our Lord calls upon us to learn from His sacred heart. This is meekness, which the Prophet Isaias foretold should be one of the characteristic marks of the future Messias. He came as a meek king; His enemies led Him to the slaughter as a lamb—the type of meekness, the symbol of all that is gentle and inoffensive. Hence, when the Baptist caught sight of Him, he said to his followers: 'Behold the Lamb of God! behold Him Who taketh away the sins of the world!' With the greatest truth could he say this; for in Our Lord the virtue of meekness was in its plenitude. It kept His mind and all the faculties of His human soul in the most profound calm. It regulated all its motions, and all its impulses. It banished thence all haughtiness, and stifled all anger. In that holy heart, where meekness sat a queen, there was no bitterness, no disdain of others, no uprising of contempt or of scorn. On the contrary, there welled up from it, as from a fountain-head, naught but mercy and beneficence.

A glance at His life will prove the truth of all this; for, in the midst of provocation the sorest that ever tried the equanimity of a human heart, His meekness always kept His soul unruffled, and in peace. When men treated Him with the utmost contumely, when they took up stones to kill Him, interrupted Him in His speech by unseemly questions, and applied to Him epithets whereat the meekest heart would have been fired with anger, Jesus remained unmoved, and answered with a degree of quiet, imperturbable dignity, which must have filled His enemies with amazement.

To those who, with Him, observed none of the courtesies of discussion, but vented in passionate abuse the baffled rage of their wicked hearts, He replied without bitterness. He did not scorn those who scorned Him, nor contemn the presumptuous impertinence of those who tried to entrap Him with captious questions.

He did not, as He might so easily have done, take summary vengeance on those who rejected Him, and strove their utmost to rob Him of His life. No; the Lamb of God being meekness incarnate, kind, gentle, and affable to all, became a refuge for those who were weak, helpless, down-trodden, and afflicted. His hands were ever stretched forth to do good. 'The bruised reed He would not break, and smoking flax He would not extinguish.'

II. Such was the meekness of Jesus Christ. It gave to Him an indescribable charm, and invested Him with a magnetic influence, which drew to Him every noble and upright heart. If you seriously reflect upon it, you, also, will not fail to be drawn to Him. You will feel your heart longing to possess a virtue which gives a boy so great strength of character, and invests him with so much power to gain a mastery over all hearts. Therefore, if you wish to acquire meekness, you must cultivate the virtues from which it springs.

These are humility and self-denial. Humility fills the boy who strives to possess it, with a very deep sense of his manifold transgressions against God. It keeps the memory of the fact that he has reviled and insulted God ever fresh in his mind, and this makes him only too glad to atone for it by every means in his power. Hence, when his companions speak injurious words against him, or insult him to his face, or attribute to him motives which he detests, or accuse him of acts which he would scorn to commit—though he may acutely feel the smart—he will, nevertheless, still the tempest of his indignation by the thought of the way in which he has treated God, of the patience with which God has borne with him, and of the meekness with which Jesus always dealt with His enemies.

Again; because he has in the past gratified himself by sinning, he will try now to deny himself, and this self-denial will cultivate in him the spirit of meekness. For what is it that most frequently causes us to sin against the virtue of meekness? It is our own overweening love of self. Our ideas and our views are our idols. We would wish all others to view things as we view them, to adopt our notions upon various points, and in no way to run counter to our will. Consequently, one of the best means for cultivating a spirit of meekness in our hearts, will be not to gratify this love which we have for our own will.

Therefore, when you are contradicted, and when others prefer to follow their own opinions, to be guided by their own lights, and to have things done in their own way, learn to keep your soul in peace. Do not suffer it to be disturbed by allowing your self-love furiously to run away with you, and make you resent as an affront what all admit to be the right of each individual. By attending to these injunctions, you will be fixing in your heart a spirit of humility and of self-denial, from the union of which there will spring up the true spirit of meekness, which will mould your heart into the likeness of the heart of Jesus.

III. Knowing, therefore, the sources whence this beautiful virtue of meekness springs, and having before you the glorious example of your Lord, you must now resolve to win it for yourself. This you cannot do, unless you practise it whenever an opportunity for so doing presents itself. Of these there will be no lack, as the experience of college-life will no doubt have abundantly proved to you. For, unhappily, owing to the many imperfections of those who, like yourself, have come to School to be trained in knowledge and in virtue, occasions for exercising humility and self-abnegation will present themselves uncalled for, and perhaps more frequently than you desire. Nevertheless, do not let one of them slip from you, for they will all contribute to build up in your heart a spirit of meekness which will make you resemble Our Lord.

For this purpose, take care to practise the following precepts: Look upon all, without exception, as equal in every respect to yourself. Be not haughty, nor distant, with them, and let not their weaknesses—their boasting, their vanity, their selfishness—make you either scorn or sneer at them. If they thwart and contradict you, keep under control the indignation which will naturally rise within you. They have just as much right to their views as you have to your own; and, if they prefer their own to yours, and, as it seems to you, without good reason, calmly endeavour to point this out to them, and then, if they do not yield, but even turn upon you to revile you, repress your anger, and suffer it not, like a tempestuous wind, to trouble the calm of your soul.

On all these occasions, let not bitterness against those who have differed from you, rankle in your heart and destroy your peace. Think not of revenging yourself upon those who have treated you contemptuously, but endeavour to bury the matter in oblivion. Your mild behaviour will make an impression upon your companions, and in time will either win them over to your side, or prepare them favourably to hear your arguments, and to yield to your suggestions. Thus you will be able to practise frequently the Christian virtues of humility and self-denial. You will be able daily to feel the weight of the Cross, and the smart of the thorns. So noble a warfare against self will end by crowning you with meekness, and giving you a command over your own heart and a mighty influence over the hearts of others.

UNSELFISHNESS OF THE SACRED HEART.

I. HUMILITY and self-denial are the parents of many beautiful virtues, but of none more beautiful and more pleasing to the hearts of men than is that of unselfishness. This virtue, which causes us to forget self, and ever to study the advantage of others more than our own, is one which shines with surpassing lustre in the sacred heart of Our Lord. In Him we perceive a total absence of self-seeking, of all thought which looked not to the task which He had come to accomplish, and to the men whom He so ardently desired to save. He aimed neither at glory nor at fame; He cared not for His own ease nor for His own convenience. He came to do Another's will, to seek that Other's advantage, and to forget personal discomfort in the attainment of that end.

But to accomplish this, He had first to embrace those hardships from which men so eagerly turn away. Poverty and toil, opposition and disgrace, torments and death, stood in His way, but could not daunt His courageous heart. He loved men too much for that, and, therefore, in all His actions we find Him regardless of His own feelings, of His own interest, and wholly occupied with that which benefited and turned to the advantage of others. In His very childhood this zeal for the good of others, and this forgetfulness of self, gleamed forth for an instant when He left His parents and gave that wondrous manifestation of His wisdom which we brought before your notice in the instruction upon the three days' loss at Jerusalem. Yet He did not satisfy that absorbing desire to care for others, because His heavenly Father willed that, for eighteen long years to come, He should first be subject to His own creatures.

When at last the moment preordained of God did actually arrive, He spared not Himself in labouring for others, but with infinite pain and inconvenience to Himself, sought out the lost sheep of the house of Israel. The search after them involved frequent and wearisome journeys, with scant food and comfortless lodging. It meant toilsome days of teaching, amid continual contradiction from malignant opponents, and that, too, when He worked astounding wonders in healing the diseases of the sick, opening the eyes of the blind, cleansing the lepers, and raising the dead to life.

But when the hour had come in which the powers of darkness were allowed to prevail over Him, His forgetfulness of self particularly shone forth in its brightest lustre. As soon as His enemies seized Him in the Garden, He thought not of Himself. He cared only for His Apostles. When His ferocious captors laid hands upon Him, He besought them to let His Apostles go free. Also, when the women of Jerusalem wept at beholding His sufferings, His thoughts were not upon His own pain, but upon the miseries which were about to fall upon the Jewish nation. Even on the Cross, while His enemies were deriding Him, mocking Him, and triumphing at His approaching death, His thoughts were filled with God, pleading with Him for pardon and for mercy. Truly did Our Jesus love Himself last; His unselfish heart put our advantage before His own; and made Him count it a gain to suffer for us. He readily endured the worst that His foes could inflict upon Him, provided only that we should reap the benefit and that He should taste all the bitterness of the wormwood and the gall.

II. Very different is the story which we should have to tell of most boys, on the score of unselfishness. Not one of them would like to be told that he is selfish. He would very probably resent the imputation as a personal insult. Yet, if any of them will take the trouble narrowly to observe his conduct for a short time, and try to note those actions in which this unlovely trait betrays itself, he will be startled by the number of selfish acts which will disclose themselves to him in the course of even a single day.

Bear in mind that it is selfishness to seek your own ease and convenience, without taking the trouble to examine whether one of your companions is not thereby annoyed, and subjected to much discomfort. It is selfishness to look only to your own gain, without trying to prevent that gain from being your neighbour's loss. It is selfishness to consult your own pleasures and your own taste, without a thought whether that which amuses you is equally amusing to your companions. It is selfishness to impose upon others either your own will or your own tastes, when they are unwilling to accept them. From these, and many other instances which might be cited, you will see how easily selfishness may hold possession of a boy's heart, and he be all the while unconscious of it.

Just look around, and observe what is daily and hourly

happening under your very eyes, and you will see many, if not all the instances of selfishness which we have mentioned, committed by the boys with whom you live. The aim of some of their lives seems to be to have the best of everything for themselves. They strive for the best and most comfortable places at the fire; they seize upon the best bats and balls, and occupy in the play-ground the best position for the games. At table, they select the best meats. In the choice of amusements which are to fill up a recreation day, they will have their likings and their dislikings taken into account, and will be angry and discontented unless their views be carried out.

But though, by their selfishness, they put their companions to much inconvenience and pain, they do not care, and they are dumb with amazement, and swell with anger, if even a hint is dropped that their conduct is selfish. When they thrust weak and delicate little boys from the fire, they do not reflect that they are guilty of a selfish act, because it is so natural for them to consult their own ease. They seem to forget that others have rights as well as they; have aims, and tastes, and views, which they would like to see attended to, as well as they. An unselfish boy would take these things into consideration, and be ingenious in devising means by which his companions might have as large a share of the good things of the College as he himself has. But not so the selfish boy. With him all charity begins at home, and stays there. He takes care to love himself, but conveniently forgets that there is a neighbour to whom he owes an equal debt of love. He is to himself first, and last, and above all things else. He never thinks of others. He cares not what pain, nor what inconvenience, nor what damage is inflicted upon them, provided that he himself is at ease, and has all that he desires. He is his own centre, his own idol, and he loves and worships himself with a devotion which, while it disgusts some, cannot fail to raise a smile, half of pity, half of scorn, upon the face of every sensible man.

III. As there is no boy that does not indignantly repudiate the accusation of selfishness, and look with contempt upon those who are selfish, let each try with a persevering effort to root from his heart this detestable fault. But while engaged in a task which is worthy of so great praise, let not the chief reason for undertaking it be, because selfishness is so unlovely in the eyes of men; but because it is displeasing to God. It is so hateful to Jesus Christ, that He will not acknowledge as His child anyone who does not deny and trample upon self. Take advantage, therefore, of every opportunity for performing any acts that will help you to break down the love of self, and make you take thought for the convenience, the comfort, and the ease of others.

For this purpose, love yourself last, and always put yourself below your neighbour. Be considerate towards those boys who are weak, or young, or in delicate health, and take care that they get the best of everything, rather than that you yourself should have it. Frequently examine your conduct, to see whether you are not a source of pain to others, and if you discover that you are, do your utmost to correct yourself. Be willing to let others, from time to time, have their way. Think a great deal more than you do about their feelings, their wishes, their likes and their dislikes, and try to accommodate yourself to them. By doing this, you will find many an occasion for thwarting yourself, and for breaking down that excessive love of your own ease which is the fruitful source of much selfishness. By acting in this way, you will find your heart becoming day by day less selfish, till at last it will be conformed in all respects to that most unselfish of hearts, the sacred heart of Our dearest Lord.

JOY OF THE SACRED HEART.

I. WHENEVER we have a sure hope of acquiring some good, or when we are actually in possession of it, our hearts are filled with a gentle emotion which we call joy. Therefore, since Our Lord had many good things, both in prospect and in actual fruition, it is certain that His sacred heart must oftentimes have been stirred to its lowest depths by the ecstasy of great joy.

He could look forwards to the time when all His labours should be finished; to that glorious day, when from the summit of the Mount He should gaze upon the earth, where He had suffered so much, and after blessing it and the disciples, whom He should there for a time leave behind Him, should be caught up into Paradise, to be for ever flooded with the joys of the beatific vision. He could peer into the ages which were yet to come, and behold the great and glorious Church filling the world and peopling the Courts of heaven with her children. He could think of the countless Saints who should love and serve Him, and glorify His Name among the nations; of the Martyrs who should confess Him before men, and give Him their hearts' best blood; of the Virgins, the Confessors, the great Popes, the Doctors, the wise men, the warriors, the leaders and guides of the world who should devote their whole lives and all their energies to His love and service. The hope of all this would, and really did fill His heart with joy.

But besides the joy of hope, He had the still more thrilling pleasure which only actual fruition can give. There were around Him those who were, so to speak, the first-fruits of that harvest of souls which had yet to be gathered into His heavenly garners. There was the spotless sanctity of His immaculate Mother. There were, as long as he lived, the sweet gentleness and humility of the lowly St. Joseph. There were the strong loving hearts of the Apostles, the innocence of the little children, the mature virtue of those who were waiting in patient hope for the dawning of the day-star of justice, and the newly-acquired purity of converted sinners, whose souls were sparkling with the diamond tears of their repentant sorrow. All these were His; they pressed round Him, they were gathered in, and held close to His sacred heart, which thrilled with so much joy, that all the Angels in heaven who beheld it, were moved to rejoice with Him over the spoils which His heart had won.

II. Dear children! you think it a privilege to be able to give joy to your parents, to your masters, and to those whom you respect and love; what happiness then may be yours, if you can give joy to the heart of Jesus Christ, your Lord and your God! You can do this, and He expects that you will do it. Let me point out to you the way.

Should any of you be so unfortunate and so wretched as to be living in a state of sin, and loaded with the crushing weight of evil habits, you can give great joy to the heart of Jesus, and to the whole Court of heaven, if you cast off your allegiance to the devil, return to God, and determine never more to leave His holy service. But as for those who are free from grievous sin, they may at every moment of the day give to Jesus very great joy. It is a pleasure for Him to look at their pure hearts, and to see that from them are carefully excluded all thoughts which would stain their spotless whiteness; to see their desires conformed to the rule of God's law, and their words honest and upright. As He sits upon His sacramental throne in the tabernacle, it gives Him great joy to see boys coming to kneel before Him, as they go to play, or to study, or when they come at the close of day to offer Him their labour. As they bow before Him, He blesses them; and while they pray, His sacred heart is quite close to them, eager to grant what they ask. When, on Sundays and on Festivals, they kneel at His table to receive Him into their souls, who shall be able to describe the transports of joy which flood His loving heart? It is the joy of a father that bends over His children and kisses them on their return from a long journey. Such as these go away taking Jesus with them. They fill His heart with joy by their regard and respect for duty, which they accomplish to please Him. They study for His sake; they are kind, and charitable, and obedient, because they know that it will please Him.

Let it, then, be the aim of every boy in the College, by visiting Jesus in the Holy Sacrament, by receiving Him, by keeping free from sin, and by manfully doing his duty, to procure this exquisite joy for the heart of Our Lord. It will be some slight compensation for the anguish which in the past he may have caused it by grievous sin.

III. Having learnt in what way you may give joy to the

sacred heart, resolve to adopt, and to put in practice, whatever will conduce to fill it with gladness. For this purpose, be determined, in the first place, not to become the slave of the devil, by consenting to mortal sin. He promises you happiness unalloyed, if you will but give yourself up to him. But happiness neither will nor can be yours, so long as you are subject to his thraldom, unless, indeed, it be that delirium which worldlings call happiness, but which, as you know very well, is not worthy of the name. It is the result of a deadly poison which obscures the light of reason, and leaves behind in the soul the germs of everlasting death.

In the next place, let no day pass without kneeling for a few moments before the altar to offer up your studies to Jesus, and to beg His blessing upon your labours. If you could see the smile of pleasure which plays like sunshine upon His face when you come before Him to salute Him and to offer Him your love, you would never begrudge the few moments so spent, but would wait with holy impatience for the time when you might again kneel in His presence, to receive the blessing of His upraised hand, and to feel the thrill of joy which His gracious smile flashes through your heart. Be diligent in your preparation to receive Him in Holy Communion, and miss no opportunity of approaching to that banquet of divine love. It is the source of life, of strength, of purity; now, you need all these, and therefore do not be so foolish as to allow mere trifles to keep you away from the fount whence they may so easily be drawn.

Finally, in order to prove to Our Lord that you really wish to give Him joy, strive to do something which will show Him that your wish is no mere sentiment, which will evaporate into thin air on meeting with the slightest difficulty. If you ask what this something is to be, we would suggest that it be the faithful accomplishment of the ordinary duties of your college-life. You can give to God no better proof of your sincerity than this.

Therefore, if in consequence of these resolutions you apply diligently to your books during all study hours, and perform your appointed task, you will give joy to the sacred heart. If you be obedient to your masters, and observe your Rule, though no eye be there to watch you, you will give joy to the sacred heart. If you be kind and charitable to your companions, and in all your relations with them try to forget self, and to remember only their convenience, profit, and pleasure, you will give joy to the sacred heart. Happy the boy who thus endeavours, in the days of his school-life, to be pleasing to Our dearest Lord. His grateful heart, which never forgets a favour done, nor a kind word spoken, nor even a cup of cold water given in His name, will reward him by giving him in this world the peace of a good conscience, and in the world to come that inestimable treasure of never-ending bliss, the magnitude of which human intelligence is inadequate to grasp, and human speech unable to express in words.

SORROW OF THE SACRED HEART.

I. A PRESENTIMENT of impending evil, or the consciousness of evil which has already laid hold of us, begets in the heart that feeling of uneasiness and disquiet which we call sorrow. Like other men, Our divine Lord felt this weakness of human nature. By a decree of His own will, He allowed the inferior part of His soul to experience all the crushing weight with which grief presses upon the sensitive hearts of men. As if to encourage them by His own example to the practice of a patience under this infirmity, He suffered so great an accumulation of sorrow to crush Him down beneath its heavy burthen, that the prophet called Him, 'The Man of Sorrows, the Man acquainted with infirmity.' How great, then, must have been the sorrow which throughout the whole of His mortal life flooded His soul, in consequence of His perfect knowledge of the fearful death awaiting Him! Only by an exercise of divine power could joy enter that heart, upon which there ever rested the gloom of Calvary and the shadow of the Cross.

But independently of the grief begotten of presentiment,

there were around Him on every side causes sufficient to steep His soul in bitterness. He came to save men; to spend Himself for them; yet in the vast majority He beheld nothing but indifference. Some treated Him with contempt; others opposed Him with obstinate and fanatical fury. Those whom He had benefited were at times ungrateful to Him. Also sin, which is so hateful to Him, so opposed to His infinite purity, held dominion in not a few of their hearts.

To add fresh fuel to the devouring grief which already consumed Him, His eyes beheld their countless miseries—the consequences and the punishments of that primeval fall, which from the days of Adam, even unto our own times, has filled the world with sighs and tears. No wonder, then, that He often sighed and groaned in spirit, that He suffered the tears of sorrow to burst from His eyes, and to stream down His cheeks. At the grave of Lazarus they flowed so unrestrainedly, that the Jews said: 'Behold how He loved him.' When He looked down upon the guilty city, and saw in the future the terrible destruction which awaited it because of its rejection of Him, His tears flowed afresh. Finally, when, in the Garden, He took upon Himself the loathsome burthen of the world's iniquity, His grief not only forced tears from His eyes, but made His blood burst through the pores of His body in a crimson sweat, which trickled down in great drops upon the dewy grass on which He knelt.

II. If that same sacred heart, which shared so largely in the woes of human nature, could now feel any sorrow, would it find no cause for grief in the conduct of some college-boys? Uunfortunately we must confess that it would! For there are not a few who inflict many a stab upon that sacred heart. If you reflect for a moment upon all that He has done for you, and then consider the return which you make to Him, you will not fail to understand the grief with which you flood His soul when you sin. For you are His dearest, most favoured children. He has done for you what He has not done except for a few privileged souls. He has put you, so to speak, in an inclosed garden, from which every occasion of scandal and of sin is carefully shut out. He has given you wise teachers, and good companions. He has set before your eyes nothing but the best examples of every virtue. The Sacraments are within your reach; God abides among you in the tabernacle; and yet, even here, in this holy place, sin is committed.

The eyes of Jesus see and mark the evil that is done. He knows those who do it. He knew, and thought of, and prayed for them, while He travelled about the dusty roads of Judea, hungry and athirst with His labour. He thought of them and saw their sin, as He knelt in the Garden, and prayed that the bitter chalice might pass away from Him. Will you dare, then, to sin, and thus renew the grief which weighed so heavily upon Him, that He declared it to be enough of itself to bring about His death? Oh! be not so cruel! Do not trample upon the blood which He so lavishly poured forth to save you. Do not, as St. Paul says, 'crucify unto yourself again the Lord of glory.' Circle not His brow with that wreath of woe; smite Him not with your hands; glare not fiercely upon Him with your eyes; speak not against Him words of reviling and of scorn; open not your ears to the speeches of His enemies. If you sin, you do all this. Nay, you do even more; you drive the nails through His quivering flesh; you make Him drink the vinegar and the gall; you pierce through and through that sacred heart which love of you rent in twain, and drenched with woe unutterable.

III. If you be wise, you will make a strong resolution never to sin again—never to wring the heart of Jesus with another pang of sorrow. For, if no other reason save that of self-interest should induce you to come to this determination, yet that alone, unworthy as it is, ought to urge you to follow this course. For, as sin, and the consequences of sin, brought sorrow and affliction of spirit upon Our Lord, so also do they plunge the hearts of men into a very sea of anguish.

Look back upon your own experience. If you have ever

had the misfortune to sin, you will know this. A boy's heart is a very paradise of pleasure, so long as the wily tempter is not listened to, and his poisoned fruit rejected with scorn. But no sooner has the devil prevailed upon him to stretch forth his hand and pluck the forbidden fruit, than there is let loose upon his heart a very tempest of raging passions. The barrier is broken down, and every beast may range at will through that which was once the garden of God.

There is then no peace for the wretched boy. For as soon as the first delirium of passion is over, his eyes are opened to see his degradation. A small voice makes itself heard in the midst of his heart, bitterly reproaching him, and saying, in accents which no amount of dissipation can drown: 'What hast thou done? Thou hast sold, for a mess of pottage, thy right to the enjoyment of God. Thou hast sacrificed the liberty of the sons of God for the slavery of the devil. Thou art now a child of hell. Let God but snap asunder the frail thread of life, and thou wouldst fall like lead into the depths of hell's fiery prison.'

If, then, you wish to have a joyous, happy life, avoid sin; be not of the number of the wicked, ' for there is no peace for the wicked, saith the Lord.' It is to be hoped, however, that higher and more unselfish motives will stir your heart to make this noble resolve. Let the memory of that tide of woe which, like the tumultuous billows of an angry sea, swept over the breast of Our Lord, soften your heart, and make it swell with those grateful feelings which the recollection of so much suffering endured for your sake will not fail to produce. Then be determined that no enticement of the devil, that no gilded bait of pleasure, shall ever again lure your heart into the commission of a grievous sin. Say to all that would tempt you from your allegiance: ' I serve a Master Who has suffered and bled for me, Whose heart has been pained and agonised for me. I will not, therefore, be so vile as to betray Him for the wretched garbage which the devil can offer me. This is my resolve; may God help me to keep it to the end of my days.'

FRIENDSHIP OF THE SACRED HEART.

I. As we meditate upon the admirable virtues of Our blessed Lord's sacred heart, we discover among them that beautiful species of love which is called the love of friendship. Those who were so highly favoured as to be the objects of it, felt that Jesus loved them in a special manner, in return for their love of Him. They were conscious that He vouchsafed to admit them to a share in His most inward thoughts, His sorrows, and His joys. This emboldened them, on their side, to confide to His loving heart all the various and conflicting emotions which either depressed their souls with sorrow, or transported them with delight. As we read the Gospel narrative, we cannot fail to notice that Martha and Mary, Lazarus and Magdalene, were of the number of these privileged ones. The Apostles, too, were His bosom friends, and this is the title by which He addressed them, after He had given them the Holy Eucharist, as the greatest pledge of His love.

But among all these, and above all these, there was one to whom the heart of Jesus linked itself in the closest bonds of friendship. This was the virginal St. John. Our Lord always treated him as a favourite, and so little did He disguise His affection for him, that His other followers were wont to call the youthful Apostle 'the disciple whom Jesus loved.' Well did he deserve that highest epithet of honour; for to him, more than to any other, the Redeemer showed the most special marks of His favour. Two others shared with John the wondrous vision upon Thabor; two others beheld with him the fearful agony in the Garden; but of no other is it recorded, that he leaned his head upon the bosom of Jesus Christ. Even St. Peter, usually so fearless in asking questions of Our Lord, did not dare to ask Him who should betray Him. But knowing His love for St. John, and the childlike affection of that disciple for Jesus, he bade him ask for the information which he so much desired to obtain. Leaning thus on the bosom of Jesus, John put the question to Him, and Our Lord at once answered it.

Furthermore, while hanging upon the Cross, Jesus turned His dying eyes towards him ; He bade His beloved Mother take John as her son; and then, in order to give His disciple the most touching mark of His personal affection, He intrusted her whom He loved more than any other creature, to the care of a heart whose tenderness He knew full well. Such was the friendship of Our Lord's sacred heart, of which the beloved disciple never wearied to speak unto men.

II. In the tabernacle, before which you so often kneel, that same sacred heart is now beating, and is filled with the same inexhaustible treasure of friendliness towards men. Each boy in the College may, if it so please him, become a bosom friend of that loving Master. Nay, Jesus is waiting there for no other purpose than to receive his love, and in return, to lavish upon him the treasures of His own undying affection. If you have the least doubt about this, reflect for a moment upon His love for the young. His very look of kindliness must have drawn them to Him, and made them press through the crowds, to be near One in Whose eyes they could see the reflection of the fire of love which burned in His heart. How did He receive them when they came to Him? He called them to Him with every sign of the most tender love, and of the most condescending friendliness. His blessed hands were laid upon their heads ; His arms enfolded them in a fatherly embrace ; and He caught them to His heart, saying: ' Suffer them to come unto Me, for of such is the kingdom of heaven.'

Each of you, therefore, both great and small may, and ought to aspire to be the friend of Jesus, and like St. John, you will be privileged to lay your head upon His bosom, where it will rest, quite close to that sacred heart which is beating with love for you. At your age you need a true friend, for without one you cannot well live. You need the kindly word, the cheering voice, the helping hand of some one who loves you, to uphold you in life's slippery way. You need some one to aid your inexperience by his wisdom, and to sustain your weakness by his strength.

Such a one you will find in Jesus Christ. He will teach

you how to subdue that spirit of revolt which is already stirring within you. He will assist you to curb the power of the devil. He will not allow him to tempt you beyond your strength. If you slip, He will catch you before you fall; and should you unhappily refuse His aid, and prefer to plunge yourself into the mire, one look from you will make Him draw you thence, and cleanse you in the bath of His most precious blood. He will admit you frequently to lay your head upon His sacred heart; nay, rather, He will give Himself to you, and rest His all-holy head upon your heart. His holy Mother will then gladly acknowledge you for her son, and the Angels of God will cluster round you, because their Lord and Master is now your friend.

III. Privileges so great, so astounding, are not given unconditionally. God has laid down His own terms, and it is only when these have been complied with that you can enter upon the enjoyment of His heavenly favours. What, then, are these terms? Summarily, they may be said to be the possession, at least in a certain degree, of those qualities which Jesus found in St. John, and in the children whom He made for ever memorable by calling them to His sacred arms.

If examined in detail, the most important will be, in the first place, simplicity, which ever attracts, and charms, and wins the hearts of all. We find it chiefly in little children, and in those childlike characters which are always so lovable. When injured, they bear no malice, but forget and forgive. In what they do, there is no self-seeking, no aiming at effect. When they want anything, they ask for it without either disguise or circumlocution. They know not how to scheme or to intrigue. If refused, they revenge not themselves; their pride is not wounded; they do not show haughtiness, nor disdain, nor scorn. Aim at their simplicity of heart, and you, too, will become very dear to the heart of Our Lord.

In the next place, you must possess that most beautiful virtue, the peerless jewel of chastity or purity. Jesus Christ will not enter a heart in which it is not to be found. If a boy has that virtue, it circles his brow with a halo of heavenly beauty and glory, which makes him very dear to God and to His holy Angels and Saints. Our Lord is drawn to him, as steel is drawn to the loadstone. He will go to him, and will take up His abode in his heart. But if that boy have foolishly cast away that bright jewel—if he have sullied the dazzling brilliancy of his baptismal robes, Jesus will avert His face; He will flee from him as from the loathsome rottenness of a putrid carcase, and naught will bring Him back but the bitter tears of true repentance. Fight, then, bravely and manfully against the inclinations of your corrupt nature. Withstand the devil, and each repulse, each victory, will increase your strength, until at last you will be able to put him to flight with as much ease as you now either open or shut your hand.

Lastly, have great confidence in the mercy and the goodness of God. Do not look upon Him as a hard task-master, a severe judge; but rather as the most kind, the most indulgent, the most loving of fathers. Imprint this notion of Our Lord deeply in your mind and heart, and in all your necessities, act towards Him as you would act towards your own father. When you feel the need of anything, ask for it with simplicity. Tell God, in prayer, that you feel this particular want; that He can relieve it, if He chooses to do so; and that you humbly hope that He will grant your request, if, in His infinite wisdom, He should see that it will be good for you. In the same way, when you are tempted to be proud or vain, angry or revengeful, disobedient or haughty, run to Him and ask Him to scatter the storm-clouds which are lowering over your heart. Should you feel the revolt of your sensual nature, flee to Him at once, as a child flees to its father when danger threatens; for worse than lion, or bear, or poisonous asp, is the demon of uncleanness.

Thus, by simplicity, by chastity, and by confidence in God, you will attract to yourself the friendship of the sacred heart. Oh! strive, dear children of Jesus Christ, to win it for yourselves, for happy both here and hereafter will that boy be who can say in his heart: 'I feel that I am the friend of Jesus Christ! His sacred heart loves me, and I love Him.'

DEVOTEDNESS OF THE SACRED HEART.

I. A MOTHER'S love is strong as death, and burns with an ardour so intense that many waters cannot extinguish its flame. To this love Jesus compares His own love for us, and promises that it will be even more intense and more lasting. 'Can a woman,' He asks, 'forget her child?' Yet if that were possible, still will I not forget thee.' Now, what is it that distinguishes a mother's love from all other species of human affection? It is its devotedness. She gives herself up entirely to the child of her bosom. She immolates herself upon the altar of her love. Her son will spring up before her eyes, and grow daily in his strength till he reaches manhood; yet if she should live to see him a gray-headed man, her love will still remain fresh and green. Amid the turmoil of life he may be separated from her, and long years may roll by, and a thousand different objects enter to occupy his heart, to cool his affections, and to blot from his mind everything but the faintest memory of home. Yet it is not so with the mother. No distance can separate her heart from her child; no length of years can slacken the fire of her love; for her heart is a treasury, stored with an inexhaustible wealth of it for the child which she has borne in sorrow and in pain. If he should prove ungrateful, her heart will still pardon and love him, because it is devoted; it forgets self and thinks only of the object beloved.

Such, also, are the sentiments of the sacred heart of Jesus towards us. That heart has loved and thought of and occupied itself with our welfare, during the long centuries which elapsed before we came into existence. When at last we were ushered in upon this busy stage of life, it yearned for our poor, cold, feeble love. We, alas! have been indifferent to it, and withheld our love from it for many a long year; but He has waited patiently and has not ceased to say: 'My son, give Me thy heart.' We have kept at a distance from Him; in our sins, in our worldly occupations and pursuits, we have not thought of Him. Yet He has persevered all the same in loving us and in asking us for our love. We have been ungrateful. We have received a thousand favours, benefits, and kindnesses, without returning Him thanks; nay, we have repaid them even with insults, offences, and injuries; still He has not turned away. He has continued to love us, and to hope for our conversion. Why is this? Because His heart has loved us with a devotedness which is well-nigh incomprehensible.

II. The contemplation of love so astounding, will surely stir up in your hearts a resolution to make the sacred heart a return of undying love. If Jesus is devotedly attached to you, try to be devotedly attached to Him. The hearts of boys are, as a rule, too full of generosity to remain cold and indifferent to such burning love; and they will, therefore, be incited to make this noble resolution. But, remember, devotedness is no easy thing. It means self-sacrifice, and a great deal of it. For, no one can pretend to love Jesus Christ without giving up much that is pleasant to the carnal man. No boy, therefore, can say that he is devoted to the sacred heart, unless he most carefully excludes from his own whatever is displeasing to God. Hence he must be ready, daily and hourly, to offer up this sacrifice. If by the aid of divine grace he be thus happily disposed, he will banish from his heart all self-esteem, all contemplation of his own excellence whether real or imaginary, and so deprive himself of that refined luxury in which proud souls delight to revel. He will abhor whatever may sully the purity of his thoughts or of his desires, and will, therefore, be careful to close the avenues of his senses against every object which might endanger the safety of that chastity which it is to be hoped he guards with unwearied vigilance. He will humbly submit to the orders of Superiors, and to the requirements of the college rules.

Sacrifices like these, though difficult enough to make, are

nevertheless easy, as long as we feel that Jesus is with us, and is watching our combat. The real test of true, devoted love, is when it is able to endure the strain which apparent separation from God puts upon it. Hence, it is no easy matter to go on loving and serving Him when all the novelty of the divine service has worn off, and all the sweetness which rewards our first efforts is withdrawn. Then we feel that God has departed from us; for we no longer experience the delight caused by His presence. The heart grows sick and faint; the love which burned so bright grows dim, and there is fear lest its smouldering embers may become utterly extinct. It is when the clouds gather over us, and there seems no hope, that the time has come to show our devoted love.

If we then persevere in God's service, we may comfort ourselves with the assurance, that our love for Jesus bears at least some faint resemblance to His love for us. It is devoted; and when we seem to be abandoned by God, and left to sit in darkness and in sorrow upon the earth, it will cause us to exclaim: 'Even though He slay me, yet I will hope in Him, love Him, and serve Him.'

III. Having seen in what devotedness to the sacred heart consists, examine in the next place how you may best put it in practice. Everything in your life that entails any kind of self-denial, and that you undertake and go on faithfully performing for the love of God, is an exercise of devotedness. Hence, the best proof that you can give to God of your heart's devotedness to Him, is in the first place strictly to observe His holy law. That law is a bridle with which you may hold in check your fallen nature. Even now in your early youth that fallen nature begins to make its existence known to you, by craving for what is gratifying to the carnal man. But there is also within you a voice, which protests loudly against the acceptance by your soul of any gratification that is not in strict accordance with the law of God. This is the voice of your spiritual nature, which pleads earnestly with you for the interests of God, and of your immortal soul.

To which of these two shall you listen? to which of them shall you give up the dominion of your heart? Shall it be to your carnal nature, or shall it be to your spiritual nature? If you be devoted to God, you will hearken to the voice of your conscience; you will take the bridle of the divine law into your hands, and with it will rein in your unruly passions. You will not suffer them to run away with you, nor to make you swerve from the line of duty, either to the right hand or to the left. This will put beyond all doubt your devotedness to Jesus Christ. It will make Him King, Lord, and Master of your heart.

A still further proof of your devotedness to the sacred heart will be your perseverance in God's holy service. It is much to serve Him for even a single day; but it is not those that begin, but those that persevere, who are crowned. Therefore, by your perseverance, prove to God and to the world that you are no mere carpet-knight, who at the first reverse sits down and gives up in despair; but rather one of God's devoted soldiers, who in the midst of hardship and rough usage, will be faithful even unto death.

Finally, show your devotedness to God, by fidelity in small things as well as in great; and therefore work hard at your books; obey the injunctions of disciplinary rules; be patient with others; always adhere to those who are in the right, and never blush to do what your conscience tells you is just, no matter who may be opposed to you, no matter what offence you may give to friends, no matter what loss and inconvenience you may bring upon yourself.

PURITY OF THE SACRED HEART.

I. GOD is holiness itself. His purity is so great that the Sacred Scripture represents the highest of the heavenly spirits as humbly veiling their faces before the dazzling splendour of its intolerable brightness. Compared with Him, they find themselves full of stains and blemishes, and therefore acknowledge by this attitude of reverential awe, their unworthiness to stand before Him. It will, then, give us some idea of the purity of the sacred heart, if we reflect that this unapproachable sanctity of God, became incarnate in the person of Jesus Christ, and that His heart is consequently the throne upon which it has taken its seat, the tabernacle in which it delights to dwell.

If a vessel which has held some precious ointment long retains the sweetness of its odour, how completely must the sacred heart be impregnated with the sanctity of the Godhead, which dwells personally within it ? With good reason, therefore, does the Church in her Liturgy say to Our Lord: 'Thou didst not abhor the Virgin's womb.' For though a special privilege of God preserved that resting-place immaculate, yet His purity is so inexpressibly great, that she deems it wonderful that He did not turn away from it in horror.

Reflecting upon this, we can well understand the lowly reverence of the saintly Baptist, when He spoke of Jesus as One, the latchet of Whose shoes he deemed himself unworthy to loose. Also, it gives us a reason why Jesus during His lifetime, though submitting to the scorn and the contumely of men, and exposing Himself to the vilest accusations which their malignant hatred could bring against Him, yet would never suffer the slightest aspersion to be cast upon this His darling attribute of purity. His very look, and gait, and person, circled Him with so bright a halo of sanctity, that His bitterest enemies, though challenged by Him to point out one speck or stain upon His character, yet dared not breathe a word which could tarnish His fair, fame.

O most pure heart of Jesus ! we cast ourselves down in humblest adoration before Thee, and with the deepest contrition bewail our sins, and ask Thee to wash us yet more and more from our iniquities.

II. This virtue, which Jesus prizes so highly, He recommends in a most special manner to you boys. Now is the spring-time of your days, the period during which you plant the seeds of those virtues which are afterwards to be the ornaments of your life, and the fruit upon which you are to live in your maturer years. At present, the soil of your heart, in which these must be cast, is soft and easily cultivated; but unless care be taken now to keep it clear, it will grow hard, and be productive of naught but noxious weeds and stinging nettles. It is for this reason, therefore, that Jesus Christ expects young boys to love and cherish this virtue. He wishes them to cultivate and tend it with the most jealous care; for its cultivation in later years is a matter of the greatest difficulty. Looking upon you with His loving, fatherly eyes, and with that winning smile which drew children nigh unto Him, He says to each of you: ' Be ye imitators of Me, as most dear children. Imitate My sanctity, My spotless purity, and let it be your chief care to defend that priceless treasure from the grasp of infernal robbers, who ever prowl about, seeking to snatch it from you, when you are least upon your guard.' God is anxious that you should be pure, because, unless you be pure, you will never see His face: ' Holiness, without which no one can see God.'

Moreover, without it you cannot pretend to be virtuous; for it is useless to try to root out other vices and defects, if the vice most opposed to holiness is left behind. It is as useless and as hopeless a task as trying to heal the gaping wounds, and dry up the running sores of a man whose blood is corrupted, for with such a one the cure must begin at the source of the evil.

In like manner, every attempt to lead a holy life will be futile, unless the heart be first thoroughly cleansed from all defilement. Consequently, each boy who would be the friend of Jesus must have the virtue of purity in his heart. God gave it to him in Baptism, and told him to wear it as a garment of honour, resplendently white. The Sacrament of Confirmation furthermore adorned it with the seal of the Holy Ghost; and in the Blessed Eucharist, Jesus Himself comes into the heart, and makes it the temple of the Most High God.

Remember, therefore, the honour with which you are clothed, the glory with which you are crowned, and never do, or say, or think, or desire anything that would tarnish your fair fame. Cultivate purity by defending it from the attacks of the devil, and by resisting the corrupt influence of the world. Then Jesus will look upon you as His most dear children, because He will see in you a likeness of Himself.

III. But you will ask, 'How are we to regain our purity if we should unhappily have lost it? or having once more regained it, how are we so faithfully to guard it as never to lose it again?' If you have lost that treasure, or sullied that white robe, or cast away that crown of glory, you must, in the first place, grieve from your heart for having thereby offended Almighty God. Then you must humbly, and with all sincerity, make unto God's minister a full confession of your sins, and resolve, with God's help, never to offend again. By these acts of repentance, the most precious blood of Our Lord will be applied to your souls. That saving stream will wash them clean from all their filth; the treasure will be restored to the centre of your hearts; the robe will again be made resplendently white; and the crown of glory be once more set upon your heads.

Lastly, if you wish to remain pure, you must pray very earnestly to God for the grace of chastity; for our nature is so weak and so prone to evil, that without the continual help of grace, obtained through prayer, no one can keep himself free from stain. Hence, each boy ought every day of his life, and frequently during the course of each day, to lift up his heart and mind to God by short and fervent prayer, saying with the Prophet: 'Create a clean heart in me, O God! and renew a right spirit within my bowels.'

In addition to prayer, there are three other most efficacious and most necessary means for preserving purity, and the boy who makes use of them will walk through the fiery furnace of this world, unscorched by its devouring flames. In the first place he must never look at dangerous objects, nor listen to wicked words, nor allow free ingress to the filthy suggestions of the devil. He must guard his eyes, which are the windows of his soul, lest through them the enemy should climb into his heart, and steal away his treasure.

In the next place, he must frequently go to the tribunal of penance, for there he will meet with a wise, experienced, and kind father to warn him of danger, to cheer him in difficulties, and to encourage him in the heat of battle.

Lastly, he must very often approach to receive the Blessed Sacrament. In that pledge of God's love for us, he will receive the sacred heart of Jesus Christ; he will receive Christ Himself, God and man, the source of all purity. His divine flesh will feed him, His blood will either quench the fierce flames of concupiscence, or so slacken them as to enable him to check their growth, and prevent them from destroying him. Therefore, let each boy who wishes to be pure, employ these means—not once or twice but continually. He will most certainly keep himself free from mortal sin; he will be clothed with honour; and purity, like a bright diadem, will circle his brow with a glory which will never fade.

FERVOUR OF THE SACRED HEART IN PRAYER.

I. Our Lord inculcated nothing more strongly, both by precept and by example, than the duty of prayer. He impressed this so deeply upon the minds of the Apostles, and made them so clearly see its utility and its necessity, that they asked Him to become their master in this science of sciences, and to teach them how to pray. He did so, and the 'Our Father,' which is the Christian's daily petition to heaven for all good things, both temporal and spiritual, is the legacy which He left to them and to us.

We all know, from our reading of the Sacred Text, how He used to go up into the solitude of the mountains, after His long and wearisome labours, to refresh His soul in sweet communion with that God Whom He taught us to regard as Our Father. There, His human heart poured forth the grief and the anguish which oppressed it. There, it felt the ecstasy of close and intimate union with the Godhead.

There, it gave an outlet to the devouring fire of love which consumed it. His was no languid, listless lip-service of God. If you would catch a glimpse of the fervour with which His heart burned in prayer, look at that awe-inspiring scene which is presented to our view in the Garden of Gethsemane. He is kneeling—nay, He is prostrate—in deep humility upon the damp earth. His whole soul has gone forth in a loud cry unto heaven for conformity of His human will to the divine decree, which dooms Him to unutterable woe. His words are few and broken with the intensity of His ardour. His confidence is unbounded in the infinite compassion and fatherly tenderness of God. He is not disheartened by dryness of spirit, nor by the withdrawal from His soul of the sensible presence of the Divinity. Like a brave, undaunted champion, who meets his enemies with calm courage, He looks upon all that He has to endure, and does not quail before it. He asks with persevering energy only that the will of heaven may be done. His feeble human nature, indeed, looked at the tide of woe which rose around Him, and shrank from it aghast; but His undaunted will never for a moment flinched: 'Father,' He cried, with redoubled fervour, 'not My will, but Thine be done.'

II. Here is an example of fervent prayer which Jesus puts before you, that you may copy it and try to act as He did whenever you come before the throne of mercy, to offer up your petitions to God. You must have already felt the necessity for prayer. If you look around you at the dangers which threaten you, and consider the weakness which makes you powerless to avert them, you ought to be earnest and eager in your prayer for all that you stand in need of. Yet, what indifference and carelessness do most boys manifest about prayer! Many of them sicken at the bare thought of it. They go to it with unwillingness; they perform it with listlessness; and they rejoice when it is over.

Now, what are the reasons for this? They may be reduced to two. The first is, that you do not remember, nor try to realise the presence of God. God is around you on every side: 'In Him,' says St. Paul, 'you live, and move, and exist.' But this is specially true when you pray, for then you direct to Him the powers of your soul and pretend to converse with Him. If you could bring this fact home to yourself, and say to your heart every time that you kneel to pray: 'God is here before me; He sees me; He is listening to me;' you would not dare to stare about you, nor to play with your fingers, nor to think of your games, of your studies, of your companions, nor in fact of anything but of that which should occupy your mind in the presence of so awful a majesty, as that before which you ought to prostrate yourself in lowliest adoration.

The next cause of your dislike for prayer is your ignorance of its necessity. You are weak, and you need strength. You are cowardly, and you need courage. You easily break down in presence of difficulty, and you need perseverance. All these necessities can be relieved only by earnest prayer. There is within you a cunning enemy who aims at enslaving your will, and making you a mere tool to do his behests. He must be crushed, and kept in subjection; but you can obtain strength to do this only by means of prayer. On all sides you are beset with other enemies, more cunning and far more cruel, who wish to compass your destruction. You cannot gain wisdom to outwit them and to frustrate their plots, except by prayer. The warfare which you have to wage against them and the vigilance which you have to exercise, in order to escape their snares, are so wearisome that unaided human nature cannot bear up against the drain which they make upon its energies. Only prayer can procure you aid from God.

Therefore, study first to realise the presence of God; and as you would not act in the presence of one of your masters with so much indifference as is that with which you sometimes act in the presence of God, let the thought that He is looking at you rouse up all your energy and force your weak human will to speak to Him in a reverent and becoming manner. Next, be convinced of your own necessities. Tremble at the terrible risk which you run of being enslaved by the devil, and then of being dragged down by him into hell. Once impress these two ideas upon your mind, and you will soon remove most of the obstacles which prevent you from praying well.

III. When you have advanced thus far in the science of prayer, you must next throw into it those qualities which render it all-powerful with God. These are humility, confidence, and perseverance. The thought of God's infinite greatness and majesty, of your own nothingness, and of the innumerable and grievous offences which you have committed against Him, will serve to inspire your heart with profound sentiments of humility. These will make you present yourself before Him with a firm conviction that you deserve nothing but punishment. Hence, your demeanour will be full of reverential fear. You will hold yourself in an attitude becoming a suppliant. All your senses will be guarded, and all your faculties absorbed in the concentrated earnestness of your appeal. From prayer of this kind God will never turn away His face. It is humble, and therefore it will pierce the very clouds and reach the throne of God.

In the next place, your prayer must be full of confidence. Though you have so grievously and so wantonly offended God, yet you must never distrust Him, nor think that your sins are too great to be pardoned. Thoughts like these, and distrust of this nature are most injurious and insulting to His divine Majesty, for they imply that you regard Him as a cruel tyrant, and not as the most loving of fathers, Who ceases not to weep over the wanderings of His child, and ardently to long for his return. Therefore, when you kneel before Him in prayer, look upon Him as One full of love and compassion for you; as waiting for the first sign of repentance; as eager to bestow His favours upon you. Then faith, or trust like this, will make Him look with pity upon your weakness, and He will open the treasures of His mercy to recompense your confiding love.

Lastly, your prayer must be persevering. You must be neither downcast nor discouraged when you do not straightway obtain what you ask. If you suffer this miserable weakness to take hold of you, you are undone, for you will leave off asking, and, consequently, will never obtain anything from God. Knowing, therefore, that God wishes to be entreated, that He does not accede at once to your requests, in order to test your faith, and make you appreciate the favours which He bestows, go on quietly and perseveringly with your petition. In the end you will obtain what you ask, for you have His word for it that whatever you ask with faith like this, you will obtain. Even if you do not obtain precisely what you ask, you will receive at least what is better adapted to your necessities. Have courage, therefore, and let your prayer to God be ever made with humility, with confidence, and with perseverance.

COMPASSION OF THE SACRED HEART.

I. DURING the course of His mortal life, Our Lord felt all the miseries of our nature, sin alone excepted, and the consequences flowing immediately from it—consequences which would have been incompatible with His divine mission upon earth. From this experimental knowledge 'He is able,' says St. Paul, 'to feel compassion for all our infirmities.' He can weep with those that weep, and pity the blindness of those that sin and err from the path of justice. Even a casual perusal of the Sacred Text will have brought out this fact in a very prominent way before us. Whenever He meets with sin, He is gentle and kind towards the wretched creature who groans under its burthen. He never allows the withering flash of His indignant anger to break forth, unless the heart of the sinner has been turned into stone, and his face has become shameless as a face of brass. When His eyes rest upon the withered limbs of the cripple, or the sightless orbs of the blind; when His ear has caught the tremulous cry of the loathsome leper, or the agonising prayer of some bereaved and wailing mother, His heart ever feels a thrill of compassion for the poor afflicted children of men; and His hand is at once stretched forth to pour in the oil and the wine of health and of joy.

Look at Him as He stands aside to allow the funeral

cortège to pass from the gates of Naim! There is a poor mother, weeping over the death of her only child. Her drooping form and streaming eyes, as she follows that shrouded figure on the bier, touch His merciful heart with pity. With that gentle voice, the very sound of which sent a thrill of joy through desolate souls, He says to her: 'Weep not.' Then, to assuage her sorrow and to show His power over death and the grave, He speaks again: 'Young man, I say to thee, Arise!' and at the word, death fled amazed; the young man sat up; and Jesus restored him to his mother.

Again; look at Him, as He sits teaching in the Temple courts. The Scribes and the Pharisees will put that merciful heart to the test. They thrust into the midst a woman taken in the act of a shameful crime, for which the law of Moses decreed the penalty of death. 'But what,' they cry, 'sayest Thou?' The poor, wretched woman stood cowering with shame and confusion before Him. Jesus bent down and wrote with His finger in the dust. He would not look at her, lest He should increase her confusion. When at last they urged Him to give His sentence, it was one of merciful compassion: 'Let him that is without spot,' said He, 'cast the first stone.' Among those present, only Jesus could say, 'I am free from stain,' and He would not raise His hand against her. Having heard these startling words, the woman's enemies, covered with shame, departed one by one; and when Our Lord found Himself alone with the poor sinner, He spoke to her with all gentleness and said, 'Hath no man condemned thee?' And she said, 'None, Lord.' Then said He, 'Neither will I condemn thee. Go in peace, and sin no more.' Well may we say with St. Paul: 'We have not a High Priest who cannot have compassion upon our infirmities.'

II. The sacred heart of Jesus is still filled with the same sentiments of compassion for the miseries of men, for that heart has not ceased to beat. It is living in our midst; for in the most Holy Sacrament it abides and loves us still. Thence He looks forth upon you, and wishes to succour you in your necessities. What a source of joy and consolation must this be to the boy who really desires to love the sacred heart! No matter how young he may be, he will not have escaped the touch of sorrow which reigns well-nigh supreme in this vale of tears; and hence he will be able to understand the joy which the presence of a consoler like Jesus never fails to bring. To be morally weak, is to be wretched; and where is the boy who has not felt what a puny creature he is in the presence of his spiritual enemies? When they attack him he cannot, without a grievous struggle, put them to flight; but that struggle is so far beyond his native strength, and must be maintained against foes so numerous, so powerful, and so subtle, that he is harassed beyond the limits of human endurance. But there is nigh at hand One Who is more tender than his own mother, more affectionate and considerate than his father; and that One sees, and knows, and compassionates his weakness. Therefore, let that boy go with confidence to the bosom of Jesus Christ, and there pour forth all his sorrows.

If he is very weak, and has not borne himself manfully before his enemies, let him with tears confess it unto Him Who never yet turned away His face from an erring child. If he is troubled and worried by temptations, let him tell them to Him, Whom the wicked spirit dared to tempt. Especially in the day of trial, let him run to Him as to a refuge, and he will gain so great strength and so great courage that the very devils will fear to encounter him.

But these are not the only trials and miseries for which the heart of Our Lord feels compassion. There are a thousand other wretchednesses and causes of misery to a college-boy, which he can tell to no one but to Our Lord. There are, for instance, on the part of his companions, acts of unkindness which cut him to the quick. At one time it is a severe and unfeeling criticism. At another it is a sneering or a contemptuous remark, or a misrepresentation of some innocent action, or some deed of petty jealousy. These things, small though they be, are nevertheless the great miseries which wring with sorrow the hearts of schoolboys. Our Lord sees them all. He feels for those who writhe under them, and is ready to heal their smart by the balm of His consolation and compassion.

Therefore, remember this, and in all your sorrows, present yourself before the tabernacle in which Jesus awaits your coming. Tell Him all that afflicts you, and ask for grace to bear yourself like a brave boy in the midst of your trials. If you do this, you will know experimentally that He is not One Who cannot have compassion on your infirmities.

III. The example of Jesus Christ ought to teach you to feel for the miseries of those around you; and your own experience of the wretchedness which the absence of sympathy has caused in your own breast, ought to make you strive to lessen the weight of woe which presses so heavily upon the hearts of those with whom you live. Bear in mind that as you have suffered from the callous indifference of others, so others may have had to carry no light burthen of grief on account of your harsh and unfeeling behaviour towards them. Strive, therefore, to have within your bosom a compassionate heart, as closely resembling that of Our Lord as it is possible for a human heart to resemble the boundless charity of the Godhead.

Be not harsh in your judgment of others, but try to remember that acts which seem to you hostile and malicious may not necessarily be so. Those who cause you annoyance are very probably not aware of it; for if they were, they would never do what arouses your ire. Try, then, to excuse their acts, by persuading yourself that their intentions are good.

In your dealings with those around you, avoid all that is rude, or rough, or offensive to them. They are keenly alive to whatever touches their honour, and look with reason for that civility with which gentlemanly boys ought to treat one another. Be considerate, and before you act reflect whether what you are about to do may not in some way either hurt the feelings, or wound the susceptibilities of your companions. All this will make you gentle and kind. It will dispose you to think more of others than you do of yourself. It will make you ready to sympathise with them, and to feel for their sorrows. You will not deride their weakness, nor scorn them, nor add to their burthens. You will rather be to them a source of happiness, a source to which in time of sorrow they will turn, that they may draw thence refreshment and courage to bear up against the trials and the miseries of life.

ZEAL OF THE SACRED HEART.

I. ZEAL is the natural outcome of great and intense love. It is an eager, earnest striving to make known unto others the object which we love, and to inspire their hearts with sentiments towards it similar to those which animate our own. If that object is ignored, we are filled with grief; if it is slighted, we are roused to indignation; if it is attacked, we are up in arms to defend it. Zeal like this filled the heart of Our Lord for the honour of His Eternal Father and the salvation of the souls of men. He loved God with an infinite love, and He loved men with all the tender fondness of a Father, who is at the same time God, the Creator and Redeemer of the creatures whom His hands have made.

Hence, the honour of God held the first place in His heart. He wished to make Him known, loved, and served with that willing homage and service which, on so many titles, are due to Him from us. Man is the image of God, capable of knowing, of loving, and of serving Him, and Jesus wished man to devote his whole being to that sweetest of tasks for which God destined him. Zeal urged Him to bring about this desire of His heart; and in all the actions of His life it shines forth most conspicuously. Zeal inspired Him, even in His childhood, to remain behind in Jerusalem, and to show His readiness to sacrifice the sweets of home, in order 'to be about His Father's business.' Zeal made Him travel about from place to place, teaching and preaching the way of salvation, healing the sick, opening the eyes of the blind, and calling back the soul to the temple of the flesh, whence the Angel of death had summoned it away. Zeal caused Him to flash forth the fire of His indignant scorn against the stony hearts and the canting hypocrisy of the Scribes and the Pharisees.

Look at Him as He enters the Temple courts, and beholds cattle tethered there, as in a market-place; the booths of the traffickers, and the tables of the money-changers! Could this be the House of God? Greed had changed it into a den of thieves. The sight filled His soul with a holy indignation. The zeal of the Lord fired His heart, and snatching up some cords which lay close at hand, He scourged the unholy crowd from the sacred precincts.

Again; look at Him as He sits, weary, footsore, and travel-stained, at the well of Samaria. His Apostles had gone to procure food, but His soul hungered after a food of which they yet knew but very little. He had come there to speak to and convert one poor soul—the soul of a woman living in the state of sin. He patiently instructed her, and finally won her back to God. Truly may we say of that sacred heart, 'the zeal of the Lord hath eaten it up.'

II. A like zeal for God's honour, and for your neighbour's salvation, ought to burn brightly in your heart. Shall only priests and religious be left to follow in the footsteps of Our Lord, in this work which is so dear to Him? No; there is much that laymen may do to promote the honour of God, and further the salvation of souls. Even boys will find that they are able to help in this work, and what is more, that they must of necessity do so, if they wish to lay claim to that proud title, 'children of God.' For, if God is your Father, you are bound by that gratitude, loyalty, and love, which you owe to Him, to be eager that all should give to Him honour, love, and obedience.

Lift up your eyes and look upon the world which is around you, and you will find motives in abundance to stir up in your heart all the zeal of which it is capable. Are there not millions of men who know not God, and bow their knees before senseless idols? Are there not countless multitudes who insult Him by their sinful lives, and vainly strive to ignore His very existence, saying in their proud hearts, 'There is no God'? Even among those who believe in Him, who profess to love Him, and to follow in His footsteps, are there not very many who, by their abominable sensuality, profane the temple of the living God? who blaspheme His holy name? who trample upon His image and do their utmost to blot it out of their souls? Yet for each of them Jesus poured forth His precious blood. By His ignominious death and bitter Passion, He paid for them a costly ransom. Shall they be lost? Shall they never be brought to repose in that sacred heart, which has loved them so much? God forbid! Each of you may help to save them. You cannot, it is true, go forth to enlighten those who sit in darkness. You cannot solve the difficulties of those who are hopelessly struggling in the meshes of error. You cannot reclaim the wicked from their dark and slippery way. Works like these are for older heads and for abler hands. Nevertheless, there is a work which you can do. You can pray.

You can beg courage and strength for some poor missioner in China or in India, who is sinking under the burthen of his labours, and desponding because of apparent failure. You can ask for light and peace for those who are tossed about upon the sea of doubt, and bewildered by the wretched philosophism of the day. You can implore the grace of repentance for those who are in sin; victory for those who are tempted; and perseverance for those who are wavering, who are inclined to look back, and to give up their chance of the kingdom of heaven.

All this you can do, and only God can tell the amount of good which your zeal may effect. Therefore, be not idle, but whatsoever your hand is able to do, do it earnestly, that is to say, do it with zeal.

III. This zeal, like well-ordered charity, must begin at home. It is upon yourself, upon your own heart, that you must first bring it to bear. In that little kingdom you will find ample work to keep you well employed. There are enemies hateful to God, and most hostile to yourself—enemies who must be conquered and thrust out of its borders. There are defects in its internal economy to be corrected; there are virtues to be won and firmly established; there are habits of vigilance and of prayer to be acquired. Therefore, turn your attention first upon yourself, and stir up all the energy of your nature to aid you in this work of zeal.

Look upon yourself as the temple of God, hallowed by His sacred presence, and adorned with His most precious gifts. Remember that the devil, with all his filthy followers, is ever prowling about, seeking to enter and spoil the beauty of that dwelling-place. Hence, be on your guard against his approach. Reject his first overtures. Have nothing whatever to do with him; for contact with him will only defile and burn. If, like a strong man armed, you can hold your ground, and keep him out, your task will not be difficult; for all your minor enemies will easily be kept in subjection.

Nevertheless, be not careless even about these; for, if you be careless, they will master you little by little, and before you are aware of it, will bind you hand and foot, and make you a scorn unto your bitterest foe. Therefore, let the fire of your zeal for God blaze forth against those movements of vanity and of pride, which boys occasionally feel in the day of their success and triumph at School. Let it check those outbursts of anger to which you sometimes give way. Let it arouse your indignation and scorn for deceit, and lying, and selfishness. Cease not your earnest efforts to be pure, humble, meek, truthful, and unselfish.

Be mindful, also, of the counsel of Our Lord to all who do not wish to be surprised by the devil: 'Watch and pray.' Always be on the alert. Be ready, like soldiers who are in the front—your arms in your hands, your senses on the watch, your courage unfaltering. Above all things, *pray:* for prayer is the fuel which keeps the fire of zeal ever burning.

Due attention to these counsels will supply you with sufficient matter upon which to exercise your zeal, and when God sees you eager to establish His kingdom in your own heart, He will fill you with zeal to extend its sway to the hearts of others, and will give you work to do which will promote the honour and the glory of His sacred heart.

GRATITUDE OF THE SACRED HEART.

I. When we say that we are grateful to anyone, we imply that we look upon ourselves as debtors to him for the benefits which we have received, and that we wish to repay him by acknowledging the gift, or by thanksgiving, or by some other benefit which we shall do him in return. From this it will be seen that we cannot affirm of Jesus Christ as God that He is grateful. For gratitude would imply that He acknowledged a benefactor and superior. But God has no superior, and no one can give Him anything that is not His by right.

Hence, it is only as man that Jesus may be regarded as grateful. His human heart can acknowledge God as His benefactor and superior. Therefore it is as man that he said: 'My Father is greater than I.' Consequently, we may say of Him: 'The sacred heart of Jesus is most grateful for benefits received.' His life and actions made this manifest, for on all occasions they proclaimed that He regarded all that He had, and all that He did, as the work of God. Whatever gifts God had bestowed upon His human nature, He employed for the promotion of God's honour and glory, and in token of His gratitude, gave thanks to Him for them. Therefore, as man, and speaking with a grateful heart, Our Lord could say to the Jews, who were amazed at His learning, knowing that He had never been taught: 'My doctrine is not Mine, but His that sent Me.'

Hence, also, before He performed any great and signal miracle, He lifted up to His heavenly Father a heart overflowing with feelings of gratitude, and gave thanks for the power bestowed upon His human nature. Before He multiplied the five barley loaves and the two fishes, which a boy chanced to have with him, He gave thanks. While standing at the grave of Lazarus, and about to astound the world by raising from the tomb one who had already been dead for the space of four days, He lifted up His eyes to His Father, and gave thanks. Also, on the night before He suffered, when about to work a miracle, compared with which all His other works pale into insignificance—when about to change the mean elements of bread and wine into His own adorable body and blood, and to leave the same astounding power in the hands of His Apostles, and of those who should succeed them in the ministry, He again lifted up His eyes and gave thanks. All these are indications of that inexhaustible source of gratitude which ever welled up from His sacred heart.

II. That heart is still among us, and can still feel the same sweet emotion of gratitude for what He is pleased to regard as a favour done to Himself. Therefore, poor and wretched as we are, we may yet console ourselves with the thought that Jesus has made us rich enough to confer benefits upon Him, and has stooped low enough to make us, in a certain sense, His benefactors. What a consolation must this be to each of you! The most obscure, the most insignificant boy in the College, can become the benefactor of Jesus Christ, and make His heart thrill with grateful emotion.

If, when the devil comes to tempt him, he turn away at once, and call upon the sacred heart for help, he will fill that abyss of love with an indescribable joy, for which Jesus will be most grateful, and will bestow upon him some fresh benefit, some further token of His love and gratitude. So, also, whenever anyone by his actions acknowledges God to be his Master, he causes the fountain of God's gratitude to well up, and to overflow in priceless gifts of grace.

Let this thought, therefore, animate you with an eager desire to give the joy of gratitude to the heart of Jesus. Bear it in mind when obedience becomes heavy, and you feel inclined to resist, or to follow your own will in preference to the will of your Superiors. Let it nerve you with that courage which will make you scorn to screen yourself from blame or from punishment, by a disgraceful lie. Let it make you generously forego the miserable gratification of pride at your success in School, and cause you to give all the glory to God. Stifle your angry feelings when you think yourself either wronged or insulted; force yourself to sacrifice your own ease in order to serve your neighbour; do not revenge yourself when you might; and by all these things you will be giving to the heart of Jesus what it desires. You will make it feel grateful to you, and that gratitude will be the fruitful source of many inestimable graces, which will help you in your career, and will build up in your soul that Christ-like spirit, which all must possess before they can enter the kingdom of eternal life.

III. Do not, however, rest satisfied with giving to Jesus the pleasure of gratitude. Try also to make your own heart like His—full of gratitude for the benefits and the favours which, every day and every hour of your life, God confers upon you. Can you say, on looking back at your past conduct, that you have been grateful, and that you have been careful to return thanks for what you have received? Alas! there are few boys who have not much to reproach themselves with on the score of ingratitude to God. They are profuse in their thanks to any schoolfellow, or to any master, who does them some trifling service; but not so to God. From Him they receive everything—life, health, social position, strength, and the rest—yet they never dream of thanking Him for these. They take them as matters of course, and forget that to be fed, and clothed, and housed luxuriously are particular favours from God—for there are thousands and millions to whom these things are not granted, who have not whereon to lay their heads, nor clothes to shelter them from the winter blast, nor food to sustain their wretched existence. O miserable forgetfulness and hardness of the human heart! Jesus remains among us, waiting to receive our thanks, and to bestow fresh favours upon us, and we actually will not sacrifice a few moments of our recreation to go to Him, and to say to Him: 'O sacred heart, so full of love for me, so bountiful to me, I thank Thee for all that Thou hast this day done for me!'

Even after boys have had the happiness of receiving God into their hearts, in Holy Communion, do they not grow weary, and look about, and allow vain thoughts to enter their minds? How is this? It is because gratitude for what they have received does not warm their hearts, and make them eloquent and profuse in the outpouring of their thanks.

What, then, ought the example of the gratitude of Jesus Christ make you do? It ought to inspire you with a resolution to let no day pass without thanking God for His innumerable blessings. You should resolve to thank Him for your food, for your instruction, for your health, for your recreation, for your life. You should go every day to the tabernacle in which He reposes, and kneeling before Him, acknowledge Him for your God, thank Him for His gifts, and tell Him that you will use them for His glory.

But it is especially after your Communion that you should pour forth your most grateful thanks for what you have received. In those golden moments, let no weariness creep over you; let no thought of books, or of studies, or of games, or of friends enter to rob you of the advantages and the joys of that sweet union with God. Be not like some giddy boys, who long for the end of the brief period which is allotted to the duty of thanksgiving. Frequently also, during the day, lift up your heart and let a fervent 'Thanks be to Thee, O sacred heart!' rise from your soul. Conduct like this will give pleasure to Our dearest Lord, and His grateful heart will open wide its treasures to enrich your poverty, and to satisfy all your wants.

OBEDIENCE OF THE SACRED HEART.

I. In the tenth chapter of St. Paul's Epistle to the Hebrews that great Apostle puts into the mouth of Our blessed Lord these prophetical words which David spoke of Him in the thirty-ninth Psalm: 'In the head of the book it is written of Me, that I should do Thy will, O God!' The end or purpose of His mission upon earth was the accomplishment of that will, very much of which the human agents chosen by God to take part in the work of our redemption made manifest to Him. For this reason Jesus gave to them an obedience as ready, as willing, and as complete as that which He gave to His Eternal Father; for they were the instruments by which God shaped the events that brought about the consummation of the great sacrifice which Jesus so ardently desired to offer.

This fact Our Lord made evident upon that ever-memorable day of His boyhood, when, unknown to His parents, He remained in Jerusalem although they had set out upon their homeward journey. As soon as they discovered His absence from them, they returned in grief to the Holy City, and after a weary search, found Him in the Temple, amazing the Doctors by the searching questions which He put to them, and by the wisdom of His own lucid answers to the questions which they addressed to Him. When our Lady, half in joyous surprise, half in loving remonstrance, said to Him : ' Why hast Thou done so to us ?' He told her that He ' must be about His Father's business,' and then at once submitting Himself to her and to St. Joseph, retired with them to the obscurity of Nazareth, and for the next eighteen years lived in the practice of the most profound obedience.

This virtue of His hidden life came out prominently also in His actions during those three brilliant years, when He shone in all the splendour of the long-looked-for Messias. To the requirements of the Mosaic Law, He gave the most willing obedience ; and the civil power found in Him One Who acknowledged its claims upon the obedience of its subjects within the due limits of its jurisdiction ; for He Himself, through St. Peter, paid the tribute money which it required.

When the time of His sacrifice had come, He obeyed, although His whole human nature shrank from the fearful suffering which that submission cost Him. He obeyed the unjust sentence of His judge; He obeyed the soldiers, and the executioners who carried out that sentence ; He stretched forth His hands to the nails; He bared His side for the lance ; He bowed His head and died, in obedience to the eternal decree. He obeyed unto death, even to the death of the Cross.

II. Contrast this love of Jesus for the virtue of obedience

with your own dislike of it. He came to do the will of His Father, not His own will. In your case it would seem as if you had come into the world for no other purpose than to do your own will. As long as the commands of your parents and of your Superiors are agreeable to you, no one is either more docile or more ready to obey. But as soon as their views and their wishes run counter to your own, at once there is an end of your docility and of your obedience.

This unwillingness to obey shows itself even in matters in which God's eternal law speaks out plainly and says: 'Thou shalt do this; thou shalt not do that.' But with these we have nothing to do at present. We are concerned now with that phase of disobedience which manifests itself by non-compliance with laws of minor importance. Your masters and your Superiors, who hold God's place in your regard, and to whom He has said: 'He that heareth you, heareth Me' make laws for your guidance and improvement; they tell you also by word of mouth to do this, and to avoid that; and you set yourself against them and do not obey. For instance, you are ordered to study, and you idle away your time; you are told not to go beyond certain limits, and you pass beyond them; you are commanded to keep silence during study-time, that both you and your companions may be able to apply to your books; and yet you speak without the slightest necessity. So is it, also, of many other little things, which need not be mentioned here. So long as you can transgress these minor points with impunity, you do not scruple to do so, and when you cannot, you obey, indeed, but with a very bad grace. You murmur, and when you dare, you become even insolent. You obey slowly, reluctantly, and with words which plainly manifest the rebellion of your heart.

How different is conduct like this from that of the boy Jesus! If He were with you in School, how, think you, would He act? He would be industrious when the time for work arrived. He would be docile and respectful to His masters. He would never transgress the limits marked out for

Him by Rule. He would obey at once, without murmuring, without showing unwillingness. Fix your eyes, therefore, upon an example so bright and so worthy of imitation, and try to copy it as far as you are able.

III. In order that you may the more easily do this, always try to keep this principle before your eyes: 'The Superiors hold the place of God in your regard, and in obeying them, you obey God.' This will help you to give to your obedience those qualities which make it perfect.

First, it will make it prompt. What the Superior orders may at times be very displeasing to you, and may cause you to rebel against his wishes, to question the justice of his commands, and the correctness of his views. Hence, if you look at him from a merely human stand-point, you will be inclined to perform only what you cannot help doing, but you will perform it slowly, without any good-will, with much internal murmuring, and even with words which show your reluctance to comply with his commands. But if you keep this principle before you, it will be as a spur to your sluggish will, to urge it on, and compel it to do what is right. You will say to yourself: 'Though this thing which is now commanded seems to me very hard, unjust, and even tyrannical, yet it is the will of God, made known to me by my Superior. God has said: "He that heareth him, heareth Me." Therefore I will obey at once, for what He commands cannot be either unjust or tyrannical.'

Secondly, it will make you obey not only promptly, but with your whole heart, for you will say: 'What God wills is sure to be for my good, though I do not now see that it is for my benefit.'

Thirdly, it will cause you to submit your intelligence, as well as your heart and will, for you will not dare to call into question, or to judge what God has deemed to be fitting and just. Thus you will submit your whole being to God, by obeying promptly, willingly, and with all your heart. Do not imagine that by acting thus, you in any way degrade yourself. On the contrary, it is degrading for a rational being to call in question the duty of subordination of power to power; to will to overturn the order which God has established in this world; and to invert it, so that, instead of being led by those whom He has appointed to be your shepherds, you should wish them to be led by you.

Therefore, never hesitate for a single moment to do what you are ordered. If it should happen to gall you, do not show temper, nor set about the accomplishment of it with a bad grace; but, above all things, do not dare to manifest your unwillingness by impertinent or by insolent words. Meekly bow down your neck under the yoke of obedience, and say: 'Thy will be done, O God! Make my heart submissive, like Thine. Let me always remember that I came into the world, not to be ministered unto, but to minister; not to do my own will, but the will of those whom Thou hast appointed to guide me.'

THE SACRED HEART, CONSOLER OF THE AFFLICTED.

I. WHILE amid the din of battle some devoted column sweeps onwards to the assault, undismayed by the death-bolts which are dealing destruction around, it leaves behind upon the torn and trampled turf many a still and many a writhing form. Filled with the rage of battle, the soldiers heed them not, but march proudly on to victory or to death. Only a few remain behind to search them out, and tend them when the fight is done. So is it also in the battle of life. Many a brave heart is stricken down by pain and sorrow before it can effectually grapple with the difficulties of the world, and falls helplessly to the earth, while the unthinking crowd rushes madly onwards, too much occupied with its own affairs and prospects to give a moment's attention to the griefs of others. What a joy and consolation it must be to the poor sufferer when some kind and gentle Samaritan stoops over him, and pours the balm of sympathy into the wounds of his aching heart!

Such a one is Jesus Christ to those who are weighed down with sorrow, and heavily burthened with the cares of life. He has a heart which can feel for all our miseries, for it has been pierced through and through with the sorrows which rack and torture the hearts of men. He has felt how like a serpent's tooth is the stinging bite of ingratitude. He knows what it is to have loved and cherished others, and then to have met with no return save coldness and indifference. He has writhed under contempt, and been indignant at slander and calumny. He has felt the hatred of malignant men, the supercilious disdain of the self-righteous, and the fanatical rage of the vulgar crowd.

He is, therefore, well qualified to console the afflicted. He can skilfully draw the poisoned shaft from the quivering flesh, and pour into the wound a healing balm which takes away its smart. He calls the poor, the weary, and the afflicted to come to Him, that He may refresh them. He sees and knows their grief, and is with them in the midst of their tribulation. If they seek consolation from Him, He will give it to them. He will scatter the dark clouds which overshadow them and shut out from them the bright sunshine of life. He will cause the light of joy to break in upon them. He will console them by His presence. He will make their burthen easy to bear, and give to their souls courage not to shrink from suffering, but even to desire it, that they may give unto Him a proof of their love.

II. Boys as well as men sometimes have their load of grief to carry, and therefore have need of a consoler to soothe them in their sorrow. Those who see them only when they are bright, joyous, and radiant with health upon the cricket-field, or in the play-ground, think that their lives are without trouble, and their hearts free from grief; but a smiling face does not always betoken a joyous heart, and a merry laugh does not always break from a soul that is free from care. There are in the far-off home troubles and cares which cast their shadows over the boy at school. They fill him with sorrow and alarm. He tells them to no one, and in secret they gnaw his heart. Or, he may be the uncomplaining victim of some petty tyrant who makes his life a burthen to him. Masters oftentimes misunderstand a boy, and see in his most innocent actions and straightforward dealing reasons for taking offence, and for inflicting punishment. Hence, they begin to dislike, to mistrust, and to treat him with great severity. Who can tell the weight of woe which these small cares fasten upon the shoulders of young boys, who are apparently so free from every cause of disquiet? Who can tell the torture which they inflict upon a high-spirited, sensitive boy?

If to these cares which press upon them from without, there are added the trials which disturb them from within, we must admit that boys need comfort and consolation as well as their elders. If a boy has come to that critical period of his life when he begins to feel the rebellion of his fallen nature, there are causes of trouble without end to harass and annoy him. Again, if he be bravely fighting against his defects, and against the evil habits which he may have contracted before coming to School, this contest will be enough to cloud his heart with anxious care. He has, perhaps, a bad temper, which makes him fly into a passion; or he has a habit of lying, and is making great and praise-worthy efforts to break through it; or he is vain, or proud, or envious of his companions. These defects bring with them their own punishment, and flood the soul of the boy with pain and sorrow.

Who then shall be his comforter? Catholic boys have a spiritual friend and guide in their Confessor, and they know the sweetness, and the peace which they carry away with them from his feet. But there is another friend to whom we recommend them. This is Jesus in the Holy Eucharist. The priest, in the tribunal of penance, is only His representative, His minister; but in the Most Holy Sacrament of the altar they have God Himself, really and truly present, saying from behind the Eucharistic veils: 'Come unto Me all ye that labour, and I will refresh you.'

III. We counsel you, therefore, to seek consolation from the sacred heart of Jesus. This will not prevent you from being quite open and childlike in your confidence with your spiritual father. If there are troubles and trials which are too insignificant to recount to him, but which nevertheless cause you real pain, these and others may be put before the compassionate heart of Our Lord. When you go into the quiet Chapel, where the lamp burns so unflickeringly, and says to you: 'The heart of Jesus is here,' cast yourself upon your knees and tell Him all that either pains or causes you grief and anguish of heart. Tell Him of the evils which are pending over your family circle, should these be the cause of your sorrow. If your companions are malicious, and take a pleasure in teasing and bullying you, offer up to God, in union with the sufferings of Our Lord, this trivial annoyance. But, while we give you this advice, we would at the same time have you so to bear yourself, that those at least of your own age may fear to play the tyrant with you.

If you are misunderstood, be patient, and remember that Our Lord's enemies maliciously misrepresented Him. Be obedient and submissive to those who mistrust you, and after doing what lies in your power to give them a right notion of your motives, trouble yourself no more about them. Submit the matter to Our Lord, and He will pour the balm of His consolation into your heart.

As for your internal trials, which bring with them disquiet, heaviness, and grief, frequently treat of them with the sacred heart. Ask Jesus to sustain you in the never-ceasing conflict which we have all to wage with our fallen nature. Beg for meekness to subdue the impetuosity of your angry heart. Ask for courage to be truthful, and be severe with yourself in order to break through the detestable and disgraceful habit of lying. Crave from the sacred heart some of its humility, and one drop of its charity. Act thus in all your troubles and trials, and you will find in that heart a well-spring of never-failing comfort and consolation. Do not seek for consolation from your earthly friends only. They have their own burthens to bear, and ordinarily are able to give but scant comfort. Go rather to the true Physician of souls. He can pluck out that which causes you pain and uneasiness. He is able to heal the most desperate wound.

THE SACRED HEART, REFUGE OF THE TEMPTED.

I. THE greatest adversary with whom the devil ever ventured to measure his strength was Our divine Lord. For in Him he found One Who turned a deaf ear to all his suggestions, and bade him begone with the authoritative voice of a master whom he did not dare to disobey. Jesus, the humble, the submissive, the obedient, came into the world to teach men how to conquer that malignant spirit, who fell from his high estate through obdurate pride and fierce rebellion against the decrees of God. Hence it followed as a natural consequence that, during His sojourn among us, He should be assaulted by His and by our adversary, with all the unwearying activity, and all the undying hate, of a nature at once so powerful and so perverse. The Man-God suffered it to be so for a time, and did not disdain, as man, 'to be tried in all things like ourselves, only without sin.'

Therefore, by the agency of this wicked spirit, the fanatical priest, the hypocritical Pharisee, and the self-sufficient doctors and rulers of Israel, were stirred up against Him, and united in a confederacy of wickedness to do Him whatever mischief they were able. In public, they interrupted His discourses and insulted Him. In their own hearts, they envied Him, because of His wisdom, His miraculous power, and the unmistakable hold which He had upon the hearts of the people. Hence they left undone nothing that could undermine His influence and throw discredit upon His motives and His aims. But, when all these efforts of the devil's agents had proved of no avail to overcome the unalterable patience and meekness of the Son of God, the great adversary of good made in person one last assault upon Him.

He held up before Him those three baits with which he best succeeds in capturing and enslaving the souls of men. First, he put before Him the lust of the flesh: 'If Thou be the Son of God, command that these stones be made bread.' Then, having failed to entrap Him by that, he tried Him with the lust of the eyes. He showed Him all the kingdoms of the earth, and the glory of them, and said: 'All these will I give Thee, if falling down, Thou wilt adore me.' Lastly, he tempted Him by the pride of life, for, having set Him upon a pinnacle of the Temple, he said, 'Cast Thyself down, for it is written: He hath given His Angels charge over Thee, and in their hands they shall bear Thee up, lest perhaps Thou dash Thy foot against a stone.' Jesus foiled him on all points, and then drove him away, covered with the confusion of a total defeat.

II. If you keep these facts well before your mind, you will be neither surprised nor alarmed when you are tempted by the devil, or by those whom his malice stirs up to do his work. For it is vain to hope that you will pass through life without undergoing the ordeal of temptation. Nay, it is even cowardly to shrink from it, because it is the test by which your loyalty to and your love of Jesus Christ are proved. Therefore nerve yourself to meet and to endure it like a brave boy.

Be not astonished, then, if at College you meet with some among your schoolfellows who will envy you the graces and the talents which God has bestowed upon you—for example, your virtuous character and the esteem in which you are held by your masters and companions. To certain natures, these advantages are motives for deep-seated hatred. They will plot against, malign, and thwart you in every possible way.

These are the trials which will come to you from without. The devil will not fail to attack you also from within. He will stir up that fund of pride which lies deep down in the heart of every child of Adam. He will strive to fire your soul with anger, and to make you pine away with envy at the good fortune of others; he will endeavour to make you false and deceitful; he will fan into a flame the corrupt nature which is smouldering within you; he will fill your thoughts with wicked images, your heart with unlawful desires, your flesh with the rebellion of the senses. All the powers of that little kingdom, which ought to be subject to the sway of your reason, will be up in arms against you, and you will be forced to fight them, and to reduce them to subjection.

This war will weary and harass you. The turmoil of the strife will daze and stun you, till your very life will become a burthen to you. You will sigh in vain for the return of those peaceful days when you basked in the sunshine of God's countenance. But be not disheartened; for, so long as all these vile images and filthy suggestions are displeasing to you, and inspire you with disgust, they are not sinful, even though they may excite some incipient pleasure in inferior nature. Let your heart, therefore, take courage and be comforted, for you have proved yourself to be a faithful follower and valiant soldier of Our Lord.

III. It is to the sacred heart of Our divine Lord that every boy ought to flee for refuge, whenever he is assaulted by the devil. For the heart of Jesus can feel for and compassionate one who is fascinated by the magical charm which evil seems to exercise upon our human nature. In Him you will find a loving friend, a sweet consoler, and a powerful defender, who will break the spell which has woven its meshes around you. He will give you courage to endure, and strength to resist. He will fill you with so noble a generosity of soul, that you will count it a gain to be able to suffer something for His sake.

But, in order to secure so happy a result, you must in moments of peril accustom yourself to turn for protection to His sacred heart You must be as a child who runs to his mother whenever danger threatens; and, like a child, you will be ever shielded from harm. Therefore, when the devil tries to conquer you by pride, and you feel your heart swelling with elation at success, turn to Jesus, and remember that all power comes from Him, and to Him, therefore, is due the glory which accrues to you from the possession of it.

On the other hand, if failure makes you envious of others who have outstripped you in the race, turn to the sacred heart, and bear in mind that God does not reward success only. He looks to your labour, and crowns that, even though its results have not been so great as you desired and expected them to be.

If your companions are unkind, or spiteful, or malicious—if they speak ill of you, and spread reports which are detrimental to your character, look to the heart of Jesus for aid to bear these trials, and reflect upon its unalterable meekness and patience in the midst of injuries the like of which no man ever suffered before. Above all, when a storm of evil thoughts rises up around you, and seems about to overwhelm you, flee for refuge to the sacred heart. The thought of its sanctity will give to your will the immobility of a rock, against which the angry billows may dash, and rage, and foam in vain.

THE SACRED HEART, A PROTECTION AGAINST THE WORLD.

I. The sacred heart of Our Lord, besides being a refuge from the assaults of the devil, is also a great source of protection against the devil's trusty ally, the world. By the world, you must not, of course, understand the material creation which surrounds you; but rather the spirit of those who have no taste, no love, no aspiration for anything either higher, or more noble, than are the perishable things of earth. This is called worldliness, and may be defined to be —a forgetfulness of God and of eternity, and a concentration of all the affections of the heart upon temporal interests and pleasures. To have this spirit, is to be of the earth, earthy, for it makes men cleave only to those goods which the earth can give, without a thought of or a desire for that glorious destiny which is the true end of their existence here below.

They who are animated by this spirit, cease to look to God and to His holy law for the rule of their lives. When called upon to decide between two lines of action, one of which is good, the other bad, they do not say to themselves: 'Which of these two will be most pleasing to God?' for God has ceased to be their guide. Their first thought is rather: 'What will the world say of me? What will it think of me? How will it treat me?' It is, therefore, no wonder that Jesus, Who came to turn heavenwards the thoughts of men, set His face so decidedly against the spirit of the world. He defied it. He embraced what the world hates and flees from, but He trampled under foot—as more worthless than the very mire of the streets—what it esteems and pursues with so untiring a zeal.

The world flees from poverty; it avoids self-humiliation; it shrinks from labour and obedience; it loves to be where there is joy; it falls down and worships wealth; it flatters the great. Jesus lived in poverty; He humbled Himself and sought after self-abasement; he loved labour and obedience; He pronounced those blessed who mourn, promising them comfort which shall never end; He cared not for wealth; and never stooped to flatter the great ones of the earth. Their wealth and their high estate were worthless in His eyes, for He looked only at the heart. Never did any one so completely set at naught all those things which the worldly-minded esteem and pursue, as if they were their last end. Therefore, He can say with truth unto those who are brought into collision with worldliness, and who shrink from encountering so formidable an enemy: 'Have confidence! I have conquered the world.'

II. There is danger of this spirit of worldliness invading the minds of even boys at College, from the simple fact that there is a tendency in the heart of every one, to fasten his affections upon the things which he sees, and to make no account of the things which he does not see. We are apt to forget that there is an invisible world around us, and an invisible destiny awaiting us, when the figure of this world shall have passed away. Hence it is, that being predisposed to catch the spirit of the world, we drink it in almost imperceptibly, when we live in an atmosphere in which it prevails, and which is, so to speak, impregnated with it.

Therefore, unless a boy keep alive within him the light of faith, and endeavour to fasten the eyes of his soul upon the great truths which it teaches him—as upon so many landmarks to guide him into the haven of rest—he will very speedily come to the same pass as that at which those worldly-minded men have arrived who have practically ceased to believe in God, and whose Gospel may be summed up in the words of the heathens of old: 'Let us eat, drink, and be merry, for to-morrow we die.' For, like the worldling, he will fear the society in which he is cast more than he fears God. He will make its maxims the rule which guides his life, and they will become for him the measure of right and of wrong. Whatsoever a few worthless boys, among whom his lot is cast, shall judge to be right—that he will cling to; and what they shall declare to be wrong—from that will he flee.

If they are wicked enough to ridicule prayer, he will lay aside this most necessary duty. If they scoff at piety, he will fear to be thought pious. If they call him a fool, for incurring punishment rather than tell a lie, he will begin to blush at the truth. He will fear to protest, and to set his face against what his conscience tells him is wrong, lest they should deem him scrupulous and weak-minded. In one word, whenever there is a question of taking either the side of God, or the side of the world, he will first ask himself: 'If I act thus, what will my companions do, or say, or think?' He will meet the cry of his conscience, and his Angel's warning voice, both which say to him: 'Non licet': it is not lawful—with the foolish excuse: 'I shall be laughed at, and slighted by society, if I do not act like the rest of men.'

III. What, then, is a boy to do, who wishes to exclude from his heart the spirit of worldliness. He must cultivate a deep and tender devotion to that heart of Jesus which so effectually contemned and conquered the world. For he cannot be devoted to it without at the same time being filled with its sentiments and its affections. Like his Divine Master he will be *in* the world, but not *of* the world; that is to say, not animated by the spirit of the world. In consequence of his union with the sacred heart, he will come to feel as Jesus felt towards the objects after which the world strives. He will learn to esteem only those things which He deemed worthy of love. Upon these he will fix his heart, and will regard all things else as vain and worthless.

Hence, the law of God will be his guide in the affairs of life. If he sees that he must either lose his dearest friends, or keep their love by breaking that law, he will not hesitate one single moment. God will be more precious to Him than are all things created. If these friends were either as dear to him as is the apple of his eye, or as necessary to him as is his right hand, he would sacrifice them rather than offend God. He will not care for the ridicule of the wicked. Their words of scorn will pass him by, harmless as the summer air. He will meet their displeasure as a man meets the irrational anger of a spoiled child.

This conduct not only will win for him the love and the esteem of God, and of all upright men, but will force even the wicked and worldly-minded to admire and respect him. The world respects courage; and to be virtuously-minded in the very teeth of an opposition as fierce as is that which the worldly-minded make, requires courage of no ordinary character. Their flippant remarks, their ridicule, their scorn, will soon cease, when they see him, conscientiously and with perseverance living up to his convictions; and they will at last pay him the homage of silent respect, and very probably regret that they dare not do what he has done.

Therefore, go to the sacred heart for strength against the spirit of the world. Very frequently ask Jesus to give you that courageous spirit by which He set the world at naught. He will gladly grant your request. He will say: 'Fear not with their fear, and be not afraid, but sanctify the Lord in your heart.'

THE SACRED HEART, A PROTECTION AGAINST THE FLESH.

I. THE devil and the world, though combined against the soul of man, are comparatively powerless, unless their efforts are seconded and their forces augmented by the flesh. Their union then has the strength of a triple cord, which is not easily broken. The chief aim, therefore, of that spirit of evil is to bring about the junction of these powers; and this junction is rendered easy, both from the inborn hostility of the flesh to the spirit, and from its natural love of the baits which the devil displays before it. Very soon, therefore, is the boy made to feel within his heart the existence of this domestic enemy. It bestirs itself and confronts the rational soul with that aggressive boldness which the consciousness of strength, and the support of powerful allies, are wont to inspire. It claims for itself absolute sovereignty over the whole man; and when its demands are refused, it rebels and rages furiously against the control which the will exercises over it.

All-important, therefore, is the decision at which the boy will arrive when he first begins to feel the rebellion of his flesh, and discovers within himself the existence of a power hostile to the power of his mind. If he should weakly yield to the imperious demands of his fallen nature, he will become the plaything of the devil; he will accomplish his behests; and by so doing, will sink himself deeply in the mire of the vilest excesses. But if he resists, and bravely grappling with this insolent rebel, forces him to obey the law of his mind, there is before him a glorious and laborious warfare. In it he has to deal with a bold and indefatigable enemy, who, at all times and in all places, will persistently attack him. Though he smite him down a thousand times, a thousand times will he rise again. He is a hydra-headed monster who never dies; and though we may contemn the devil, and laugh at the world, we must always be on our guard against the flesh, and fight out the battle against it to the bitter end. The sword must ever be in our hands, and our harness ever on our backs. We must always be on the alert, and never suffer any fancied security to lull us into forgetfulness. Hence, we shall find that life is, in very truth, ' a warfare ' in which there may be periods of truce, but no lasting peace.

II. Therefore, it is of the most vital importance that the boy's spiritual strength, or power of resistance, should be constantly renewed, and his soul made proof against the insidious attacks of this most wily and relentless enemy. This desirable end will be secured, if he go frequently to the sacred heart of Jesus, in the Most Holy Sacrament. There he will receive Our Lord, the source of strength, into the sanctuary of his heart, and will be endowed by Him with might, which will make him formidable to the enemies of his soul. For this very purpose God, by an astounding miracle of wisdom and of power, instituted the Holy Eucharist. He wished to be our food, that He might unite Himself to our hearts; and He gave Himself to us under the symbols of bread and wine, that He might indicate to us the wondrous effects which He intended that divine mystery to produce in our souls. For, as meat and drink preserve the spark of life, and keep up our natural strength, so do that heavenly bread and that heavenly drink sustain our spiritual life.

They do not *give* us spiritual life, for we must be spiritually alive in order to partake worthily of the Sacrament; but they *feed* and sustain the life which we already possess, and they are to our souls what fuel is to a fire. But they do more than simply feed; they preserve us from the poison of sin. For in that Holy Sacrament we receive Jesus Himself, true God and true Man. We receive that same Jesus Whose touch cleansed the leper and opened the eyes of the blind; Whose very words banished disease from the bodies of men, and called back life into their inanimate clay. If mere contact with even His garments could heal incurable disease, if the touch of His hand, or the indication of His will, could work wondrous miracles, what will not the actual possession of His sacred Person be able to effect for the souls of those who, with due dispositions, receive Him into their hearts? It will supply them with strength to resist all their foes, and be a most powerful antidote against the poison of sin.

III. If, then, you wish to be free, with that freedom wherewith Christ has made us free; if you desire to live a noble, upright, spotless life; if you do not wish to be the slave of your own body, but aspire rather to be king in your own heart, and to rule over it with absolute sway, do not neglect to go very often to unite yourself to Jesus Christ in Holy Communion. He is the strong man armed, Who keepeth His court, and hath all His possessions in peace. He is the conqueror of the devil and of the world. Unite yourself to Him, and you will feel that He is the conqueror of the flesh also. For, when joined to Him, you no longer contend single-handed, and with your own native strength, against your powerful enemies. You have on your side the might of God, and conscious of this, you go from the Holy Table like a lion, says St. John Chrysostom, breathing fire against your enemies. Yes, for you go forth from the house of God, bearing away in your bosom Jesus Christ, the Strong One. Your lips are empurpled with the blood of the Lamb; your flesh is purified and made proof against the poison of sin; and, as the destroying Angel turned aside his avenging sword from the dwellings which were sprinkled with the blood of the Paschal Lamb, so will the evil spirits turn away from you. If they dare to assault you, they will make their attack with fear and trembling. Therefore, you will be able easily to rout them; for feeble is the onslaught of an adversary whose heart is full of fear; he turns and flees when the slightest resistance is offered.

But in order that you may reap to the full all the advantages of Holy Communion, you must *frequently* approach to the altar of God. The Sacred Body and Blood, which you there receive, is the food of your soul; and, as only those are strong who eat regularly and every day, so is it also with those who partake of Holy Communion. Furthermore, you must prepare yourself for the worthy reception of so great a guest. Dispose your heart thereunto by most fervent acts of sorrow for past sins, by humble confession of your daily defects, and by devout and earnest prayer immediately before you draw nigh to your Lord. Then with a lively faith go to receive Him, and when He is actually in your breast, speak lovingly to Him, as a child would speak to its father. Ask Him for all that you stand in need of; for strength, for perseverance, and for grace never to be overcome by the devil, or by the world, or by your own flesh.

THE SACRED HEART, HELP OF THE DYING.

I. WE all hope that the happiness of heaven shall one day be ours, and that we shall for evermore gaze, with joy unutterable, upon the vision of God. But before our eyes can drink in the ravishing beauty of that countenance, the charms of which will never tire, we have first to pass through the grim portals of death; we have to take that step into the darksome land, that step from which all men recoil with natural horror, even though everlasting joy, and the possession of God, lie beyond. As far as it is possible, men try to forget the inevitable destiny which awaits them. They do not like to face and calmly view it in its various bearings. Hence, when the summons comes, and the hand of the great leveller is laid upon their shoulders, and his voice whispers in their ears: 'Come away,' the poor heart is terror-stricken, and flutters, and tries in vain to escape.

We need not wonder at this; for an eternity depends upon that moment of death, upon that step which must be taken in the dark. The issue of it is all-important for us; the risk tremendous; for we know not whether we are worthy of love or of hatred!

If we look into the past, there is unfolded before our view a long list of transgressions; years of lukewarmness and indifference in the service of God; means of grace neglected; opportunities lost; the work of life done in a way which will call forth the stern rebuke of the great Master.

If we examine the present, it is full of fear and confusion. All things are slipping away from us—our friends, our property, our bodily frame. The future, if we give it a thought, and do not rather try to exclude it from our mind, is terrible to contemplate. We know that eternity is before us; that judgment and a sentence await us. We feel that we are gradually being thrust nearer and nearer the border line, where life ends and eternity begins. We must step across it, whether we will or not.

Earth seems to be sinking from beneath us. Darkness has gathered round us. Slower and slower beats our poor fluttering, terrified heart. Now the shadow of the great throne of God is upon us! One sigh, one faint, feeble effort, and the step has been taken! We have passed out of the shadows and the mists of time, into the never-fading day of eternity. We look upon the face of God!

II. Surely this is a moment when we shall need a kind and compassionate heart to soothe our anxiety, to calm our fears, and to sustain our failing courage. In that dread hour of man's direst need, happy will it be for him who has put his trust in the sacred heart of Our Lord; for Jesus will stand by him to be his helper. His own most holy heart has felt all the terror of death. To Him also there came a moment, when this ingredient of human sorrow entered into His chalice of suffering. He tasted all its bitterness when the Roman governor showed Him to the people and said: 'Behold the Man,' and they, with one accord, sent up a loud, ferocious cry for His blood, saying: 'Away with Him! Crucify Him! His blood be upon us and upon our children.' Then Pilate handed Him over to their fury, and told Him that He must die.

Like the rest of men, the moment of terror had come for Him. He stood face to face with death, and His human nature shrank in horror from the embrace of that king of terrors. Fearful must have been the anguish which it caused Him; for the foreknowledge of this moment felled Him to the earth in the Garden, and forced through His panting frame a miraculous sweat of blood. For though He had no dark past to rise up before His eyes and accuse Him—no future with its dread uncertainties—yet the natural fear of death, and of *such* a death, caused Him to pray with all the energy of His soul, ' that the chalice might pass away.' He did not, like other men, breathe forth His soul in the midst of sorrowing friends. His was a death of ignominy, and of unutterable pain. He died amid the shouts and the blasphemies of a rabble which hated Him, and gloated over His sufferings, and triumphed in His destruction.

Jesus, therefore, has had personal experience of the anguish which settles down upon the soul at the approach of death. He bears it in mind when those who have loved Him, and served Him well, are made to feel the sorrows of death. When they cry to Him He is at hand, like a gentle mother, to fold them in His protecting arms, to lay their heads against His loving heart, and thus to hush them to sleep, that they may, without fear, pass through the dark portals, and awake joyously in His sacred presence.

III. If we desire to have so great a privilege, we must try to make ourselves worthy of it, by leading a good life. If our life have been a life of lukewarmness, death will probably find us in that state; if our life have been good, so also will be our death. Therefore, try to lead a holy life, and death will be shorn of half his terrors. Fight hard and well against your enemies, now that you are in health, and when the summons comes to call you hence, you will look back upon a way on which you have left behind no enemies to close in upon you, and attack you when you are least able to repel their assault.

If, upon looking back now, you discover that there is any place from which you have reason to think that they have not been ejected, and in which they may be lurking in ambush to destroy you, examine it carefully, and leave nothing undone to make your position perfectly secure.

Having satisfied yourself upon this point, you must, in the next place, entirely submit yourself to the divine will. Offer up the life which God has given you, as a sacrifice which you will gladly immolate to Him, in the manner which He wills, in the place which He shall appoint, and at the time when He may think fit.

Have no anxiety whatever about those whom you leave behind. Ask yourself: 'What advantage will my grief about them bring either to myself or to them?' None whatever. Therefore cast it aside, as an obstacle thrown in your way by the devil, for the purpose of making you employ the few remaining moments of life in useless sorrows and regrets.

With these dispositions, go on serving God to the best of your power, and He will not desert you when the supreme moment shall arrive. You will, no doubt, experience for a short time, some little of that natural dread and shrinking from death, which weak human nature cannot avoid; but Jesus, Our good, kind Master, will quickly reassure you. He will give you so great strength that you will smile at your terrors, as a child does when it clasps the hand of its father; and, under the shadow of God's protecting wings, you will step without fear over the threshold of death, into a bright and glorious immortality.

DUTY OF REPARATION TO THE SACRED HEART.

I. When a parent or a dear friend has been either injured or affronted, we do our utmost to soothe his wounded feelings, and to calm his ruffled temper. We express our sorrow at what has occurred, and we endeavour, by greater respect and by more devoted love, to atone for the insult which has been offered. Should we ourselves, by some mischance, have been the occasion of his sorrow, we try by a more ready obedience, a more tender love, and a more filial devotion, to remove the bad impression which our misconduct has left upon his mind. Such, also, should our behaviour be towards the sacred heart of Jesus, both on account of the injuries which we ourselves have done to it, and of the numberless outrages which it has suffered from the hands of our fellow men. To act thus, is to make reparation for our own transgressions, and to atone, in some slight degree, for the sins of others.

We cannot, of course, pretend adequately to do this, for no one but God can atone for the least sin; but we may, in a certain sense, do so through the gracious condescension of Our Lord, Who out of regard for His own infinite merits, will accept our good intention, and impart to our worthless actions some of the merits purchased for us by His bitter Passion and death.

If we take the trouble to look around us, we shall discover reasons without end for devoting ourselves, heart and soul, to the work of reparation. Jesus, Our God, Our Father, is ignored by many men. He is blasphemed and treated with contumely, worse than was even that which He suffered from the Jews. His love is set at naught; His living temples are changed into the abodes of devils, and devoted to the vilest uses.

In the Holy Sacrament, in which He dwells corporally, in which that heart which the Jews pierced for us lives and loves us still, He is most horribly profaned. We speak not of the impiety of heretics, who trample upon the sacred species; like the rabble on Calvary, they know not what they do. But we speak of those so-called Christians, who, after telling in the tribunal of penance a lie to the Holy Ghost, presume to approach with sinful hearts to the Holy Table, where Judas-like, they give Our Lord the traitor's kiss, and deliver Him up to His enemies. They unite Him to their foul hearts which the devil has already entered; and as far as in them lies, they make Him the sport of His bitterest foe. He is derided; He is mocked; He is spit upon; He is scourged, trampled under foot, and as St. Paul expresses it, 'crucified again' by those whom He has redeemed by His precious blood.

II. If you love the sacred heart, the thought of these outrages will fire your breast with zeal, to do something that will atone for these horrible profanations. First, it will bring back to your mind the memory of what you yourself have done, to injure that much-enduring and ever patient heart. Looking back into the past, you will perhaps remember a time when you gave to God a lukewarm service. You were negligent, dissipated, and giddy at prayer. You were irreverent in the presence of God. You suffered weeks and months to pass by with scarce one uplifting of your heart to Him. You were haughty and disdainful towards the poor. You were deceitful, disobedient, and untruthful to your parents and your Superiors. You did not always respect, in yourself, the temple of the living God, but forgot that His all-holy eyes were looking at you. Then, with regard to the holy Sacraments? Have you been sincere in your confessions? Have your Communions been worthily made? On all these points, or at least, on some of them, you may, perhaps, have much with which to reproach yourself. Yet God, Whom you insulted and outraged, has favoured you far more than He has favoured the vast majority of other boys.

Therefore, now that you understand how evil all these things are, try to repair your past lukewarmness by fervour, and by diligence in the service of God. Be reverent in His holy temple, and by frequent aspirations of love lift up your heart to Him. Be kind and considerate to your inferiors and to the poor. Love truth in all your dealings with others. Obey your parents and masters as God's representatives, and always bearing in mind that you live, move, and exist in the presence of God, never suffer any thought to enter your mind, nor desire to take posession of your heart, nor word to pass your lips, nor act to be done by you, which you would be ashamed of if it came to the knowledge of your parents, or masters, or companions. To act thus will be the best kind of reparation that you can possibly make to the sacred heart for any insult which you may have offered to it, or for any grief which you may have caused it in the past.

III. Besides making reparation for your own sins, you should endeavour to make amends to the sacred heart, also for the grievous sins of the world at large. For, just consider how it forgets and ignores God. Vast multitudes of men are so blinded by pride of intellect, that they rise up insolently to question God's very existence. Others, bolder still, stop not at merely doubting this fundamental truth; they go farther, and deny it altogether. Having rid themselves of God, they next cast aside His moral law, which puts a check upon their evil passions; or rather, it would, perhaps, be more correct to say that, having first thrown off the trammels of conscience, and of the moral law, they are stricken with blindness of intellect, as a punishment for their corruption of heart. Consequently, being unable to see either the sophisms of their false logic, or the turpitude of their wicked lives, they fall under the dominion of their flesh and are condemned by that pitiless task-master to feed its animal passions with all the filthy garbage for which these latter crave. Others, again, rage with diabolical fury against the Church of God, against her ministers, and against her children. Others profane the Sacraments, and turn those sources of spiritual health and life into the most deadly poison.

What shall we say of the pride, the falsehood, the hatred, the injustice, and the cruelty of the human heart? What shall we say of its forgetfulness of God and its pursuit of earthly things? Alas! all these crimes and sins are so many cruel stabs to the sacred heart of Jesus! For all the souls which flout and scorn Him, He has poured forth His heart's best blood, has loved them with an infinite, everlasting love, and when He beholds them thus madly rejecting His salvation, stubbornly refusing to submit to Him, and thereby exposing themselves to eternal torments, He would, if it were possible, grieve with a mighty sorrow, and be straitened with the intensity of His anguish.

You must, therefore, try to make amends to the loving heart of Our Lord for the negligence, the indifference, and the sins of men. For this purpose go frequently into His presence, and kneel before the altar on which for love of you He remains by night and by day. There pour forth your heart in prayer to Him. Pass in review all the evil that is done in the world, and make acts of sorrow for it. Tell Him how it grieves you to see Him forgotten and ignored by men. Say with what horror the contemplation of their frightful sins inspires your soul. Make up by your love, for their hatred; by your frequent and devout reception of the Sacraments, for the sacrileges which they commit; by your Christian life, your humility, your gentleness, your obedience, your truthfulness, and your purity of heart, for all the lust, the deceit, the rebellion, the fierce anger, and the diabolical pride of the human heart. Set aside certain days on which, approaching the most Holy Sacrament, you will try to satisfy for these various sins; and let there not pass a single day upon which you will not frequently lift up your heart, and offer it to Jesus for these various intentions.

If you do this you will fill the sacred heart with gladness; you will make the Angels rejoice; you will do the work of an Apostle; and the day may come when, in the courts of heaven, God will point out to you many whom your acts of reparation have saved from eternal perdition.

UNION WITH THE SACRED HEART.

I. To fill the hearts of boys with a tender love of Jesus Christ, is one of the chief motives for so strongly recommending to them the practice of devotion to the sacred heart. For, if that love be enkindled in their souls, they will run the way of God's commandments without either stumbling or turning aside. The reason of this is manifest; love tends to union; therefore, if he who follows Christ walketh not in darkness but hath the light of life, with how much greater reason may we say this of all who are closely united to Him? Hence it must be one of Our Lord's most ardent desires that your hearts should be united to Him. He wishes them to be one with His own—one in aim, one in desire, one in will.

So intense is this desire on His part, that He has not left us to deduce it either from His words or from His acts, but has given expression to it by the mouth of the Wise Man: 'My delights are to be with the children of men.' He proved this to be no inefficacious wish, but a settled determination, which had its effect in act. For He came among us, not in the form of God—for that would not, perhaps, have attracted our love—but in the form of man, that we might be able to love Him and to unite ourselves to Him.

When, after accomplishing His mission, He returned to the Father, He did not leave us orphans; but by a most stupendous miracle of wisdom and of power, contrived a means by which He might still be with us, and enter into the closest of unions with us. This is the Most Holy Sacrament of the altar, by which there is established between ourselves and Jesus Christ a union so close, so intimate, that St. Cyril does not hesitate to compare it to the fusion of two pieces of molten wax.

When we think of this, we are struck with amazement, and ask ourselves: 'Why does Jesus show unto us such gracious condescension? Why should He wish to be united to us? We are unknown to the world. We have never done anything great, anything heroic. Yet He knows us, loves us, and wishes to be united even unto us!' As we revolve these things in our minds, we are constrained to cry out in joyous humility: 'What is man that Thou art mindful of him, or the son of man that Thou shouldst visit him? Thou hast made him a little less than the Angels. Thou hast crowned him with glory and honour, and hast set him over the works of Thy hands.'

II. Since, then, the sacred heart of Jesus, so earnestly desires to be united to your heart, endeavour to appreciate the greatness of the honour which He confers upon you, that you may show, on your part, a corresponding eagerness to comply with His wishes. For this end, try to impress upon your mind a notion of the great advantages which must of necessity flow from this union. You unite yourself to the heart of a most loving Father, compared with Whose love, the intense, never-dying love of your earthly mother, is cold and inactive. He holds in His hands the power which rules and guides the universe, and therefore, when united to Him, you may rest secure, like one who sleeps in an impregnable fortress, upon the granite walls of which the prowling robber and the marauding thief can make no impression. True, you will, to a certain extent, feel the attacks of your enemies, but they will never be able to harm you, for God will keep you as the apple of His eye.

Whatever you see that is noble, or grand, or heroic, in the men with whom you come in contact, is to be found in its plenitude in Him; and from that ever-flowing fountain, you may drink your fill of lofty aims, of noble resolves, and of power to do glorious deeds. You will find in that sacred heart all that is good, and generous, and lovable. From it has flowed out upon the world all that makes men happy, all that makes them admirable, all that makes them virtuous. The Sacraments, which lift up poor weak mortals from the mire of earth into the glorious courts of heaven, issued from that inexhaustible treasure-house, and chief among them all, that Sacrament of love, in which God, though infinite, eternal, omnipotent, 'empties Himself,' and takes upon Himself even less than the form of a servant. To that heart you unite yourself! Into that sanctuary of the Divinity you are admitted, for in that heart 'there dwelleth all the fulness of the Godhead corporally.'

There, you will find humility, to cast out of your heart the wretched vanity and pride which rob you of your merit, and make you hateful to God. There you will be brought in contact with the fire of charity which inflames and softens the heart with love, and takes away from it the multitudinous defects which make it displeasing to God. There you will imbibe that spotless purity which crowns the soul with glory and honour. Therefore, be eager to unite yourself to Jesus, that you may draw all these inestimable virtues and favours from the fountains of your Saviour.

III. But, you will ask, how is this union to be brought about? First, by removing those obstacles which stand between you and God. These are your defects and your grievous sins. The latter will exclude you altogether from the loving embraces of your Father; for they rise up between you and Him as a wall of brass; the former will draw between you and Him a veil, which will hinder you from beholding the beauty of His face. Therefore, if you wish to be united to Jesus, you must cleanse your heart from all grievous sin and from all affection to it, and having once and for ever broken with it—having cast aside its yoke, and escaped from its slavery, let not the deceptive baits of the devil ever again lure you back. Then go with confidence to Our Lord, and you will be received into the closest union with His heart. That union will become daily more intimate in proportion as you divest yourself of all affection to sin.

As for your defects, endeavour to rid your heart of them,

for they cool the love of Our Lord, just as selfishness, or conceit, or meanness would estrange from you the affection of a friend. Hence, you cannot expect Our Lord to admit you to a close union with His heart, if you are sharp-tempered with your companions, if you speak ill of them, if you are proud, or vain, or disobedient, or idle. He cannot take to His bosom a boy who is false and deceitful; nor can He smile upon one who keeps enmity in his heart, and shows by sulky looks and childish anger that he resents correction. Therefore, try to overcome these faults.

In the next place, have a great love and esteem for purity. Put modesty as a guard before that treasure of your youthful heart. Be watchful. Shun danger. Show God that you esteem, respect, love, and are ready even to die for it; then, because by these means you become a faint image of Him Who is sanctity itself, He will acknowledge you as His child, and love you with all the ardour of His sacred heart.

Lastly, be assiduous in approaching to the Most Holy Sacrament of the altar; for by partaking of it, the union between your heart and the heart of Jesus is consummated. There Jesus admits you to His fond embrace. There, you rest your head upon His bosom, and nestle close to His sacred heart. As you recline there, always ask to grow daily more and more pure; so that you may never offend God, and never be separated from Him, either here or hereafter.

HOW WE OUGHT TO ENTERTAIN OURSELVES WITH THE SACRED HEART AFTER COMMUNION.

I. IF you wish to triumph over the three great enemies who are continually plotting your destruction, your victory will depend in great measure upon the manner in which you behave yourself after Holy Communion. For then the heart of Jesus is with you, and is most closely united to you. That treasury of virtues and of strength is thrown wide open, and you are told to ask for what you please. But if, instead of exposing your necessities to Our Lord, and beseeching Him to relieve them, you begin to look about you, to fill your mind with thoughts of games, or of studies, or of other things still more frivolous, Jesus will give you nothing, and you will go away from Communion well-nigh empty-handed. In order, then, that this may not happen, learn what you ought to do whenever you receive the Holy Eucharist.

After approaching with the greatest reverence to the altar, and receiving the adorable Sacrament from the hands of the priest, return with great modesty and recollection to your place. There, casting yourself upon your knees, and closing your eyes to all external objects, reflect for an instant upon the majesty of the Guest Whom you have received. You have Jesus Christ, Who always treated children with gentleness and condescension, now present within you. His arms are twined around you. He holds you close to that burning heart which has loved you so much.

What will you say to Him? Pour forth your most grateful thanks to Him for having come to visit you. Tell Him how unworthy you are of so much love, and how unable you are adequately to express in words the deep gratitude of your heart.

Then, turning to the Blessed Virgin, and to her holy spouse St. Joseph, ask them to join their voices with the voice of your guardian Angel, in praising and thanking Our dear Lord for His unutterable love. Unite your own poor, weak, human heart with theirs, and then with all the heavenly hosts, with all the righteous men upon earth, with all the imprisoned just in Purgatory, adore, praise, and thank Him for all His mercies, and for all His exceeding great kindness to you.

II. In the next place, looking into the wants of your soul, expose them all to the compassionate eyes of your Saviour, and ask Him to relieve them. You may, perchance, have a hot temper, which causes you frequently to break forth into fits of anger, and to be guilty of many imperfections. Or you may have contracted the wicked and detestable habit of not telling the truth. Also, your heart may very often swell with pride, and your mind be full of vain thoughts. Knowing, then, your many shortcomings, do not let these precious moments pass by while you have with you Him Who is the Truth itself, Who is the meekest among the children of men, and the most humble of heart. He will help you to keep your temper within due bounds; to repress the uprisings of foolish pride and vanity; and, to have so great a love for truth, that you will prefer any punishment rather than disgrace yourself by a cowardly lie.

Never forget to ask Him for a still greater love of that beautiful virtue of purity, which He values so highly, and so earnestly wishes boys to cultivate. If you find the powers of evil pressing upon you, and threatening to pluck it from your heart, ask him for courage to resist, and for strength to prevail over them.

Then offer to Him your whole heart, and your whole self—your memory, that it may be filled with His image; your understanding, that it may ever reflect upon Him; your will, that it may be constantly turned to do His holy bidding. In return for the little offering which you make to Him, ask Him to aid you in your studies, by making your memory and your intelligence quick, far-reaching, and tenacious of grasp. Also, beseech Him to support your moral nature, by endowing your will with so great pertinacity of purpose, that nothing may be able to move it from its fixed resolve.

He will not turn a deaf ear to these requests, but will bestow upon you an abundance of graces and favours, which will be useful to your own soul, and beneficial to the souls of those who may afterwards be brought within the reach of your influence.

III. Lastly, after thus observing the due order of charity, which always begins at home, do not forget, in your prayers, the necessities of those who are near and dear to you. Beg the blessing of the sacred heart for each and all the members of your family, but most particularly for your parents, because of the good that they have done to you.

Then, remembering that your College is your 'Alma Mater,' or loving mother, recommend to the sacred heart those who are living with you under her protecting care—the masters, who labour so earnestly, and watch with so much solicitude over you welfare; and the boys, who together with you, are being trained in the paths of knowledge and of virtue. Ask Jesus to bestow His grace upon them, and to banish from among them even the faintest shadow of vice.

Let not your charity stay here. Pour it forth unsparingly upon all the faithful at large. There are, stretched upon their beds of pain, thousands of the sick poor, for whom you must ask patience and resignation to the holy will of God. There are passing away from this world of sense to the world of spirits souls who will need a helping hand to bear them safely through their last agony, a friendly arm to sustain them as they enter within the shadow of the awful throne, and a compassionate heart to plead for them when they stand in the dread presence of the Almighty Judge. There are numberless souls struggling bravely against temptations, and courageously wrestling with their evil habits. Pray very earnestly for all these, and it may be that through the efficacy of your prayer, Our dear Lord will be kind and gentle to the dying. He will calm their fears, and receive them with a serene and smiling countenance when they have crossed the threshold of eternity; He will stand by the soul that is harassed by temptation; He will strike off the fetters of evil habits from the limbs of those who by long years of licence have forged them for themselves, and will snatch from the brink of destruction those who are wavering between good and evil. He will do all this because of your timely prayer.

Lastly, before you quit the Chapel, offer up a fervent supplication to the sacred heart of Jesus for the poor prisoners who are detained in the penal fires of Purgatory, and who wait so patiently for God to remember them. Not one word that you utter either in their behalf, or in behalf of any soul that is in need, will be lost upon those ears which catch the faintest sigh of the human heart. Our Lord will graciously accede to your request, and many a bright soul will enter heaven on the days when you communicate; many a mortal sin will be prevented; many a temptation overcome; many a good habit strengthened, and the kingdom of God established in the hearts of men.

Therefore, be diligent during those precious moments which follow communion. God's treasure-house is thrown open, and you are bidden to take thence precious jewels, with which to adorn your own soul, and to ransom the souls of others from danger and destruction.

CONCLUSION OF THE MONTH OF THE SACRED HEART.

I. As one who has minutely examined the several beauties of some splendid work of art steps back to view them as a whole, so must we also pause awhile to consider the united excellences of the sacred heart, upon which our thoughts have been centred during the month, which is now fast drawing to a close. One by one the attributes which grace that masterpiece of God's creative hand have been the objects of our study, and are stored up in the faithful memory, as in a treasure-house, whence they may be drawn for our support in time of need. We can, therefore, now sum up the knowledge which we have gained about the sacred heart, and view it as a whole.

That knowledge may be briefly formulated thus: ' The heart of Jesus is the source of all our good, and the model upon which our own hearts must be fashioned to every virtue.' In the first place, it is the source of all our good, because it is the well-spring whence the waters of life flow in copious streams into the hearts of men. For, as theologians tell us, and as the Church distinctly teaches, the heart of Our Lord is hypostatically united to the Divine Nature; that is to say, it is the heart of a Divine Person, namely, God the Son, the second Person of the Most Holy Trinity. Consequently, it possesses—if we may use such an expression—what is divine, what is infinite; and therefore, there is poured forth from it upon the souls of men, whatever good they either desire or can hope for.

The lukewarm, and those who have long grown cold must thence expect the grace which will infuse into their torpid veins a new element of life, to quicken their hearts, and set them on fire with love.

The habitual sinner, whose wicked life has filled him with fear and shame, must thence expect that true contrition, which will blot out all his misdeeds, and inspire him with a loving trust in God.

Thence, too, the fervent few derive their zealous spirit, which upholds them amid the difficulties of this weary life, and enables them to labour on perseveringly till the cool eventide, when the good Master will come to give them their exceeding great reward. In times of doubt the heart of Jesus is their prudent counsellor; in fear, their courageous helper; in despondency, their soothing comforter, whose genial smile pours sunshine into their darkened souls, giving them courage to advance with firm and manly stride in the ways which lead to God.

II. Besides being an inexhaustible treasury, whence you may draw supplies to satisfy all your needs, the sacred heart is, in the second place, a glorious model, the many beauties of which you must try to imprint upon your own soul.

What do you behold in the Man-God, Christ Jesus? You see one who perfectly fulfilled the law which He came on earth to teach unto men. A single glance at His all-holy life will convince you of this. When men injured and affronted Him, He bore their insults and injustice with imperturbable patience, showing kindness and gentleness to all, without exception. Though Lord and Master of the world, His humility resembled that of a child. No injurious treatment roused Him to anger or to resentment. He thought not of self and of self-interest, but always showed Himself careful about the interests of others. He obeyed the very creatures whom His hands had made. His purity shone so brightly that He could challenge His bitterest enemies to point out one single stain in His character. His fervour and zeal in the service of God surpassed the fervour and zeal of all others. His gratitude for the slightest favour, not only to His Eternal Father, but to even the lowliest of men, far outstripped the gratitude of the holiest of His creatures.

These are but a few of the good deeds commanded by the law of God, and we have specially selected them, because they are suited to your state, and may easily be performed by you. You will find them all in Jesus. He stands before you as a model. Therefore mark Him well, and endeavour to transfer to your own heart the virtues which you see in His. You will soon do so, if you begin at once to practise them.

Try, for instance, to bear patiently with your companions, and not to resent that thoughtlessness which sometimes makes them do things which are displeasing to you. Always treat them with unvarying kindness and gentleness. Be neither overbearing nor haughty in your conduct towards them. Endeavour to put their interest and convenience before your own, in order to gain an unselfish spirit. Towards all Superiors be very submissive and obedient. Remember the Child Jesus at Nazareth, and how He loved that lowly virtue, even to the death of the Cross. Try always to serve God with a fervent, devoted spirit, and the sum of these virtues will be purity of heart, of soul, of mind and of body—a purity which will make you an exact counterpart of Jesus Christ.

III. Therefore, the fruit which you are to gather from all that has been said about the sacred heart of Jesus is a fixed determination, in the first place, always to have recourse to that source of grace and virtue. You have not to incur any great risk, nor to put yourself to any great inconvenience in order to seek it. It is literally at your very door—oftentimes under the same roof that covers you. Be diligent, therefore, in paying frequent visits to the Tabernacle in which the sacred heart of Jesus rests, and from which He watches over and protects you. There He slumbers not, nor sleeps, but waits your coming, and is glad to accept at the beginning of the day the offering which you make to Him of your labours and your trials. He longs for the moment of your next visit when, in the early afternoon, you return to consecrate the rest of the day to His service; and He lifts up His hands and blesses you as a father blesses his children before they retire to rest, when you kneel before Him in the evening to offer Him your work, and humbly beseech Him to pardon the defects which have crept into it. On these occasions bear in mind that the treasury of God is thrown open to you, and that He will give you whatever you ask, if the petition be made with a humble heart and a fervent spirit. Especially remember this when you go to Holy Communion, and receive Him into your heart. Do not fail when that privilege is granted you to ask for all that you need.

In the next place, resolve to behave towards your companions as Jesus would behave if He were living and studying at College. What would He do if He were teased, or contradicted, or injured? He would endure it patiently, and in silence. How would He act towards His companions? He would be kind and considerate to them; He would be humble in the midst of success and praise; unselfish in His dealings with others, and obedient to all the commands and the wishes of His masters. He would be modest in all His looks and actions; pure in thought, in desire, in act and in word; an example to which all eyes would be turned, and a centre whence the sweet aroma of sanctity would be diffused around.

Aim at making yourself like unto Jesus Christ. Pray fervently to Him for this great grace, and then your study of the sacred heart, and your pious practices during this holy month will be productive of results which will be beneficial to yourself, and to all with whom you may be brought in contact.

BY THE SAME AUTHOR.

Price 3s. 6d.
LIFE OF GREGORY LOPEZ, THE HERMIT.

Price 10s. 6d.
PRINCIPLES OF RELIGIOUS LIFE.

Price 7s. 6d.
THE GATES OF THE SANCTUARY.

Price 5s. 6d.
THE TEACHING OF ST. BENEDICT.

Price 6s.
INTRODUCTION TO THE STUDY OF RHETORIC.

VOL. II.
LECTURES FOR BOYS
Will be ready in 1897.

LONDON:
R. WASHBOURNE, 18 PATERNOSTER ROW.

www.ingramcontent.com/pod-product-compliance
Lightning Source LLC
Chambersburg PA
CBHW030259010526
44108CB00038B/633